NEW PERSPECTIVES ON

Microsoft® Expression® Web 3.0

INTRODUCTORY

NEW PERSPECTIVES ON

Microsoft® Expression® Web 3.0

INTRODUCTORY

Henry Bojack

COURSE TECHNOLOGY
CENGAGE Learning™

Australia • Brazil • Japan • Korea • Mexico • Singapore • Spain • United Kingdom • United States

COURSE TECHNOLOGY
CENGAGE Learning™

New Perspectives on Microsoft Expression Web 3.0, Introductory

Vice President, Publisher: Nicole Jones Pinard
Executive Editor: Marie L. Lee
Associate Acquisitions Editor: Brandi Shailer
Senior Product Manager: Kathy Finnegan
Product Manager: Leigh Hefferon
Associate Product Manager: Julia Leroux-Lindsey
Editorial Assistant: Jacqueline Lacaire
Director of Marketing: Cheryl Costantini
Senior Marketing Manager: Ryan DeGrote
Marketing Coordinator: Kristen Panciocco
Developmental Editor: Sasha Vodnik
Content Project Manager: Jennifer Feltri
Composition: GEX Publishing Services
Art Director: GEX Publishing Services
Text Designer: Althea Chen
Cover Designer: Roycroft Design
Cover Art: © Jennifer Smith/Flickr/Getty Images
Copyeditor: Karen Annett
Proofreader: Chris Clark
Indexer: Alexandra Nickerson

Library of Congress Control Number: 2010929657

ISBN-13: 978-0-538-74675-5

ISBN-10: 0-538-74675-0

Course Technology
20 Channel Center Street
Boston, MA 02210
USA

Cengage Learning is a leading provider of customized learning solutions with office locations around the globe, including Singapore, the United Kingdom, Australia, Mexico, Brazil, and Japan. Locate your local office at:
international.cengage.com/global

Cengage Learning products are represented in Canada by Nelson Education, Ltd.

To learn more about Course Technology, visit **www.cengage.com/course technology**

To learn more about Cengage Learning, visit **www.cengage.com**

Purchase any of our products at your local college store or at our preferred online store **www.cengagebrain.com**

Printed in the United States of America
1 2 3 4 5 6 7 8 9 14 13 12 11 10

Preface

The New Perspectives Series' critical-thinking, problem-solving approach is the ideal way to prepare students to transcend point-and-click skills and take advantage of all that Microsoft Expression Web 3.0 has to offer.

In developing the New Perspectives Series, our goal was to create books that give students the software concepts and practical skills they need to succeed beyond the classroom. We've updated our proven case-based pedagogy with more practical content to make learning skills more meaningful to students.

With the New Perspectives Series, students understand *why* they are learning *what* they are learning, and are fully prepared to apply their skills to real-life situations.

"This text engages students by providing workplace scenarios designed to help them personally connect with the concepts and applications presented. The new visual overviews greatly enhance each tutorial as they provide a snapshot to the lessons."

—Paulette Comet
The Community College of Baltimore County

About This Book

This book provides thorough coverage of the new Microsoft Expression Web 3.0 software, and includes the following:

- Hands-on instruction of the new Expression Web 3.0 features such as SuperPreview, giving students the opportunity to review and compare Web pages in multiple browsers
- Detailed coverage of the Expression Web 3.0 workspace and editing window, increasing student familiarity with the Expression Web 3.0 environment
- Exploration of the powerful tools available in Expression Web 3.0 that allow students to create and manage CSS styles

New for this edition!

- Each session begins with a Visual Overview, a new two-page spread that includes colorful, enlarged screenshots with numerous callouts and key term definitions, giving students a comprehensive preview of the topics covered in the session, as well as a handy study guide.
- New ProSkills boxes provide guidance for how to use the software in real-world, professional situations, and related ProSkills exercises integrate the technology skills students learn with one or more of the following soft skills: decision making, problem solving, teamwork, verbal communication, and written communication.
- Important steps are now highlighted in yellow with attached margin notes to help students pay close attention to completing the steps correctly and avoid time-consuming rework.

System Requirements

This book assumes a typical installation of Microsoft Expression Web 3.0 using an Aero theme. The browser used for any steps that require a browser is Internet Explorer 8.

"The clear step-by-step instructions, real-world data files, and helpful figures make New Perspectives texts excellent for courses taught in the classroom, the hybrid/blended format, or entirely online."
—Sylvia Amito'elau
Coastline Community College

The New Perspectives Approach

Context

Each tutorial begins with a problem presented in a "real-world" case that is meaningful to students. The case sets the scene to help students understand what they will do in the tutorial.

Hands-on Approach

Each tutorial is divided into manageable sessions that combine reading and hands-on, step-by-step work. Colorful screenshots help guide students through the steps. **Trouble?** tips anticipate common mistakes or problems to help students stay on track and continue with the tutorial.

VISUAL OVERVIEW

Visual Overviews

New for this edition! Each session begins with a Visual Overview, a new two-page spread that includes colorful, enlarged screenshots with numerous callouts and key term definitions, giving students a comprehensive preview of the topics covered in the session, as well as a handy study guide.

PROSKILLS

ProSkills Boxes and Exercises

New for this edition! ProSkills boxes provide guidance for how to use the software in real-world, professional situations, and related ProSkills exercises integrate the technology skills students learn with one or more of the following soft skills: decision making, problem solving, teamwork, verbal communication, and written communication.

KEY STEP

Key Steps

New for this edition! Important steps are highlighted in yellow with attached margin notes to help students pay close attention to completing the steps correctly and avoid time-consuming rework.

INSIGHT

InSight Boxes

InSight boxes offer expert advice and best practices to help students achieve a deeper understanding of the concepts behind the software features and skills.

TIP

Margin Tips

Margin Tips provide helpful hints and shortcuts for more efficient use of the software. The Tips appear in the margin at key points throughout each tutorial, giving students extra information when and where they need it.

REVIEW
APPLY

Assessment

Retention is a key component to learning. At the end of each session, a series of Quick Check questions helps students test their understanding of the material before moving on. Engaging end-of-tutorial Review Assignments and Case Problems have always been a hallmark feature of the New Perspectives Series. Colorful bars and brief descriptions accompany the exercises, making it easy to understand both the goal and level of challenge a particular assignment holds.

REFERENCE
TASK REFERENCE
GLOSSARY/INDEX

Reference

Within each tutorial, Reference boxes appear before a set of steps to provide a succinct summary and preview of how to perform a task. In addition, a complete Task Reference at the back of the book provides quick access to information on how to carry out common tasks. Finally, each book includes a combination Glossary/Index to promote easy reference of material.

www.cengage.com/ct/newperspectives

Our Complete System of Instruction

BRIEF
INTRODUCTORY
COMPREHENSIVE

Coverage To Meet Your Needs

Whether you're looking for just a small amount of coverage or enough to fill a semester-long class, we can provide you with a textbook that meets your needs.

- Brief books typically cover the essential skills in just 2 to 4 tutorials.
- Introductory books build and expand on those skills and contain an average of 5 to 8 tutorials.
- Comprehensive books are great for a full-semester class, and contain 9 to 12+ tutorials.

So if the book you're holding does not provide the right amount of coverage for you, there's probably another offering available. Go to our Web site or contact your Course Technology sales representative to find out what else we offer.

CourseCasts – Learning on the Go. Always available…always relevant.

Want to keep up with the latest technology trends relevant to you? Visit our site to find a library of podcasts, CourseCasts, featuring a "CourseCast of the Week," and download them to your mp3 player at http://coursecasts.course.com.

Our fast-paced world is driven by technology. You know because you're an active participant—always on the go, always keeping up with technological trends, and always learning new ways to embrace technology to power your life.

Ken Baldauf, host of CourseCasts, is a faculty member of the Florida State University Computer Science Department where he is responsible for teaching technology classes to thousands of FSU students each year. Ken is an expert in the latest technology trends; he gathers and sorts through the most pertinent news and information for CourseCasts so your students can spend their time enjoying technology, rather than trying to figure it out. Open or close your lecture with a discussion based on the latest CourseCast.

Visit us at http://coursecasts.course.com to learn on the go!

Instructor Resources

We offer more than just a book. We have all the tools you need to enhance your lectures, check students' work, and generate exams in a new, easier-to-use and completely revised package. This book's Instructor's Manual, ExamView testbank, PowerPoint presentations, data files, solution files, figure files, and a sample syllabus are all available on a single CD-ROM or for downloading at http://www.cengage.com/coursetechnology.

SAM: Skills Assessment Manager

SAM is designed to help bring students from the classroom to the real world. It allows students to train and test on important computer skills in an active, hands-on environment.

SAM's easy-to-use system includes powerful interactive exams, training, and projects on the most commonly used Microsoft Office applications. SAM simulates the Office application environment, allowing students to demonstrate their knowledge and think through the skills by performing real-world tasks, such as bolding text or setting up slide transitions. Add in live-in-the-application projects, and students are on their way to truly learning and applying skills to business-centric documents.

Designed to be used with the New Perspectives Series, SAM includes handy page references, so students can print helpful study guides that match the New Perspectives textbooks used in class. For instructors, SAM also includes robust scheduling and reporting features.

Content for Online Learning

Course Technology has partnered with the leading distance learning solution providers and class-management platforms today. To access this material, visit www.cengage.com/webtutor and search for your title. Instructor resources include the following: additional case projects, sample syllabi, PowerPoint presentations, and more. For students to access this material, they must have purchased a WebTutor PIN-code specific to this title and your campus platform. The resources for students might include (based on instructor preferences): topic reviews, review questions, practice tests, and more. For additional information, please contact your sales representative.

Acknowledgments

The author wants to thank:

Marie Lee, Executive Editor, New Perspectives Series, Computer Science & Programming, for initiating this project.

Jennifer Feltri, Content Project Manager, for the extremely professional manner in which she kept everyone on task and on schedule.

Leigh Hefferon, Product Manager, Christian Kunciw, Manuscript and Quality Assurance, and his superb team of quality assurance testers, Susan Whalen and John Freitas; Karen Annett, copyeditor, and Chris Clark, proofreader. I also want to thank Vickie Legier at GEX for her outstanding work on the page composition and Jackie Bates at GEX for her design work.

I want to give a special thanks to Sasha Vodnik, Development Editor, for his attention to detail and patient guidance, which were instrumental in making this project a success.

I also want to thank the Cengage "team" for their work on this project: Justin Palmeiro, Julia Leroux-Lindsey, Jacqueline Lacaire, and Alexandra Nickerson.

I would like to dedicate this text to the three people who matter most in my life: my loving wife, Liliana; my handsome son, Mark; and my still "favorite daughter, " Lauren.

BRIEF CONTENTS

EXPRESSION WEB

TABLE OF CONTENTS

OBJECTIVES

- Identify the changes in Expression Web 4.0
- Apply Search Engine Optimization
- Explore the SuperPreview online service and the Insert Symbol dialog box
- Review the changes to the Menu Bar
- Identify the differences in the dialog boxes

Introduction to Expression Web 4.0

What's New in Expression Web 4.0

During the development of the New Perspectives on Microsoft Expression Web 3.0 text, Microsoft released the new version of Expression Web 4.0 as a free download. Although the differences between the two versions of Expression Web are minimal, this section is designed to identify and describe those differences. This textbook was written and tested using the Expression Web 3.0 software; however, students and instructors using Expression Web 4.0 can complete the tutorials and exercises in this book without difficulty. This book is now fully compatible with the Expression Web 3.0 and 4.0 versions of the software.

The information in this section explains and shows the differences between the two versions and also describes the new features added to the 4.0 release. Students using the 4.0 software should read this section before they begin working through the tutorials so that they are familiar with the minor differences they will encounter in the text.

STARTING DATA FILES

There are no starting Data Files needed for this section.

Search Engine Optimization (SEO)

The Search Engine Optimization feature of Expression Web 4 is designed to help Web browsers improve the search-engine ranking of your site.

Although each of the major contemporary browsers has a proprietary (and highly secret) method for ranking Web sites, the search-engine ranking of a site is determined by several factors. The Microsoft Expression Web SEO checker helps you analyze the HTML code of your Web page to maximize the search-engine ranking of your site.

Among the HTML elements the SEO checker analyzes are the title tags, the page description, the keywords, and the h1 heading element. When you create an Expression Web document, Expression Web automatically inserts certain HTML elements into the HTML code, but it is up to you, the Web page developer, to assign corresponding values to these elements. The SEO checker will see you have assigned values to these elements in the Page Properties. Figure 1 shows the result of an SEO check on an Expression Web document.

Figure 1 An SEO Check on an Expression Web document

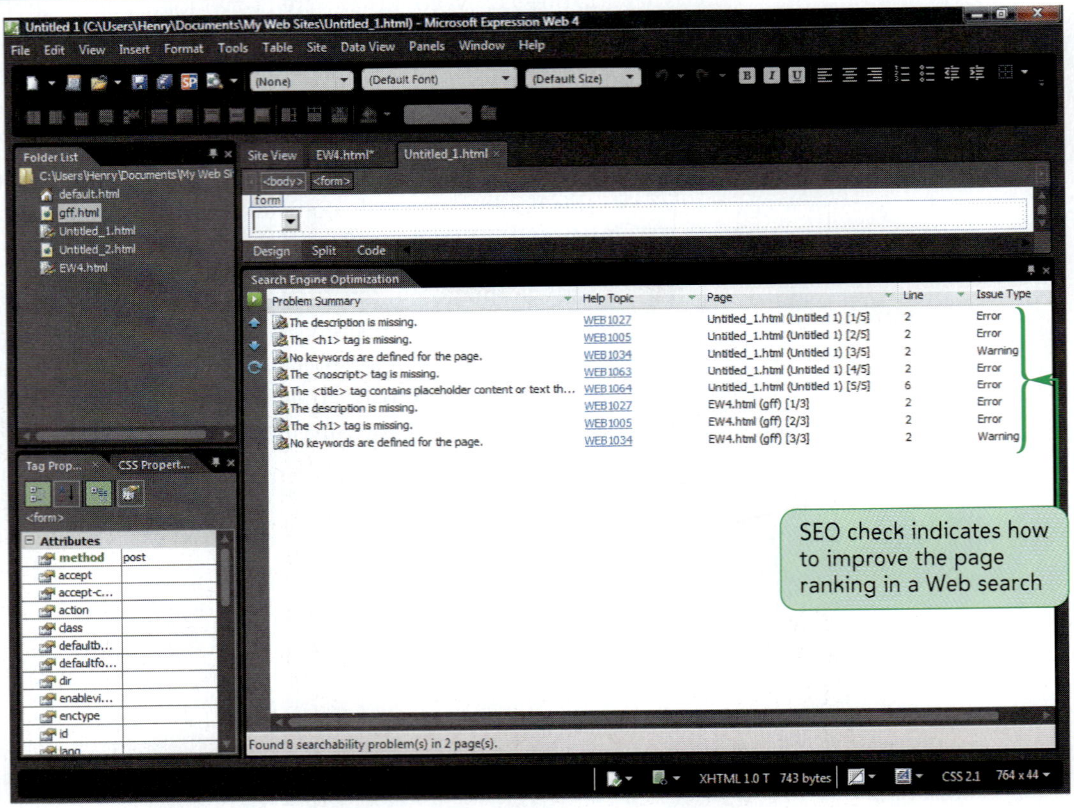

SuperPreview Online Service

The Microsoft Expression Web SuperPreview online service is a service that extends the capability of SuperPreview to include support for additional browsers and operating systems. With online support, you will be able to use SuperPreview to compare your documents in browsers and browser versions that you do not have installed locally on your computer. You need a valid email address in order to use the SuperPreview online service.

To activate the SuperPreview online service:

1. Create or open an existing Expression Web document. If this is a new document, save the file.
2. Press the **Shift+F12** keys to open SuperPreview.
3. In the toolbar, click the **Sign-up** button. A new email message opens.
4. Type a valid email address, and then click the **Send e-mail**. An activation email will be sent to the email address you typed.
5. Exit Expression Web and log in to your email. Look for the email from Microsoft regarding your online activation.
6. Open the activation email message and follow the instructions to activate the SuperPreview online service.
7. Start Expression Web. Open an existing file, and then press the **Shift+F12** keys to open SuperPreview.
8. In the SuperPreview toolbar, click the **Activate** button.
9. Position the insertion point where you want to insert an HTML special character.
10. Click the **Insert** menu, and then click **Symbol**. The Symbol dialog box opens. What you see next depends on whether you have made a new install or not. An example of what might occur for a new install of Expression Web 4 is shown in Figure 2. In this instance, new icons for the Safari browser have been added.

Figure 2 Preview with Remote Browsers

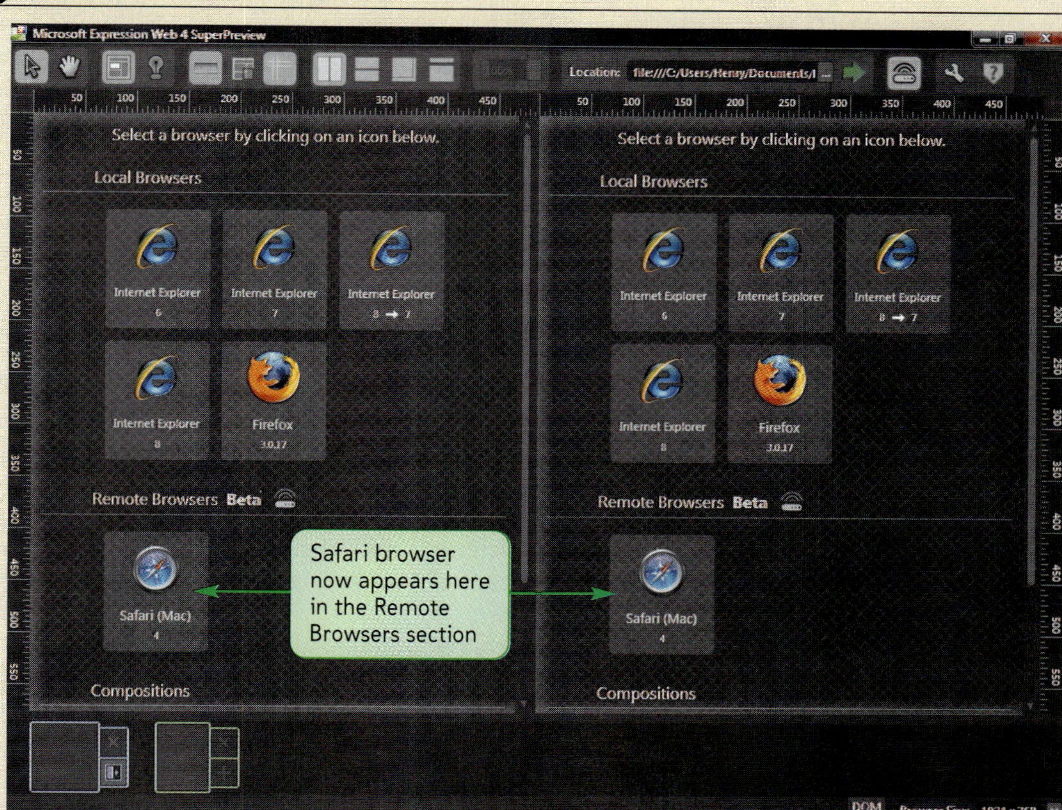

The Online Community

Expression Web 4 makes it easy to access the Microsoft Expression Web online community home page. In Expression Web, click Menu, and then click Online Community. The Online Community home page will open. The home page includes articles on the available software, related books, and the new features for Expression Studio. There also are additional links to learn more about Expression Web, participate in online forums, and post your work to an online gallery. Although the home page changes quite often, Figure 3 shows an example of the online community home page. Note the navigation bar near the top of the page, which provides links to other interesting topics.

Figure 3 **The Expression Web Online Community home page**

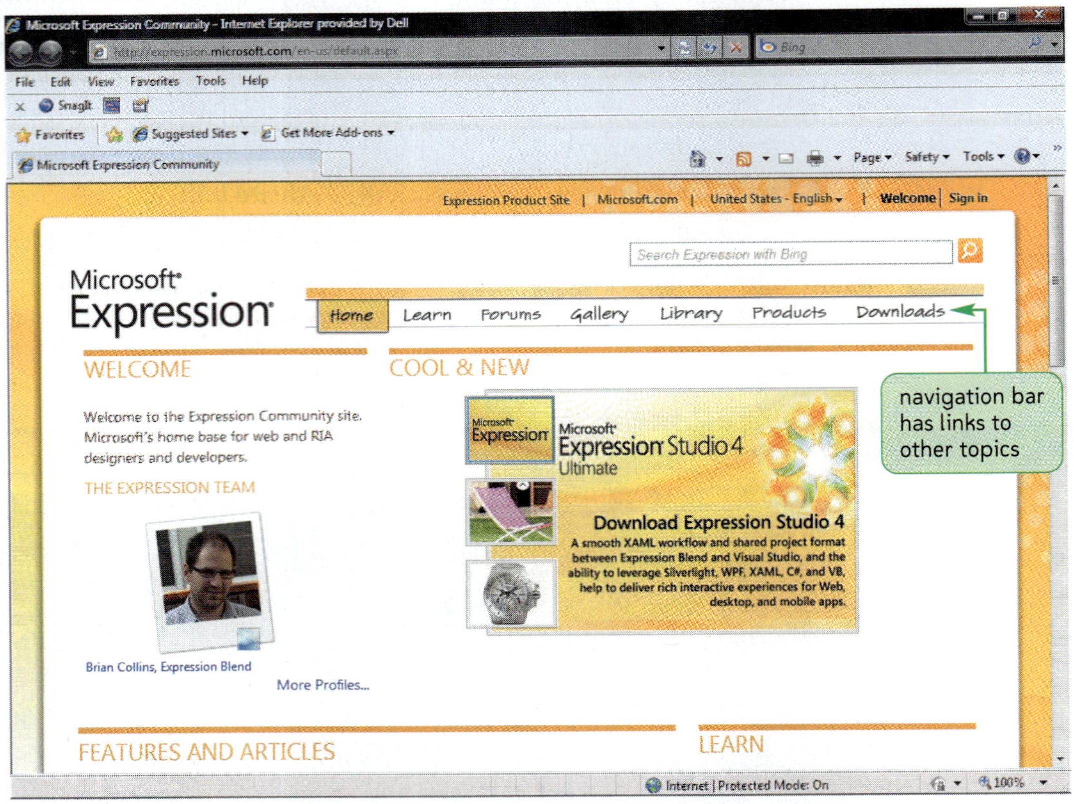

What's Different in Expression Web 4.0

The Symbol Dialog Box

A special character is any character in a document that you cannot type from the keyboard. HTML code must be used to display special characters on a Web page. Examples of special characters are the copyright symbol ©, the Yen sign ¥, and the cent sign ¢. Expression Web 4 has redesigned the Symbol dialog box to make it easier to locate and insert the most commonly used special characters. Figure 4 shows the Symbol dialog box.

Figure 4 The Symbol dialog box

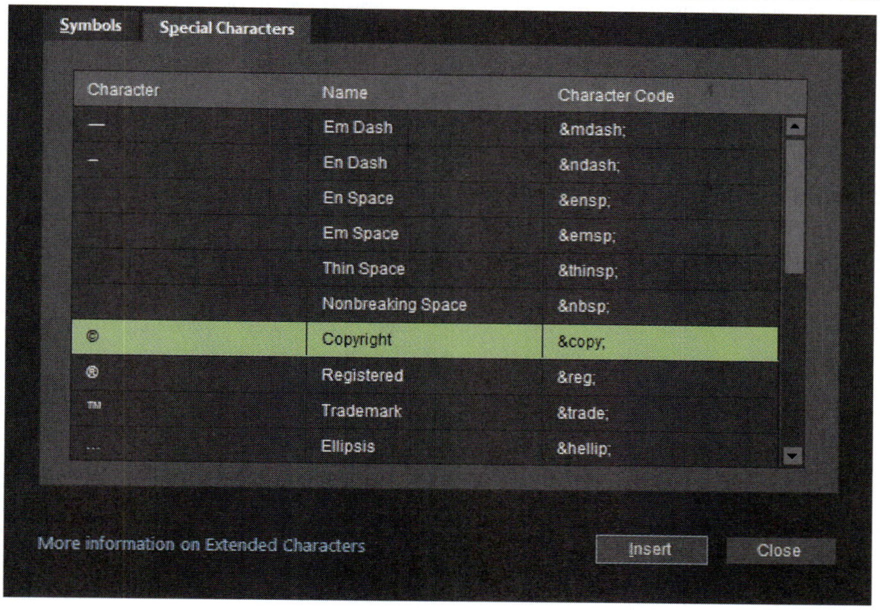

In Expression Web 4, the steps to insert a special character have changed. Use the following steps to insert a special character.

To insert a special character:

1. Position the insertion point where you want to insert an HTML special character.
2. Click the **Insert** menu, and then click **Symbol**. The Symbol dialog box opens.
3. Click the **Special Characters** tab.
4. In the character list, locate the HTML special character you want to insert. Click in any of the three columns (Character, Name, or Character Code) for that character.
5. Click the **Insert** button.
6. Click the **Close** button.

The Menu Bar

There were several changes to the menu bar in Expression Web 4 that include new functionality and functionality that was removed. Figure 5 shows which menu and function changed and how.

Figure 5 Changes to the Menu Bar

Menu	Function	Added/Removed
Help	Microsoft Expression Web Online	Removed
Help	Online Community : • Expression Web Community Home • Expression Web Online Forums • Learn Expression Web • Add-ins Community Gallery • Microsoft Web Platform Installer • Expression Web Team Blog	Added
Help	SDK Expression Web User Guide	Added
Panels	Layout Tables	Removed
Panels	SEO Panel	Added
Tools	SEO Reports	Added
Table	Layout Tables	Removed
Site	• Publish Current File • Publish Changed Files • Publish All Files	Added
Window	Site View	Added

The Apply Styles and Manage Styles Panels

Microsoft Expression Web creates styles automatically as you perform certain tasks when creating a Web page. These automatically created styles ("autostyles") are listed in both the Apply Styles and Manage Styles panels. In Expression Web 3, autostyles used the format .style#, for example, .style1. In Expression Web 4, autostyles use the format .auto-style#, such as .auto-style1 and .auto-style2. Figure 6 shows how autostyles appear in Expression Web 4.

Figure 6 Autostyles in the Apply Styles panel

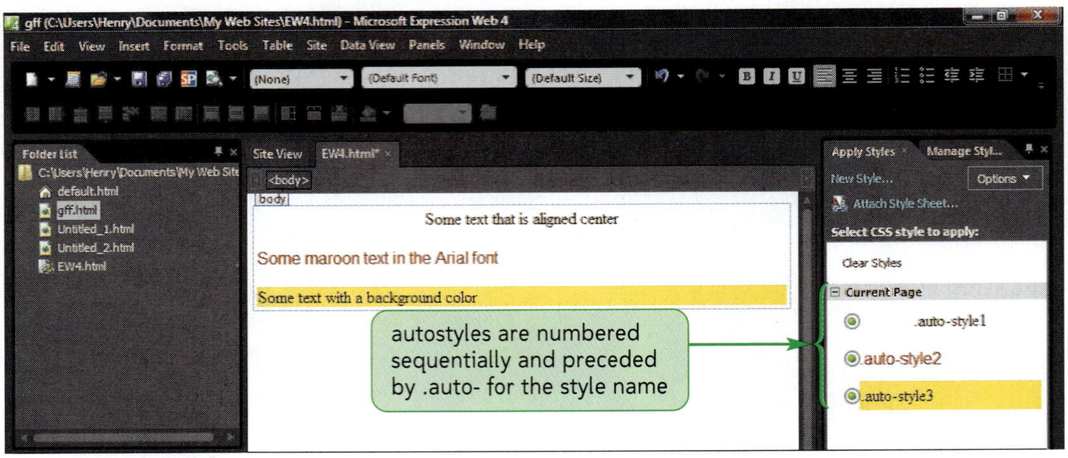

Dialog Box Default Choices

In Expression Web 3, dialog box default choices appeared as black text on a white background. In Expression Web 4, default choices appear as black text on a silver background. Figure 7 shows how default choices appear in Expression Web 4.

Figure 7 Default choices in a dialog box

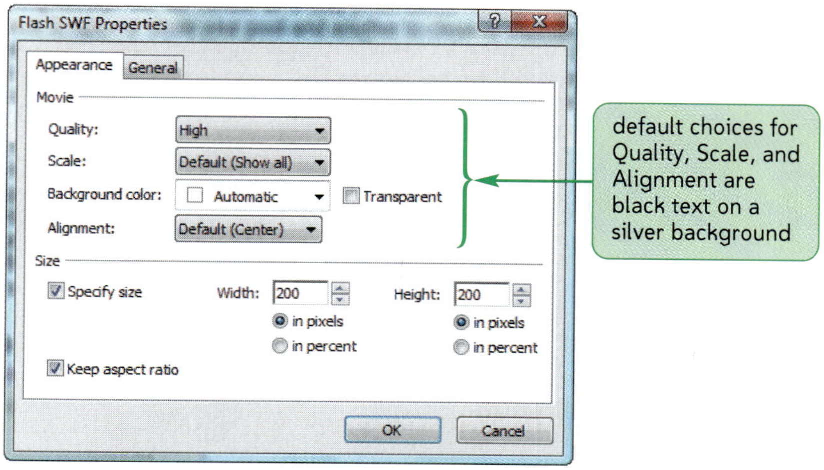

The Insert Hyperlink and Edit Hyperlink Dialog Boxes

The Browse the Web button has been removed from both the Insert Hyperlink and Edit Hyperlink dialog boxes. Figure 8 shows the Insert Hyperlink dialog box in Expression Web 4.

Figure 8 Hyperlink buttons in Expression Web 4

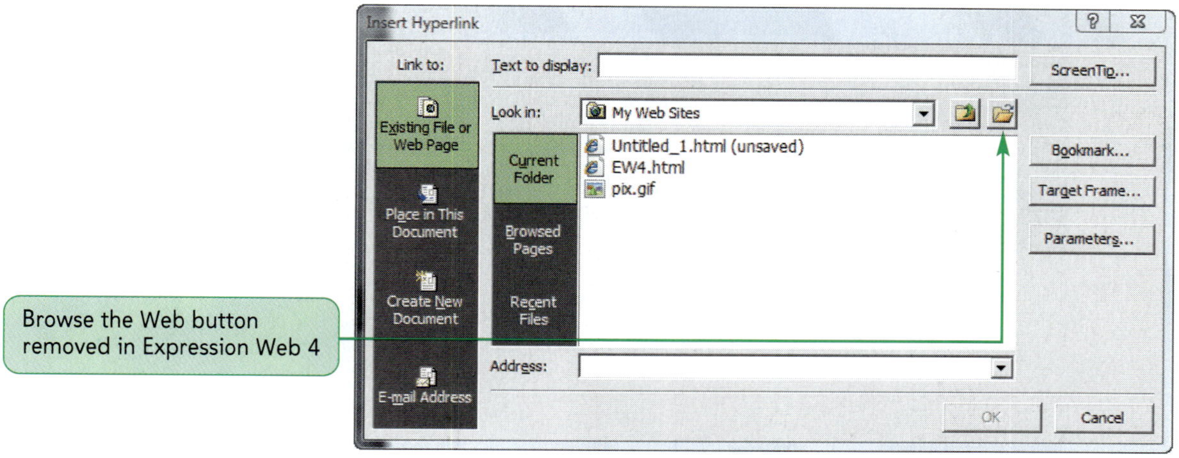

Layout Tables

Layout tables have been removed from Expression Web 4. Use Code view and enter CSS code for page layout or use the Expression Web layout templates for page layout. The Show Layout Tool, Draw Layout Table, and Draw Layout Cell buttons have been removed from the Tables toolbar. Figure 9 shows the Tables toolbar as it appears in Expression Web 4.

Figure 9 **The tables toolbar in Expression Web 4**

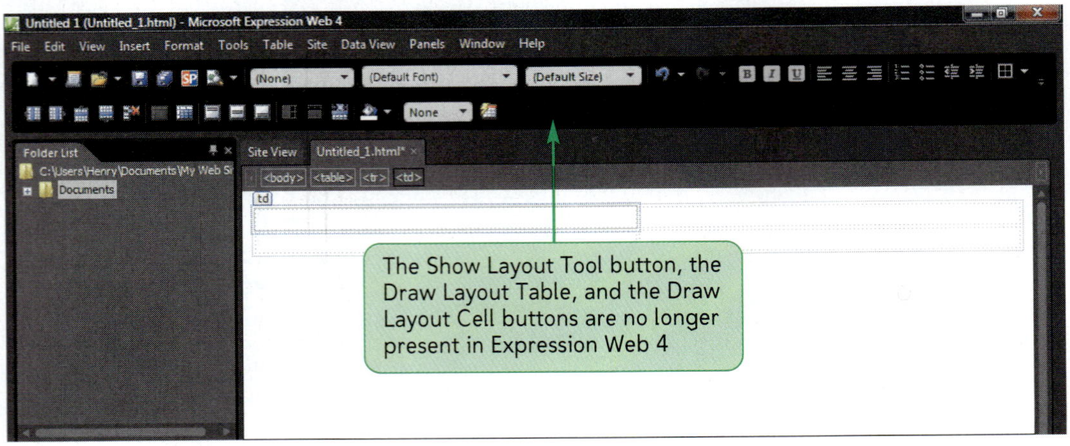

The Pictures Toolbar

The Pictures Toolbar no longer has the Color button. The two choices that were available from the Color button arrow, Grayscale and Wash Out, are no longer available. Figure 10 shows the new Pictures Toolbar in Expression Web 4.

Figure 10 **The Pictures toolbar in Expression Web 4**

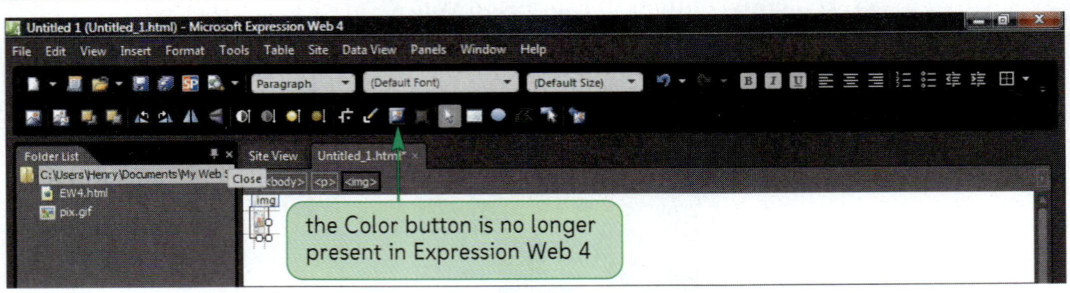

TUTORIAL 1

Getting Started with Expression Web 3

Exploring the Expression Web 3 Workspace

EXPRESSION WEB

OBJECTIVES

Session 1.1
- Identify the purpose of HTML and CSS
- Change views in the editing window
- Position, close, and open panels
- Describe the function of the status bar

Session 1.2
- Use the Expression Web editing tools
- Cut and paste text
- Enter page properties for search engines
- Use the SuperPreview feature

Case | *The Web Page Design Club*

Norma Velasquez, president of the campus Web Page Design Club at East Shore College in Prestonville, Rhode Island, has asked for your help in getting started with Microsoft Expression Web 3, which you refer to simply as *Expression Web*. The club designs and maintains Web sites for several academic departments on campus. Membership in the club provides a valuable opportunity for members to hone their Web design skills and gain practical work experience. Until now, Norma and her fellow Web page designers have been creating and revising Web pages using Windows Notepad. Although Norma and the other club members are well versed in how to write Web page computer code, the club is considering using Web page design software to streamline the development process for creating and maintaining the club's Web pages. Norma feels that a software program like Expression Web is just what the club members have been looking for. Because Expression Web writes all the code to create and design Web pages, Norma feels that the ease of using Expression Web will attract new members to the club. Norma has installed Expression Web on her computer and is eager to begin creating her first Web page. In this tutorial, you'll show Norma how to start Expression Web and create a Web page.

STARTING DATA FILES

There are no starting Data Files needed for this tutorial.

SESSION 1.1 VISUAL OVERVIEW

The **title bar** shows the current Web site or page.

The **menu bar** provides editing and formatting choices.

The **Common toolbar** is the default toolbar and contains options for the most common tasks.

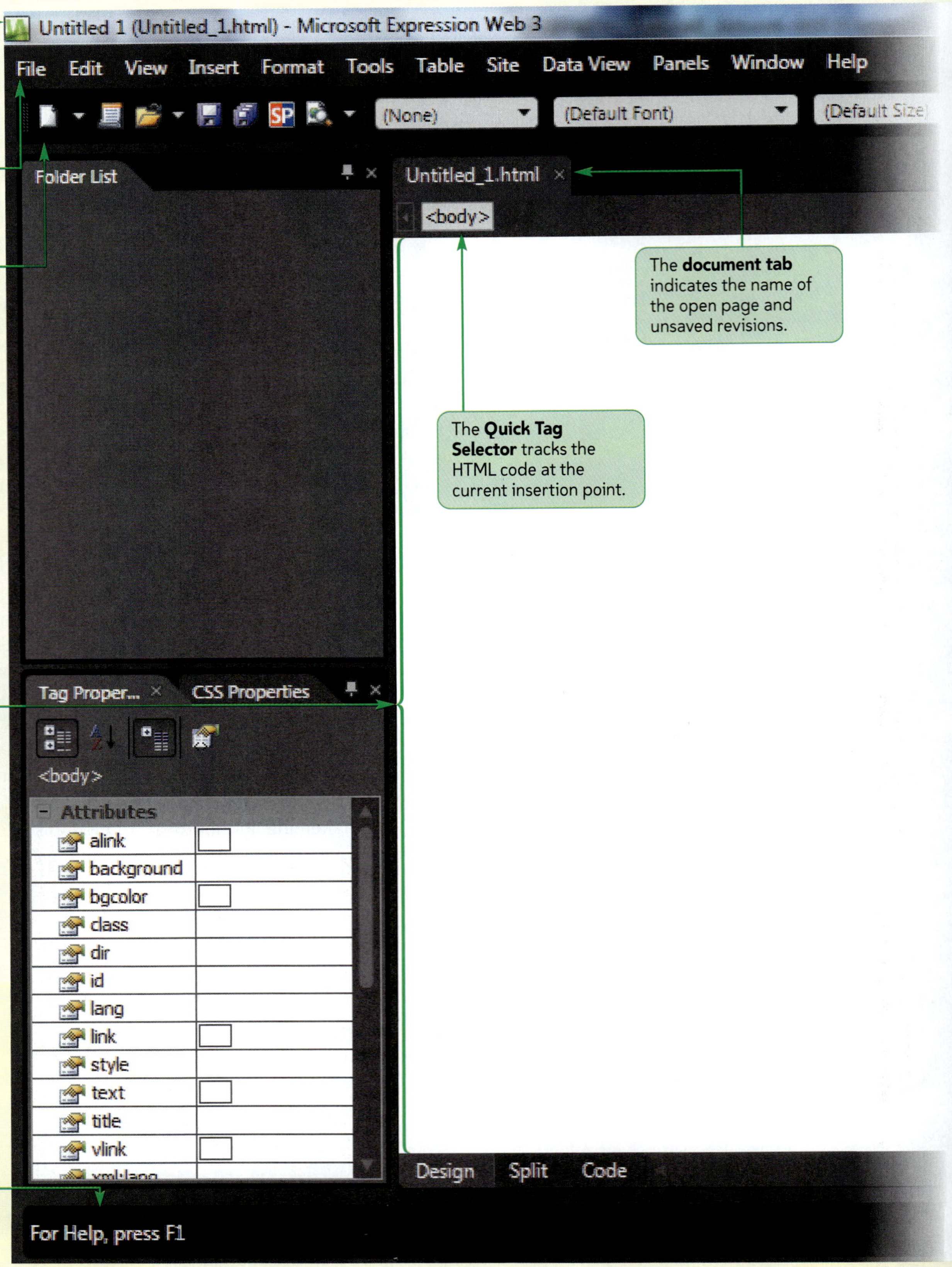

The **document tab** indicates the name of the open page and unsaved revisions.

The **Quick Tag Selector** tracks the HTML code at the current insertion point.

The **editing window** is used to enter and revise the Web page content.

The status bar provides shortcuts for useful tools, like the Help menu.

THE EXPRESSION WEB WORKSPACE

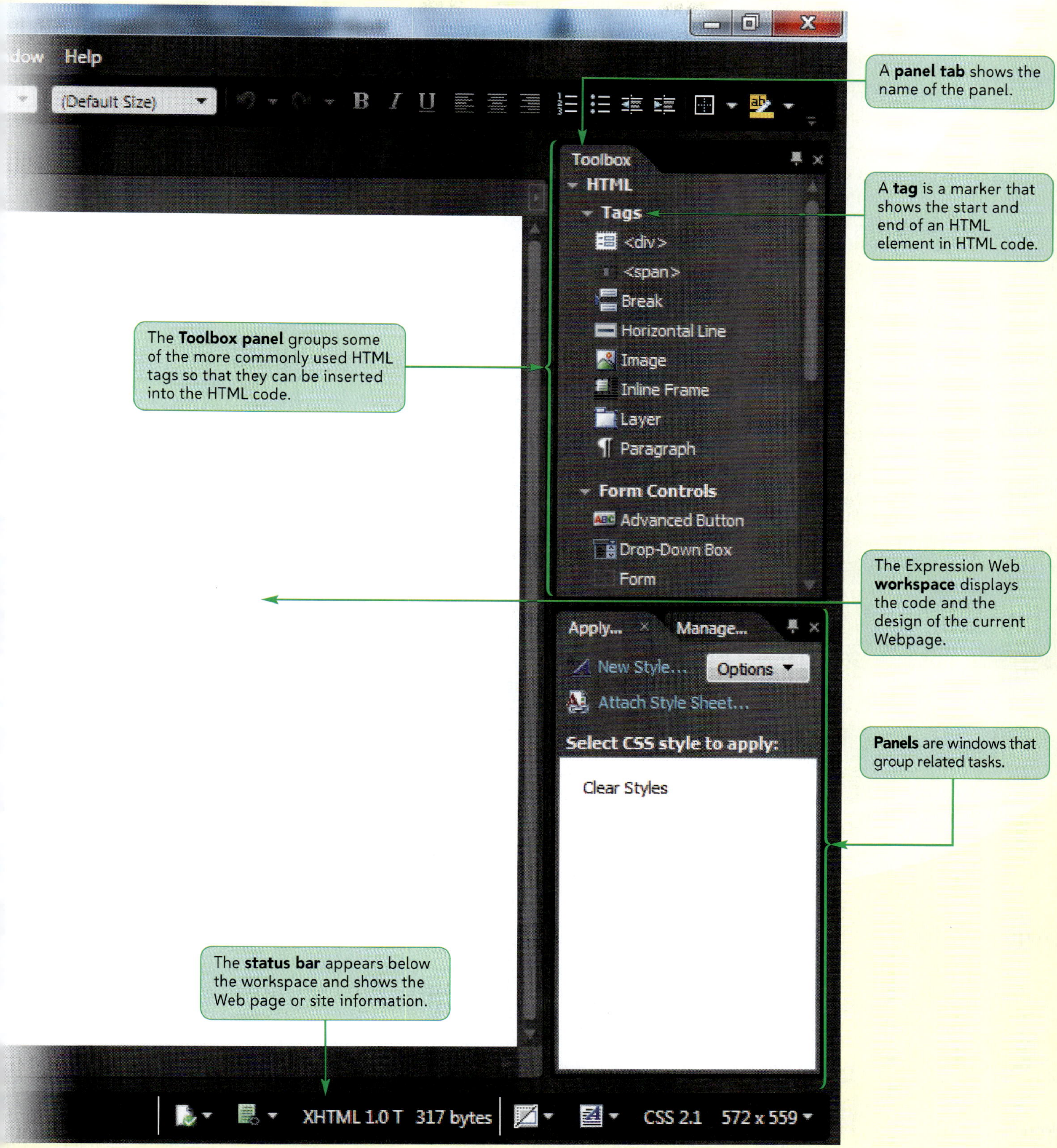

How Web Pages Are Created

You've probably used word-processing software, such as Microsoft Word, to compose a term paper or a report that has text, tables, and graphics. When you use Microsoft Word, you just type the text and format it using buttons or the Ribbon. You don't have to consider how text is made bold or italic or centered. You select the text, click a button, and the program formats the text. In contrast, Web pages are formatted using several computer languages. The two computer languages you will use in this text are HTML and CSS. **HTML** stands for **Hypertext Markup Language**. (In recent years, HTML has also been referred to as **XHTML**, **Extensible Hypertext Markup Language**, which is a stricter method of writing HTML code.) **CSS** stands for **Cascading Style Sheets**. CSS separates the structure of a Web page from the presentation (the appearance) of the page. HTML and CSS are markup languages, not programming languages. A **markup language** is solely a means to **render** (prepare the display of) Web page content. Markup languages are much easier to learn than programming languages.

Working with Expression Web

Norma is curious to know the advantages of working with a program like Expression Web. Expression Web simplifies the process of creating and formatting Web pages because it enters all of the HTML and CSS code for you. To create Web pages in Expression Web, you do not have to know the underlying HTML and CSS code. However, if you prefer working with code, Expression Web lets you develop Web pages using code. Whether you are a novice or a pro at creating Web pages, you will feel comfortable using Expression Web.

Another advantage of using Expression Web is that you can create your Web pages as they will appear in the browser. If you were using a text editor, such as Notepad, to create your Web pages, you would only see the text and the HTML code on your screen. You would have no idea how the page would appear in the browser until you saved the page, switched to your browser, and then opened the page in the browser. An example of code entered for a Web page in Notepad appears in Figure 1-1.

Figure 1-1 **Sample Web page code in Notepad**

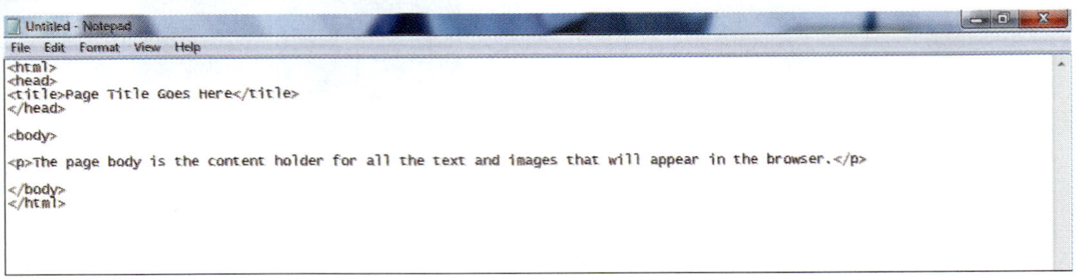

Expression Web, however, allows you to develop and view your Web pages as they will appear in the browser, which makes it much easier to revise and preview your work. There is no delay and no guesswork about how your pages will appear in the browser. When you purchase Expression Web 3, you also receive two other development tools, Expression Encoder 3 and Expression Design 3. **Expression Encoder** is a program that creates high-quality audio and video. **Expression Design 3** is a professional illustration and graphic design tool, which you can use to create banners, logos, and other illustrations.

A **Web site** is a collection of Web pages, files, and folders that you publish (upload) for presentation on the Web. One of the more powerful and time-saving features of Expression Web is its file management tools. Expression Web relieves you from having to keep track of the location of files used to create your Web site. You use Expression Web to create, delete, move, copy, rename, and organize the files in your Web site.

Web pages can have numerous links to other pages or other Web sites. Keeping track of those links and updating them can be a daunting task, but Expression Web makes creating links easy. If you change a link, such as moving a linked file to a different folder, Expression Web automatically updates the link code for every document linked to that Web page—an extraordinary time-saving feature.

After you have created your Web site, you have to publish the Web pages to a Web server so that your pages can be displayed on the Internet. Expression Web makes publishing your Web site a simple task.

Expression Web has a full range of editing tools not found in many text editors. You can check the spelling, use the Thesaurus feature, and use the Find and Replace feature to make global changes to one or all of the pages at your Web site.

Starting Expression Web

You'll show Norma how to create her first Web page in Expression Web. You start Expression Web as you would any other Windows program.

To start Expression Web:

1. Click the **Start** button on the taskbar, point to **All Programs**, click **Microsoft Expression**, or click the **Expression Web** folder, and then click **Microsoft Expression Web 3**. The Expression Web main window (the workspace) opens. You might not see the vertical and horizontal rulers, depending on whether the last user had them displayed.
2. If necessary, click the **Maximize** button to maximize the window.

   Trouble? If you encounter an error message that a file or Web site is not available on the server, click the OK button.

   Trouble? If the screen is split horizontally, click the Design button near the lower left of the screen.

   Trouble? If a list of files and folders appears on the screen, click the Site menu, and then click Close.

PROSKILLS

Teamwork: Opening and Closing the Last Used Web Site

When you start Expression Web, it automatically opens (or attempts to open) the last Web site that was open. In a classroom setting, where many students share the same computer, it might be quite common for you to encounter an alert message when you first start Expression Web stating that the program can't locate the last site that was open (more than likely because it resides on another student's flash drive). In a workplace setting, though, the ability to continue working with the same Web site at the same computer can be a real time-saver and a valuable tool when working with teams. Because the default setting in Expression Web is to open the most recently used Web site, any team member can quickly access the file and see any changes made to the site. To disable the choice to open the last open Web site, click Tools on the menu bar and then click Application Options. In the Application Options dialog box, click the check box for "Open last site automatically when Expression Web starts" to uncheck that option.

Expression Web arranges the toolbars just as you left them when you last exited the program. By default, only the Common toolbar (and depending on the install, the Pictures toolbar) appears in the workspace. If you are using a shared workspace, the toolbars you see might look different each time you open Expression Web. In this session, you'll only work with the Common toolbar, so you'll show Norma how to reset the workspace layout, which restores the workspace to its default settings, and also display just the Common toolbar.

To restore the default workspace layout:

1. Click the **Panels** menu, and then click **Reset Workspace Layout**. The Expression Web workspace is reset to the default layout. (You won't see any change on the screen if the default layout was already selected.)
2. Click the **View** menu, and then point to **Toolbars**. On the cascading menu, make sure that only the choice for **Common** is checked. If other toolbars are checked, click that name in the list to deselect it. Repeat this step until the Common toolbar is the only one that appears in the workspace, and then press the **Esc** key twice to close the menu.
3. If the Tags are collapsed in the Toolbox, there will be an arrow pointing toward the word Tags. Click the arrow, expand that section to see the HTML tags as well. The workspace should now appear, as shown in Figure 1-2.

Figure 1-2 Restoring the default workspace

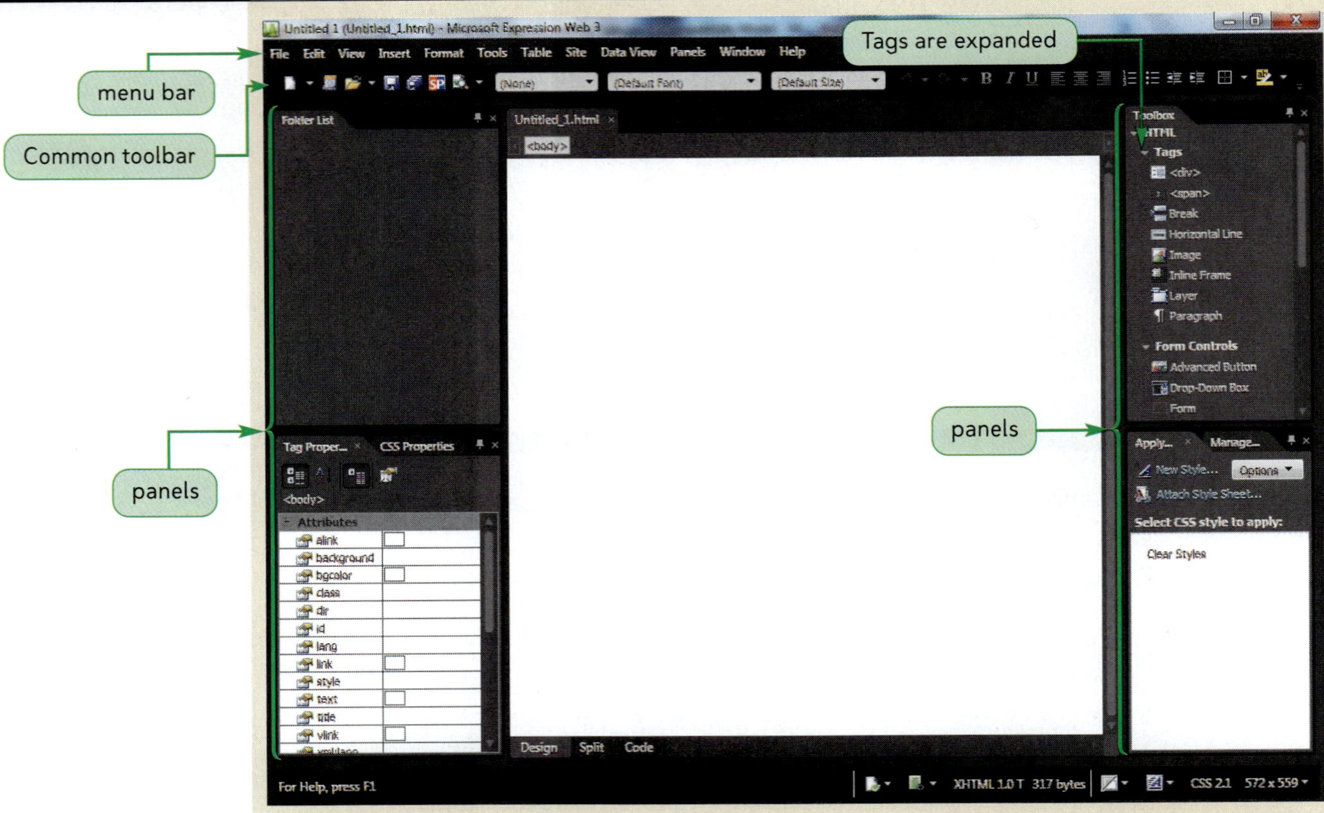

Next, you'll show Norma the components of the Expression Web workspace, which is where you create and revise Web pages.

Navigating the Expression Web Workspace

The Expression Web **workspace** establishes the overall user interface for the Expression Web program. The workspace has several components, as shown in the Session 1.1 Visual Overview.

Expression Web provides a menu bar and 11 toolbars. It does not include the Ribbon, as you would find in other Microsoft products such as Microsoft Office. Although you work with the other toolbars in upcoming tutorials, you'll focus primarily on the functions of the Common toolbar in this tutorial. The menu bar and the Common toolbar are shown in Figure 1-2.

The workspace is completely customizable. You can **dock** (drag a toolbar to the top, bottom, or side of the window until it snaps to the edge of the main window) and resize toolbars. Now that a new file is open and the default settings have been restored, you'll show Norma how to name and save the file.

TIP

Resetting the workspace layout applies only to the appearance and placement of the panels. If you added or removed toolbars, Expression Web does not restore those changes.

Saving and Renaming a File

An asterisk to the right of the filename on the document tab indicates revisions have been made to the document, but not yet saved. By default, Expression Web names the first file in a new editing session "Untitled_1.html." You can have several documents open at the same time in Expression Web.

If you have created a Web site and have the site open, the Site View tab appears to the left of the first document tab. You can use the Site View tab to display the file structure for the site. Creating a Web page in Expression Web is different from creating an entire Web site. You learn how to create and manage a Web site in later tutorials.

By default, a file created in Expression Web has the filename extension ".html." If you want, you can use the Page Editor options and choose to have the filenames you create end with the filename extension ".htm." Both .html or .htm filename extensions are correct; just be consistent in using the same filename extension you prefer. Next, you'll show Norma how to save the new Website and give it a new filename.

To save the file with a new filename:

1. Make sure you have created your copy of the Data Files and that your computer can access them. Right now, there are no files in the Tutorial 1 folder, but you will be saving your file in the Tutorial folder.

   Trouble? If you haven't copied the Data Files, you need to copy them before you can proceed. Your instructor will either give you the Data Files or ask you to obtain them from a specified location (such as a network drive). If you have any questions about the Data Files, see your instructor or technical support person for assistance.

2. Click the **File** menu, and then click **Save As**. The Save As dialog box opens.
3. Navigate to the Tutorial.01\Tutorial folder.
4. In the File name text box, type **webclub**.
5. Click the **Save** button. The file is saved. The document tab now indicates webclub.html as the filename, as shown in Figure 1-3.

Be sure to use lower case when naming the file, because Expression Web doesn't recognize capital letters in filenames.

Figure 1-3 **New filename displayed in the document tab**

document tab indicates the file has been saved as webclub.html

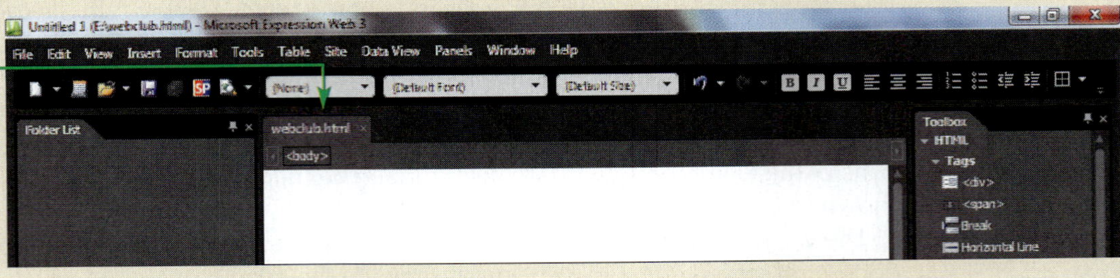

Next, you show Norma how to use the editing window.

Using the Editing Window

You will spend most of your time working in the editing window. The editing window is the largest window in the workspace. You use the editing window to create, revise, and format the content for your Web pages. The editing window has three views:

- **Design view** lets you design a page without seeing any of the underlying HTML and CSS code. Keep in mind, though, that Design view offers only a close *approximation* of how the page will appear in the browser. Your browser, its version, monitor size, and screen resolution all affect how a Web page will actually appear.
- **Code view** displays only the HTML and CSS code for the Web page. If you like to work directly with markup language code, you will prefer this view. The code for a Web page tells the browser where and how to display the text and images on a Web page. The code contained in an HTML document provides the back-end information necessary in order to get the Web page to display correctly. Historically, it was necessary to manually enter the code for each Web page, but that is no longer the case. Whenever you create a new document, Expression Web automatically creates all the code necessary to create a valid HTML document. You'll learn more about code a little later in this Session.
- **Split view** creates a split screen with two panes. The Code pane is on top, and the Design pane is on the bottom. If you make any changes to the document in the Design pane, the code is automatically updated. If you make any changes in the Code pane, save the file. Pressing the F5 (Refresh) button updates the Design pane. You can use the **split bar** to resize the Code view or Design view. As you move the mouse pointer over the area that divides the Code pane from the Design pane, the mouse pointer turns into the **resize pointer** ⇕, a pointer that points both up and down. You can click and drag the split bar up or down to see more or less of either pane. If you have trouble locating the split bar, right-click in the Design pane, and then click Move Split. A light gray patterned horizontal line appears between the panes. Repeatedly press the Up or Down arrow keys to increase or decrease your view of the Design pane, and then press the Enter key. Figure 1-4 shows the current document in Split view. (The screen might not be evenly split, depending on how the last user adjusted the split.)

Figure 1-4 Split view

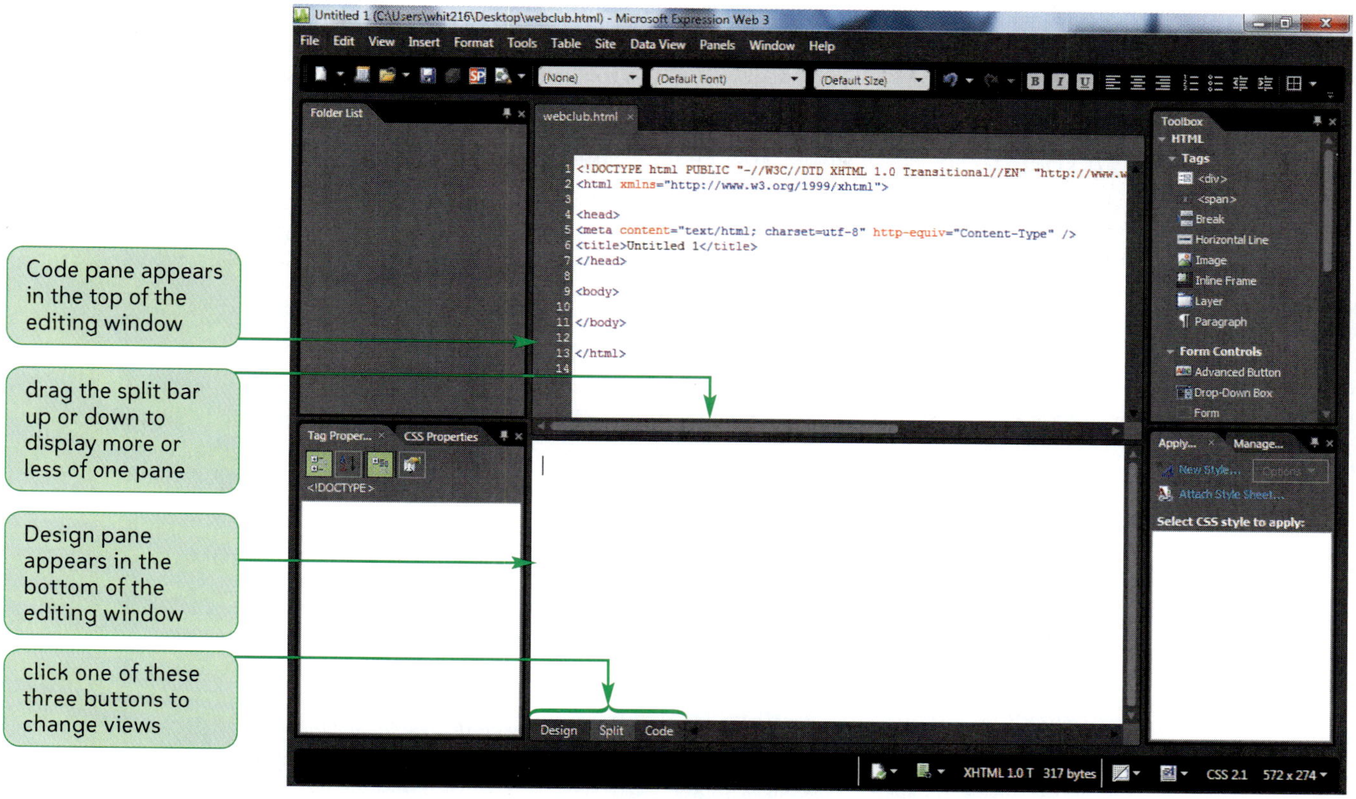

A **View button** is used to switch to a different view. The three View buttons appear at the lower left of the editing window, as shown above.

REFERENCE

Changing Views

- Click the Design button to show Design view.
- Click the Split button to show Split view. If necessary, click and drag the split bar to show more or less of either pane in Split view.
- Click the Code button to show Code view.
- Press the Ctrl+Page Down keys to cycle forward through views.
- Press the Ctrl+Page Up keys to cycle backward through views.

Currently, the editing window displays Design view. You'll show Norma how to switch to Split view, where she can see both the HTML code for the document and Design view at the same time in a split screen. You'll also show Norma how to drag the split bar to change the size of the two panes in Split view.

To change to Split view and resize the panes:

1. At the bottom of the editing window, click the **Split** button to show Split view. The editing window is now divided horizontally into two panes, with the Code pane on top and the Design pane on the bottom.
2. Move the pointer over the bottom of the black horizontal band that divides the pane and look for the split bar.

   Trouble? If you have trouble locating the split bar, right-click anywhere in the Design pane, and then click Move Split. The split bar should now be visible (it's a light gray patterned horizontal bar). Repeatedly press (or hold down) either the Up arrow key or the Down arrow key to move the split bar, and then press the Enter key.
3. When the pointer turns into a double arrow, click and drag the split bar up approximately one inch, as shown in Figure 1-5.

> **TIP**
> You can use the Alt+Page Down keys or the Alt+Page Up keys to switch between panes in Split view.

Figure 1-5 The Design pane resized in Split view

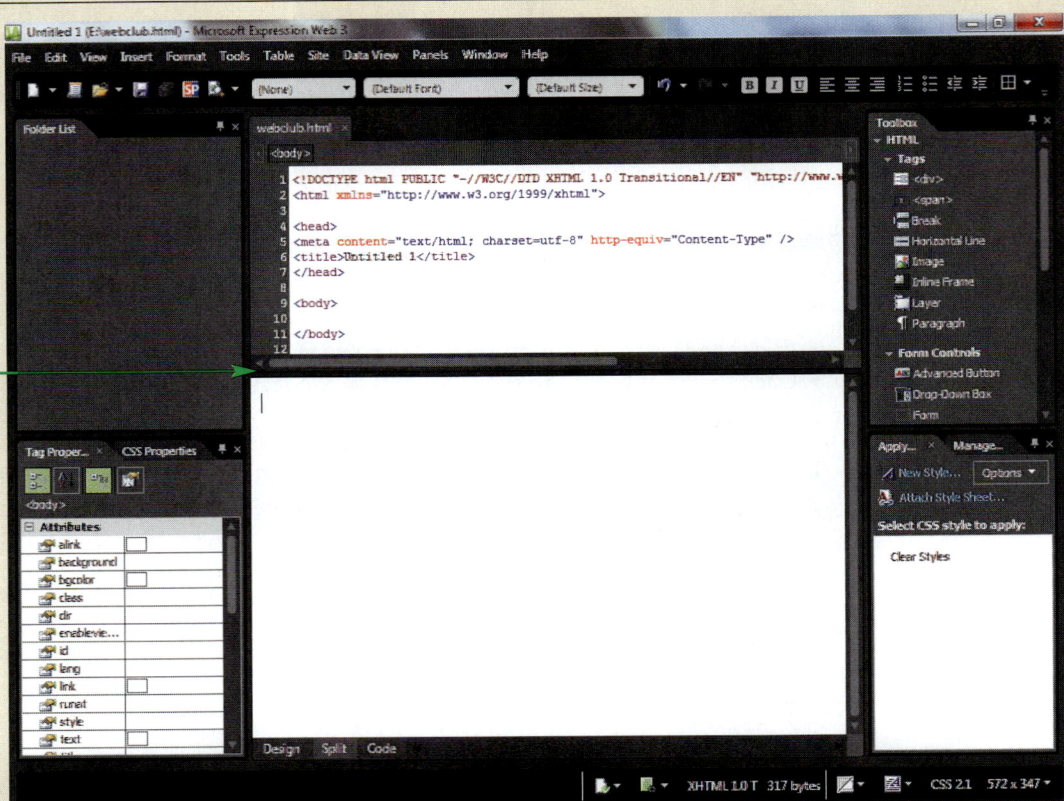

4. Click and drag the split bar down approximately three inches.
5. Click and drag the split bar to return it to its original position.

> **TIP**
> Double-click the split bar in Split view to return to Design view.

The third view is Code view. Once you become familiar with HTML and CSS code, you will feel comfortable working in Code view because it allows you to work solely with the code. In Code view, you do not see Design view at all. Initially, in Code view, you see only the HTML and CSS code that Expression Web automatically creates for you. You show Norma Code view now.

To change to Code view:

1. At the bottom of the editing window, click the **Code** button to show Code view. Only the HTML code now appears in the editing window, as shown in Figure 1-6.

Figure 1-6 Code view

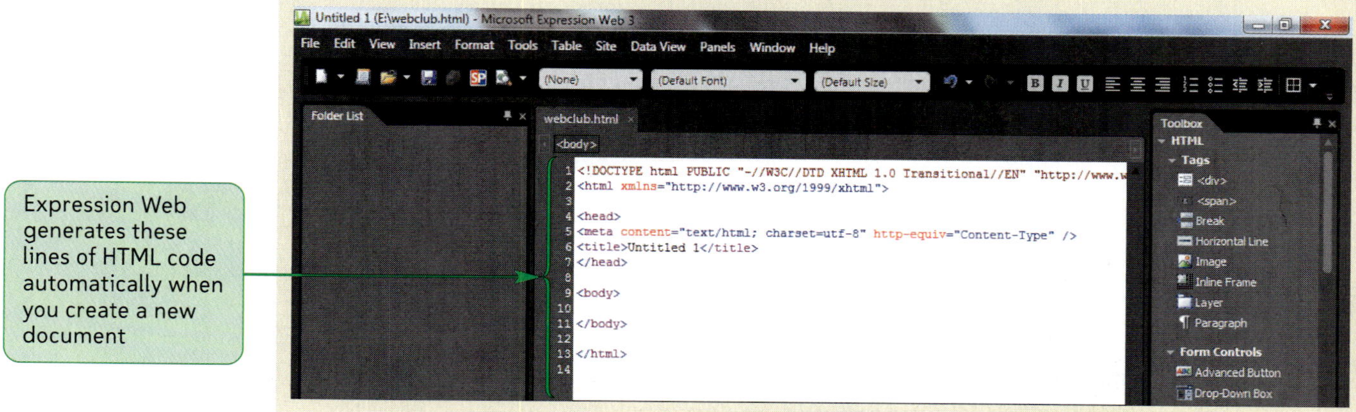

2. At the bottom of the editing window, click the **Design** button to display Design view in the editing window.

Norma is curious to know a little bit about the HTML code she saw in Code view, so you'll spend a little time explaining to her what HTML code is all about.

Working with Web Page Code

The **World Wide Web Consortium (W3C)** is the international organization that controls the HTML and CSS standards. The **DOCTYPE**, the document type declaration, is an instruction that identifies a Web page as using a particular version of the HTML standard.

An HTML **element** is an HTML structure that creates content, such as a heading, a paragraph, or a list. A tag is a marker that shows the start and end of an HTML element in HTML code. Tags usually appear in pairs; there is a **start tag**, a marker that indicates the beginning of an instruction, some Web page content, and then a corresponding **end tag**, which indicates the end of an instruction. Start tags are preceded and followed by angle brackets like this: <p>. End tags also have angle brackets, but they also contain a forward slash character like this: </p>.

The start <html> tag appears below the document type declaration. The document ends with the end </html> tag. The start <title> and end </title> tags are used to identify what appears in the title bar above the document window in the browser. All content for the Web page that appears in the browser is placed between the start <body> and end </body> tags. Just the content for the Web page, and not the HTML or CSS code, appears in the browser. Next, you show Norma how to use some of the design guides in Expression Web.

Using the Design Guides

In Design view, it's often useful to see the screen position of the elements you are creating. Expression Web has two design guides. The **vertical ruler**, which indicates measurements down the editing window, appears along the left side of the editing window. The **horizontal ruler**, which indicates measurements across the editing window, appears along the top edge of the editing window.

You can also display a **grid**, an arrangement of vertical and horizontal lines that help position and align objects in the editing window. You can only see the rulers and the grid in Design view or Split view.

REFERENCE

Displaying Rulers and Grids

- To display vertical and horizontal rulers, click View on the menu bar and point to Ruler and Grid. Then click Show Ruler.
- To display the grid, click View on the menu bar, and point to Ruler and Grid. Then click Show Grid.

You'll show Norma how to display the rulers (if they are not already present) and the grid in Design view.

To display the rulers and the grid:

1. If the rulers do not already appear on the workspace in Design view, click the **View** menu, point to **Ruler and Grid**, and then click **Show Ruler**. The rulers appear, as shown in Figure 1-7.

Figure 1-7 The rulers

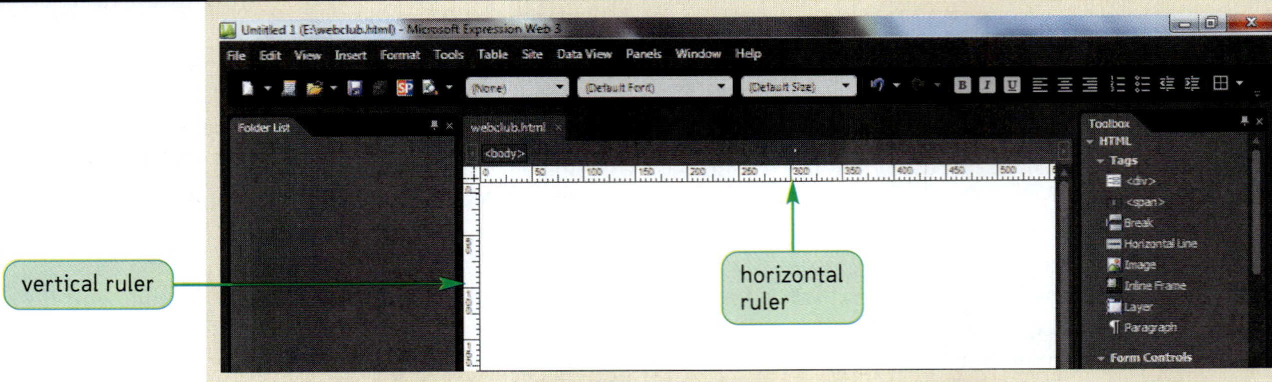

2. Click the **View** menu, point to **Ruler and Grid**, and then click **Show Grid**. A grid appears, as shown in Figure 1-8. (Your grid might not appear exactly as the one shown in Figure 1-8, depending on how the last user set the grid size.)

Figure 1-8 **The grid**

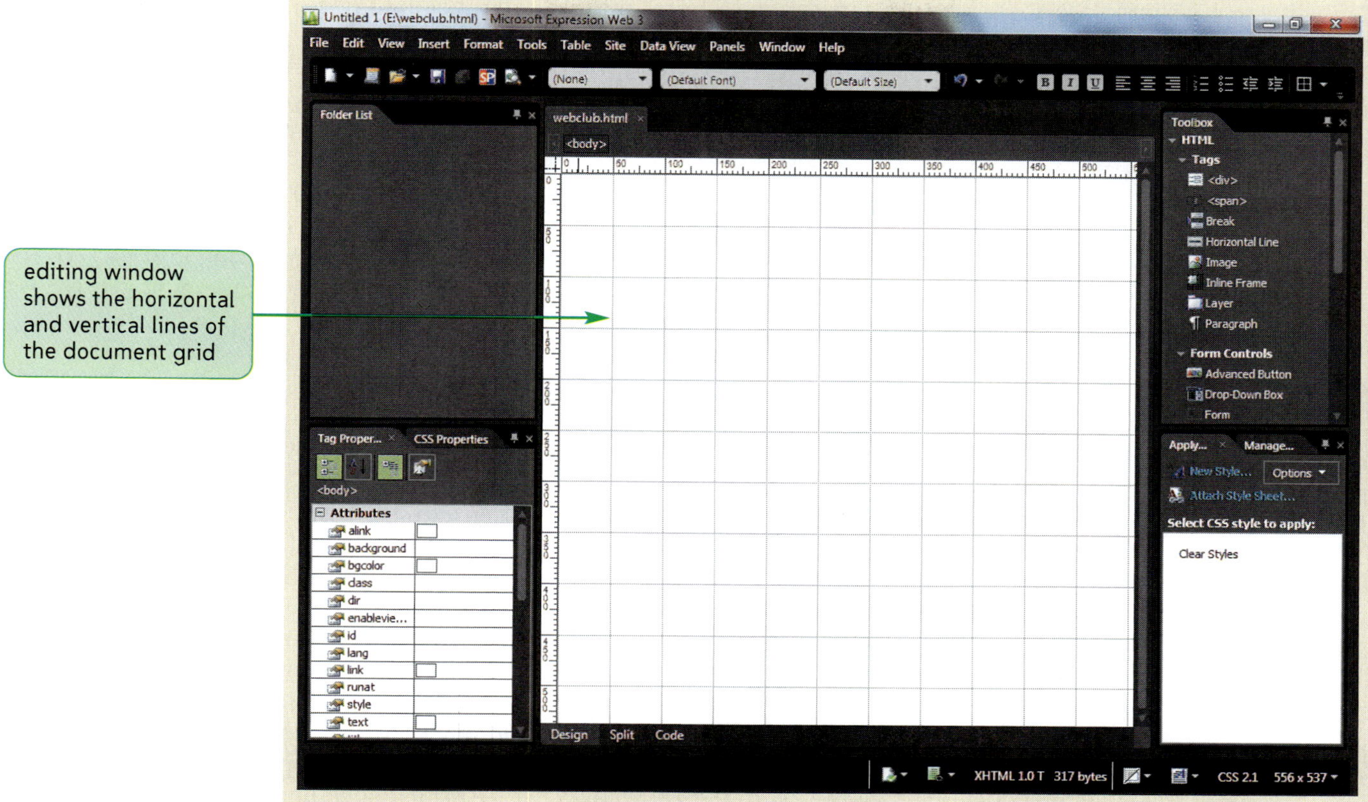

3. Click the **View** menu, point to **Ruler and Grid**, and then click **Show Grid**. The grid no longer appears. The rulers remain on the workspace.

INSIGHT

Configuring the Rulers and the Grid

You can use the Page Editor Options dialog box to change the appearance of either the rulers or the grid. Click Tools on the menu bar, and then click Page Editor Options to display the Page Editor Options dialog box. Click the Ruler and Grid tab. You can set the following ruler and grid units:

- Pixels
- Inches
- Centimeters
- Points

You can also set the number of units for either the ruler or the grid, set the spacing between gridlines, select the type of line style for the grid (solid, dashes, or dots), and set the line color for the grid. Changing the line color from the default gray to another color helps to make the grid stand out against the text and the other content on the Web page.

Next, you'll show Norma how to use several of the panels that appear in the editing window.

Working with Panels

The editing window is surrounded by several panels, which you can use to group related tasks together. Panels can be opened, closed, moved, and resized. To dock a panel is to move a panel to a different part of the workspace. The Folder List panel appears in the upper-left corner of the workspace. When you create a Web site in Expression Web, the **Folder List panel** lists all of the files and folders in your Web site. Because you have thus far only saved a new Web page and not a Web site, the Folder List panel is empty. You'll create a Web site in later tutorials.

The Tag Properties panel is directly below the Folder List panel. The **Tag Properties panel** lists all of the ways you can modify an HTML tag at the current location of the insertion point. Note that this area of the workspace has two panel tabs: one for the Tag Properties panel and another for the CSS Properties panel. Clicking the CSS Properties tab displays the **CSS Properties panel**, which lists the CSS code in effect for that part of the page where the insertion point currently is positioned.

TIP

The same options for inserting HTML code in the Toolbox panel are available when you click Insert on the menu bar and then point to HTML.

The panels to the right of the editing window are the Toolbox panel and the Apply Styles panel. The Toolbox panel contains two task groups. The HTML group contains Tags, Form Controls, and Media. The second group is ASP.NET Controls. You work with Form Controls and Media in later tutorials. The Apply Styles panel and the Manage Styles panel are grouped beneath the Toolbox panel. You use the **Apply Styles panel** to create and modify CSS styles, and you use the **Manage Styles panel** to modify and organize your CSS styles. In later tutorials, you'll create and apply CSS styles to a section of your document or to several documents.

If you click and drag a panel into either the top quarter or the bottom quarter of the screen in Design view, the panel appears horizontally across the editing window. You can maximize panels so you can view more of the available options and choices in the panel. You can close a panel to remove it from the screen. You can also hide one or more panels or hide all the panels. When you hide a panel, a panel tab appears in place of the full panel on either the left or right edge of the workspace (depending on the default location of the panel). The panel reappears for as long as you hover the mouse pointer over the panel tab. You can click the Turn off AutoHide button to restore the panel to the workspace. You'll show Norma how to **undock**, or pull a panel away from the top, bottom, or side of the main window, and close the Folder List panel.

To undock and close the Folder List panel:

1. Click the **Folder List** panel tab (or the gray area to the right of the tab) and drag the **Folder List** panel to the approximate center of the editing window to undock it, as shown in Figure 1-9.

Figure 1-9 **The Folder List panel undocked**

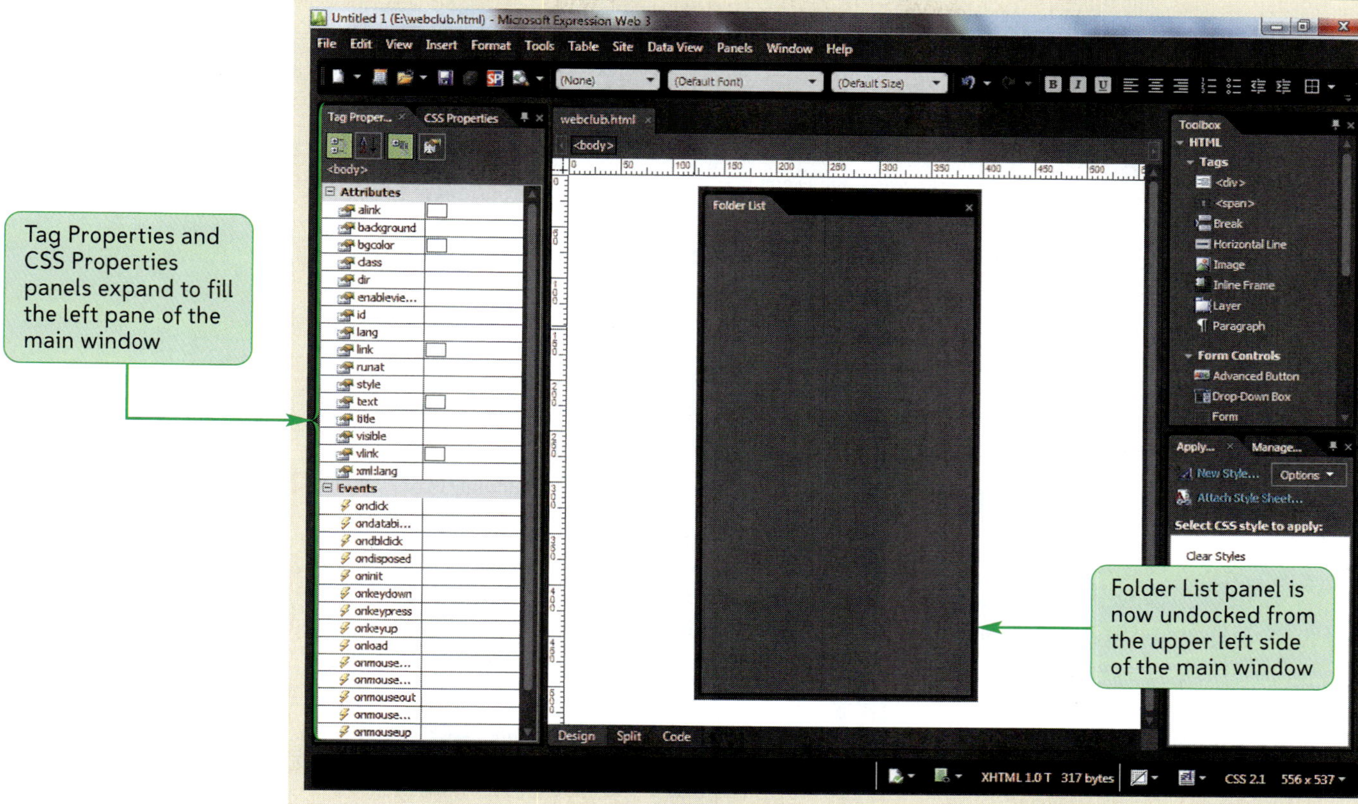

2. Click the **Close** button in the upper-right corner of the Folder List panel to close it.

Now, you show Norma how to hide all the panels, view the panels by moving the mouse pointer over the panel tabs, and reset the workspace layout.

To hide the panels:

1. Click the **Panels** menu, and then click **AutoHide All Panels**. All panels are now hidden, as shown in Figure 1-10. Note that panel tabs now appear on both the upper-left and upper-right sides of the workspace.

Figure 1-10 **Hidden panels**

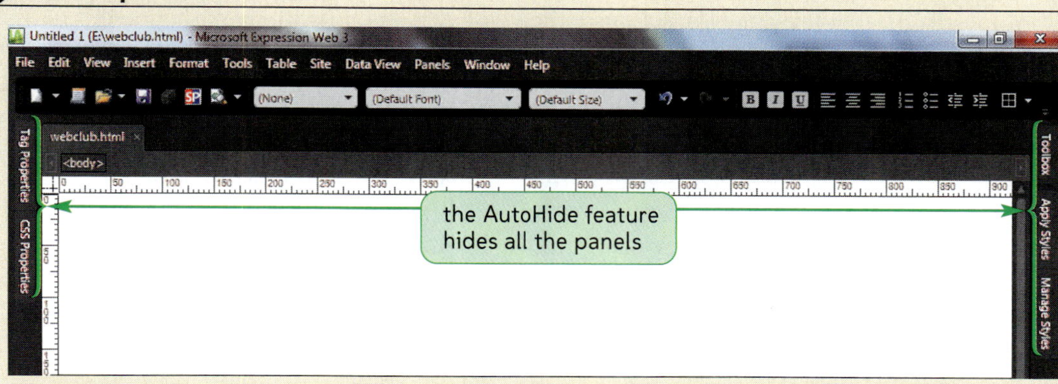

2. On the upper-left side of the workspace, move the mouse pointer over the Tag Properties and CSS Properties panel tabs. Each panel reappears as you position the mouse pointer over each tab.
3. On the right side of the workspace, position the mouse pointer over the Toolbox panel tab. The Toolbox reappears.
4. Click the **Panels** menu, and then click **Reset Workspace Layout**. The default workspace arrangement for the panels is restored.

Next, you'll show Norma how to use the status bar in Expression Web.

Using the Status Bar

The Expression Web status bar appears at the bottom of the workspace. The status bar is divided into several sections, each of which shows information about the current state of the window or the Web page, as shown in Figure 1-11.

Figure 1-11 **The status bar buttons**

Button		Function
HTML Incompatibility		Checks to see if your document is compatible with a particular browser and browser version.
Code Errors		If there is a code error in the file, the icon will change to that of an exclamation point. Click the list arrow and then click Go To Error to position the insertion point in Split view at the point of the code error.
Doctype and Schema	XHTML 1.0 T	Determines which version of (X)HTML the document code is compatible with.
Download Size	317 bytes	Indicates the byte size of the file.
Visual Aids		Determines whether the Visual Aids feature is on or off.
CSS Mode		Sets the CSS authoring mode. If the authoring mode is set to Manual, you can write our own CSS code. If the authoring mode is set to Auto, Expression Web will write the CSS code for you. CSS, use Auto mode.
CSS Schema	CSS 2.1	Determines which version of CSS the document code is compatible with.
Page Size	556 x 543	Indicates the current pixel height and width of the editing window.

The first two buttons indicate HTML incompatibility and code errors. These two buttons alert you if there is an error in the HTML code. Note that the Download Size is also included in the status bar and indicates the size of the file in bytes. **Visual Aids** are controls used to display *white space*, such as margins, that are useful to ensure that your text has **breathing room**, separation between text or picture objects on the page, which makes the page easier to read. To get an accurate indication of your Web page layout, you should always work with Visual Aids on, which is the default choice. If Visual Aids are off, click the Visual Aids list arrow and then click Show.

TIP

You can also press the Ctrl+/ keys to enable or disable Visual Aids.

On the far-right side of the status bar is a measurement for Page Size, such as 955 × 600. The page size is also referred to as the screen resolution. The numbers correspond to the physical number of rows of **pixels** (or picture elements, which are the units of measurement for pictures and images on computer and television screens) that create the display in the editing window. Today, most users have their page size set to 1024 × 768 or higher. The default setting is Current Page Size, which is a good choice; it causes text to wrap as you type paragraph text in the editing window in Design view. The Page Size value has no effect on how the document appears in the browser. If you choose a lower resolution (for example, 955 × 600), the text wraps in Design view; however, unless you have a wide-screen monitor or have closed several panels, you do not see the entire line of text in the editing window. It appears that the text is not wrapping.

You are not limited to the list of screen resolutions you see when you click the Page Size list arrow. To enter a different screen size, click the Page Size list arrow and then click Modify Page Sizes. You can also create a custom screen size by clicking View on the menu bar, pointing to Page Size, and then clicking Modify Page Sizes. Use the Modify Page Sizes dialog box to change the screen size.

The notation for CSS 2.1 is the CSS schema indicator. This indicator shows that Expression Web is creating code based on the current code standards of CSS version 2.1. Last, you show Norma how to close the file and exit Expression Web.

To close the Web page:

1. Click the **File** menu, and then click **Close**.
2. If you are prompted to save your changes, click the **No** button.

REVIEW

Session 1.1 Quick Check

1. What do the letters HTML stand for? hypertext mark up language
2. What do the letters CSS stand for? cascading style sheets
3. What are the main components of the workspace? menubar + 11 tool bars
4. What toolbar should always be visible in the workspace? common toolbar
5. What are the three workspace views? design | code | split
6. What can you display in the workspace to assist you in positioning and aligning page content? gridlines + rulers / vertical ruler + horizontal ruler
7. What bar appears at the bottom of the workspace? status bar

SESSION 1.2 VISUAL OVERVIEW

Toggle Thumbnail Visibility shows a very small thumbnail image of the page in the lower-right corner of the preview window.

Vertical Split Layout compares browser views side by side.

Horizontal Split Layout compares browser views with one browser view on the top and the other on the bottom.

Single Layout displays a single browser view, similar to pressing the F12 key.

Panning Mode lets you drag the page upward or downward.

Selection Mode allows you to select individual sections for comparison.

Box Highlighting Mode highlights the selected element in blue in the baseline browser view and in green in the comparison browser view.

Lights-Out Highlighting Mode highlights the selected element and dims the rest of the page.

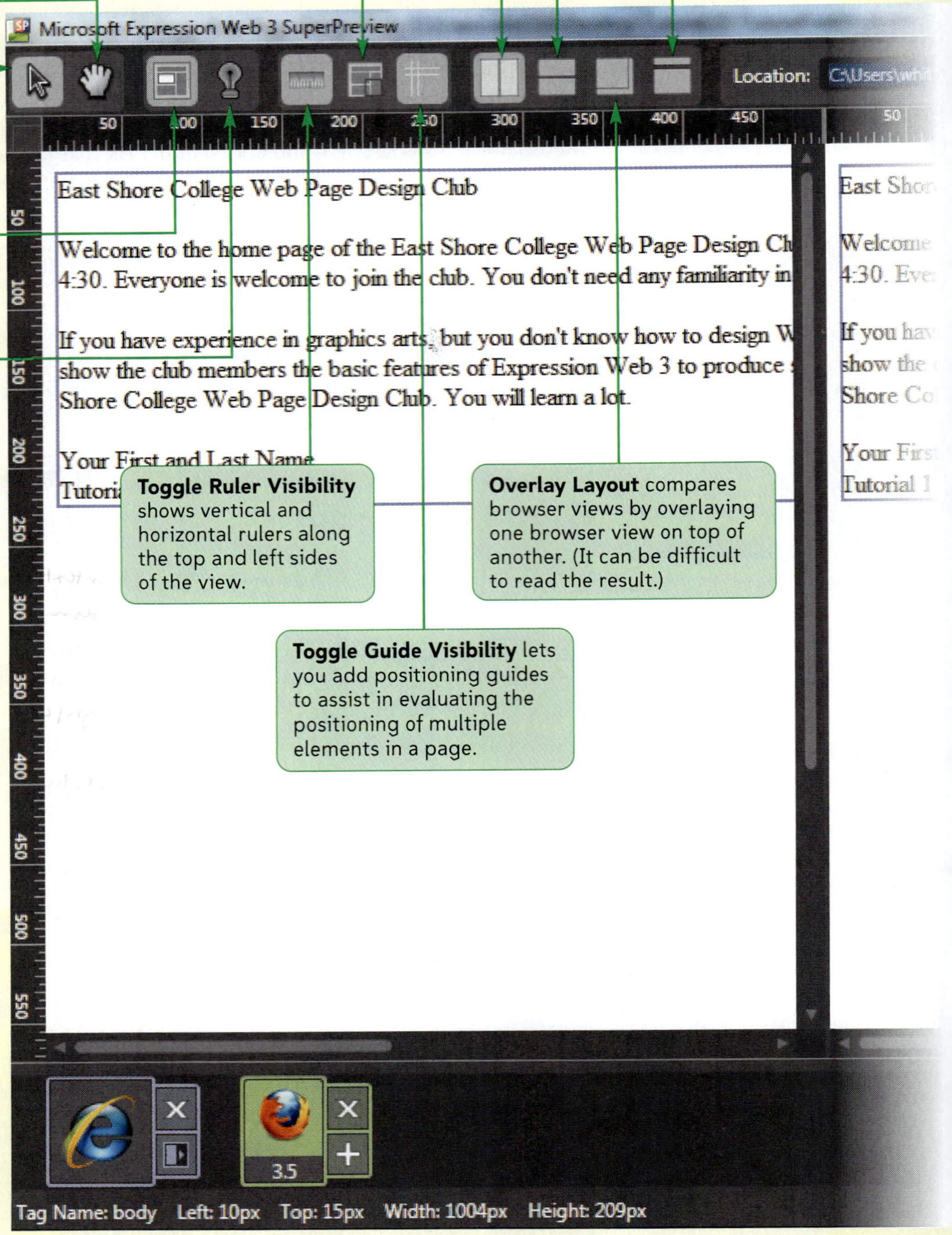

Toggle Ruler Visibility shows vertical and horizontal rulers along the top and left sides of the view.

Overlay Layout compares browser views by overlaying one browser view on top of another. (It can be difficult to read the result.)

Toggle Guide Visibility lets you add positioning guides to assist in evaluating the positioning of multiple elements in a page.

THE SUPERPREVIEW WINDOW

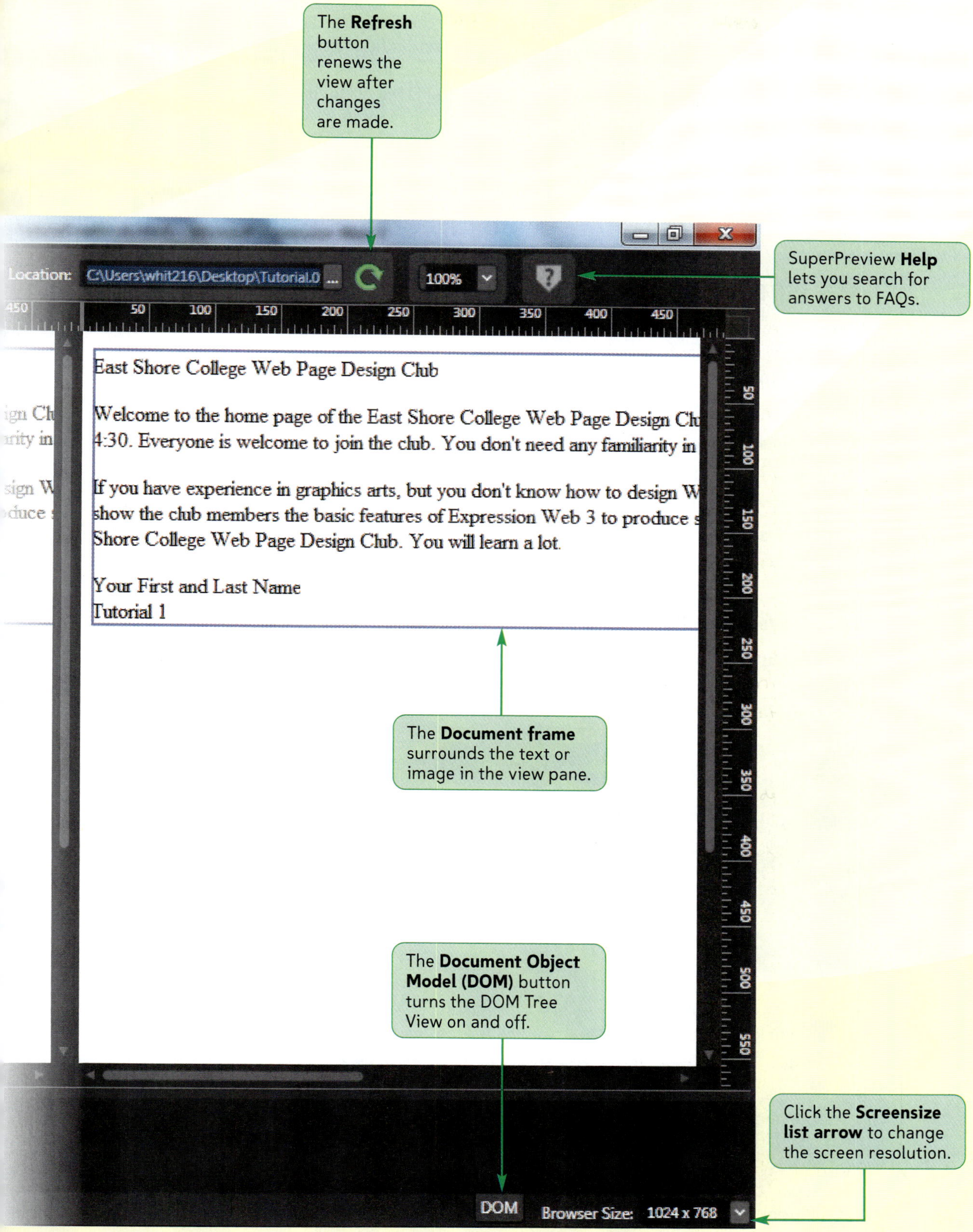

Entering Text

You type text in Expression Web just as you would if you were typing text in Microsoft Word. As you type the text, let the text wrap. You press the Enter key to create a blank line between paragraphs; press the Shift+Enter keys to end a line short of the right margin, just as if you were typing several lines for the inside address of a business letter.

Recall that a tag is a representation of an element in HTML code. A **Code tab** in the Expression Web editing window indicates what HTML tag is in effect. Because you haven't as yet created any content for the Web page, the insertion point is within the body tag. The **body tag** begins the content for your Web page. The first line of text you show Norma how to enter is the heading for the page, which is the name of the Web Page Design Club.

To enter the first line of text:

1. If necessary, start Expression Web. If the webclub.html filename appears in the Folder List panel, double-click the **webclub.html** filename to open that file, or click the **File** menu, and then click **Open File**. The Open File dialog box opens.
2. Navigate to the Tutorial.01\Tutorial folder.
3. Double-click the **webclub.html** filename. The file opens.
4. If necessary, click the **Design** button near the lower left of the screen to display Design view.
5. Click the **Panels** menu, and then click **Reset Workspace Layout**.
6. If necessary, close all toolbars other than the Common toolbar.
7. If necessary, click anywhere in the editing window, and then type **East Shore College Web Page Design Club**.
8. Press the **Enter** key. Your document should look similar to Figure 1-12.

Figure 1-12 Entering text

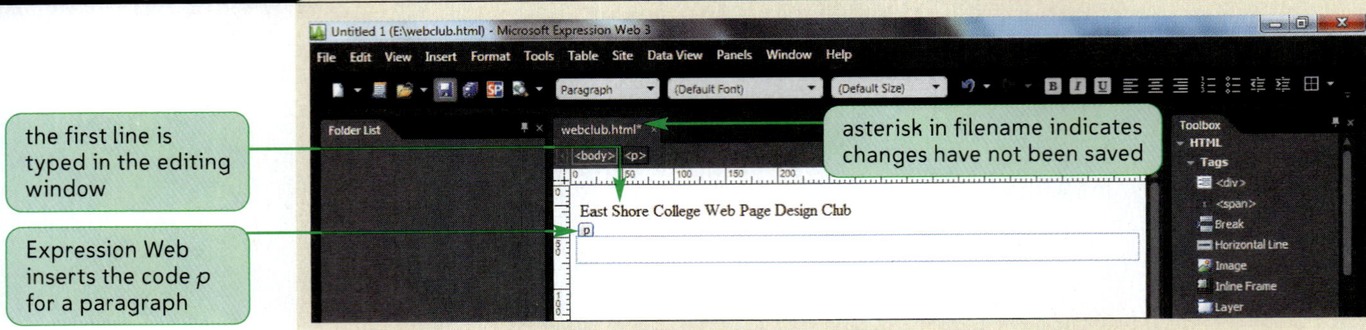

Trouble? If the line of text you just typed has a shaded background on your screen, click the View menu, point to Visual Aids, and then click Margins and Padding.

If you look closely at the editing window, you will see that several actions have occurred. Note that a *p* appears above the line where the insertion point is now positioned. The *p* is the Code tab that indicates you have typed a paragraph. Even though you have typed only one line, Expression Web considers it a paragraph unless you format the text differently. When you look at the webclub.html document tab, you'll note that an asterisk now appears to the right of the filename. The asterisk indicates that revisions have been made to the file, but have not yet been saved.

Next, you'll type two short paragraphs so that Norma can see how the text wraps as you type. It is important that you enter only one space after any punctuation mark that ends a sentence. If you enter more than one space at any time while typing, Expression Web adds the HTML special character * * to the HTML code. The * * special character is the HTML code for a nonbreaking space, and that special character enters an extra space even when the document appears in the browser. In general, you don't want your HTML code to be populated—and perhaps even overwhelmed—by nonbreaking space characters. To keep your code as simple as possible for someone who might later be using Code view to edit your document, enter only one space after any punctuation mark that ends a sentence.

Expression Web also adds the characters *'* to the code whenever you type an apostrophe. That is the HTML code for an apostrophe. In Design view, you only see the apostrophe, but if you view the file in Code view, you see *'*.

Now you'll enter the first and second paragraphs of the webclub.html Web page. Later, you'll show Norma how to use some of the editing tools in Expression Web to correct errors, so be sure to type the text exactly as you see it in the following steps, which contains intentional errors.

To enter the text for the first and second paragraphs:

1. Type the following paragraph exactly as shown, including the intentionally misspelled words "foward" and "alot." Let the text wrap as you type the paragraph:

   If you have experience in graphics arts, but you don't know how to design Web pages, please join us as well. We look foward to seeing you at the next club meeting of the East Shore College Web Page Club. You will learn alot. At our next meeting, we will have a guest speaker who will show the club members the basic features of Expression Web 3 to produce good Web pages.

2. Press the **Enter** key and then type the second paragraph exactly as shown; again, let the text wrap as you type the paragraph:

   Welcome to the home page of the East Shore College Web Page Club. We meet during the campus common hours on Tuesdays and Thursdays from 3:30 till 4:30 p.m. Everyone is welcome to join the club. You don't need any experience in creating Web pages to become a member.

3. Press the **Enter** key.
4. Type your first and last name.
5. Press the **Shift+Enter** keys.
6. Type **Tutorial 1**. Based on your monitor size, the line endings of the paragraph text might be different, but your document should look similar to the one shown in Figure 1-13.

Figure 1-13 **Document after entering text**

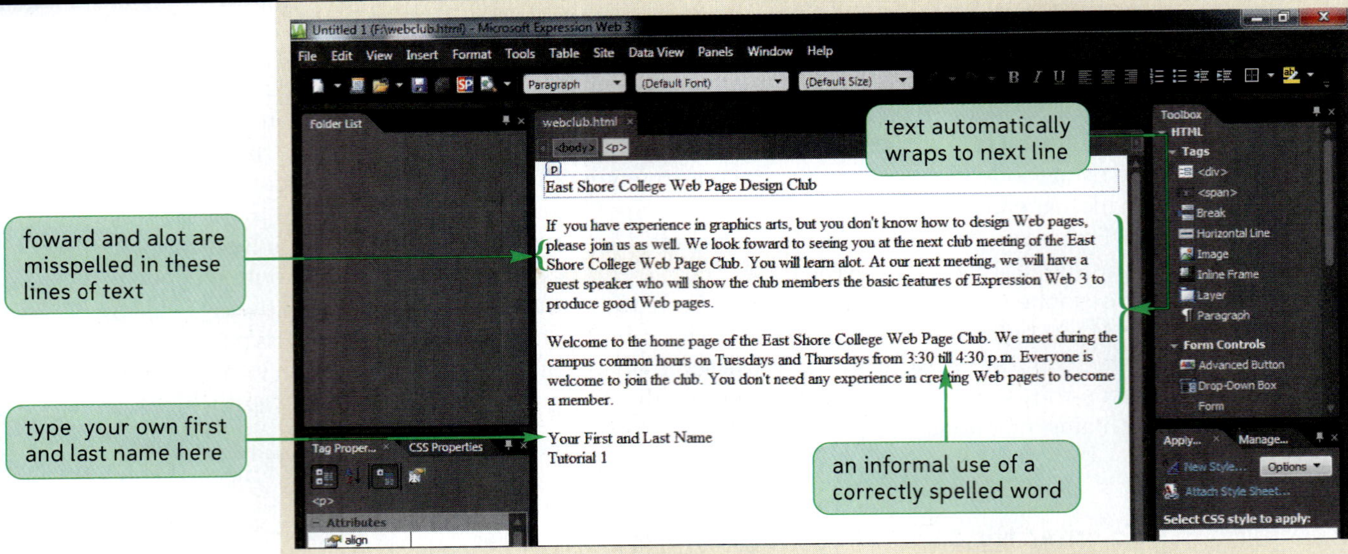

Whenever you enter new text, it is always a good idea to check it for spelling and grammar mistakes. In addition to these editing tools, Expression Web has other tools to make editing easier, which you show Norma later. You begin by showing Norma how to correct spelling errors in the document.

Using the Editing Tools

Expression Web provides editing tools that enable you to check the spelling of an Expression Web document, use the Thesaurus feature, and find and replace text or code. These editing features work very similarly to the same features found in Microsoft Word, so if you have worked with some or all of these editing tools in Microsoft Word, you should have no trouble using these features in Expression Web.

Checking the Spelling

It's always a good idea to check the spelling in text that you have entered. Web pages must be error free. Even one typographical error on a Web page can damage the credibility of the Web page. In Design view, Expression Web places a red wavy line under a word that the system dictionary identifies as misspelled, assuming the option for "Check spelling as you type" is on.

You can right-click a word that has been marked as a possible spelling error and click to replace the word with one of the choices from the shortcut menu's list of suggested words. To check the spelling of the entire document, however, it is more efficient to use the Spelling tool feature.

It is a good idea to display the Standard toolbar now because it has a button that you can click to check the document for spelling errors. The Standard toolbar contains some buttons that you won't find on the Common toolbar: Spell, Cut, Copy, Paste, and the Format Painter. You can also use the Show Formatting Marks button on the Standard toolbar to reveal nonprinting characters.

You'll display the Standard toolbar and then check the spelling of the document.

To check the spelling of the document:

1. Press the **Ctrl+Home** keys to position the insertion point at the top of the page.
2. Click the **View** menu, point to **Toolbars**, and then click **Standard**.
3. If the Standard toolbar is now on your screen as a floating toolbar, click and drag the **Standard** toolbar to a position just below the Common toolbar so that the Standard toolbar appears, as shown in Figure 1-14.

Figure 1-14 The Standard toolbar

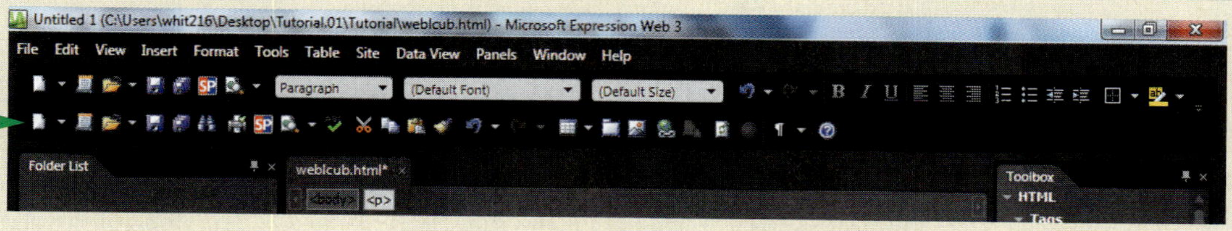

4. Click the **Spelling** button on the Standard toolbar. The Spelling dialog box opens, as shown in Figure 1-15.

Figure 1-15 The Spelling dialog box

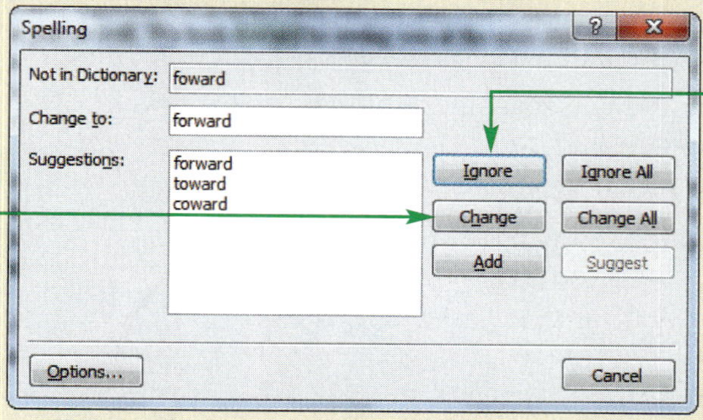

TIP

To see spelling options, click the Options button in the Spelling dialog box.

Trouble? If necessary, click and drag the title bar of the Spelling dialog box out of the way so you can see the paragraph text.

5. Currently, the word *foward* is highlighted. The word *foward* should be *forward*, so, if necessary, click **forward** in the Suggestions list, and then click the **Change** button.
6. The word *alot* should be marked next. Click **a lot** in the Suggestions list, and then click the **Change** button.
7. If the spelling check queries either or both of your first and last names, click the Ignore All button as many times as necessary.
8. When you are prompted that the spelling check is complete, click the **OK** button.

The next editing tool you'll use is the Thesaurus feature.

Using the Thesaurus Feature

The Thesaurus feature lets you look up the synonyms of a word or phrase and replace that word or phrase from a list of words that have the same or similar meaning. The Thesaurus feature is a great tool for introducing word variety in your documents. Your documents will appear more professional if you have used the appropriate word in your content and not overused that word. Norma would like to choose a more interesting word than *good,* which appears near the end of the first paragraph.

REFERENCE

Using the Editing Tools

- To access the Spelling feature, press the F7 key.
- To access the Thesaurus feature, position the insertion point within a word and then press the Shift+F7 keys.
- To access the Find and Replace feature, click the Find button on the Standard toolbar.

or

- Press the Ctrl+F keys (to Find) or the Ctrl+H keys (to Replace).

or

- Click the Edit menu, and then click Find (to Find) or click Replace (to Replace).

Although there is a button on the Standard toolbar to check spelling, the Standard toolbar does not have a button to access the Thesaurus feature. You show Norma how to use the Thesaurus feature to choose a different word to replace *good*. Norma also sees that she has used the word *experience* twice, so she also replaces the word *experience* in the last sentence of the document.

To use the Thesaurus feature:

1. In the last sentence of the first paragraph, click anywhere in the word **good**.
2. Press the **Shift+F7** keys. The Thesaurus dialog box opens, as shown in Figure 1-16.

Figure 1-16 **The Thesaurus dialog box**

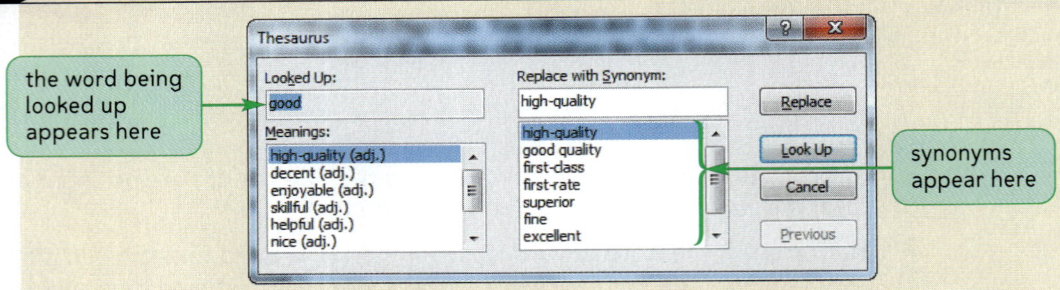

3. In the Replace with Synonym text box, click **superior**.
4. Click the **Replace** button. The word *good* is replaced with the word *superior*.
5. In the last sentence of the document, click anywhere in the word **experience**.
6. Press the **Shift+F7** keys. The Thesaurus dialog box opens again.
7. In the Replace with Synonym text box, click **familiarity**.
8. Click the **Replace** button. The word *experience* is replaced with the word *familiarity*.

The Find and Replace feature is a great tool for making global (document-wide) changes to a document. Next, you'll use the Find and Replace feature.

Using the Find and Replace Feature

Like many other Microsoft products, Expression Web has a robust Find and Replace feature. However, in addition to searching for text, you can use the Find and Replace feature to find and replace HTML code. Norma has brought to your attention that on two occasions the name of the club has not been entered correctly. It should be the "Web Page *Design* Club." You show Norma how to use the Expression Web Find and Replace feature to make the global change she wants to make.

To use the Find and Replace feature:

1. Press the **Ctrl+Home** keys to position the insertion point at the top of the page.
2. Click the **Find** button on the Standard toolbar. The Find and Replace dialog box opens. If necessary, click and drag the title bar of the Find and Replace dialog box out of the way so you can see paragraph text, as shown in Figure 1-17. (Your Find what text box might already have text or code entered from a previous user.)

Figure 1-17 The Find and Replace dialog box

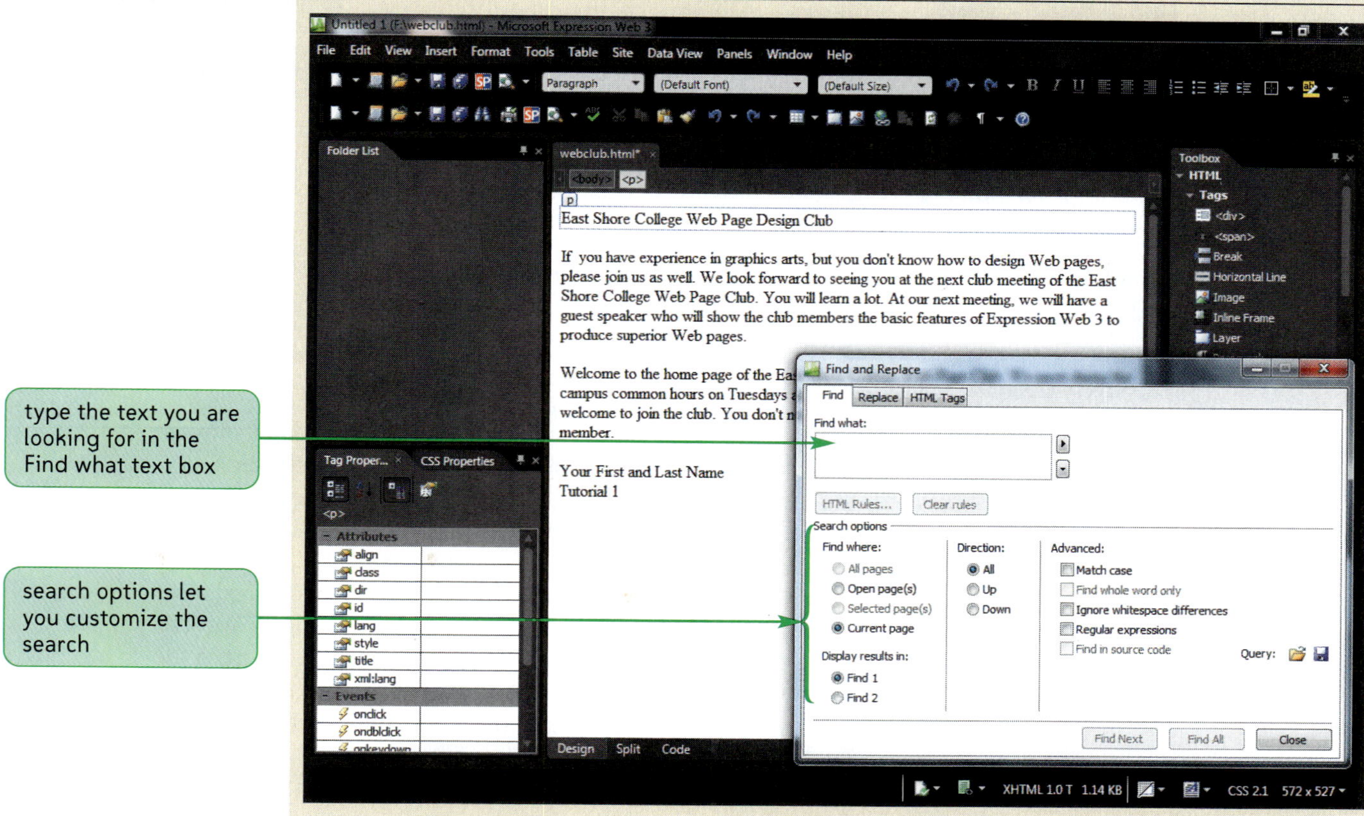

3. Click the **Replace** tab.
4. In the Find what text box, type **Web Page Club**.
5. Click in the Replace with text box. If necessary, delete any text or code in that text box.
6. Type **Web Page Design Club**.
7. Click the **Replace All** button.
8. Click the **OK** button to accept the alert that two occurrences have been replaced.
9. Perform the same steps to change "graphics arts" to "graphic arts."

10. Click the **Close** button to close the Find and Replace dialog box. Your document should look similar to Figure 1-18.

Figure 1-18 **The replaced text**

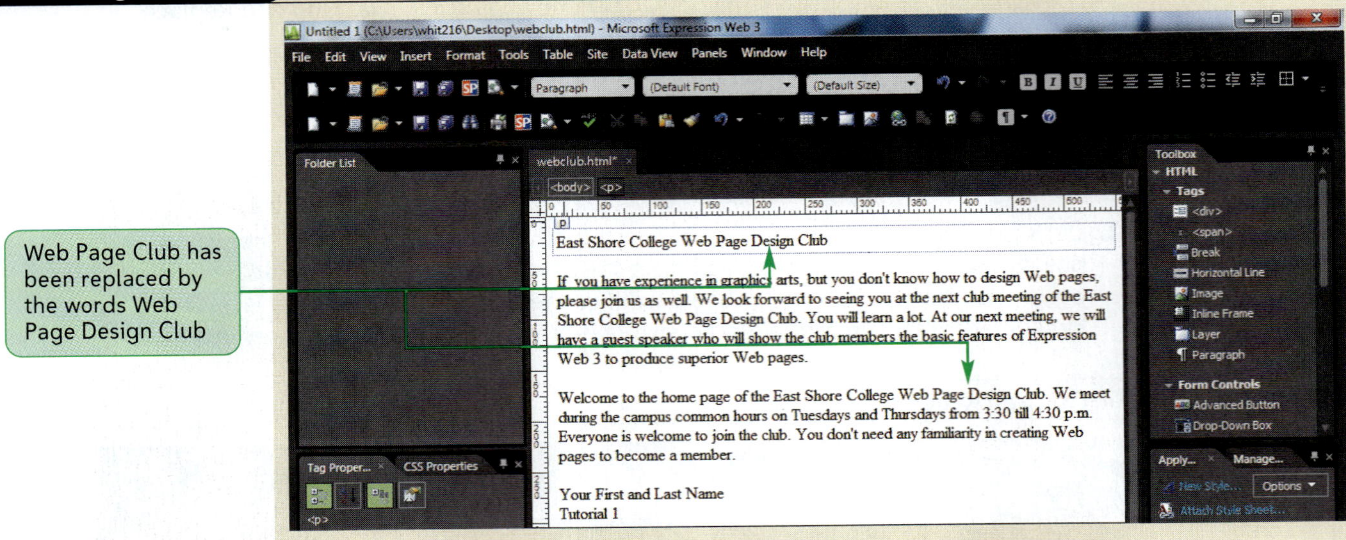

11. Click the **View** menu, point to **Toolbars**, and then click **Standard** to close the Standard toolbar.

Other convenient tools for working with text are the copy and paste tools. You'll work with these tools next.

Using Copy, Cut, and Paste

Expression Web has the same features to cut, copy, and paste text as most other software programs. However, when you cut or copy a block of text in Expression Web, such as a paragraph or a heading, you must also be mindful to select not only the text, but also the surrounding HTML code that provides the formatting for the text. You can use the Quick Tag Selector bar, often referred to as the *breadcrumb bar*, to select just the text or both the text and the surrounding HTML code. Similar to all Microsoft Office products, you can cut, copy, and paste text in Expression Web using a variety of methods. You can use keyboard shortcuts, choose options from a shortcut menu, make selections from the menu bar, and so forth. You first show Norma how to cut and paste a sentence within the same paragraph, and then you show her how to cut and paste an entire paragraph.

TIP

Clicking the Find All button in the Find and Replace dialog box creates a list of all occurrences of the search string at the bottom of the screen.

To cut and paste a sentence:

1. In the last sentence of the first paragraph, click before the letter **A** in the words, "At our next meeting . . ."
2. Click and drag to select all the words in that sentence (including the period that follows the sentence).
3. Right-click anywhere within the selected text.
4. Click **Cut** on the shortcut menu.

5. In the second sentence of the first paragraph, click before the letter **W** in the words "We look forward to seeing you . . ."
6. Right-click, and then click **Paste** on the shortcut menu.
7. Press the **spacebar** once to add a space after the period. The sentence text is pasted, as shown in Figure 1-19. (Depending on your settings, the Paste Options icon might also appear near the pasted text.)

Figure 1-19 The cut-and-pasted sentence

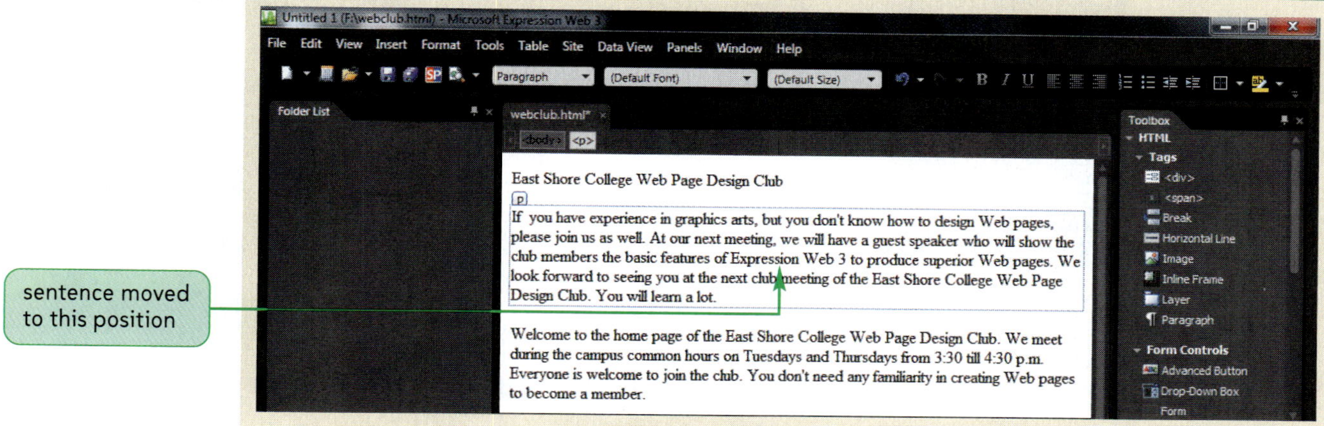

Now that the sentence has been cut and pasted, you'll cut and paste the first full paragraph of text and make it the second paragraph.

To cut and paste a paragraph:

1. If necessary, click anywhere in the first paragraph to reveal the <p> Code tab above the paragraph.
2. Click the **<p> Code tab** for the paragraph that begins with the words "If you have experience in graphic arts ... Note that the entire paragraph and the space above and below the paragraph, indicated by a shaded area, are now selected.
3. Right-click anywhere in the paragraph, and then click **Cut** on the shortcut menu.
4. Position the insertion point at the start of the line with your name.
5. Right-click, and then click **Paste** on the shortcut menu. The paragraph text is pasted, as shown in Figure 1-20. (Depending on your settings, the Paste Options icon might also appear near the pasted text.)

Figure 1-20 The cut-and-pasted paragraph

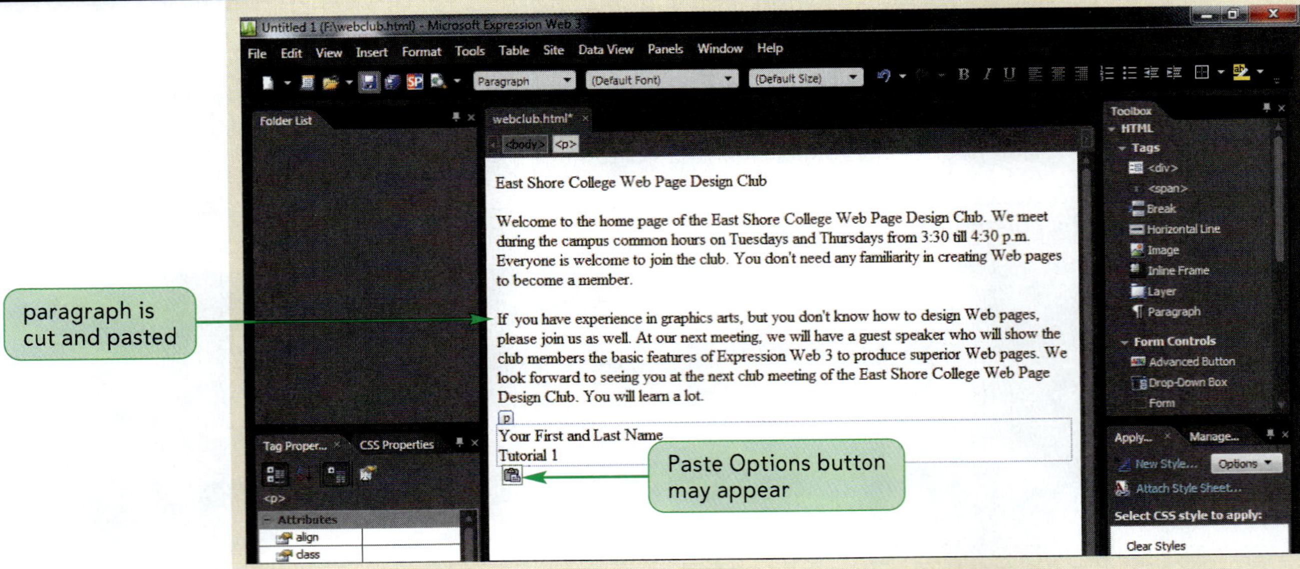

INSIGHT

Copying and Pasting from Other Applications

You can copy and paste text from another application, such as Microsoft Word, into Expression Web. Select the text in the source file, and then choose Cut or Copy. Switch to Expression Web. In Expression Web, position the insertion point where you want to paste the text. Click Edit on the menu bar, and then click Paste Text. The Paste Text dialog box opens, where you can select five options in the Paste Text dialog box. The three you will most often choose are as follows:

- *Plain text*—Pastes all of the text and removes paragraph, row, or other types of line breaks by replacing them with spaces.
- *Normal paragraphs with line breaks*—Pastes all of the text and maintains paragraph, row, or other types of line breaks by replacing them with the HTML line break tag.
- *Normal paragraphs without line breaks*—Preserves paragraph breaks, but removes line breaks. This choice is usually the best option.

TIP

To remove formatting from text within an Expression Web document, select the text, click Format on the menu bar, and then click Remove Formatting.

Next, you'll show Norma how to give the page a title that will display in the title bar when the document displays in the browser. You'll also show her how to add some identifying information—in this instance, a page description and some keywords, to the webclub.html page. This page description will not appear in either the editing window or the browser. The page description is strictly information to be used by Web page search engines. A **search engine** is specialized software whose primary function is to locate information on the Web. Popular search engines include Google and Bing.

Changing the Page Properties

The **Page Properties** dialog box allows you to enter a title for the Web page, keywords, and a description so that search engines can locate your page once it has been stored on a file server. The text you type in the Title text box is the title for your Web page, and that text will appear in the title bar at the top of the browser screen. The title should be fewer than 70 characters and briefly describe your Web page, for example, the "Web

Page Design Club." The words you type in the Keywords text box are the words that are most frequently used (or the most important words) on your Web page, such as "Web page design club Expression college meeting." Search engines use these keywords to locate your Web page. Because someone might type a misspelling when entering text in a search text box, it's a good idea to also type a few common misspellings for the keywords. The text you type in the Page description text box should be a brief summary (of one or more sentences) describing what your page is about, such as "This is the home page for the Web Page Design Club for East Shore College in Prestonville, Rhode Island."

You show Norma how to add a title, keywords, and a description to the Web page she is creating. Keywords and a description are optional, but are almost always added to every Web page.

To enter page properties:

1. In Design view, right-click a blank section of the editing window.
2. On the shortcut menu, click **Page Properties**. The Page Properties dialog box opens, as shown in Figure 1-21.

Figure 1-21 The Page Properties dialog box

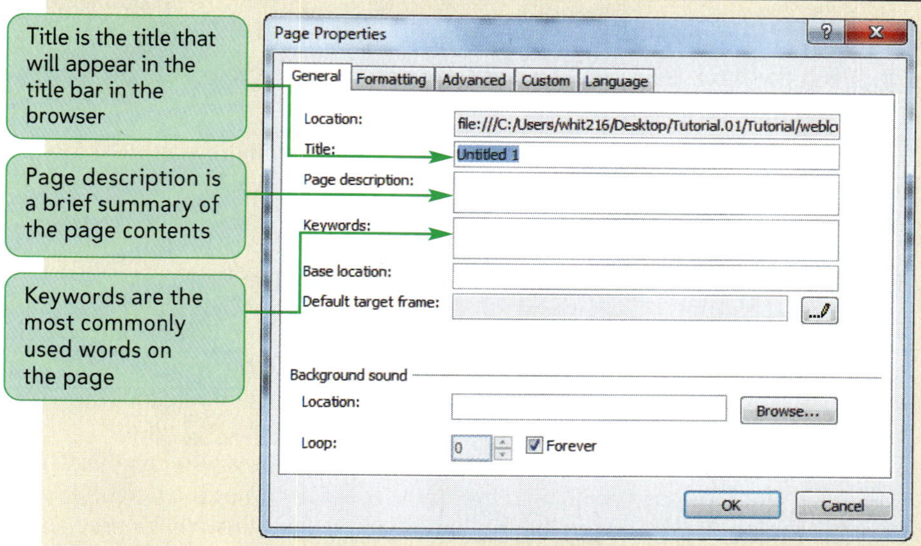

3. In the Title text box, type **East Shore College Web Page Design Club**.
4. Click in the **Page description** text box. Type **This is the home page for the Web Page Design Club**.
5. Click in the **Keywords** text box. Type **East Shore College Web Page Design Club Prestonville Rhode Island**.
6. Compare the text you typed with that shown in Figure 1-22. If necessary, correct any errors.

Figure 1-22 **The Page Properties dialog box with data**

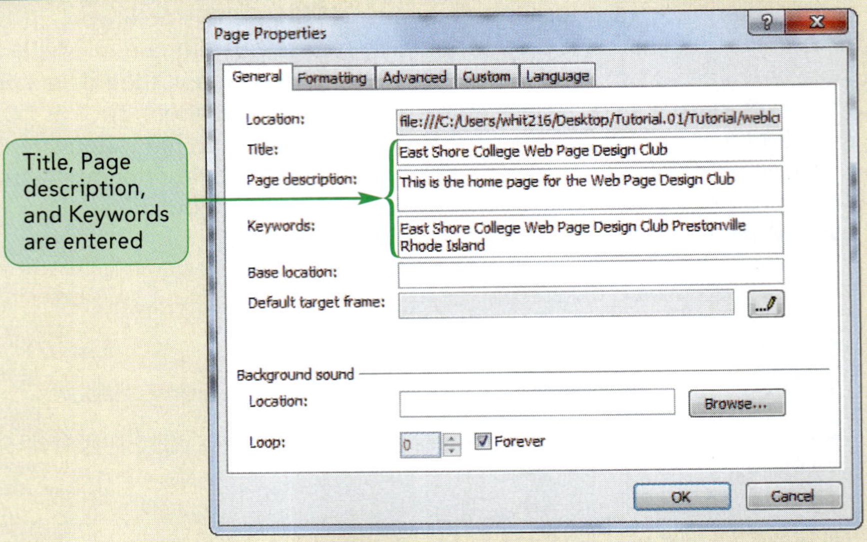

7. Click the **OK** button.
8. Click the **Save** button on the Common toolbar.

Now that you have saved the file, you can show Norma how to view the file in the default browser.

Viewing the File in the Browser

You have several options for viewing the file in the browser. Which one you choose is mostly a matter of preference. The **default browser** is the browser you select to preview a page. By default, Internet Explorer is selected. To change the default browser, click the list arrow to the right of the Preview in Browser button on the Common toolbar. The **browser list** is the list of browsers and browser versions you have installed on your computer. The browser you click in the browser list becomes the default browser. You have the option of previewing the file only in the default browser or previewing the file in all of the browsers you have installed on your computer. You must save the file before you preview a file in the browser.

REFERENCE

Previewing a File in the Browser

- To preview a file in the default browser, save the file, and then press the F12 function key.
- Click the File menu, point to Preview in Browser, and then click any of the browsers in the browser list.

or

- Click the Preview in Browser button on the Common toolbar. Click the drop-down list to the right of the Preview button to select the default browser.

or

- To preview a file in split screen, click the Panels menu, and then click Snapshot.
- To view the file in another installed browser, click the list arrow to the right of the browser name on the Browser tab.

You'll show Norma how to preview the file in the default browser.

To view the file in your default browser:

1. Press the **F12** key. The document appears in your default browser. Norma's default browser is Internet Explorer 8, as shown in Figure 1-23.

Figure 1-23 The document in the default browser

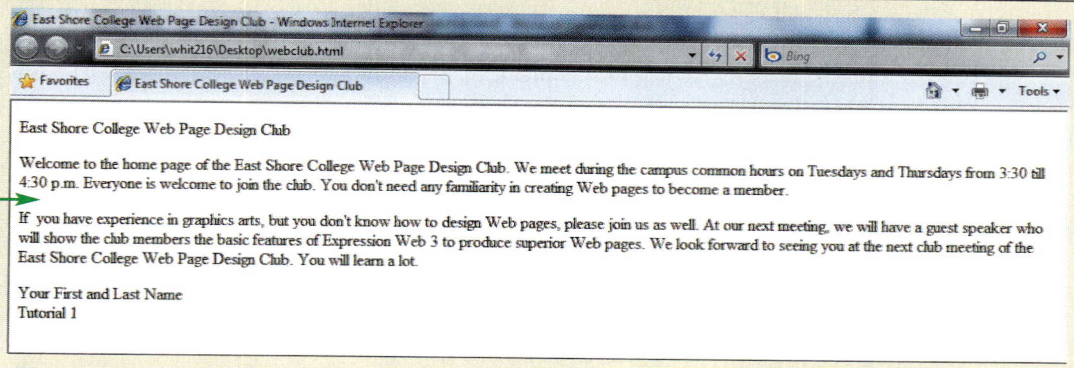

document shown in Internet Explorer 8; your document might differ

2. Close the browser.

Next, you'll use Snapshot view to view, the file in the browser without having to close the Design view window.

Using the Snapshot View

Snapshot view previews your file in the default browser, but it does so in a split screen mode, which makes document comparisons much easier than having to switch between browsers using the Windows taskbar. In Snapshot view, the top pane shows your document in Design view. The bottom pane shows your document as it would appear in your default browser. You can change the size of the split screen by passing the mouse pointer over the gray area between Design view and Snapshot view.

When you see the resize pointer ↕, you can click and drag to see more (or less) of the document in Snapshot view. You'll show Norma how to enter Snapshot view now.

TIP

In addition to using the vertical scroll bar, you can drag the hand cursor to scroll up or down in Snapshot view.

To view the file in Snapshot view:

1. If necessary, save the file.
2. In Design view, click the **Panels** menu, and then click **Snapshot**. The document appears in split screen, as shown in Figure 1-24.

Figure 1-24 The document split screen Snapshot view

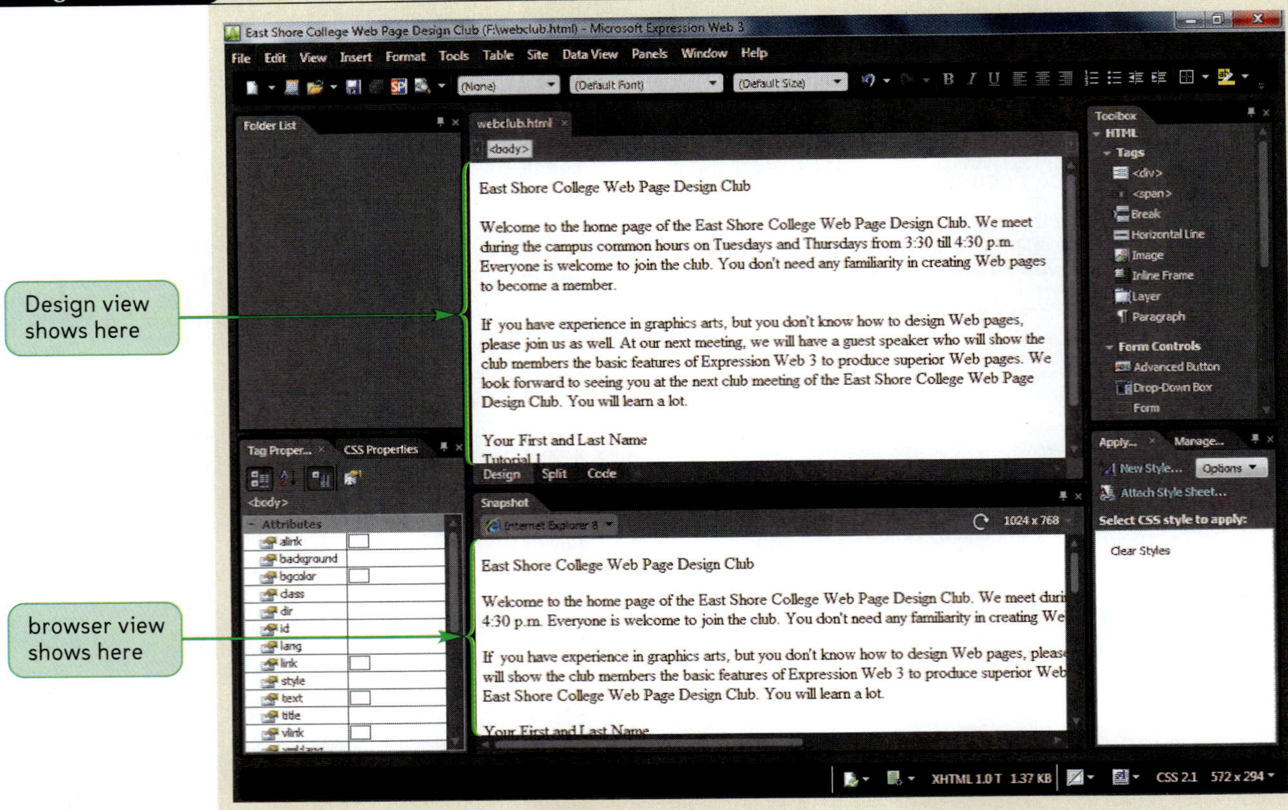

3. In the upper-right corner of the Snapshot view pane, click the **Close** button.

Now that you have shown Norma how to view the file in the default browser and shown her Snapshot view, you'll now show her an even more powerful feature, the SuperPreview feature.

Using SuperPreview

Expression Web has several methods of previewing a file in multiple browsers. For example, if you click File on the menu bar, point to Preview in Browser, and then click Preview in Multiple Browsers, the file first opens in the default browser and then opens in the most recent version of each browser you have installed. When you choose this method, only one browser occupies the screen at a time.

REFERENCE

Previewing a File in SuperPreview

- To preview a file in SuperPreview, save the file.
- Press the Shift+F12 function key.
- Click the Display in SuperPreview button on the Common toolbar.

or

- Click File on the menu bar, and then click Display in SuperPreview.

Unlike other methods of previewing the same file in multiple browsers, SuperPreview makes comparing how your document will appear in different browsers or browser versions a very simple task. **SuperPreview** allows you to view the same document in different browsers or different versions of the same browser in a split screen. The **Baseline browser** is the default browser. The **Comparison browser** is the browser against which you are comparing the presently opened file. Figure 1-25 shows the webclub.html file in SuperPreview as it appears in Internet Explorer and the Firefox browsers.

Figure 1-25 **SuperPreview of the webclub file**

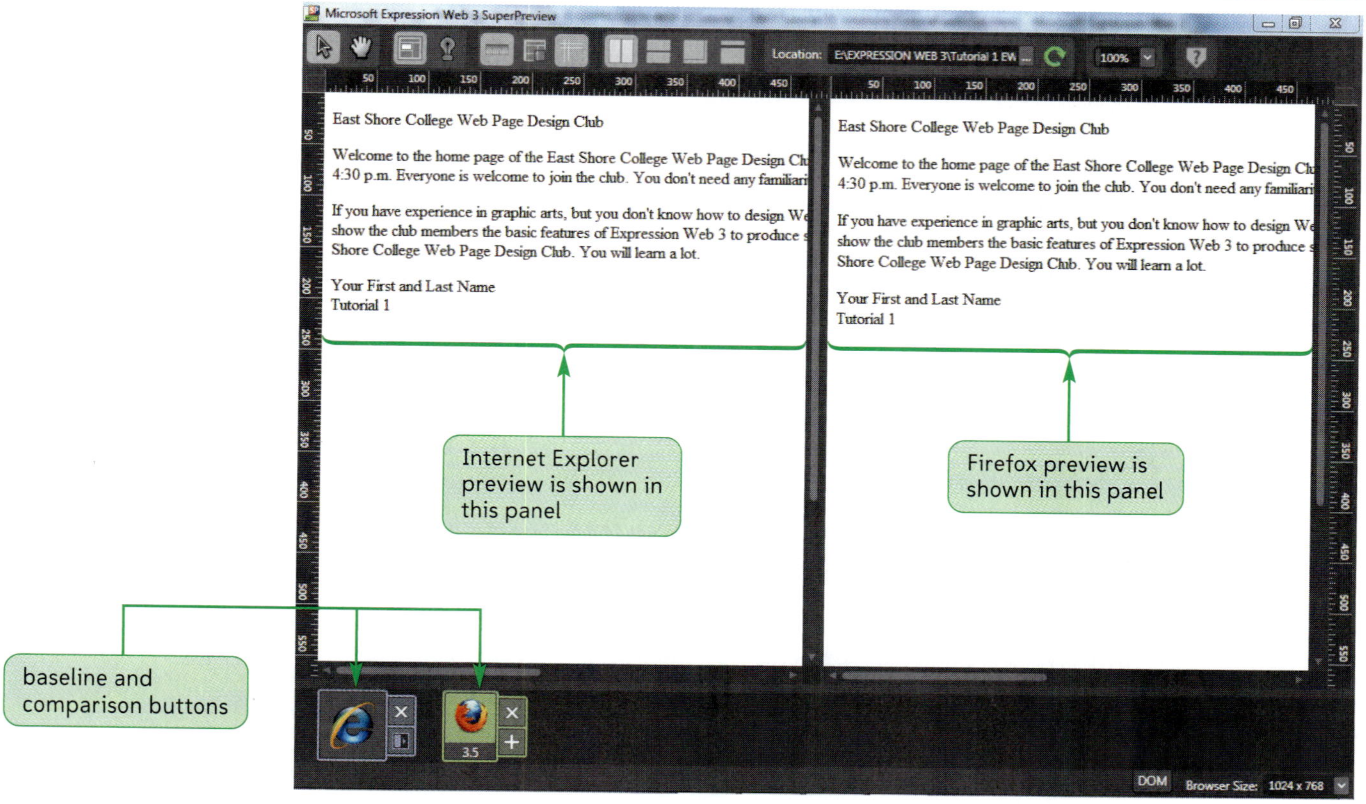

If your screen does not match, it's because the settings made by the last user are still in effect. You change the settings in the next steps. If you have a new installation of Expression Web 3 and this is the first time you are using SuperPreview, you will have to manually select a browser and version in both the Baseline and Comparison panes, and then click the Submit button (green arrow) to the right of the Location text box. Just right-click either pane and click Close Browser. Click the Baseline browser location button and then click the icon of the installed browser you want as the baseline browser. Follow the same steps for the Comparison browser, except just click a browser icon to select the Comparison browser.

The SuperPreview toolbar is divided into four groups of buttons. The functions of the first group, which control selection, are as follows:

- *Selection Mode* allows you to select individual sections for comparison.
- *Panning Mode* lets you drag the page upward or downward.

The second group of buttons controls highlighting. The functions of the second group are as follows:

- *Box Highlighting Mode* highlights the selected element in blue in the Baseline browser view. The selected element is highlighted in green in the comparison browser view.
- *Lights-Out Highlighting Mode* highlights just the selected element while dimming (graying out) the remainder of the page.

The third group of buttons is the Toggle buttons. Clicking a Toggle button activates the function; clicking the Toggle button again deactivates the function. One or more of the buttons can be active at any time. If the button has a light gray background, the button feature is active. If the button does not have a light gray background, the feature is toggled off. The functions of this group of buttons are as follows:

- *Toggle Ruler Visibility* shows vertical and horizontal rulers along the top and left sides of the view.
- *Toggle Thumbnail Visibility* shows a very small thumbnail image of the page in the lower-right corner of the preview window. Click anywhere on the thumbnail image to view only that region of the page.
- *Toggle Guide Visibility* lets you add positioning guides to assist in evaluating the positioning of multiple elements in a page.

The fourth group of buttons controls the split and layout. By default, the comparison appears as a vertical split layout. The functions of these buttons are as follows:

- *Vertical Split Layout* compares browser views side by side.
- *Horizontal Split Layout* compares browser views with one browser view on the top and the other on the bottom.
- *Overlay Layout* compares browser views by overlaying one browser view on top of another. (It can be difficult to read the result.)
- *Single Layout* displays a single browser view, similar to pressing the F12 key.

PROSKILLS

Decision Making: Previewing Pages in Multiple Browsers

In the workplace, follow your firm's best practices for determining to what extent your pages should be compatible across all browsers. The leading contemporary browsers are Microsoft Internet Explorer, Mozilla Firefox, Google Chrome, Apple Safari, and Opera. If you are designing pages for a corporate intranet, a Web site that will only be viewed by workers within your own company, you need to design your pages to be compatible with the most recent and perhaps the previous version of the preferred browser within that company. When designing pages for the Internet, you should develop your pages to display correctly in at least the most recent version of all of the contemporary browsers. To widen your audience even further, you might want to also design your pages to be compatible with the previous versions of the contemporary browsers as well. Keep your target audience in mind when deciding which browsers to support.

The Baseline and Comparison buttons are in the lower-left corner of the preview window. The Baseline button allows you to switch the location of the baseline and comparison browsers, such as moving the comparison browser to the left and the baseline browser to the right. Clicking the plus sign in the comparison browser button lets you add other browsers or browser versions to the screen (up to eight comparisons can be displayed at one time). Clicking the Close button allows you to choose different browsers for each window.

The Location text box shows the URL of the file being shown as the baseline file. To view a different file, click the ellipsis to the right of the text box. Click the DOM button in the status bar to view the document tree. You show Norma how to obtain a comparison between the Internet Explorer browser and the Firefox browser.

Complete the following steps only if there is more than one browser or more than one version of the same browser installed on your computer.

TIP

To revise the setup comparison, right-click either browser window, click Close Browser, and then click a browser icon.

To view the file in different browsers:

1. Click anywhere in the document.
2. Press the **Shift+F12** keys. The document appears in SuperPreview.
3. Click the **Lights-Out Highlighting Mode** button at the top of the screen. Click anywhere in the first paragraph. Note that only the first paragraph is now highlighted; the remainder of the document is dimmed.
4. Click anywhere outside the first paragraph. The view returns to normal.
5. Click the **Horizontal Split Layout** button at the top of the screen. The documents appear at the top and bottom of the screen.
6. Click the **Vertical Split Layout** button at the top of the screen. The documents appear side by side.
7. Click the **Single Layout** button at the top of the screen. Only the Baseline browser view appears (only one document appears on the screen).
8. Press the **Alt+F4** keys to close SuperPreview and return to Design view.

You'll explore the Expression Web Help feature to learn more about the program and do troubleshooting on your own.

Accessing the Help Feature

Expression Web has an excellent Help feature that can assist you in learning about any aspect of Expression Web. Help has a toolbar with buttons that allow you to view or print a Help topic. The Help screen has three tabs: Contents, which has folders on major topics that you can expand to see greater detail; Index, where you can see an index of all the topics; and Search, where you can input keywords to search for help on a topic.

To access Expression Web Help:

1. Press the **F1** key. The Expression Web Help screen appears, as shown in Figure 1-26.

Figure 1-26 The Expression Web Help screen

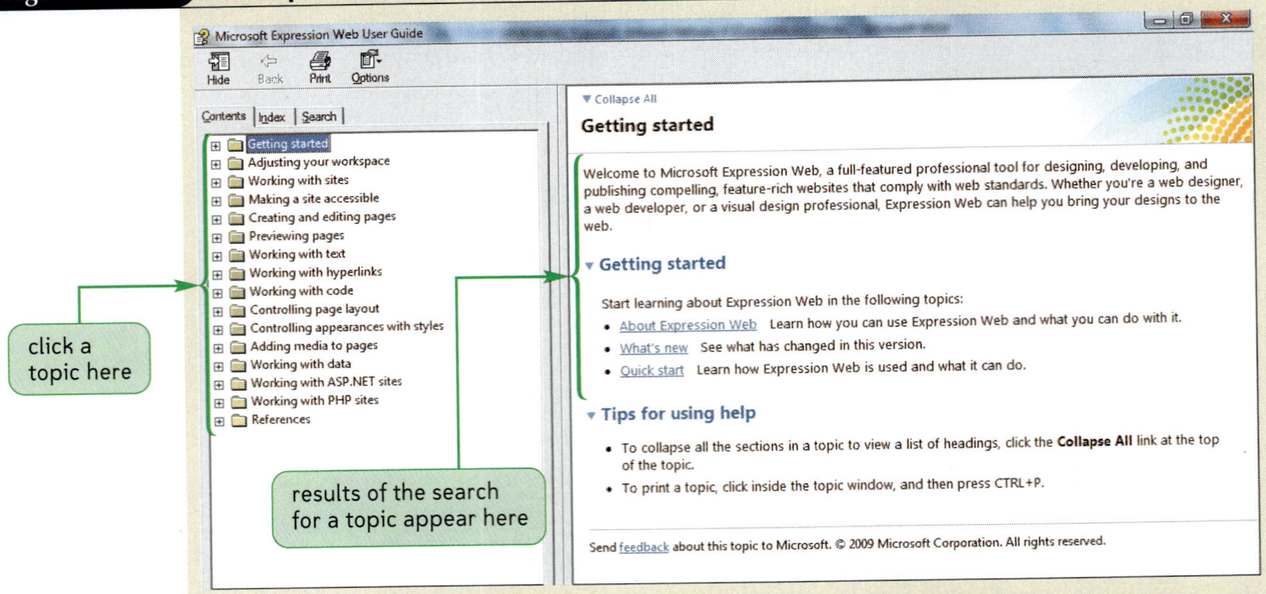

2. If necessary, click the **Index** tab.
3. In the Type in the keyword to find text box, type **undoing**.
4. Press the **Enter** key. The Undo or redo actions Help panel opens, as shown in Figure 1-27.

Figure 1-27 Help for undoing and redoing

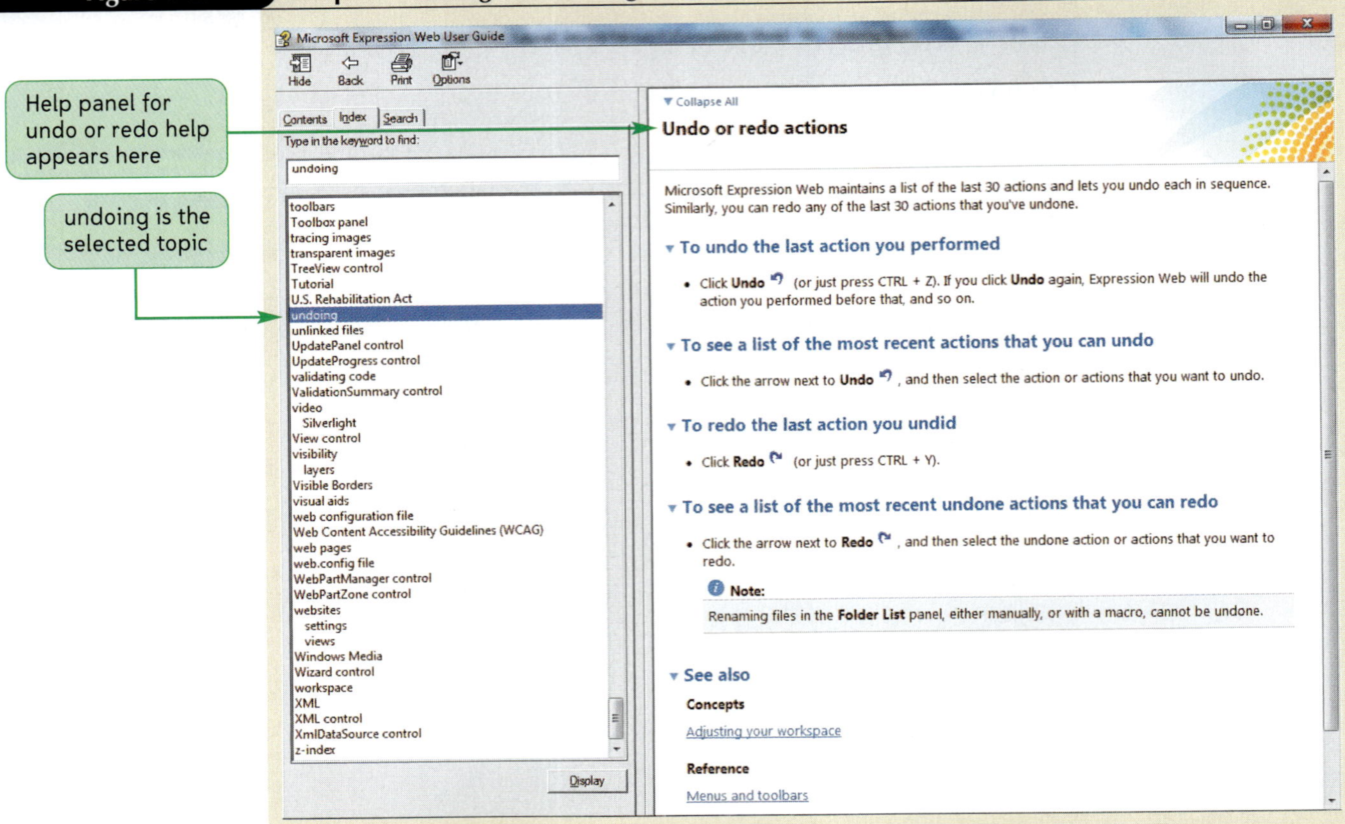

5. When you are done reviewing the Help panel, press the **Alt+F4** keys to exit Expression Web Help.

Finally, you'll show Norma how to print the document in Expression Web.

Printing a File

You can print a file in Expression Web as you would in many other Windows programs, such as by pressing the Ctrl+P keys. You'll use the keyboard shortcut to print the file in Design view.

To print the file:

1. In Design view in Expression Web, press the **Ctrl+P** keys.
2. When the Print dialog box opens, click the **OK** button.
3. Submit the completed file to your instructor, either in printed or electronic form, as requested.

You have successfully created, saved, displayed, and printed your first Web page. Now, you'll close the page.

To close the Web page:

1. On the menu bar, click **File**, and then click **Close**. (If you are prompted to save your changes, click the Yes button.)
2. If you will not be completing the Review Assignment, exit Expression Web.

REVIEW

Session 1.2 Quick Check

1. What two commonly used editing tools are available in Expression Web?
2. Can you access the Find and Replace feature from the Common toolbar?
3. If you are moving or copying a paragraph or several paragraphs, what must you also select in addition to the text?
4. In what dialog box do you enter information about the keywords and a document description?
5. What is the purpose of entering keywords and a document description?
6. What function key do you press to preview the document in the default browser?
7. How do you set the choice for the default browser?
8. Which feature allows you to view your document in more than one browser using a split screen view?

Practice the skills you learned in the tutorial.

PRACTICE

Review Assignments

There are no Data Files needed for these Review Assignments.

Norma would like to create another Web page for the Web Page Design Club. She will be introducing Expression Web to the club members at the next meeting, and wants to compose an announcement for the meeting. Figure 1-28 shows a preview of how the completed document should appear after you have typed it, but before you edit it.

Figure 1-28

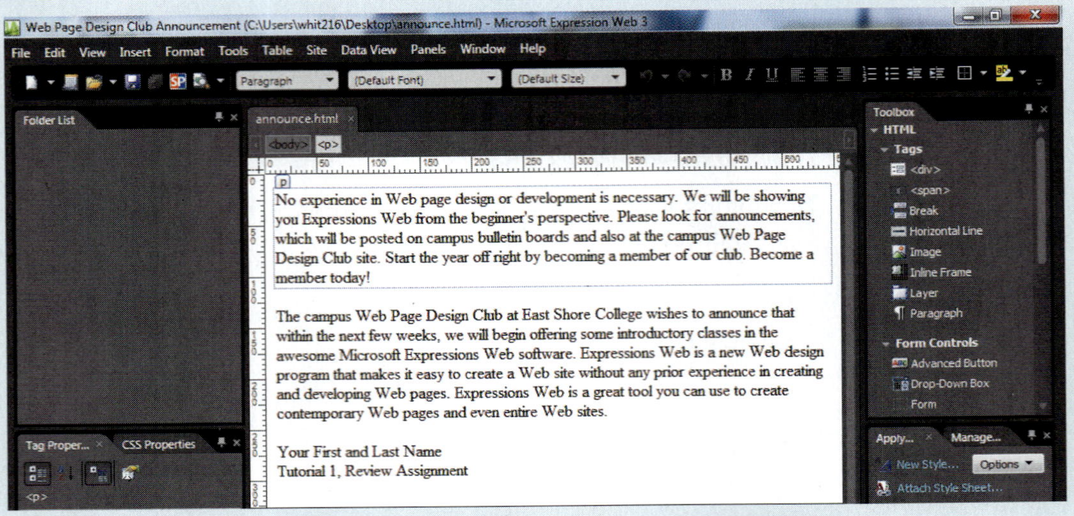

Complete the following:

1. If necessary:
   - Start Expression Web.
   - Close any open sites.
   - If necessary, create a new document.
   - Reset the workspace layout.
   - Close any toolbars other than the Common toolbar.
   - Switch to Design view.
2. In Design view, open the Page Properties dialog box. In the Title text box, type **Web Page Design Club Announcement**.
3. In the Page description text box, type your first and last name, type /, and then type **Tutorial 1, Review Assignment**. Click the OK.
4. In Design view, type the following two paragraphs. Press the Enter key after you type the first paragraph; otherwise, let the text wrap as you type the two paragraphs. (*Note*: Text you need to type is shown in bold for ease of reference only; do not bold the text unless otherwise instructed.)

   No experience in Web page design or development is necessary. We will be showing you Expressions Web from the beginner's perspective. Please look for announcements, which will be posted on campus bulletin boards and also at the campus Web Page Design Club site. Start the year off right by becoming a member of our club. Become a member today!

The campus Web Page Design Club at East Shore College wishes to announce that within the next few weeks, we will begin offering some introductory classes in the awesome Microsoft Expressions Web software. Expressions Web is a new Web design program that makes it easy to create a Web site without any prior experience in creating and developing Web pages. Expressions Web is a great tool you can use to create contemporary Web pages and even entire Web sites.

5. After you type the second paragraph, press the Enter key.
6. Type the following text as shown.
   Your First and Last Name
   Tutorial 1, Review Assignment
7. Save the file as **announce** in the Tutorial.01\Review folder.
8. Use the Thesaurus feature and replace the word *awesome* in the first sentence of the second paragraph with a word similar in meaning.
9. Position the insertion point at the top of the page. Use the Find and Replace feature to replace all instances of *Expressions Web* with *Expression Web 3*.
10. Check the spelling in the document and correct any typographical errors you find.
11. Use the cut-and-paste feature to make the first paragraph the second paragraph. (Click the p Code tab to select the first paragraph and cut the paragraph. Paste the paragraph at the start of the line with your name.)
12. Save the file. Open the **announce.html** file in your default browser.
13. Close the browser.
14. If your computer has more than one browser or browser version installed, view the file in SuperPreview. Click each one of the four Layout buttons to preview your file in the different layout views. Close SuperPreview.
15. Close all documents.
16. Submit the completed file to your instructor, either in printed or electronic form, as requested.

Create a Web page about Benjamin Franklin.

APPLY

Case Problem 1

There are no Data Files needed for this Case Problem.

The Legacy of Ben Franklin You have been asked to create a Web page that briefly describes the accomplishments of Ben Franklin, one of America's most famous founding fathers. Although your file might appear somewhat differently, a preview of the file (before revisions) appears in Figure 1-29.

Figure 1-29

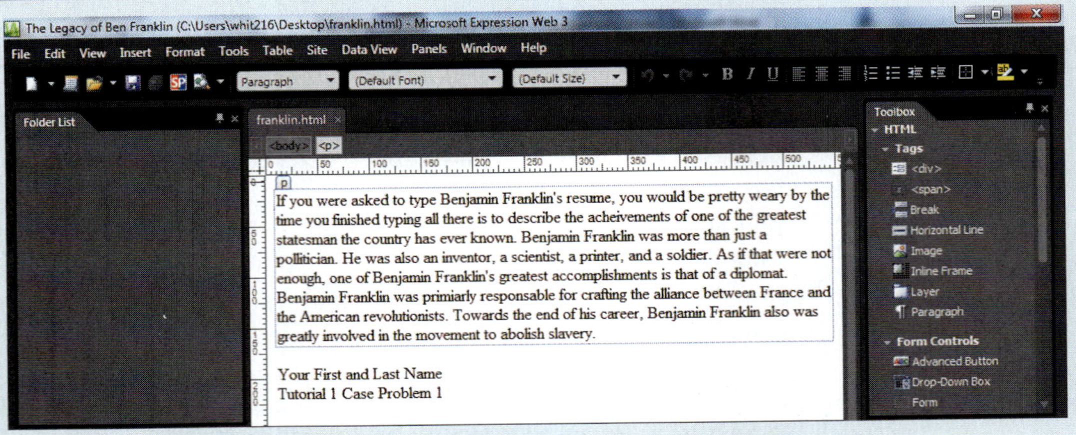

Complete the following:

1. If necessary, start Expression Web and close any open sites. Reset the workspace layout.
2. If a new blank page is not already on your screen in Design view, click the New Document button on the Common toolbar to create a new document. If necessary, switch to Design view.
3. In Design view, open the Page Properties and type the title **The Legacy of Ben Franklin**. In the Page description text box, type your first and last name, type / (a forward slash character), and then type **Tutorial 1, Case Problem 1**.
4. In Design view, type the following paragraph exactly, including the spelling errors. Let the text wrap as you type the paragraph. (*Note*: Text you need to type is shown in bold for ease of reference only; do not bold the text unless otherwise instructed.)

   If you were asked to type Benjamin Franklin's resume, you would be pretty weary by the time you finished typing all there is to describe the acheivements of one of the greatest statesman the country has ever known. Benjamin Franklin was more than just a pollitician. He was also an inventor, a scientist, a printer, and a soldier. As if that were not enough, one of Benjamin Franklin's greatest accomplishments is that of a diplomat. Benjamin Franklin was primiarly responsable for crafting the alliance between France and the American revolutionists. Towards the end of his career, Benjamin Franklin also was greatly involved in the movement to abolish slavery.
5. After you type the paragraph, press the Enter key.
6. Type the following text.

   Your First and Last Name
   Tutorial 1, Case Problem 1
7. Save the file as **franklin** in the Tutorial.01\Case1 folder.
8. Position the insertion point at the top of the page.
9. Display the Standard toolbar.
10. Check the spelling in the document. Correct all errors.
11. Use the Find and Replace feature to replace all instances of *Benjamin* with *Ben*.
12. Hide the Standard toolbar.
13. Save the file.
14. View the document using the Snapshot panel. Click the Close button in the Snapshot panel to close it.
15. Close the **franklin.html** document.
16. Submit the completed file to your instructor, either in printed or electronic form, as requested.

Create a Web page about a marketing principle.

APPLY

Case Problem 2

There are no Data Files needed for this Case Problem.

The Window of Opportunity You have been asked to write a Web page about the marketing principle known as the window of opportunity. Although your file might appear somewhat differently, a preview of the file before revisions appears in Figure 1-30.

Figure 1-30

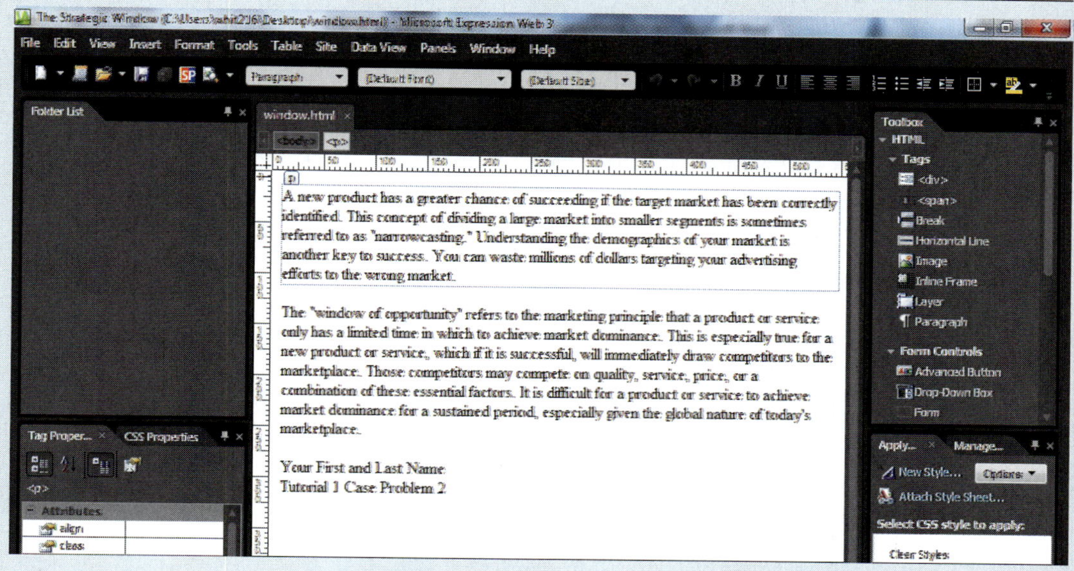

Complete the following:

1. If necessary, start Expression Web. If necessary, in Expression Web, close any open sites and create a new document. Reset the workspace layout.
2. In Design view, open the Page Properties and type the title **The Strategic Window**. In the Page description text box, type your first and last name, type / (a forward slash character), type **Tutorial 1, Case Problem 2**.
3. In Design view, type the following two paragraphs. Press the Enter key after you type the first paragraph; otherwise, let the text wrap as you type the two paragraphs. (*Note*: Text you need to type is shown in bold for ease of reference only; do not bold the text unless otherwise instructed.)

   A new product has a greater chance of succeeding if the target market has been correctly identified. This concept of dividing a large market into smaller segments is sometimes referred to as "narrowcasting." Understanding the demographics of your market is another key to success. You can waste millions of dollars targeting your advertising efforts to the wrong market.

   The "window of opportunity" refers to the marketing principle that a product or service only has a limited time in which to achieve market dominance. This is especially true for a new product or service, which if it is successful, will immediately draw competitors to the marketplace. Those competitors may compete on quality, service, price, or a combination of these essential factors. It is difficult for a product or service to achieve market dominance for a sustained period, especially given the global nature of today's marketplace.
4. After you type the second paragraph, press the Enter key.
5. Type the following text.

   Your First and Last Name
   Tutorial 1, Case Problem 2

6. Save the file as **window** in the Tutorial.01\Case2 folder.
7. Check the spelling in the document. Correct all errors you find, and then close the dialog box when the spelling check is complete.
8. Use the cut-and-paste feature to make the second paragraph the first paragraph.
9. Position the insertion point at the beginning of the document.
10. Switch to Code view. In Code view, delete the letter *b* in the start <body> tag. Note the color of the end </body> tag and the end </html> tag, which signifies there is an error in the HTML code.
11. Retype the letter **b** to restore the start <body> tag. The code should no longer indicate an error.
12. In Code view, position the insertion point on the blank line below the start <body> tag. Press the Ctrl+/ (the forward slash) keys to enter the code for an HTML comment. Type your first and last name between the <!-- and --> HTML comment characters.
13. In Code view, and between the start <title> and end </title> tags, change the document title from "The Strategic Window" to "The Window of Opportunity."
14. In Code view, delete any instances (if any) of " " that might be in your code. When you are done, switch back to Design view.
15. Save the file.
16. View the file in your default browser and then close the browser.
17. Close the **window.html** document.
18. Submit the completed file to your instructor, either in printed or electronic form, as requested.

Expand your skills to create and style a Web page about academic integrity.

CREATE

Case Problem 3

There are no Data Files needed for this Case Problem.

Academic Integrity The Computer Science Department at Villone Community College in Charleston, Nebraska, is creating a Web page to be posted at the department's Web site. You have been asked to enter some text for a document that will highlight the importance of students maintaining academic integrity. Although your file might appear somewhat differently, a preview of the file before revisions appears in Figure 1-31.

Figure 1-31

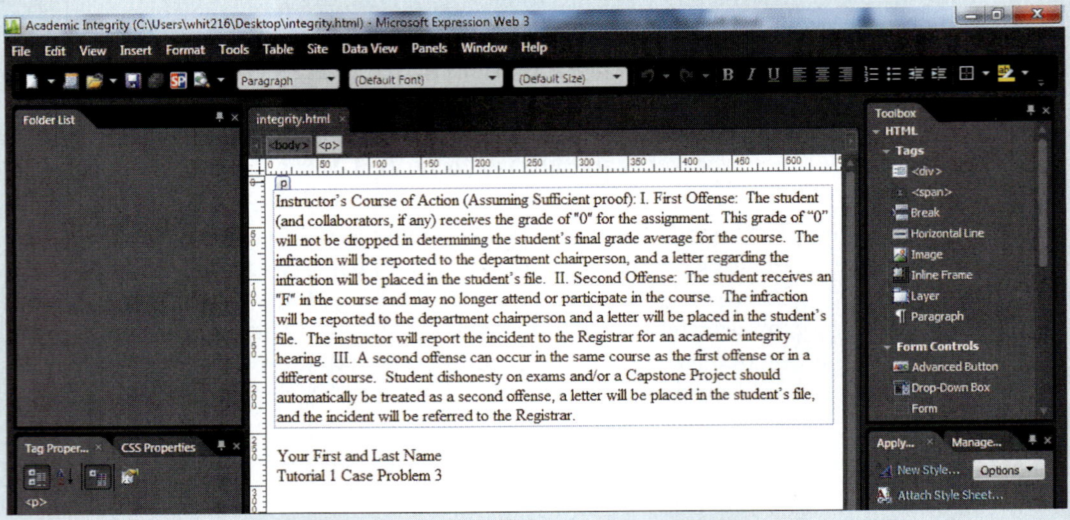

Complete the following:

1. If necessary, start Expression Web. If necessary, in Expression Web, close any open sites and create a new document. Reset the workspace layout.
2. In Design view, name the page **Academic Integrity**. In the Page description text box, type your first and last name, type / (a forward slash character), and type **Tutorial 1, Case Problem 3**.
3. In Design view, type the following paragraph. Let the text wrap as you type the paragraph. (*Note*: Text you need to type is shown in bold for ease of reference only; do not bold the text unless otherwise instructed.)

   Instructor's Course of Action (Assuming Sufficient proof): I. First Offense: The student (and collaborators, if any) receives the grade of "0" for the assignment. This grade of "0" will not be dropped in determining the student's final grade average for the course. The infraction will be reported to the department chairperson, and a letter regarding the infraction will be placed in the student's file. II. Second Offense: The student receives an "F" in the course and may no longer attend or participate in the course. The infraction will be reported to the department chairperson and a letter will be placed in the student's file. The instructor will report the incident to the Registrar for an academic integrity hearing. III. A second offense can occur in the same course as the first offense or in a different course. Student dishonesty on exams and/or a Capstone Project should automatically be treated as a second offense, a letter will be placed in the student's file, and the incident will be referred to the Registrar.
4. Press the **Enter** key.
5. Type the following text (press the Shift+Enter keys after you type your name).

   Your First and Last Name
   Tutorial 1, Case Problem 3
6. Check the spelling in the document. Correct any errors you might find.
7. Position the insertion point at the top of the page. Use the Find and Replace feature to replace all instances of *Registrar* with *Dean of Students*.
8. There are three instances of the word *infraction* in the document. Use the Thesaurus feature to find an appropriate synonym for *infraction* so that the word *infraction* is used not more than twice in the document.
9. Insert blank lines before the first, second, and third Roman numerals so that each Roman numeral starts a separate paragraph.
10. Save the file as **integrity** in the Tutorial.01\Case3 folder.
11. View the file in your default browser and then close the browser.
12. Submit the completed file to your instructor, either in printed or electronic form, as requested.

Use the Help feature to create an information Web page on SuperPreview.

RESEARCH

Case Problem 4

There are no Data Files needed for this Case Problem.

Using the Help Feature Use the Help feature to compose several paragraphs about how to use the SuperPreview feature.

Complete the following:

1. If necessary, start your browser and then start Expression Web. If necessary, in Expression Web, close any open sites, and create a new document. Reset the workspace layout.
2. In Design view, open the Page Properties dialog box, then in the Title text box, type **Using the Help Feature**. In the Page description text box, type your first and last name, type / (a forward slash character), and type **Tutorial 1, Case Problem 4**.
3. EXPLORE In Design view, type several paragraphs about how to use the SuperPreview feature. In your document, include information about how to display a page in SuperPreview, pointer modes, DOM highlighting, ruler display, and thumbnail display. Press the Enter key after you type each paragraph. Let the text wrap as you type each paragraph.
4. After you have composed your document, type the following text as indicated. (*Note*: Text you need to type is shown in bold for ease of reference only; do not bold the text unless otherwise instructed.)

   Your First and Last Name
   Tutorial 1, Case Problem 4
5. Check the spelling in the document. Correct all errors you might find.
6. Save the file as **help** in the Tutorial.01\Case4 folder.
7. View the file in your default browser and then close the browser.
8. Close all documents.
9. Submit the completed file to your instructor, either in printed or electronic form, as requested.

ENDING DATA FILES

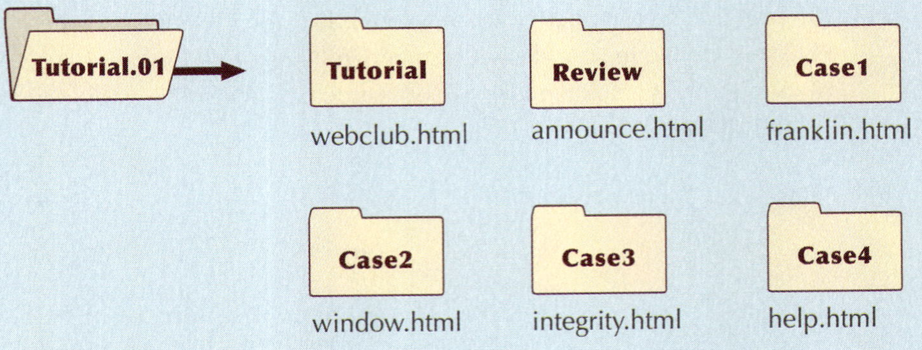

TUTORIAL 2

Formatting Text

Using the Common Toolbar to Format Text

OBJECTIVES

Session 2.1

- Learn the functions of the Common toolbar
- Change the size of text
- Discern which fonts to use on a Web page
- Check the document for spelling

Session 2.2

- Create a list
- Insert a horizontal line
- Insert symbols
- Format text using the Font dialog box

Case | *The Flynn and Flynn Insurance Company*

Flynn and Flynn Insurance Company is a regional insurance provider primarily for residents of Texas and Oklahoma. Headquartered in Galveston, Texas, Flynn and Flynn has been providing its customers with insurance for more than 50 years. The company originally started selling insurance to boat owners, but since then the company has expanded to sell other types of insurance, including life, auto, health, and homeowner's insurance. The company is now considering opening new offices in both New Mexico and Arizona. Sandeep Singh, the marketing director for the suburban Galveston region, has approached you about creating a new home page for one of the region's local offices in Riordan, Texas. Sandeep has already provided you with some promotional material, which you have entered into a file named insure.html. In this session, you work with Sandeep on developing the Flynn and Flynn Web page for this regional office.

STARTING DATA FILES

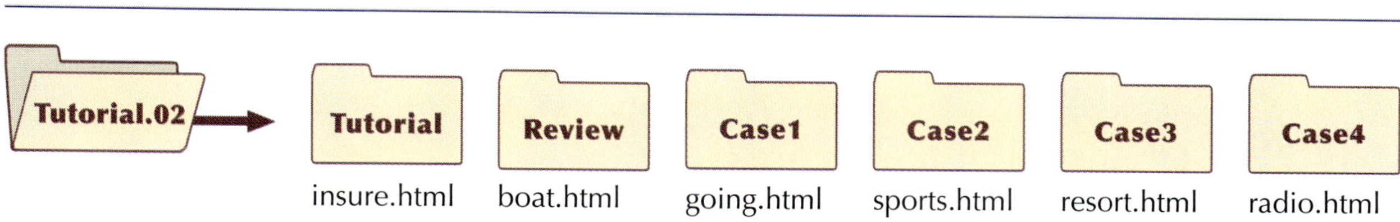

SESSION 2.1 VISUAL OVERVIEW

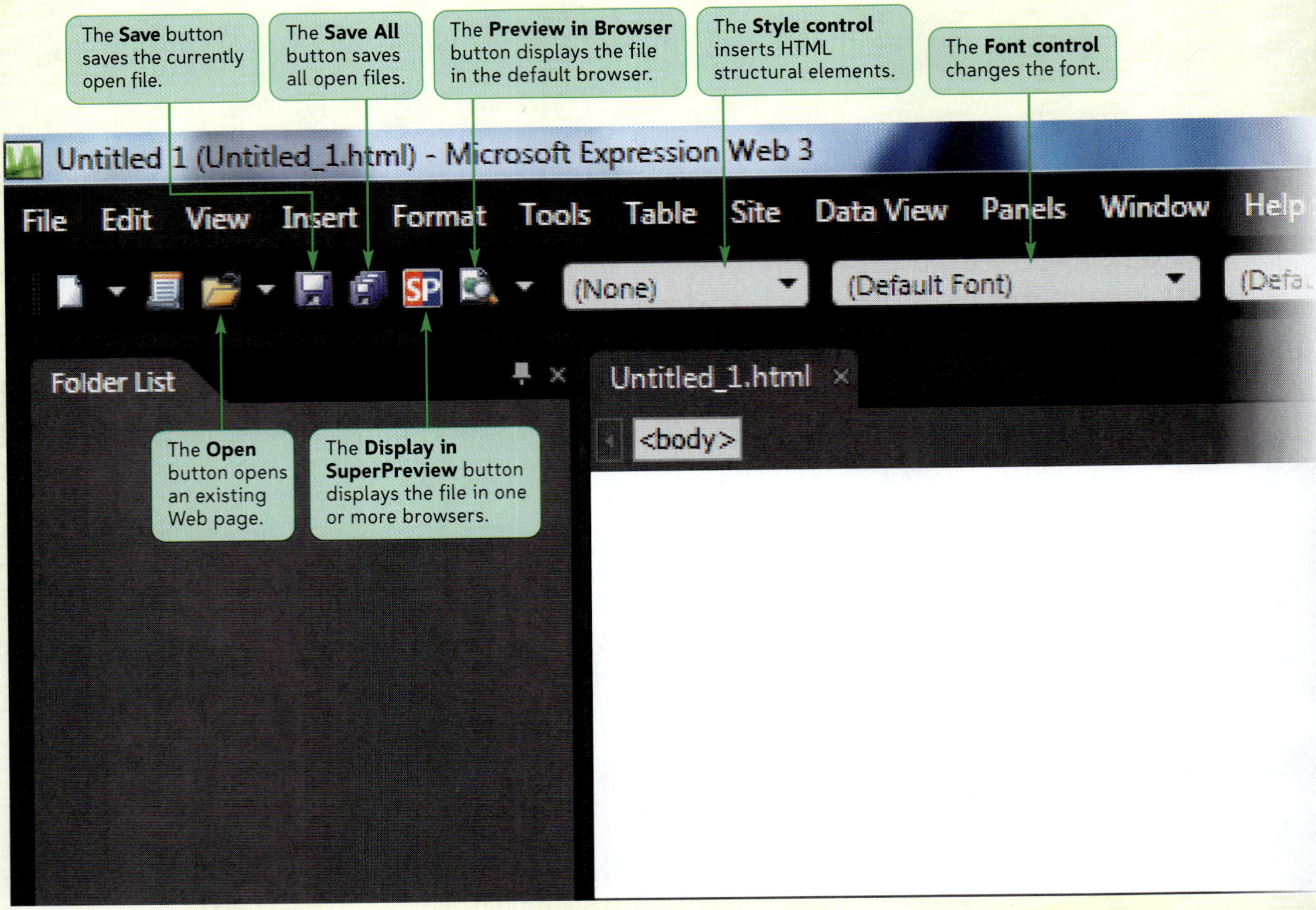

FILE MANAGEMENT AND FONT BUTTONS

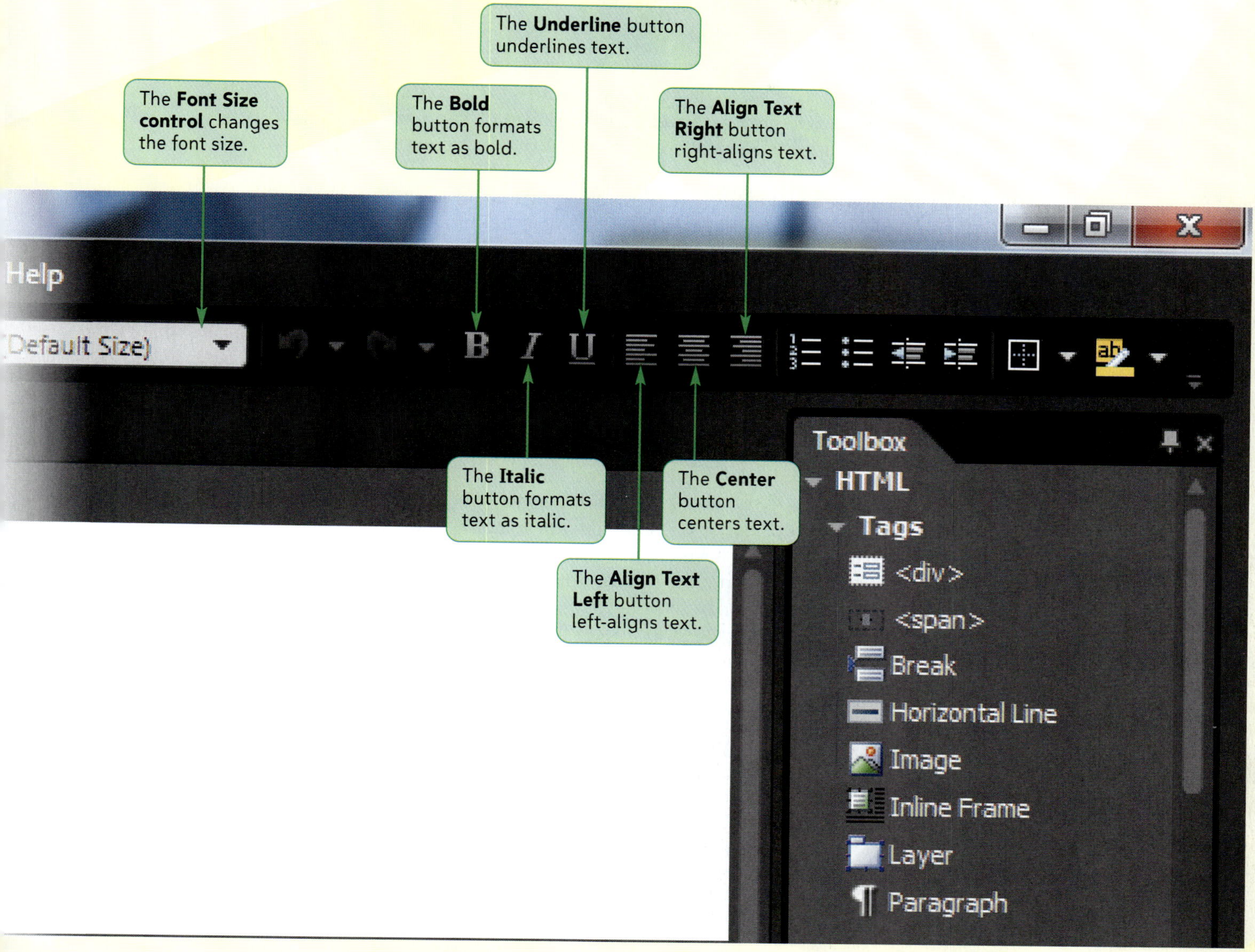

Opening an Existing Web Site

In Expression Web, a Web site is a collection of Web pages, files, objects, and folders that will be published for presentation on the Web. Creating an Expression Web site offers many advantages. With Expression Web, you can do the following:

- Use the Folder List panel to organize all your files.
- Update links to other files automatically. Expression Web rewrites all the HTML link code whenever you create, move, copy, or delete files in your Web site.
- Automatically apply CSS code to as few or as many documents in your Web site as you want.
- Find and replace text in multiple documents within your Web site.
- Perform a spelling check on multiple documents within your Web site.
- Create template documents that standardize the appearance of pages in your Web site.

To ensure that the relationship among the files and folders is always maintained (especially for linked documents), it is important that you perform all of your Web site file management within Expression Web using the Folder List panel, rather than using the file management utilities of Windows. Expression Web has a default root folder for you to store your Web sites. The default folder is most commonly C:\Users\Name\Documents\My Web Sites (where *Name* is the user name assigned to that computer). However, you can store a Web site on any storage device you want. After you create a Web site, the Folder List panel will display the folders and files you create for the site.

Once you create a Web site, you should revise all of the files for that Web site within Expression Web so that you can take advantage of the time-saving features that Expression Web offers. You have created a Web site for Sandeep in Expression Web, and you have stored the insure.html file in the Tutorial folder in that Web site. You'll start by showing Sandeep how to open the Web site you've created for him. After he has become familiar with working within an Expression Web site, later you'll show him how to create a Web site.

To open the Tutorial.02 Web site:

1. If necessary, start Expression Web. If another Web site from a previous user is open, click the **Site** menu, and then click **Close**.
2. Click the Panels menu, and then click **Reset Workspace Layout**.
3. Click the **Site** menu, and then click **Open Site**. The Open Site dialog box opens, as shown in Figure 2-1.

Figure 2-1 The Open Site dialog box

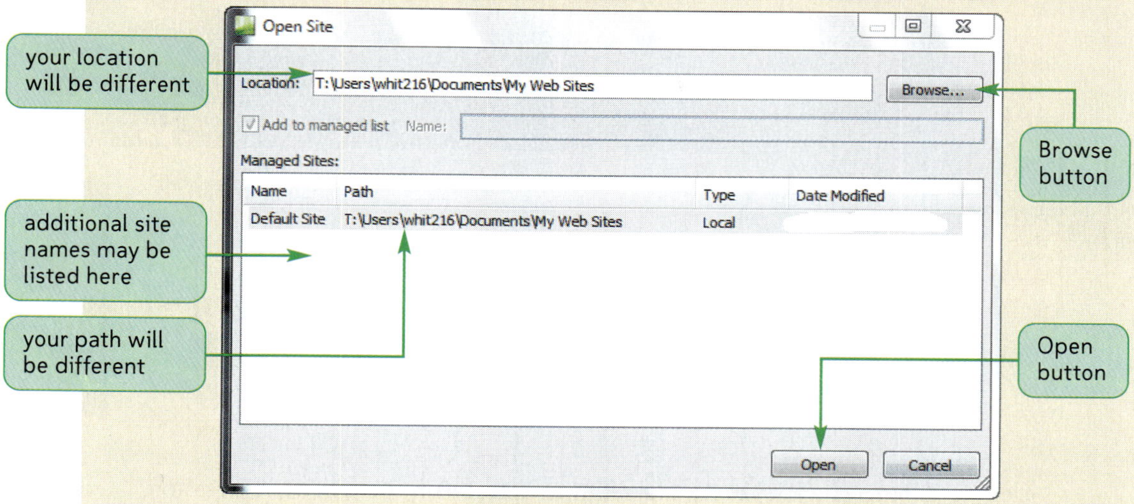

4. Click the **Browse** button and then navigate to the location of the Tutorial.02 Web site.
5. Click the **Tutorial.02** Web site to select it.
6. Click the **Open** button. The Open Site dialog box opens again.
7. Click the **Open** button again. The Tutorial.02 Web site opens. The Folder List panel shows the root folder and the Data Files folder, as shown in Figure 2-2. Your root folder name will be different.

Figure 2-2 The Web site opens

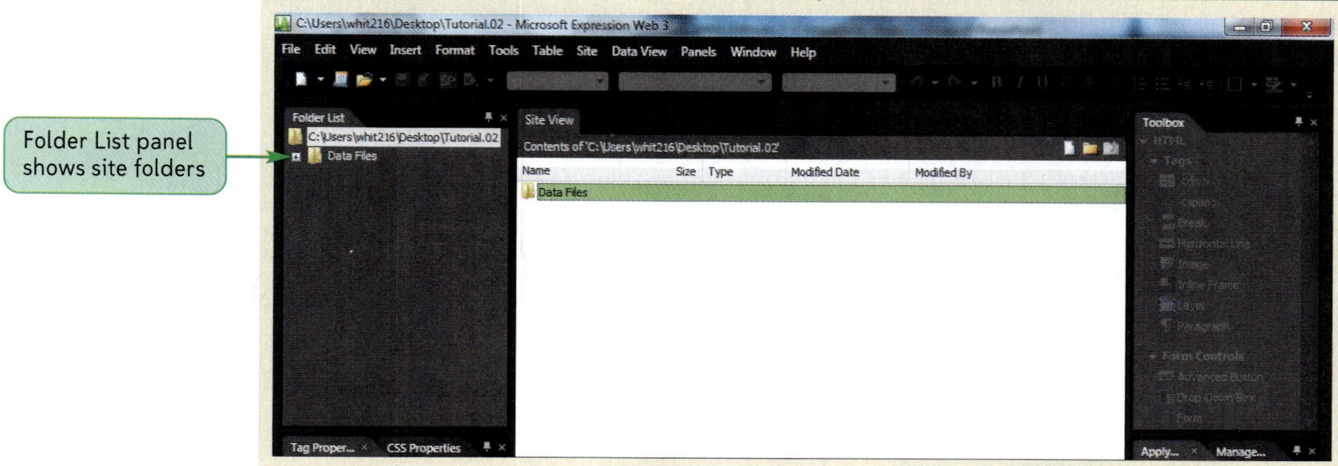

8. Click the **+ sign** to the left of the Data Files folder to show the contents of that folder.
9. Click the **+ sign** to the left of the Tutorial folder to show the contents of that folder, as shown in Figure 2-3.

Figure 2-3 Folder List panel contents

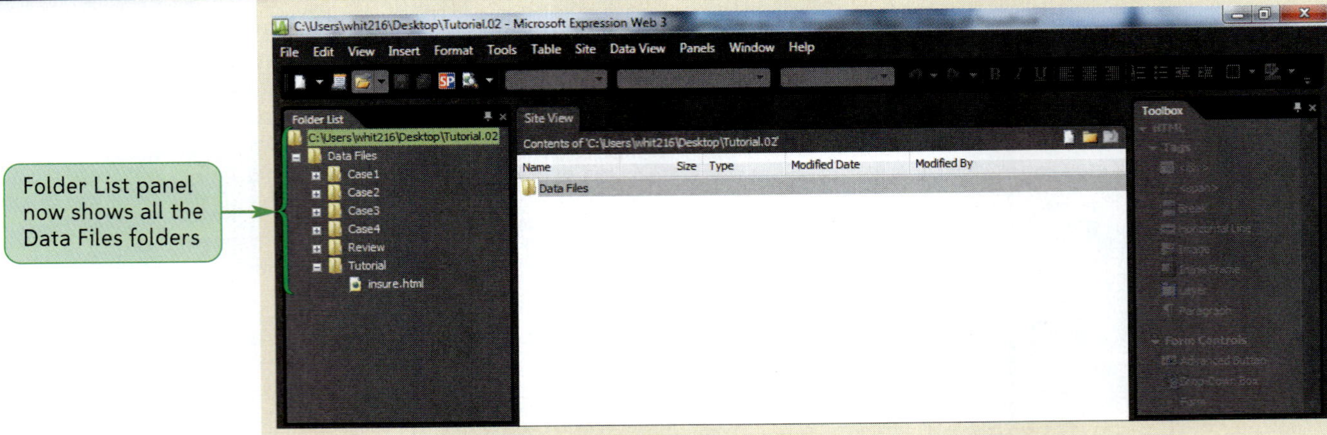

Now you'll show Sandeep how to open the insure.html file and restore the default settings.

To open the insure.html file and restore the default settings:

1. In the Folder List panel, double-click the **insure.html** filename.
2. If necessary, click the **Design** button to display Design view.
3. If necessary, close any toolbars other than the Common toolbar. The workspace should look similar to Figure 2-4.

Figure 2-4 The original insure.html file

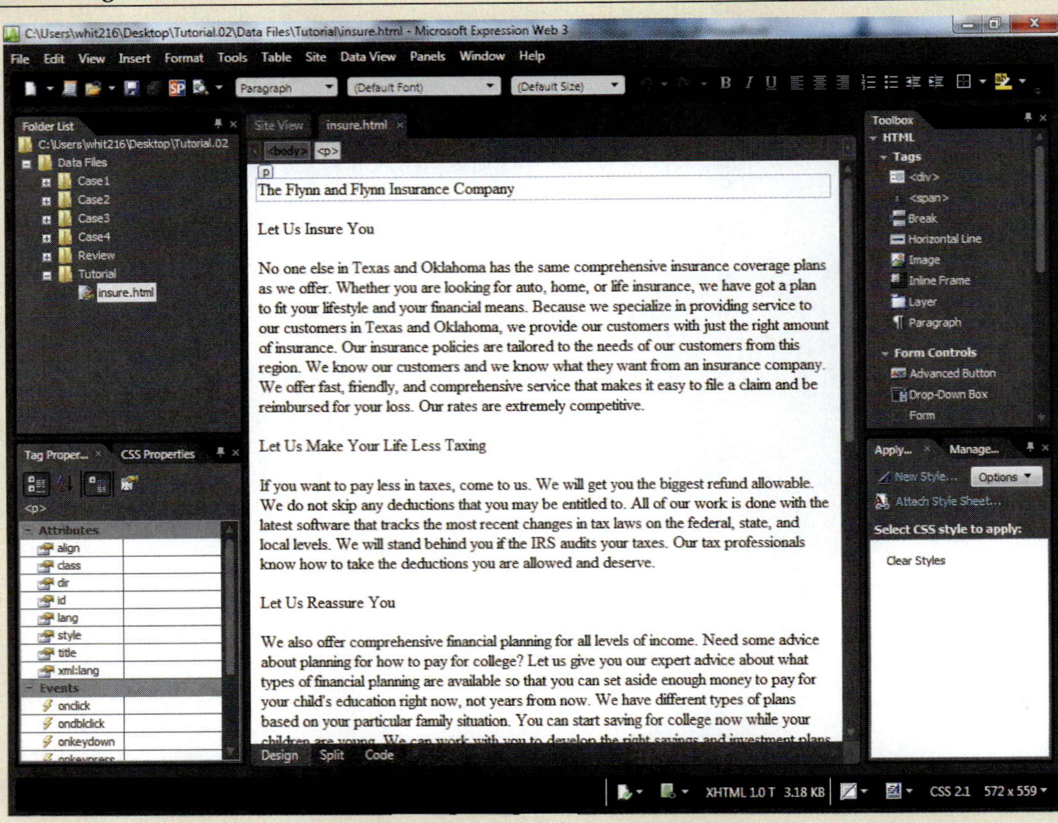

INSIGHT

Managing the Open Sites List

When you open the Open Site dialog box, the box is populated by a list of sites that either you or someone else using the same computer have recently accessed. Over time, this list of recently opened sites can become quite long. You can delete a site from the Managed Sites list by clicking Site on the menu bar and then clicking Manage Sites List. Click a site name on the list and then click the Remove button to remove the site from the list. Clicking the Remove button does not delete the site; it only deletes the site name from the list. You can clear the entire list by clicking the site name at the top of the list, holding down the Shift key, clicking the last site name in the list, and then clicking the Remove button to delete all the site names. You can also click the Add button to add a site to the list.

You'll now save the file with a new filename in the same file folder. You won't be using the two Properties panels, so you close those panels, which allows you to see more data in the Folder List panel.

To save and rename the insure.html file:

1. On the menu bar, click **Panels**, and then click **Tag Properties**. The Tag Properties panel closes.
2. On the menu bar, click **Panels**, and then click **CSS Properties**. The CSS Properties panel closes.
3. On the menu bar, click **File**, and then click **Save As**. The Save As dialog box opens.
4. In the File name text box, type **insurenew**.
5. Click the **Save** button. The file is saved as **insurenew.html**, and the filename is added to the bottom of the list of filenames in the Folder List panel.

Every Web page should have a title that will display in the title bar at the top of the browser window. To ensure that Web search engines can locate your page, each page should also have a page description and keywords. You'll show Sandeep how to add a title, a page description, and several keywords to his Web page. Substitute your first and last name as indicated. The keywords will include two intentionally misspelled words.

To create a title, a page description, and keywords:

1. Right-click anywhere in the editing window. On the shortcut menu, click **Page Properties**. The Page Properties dialog box opens.
2. In the Title text box, type **Riordan Texas Insurance Office**.
3. Click in the **Page description** text box. Type Your First and Last Name/**Tutorial 2**.
4. Click in the **Keywords** text box. Type **flynn flyn insurance company compnay**.

   Your screen should look similar to Figure 2-5.

TIP

Alternatively, you can display the page properties by clicking File on the menu bar, and then clicking Properties.

Figure 2-5 **Entering Title, Page Description, and Keywords**

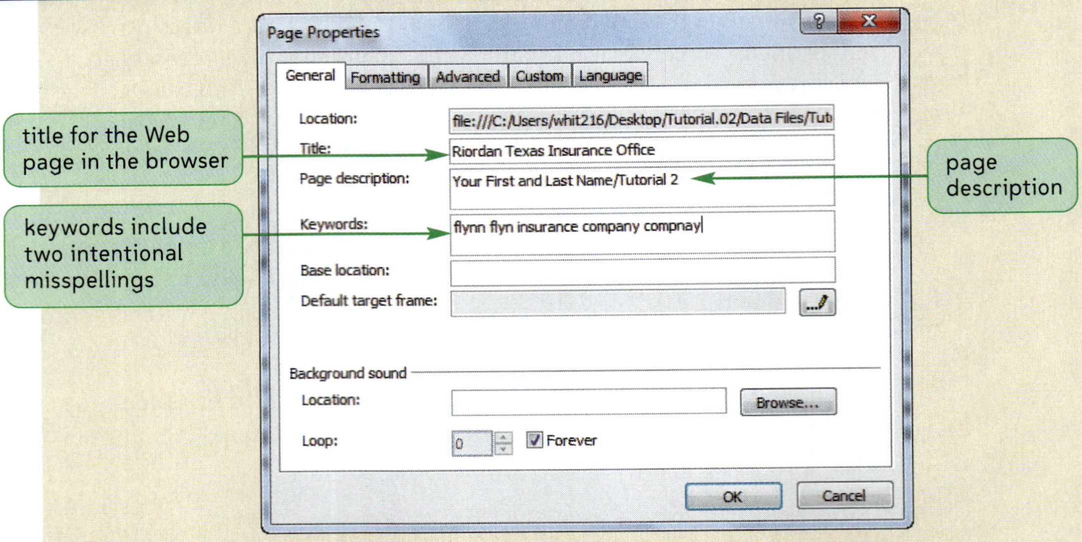

5. Click the **OK** button.

Next, you'll show Sandeep how to change the background color for the page.

Changing the Background Color for the Page

Sandeep wants to change the background color of the Web page. You can use the page properties to change both the text color and the background color. The default is black text on a white background. If you decide to change the text color or the background color of the page, be mindful of contrast. For example, you don't want dark text on a dark background. Also, don't have too bright a background, such as bright yellow or orange, which might be distracting to the reader.

To change the color, you click a **swatch**, a block of color that represents a sample of that color choice. You'll show Sandeep how to change the background color for the insurenew.html page.

TIP

Alternatively, you can change the page background by clicking Format on the menu bar, and then clicking Background.

To change the background color:

1. Right-click anywhere on the page. Click **Page Properties** on the shortcut menu.
2. In the Page Properties dialog box, click the **Formatting** tab. The Formatting choices appear, as shown in Figure 2-6.

Figure 2-6 The Page Properties dialog box

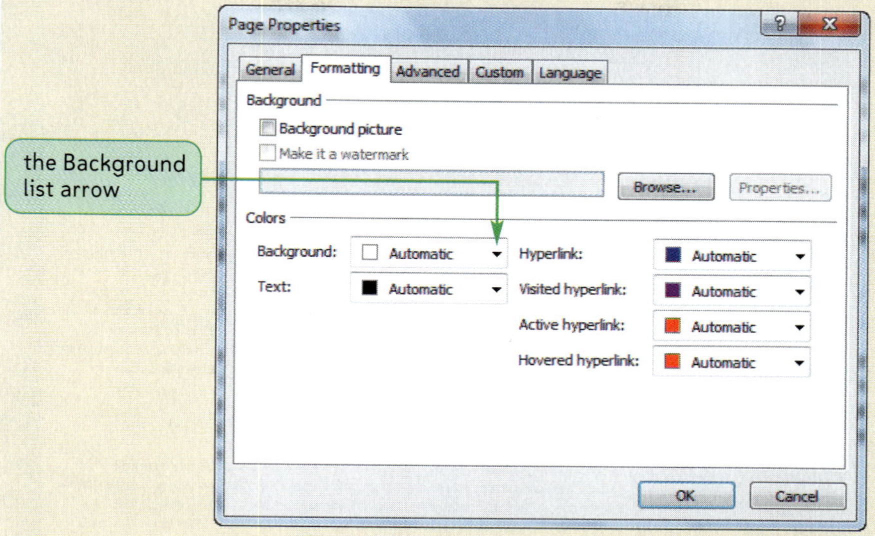

3. Under Colors, click the **Background** list arrow.
4. Click **More Colors**. The More Colors color gallery opens.
5. In the color gallery, the colors do not have names, but click the **light yellow** swatch for hex code color #FFFFCC near the center of the color gallery, as shown in Figure 2-7. In the Value box, Hex={FF,FF,CC} appears, as shown in Figure 2-7.

Figure 2-7 The More Colors color gallery

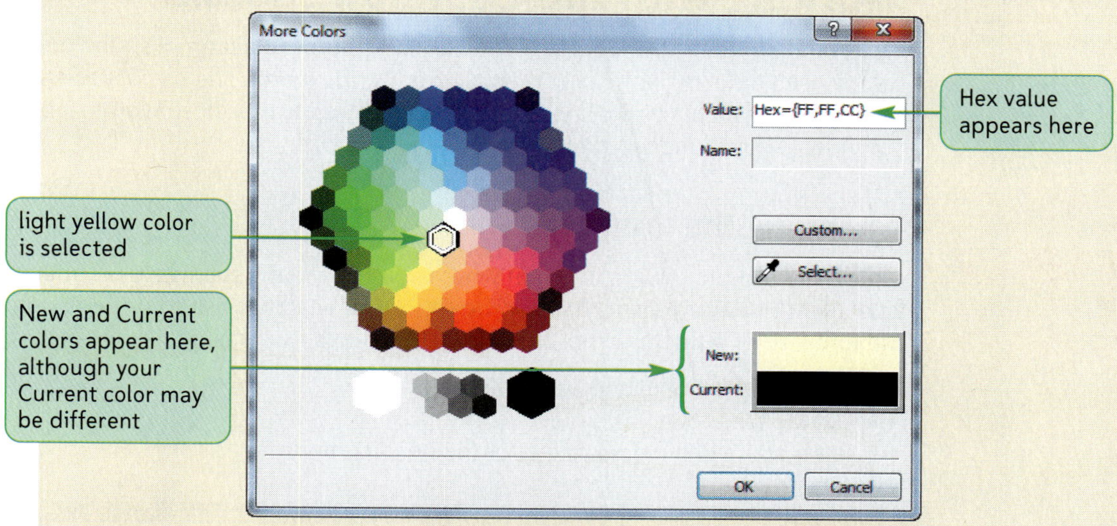

Trouble? If the choice for Hex={FF, FF, CC} does not appear in the Value box, delete any content in that box, type FFFFCC, and then press Enter.

6. Click the **OK** button. The Page Properties dialog box opens.
7. Click the **OK** button again to display the editing window. The background color of the editing window is light yellow, as shown in Figure 2-8.

Figure 2-8 **The new background color**

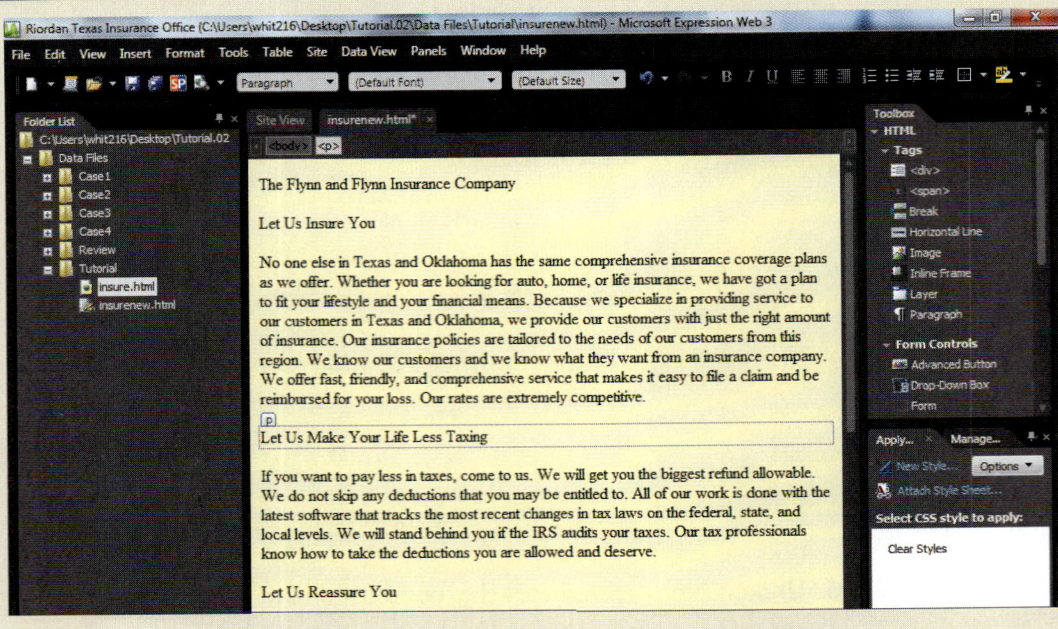

Sandeep is eager to begin formatting the text, and he wants the company name to stand out from the rest of the text. You'll show Sandeep how he can use the Common toolbar to format a Web page.

Working with the Common Toolbar

As its name implies, the Common toolbar has buttons to accomplish the most commonly used tasks in Expression Web. Currently, the words *The Flynn and Flynn Insurance Company* do not have much visual appeal. Sandeep wants those words to be larger, so you'll first show Sandeep how to change the font size.

Changing the Font Size

Unlike a word-processing program where you have many settings for changing the text size, HTML has only six font sizes. The six HTML headings are commonly used to change the font size of a single line of text. HTML headings can accomplish the following:

- Change the size of text to one of six sizes.
- Make the text bold.
- Insert a blank line before and after the heading text.

REFERENCE

Changing the Font Size

- Click the Style list arrow on the Common toolbar.
- Click any one of the six heading sizes Heading 1 through Heading 6.

Expression Web also allows you to change the font size by choosing from seven CSS keywords in the Font Size box on the Common toolbar. An HTML **keyword** is a word that has special meaning in Web page code. Do not confuse HTML keywords with the document keywords you entered earlier in the Page Properties dialog box. Those keywords could be *any word* that describes your Web page, and those words have no special meaning in HTML code. There are seven keywords that are used to change the text size. Figure 2-9 shows the relationships between the six heading sizes and the seven text size keywords, which are used strictly to change the size of text. Note that there is no corresponding HTML heading size for the keyword xx-large. In typography, a **point** is 1/72 of an inch in height. The font sizes are approximate and vary depending on the browser and browser version.

Figure 2-9 **Headings, keywords, and font sizes**

Heading	Keyword	Font Size (in points)
-	xx-large	36pt
h1	x-large	24
h2	large	18
h3	medium	14
h4	small	12
h5	x-small	10
h6	xx-small	8

there is no corresponding value for this choice

a point is 1/72 of an inch in height

You'll have Sandeep format the words *The Flynn and Flynn Insurance Company* as an h1 heading, which is the largest heading size.

To apply the h1 heading to the first line of text:

1. Click anywhere inside the words **The Flynn and Flynn Insurance Company**.
2. Click the **p Code tab** above the words *The Flynn and Flynn Insurance Company* to select that line of text.
3. With *The Flynn and Flynn Insurance Company* text selected, on the Common toolbar, click the **Style** list arrow (the current setting is Paragraph style), and then click **Heading 1 <h1>**. The text now appears much larger than before. Note also that the p Code tab has now been replaced by an h1 Code tab, indicating the text is now an h1 heading.
4. In the editing window, click anywhere below the words **The Flynn and Flynn Insurance Company** to deselect the heading. The text should appear as shown in Figure 2-10.

Figure 2-10 **The Heading 1 text**

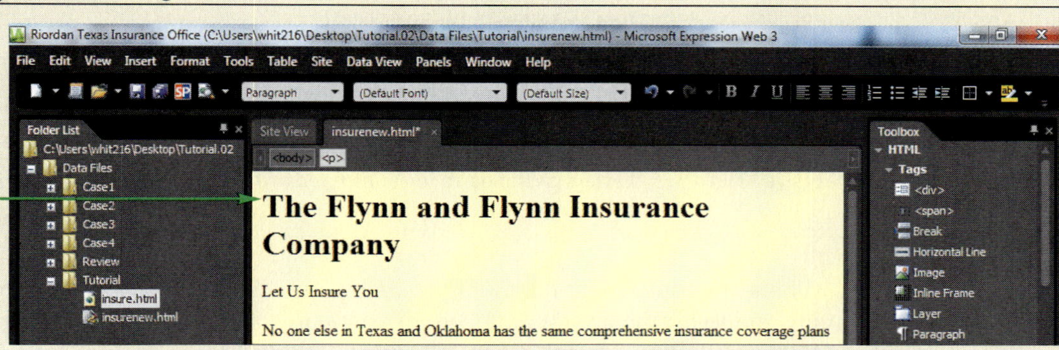

the heading 1 style is applied to the first line of text

Sandeep is not exactly sure what fonts are and how they are used with text, so you'll take some time to explain to him how Expression Web uses fonts with text.

Working with Fonts

A **font** is a particular design given to the appearance of text. A **serif font** is a font embellished with stroke endings that resemble hooks or tails. A **sans-serif font** does not have stroke embellishments. Times New Roman and Arial are two very commonly used fonts. Times New Roman is an example of a serif font, and it is the default font for most browsers. Arial is an example of a sans-serif font.

Courier is an example of a **monospace font**, which is a font where each character occupies the same amount of space, similar to print from an old-fashioned typewriter. Serif, sans-serif, and monospace fonts are the most commonly used fonts installed on most computers. A **cursive font** is a font in which the characters resemble handwriting or script. A **fantasy font** is a font that is designed to appear whimsical and artistic. Fantasy fonts are not as widely installed on computers, so what one computer interprets as a fantasy font might not be interpreted the same way on another computer. In general, then, you should limit or avoid using fantasy fonts on your Web pages. A common solution to this problem is to compose text in a fantasy font in a graphics design program such as Expression Design, save the text as an image, and then display the text as an image on your Web page.

REFERENCE

Changing the Font

- Select the text.
- Click the Font list arrow on the Common toolbar.
- Click any one of the font families.

A **font face** is a particular type of font, such as Arial. A **font family** is a group of variations on the same font face, such as Arial, Arial Narrow, and Arial Black. A font family can also be a group of fonts with a similar appearance but different names, such as Arial or Helvetica. The Arial font is commonly found on Windows systems. The Helvetica font is commonly found on Apple computers. The **generic fonts** are the five major categories of HTML fonts. The five generic fonts are serif, sans-serif, monospace, fantasy, and cursive. Figure 2-11 illustrates the differences among these five categories.

Figure 2-11 **The five generic fonts**

Generic Name	Description	Example
Serif	Letters have strokes (serifs) that finish the top or bottom of the letter form	Times New Roman
Sans-serif	Letters do not have finishing strokes	Arial
Monospace	Fixed-width letters	Courier New
Fantasy	Decorative letters	Broadway
Cursive	Letters designed to look like handwriting or script	Lucida Handwriting Brush Script MT

Whenever you change the font for a Web page, it's always a good idea to list a font family and to list the appropriate generic font name at the end of the list of fonts. By doing so, you ensure that the font will appear as you intended in the browser on the user's monitor. If you have chosen an unusual font and the user does not have the specified font installed on his or her computer, the browser will display the most similar font it has installed from one of the five generic fonts that you specified. The **font list** is the preferred list of fonts. A font list looks like this: Arial, Helvetica, sans-serif.

Sandeep wants the h1 heading text to appear in a contemporary font. You'll show him how to change the font from the default Times New Roman font to the Arial font.

To change the font for the h1 heading to Arial:

1. Select the h1 heading text **The Flynn and Flynn Insurance Company**.
2. On the Common toolbar, click the **Font** list arrow (the current setting is Default Font) on the Common toolbar, and then click **Arial, Helvetica, sans-serif**.
3. In the editing window, click anywhere below the words *The Flynn and Flynn Insurance Company* to deselect them. The words appear in the Arial font, as shown in Figure 2-12.

Figure 2-12 The Arial font is applied to the h1 text

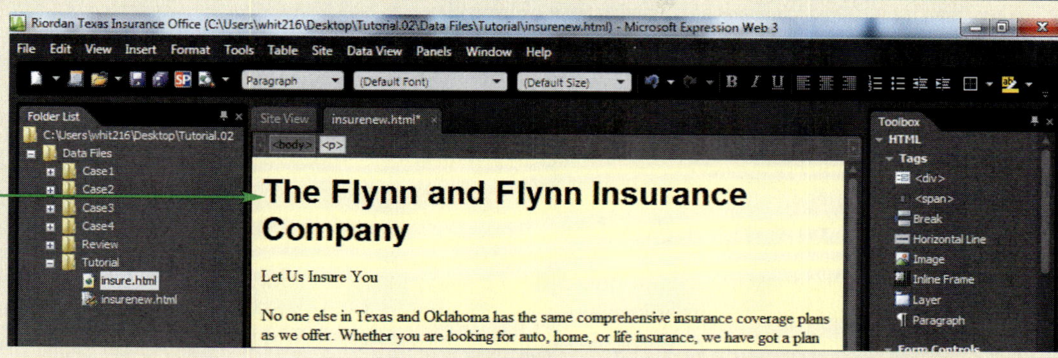

Arial font gives the text a more modern appearance

4. On the Common toolbar, click the **Save** button to save the file.

In the Apply Styles panel in the lower-right corner of the screen, you now see that Expression Web has created a style named *.style1* for the font style you just created. **Styles** are a means of consistently applying formatting characteristics to Web page content. You'll learn about styles in a later tutorial.

Sandeep is pleased with the look of the h1 heading text, but he wonders if the text could be given more visual appeal. Expression Web, like most other Microsoft products, allows you to position text left-aligned, centered, or right-aligned. Sandeep is not sure if he would prefer to have the h1 heading text appear centered or flush right. You'll show Sandeep how to align the text so that he can choose the text alignment he prefers.

To change the text alignment:

1. Click anywhere inside the words **The Flynn and Flynn Insurance Company**.
2. On the Common toolbar, click the **Center** button.
3. On the Common toolbar, click the **Align Text Right** button.

   After looking at both alignments, Sandeep would prefer the text in the heading to be centered.
4. On the Common toolbar, click the **Center** button.
5. In the editing window, click anywhere below the h1 heading to deselect the header. The heading now appears as shown in Figure 2-13.

Figure 2-13 **The text is centered**

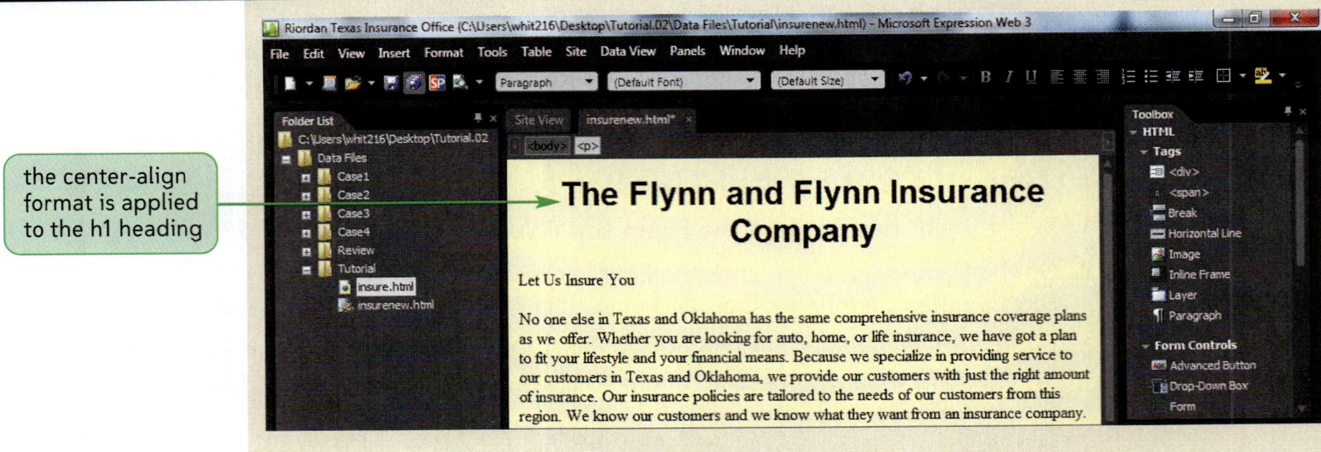

6. Save the file.

Sandeep likes the positioning of the h1 text. He does, however, want to separate the heading from the rest of the document. You suggest that a decorative border around the h1 text would accomplish this task. You'll show Sandeep how to create a border around the h1 text.

Creating a Border

One way to call attention to text is to place a border around it. Expression Web has two methods to apply borders. Sandeep wants to create a thin outside border on all four sides of the heading. If you select just the text, Expression Web places a border around the text only. If you select the container, which in this instance is the h1 Code tab, Expression Web creates a border across the entire page, not just around the text.

To create an outside border:

1. Click anywhere inside the h1 text **The Flynn and Flynn Insurance Company**.
2. Click the **h1.style1 Code tab** to select the h1 container.
3. On the Common toolbar, click the **Outside Borders** list arrow and then click **Outside Borders**.
4. Click anywhere outside the h1 text. The h1 container now appears with a thin border on all four sides, as shown in Figure 2-14.

Figure 2-14 **The outside border**

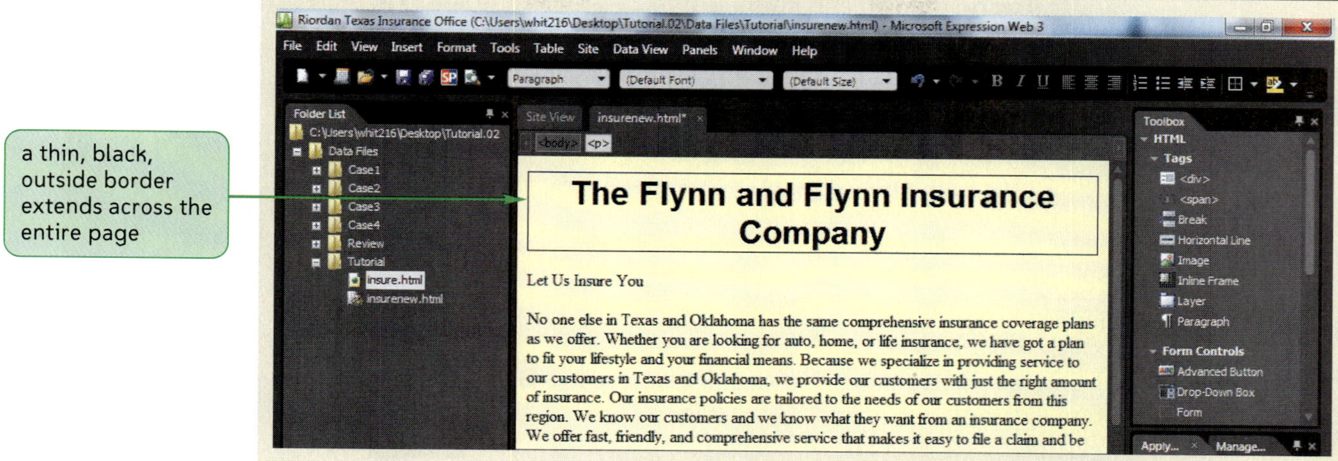

You can create more complex borders by changing the border style, the border color, and the border width. You cannot, however, make these changes by using the Outside Borders button on the Common toolbar. To make these more complex changes, you need to use the Borders and Shading dialog box.

REFERENCE

Changing the Border Style, Color, and Width

- Select the text or the container tab.
- Click Format on the menu bar.
- Click Borders and Shading.
- For the Setting, click either Default, Box, or Custom.
- In the Style box, click a border style.
- Click the Color list arrow and then click a color.
- For the Width, repeatedly click the top spin button until you find the value you want.
- Optionally, set the padding choices for Left and Right and for Top and Bottom.

You'll show Sandeep how to change the border color, and you'll show him how to change the thickness of the border. In addition, you'll create some padding between the text in the heading and the border so the text and the border are not too crowded.

To change the border style, color, and width:

1. Click anywhere inside the h1 text, **The Flynn and Flynn Insurance Company**.
2. Click the **h1.style1 Code** tab to select the h1 container.
3. Click the **Format** menu, and then click **Borders and Shading**. The Borders and Shading dialog box opens.
4. If necessary, click the **Box** icon as the Setting.
5. In the Style section, click **outset**.
6. Click the **Color** list arrow and then click the **Red** swatch third from the right in the bottom row of colors.
7. Click the **Width** top spin button until **5px** appears.

8. For Padding, make sure that the choices are set to **4px** on the Left and Right, and to **4px** on the Top and Bottom. If those are not the settings, adjust those settings accordingly, and then compare your dialog box with Figure 2-15.

Figure 2-15 **The Borders and Shading dialog box**

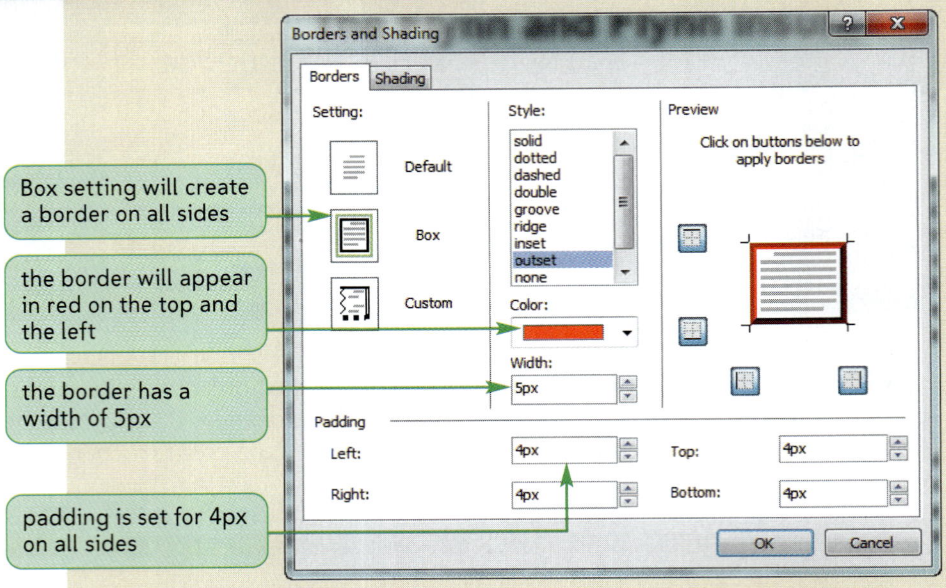

9. Click the **OK** button.
10. In the editing window, click anywhere outside of the h1 text. The h1 heading text has a decorative border, as shown in Figure 2-16.

Figure 2-16 **The formatted border**

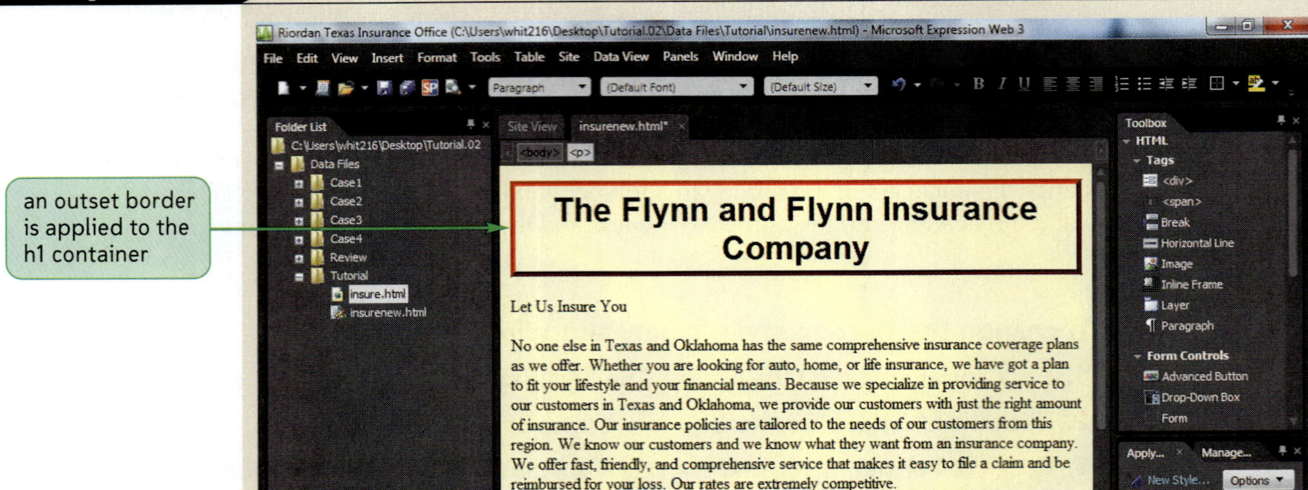

INSIGHT

Formatting Borders Individually

You can format each border side individually by using the Borders and Shading dialog box. When the Borders and Shading dialog box opens, in the Preview pane, click the icon for the border side you want to format. Enter your choices for Style, Color, Width, or Padding. Click the same border icon again to apply the formatting to that border.

Sandeep is impressed with the changes that have been made to the appearance of the h1 heading. He now wants to liven up the page by using some vibrant colors. You'll show Sandeep how to work with color on a Web page.

Working with Color

Sandeep feels that the heading would get more attention if the text color (the foreground color) and the background color had greater contrast. You can modify both the foreground color and the background color using buttons on the Common toolbar. Expression Web refers to the foreground color as the **font color**, and refers to the background color as the **highlight color**. When changing either the font color or the highlight color, it is important to have sufficient contrast between the two colors.

INSIGHT

Understanding Color

On computer monitors, color is actually a combination of three colors: red, green, and blue. Mixing these three colors and varying their strength (their intensity) is what produces the color gallery you see in the world around you. Computer monitors do the same thing; they vary the intensity (in voltage) of red, green, and blue. The greatest intensity of red, green, and blue creates the color white; the absence of those colors produces black.

Colors used in HTML code are usually described by either their name or by a hexadecimal value. Referring to a color by its name is easy. Some of the Web color names, such as white, red, and navy, are familiar to you. Other Web color names, such as *aliceblue* or *burlywood*, probably are not. There are two great disadvantages to using named colors. First, there are only 216 named colors, and second, with the exception of 17 of these named colors, computer monitors do not always display these named colors the same way.

The **Web-safe colors** are those colors that are so common that all monitors should be able to display them correctly. A list of the 17 Web-safe colors, their RGB triplet values, and their hexadecimal values are shown in Figure 2-17.

Figure 2-17 The 17 Web-safe colors

Name	Hexadecimal Value	Name	Hexadecimal Value
aqua	#00FFFF	olive	#808000
black	#000000	orange	#FFA500
blue	#0000FF	purple	#800080
fuchsia	#FF00FF	red	#FF0000
gray	#808080	silver	#C0C0C0
green	#008000	teal	#008080
lime	#00FF00	white	#FFFFFF
maroon	#800000	yellow	#FFFF00
navy	#000080		

The primary advantage to using hexadecimal values to refer to colors is that there are millions of hexadecimal color values. You do not have to remember the hexadecimal values for each color, but you should know how hexadecimal values are derived. The decimal system is based on the number 10. In the decimal system, we use the numbers 0–9, and then we start repeating those numbers. The **hexadecimal system** is a numbering system based on the number 16. After the number 9, the letters A, B, C, D, E, and F are used to represent the numbers 10, 11, 12, 13, 14, and 15, as shown in Figure 2-18.

Figure 2-18 Decimal and hexadecimal systems

Decimal	0–9	10	11	12	13	14	15
Hexadecimal	(Same)	A	B	C	D	E	F

The hexadecimal values for color are based upon the intensity of red, green, and blue. In hexadecimal representation, 00 is the lowest intensity and FF is the highest. The hexadecimal number is preceded by a flag character, the # symbol. A **flag character** is a character that has special significance in HTML or CSS code. In this instance, the numbers that follow the flag character are treated as code, not as numbers. The flag character is followed by three **RGB triplets**, which are three two-character groups of hexadecimal numbers representing the intensity of red, green, and blue. For example, the hexadecimal notation for the color navy is #000080. The hexadecimal notation for the color yellow is #FFFF00.

PROSKILLS

Written Communication: Writing for Your Intended Audience

In the workplace, you often will be asked to explain a technical concept to others who are not familiar with a task or the features of a software application. Your goal is to have others understand the points you are trying to get across. Put yourself in the position of the person who is not familiar with what you have to say. If you are explaining a procedure to a group of executives who might not be technically savvy, spend the time to define terms that are familiar to you, but not to them. If your audience is a group of your peers, outline your ideas in a logical order. There is no need to explain terminology to this group, unless you are setting forth a new plan for a new software procedure. Always bear in mind the technical competence of your audience. Go slow and be patient with those who do not share the same technical background as you, and yet don't try the patience of those who will quickly grasp what you have to convey.

TIP

You can enter a hexadecimal value for color in either uppercase or lowercase letters.

Most Web developers simply refer to hexadecimal numbers as **hex code**. **Short hex** is a shorthand notation for representing repeating values in hex code. For example, the color yellow has three repeating pairs of letters and numbers: FF, FF, and 00. So instead of entering the code for yellow as #FFFF00, some Web developers use the short hex notation of #FF0 instead. To differentiate between letters and numbers, it's a good idea to type the letters in lowercase. Sandeep wants the font color to be yellow and the background color to be maroon. When you make a selection for a color, you have to click the appropriate color swatch in the row of color swatches. You'll show Sandeep how to apply those colors to the h1 heading text.

To change the font color and the highlight color:

1. Click anywhere inside the h1 text **The Flynn and Flynn Insurance Company**.
2. Click the **h1.style1 Code** tab.
3. On the Common toolbar, click the **Highlight** button list arrow.
4. Click the **teal #008080** color swatch (the last color swatch in the row), and then click the **Apply** button.
5. With the contents of the h1 heading text still selected, on the Common toolbar, click the **Font Color** list arrow.

   Trouble? If because of your monitor size or screen resolution, you cannot see buttons on the Common toolbar to the right of the Highlight button, click the More Buttons list arrow at the end of the Common toolbar, and then click the Font Color list arrow.
6. Click the **yellow #FFFF00** color swatch, which is the eighth swatch from the right, and then click the **Apply** button.
7. Click anywhere outside of the h1 heading text to deselect the text. The words *The Flynn and Flynn Insurance Company* now appear as yellow text on a teal background, as shown in Figure 2-19.

Figure 2-19 The font color and the highlight color

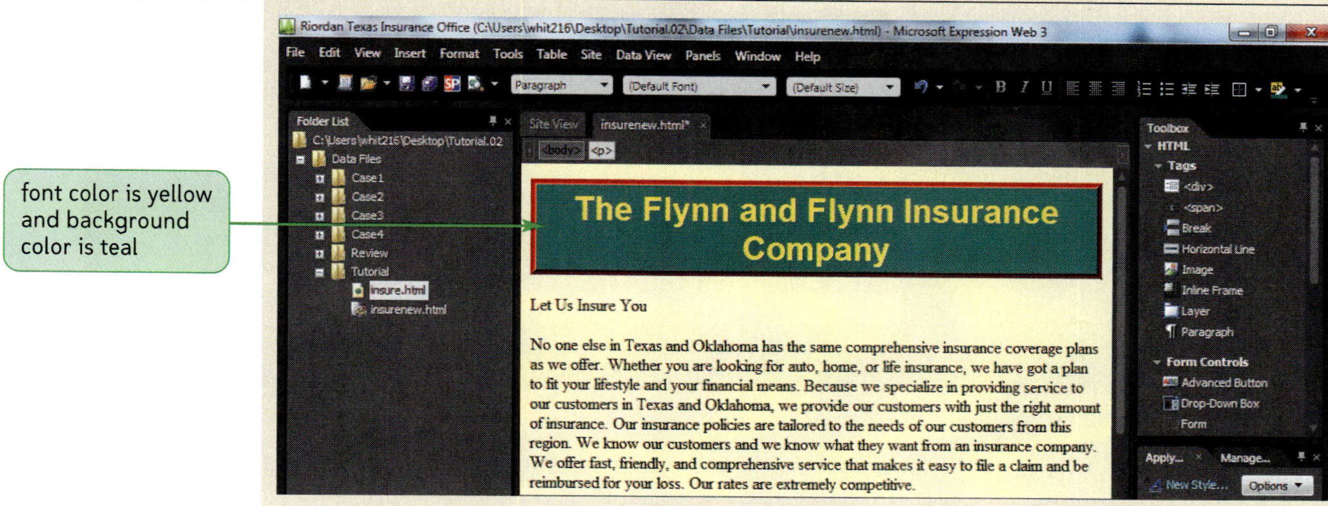

Sandeep also wants the subheading text, such as "Let Us Insure You," in the body of the document to be formatted as headings. He wants these subheadings to be in a smaller point size than the heading 1 text at the top of the page. For these subheadings, a heading 2 style would be appropriate, so you'll show Sandeep how to apply the heading 2 style to the subheading in the document. You'll have him change the font to the Arial font for the subheadings as well.

To apply the heading 2 style to the subheadings:

1. In the editing window, select the words **Let Us Insure You**.
2. On the Common toolbar, click the **Style** list arrow (the current setting is Paragraph).
3. Click **Heading 2 <h2>**. The subheading now appears in 18-point bold type, which is the font size for an h2 heading.
4. With the heading 2 text still selected, click the **Font** list arrow and then click **Arial, Helvetica, sans-serif**.
5. Repeat the preceding steps to format the other subheadings: "Let Us Make Your Life Less Taxing," "Let Us Reassure You," and "Here Are Some of the Advantages We Offer."
6. Press the **Ctrl+Home** keys to position the insertion point at the top of the page. The document should appear similar to Figure 2-20.

TIP

You can also access the Font dialog box by clicking Format on the menu bar and then clicking Font.

Figure 2-20 The heading 2 style

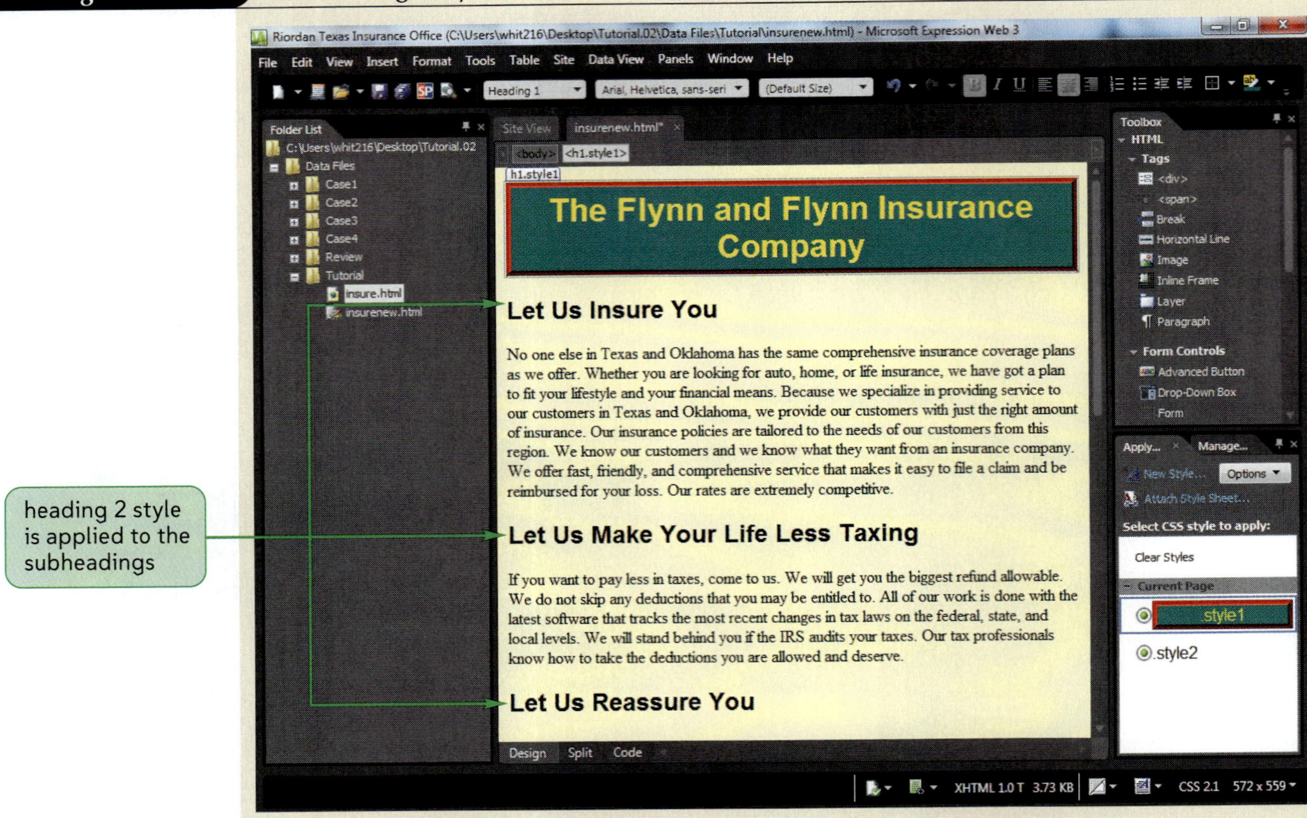

Finally, you'll show Sandeep how to use the Common toolbar to emphasize text.

Emphasizing Text

Text emphasis is applied to text in the same manner as it is in many other Microsoft programs. The Common toolbar has a button to make text bold and a button to make text italic. You can also make text bold or italic by using keyboard shortcuts or by making selections in dialog boxes.

REFERENCE

Emphasizing Text

- Select the text.
- Click the Bold button on the Common toolbar to make text appear in bold.
- Click the Italic button on the Common toolbar to make text appear in italic.

Sandeep wants the first sentence of each of the first three paragraphs to appear in italic, so you'll emphasize the text in those three sentences.

To make text appear in italic:

1. Select the **first sentence** of the paragraph below the "Let Us Insure You" h2 heading.
2. On the Common toolbar, click the **Italic** button.
3. Select the first sentence of the text below the "Let Us Make Your Life Less Taxing" h2 heading.
4. On the Common toolbar, click the **Italic** button.
5. Select the first sentence of the paragraph below the "Let Us Reassure You" h2 heading.
6. On the Common toolbar, click the **Italic** button.

Sandeep wants the address and phone number at the bottom of the page to stand out, so you'll show him how to make that text bold.

To make text appear in bold:

1. Scroll down to the bottom of the page, and then click anywhere in the Flynn and Flynn address.
2. Click the **p Code tab** for the paragraph that contains the address.
3. Press and hold down the **Ctrl** key, and then click anywhere in the phone number. Both the address and the phone number are now selected.
4. On the Common toolbar, click the **Bold** button. Click anywhere outside those two paragraphs to deselect the text. The document should appear similar to Figure 2-21.

Figure 2-21 **Bold text**

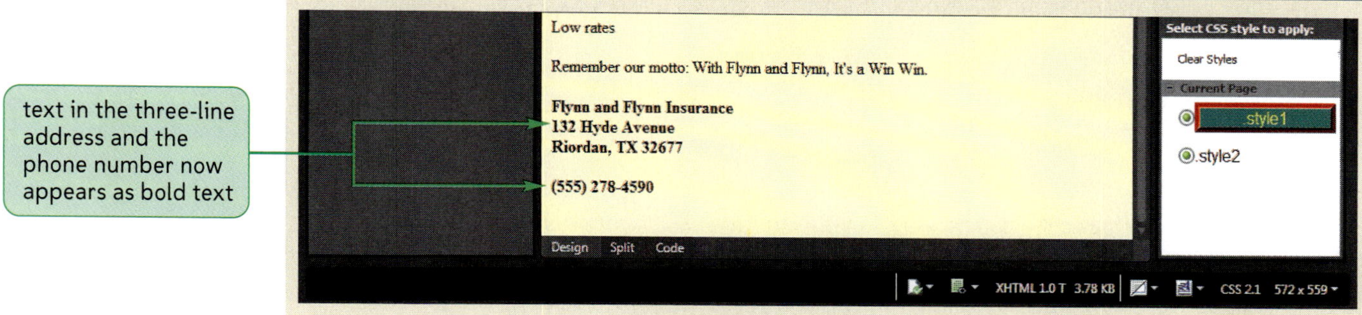

Sandeep wants the motto text to be the most emphasized, so you show him how to apply both bold and italic to the motto text.

To make text appear both bold and italic:

1. Select the line of text that begins "Remember our motto . . . "
2. On the Common toolbar, click the **Bold** button **B**.
3. On the Common toolbar, click the **Italic** button *I*. Click anywhere outside the line to deselect the text. The line of text should appear similar to that shown in Figure 2-22.

TIP

Alternatively, press the Ctrl+B keys to make text bold; press the Ctrl+I keys (the letter *i*) to make text italic.

Figure 2-22 Bold and italic text

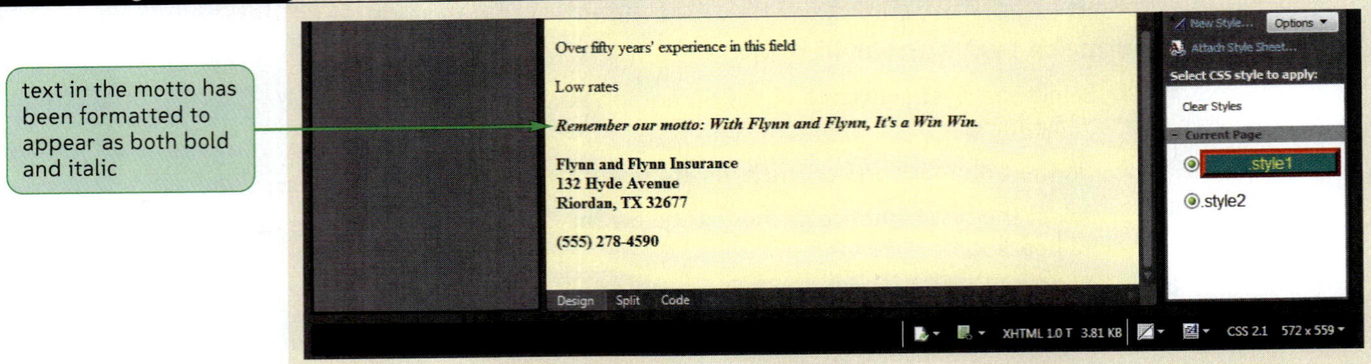

Now you'll have Sandeep save the insurenew.html file and display the file in the browser to view the results of the formatting so far.

To view the revised file in the browser:

1. Save the file.
2. Press the **F12** key to display the file in your default browser. Your screen should look similar to Figure 2-23.

Figure 2-23 **The revised insurenew.html file in the browser**

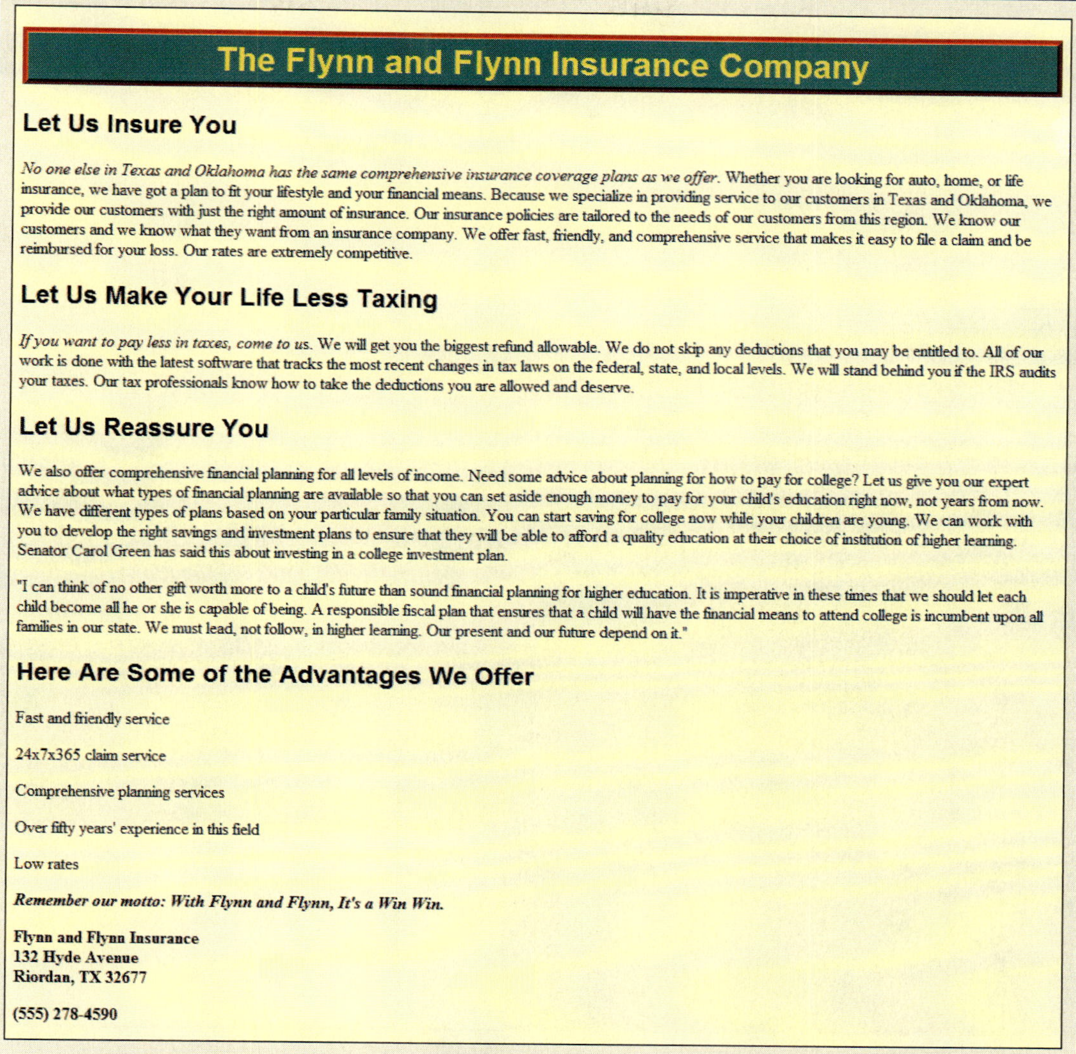

The Flynn and Flynn Insurance Company

Let Us Insure You

No one else in Texas and Oklahoma has the same comprehensive insurance coverage plans as we offer. Whether you are looking for auto, home, or life insurance, we have got a plan to fit your lifestyle and your financial means. Because we specialize in providing service to our customers in Texas and Oklahoma, we provide our customers with just the right amount of insurance. Our insurance policies are tailored to the needs of our customers from this region. We know our customers and we know what they want from an insurance company. We offer fast, friendly, and comprehensive service that makes it easy to file a claim and be reimbursed for your loss. Our rates are extremely competitive.

Let Us Make Your Life Less Taxing

If you want to pay less in taxes, come to us. We will get you the biggest refund allowable. We do not skip any deductions that you may be entitled to. All of our work is done with the latest software that tracks the most recent changes in tax laws on the federal, state, and local levels. We will stand behind you if the IRS audits your taxes. Our tax professionals know how to take the deductions you are allowed and deserve.

Let Us Reassure You

We also offer comprehensive financial planning for all levels of income. Need some advice about planning for how to pay for college? Let us give you our expert advice about what types of financial planning are available so that you can set aside enough money to pay for your child's education right now, not years from now. We have different types of plans based on your particular family situation. You can start saving for college now while your children are young. We can work with you to develop the right savings and investment plans to ensure that they will be able to afford a quality education at their choice of institution of higher learning. Senator Carol Green has said this about investing in a college investment plan.

"I can think of no other gift worth more to a child's future than sound financial planning for higher education. It is imperative in these times that we should let each child become all he or she is capable of being. A responsible fiscal plan that ensures that a child will have the financial means to attend college is incumbent upon all families in our state. We must lead, not follow, in higher learning. Our present and our future depend on it."

Here Are Some of the Advantages We Offer

Fast and friendly service

24x7x365 claim service

Comprehensive planning services

Over fifty years' experience in this field

Low rates

Remember our motto: With Flynn and Flynn, It's a Win Win.

Flynn and Flynn Insurance
132 Hyde Avenue
Riordan, TX 32677

(555) 278-4590

3. Close the browser.
4. If you will not be completing the next session, click the **Site** menu, and then click **Close**.

REVIEW

Session 2.1 Quick Check

1. What heading size creates the largest size of type?
2. In typography, how large is a point?
3. How many heading sizes are available in HTML?
4. What are the names of the five generic font families?
5. Which font family has strokes on each letter?
6. Which font family has characters that are all the same width?

SESSION 2.2 VISUAL OVERVIEW

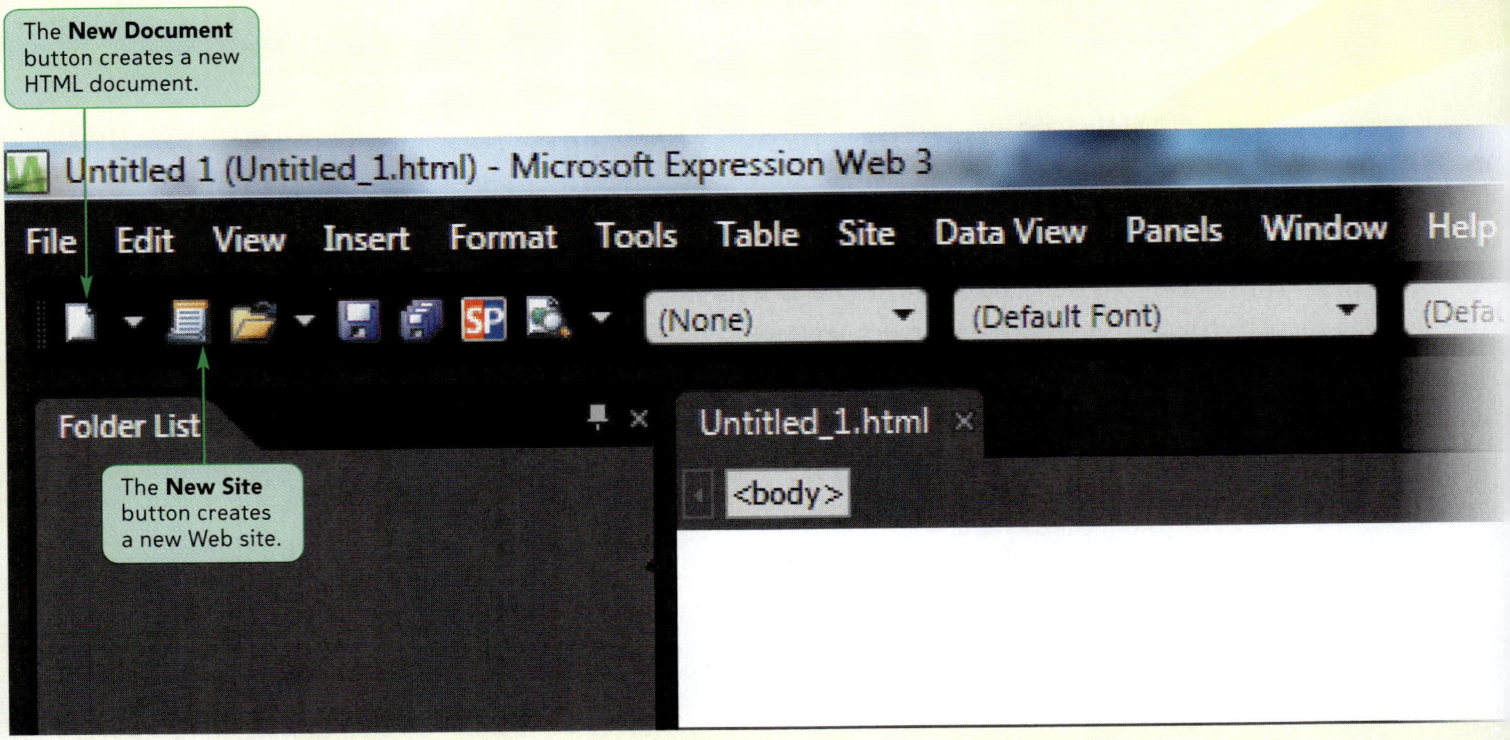

FORMATTING BUTTONS

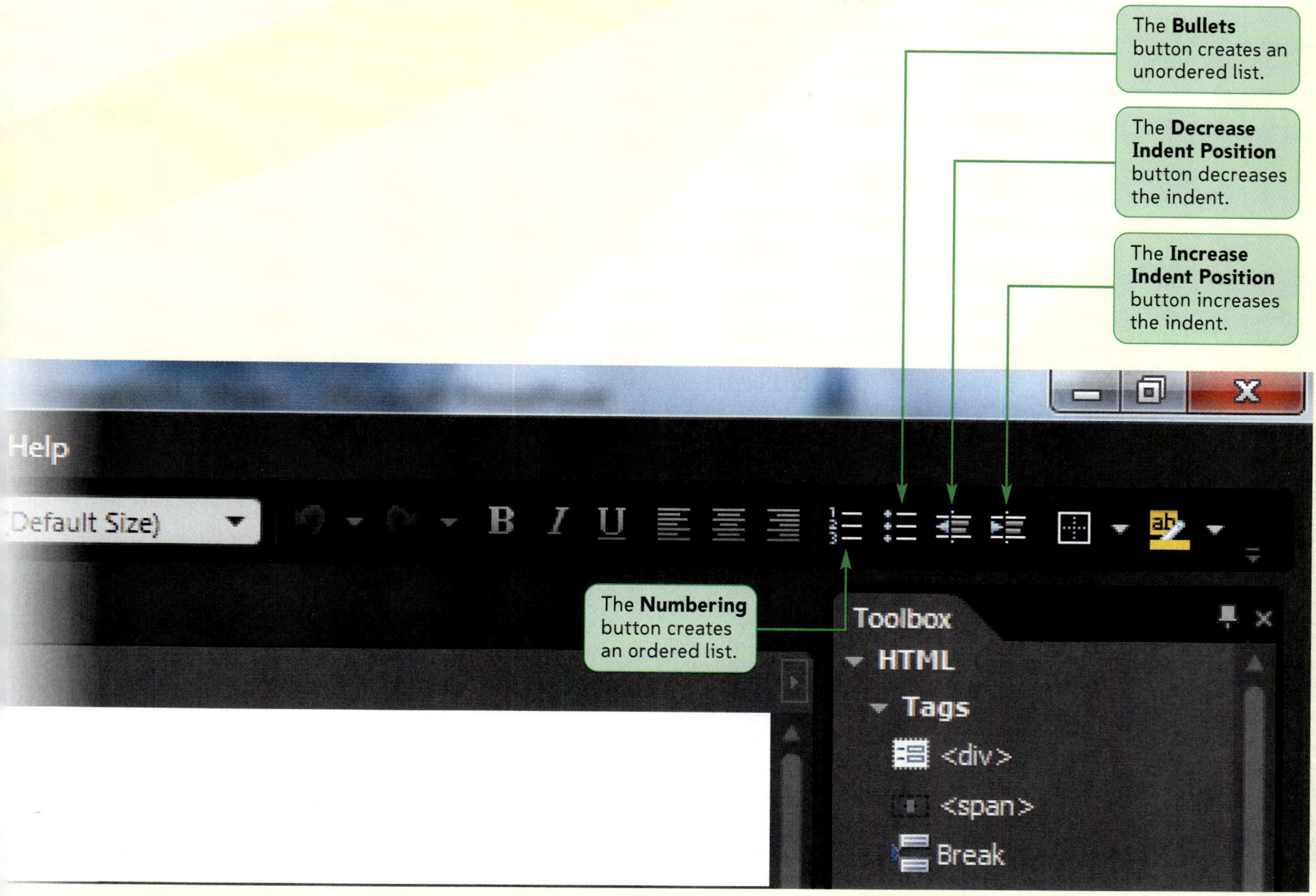

Creating Lists

Bulleted lists and numbered lists are created in Expression Web in the same manner as you would create a list in Microsoft Word, which is to click toolbar buttons. In HTML code, an **unordered list** is a list with bullets as the list marker, and an **ordered list** is a list with letters or numbers as the list marker. Create an unordered list when the items in a list have no order of importance and do not need to appear in sequence. For example:

- Banana
- Automobile
- Paper clip

Create an ordered list when the items in a list have a particular order of importance or should appear in sequence. For example:

1. Unplug the appliance.
2. Remove the charger.
3. Check for defects.

In Expression Web, the Bullets button on the Common toolbar is used to create an unordered list, and the Numbering button on the Common toolbar is used to create an ordered list.

REFERENCE

Creating a Bulleted or Numbered List

- Select the text that will be the list item.
- Click the Bullets button on the Common toolbar to create an unordered list.

or

- Click the Numbering button on the Common toolbar to create an ordered list.

Following the h2 heading, "Here Are Some of the Advantages We Offer" is a series of items that the Flynn and Flynn Insurance Company cites as advantages for becoming one of its customers. Because the items in this list are not in any particular order, you'll show Sandeep how to convert these items into a bulleted list.

To create an unordered list:

1. If necessary, start Expression Web, close any open sites, and close any toolbars other than the Common toolbar. If necessary, close the Tag Properties and CSS Properties panels.
2. If necessary, click the **Site** menu, and then click **Open Site**. The Open Site dialog box opens.
3. Navigate to the Tutorial.02 Web site, click the **Tutorial.02** Web site to select it, and then click the **Open** button.
4. If necessary, in the Folder List panel, click the **+ sign** to the left of the Data Files folder to expand the contents to display all folders. If necessary, in the Folder List panel, click the **+ sign** to the left of the Tutorial folder to expand and display its contents.
5. If necessary, double-click the **insurenew.html** file to open it.
6. In the editing window, select the five lines beginning with "Fast and friendly service," and ending with "Low rates."

7. On the Common toolbar, click the **Bullets** button.
8. In the editing window, click anywhere outside the bulleted list. The paragraphs you selected have bullets and appear as a bulleted list, as shown in Figure 2-24.

Figure 2-24 Newly created bulleted list

a bulleted list has been created from the five paragraphs

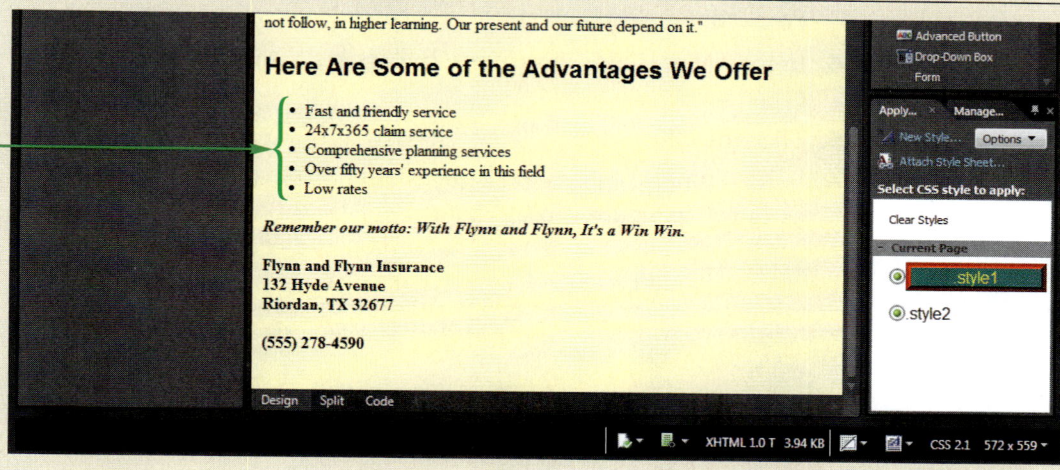

Sandeep wonders if the bulleted list could be made more visually appealing. He also wonders if there are any choices for bullets other than a solid round bullet. Next you'll show him how to customize the appearance of a list.

Customizing the Appearance of Lists

You can use options in the List Properties dialog box to change the appearance of bullets. A solid bullet is the default choice for bullets, but you can select a hollow circle or a square.

REFERENCE

Changing the Bullet Type

- Select the list contents.
- Click Format on the menu bar, and then click Bullets and Numbering.
- If necessary, click either Picture Bullets, Plain Bullets, or Numbers.
- For Plain Bullets, click a bullet style from those shown in the style gallery.

or

- For Numbers, click a bullet style from those shown in the style gallery. Optionally, set a starting number.
- Click the OK button.

A **gallery** is a set of choices, arranged as graphics in a line or table, from which you may click to make a selection. You'll show Sandeep how to change the bullets from round solid bullets to square bullets.

TIP

You can also use an image as a bullet.

To change the appearance of the bullets:

1. Click anywhere in the bulleted list.
2. In the Tag selector (just below the insurenew.html document tab) click the **<ul>** tag to select the bulleted list.
3. On the menu bar, click **Format**, and then click **Bullets and Numbering**. The List Properties dialog box opens. If necessary, click the **Plain Bullets** tab.
4. In the gallery, click the **square bullets** style (the image in the lower-right corner of the gallery) to select it.
5. Click the **OK** button.
6. In the editing window, click anywhere outside the list. The list has square bullets, as shown in Figure 2-25.

Figure 2-25 Modified bulleted list

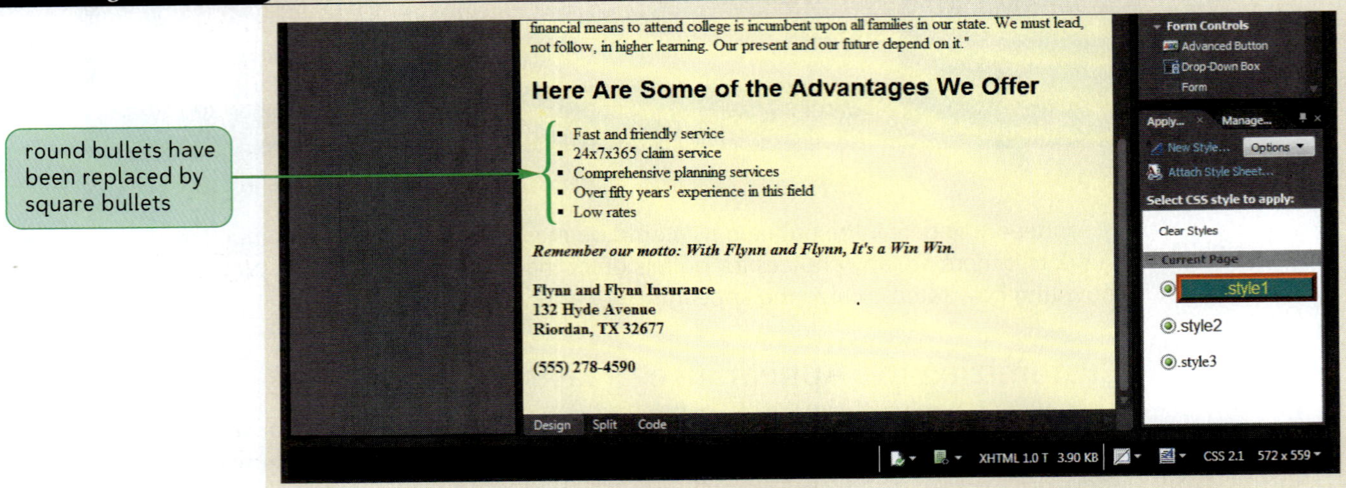

For an ordered list, you can choose from among five types of numbers or letters. The **list style type** sets the type of the list-item marker. The five list style types for letters and numbers are as follows:

- Arabic numbers (the default)
- Lowercase Roman numerals (i, ii, iii, and so on)
- Uppercase Roman numerals (I, II, III, and so on)
- Lowercase letters (a, b, c, and so on)
- Uppercase letters (A, B, C, and so on)

You also have the option of restarting the numbering or lettering of the list if text or images fall between the list items. Next you'll show Sandeep how to create one other type of list, a definition list.

Creating a Definition List

Definition lists do not create a list marker such as a bullet or a number; instead, a **definition list** is used to create a hanging indent format. Definition lists are commonly used to create a **chronology**, which is a list of events in time or date order from first to last, as shown in the following text:

2013 Championship Year!
 This was the year the Royals did it all. They beat the Seals in the championship series, winning the series by a 4–0 margin. It's the first time any team has swept the Seals in championship play.

2012 The Royals Finish in Second Place
 During this season, the team boasted its best record in nearly 10 years. The highlight of the season came on June 14 in a come-from-behind extra-inning win over the Clippers.

A definition list is also commonly used to create a Works Cited page, containing an alphabetical list of author names and other references. Definition lists are often used to create a question-and-answer layout, where the question is on the first line and the answer is below the question. Another common use of definition lists is to create a glossary, where a glossary item appears on one line and the definition of the glossary term is placed on the lines below it in a hanging indent format.

In the HTML code, a definition list begins with the start <dl> tag. The start <dl> tag is followed by the defined term. The defined term is preceded by a start <dt> tag and ended with an end </dt> tag. The definition data is preceded by a start <dd> tag and ended with an end </dd> tag.

TIP

The defined term can be any text. It does not have to be a definition.

Expression Web makes it very easy to compose a definition list and creates all of the HTML code for you. You'll show Sandeep how simple it is to create a definition list in Expression Web by creating one just above the "Remember our Motto . . . " text.

To enter the first definition list entry:

1. In Design view, click at the start of the paragraph that begins "Remember our motto . . . "
2. Press the **Enter** key once. Press the **Up arrow** key once.
3. Click the **Style** list arrow on the Common toolbar and then click **Defined Term <dt>**. A dt Code tab now replaces the p Code tab.
4. Type **Q. Have rates gone up because of Hurricane Grace?**
5. Press the **Enter** key. A dd Code tab now appears. A hanging indent also has been created.
6. Type **A. No. In fact, our rates have remained the same, and in many cases, our rates have even declined over the past year. You can trust us to continue offering the most efficient service and the most affordable insurance in the region.**
7. Press the **Enter** key. The text is entered. The insertion point returns to the left margin, where another dt Code tab now appears.

Now that you have typed the first entry, you'll show Sandeep how to enter the second entry in the definition list.

To enter the second definition list entry:

1. Type **Q. Can I get discounted auto insurance if I purchase an alternative energy vehicle?**
2. Press the **Enter** key. A dd Code tab now appears.
3. Type **Yes. We are offering discounts if you purchase an electric-powered vehicle or hydrogen fuel cell vehicle. These discounts do not cover hybrid gas-powered vehicles, but we have competitive rates for those vehicles as well. Call us for more details on insuring any of these types of high-mileage vehicles.**
4. Click anywhere outside the definition list. The list appears as shown in Figure 2-26.

Figure 2-26 Definition list

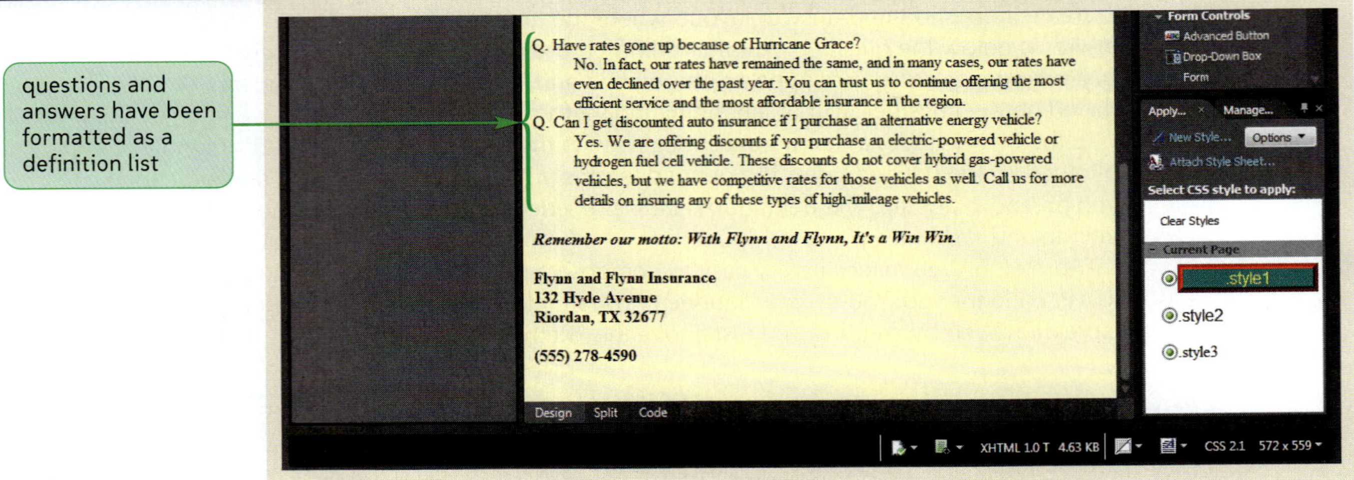

Next, you'll show Sandeep another means of formatting text besides using the Common toolbar: you'll show him some of the features of the Font dialog box.

Using the Font Dialog Box

Sandeep wants the list to stand out on the page. He wants the list to appear bold and italic and to appear in a different color from the other text. You have formatted text by using the Common toolbar. You can also use the Font dialog box to format text. The Font dialog box has several unique means to format text, such as making text appear in all capitals and creating superscripts and subscripts. You now show Sandeep how to use the Font dialog box to make several formatting changes to the document.

To use the Font dialog box to format text:

1. Select the five lines of the unordered list.
2. Right-click anywhere on the unordered list and then click **Font** on the shortcut menu.
3. In the Font list box, click **Arial, Helvetica, sans-serif**.
4. In the Font style list, click **Bold**.

5. In the Size list box, click **medium (14 pt)**.
6. Click the **Color** list arrow, and then click **Maroon** (the fourth color in the first row).
7. In the Effects group, click the **Small caps** check box. The choices in the Font dialog box appear as shown in Figure 2-27.

Figure 2-27 Choices for the Font dialog box

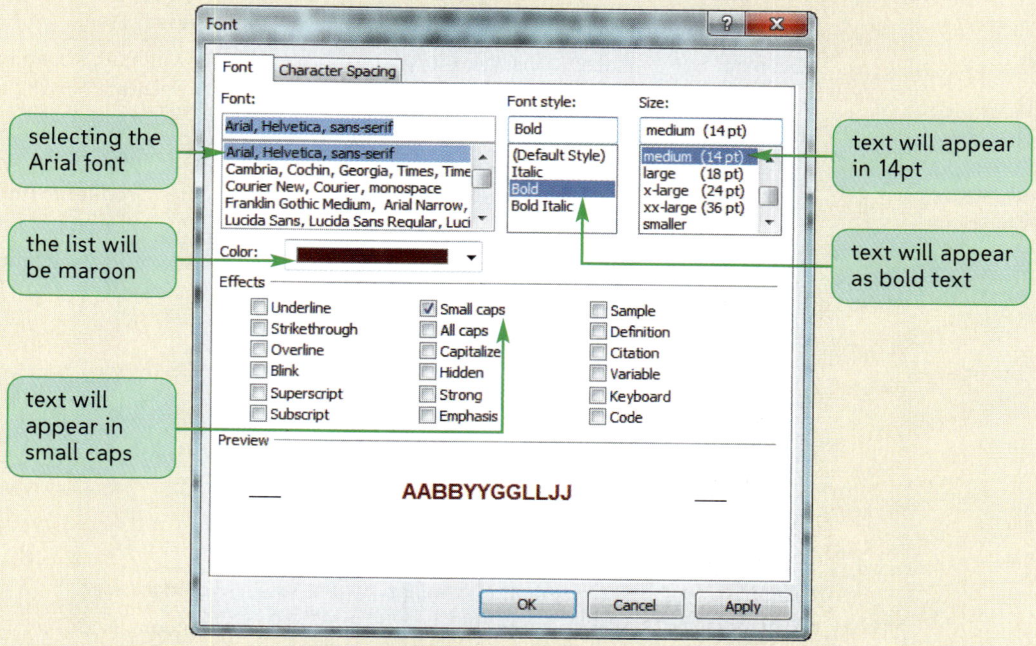

8. Click the **OK** button.
9. In the editing window, click anywhere outside the list. The list should now appear as shown in Figure 2-28.

Figure 2-28 Using the Font dialog box to format text

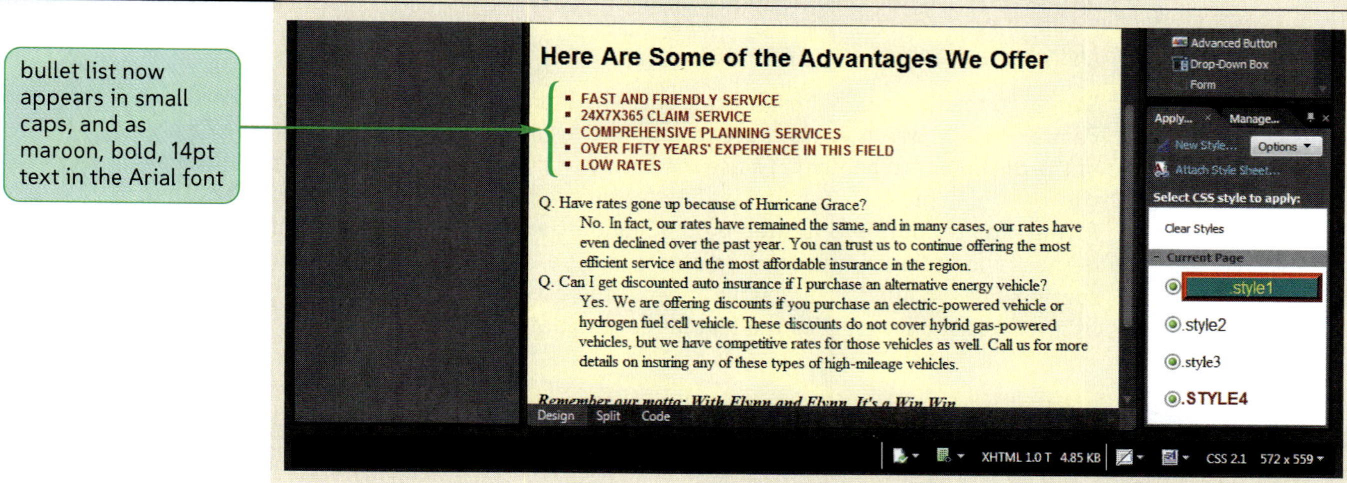

You can apply many effects using the Font dialog box, as shown in Figure 2-29.

Figure 2-29 **Effects available from the Font dialog box**

Effect	Result	Comment
Underline	Underlines text	Do not use for text emphasis in body text (underlined text might be confused with a link)
Strikethrough	Places a line through text	Seldom used
Overline	Places a line above text	Use in math equations and with underline to decorate headings
Blink	Makes text blink on and off	Do not use (considered amateurish and distracting)
Superscript	Raises text one-half line above the line of type	Often used for footnotes
Subscript	Lowers text one-half line below the line of type	Used often in chemical formulas and math equations
Small caps	Displays text in a slightly smaller point size and in all capitals	
All caps	Capitalizes all letters in the text	
Capitalize	Capitalizes the first letter of each word	
Hidden	Hides text	
Strong	Makes text bold	
Emphasis	Makes text italic	
Sample	Displays text in a monotype font face	Seldom used
Definition	Makes text italic	Seldom used
Citation	Makes text italic	Seldom used
Variable	Makes text italic	Seldom used
Keyboard	Displays text in a monotype font face	Seldom used
Code	Displays text in a monotype font face	Seldom used

INSIGHT

Using the Format Painter Tool

Similar to many other Microsoft programs, the Standard toolbar also has a Format Painter button, which you can use to copy the formatting characteristics from one area of the document to another. To use the Format Painter, click in the text whose format you want to copy. Click the Format Painter button once to copy the format once. The Format Painter button is located on the Standard toolbar, not on the Common toolbar. Because the Format Painter button creates a type of CSS style that you should use very sparingly, it is a good idea to limit or avoid the use of the Format Painter button. To turn off the Format Painter, click the Format Painter button again.

Sandeep wants to make the quoted material stand out by being indented on either the left or right. You'll show him how to indent the quoted material that appears at the end of the "Let Us Reassure You" paragraph.

Indenting Text

Expression Web has two buttons on the Common toolbar that change a text indent. Each click of the Decrease Indent Position button decreases the indent by approximately 50 pixels. Each time you click the Increase Indent Position button, Expression Web increases the indent by 50 pixels. These two buttons increase or decrease the indent on one side only. The HTML **blockquote element**, however, indents text on both sides.

You can access the blockquote style by clicking the Style list arrow on the Common toolbar. Sandeep wants to indent the text on the left only, but he's not sure how much of an indent he wants. You'll show him several ways to create an indent and let him decide on how much of an indent he wants. The first method you'll show him is how to create an indent using the buttons on the Common toolbar.

TIP

The blockquote element is seldom used in HTML code.

To create indented text:

1. In the editing window, click anywhere in the quoted paragraph that begins with the words, "I can think of no other gift . . . "
2. Click the **p Code** tab above the paragraph to select the paragraph.
3. On the Common toolbar, click the **Increase Indent Position** button. Sandeep wants to see more of an indent.
4. With the paragraph text still selected, again click the **Increase Indent Position** button. Sandeep now feels the text is indented too much.
5. With the paragraph text still selected, click the **Decrease Indent Position** button twice on the Common toolbar. The paragraph text is no longer indented.

PROSKILLS

Teamwork: Getting a 360-Degree View

Web development traditionally has fallen as a task shared by two distinct groups. On the one hand are Web page designers, whose primary focus is to design an attractive and attention-getting Web page. On the other hand are Web page developers, who write software that supports the underlying features of a Web page, such as accessing a database and retrieving that information for display on the user's screen. The two groups often possess different skill sets, with the designers being well versed in such software programs as Adobe Photoshop or Adobe Illustrator. The developers are more likely to be familiar with programming languages that are used with the Web, such as XML or JavaScript. Today, there is a growing convergence of these two skills. The term **devsigner** is used to describe a person who has both design and development skills. When developing a Web page, each group must keep in mind that there has to be a balance between the priorities of both groups. The designers might want a page whose chief advantage is attractive design and layout, whereas the developers might want a page whose focus relies on accessing data allocation and retrieval. The goal of everyone on the development team should be to design a Web site that is both well designed and functional. You are not creating the Web page to please yourself; you are creating the Web page to please the visitors to your Web site.

Next you'll show Sandeep how to use the Paragraph dialog box to create several formatting changes, including indenting text.

Using the Paragraph Dialog Box

You can use the Paragraph dialog box to create multiple formatting changes. You can also use it to make formatting changes that cannot be made from the Common toolbar. Sandeep wants to have the following text effects:

- Indent the paragraph text on both sides, not just on the left or just on the right.
- Create an additional indent for just the first line of the paragraph.
- Change the line spacing for the paragraph to double spacing.
- Create some extra spacing before and after the paragraph.

You'll show Sandeep how to make these formatting changes using the Paragraph dialog box.

To format text using the Paragraph dialog box:

1. With the text in the quoted paragraph selected, click **Format** on the menu bar, and then click **Paragraph**. The Paragraph dialog box opens.
2. In the Indentation group, click in the **Left side** box. Delete any value presently in the box, and then type **20**.
3. Click in the **Right side** text box. Delete any value presently in the box and then type **20**.
4. Click in the **Indent first line** text box and then type **10**.
5. In the Spacing group, click in the **Before** text box and then type **12**.
6. Click in the **After** text box and then type **12**.
7. Click the **Line spacing** list arrow and then click **Double**. Your choices should appear similar to those in Figure 2-30.

Figure 2-30 Choices entered in the Paragraph dialog box

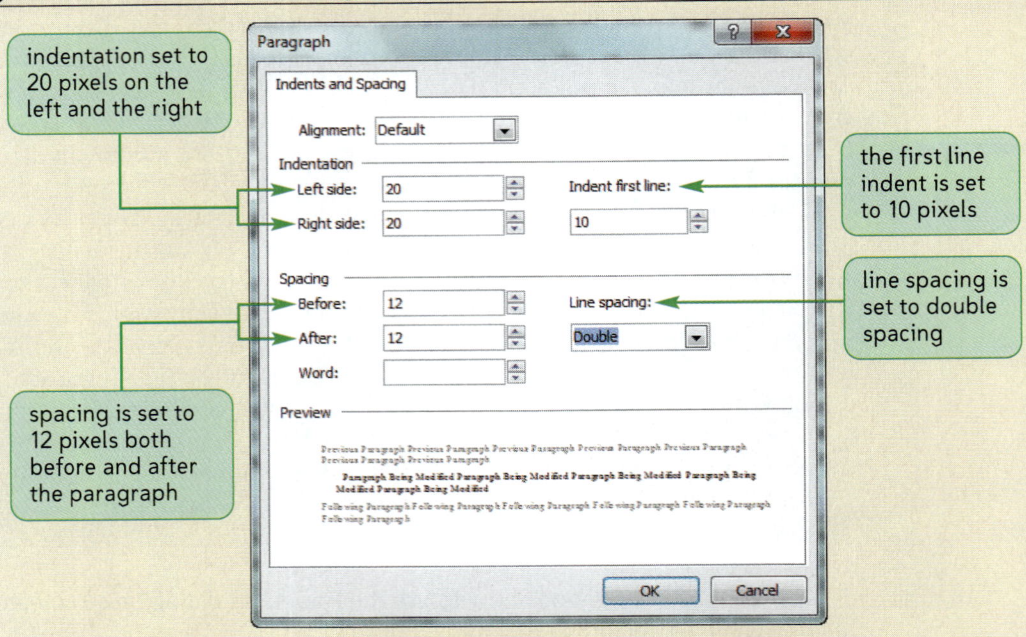

8. Click the **OK** button to close the Paragraph dialog box.

9. Click anywhere outside the paragraph. The quoted paragraph should look similar to the one shown in Figure 2-31. If necessary, scroll down to see the entire quoted paragraph. Note that the indent and the line spacing have now changed.

Figure 2-31 **The quoted paragraph formatted**

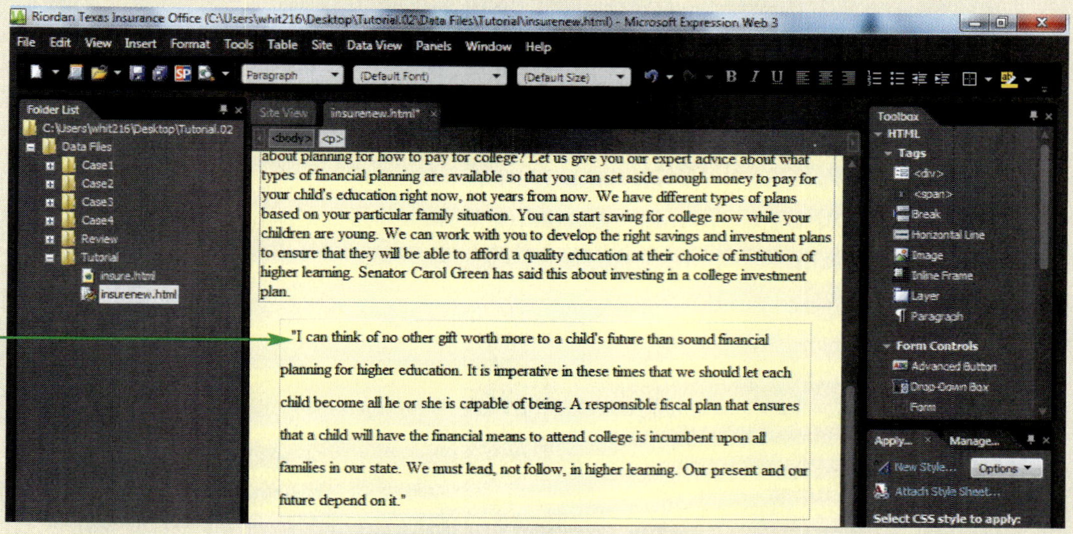

You can use other methods to call attention to heading text. Word spacing and character spacing create an artistic effect that draws attention to a heading. You'll explore how these features work in Expression Web.

Creating a Spread Heading

Word spacing is a feature in Expression Web that creates extra space between words. Similarly, **character spacing** is a feature that creates extra space between characters. Of course, you could use the spacebar to create word or character spacing in text, but you have much greater precision in spacing letters or words by using the word spacing and character spacing features of Expression Web.

REFERENCE

Changing the Character Spacing

- Select the text.
- Right-click and then click Font on the shortcut menu.
- In the Font dialog box, click the Character Spacing tab.
- Click the Spacing list arrow, and then click Expanded.
- In the By box, type a point value.
- Click the OK button.

A **spread heading** is a heading that uses either word or character spacing. You use the Paragraph dialog box to add word spacing, and the Font dialog box to establish character spacing. You do not, however, see the effect of word spacing in Design view; you see word spacing only when you preview a document in the browser. This is one of the few times that you do not see formatting take effect in Design view. You do, however, see character spacing in Design view. You'll show Sandeep how to add some character spacing to the h1 heading at the top of the page.

To create character spacing in the h1 heading:

1. Press the **Ctrl+Home** keys to position the insertion point at the top of the page.
2. Select the h1 heading text **The Flynn and Flynn Insurance Company**.
3. Right-click anywhere inside the h1 heading text, and then on the shortcut menu, click **Font**. The Font dialog box opens.
4. In the Font dialog box, click the **Character Spacing** tab.
5. Click the **Spacing** list arrow, and then click **Expanded**.
6. Click in the **By** text box. Delete any existing value and type **3 px**.
7. Click the **OK** button.
8. Click anywhere outside the h1 heading text. The h1 heading text is spaced out more across the page, as shown in Figure 2-32.

Figure 2-32 Character spacing

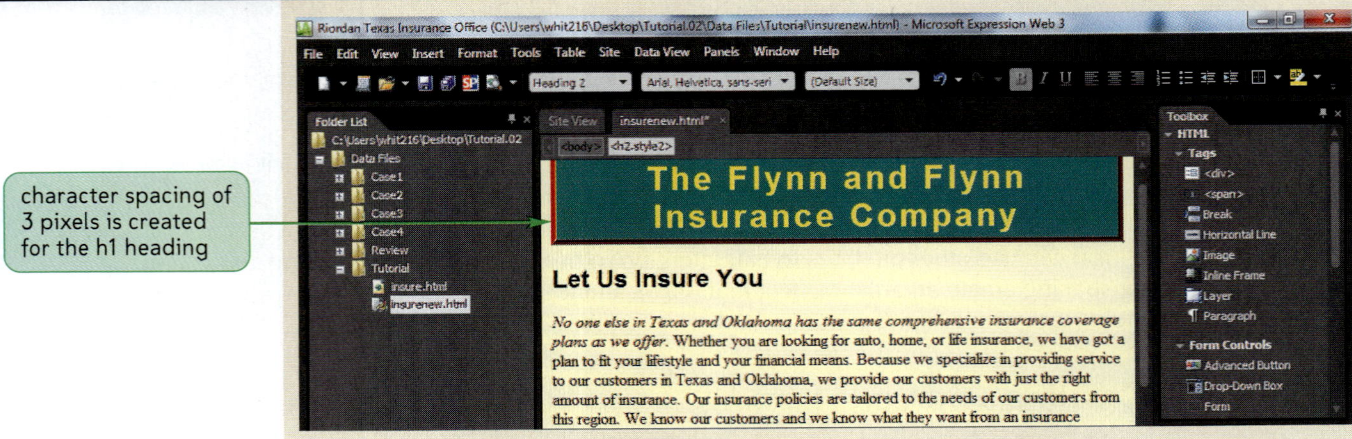

Sandeep wants to make sure that the list is separated from the address at the bottom of the Web page. You'll show Sandeep how to create a horizontal line to accomplish this.

Creating a Horizontal Line

Horizontal lines serve as content dividers for Web pages. By default, a horizontal line is gray and occupies 100% of the screen width. You can change the width, the height, and the color of the line, but bear in mind that browsers differ in how they display horizontal lines.

INSIGHT

Creating Horizontal Lines

Horizontal lines are referred to in HTML as horizontal rules. Horizontal lines appear differently depending on the browser and browser version. For example, don't be concerned if your single horizontal line appears in another browser as a double line. Again, depending on the browser and browser version, a custom line color might not show. In addition, a line might have sharp corner endings in one browser, but rounded edges in another. Again, you will see substantial difference among browsers in the appearance of a line if you choose to format it to appear with no shading. Horizontal lines are not used on Web pages as much as they were a few years ago. Today, if you see a horizontal line on a Web page, it usually is there as an image or as a line that was created using CSS.

You'll show Sandeep how to insert a horizontal line by using the menu bar, as well as how to change some of the characteristics of the horizontal line.

To insert a horizontal line:

1. Press the **Ctrl+End** keys to position the insertion point at the bottom of the page.
2. Position the insertion point at the start of the first line of the Flynn and Flynn Insurance address.
3. Click the **Insert** menu, point to **HTML**, and then click **Horizontal Line**. A default horizontal line, which is thin and gray, extends across the full screen width above the address.

   Trouble? If the horizontal line is not thin and gray and does not extend across the full screen width, it's because Expression Web "remembers" how the last user styled horizontal lines. You'll format the line in the next set of steps.
4. Double-click anywhere on the horizontal line. The Horizontal Line Properties dialog box opens.
5. In the Width text box, type **90**.
6. Click in the **Height** text box, delete any value already present, and type **4**.
7. If necessary, click the **Solid line (no shading)** check box to select that choice.
8. Click the **OK** button.
9. Click anywhere outside the horizontal line to deselect the line. The horizontal line should appear as shown in Figure 2-33. (The line is shown in Internet Explorer. Not all browsers, such as the Firefox browser, will display the horizontal line with no shading in the same manner as shown in Figure 2-33.)

Figure 2-33 A horizontal line

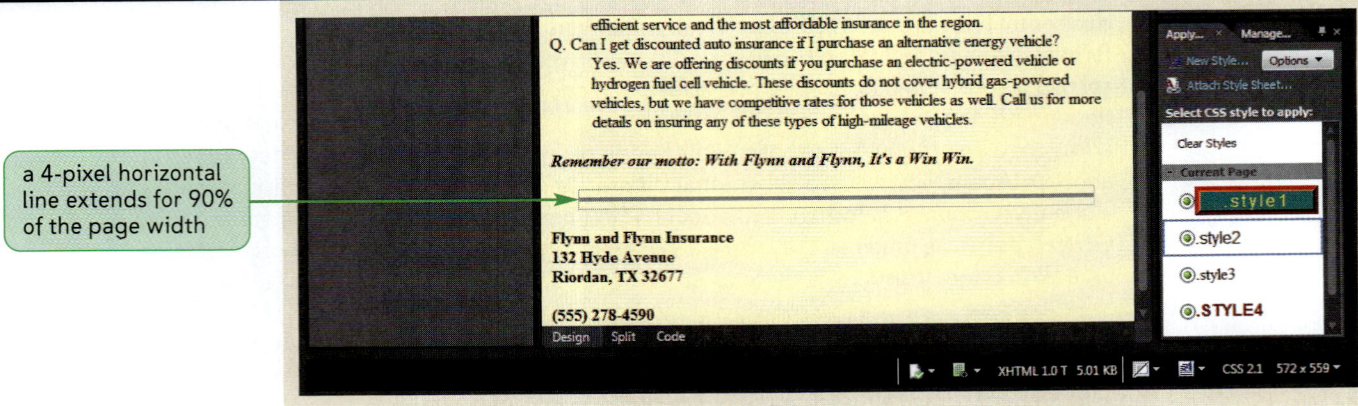

Sandeep wants to create a line of text at the bottom of the Web page that places a copyright on the Web page. He also wants the line to be centered and in a different color. The **document footer** is the last line (or several lines) of a Web page, and usually includes contact information or a list of links to other pages at the same Web site. You'll work with Sandeep to format the document footer, including inserting the copyright symbol.

Inserting Symbols

Symbols are characters that cannot be entered from the keyboard, such as the registered trademark symbol (®) and the copyright symbol (©). You'll enter a copyright symbol in the document footer. You'll also center the footer and change the text color by using the Font Color box on the Common toolbar. If you are using Expression Web 4, you will find the Symbol dialog box to be quite different. Please review the *Introduction to Expression Web 4* pages in the front matter of this text.

To insert a new paragraph and enter a symbol:

1. Position the insertion point after the number ***0*** in the phone number (555) 278-4590.
2. Press the **Enter** key to create a new paragraph.
3. Click the **Insert** menu, and then click **Symbol**. The Symbol dialog box opens.
4. If necessary, click the **Subset** list arrow and then click **Basic Latin**. The dialog box should appear as shown in Figure 2-34, although your Recently used symbols may be different.

Figure 2-34 **The Symbol dialog box**

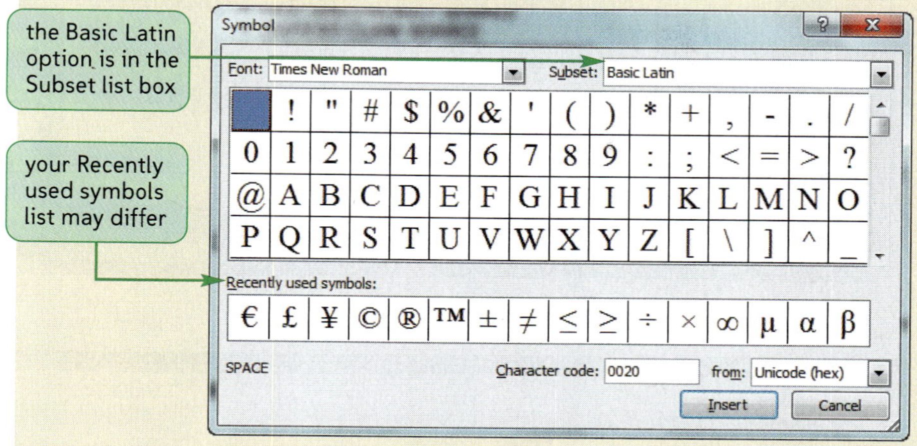

5. If the copyright (©) symbol is not shown among the Recently used symbols, scroll down and find the copyright symbol, which should be in the middle of the seventh row.
6. Click the copyright symbol, ©.
7. Click the **Insert** button.
8. Click the **Close** button. The copyright symbol is inserted.

Next, you enter and format text for the footer. Recall that to enter text on a new line without creating a paragraph, you press the Shift+Enter keys.

To enter and format text for the footer:

1. Type the current year.
2. Press the **Shift+Enter** keys.
3. Type Your First and Last Name, **Tutorial 2**.
4. If the text in the two lines is not already bold, select the two lines of text you just typed and format the text so that those lines are bold.
5. Click the **p Code tab** to select the two lines you just typed. On the Common toolbar, click the **Center** button.
6. With the lines still selected, on the Common toolbar, click the **Font Color** list arrow. Click the **blue #0000FF** color swatch, which is the next-to-last color swatch in the row. Depending on your monitor size and your resolution, you may have to click the More Buttons list arrow to access the Font Color.
7. Click the **Apply** button.
8. Click anywhere outside the lines to deselect the text. The footer lines should look similar to those shown in Figure 2-35.

Figure 2-35 The footer

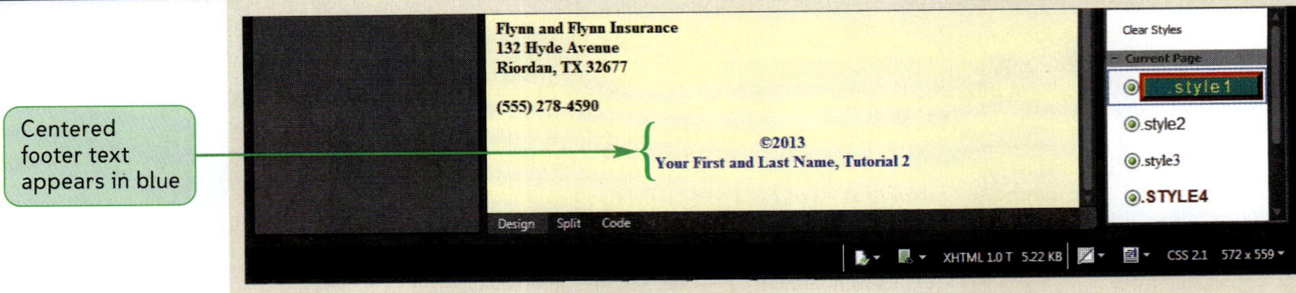

INSIGHT

Inserting HTML Code

It is sometimes necessary to insert some HTML code, particularly in the document footer area. By default, Expression Web carries over the present style. Usually, that's a benefit. If you type one paragraph, Expression Web creates another paragraph (the paragraph style) when you press the Enter key. For example, if you created and styled an h1 heading and then pressed the Enter key after that heading, the next paragraph would have the h1 heading style, which might not be what you want. To insert HTML code, click Insert on the menu bar, point to HTML, and then click the HTML code you want to insert. If you position the insertion point past the last HTML tag that formats text on the page, *Expression Web stops generating code*. You must insert HTML code using the preceding steps.

Next, you'll have Sandeep save and view the completed file in the browser. In addition to the other methods you have used to save a file, you can also save a file by right-clicking the document tab.

To save the file and view the completed file in the browser:

1. Right-click the **insurenew.html** document tab.
2. Click **Save**.
3. Press the **F12** key to display the file in your default browser.
4. If necessary, press the **Ctrl+Home** keys to position the insertion point at the top of the page in the browser. Your file should look similar to the one shown in Figure 2-36.
5. Close the browser.

Figure 2-36 The completed page

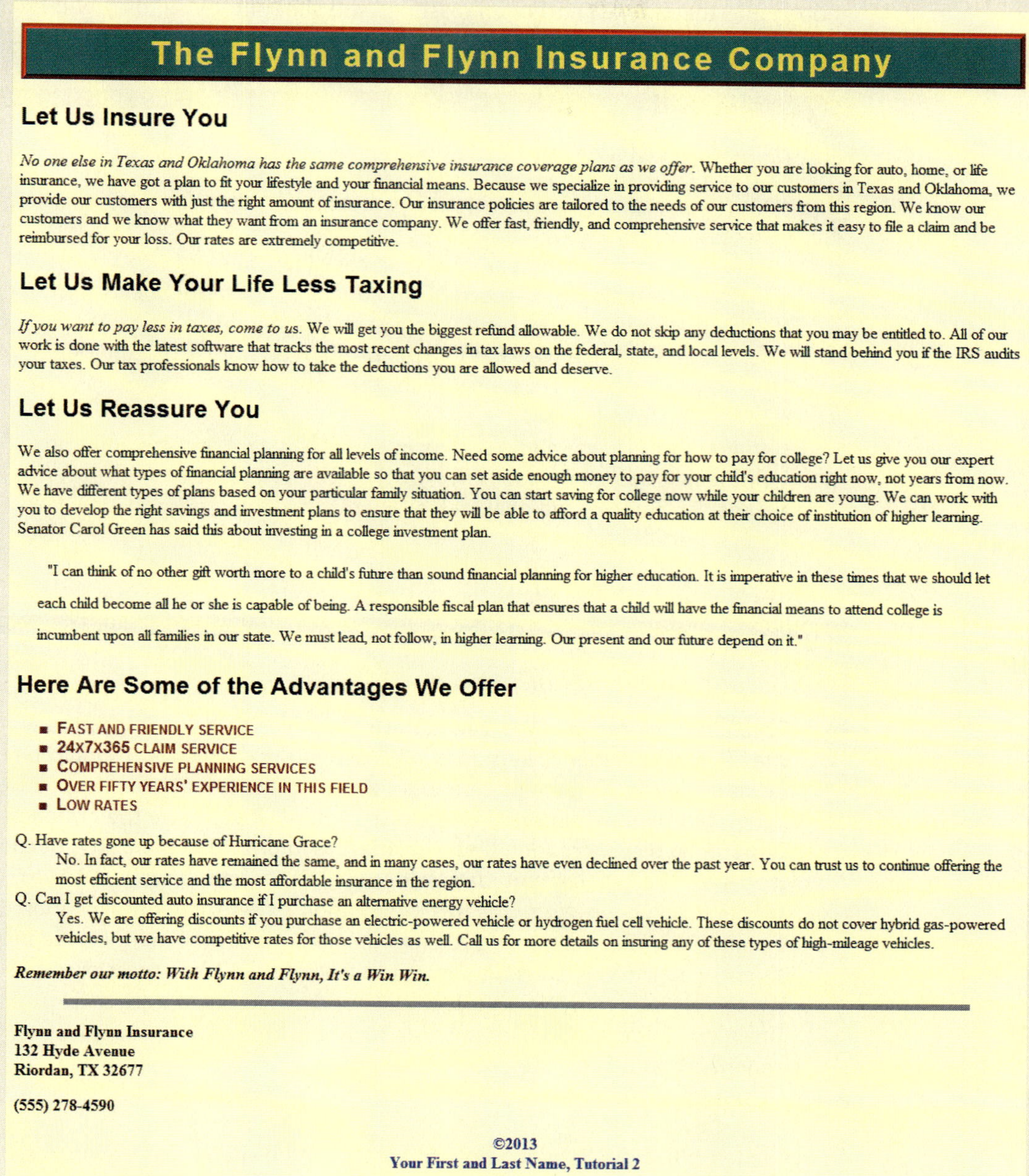
The Flynn and Flynn Insurance Company

Let Us Insure You

No one else in Texas and Oklahoma has the same comprehensive insurance coverage plans as we offer. Whether you are looking for auto, home, or life insurance, we have got a plan to fit your lifestyle and your financial means. Because we specialize in providing service to our customers in Texas and Oklahoma, we provide our customers with just the right amount of insurance. Our insurance policies are tailored to the needs of our customers from this region. We know our customers and we know what they want from an insurance company. We offer fast, friendly, and comprehensive service that makes it easy to file a claim and be reimbursed for your loss. Our rates are extremely competitive.

Let Us Make Your Life Less Taxing

If you want to pay less in taxes, come to us. We will get you the biggest refund allowable. We do not skip any deductions that you may be entitled to. All of our work is done with the latest software that tracks the most recent changes in tax laws on the federal, state, and local levels. We will stand behind you if the IRS audits your taxes. Our tax professionals know how to take the deductions you are allowed and deserve.

Let Us Reassure You

We also offer comprehensive financial planning for all levels of income. Need some advice about planning for how to pay for college? Let us give you our expert advice about what types of financial planning are available so that you can set aside enough money to pay for your child's education right now, not years from now. We have different types of plans based on your particular family situation. You can start saving for college now while your children are young. We can work with you to develop the right savings and investment plans to ensure that they will be able to afford a quality education at their choice of institution of higher learning. Senator Carol Green has said this about investing in a college investment plan.

> "I can think of no other gift worth more to a child's future than sound financial planning for higher education. It is imperative in these times that we should let each child become all he or she is capable of being. A responsible fiscal plan that ensures that a child will have the financial means to attend college is incumbent upon all families in our state. We must lead, not follow, in higher learning. Our present and our future depend on it."

Here Are Some of the Advantages We Offer

- FAST AND FRIENDLY SERVICE
- 24X7X365 CLAIM SERVICE
- COMPREHENSIVE PLANNING SERVICES
- OVER FIFTY YEARS' EXPERIENCE IN THIS FIELD
- LOW RATES

Q. Have rates gone up because of Hurricane Grace?

: No. In fact, our rates have remained the same, and in many cases, our rates have even declined over the past year. You can trust us to continue offering the most efficient service and the most affordable insurance in the region.

Q. Can I get discounted auto insurance if I purchase an alternative energy vehicle?

: Yes. We are offering discounts if you purchase an electric-powered vehicle or hydrogen fuel cell vehicle. These discounts do not cover hybrid gas-powered vehicles, but we have competitive rates for those vehicles as well. Call us for more details on insuring any of these types of high-mileage vehicles.

Remember our motto: With Flynn and Flynn, It's a Win Win.

Flynn and Flynn Insurance
132 Hyde Avenue
Riordan, TX 32677

(555) 278-4590

©2013
Your First and Last Name, Tutorial 2

6. Click the **File** menu, and then click **Close**.
7. Submit the completed file to your instructor, either in printed or electronic form, as requested.

Creating a Web Site

Now that you have familiarized Sandeep with opening and working with an Expression Web site, you'll show him how to create one. The home page for most Web sites is a file named default.htm or index.htm. Expression Web automatically creates a file named default.htm for you. Filenames for Web sites should be lowercase, should not include any punctuation other than the underscore character, and should begin with a letter. Filenames should be brief, preferably not more than eight characters, and should not include spaces. Before you create a Web site, you should close any pages that might be open and that are not part of an existing Web site; otherwise, they will be added to the new Web site.

REFERENCE

Creating a Web Site

- Choose a storage location on your computer for the Web site; insert storage media if necessary.
- Click Site on the menu bar, and then click New Site.
- In the New dialog box, specify One Page Site or Empty Site.
- Click the Browse button and navigate to the storage location you have chosen for the Web site. Click the New Folder icon or the New Folder button (depending on your operating system). Type a name for the new folder.
- Click the Open button.
- In the "Specify the name and location of the new Web site" text box, click to the right of the last backslash.
- Type the name of the new Web site.
- Click the OK button.

INSIGHT

Hidden Files and Folders

Recall that Expression Web keeps track of all files that are associated with your Web site. This information is kept in two hidden folders, which you should be careful not to move or delete. These hidden folders and their contents do *not* appear in the Folder List panel, but they *will* appear in Windows Explorer if you have the option set in Windows Explorer to display hidden files. Metadata is information about the documents in your Web site. The *_vti_cnf* metadata folder contains information about every file in a particular site. Expression Web uses this information to determine the location of links within the site. The *_vti_pvt* metadata folder stores several files that provide information, among other things, to configure the initial settings for Expression Web. Just remember not to delete or move these two folders or their contents from an Expression Web site. These two folders, although invisible to you in the Folder List panel, are important components of your Web site.

Next you'll show Sandeep how to create a Web site in Expression Web.

To create a new Web site:

1. Click the **Site** menu, and then click **Close**. The editing window should now be dark gray.
2. Click the **Site** menu, and then click **New Site**. The New dialog box opens, as shown in Figure 2-37. (There might already be values in the Location and Name boxes.)

Figure 2-37 The New dialog box

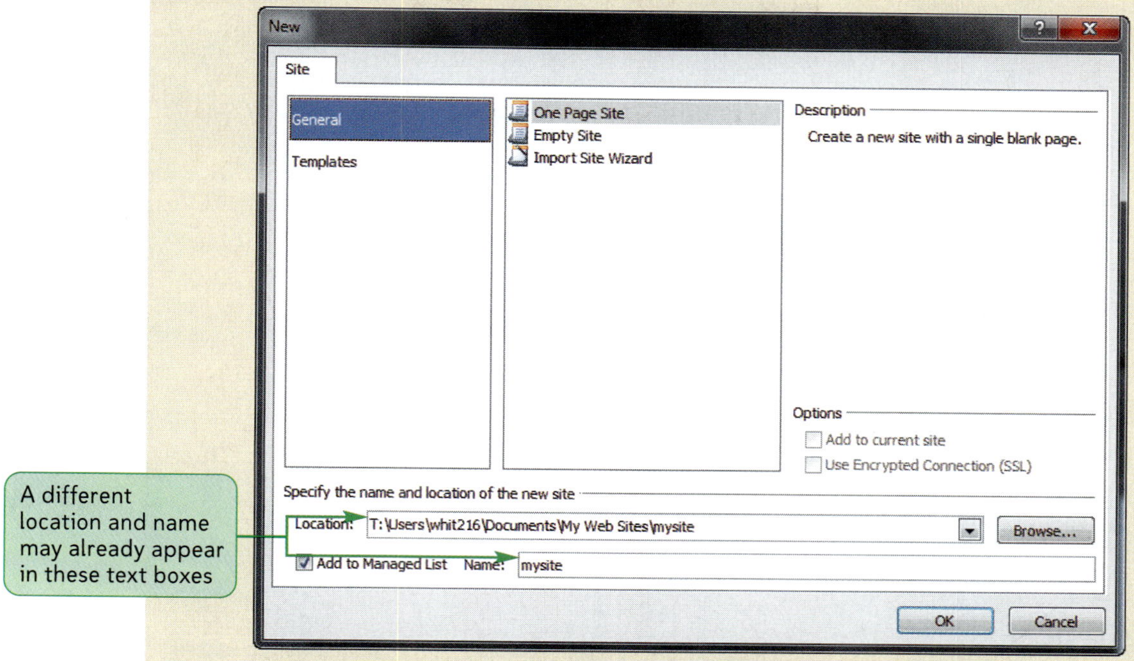

3. Click **One Page Site**. You now need to determine a storage location for the Web site. Click the **Browse** button. The New Site Location dialog box opens.
4. Click **Computer**. Navigate to the drive letter of your flash drive (or other storage location where you will store the file).
5. Double-click the **drive letter**. Click the **New folder** button, type **flynn**, and then press the **Enter** key.
6. Click the **Open** button. The New dialog box opens.
7. In the Location text box, click to the right of the last backslash. Make sure the path is not selected (reverse highlighted). If necessary, click again to the right of the last backslash so that none of the path is selected.
8. Type **myfirstsite**. The New dialog box should appear similar to that shown in Figure 2-38, although your path will be different.

Figure 2-38 The new Web site location

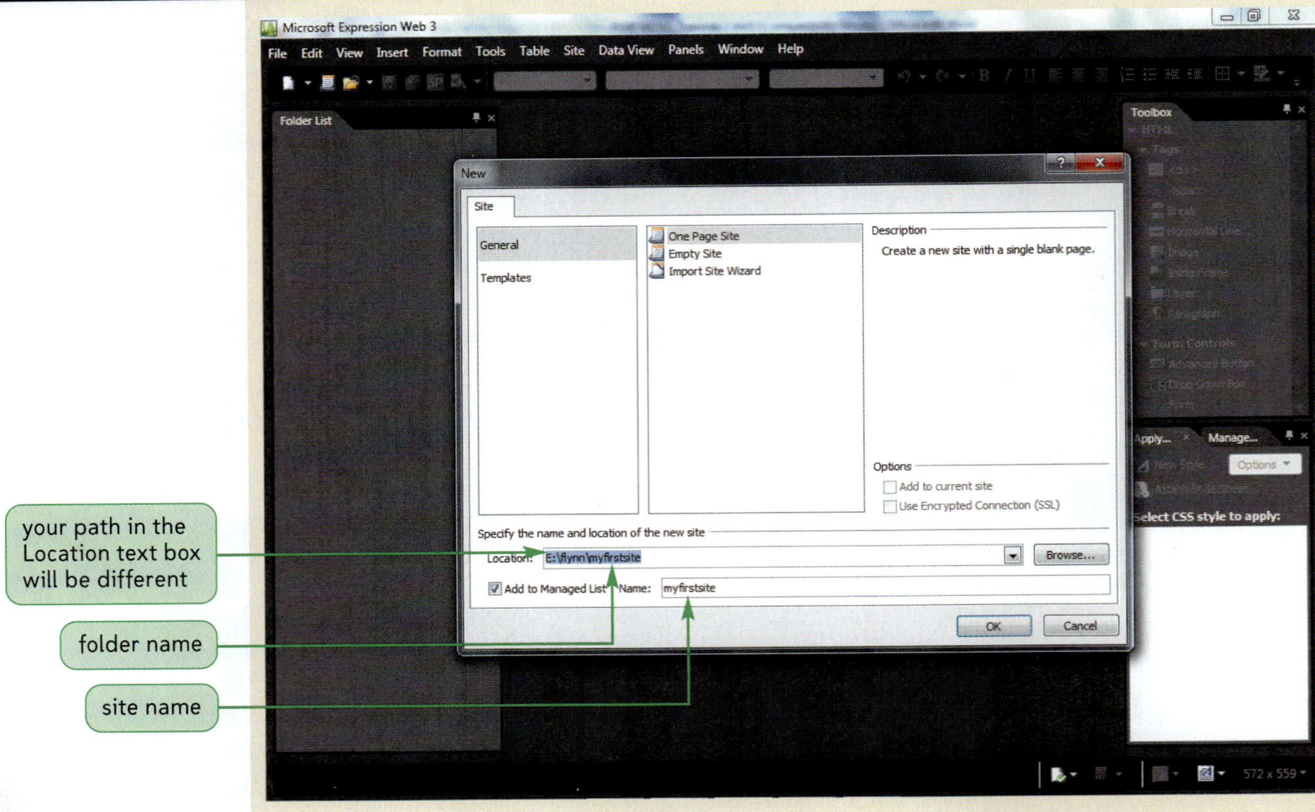

9. Click the **OK** button. In a few seconds, Expression Web creates the Web site. Your screen should look similar to Figure 2-39.

Figure 2-39 The New Web site screen

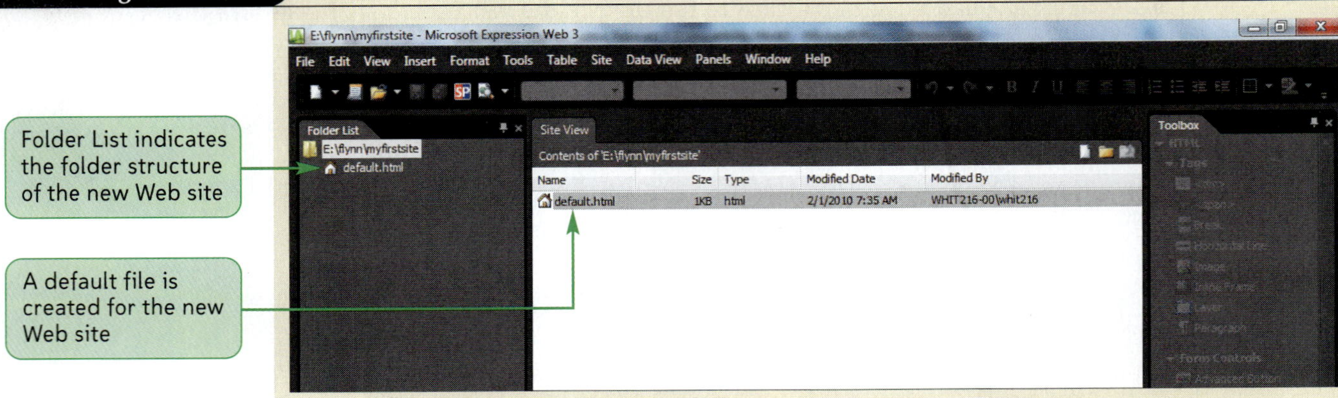

TIP

You can open a recently created or revised Web site by clicking Site on the menu bar, pointing to Recent Sites, and then clicking the site you want to open.

A default home page, default.html, has been created for you. The default.html filename appears both in the Folder List panel and in the Web site window. Although you could click either filename to open the default.html file, you'll open the file from the Folder List panel because it is the window that manages all of the files for the Web site.

To open the default home page:

1. In the Folder List panel, double-click the **default.html** filename. A blank page opens in Expression Web.
2. If the page is displayed in Split view or Code view, click the Design button.
3. Click **Site** and then click **Close** to close the Web site.
4. If you will not be completing the Review Assignments or the Case Problems, exit Expression Web.

REVIEW

Session 2.2 Quick Check

1. What are three types of lists that can be created?
2. Name two font effects that you should avoid using.
3. What is the term used to refer to an indent on both sides?
4. What is the default appearance of a horizontal rule?
5. What is a symbol?
6. On the menu bar, which command would you click to create a new Web site?

Practice the skills you learned in the tutorial.

PRACTICE

Review Assignments

Data Files needed for the Review Assignment: boat.html

Sandeep was pleased with the Web page you created for The Flynn and Flynn Insurance Company. Sandeep wants to add another page that calls attention to boat insurance, which is another type of insurance that the company offers to its customers. Although your document might appear somewhat differently, depending on your browser and browser version, a preview of the completed document appears in Figure 2-40.

Figure 2-40 **Completed boat insurance Web page**

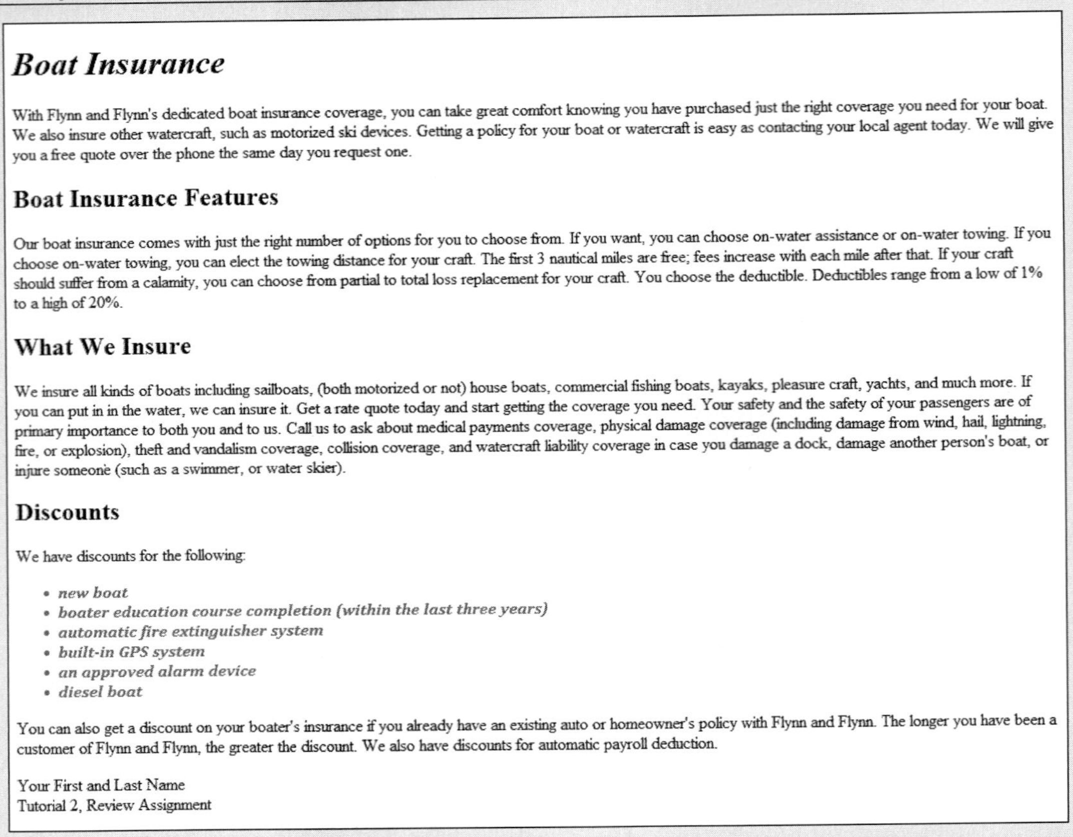

Boat Insurance

With Flynn and Flynn's dedicated boat insurance coverage, you can take great comfort knowing you have purchased just the right coverage you need for your boat. We also insure other watercraft, such as motorized ski devices. Getting a policy for your boat or watercraft is easy as contacting your local agent today. We will give you a free quote over the phone the same day you request one.

Boat Insurance Features

Our boat insurance comes with just the right number of options for you to choose from. If you want, you can choose on-water assistance or on-water towing. If you choose on-water towing, you can elect the towing distance for your craft. The first 3 nautical miles are free; fees increase with each mile after that. If your craft should suffer from a calamity, you can choose from partial to total loss replacement for your craft. You choose the deductible. Deductibles range from a low of 1% to a high of 20%.

What We Insure

We insure all kinds of boats including sailboats, (both motorized or not) house boats, commercial fishing boats, kayaks, pleasure craft, yachts, and much more. If you can put in in the water, we can insure it. Get a rate quote today and start getting the coverage you need. Your safety and the safety of your passengers are of primary importance to both you and to us. Call us to ask about medical payments coverage, physical damage coverage (including damage from wind, hail, lightning, fire, or explosion), theft and vandalism coverage, collision coverage, and watercraft liability coverage in case you damage a dock, damage another person's boat, or injure someone (such as a swimmer, or water skier).

Discounts

We have discounts for the following:

- *new boat*
- *boater education course completion (within the last three years)*
- *automatic fire extinguisher system*
- *built-in GPS system*
- *an approved alarm device*
- *diesel boat*

You can also get a discount on your boater's insurance if you already have an existing auto or homeowner's policy with Flynn and Flynn. The longer you have been a customer of Flynn and Flynn, the greater the discount. We also have discounts for automatic payroll deduction.

Your First and Last Name
Tutorial 2, Review Assignment

Complete the following:

1. If necessary, start Expression Web, close any open sites, and close any toolbars other than the Common toolbar. Reset the workspace layout.
2. If necessary, open the Tutorial.02 Web site. If necessary, expand the Review folders.
3. Open the **boat.html** file from the Review folder in the Folder List panel. Save the file as **boatnew.html** in the same folder.
4. In Design view, right-click anywhere on the page. Open the Page Properties dialog box, then in the Page description box, type your first and last name, type / (a forward slash character), and type **Tutorial 2, Review Assignment**. Close the Page Properties dialog box and return to Design view.
5. Position the insertion point at the top of the page. Use the Find and Replace feature to replace each instance of the word *protect* with the word *insure*.

6. At the top of the page, select the words *Boat Insurance* and format those words as a Heading 1 <h1> heading. Also have the h1 heading text appear in italic.
7. Use the Thesaurus feature to find a synonym for the word *specialized* in the first sentence below the h1 heading.
8. One by one, select the remaining three subheadings ("Boat Insurance Features," "What We Insure," and "Discounts") and format those headings as Heading 2 <h2> headings.
9. Select the six items from "new boat" through "diesel boat". Format those items as a bulleted list.
10. With the list items still selected, use the Font dialog box to format the list items to appear in the Cambria font, and as bold, italic, green text.
11. Perform a spelling check on the document. Correct any errors. (There are some words in the document that have been deliberately misspelled.)
12. Press the **Ctrl+End** keys to position the insertion point at the end of the document. On two lines, type the following (substitute your name as appropriate). Press the Shift+Enter keys after you type your name. (*Note*: Text you need to type is shown in bold for ease of reference only; do not bold the text unless otherwise instructed.)
    Your First and Last Name
    Tutorial 2, Review Assignment
13. Save the **boatnew.html** file.
14. Open the **boatnew.html** file in your browser. The document should be similar to the one shown in Figure 2-40.
15. Close the document.
16. Submit the completed file to your instructor, either in printed or electronic form, as requested.

Use the skills you learned in the tutorial to create a Web page about reducing energy consumption in new homes.

APPLY

Case Problem 1

Data File needed for this Case Problem: going.html

Going Green to Make Green The housing slump that has affected most of the country has had an unusual side effect. Home sellers are turning to environmental issues to give themselves an advantage when the time comes to sell a home. The overall cost of home ownership is a major issue, especially for first-time homebuyers. You have been asked to create a Web page for a home-building company that outlines the advantages of having an environmentally friendly home. Although your file might appear somewhat differently, a preview of the completed document appears in Figure 2-41.

Figure 2-41 **Completed green homes Web page**

Going Green to Make Green

Today, companies are thinking of improving the bottom line by entering the energy business. Many manufacturing companies are drawing up or even implementing plans that will lead to energy independence. It may be that within 10 years or so, our abundant resources for wind, wave, solar, geothermal, hydroelectric and hydrogen technology will lead to greater energy independence for our nation.

The home building industry is getting remarkable incentives to go green. It used to be that green homes referred to the lush landscaping that surrounded a home. Green homes had more to do with culturing a great lawn than it did the home itself. Much of that has changed since the home building bubble has burst. During the boom times in new home construction in the early part of this century, it was a mere convenience to build homes that are more energy efficient. There was an interest in making homes more affordable, but there was no real passion about it. Now that the new home market has fallen into more troubled times, home builders are recognizing that building an energy-efficient home can serve as a point of differentiation. If two homes are of similar price and size, the green home would offer the prospective buyer a real incentive to buy. Even today, there are varying degrees of how homes are considered to be energy-efficient and environmentally friendly. Those homes who feature the greatest energy savings and are the most environmentally friendly are now often referred to as deep green homes, super green, or mega green homes.

What Is a Green Home?

What makes a home green? To start with, a green home keeps itself warm in the winter and cool in the summer. Windows that reflect light (and also dampen sound) do a great job in keeping the inside temperature of a home from having drastic highs and lows. Insulation material like TruTechno® in the walls and roofing certainly make a difference as well. Homes with snow on the roof in winter time aren't just reminiscent of a Christmas greeting card; that's a sign that the home is energy efficient and heat isn't being lost through the roof.

The Source of Energy

How the home derives its source of heating and cooling is certainly a factor as well. Geothermal systems, which rely on circulating hot water from underground tanks, and solar panels are technologies have been around for many years. These technologies are now getting a second and even a third look as the price of these systems has dropped and the technology behind them has improved and become far less complex and far more reliable than in the past.. Green homes give the added value that new home buyers are looking for. A new idea for keeping a home from exhibiting temperature extremes is actually an old one, which is the concept of using metal roofs, rather than shingles. The metal roofs reflect the heat during the summer, so metal roofs are ideal in the Southwest and the deep Southern states, where the temperatures tend to be on the warm side for 9 or 10 months a year. Cooling costs can be dramatically reduced as a result.

Construction

The construction of the home also lends to being more socially responsible in taking care of our planet for future generations. Using recycled wood cuts down on the need to harvest virgin forest. Even the type of wood can invoke a sense of social responsibility. Using maple instead of other hardwoods that are less abundant, such as teak or bamboo, puts lets pressure on the forests of those countries that supply such boutique building materials.

Appliances

Home appliances, of course, make a contribution as well. Using appliances that are the most energy-efficient will certainly reduce the overall monthly cost of operation. Air conditioners and heating units that are at the top of their ranking in efficiency further reduce monthly energy costs. Of course, using fluorescent lighting instead of incandescent lighting can have a huge impact on the cost of lighting the home.

Green Computing

Of course, computing technology can further reduce the cost of energy in a home. Computers can be used to program lights on and off (both inside and outside) based upon the solar calendar. Thermostats can be programmed to be lowered during the day (if no one is home) and to be raised about half an hour before the first person to arrive home walks through the door. Most families these days have more than one computer, so having a computer that saves energy is still yet another way to reduce energy costs. So is having an eco-friendly computer; one that uses newer materials other than plastic, which is petroleum based, for the computer case as well as internal parts.

Your First and Last Name
Tutorial 2, Case Problem 1

Complete the following:

1. If necessary, start your browser and then start Expression Web. If necessary, in Expression Web, close any open sites. Reset the workspace layout.
2. If necessary, open the Tutorial.02 Web site. If necessary, expand the Case1 folder.
3. Open the **going.html** file and then save the file as **goingnew.html** in the same folder.
4. In Design view, open the Page Properties. In the Title box, type **Green Energy Favors Buyers and Sellers**. In the Page description box, type your first and last name, type / (a forward slash character), type **Tutorial 2, Case Problem 1**, and then close the dialog box and return to Design view.
5. In Design view, position the insertion point at the top of the goingnew.html page.
6. Select the text *Going Green to Make Green* and format those words as a Heading 2 <h2> heading.
7. Use the Common toolbar to center the words in the h2 heading.

8. Use the Common toolbar to change the color of the h2 heading to maroon (#800000).
9. Use the Common toolbar to change the font of the h2 heading to Cambria.
10. Use the Common toolbar to change the font size of the h2 heading to 36 points (xx-large).
11. Insert a horizontal line below the h2 heading. Format the horizontal line to be 80% of the window, 6 pixels high, center-aligned, navy, and without shading.
12. Starting with the side heading "What Is a Green Home?" and proceeding one by one, select the five side headings and format them as Heading 3 <h3> headings.
13. In the paragraph below the heading "What is a Green Home?", insert the registered trademark symbol after the word *TruTechno*.
14. Use the Thesaurus feature to find a synonym for the word *tremendous* in the first sentence of the second paragraph.
15. Display the Standard toolbar.
16. Perform a spelling check on the document. You will find numerous spelling errors. Correct any errors. The word *TruTechno* is spelled correctly.
17. Close the Standard toolbar.
18. Press the **Ctrl+End** keys to position the insertion point at the end of the document. On two lines, type the following (substitute your name as appropriate). Press the Shift+Enter keys after you type your name. (*Note*: Text you need to type is shown in bold for ease of reference only; do not bold the text unless otherwise instructed.)
    Your First and Last Name
    Tutorial 2, Case Problem 1
19. Save the **goingnew.html** file.
20. Open the **goingnew.html** file in your browser. The document should be similar to the one shown in Figure 2-41.
21. Close the document.
22. Submit the completed file to your instructor, either in printed or electronic form, as requested.

Explore how to create and style a Web page about how teams become winners.

CHALLENGE

Case Problem 2

Data File needed for this Case Problem: sports.html

The Chemistry of Winning Although much has been said of late about athletes taking performance-enhancing drugs, no one has yet been able to figure out how a professional sports team is affected by the group dynamics surrounding the entire team. You have been asked to write a Web page for a local high school that outlines the dangers of being too competitive at too early an age. Although your file might appear somewhat differently, a preview of the completed file appears in Figure 2-42.

Figure 2-42 The Chemistry of Winning Web page

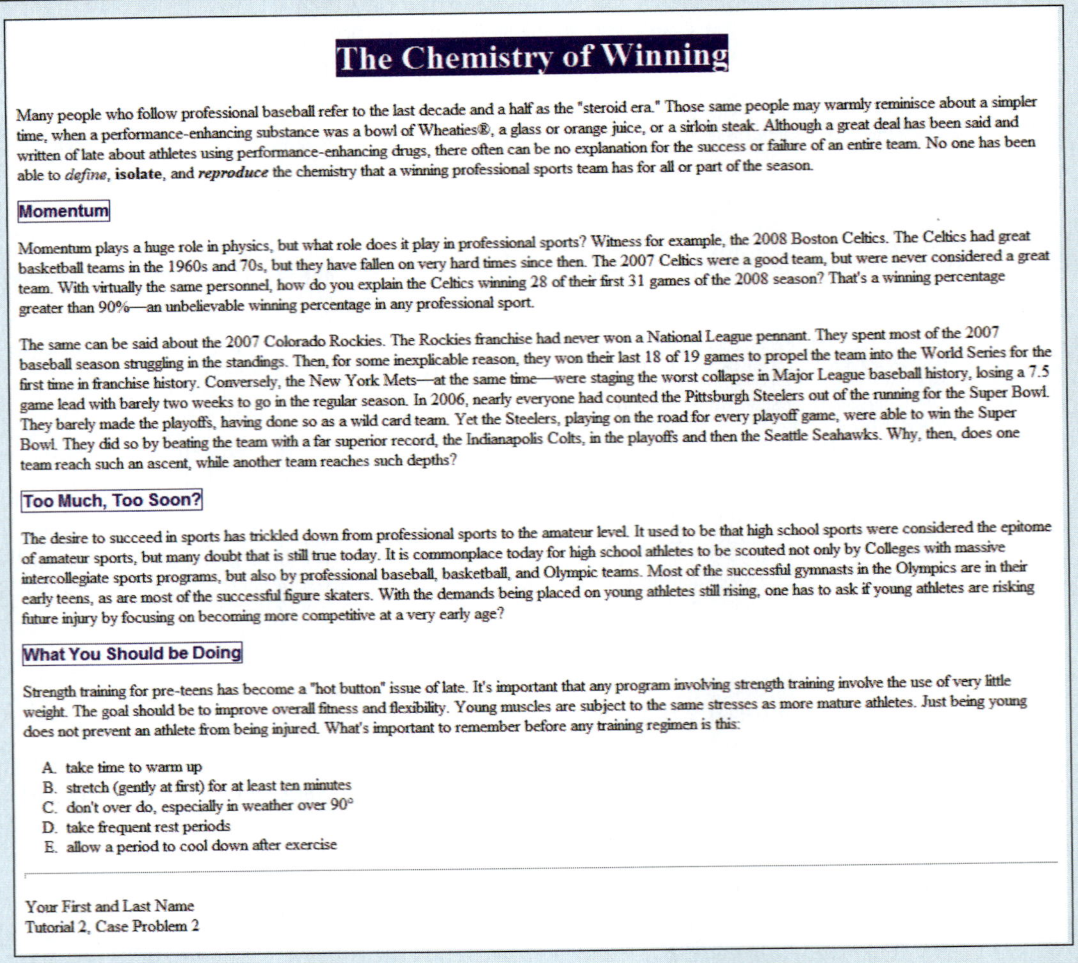

The Chemistry of Winning

Many people who follow professional baseball refer to the last decade and a half as the "steroid era." Those same people may warmly reminisce about a simpler time, when a performance-enhancing substance was a bowl of Wheaties®, a glass or orange juice, or a sirloin steak. Although a great deal has been said and written of late about athletes using performance-enhancing drugs, there often can be no explanation for the success or failure of an entire team. No one has been able to *define*, **isolate**, and ***reproduce*** the chemistry that a winning professional sports team has for all or part of the season.

Momentum

Momentum plays a huge role in physics, but what role does it play in professional sports? Witness for example, the 2008 Boston Celtics. The Celtics had great basketball teams in the 1960s and 70s, but they have fallen on very hard times since then. The 2007 Celtics were a good team, but were never considered a great team. With virtually the same personnel, how do you explain the Celtics winning 28 of their first 31 games of the 2008 season? That's a winning percentage greater than 90%—an unbelievable winning percentage in any professional sport.

The same can be said about the 2007 Colorado Rockies. The Rockies franchise had never won a National League pennant. They spent most of the 2007 baseball season struggling in the standings. Then, for some inexplicable reason, they won their last 18 of 19 games to propel the team into the World Series for the first time in franchise history. Conversely, the New York Mets—at the same time—were staging the worst collapse in Major League baseball history, losing a 7.5 game lead with barely two weeks to go in the regular season. In 2006, nearly everyone had counted the Pittsburgh Steelers out of the running for the Super Bowl. They barely made the playoffs, having done so as a wild card team. Yet the Steelers, playing on the road for every playoff game, were able to win the Super Bowl. They did so by beating the team with a far superior record, the Indianapolis Colts, in the playoffs and then the Seattle Seahawks. Why, then, does one team reach such an ascent, while another team reaches such depths?

Too Much, Too Soon?

The desire to succeed in sports has trickled down from professional sports to the amateur level. It used to be that high school sports were considered the epitome of amateur sports, but many doubt that is still true today. It is commonplace today for high school athletes to be scouted not only by Colleges with massive intercollegiate sports programs, but also by professional baseball, basketball, and Olympic teams. Most of the successful gymnasts in the Olympics are in their early teens, as are most of the successful figure skaters. With the demands being placed on young athletes still rising, one has to ask if young athletes are risking future injury by focusing on becoming more competitive at a very early age?

What You Should be Doing

Strength training for pre-teens has become a "hot button" issue of late. It's important that any program involving strength training involve the use of very little weight. The goal should be to improve overall fitness and flexibility. Young muscles are subject to the same stresses as more mature athletes. Just being young does not prevent an athlete from being injured. What's important to remember before any training regimen is this:

A. take time to warm up
B. stretch (gently at first) for at least ten minutes
C. don't over do, especially in weather over 90°
D. take frequent rest periods
E. allow a period to cool down after exercise

Your First and Last Name
Tutorial 2, Case Problem 2

Complete the following:

1. If necessary, start your browser and then start Expression Web. If necessary, in Expression Web, close any open sites. Reset the workspace layout.
2. If necessary, open the Tutorial.02 Web site. If necessary, expand the Case2 folder.
3. Open the **sports.html** file and then save it as **sportsnew.html** in the same folder.
4. In Design view, open the Page Properties dialog box, and then in the Title box, type **The Chemistry of Winning**. In the Page description box, type your first and last name, type / (a forward slash character), type **Tutorial 2, Case Problem 2**, and then close the dialog box and return to Design view.
5. In Design view, in the Editing window, position the insertion point at the top of the sportsnew.html page. Select the text "The Chemistry of Winning" and format those words as a Heading 1 <h1> heading. Change the background color to navy (#000080). Change the text color to white. Center the heading.
6. Select the text in the next side heading, "Momentum." Format that text as a Heading 2 <h2> heading. Change the font to Arial, Helvetica, sans-serif. Change the size of the text to medium (14 points). Change the color of the heading to navy. Format the heading so that it has Outside Borders.

EXPLORE

7. If necessary, display the Standard toolbar. Use the Format Painter to format the other side headings in the same style as the Momentum heading. (*Note*: you may have to apply the Outside border individually to each side heading.)
8. In the last sentence of the first paragraph, format the word *define* to appear as italic, and format the word *isolate* to appear as bold. Format the word *reproduce* to appear as both bold and italic.
9. In the first paragraph, insert the registered trademark symbol after the word *Wheaties*. Insert a degree symbol (character code 0080) after the number 90 in the third line of text from the bottom of the page.

EXPLORE

10. Select the five items in the list at the bottom of the page. Use the Numbering button on the Common toolbar to make the five items into an ordered list. With the list still selected, use the List Properties dialog box to change the list style type to capital letters: A, B, C, D, and E.
11. Insert a horizontal line below the list. Format the horizontal line as necessary so that the line is 100% of the window, 4 pixels high, black and with no shading.
12. Use the Thesaurus feature to find a synonym for the word *fondly* in the first paragraph.
13. Perform a spelling check on the document. Correct any errors.
14. Close the Standard toolbar.
15. Click below the horizontal line. On two lines, type the following (substitute your name as appropriate). Press the Shift+Enter keys after you type your name. (*Note*: Text you need to type is shown in bold for ease of reference only; do not bold the text unless otherwise instructed.)

    Your First and Last Name
    Tutorial 2, Case Problem 2
16. Save your **sportsnew.html** file.
17. Open the **sportsnew.html** file in your browser. The document should be similar to the one shown in Figure 2-42.
18. Close the document.
19. Submit the completed file to your instructor, either in printed or electronic form, as requested.

Expand your skills to create and style a Web page for a mountain resort area.

CHALLENGE

Case Problem 3

Data File needed for this Case Problem: resort.html

The Johnson Mountains The Johnson Mountains in West Virginia span two counties in the center of the state. The area has shifted from being heavily reliant on mining to now being a tourist attraction for the mid-Atlantic region. You have been asked to develop a Web page for the local chamber of commerce that speaks to the natural beauty of the region and the many attractions that can be found there. Although your file might appear somewhat differently, a preview of the completed file appears in Figure 2-43.

Figure 2-43 The completed Johnson Mountain Web page

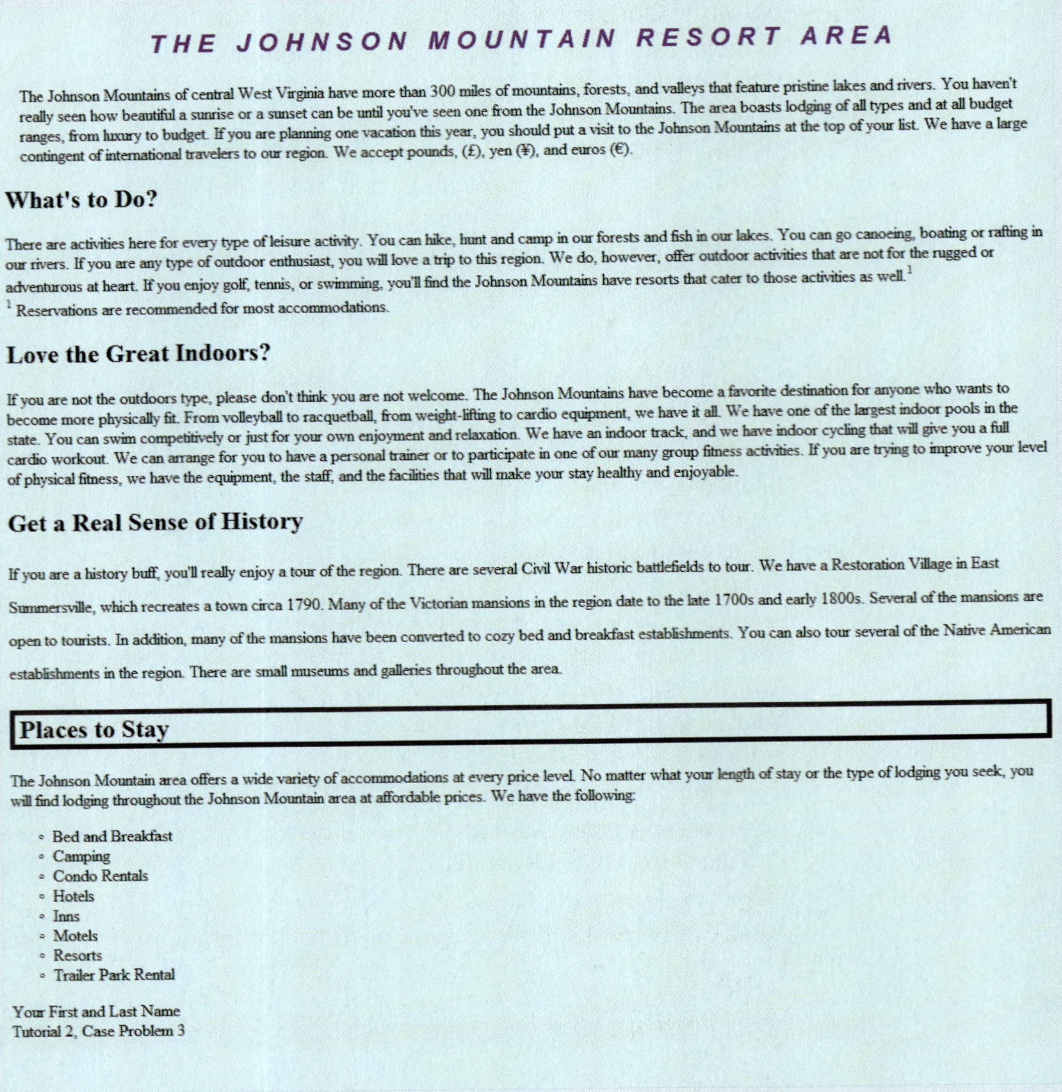

THE JOHNSON MOUNTAIN RESORT AREA

The Johnson Mountains of central West Virginia have more than 300 miles of mountains, forests, and valleys that feature pristine lakes and rivers. You haven't really seen how beautiful a sunrise or a sunset can be until you've seen one from the Johnson Mountains. The area boasts lodging of all types and at all budget ranges, from luxury to budget. If you are planning one vacation this year, you should put a visit to the Johnson Mountains at the top of your list. We have a large contingent of international travelers to our region. We accept pounds, (£), yen (¥), and euros (€).

What's to Do?

There are activities here for every type of leisure activity. You can hike, hunt and camp in our forests and fish in our lakes. You can go canoeing, boating or rafting in our rivers. If you are any type of outdoor enthusiast, you will love a trip to this region. We do, however, offer outdoor activities that are not for the rugged or adventurous at heart. If you enjoy golf, tennis, or swimming, you'll find the Johnson Mountains have resorts that cater to those activities as well.[1]

[1] Reservations are recommended for most accommodations.

Love the Great Indoors?

If you are not the outdoors type, please don't think you are not welcome. The Johnson Mountains have become a favorite destination for anyone who wants to become more physically fit. From volleyball to racquetball, from weight-lifting to cardio equipment, we have it all. We have one of the largest indoor pools in the state. You can swim competitively or just for your own enjoyment and relaxation. We have an indoor track, and we have indoor cycling that will give you a full cardio workout. We can arrange for you to have a personal trainer or to participate in one of our many group fitness activities. If you are trying to improve your level of physical fitness, we have the equipment, the staff, and the facilities that will make your stay healthy and enjoyable.

Get a Real Sense of History

If you are a history buff, you'll really enjoy a tour of the region. There are several Civil War historic battlefields to tour. We have a Restoration Village in East Summersville, which recreates a town circa 1790. Many of the Victorian mansions in the region date to the late 1700s and early 1800s. Several of the mansions are open to tourists. In addition, many of the mansions have been converted to cozy bed and breakfast establishments. You can also tour several of the Native American establishments in the region. There are small museums and galleries throughout the area.

Places to Stay

The Johnson Mountain area offers a wide variety of accommodations at every price level. No matter what your length of stay or the type of lodging you seek, you will find lodging throughout the Johnson Mountain area at affordable prices. We have the following:

- Bed and Breakfast
- Camping
- Condo Rentals
- Hotels
- Inns
- Motels
- Resorts
- Trailer Park Rental

Your First and Last Name
Tutorial 2, Case Problem 3

Complete the following:

1. If necessary, start your browser and then start Expression Web. If necessary, in Expression Web, close any open sites. Reset the workspace layout.
2. If necessary, open the Tutorial.02 Web site. If necessary, expand the Case3 folder.
3. Open the **resort.html** file and save the file as **resortnew.html** in the same folder.
4. In Design view, open the Page Properties dialog box, then in the Title box, type **Johnson Mountain Resorts**. In the Page description box, type your first and last name, type / (a forward slash character), type **Tutorial 2, Case Problem 3**, and then close the dialog box and return to Design view.
5. Change the background color of the page to a light shade of green or blue. Click the OK button enough times to return to Design view.

EXPLORE

6. Select the text "The Johnson Mountain Resort Area." Click Format on the menu bar, and then click Font. Change the appearance of this text to appear as follows:
   - Have the text appear in the Arial font.
   - Make the text appear as both bold and italic.

- The text should appear in all caps.
- The text should appear purple.
- Change the font size to x-large.
- In the Font dialog box, click the Character Spacing tab. Change the Spacing to Expanded and By 5pt. Click the OK button to return to Design view.

7. Center the words "The Johnson Mountain Resort Area."
8. Select the eight items at the bottom of the page and make those items into an unordered list. With the list still selected, use the List Properties dialog box to change the list style type to hollow bullets.
9. At the end of the first paragraph, insert the British pound (£) (character code 00A3), the Japanese yen (¥) (character code 00A5), and the euro (€) (character code 20AC) symbols between the appropriate set of parentheses.

EXPLORE

10. At the end of the second paragraph, select the number 1 after the word *well*. Use the Font dialog box to format that number as a superscript. Do the same for the number 1 that precedes the footnote text, "Reservations are recommended for most accommodations."
11. Format all the headings (except the first one) as Heading 2 <h2> headings.
12. Select the text in the first paragraph. Format this text so that it is indented on both sides by 15 pixels. (Use the Paragraph dialog box to do this task.)
13. Select the text in the "Places to Stay" h2 heading. Use the Borders and Shading dialog box to change the border to Box, Outset, with a width of 5px.
14. Select the text in the "Get a Real Sense of History" paragraph. Use the Paragraph dialog box to change the line spacing for this paragraph to double space.
15. Press the **Ctrl+End** keys to position the insertion point at the end of the document. On two lines, type the following (substitute your name as appropriate). Press the Shift+Enter keys after you type your name. (*Note*: Text you need to type is shown in bold for ease of reference only; do not bold the text unless otherwise instructed.)

    Your First and Last Name
    Tutorial 2, Case Problem 3
16. Perform a spelling check on the document. Correct any errors.
17. Save your **resortnew.html** file.
18. Open the **resortnew.html** file in your browser. The document should be similar to the one shown in Figure 2-43.
19. Close the document.
20. Submit the completed file to your instructor, either in printed or electronic form, as requested.

Using the files provided, create and style a Web page for a campus radio station.

CREATE

Case Problem 4

Data File needed for this Case Problem: radio.html

The Mirrow Vista College Radio Station Mirrow Vista College is located south of Reno, Nevada. The campus radio station plays several types of formats, including country and western, modern rock, adult contemporary, oldies, R & B, contemporary urban, hip-hop, and disco. The station also has a series of public information shows that center around campus and community life. Professors also lecture about special topics of interest to their students and the campus community as a whole. A *Chat with the President* show is broadcast once a week. Other shows feature lively discussions of campus, regional, national, and world issues. You have been asked to compose a Web page for the campus radio station. Complete the following:

1. If necessary, start Expression Web. If necessary, close any open sites. If necessary, open the Tutorial.02 Web site. Reset the workspace layout.

2. If necessary, open the Tutorial.02 Web site. If necessary, expand the Case4 folder.
3. Open the **radio.html** file and save the file as **radionew.html** in the same file folder.
4. In Design view, open the Page Properties dialog box, and then in the Title box, type **Campus Radio Station**.
5. In the Page description box, type your first and last name, type a **/** (a forward slash character), type **Tutorial 2, Case Problem 4**, and then close the dialog box.
6. In the body of the document, include examples of the following:
    - Headings <h1>, <h2>, and <h3>
    - Bold text
    - Italic text
    - Bold and italic text
    - A symbol
    - Text color
    - A text color and a background color
    - An ordered or unordered list
    - A font change
    - A font size change for the last paragraph (the last line of the page)
    - A horizontal line (change the width and the height of the line)
    - Text surrounded with a border that has a different border style, color, and width
    - Centered text
    - Text that is indented on one or both sides
7. Perform a spelling check on the document. Correct any errors.
8. At the bottom of the page and on two lines, type the following (substitute your name as appropriate). Press the Shift+Enter keys after you type your name. (*Note*: Text you need to type is shown in bold for ease of reference only; do not bold the text unless otherwise instructed.)

    Your First and Last Name
    Tutorial 2, Case Problem 4
9. Save the **radionew.html** file.
10. Open the **radionew.html** file in your browser. Observe the result. Correct any errors.
11. Close the browser, close all documents, and then close the Web site.
12. Submit the completed file to your instructor, either in printed or electronic form, as requested.

ENDING DATA FILES

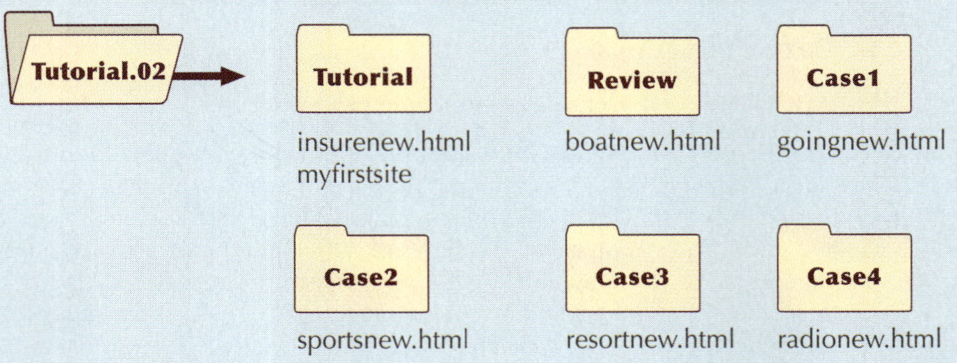

TUTORIAL 3

Working with Images

Using Images on a Web Page

OBJECTIVES

Session 3.1

- Identify the differences among image file types
- Evaluate the purpose of alternate text
- Position an image
- Wrap text around images
- Identify the picture properties
- Create a border and white space around images

Session 3.2

- Change the size of an image
- Modify the contents of an image
- Explore the functions of the Pictures toolbar
- Create a thumbnail image

Case | ***Hilson Lake Landscape Design***

Hilson Lake Landscape Design, located in Butler, Minnesota, has served the local community for more than 60 years. The company has several hundred acres devoted to a tree farm and growing sod. The company grows and installs sod for the athletic fields of many colleges in Minnesota. Throughout the years, the company has relied on its loyal customer base for most of its business. With a recent economic downturn, however, Hilson Lake Landscape Design is turning to the Web to expand its business and to provide better service to its existing customers. You'll be working with the owner, Renee Davis, to develop a Web page for the company. Renee has started the Web page with some promotional copy, but she needs your help in inserting and positioning the images she wants to use for the Web page.

STARTING DATA FILES

Tutorial.03 →

Tutorial	Review	Case1	Case2	Case3	Case4
back.png	field.html	burger.jpg	east.html	cola.jpg	judd.gif
bullet.png	lakelogo.png	cake.jpg	eastlogo.gif	movie.html	judd.html
garden.jpg	sod.jpg	steer.html	hours.gif	movielogo.gif	london.gif
hardscape.jpg			pine.jpg	popcorn.jpg	madrid.gif
lake.html			walkway.jpg		paris.gif
lakelogo.png					rome.gif
rule.png					

SESSION 3.1 VISUAL OVERVIEW

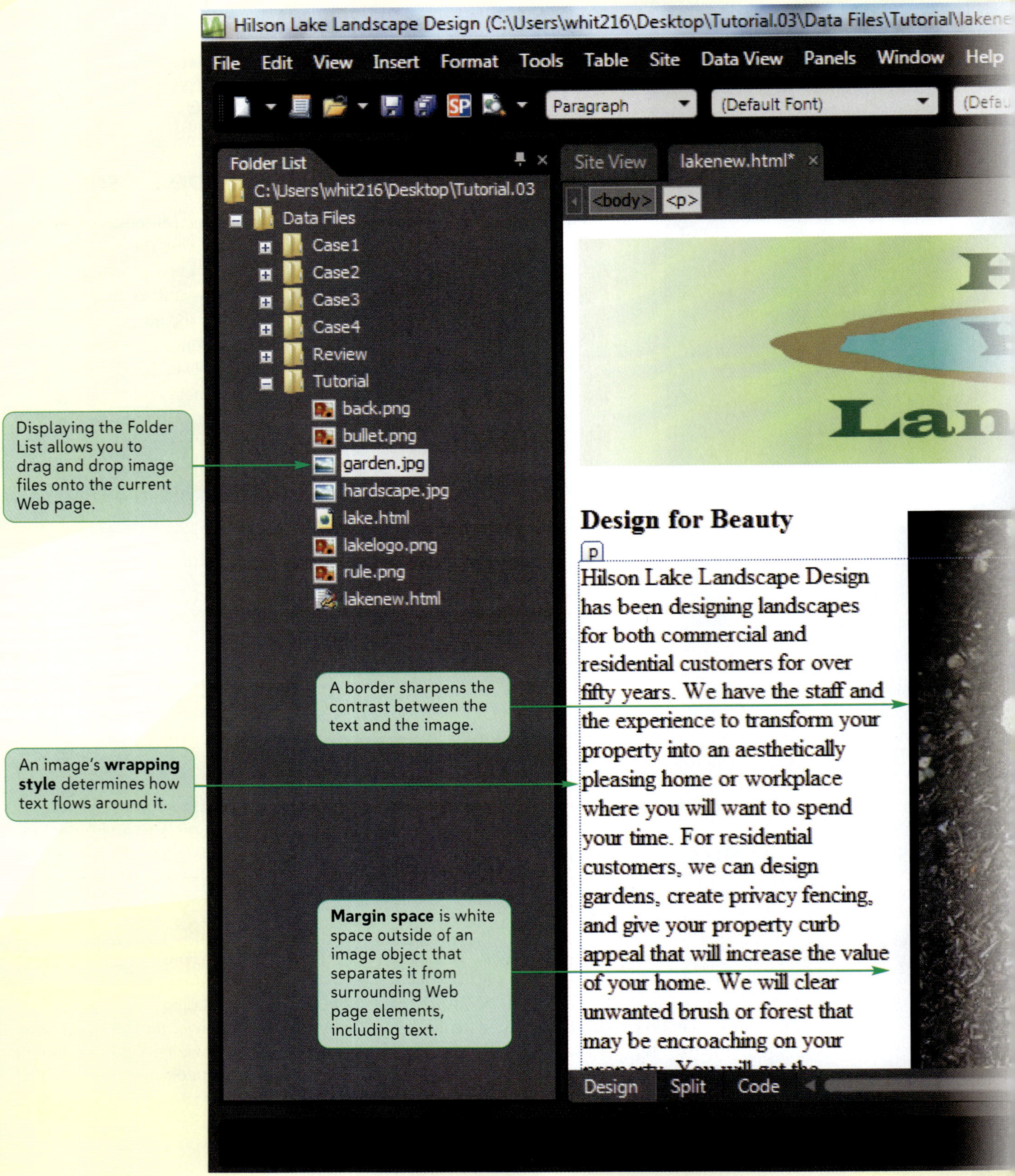

PLACING IMAGES

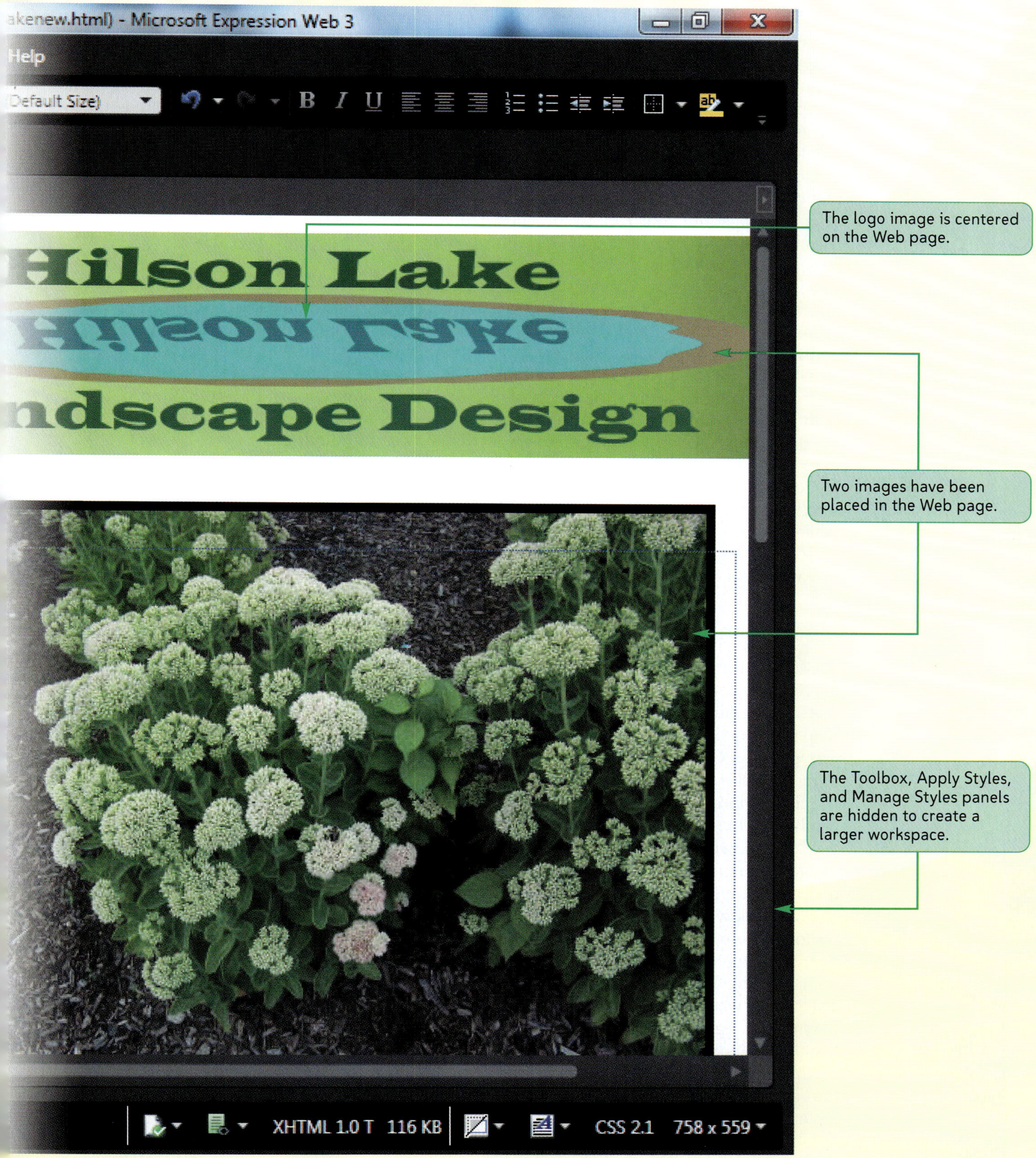

Using Images on a Web Page

A Web page that has only text is quite informative, but it lacks visual interest. You can expect, therefore, that nearly all of the Web pages you create will have one or more images. You will generally find a corporate logo or banner image at the top of a Web page. At the bottom of many Web pages, you will see **navigational icons**, which are images such as a picture of a house, a hand pointer, or an arrow that are used as links to other pages at the same Web site. For example, many Web sites use images of arrows that point to the left or right as links to display the previous or next page. Besides a logo image and navigational icons, you also want your Web pages to include some images in the document body to convey information or add compelling visual appeal.

Depending on the image file format, images can substantially increase the file size of a Web page, which makes the page slower to download. Therefore, be judicious in selecting images for your Web pages, and be mindful of their file size. In general, do not use an image on a Web page unless the image enhances the page appearance or conveys useful information.

When you use images on your Web pages, you need to devise a plan for the page layout. Your Web page layout should strike a balance between the amount of screen space used for text and that used for images. A page with a design composed mostly of images and very little text is amateurish. On the other hand, a page that is all text will not capture the interest of visitors to your Web pages.

You also need to balance the layout of your Web page. For example, do not fill the top of the page with images and the remainder of the page entirely with text. Be mindful of the flow of text around the images. You want the text that surrounds an image to be easy to read, so you need to leave some margin space between the image and the surrounding text so that the image and the text that wraps around it are not competing for the same screen space. You want your Web pages to have breathing room, planned areas of white space on the screen, so that the text and the images do not appear too crowded. As you instruct Renee how to use images on her Web page, you also remind her of the importance of these Web page design principles.

Understanding Image File Formats

The filename extension determines whether a particular program can open and use that file. In using image files on the Web, you will encounter several file formats, but the three most common file formats you will use are .gif, .jpg, and .png. GIF is an acronym for **Graphics Interchange Format**, an image format originally devised by AOL/CompuServe. GIF is most often pronounced with a hard "g" sound, although the creators of this file format (and many others) pronounce "gif" with a "j" sound ("jif"). GIF files use **file compression**, the process of encoding information in the file to use fewer bits, resulting in the file having a much smaller file size. Because of file compression, .gif files are fast to download, which, of course, makes them ideal for use on Web pages. Many images used on the Web are drawings (sketches), referred to as **line art** or **clip art**. Line art images are usually stored in a .gif file format.

Photos, however, are stored in a .jpg file format. JPG (pronounced "jay peg") stands for **Joint Photographic Experts Group**, which is the international committee that created the .jpg image file format standard. Although you can convert a .gif file to a .jpg file (or convert a .jpg file to a .gif file), you must exercise caution. GIF files can have as many as 256 colors, whereas .jpg files can have several million colors. When converting an image file from a different file format, carefully check the result of the conversion to see if the result is desirable.

The **Portable Network Graphics** format is another format used for line art. PNG files (pronounced "ping") have somewhat better file compression than .gif files, and these files are not limited to 256 colors. You can use GIF files to create animation, but .png files do not support animation.

TIP

You can open a .bmp file in Expression Web, but not a .tif file.

Windows Bitmap files are standard Windows graphics files. These files have the filename extension of .bmp. **Tagged Image File Format** is a standard graphic image file format usually generated by optical scanners or digital cameras. Screen captures are often stored in this file format. These files have the filename extension of .tif. In general, you should avoid using .bmp and .tif files on your Web pages because they tend to have much larger file sizes than .gif, .jpg, or .png formats.

Figure 3-1 lists the three most common image file types used on the Web.

Figure 3-1 **Common Web image file types**

File Type	Pronounced As	Stands for	Used for
.gif	Either gif (hard g) or jif (soft g)	Graphics Interchange Format	Line art/clip art
.jpg	Jay peg	Joint Photographic Experts Group	Photographs
.png	Ping	Portable Network Graphics	Line art/clip art

Renee is curious to know where she can obtain images for her Web pages, so you work with her to get images for the Web page she wants to create.

Learning About Where to Obtain Images

Plenty of sources are available for obtaining images to use on your Web pages. Many Web sites offer free clip art and photos in .gif and .jpg file formats. You should be mindful that even "free" images have copyright restrictions regarding their use, particularly for commercial use. You can also buy images and clip art on CDs or DVDs or obtain images as part of an Office suite, such as Microsoft Office. You can buy images online by purchasing a subscription from an image service. Again, be mindful of restrictions on the use of these images.

You can also use your digital camera and your cell phone as sources for images, but some preparation is involved. Expression Web can import images from a digital camera or cell phone, but images taken with these devices tend to be large and have a large file size. You will have to resize the picture, but that is an easy task in Expression Web.

INSIGHT

Establishing Accessibility

An important issue in Web page design is accessibility. Both in the workplace and outside it, your Web pages need to accommodate the needs of people with visual impairments. So that everyone can benefit from your image files, every image must have a description that can be read aloud to people who have trouble seeing the screen or who cannot read it. Many people with visual impairments browse the Web using a **screen reader**, which is a hardware device or software program that reads aloud the Web page content and descriptions of Web page content. One of the more commonly used screen reader is JAWS, which is an acronym for *Job Access With Speech*. Produced by the Blind and Low Vision Group at Freedom Scientific of St. Petersburg, Florida, JAWS is used to make personal computers running Microsoft Windows accessible to blind and visually impaired users. Many other programs are also used to bring the wealth of information on the Web to all who use and view Web pages.

TIP

An image can also serve as the background for the entire Web page.

You will also see images used on the Web in other ways. It is common today for Web pages to have images that serve as horizontal lines, dividing a page into different sections to group related topics. Images are also frequently used instead of solid black bullets to call attention to items in an unordered list. An image can be used as a background for text as well, as you often see in a banner at the top of a Web page.

Entering Alternate Text

When you insert an image using Expression Web, the Accessibility Properties dialog box opens. This dialog box contains two text boxes. The first text box is for **alternate text**, also known as **alt text**, which is the text you type to provide a description of the image for screen readers. Besides creating text for a description of the image for screen readers, alternate text also appears before the image fully downloads. In some browsers, such as Internet Explorer, alternate text also appears as a ScreenTip when a visitor to your Web site passes the pointer over an image. If an image fails to download, some browsers display the alternate text beside a **placeholder icon**, which is a standardized visual representation that a problem in downloading an image has occurred.

> **TIP**
> A placeholder icon does not appear if there is a problem with an image used as a bullet or with an image used as a horizontal line.

To provide for accessibility, and for the other reasons mentioned, you should always provide alternate text for every image that conveys information on your Web pages. The alternate text should be brief, but descriptive. For example, if you insert a photo of a 1958 Cadillac DeVille, alternate text such as "car photo" would not be very useful to a visually impaired person. Put yourself in the position of the person who will hear the alternate text read aloud. In this instance, a better description of the image is "photo of classic pink 1958 Cadillac DeVille with enormous tailfins and chrome bumpers."

In the Accessibility Properties dialog box, you use the **Long description** box to assign a link to a file that provides a more detailed description of an image. Long descriptions are not fully supported by all browsers and browser versions, so if you use a long description, be sure to test for browser support of this attribute. At times, however, using alternate text does not provide useful information to the reader. For example, it does not make much sense to provide alternate text for an image used as a list bullet. You'll show Renee how to open the lake.html file so she can begin using images on her Web page.

To open the Tutorial.03 Web site:

1. If necessary, start Expression Web. If another Web site from a previous user opens, on the menu bar, click **Site**, and then click **Close**.
2. On the menu bar, click **Panels**, and then click **Reset Workspace Layout**.
3. On the menu bar, click **Site**, and then click **Open Site**. The Open Site dialog box opens.
4. Click the **Browse** button and navigate to the location where you store the Tutorial.03 Web site.
5. Click the **Tutorial.03** Web site to select it, and then click the **Open** button.
6. Click the **Open** button again.

   The Tutorial.03 Web site opens. The Folder List panel shows the root folder and the Data Files folder.
7. Click the **+ sign** to the left of the Data Files folder to expand and show the contents of that folder.
8. Click the **+ sign** to the left of the Tutorial folder to expand and show the contents of that folder.
9. In the Folder List panel, double-click the **lake.html** filename to open that file. The original lake.html file opens, as shown in Figure 3-2.

Figure 3-2 **The Hilson Lake Landscaping Design Web page**

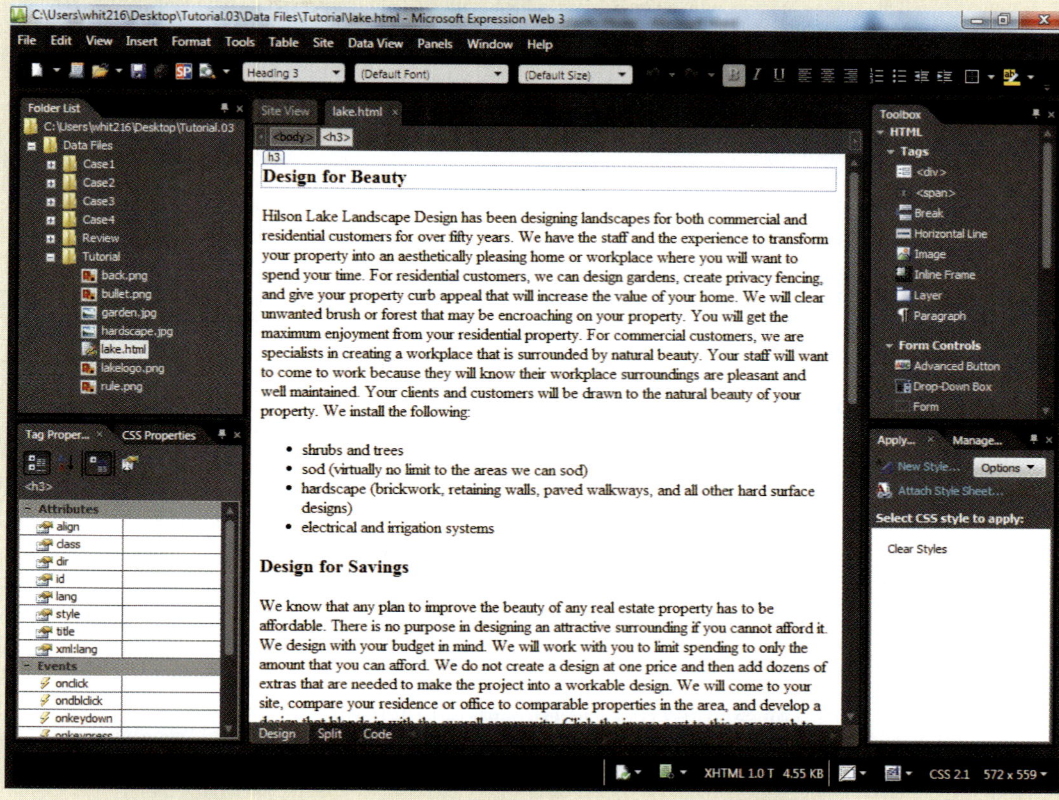

You'll show Renee how to customize the workspace. Because you will be working with several files, you'll show Renee how to close the Tag Properties and CSS Properties panels. By closing these two panels, you will have no trouble seeing all of the filenames in the Folder List panel.

To customize the workspace:

1. If necessary, click the **Design** button at the bottom of the editing window to display Design view.
2. Only the Common toolbar should appear on the screen. If necessary, close any other toolbars other than the Common toolbar.
3. On the menu bar, click **Panels**, and then click **Tag Properties**.
4. On the menu bar, click **Panels**, and then click **CSS Properties**.

You'll have Renee save the lake.html file under a new filename. Recall that every Web page should have a title that will display in the title bar at the top of the browser window. You can create a page title when you save a file. You'll show Renee how to enter a page title as part of saving the file.

After you enter the filename, do not click the Save button.

To rename the lake.html file and give the page a title:

1. On the menu bar, click **File**, and then click **Save As**. The Save As dialog box opens.
2. In the File name box, type **lakenew**.
3. In the Save As dialog box, click the **Change title** button. The Set Page Title dialog box opens. In the Page title box, type **Hilson Lake Landscape Design**.

   Compare your text with that shown in Figure 3-3.

Figure 3-3 Set Page Title dialog box

type the page title in this box

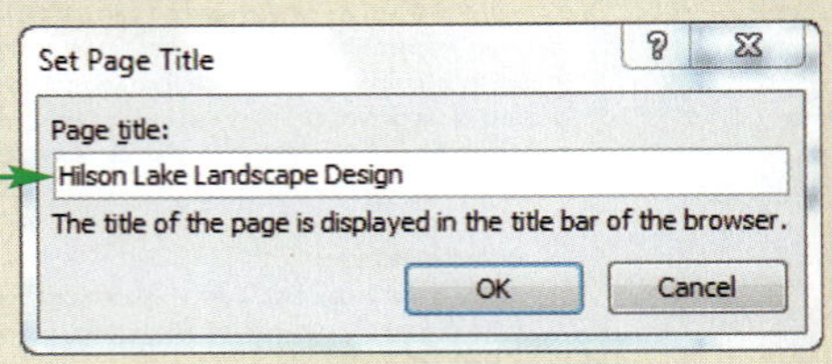

Trouble? If you pressed the Enter key before typing the title, right-click any portion of the editing window and then click Page Properties to access the Page Properties dialog box. Type the title and then Press the Enter key.

4. Click the **OK** button.

   The Save As dialog box appears by itself.
5. Click the **Save** button to save the file as **lakenew.html**.

Expression Web offers several options for inserting an image into a Web page in Design view. You can use the menu bar, the Pictures toolbar, or you can just paste an image onto the workspace or Folder List panel in Design view. The method you use depends on your preference and the current location of the image file. You'll start by showing Renee how to use the Folder List panel to insert an image.

Inserting an Image Using the Folder List Panel

Renee wants to use a logo image at the top of her Web page. You have been working on a logo and have created a file named lakelogo.png.

REFERENCE

Inserting an Image from the Folder List Panel

- Click and drag the image filename to the desired location in the editing window.
- Release the mouse button.
- When the Accessibility Properties dialog box opens, type alternate text for the image.
- Click the OK button or press the Enter key to insert the image.

You'll show Renee how to create some space at the top of the document so there is room for the image.

To insert the logo image:

1. In Design view, if necessary, press the **Ctrl+Home** keys to position the insertion point at the top of the document.
2. Press the **Enter** key once, and then press the **Up arrow** key once.
3. Click the **h3** Code tab at the top of the page.
4. On the Common toolbar, click the **Style** arrow, and then click **Paragraph <p>**.
5. In the Folder List panel, click and drag the **lakelogo.png** file anywhere in the blank paragraph at the top of the page, and then release the mouse button.

   The Accessibility Properties dialog box opens.
6. In the Alternate text box, type **Hilson Lake logo image**.

   Leave the Long description box blank, as shown in Figure 3-4.

Figure 3-4 The Accessibility Properties dialog box

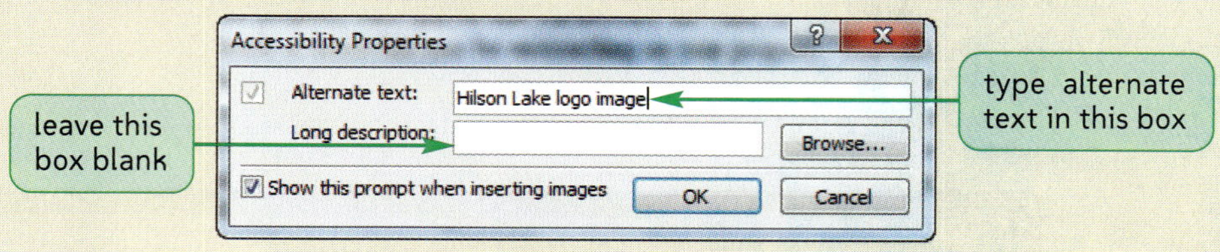

7. Click the **OK** button to insert the lakelogo.png image in Design view in the Web page, as shown in Figure 3-5.

Figure 3-5 Logo image is inserted at the top of the page

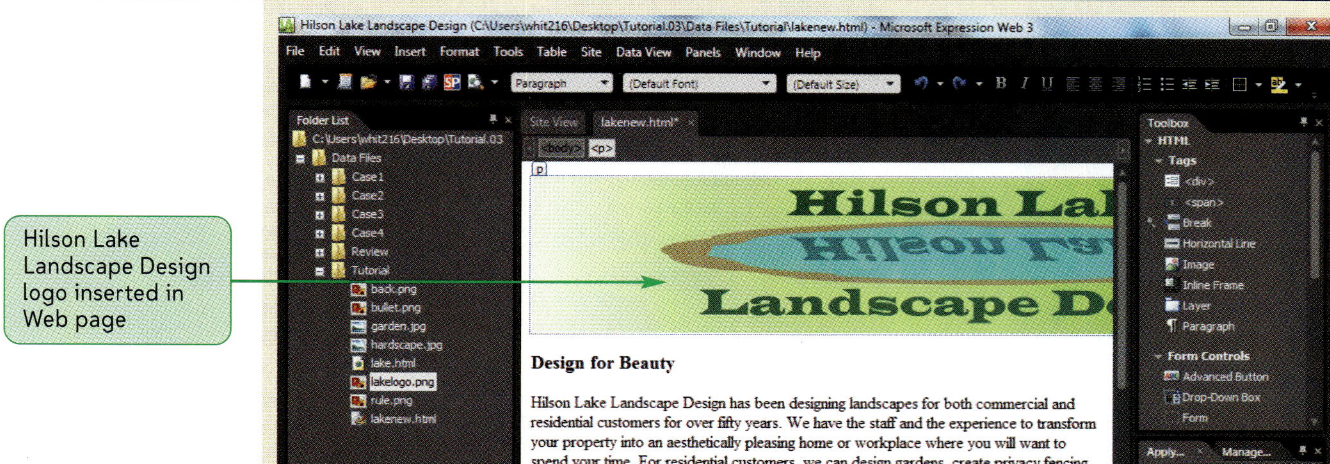

8. On the Common toolbar, click the **Center** button to center the image.

   Trouble? Depending on your monitor size and screen resolution, you might not see any change in the positioning of the image.
9. Right-click the **lakenew.html Document** tab and click **Save** on the shortcut menu.
10. Press the **F12** key to view the file in the default browser. Your screen should look similar to Figure 3-6.

Figure 3-6 The Web page in the browser

logo image in the default browser

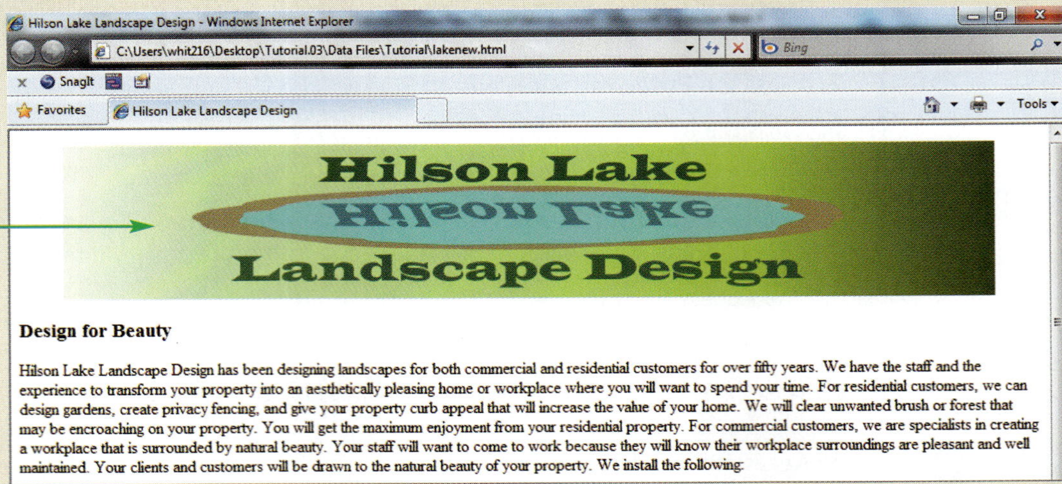

11. Close the browser.

INSIGHT

Using Expression Design to Edit Images

Expression Design, which is a program included in Expression Studio, can also be used to edit images. One of the more interesting editing effects is to change the opacity of an image, which is the degree to which light is blocked. As you lower the image opacity, you can start to see through the image. Setting the image opacity to a very low percentage, such as 10 percent, creates a watermark effect, where you can use the image as a page background and overlay text on top of the background image.

Renee wants to add another image to the document. She has given you an image of some garden plantings that she recently designed for a client. You'll show her how to insert the image, named garden.jpg, just before the "Design for Beauty" heading. You'll also show her how to close the panels on the right side of the workspace so that you can see more of the editing window.

To insert the garden.jpg image:

1. On the menu bar, click **Panels**, and then click **Toolbox**.
2. On the menu bar, click **Panels**, and then click **Apply Styles**.
3. On the menu bar, click **Panels**, and then click **Manage Styles**.
4. In the Folder List panel, click and drag the **garden.jpg** filename to the start of the "Design for Beauty" h3 heading, and then release the mouse button. The Accessibility Properties dialog box opens.
5. In the Alternate text box, type **image of garden plants**.
6. Click the **OK** button to insert the garden.jpg image into the Web page, as shown in Figure 3-7.

Figure 3-7 **The garden.jpg image**

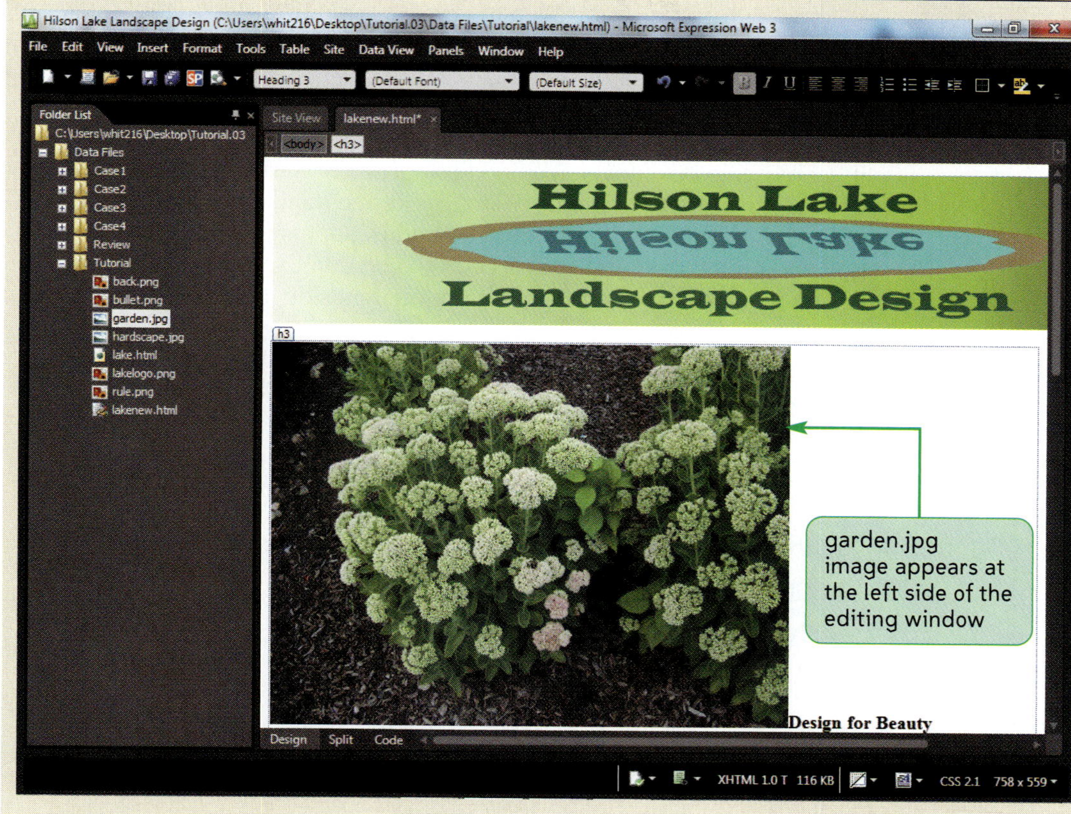

7. Right-click the **lakenew.html Document** tab and then click **Save**.

Renee likes the image, but she feels that it looks awkward on the Web page—there is a great deal of white space to the right of the image. She wants to know how to make the text wrap around the image. You'll show Renee how to use the Picture Properties dialog box to position and size an image.

Setting the Picture Properties

Although Expression Web does not have the wealth of image-editing tools found in dedicated image-editing software, Expression Web has more than 20 tools that you can use to change the size, position, and appearance of an image as well as to convert an image into a link.

REFERENCE

Setting Picture Properties

- Right-click the image and then click Picture Properties on the shortcut menu.
- In the Picture Properties dialog box, click the Appearance tab.
- Set the Wrapping style to None, Left, or Right.
- Set the Layout for Alignment, Border thickness, and the Horizontal and Vertical margins.
- Set the Height and the Width to either a percent or pixel value.
- Click the OK button.

Currently, the garden.jpg image has a large block of undesirable white space to its right. By default, an image appears at the left edge of the page, and text does not wrap around the image.

TIP

By default, the first line of text that appears next to the image appears near the base of the image.

You can use Expression Web to create a wrapping style that positions an image at either the left or the right edge of the page. If you set the Wrapping style to Left, the image is positioned at the left edge of the screen, and the text wraps to the right of the image. If you set the Wrapping style to Right, the image is positioned at the right edge of the screen, and the text wraps to the left of the image. When you click an image to select it, a bounding box and resize handles appear. A **bounding box** is a rectangular box that defines the outside border of an image. **Resize handles** are controls that modify the box size. In most other programs, resize handles appear as small boxes in each corner of the box and on the center of each side of the box. In Expression Web, however, an image has only three resize handles: one on the right side, one on the bottom, and one in the lower-right corner.

Renee wants the image positioned on the right with the text wrapping to the left of the image. You'll show Renee how to change the wrapping style now.

To change the wrapping style:

1. Right-click anywhere on the **garden.jpg** image.
2. Click **Picture Properties** on the shortcut menu.

   The Picture Properties dialog box opens.
3. Click the **Appearance** tab.
4. In the Wrapping style gallery, click the **Right** option.

   The Picture Properties dialog box appears as shown in Figure 3-8.

Figure 3-8 **Selecting a wrapping style in the Picture Properties dialog box**

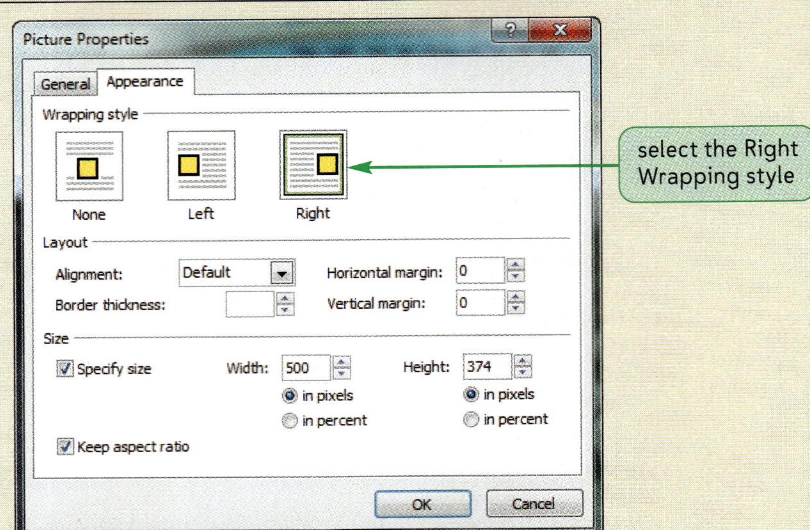

5. Click the **OK** button.
6. The image appears in Design view at the right edge of the screen, but the image is dimmed as a visual indicator that you have selected it.
7. Click anywhere outside the garden.jpg image. The image is no longer selected, as shown in Figure 3-9.

Figure 3-9 **Positioning an image for text wrap**

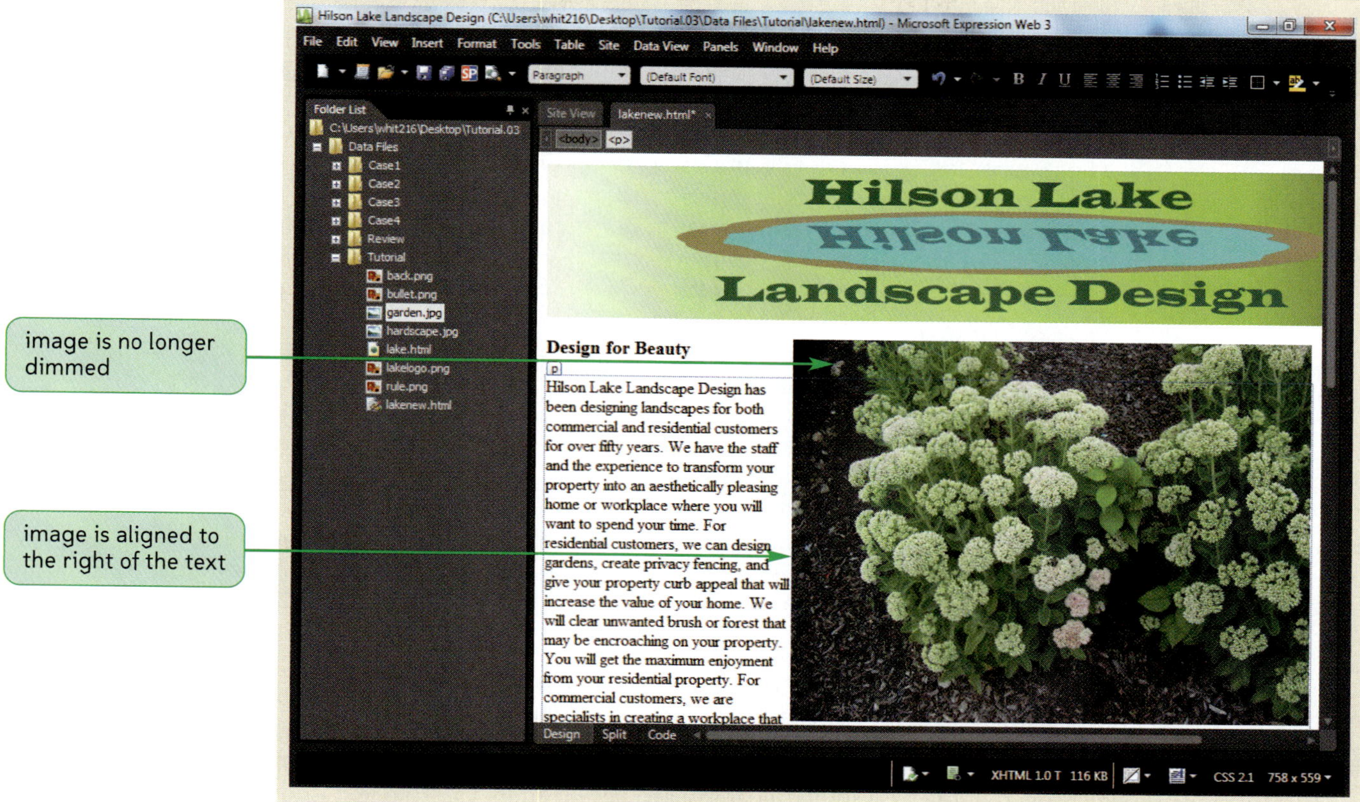

Now that you have wrapped text around the image, you mention to Renee that it is a good idea to have some margin space around an image so that the text beside the image and the image itself do not seem too crowded. Having margin space around an image makes the page easier to read because it provides some visual separation between the image and the text that is wrapping around it. You can also make an image stand out by applying a border to the image. You'll work with Renee on creating some margin space and adding a border for the image.

PROSKILLS

Verbal Communication: Rehearsing a Presentation

In the workplace, it might be necessary to give a presentation to clients or other members of your organization. For example, you might need to discuss layout revisions to an existing Web site or to discuss the launch of a new Web site. If you have created a **prototype**, or a working model, of the revised or the proposed Web site, make sure you know what features work in your prototype and what features do not work. You do not want to embarrass yourself in front of a group of your peers or superiors by demonstrating your lack of familiarity with your proposal. To gain a sense of confidence, rehearse what you have to say several times before you make your actual presentation. If you plan to use a slide presentation, such as PowerPoint, rehearse your presentation and pay attention to the order and content of the slides.

Rearrange the content so that it follows a logical progression. Notice and correct any slides that contain typos or other factual errors. Anticipate that those in attendance might ask questions about the slide content. Be sure of your facts and be ready to back them up. Establish a plan in case there are technical difficulties with the slide show or the projection media. Even if you do not plan to distribute them, always bring printouts of the slides so you can distribute your paper copies in case there are unforeseen difficulties. You can always email your slide show to the attendees later. If you rehearse your speech, you will have a greater sense of confidence and be more relaxed when you give the presentation.

Creating Margin Space and Adding a Border

In Expression Web, you can control the horizontal margin, which is the space to the left or right of an image, and you can control the vertical margin, which is the space above and below the image. Another means of separating an image from text is to place a border around the image. You can change the border thickness (in pixel values). By default, the border color matches the text color. Because the text color is black by default, the border color for an image will also be black unless you change the text color or change the border color.

REFERENCE

Moving an Image

- Click anywhere in the image.
- Pass the mouse pointer over an image border.
- When the pointer turns into the move pointer, click and drag the image to the desired location.
- Release the mouse button.

or

- Click and drag the image to the new location.

In the Picture Properties dialog box, you can add white space and create a border in the Layout section. You'll show Renee how to change the picture layout by adding margin space for the image and creating a border around the image. You'll also show her a shortcut for opening the Picture Properties dialog box.

To change the margin space and add a border:

1. Double-click the **garden.jpg** image.

   The Picture Properties dialog box opens.

2. Click the **Appearance** tab.
3. Click in the **Border thickness** box and type **6**.
4. Click in the **Horizontal margin** box, delete any value in the box, and then type **12**.
5. Click in the **Vertical margin** box, delete any value in the box, and then type **6**.
6. Click the **OK** button.
7. Click anywhere outside the garden.jpg image. The image now has a black border. It is also surrounded by white space, as shown in Figure 3-10.

Figure 3-10 Margin space and a border

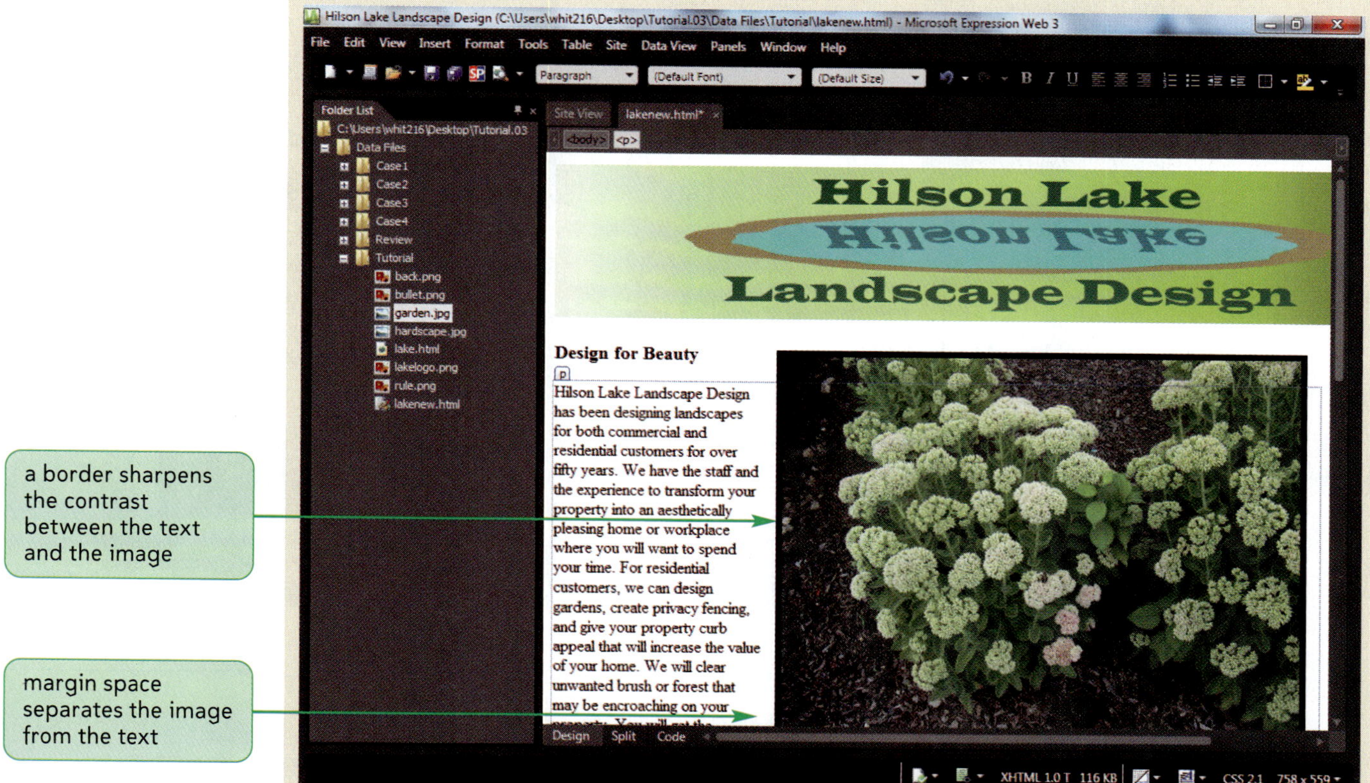

Renee wants to know if it is possible to move an image. She would prefer to have the first paragraph extend the full screen width. She wants the garden.jpg image placed to the right of the second paragraph, rather than the first. You'll show Renee how easy it is to move an image in Expression Web.

To move the garden.jpg image:

1. If necessary, scroll down a bit to see the "Design for Savings" h3 heading.
2. Click the **garden.jpg** image to select it. The image is dimmed.
3. Press and hold down the mouse button, and then drag the **garden.jpg** image to the start of the second h3 heading, "Design for Savings."

4. **Release the mouse button.**

   The garden image now appears to the right of the "Design for Savings" heading and the second paragraph, as shown in Figure 3-11.

Figure 3-11 **New image location after changing Picture Properties**

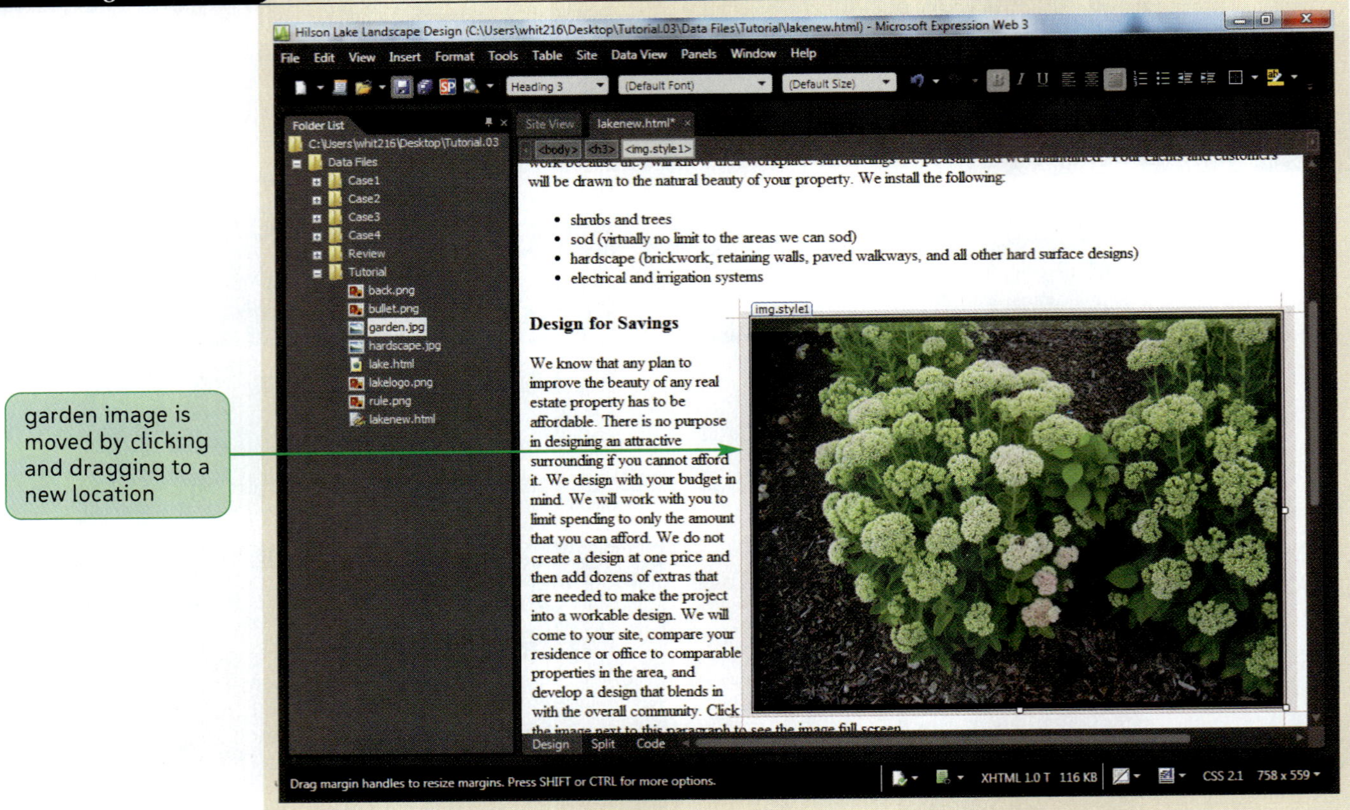

5. **Click anywhere outside the garden.jpg image.**

INSIGHT

Aligning an Image with a Single Line of Text

To align an image with a single line of text, you do not set the alignment as Left or Right; instead, you set the vertical alignment for the image. It is important to remember that you are aligning the image, not the text. Although you have several choices for alignment in the Picture Properties dialog box, it's best to choose either Top, Middle, or Bottom as the choice for image alignment, as not all browsers support the Baseline, Text-top, and Text-bottom alignment choices. "Top" aligns the top of the image with the single line of text, "Middle" aligns the image in the middle of the text, and "Bottom" aligns the bottom of the image with the line of text. The "Sub" and "Super" choices, which are also present in the box, are used to create subscripts and superscripts.

Although you can view the image in Design view, it is always a good idea to view the document in the browser. Recall that Design view presents only a close approximation of how the page will appear in the browser. You'll have Renee save the file and then view it in the default browser.

To save and view the file in the default browser:

1. Save the **lakenew.html** file.
2. Press the **F12** key.

   The Web page opens in the default browser.
3. If necessary, scroll down until you can see the garden.jpg image.

   Figure 3-12 shows the newly formatted image in the browser.

Figure 3-12 **The garden image in the browser**

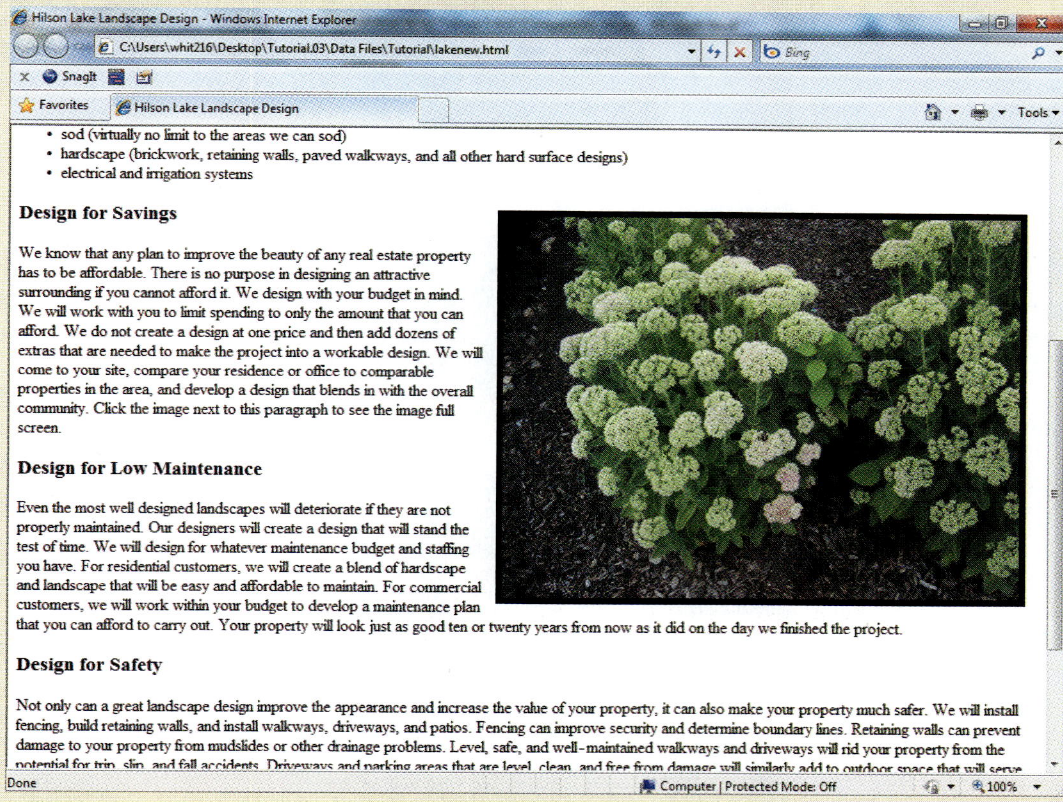

4. Close the browser and then return to Design view in Expression Web.

REVIEW

Session 3.1 Quick Check

1. What are navigational icons?
2. When should you use an image on your Web page?
3. Which image file formats should you use for line art? Which image format should you use for photos?
4. Which image file formats should you *not* use on a Web page?
5. If you want to use an image captured with a digital camera or cell phone, what should you do before using the image on your Web page?
6. What is the purpose of providing alternate text?
7. What are the three wrapping styles for an image?

SESSION 3.2 VISUAL OVERVIEW

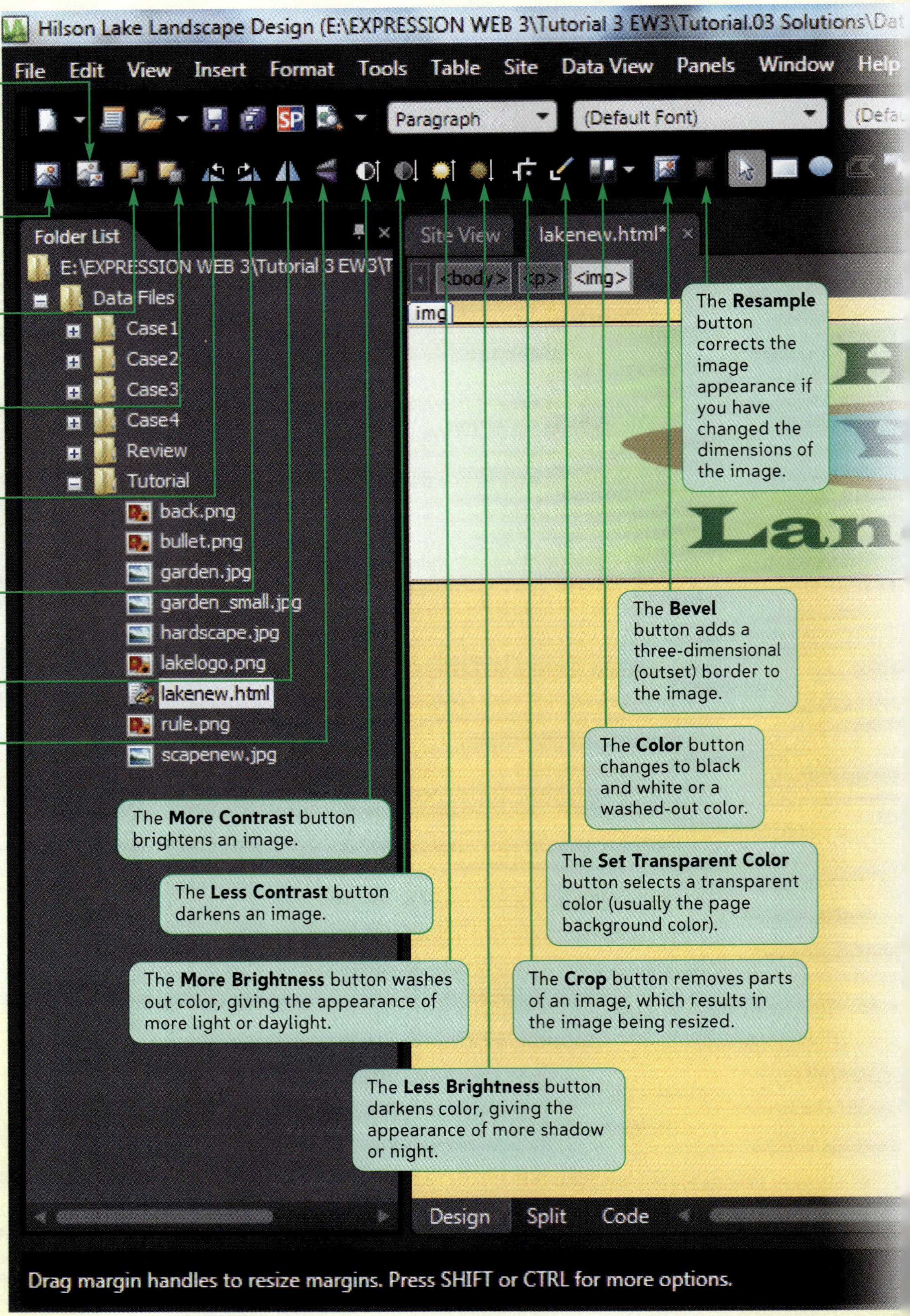

The **Auto Thumbnail** button makes a larger picture smaller so that, when clicked, it is restored to its original size, but on a new Web page.

The **Insert Picture from File** button inserts an image from a storage location on your computer or storage device.

The **Bring Forward** button places an image on top of another image.

The **Send Backward** button places an image under another image.

The **Rotate Left 90°** button rotates the image left 90 degrees.

The **Rotate Right 90°** button rotates the image right 90 degrees.

The **Flip Horizontal** button flips the image horizontally.

The **Flip Vertical** button flips the image vertically.

The **More Contrast** button brightens an image.

The **Less Contrast** button darkens an image.

The **More Brightness** button washes out color, giving the appearance of more light or daylight.

The **Less Brightness** button darkens color, giving the appearance of more shadow or night.

The **Crop** button removes parts of an image, which results in the image being resized.

The **Set Transparent Color** button selects a transparent color (usually the page background color).

The **Color** button changes to black and white or a washed-out color.

The **Bevel** button adds a three-dimensional (outset) border to the image.

The **Resample** button corrects the image appearance if you have changed the dimensions of the image.

PICTURES TOOLBAR

Editing Images

Renee wants to add a third image to the lakenew.html page. To balance the page content, she wants to align this image at the left edge of the screen and have the text wrap to its right, with some margin space around the image. She wants this image to appear to the left of the "Design for Safety" heading.

The image you will insert was taken with a digital camera and downloaded to the computer. Unless you have edited the image in image-editing software, it is common for a digital photo to be quite large when you insert it on the Web page. After you show Renee how to insert the image, you'll show her how to resize the image to a more manageable size.

To insert the hardscape.jpg image:

1. If necessary, start Expression Web, close any open sites, open the **Tutorial.03** Web site, and then open the **lakenew.html** file. If necessary, display Design view, close any toolbars other than the Common toolbar, and then close all panels other than the Folder List panel.
2. If necessary, scroll down until you see the "Design for Safety" h3 heading in the editing window.
3. In the Folder List panel, click and drag the **hardscape.jpg** filename to just before the "Design for Safety" h3 heading, and then release the mouse button.

   The Accessibility Properties dialog box opens.
4. For the Alternate text, type **photo of building with hardscape design**.
5. Click the **OK** button. The picture is inserted, but the picture fills the entire editing window, as shown in Figure 3-13. You'll correct this problem in the next section.

Figure 3-13 hardscape.jpg image is inserted

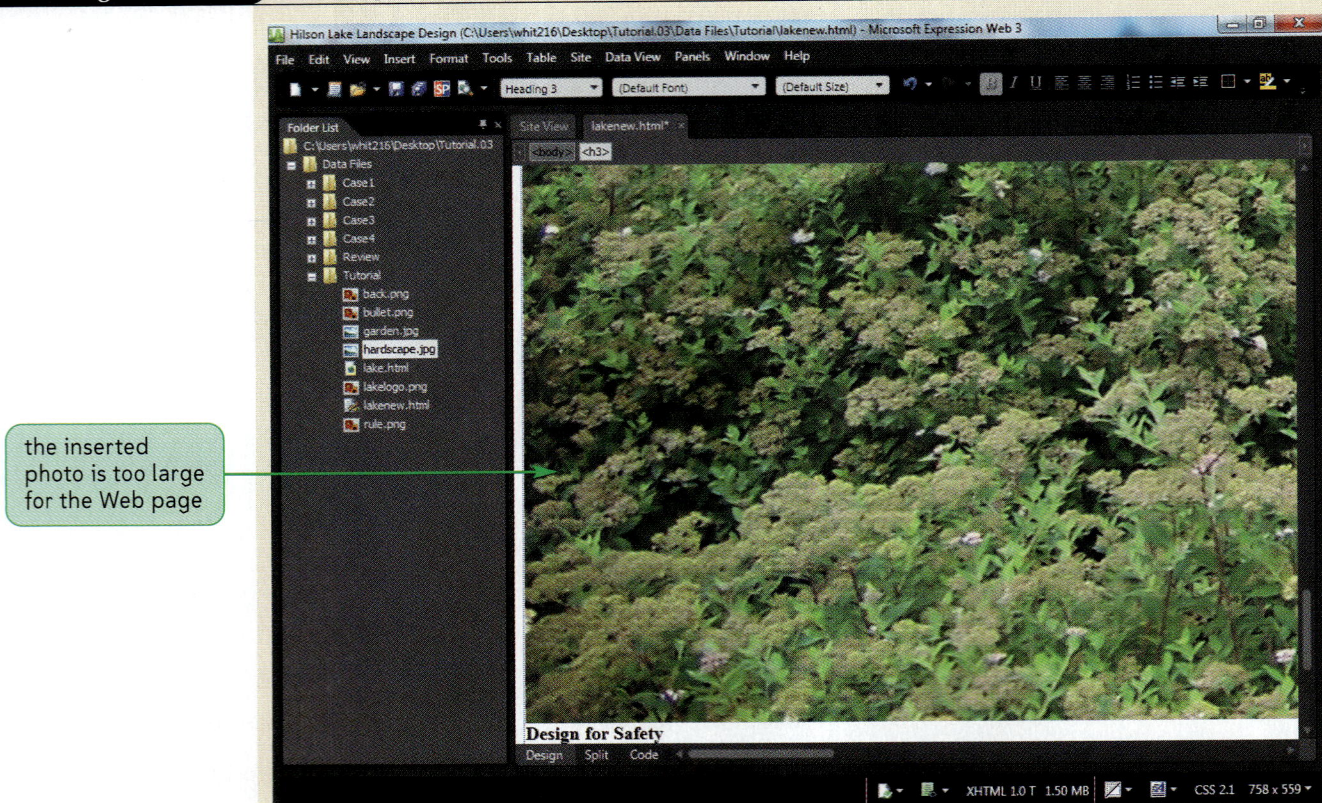

Next, you'll show Renee how to scale an image. Your first task is to show her how to make the hardscape.jpg image smaller.

Scaling an Image

Making an image smaller does not change the image quality. However, if you try to enlarge an image, the image quality degrades, and the image tends to look grainy. As a rule of thumb, never try to enlarge an image more than 10 percent of its original size. **Scaling** an image is changing the width and the height of an image. When scaling an image, it is very important to maintain the **aspect ratio**, which is to keep both the width and the height in the same proportion. For example, if you had an image with a width of 400 pixels and a height of 200 pixels, you could scale the image to be 200 pixels wide and 100 pixels in height (decreasing the width and the height both by 50%). If you scale an image without maintaining the aspect ratio, the image might appear distorted or out of focus. Renee wants the hardscape.jpg image to be smaller, so you'll show her how to scale the image now.

To scale the image:

1. Double-click anywhere on the **hardscape.jpg** image.

   The Picture Properties dialog box opens.
2. Click the **Appearance** tab.
3. In the Size section, make sure the Specify size check box and Keep aspect ratio check box are checked. If necessary, click in each check box to insert a check.
4. Click in the **Width** text box. Delete the number in the text box, and then type **500**.

   Because the Keep aspect ratio check box is checked, the value for the Height changes automatically to 375, as shown in Figure 3-14.

Figure 3-14 **Picture Properties dialog box**

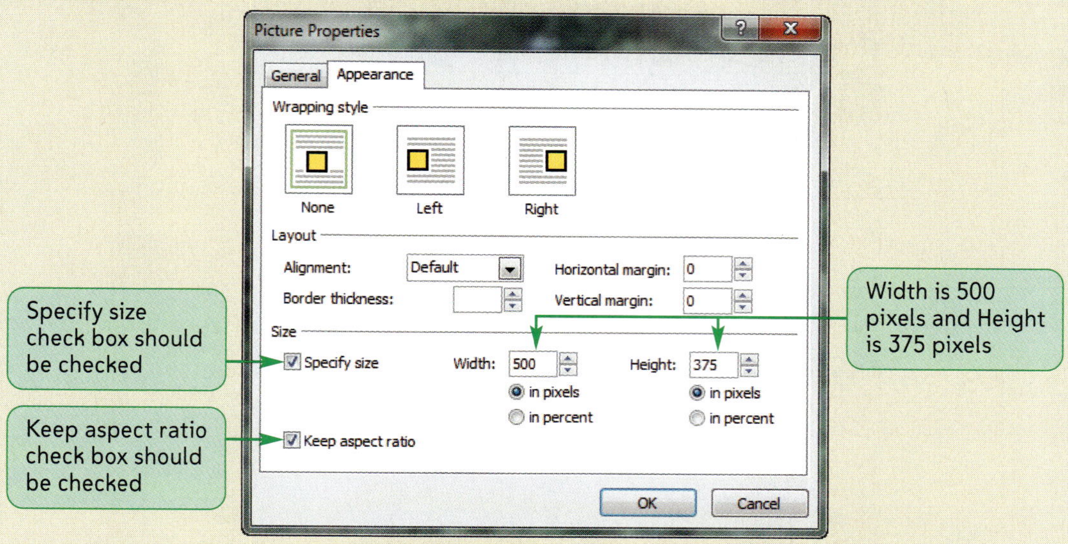

5. Click the **OK** button to resize the image. If necessary, scroll up to view the image.
6. Click anywhere outside the hardscape.jpg image. The image should appear similar to Figure 3-15.

Figure 3-15 The scaled image

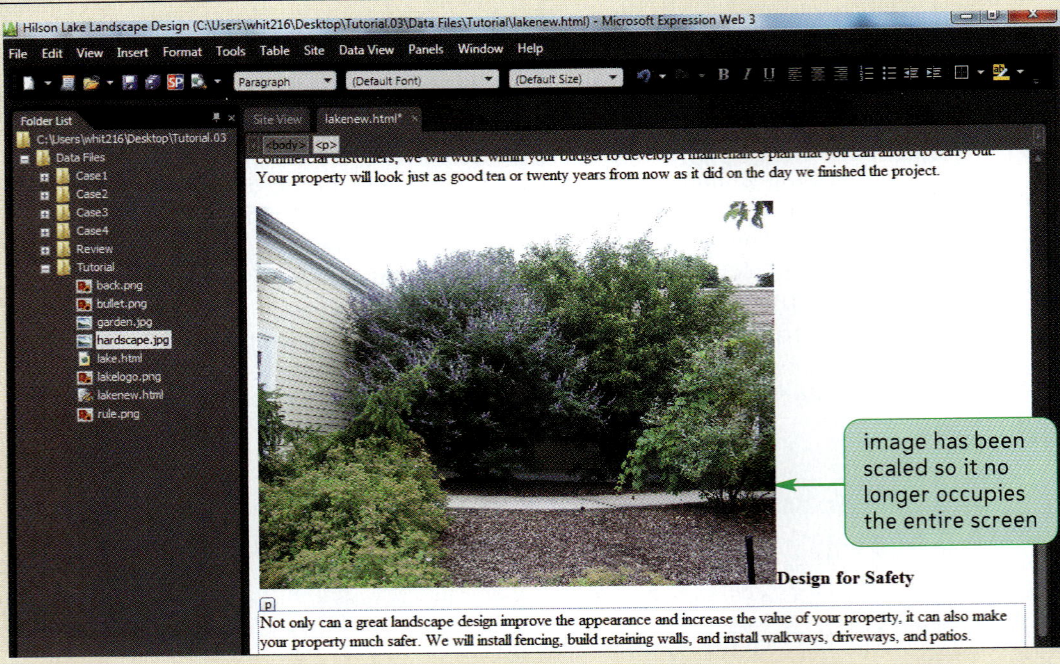

Because the text does not wrap around the image, a great deal of white space appears to the right of the image. You'll set the Wrapping style to have the text wrap and create some margin space for the image.

To set the Wrapping style and create margin space:

1. Double-click the **hardscape.jpg** image.

   The Picture Properties dialog box opens.
2. Click the **Appearance** tab.
3. For Wrapping style, click **Left**.
4. Click in the **Border thickness** box and then type **6**.
5. Click in the **Horizontal margin** box, delete any existing value, and then type **10**.
6. Click the **OK** button.
7. Click anywhere outside the image.

   Note that the text wraps to the right of the hardscape.jpg image and margin space has been added, as shown in Figure 3-16.

Figure 3-16 The repositioned image

Now that Renee is familiar with inserting an image and changing some of the picture properties, you'll show her how to use the Expression Web design tools to edit the appearance of an image itself.

Using the Pictures Toolbar

You can use the Pictures toolbar to change many aspects of the appearance of an image. You can edit an image to rotate and flip it, change its brightness and contrast, and to crop it. If you are not pleased with the edits you make to an image, or if you change your mind about the edits, you can undo any unsaved changes by clicking the Restore button, which is the last button on the right on the Pictures toolbar. You'll learn more about the five buttons to the left of the Restore button, which you use for image maps, in a later tutorial. Figure 3-17 shows the functions of the Pictures toolbar buttons.

Figure 3-17 **The Pictures toolbar buttons**

Button	Function
Insert Picture from File	Inserts a picture into the Web page from a file storage device
Auto Thumbnail	Makes a larger picture smaller so that, when clicked, it is restored to its original size, but on a new Web page
Bring Forward	Places an image on top of another image
Send Backward	Places an image under another image
Rotate Left 90°	Rotates the image left 90 degrees
Rotate Right 90	Rotates the image right 90 degrees
Flip Horizontal	Flips the image horizontally
Flip Vertical	Flips the image vertically
More Contrast	Brightens an image
Less Contrast	Darkens an image
More Brightness	Washes out color, giving the appearance of more light or daylight
Less Brightness	Darkens color, giving the appearance of more shadow or night
Crop	Removes parts of an image, which results in the image being resized
Set Transparent Color	Selects a transparent color (usually the page background color); use on .gif files only
Color	Changes to black and white or a washed-out color
Bevel	Adds a three-dimensional (outset) border to the image
Resample	Corrects the image appearance if you have changed the dimensions of the image
Restore	Restores changes that have not been saved

INSIGHT

Setting a Transparent Color

Very often, round or irregularly shaped images are actually contained within a square or a rectangle. To make the round image appear on the page without its background color, you can set a transparent color (the color that surrounds the image). To do so, click the image and then click the color you want to make transparent. As you move the cursor over the image, the pointer appears as a pencil eraser. Click the pencil eraser on the color you want to be transparent. The selected color becomes transparent, which allows the background color of the page to show through. You can only make a color in a .gif file transparent. If you select a .jpg image to have a transparent color, a Windows alert dialog box opens, and prompts you to convert the .jpg file into a .gif file.

To **resample** an image means to improve the picture quality of the image once it has been scaled. Resampling an image often reduces the file size, which makes the image download faster. When you save an edited image, the Save Embedded Files dialog box opens. You can keep the original file by renaming the image file, or you can overwrite the original image. When you overwrite an image, any changes you have made to the image by using the Pictures toolbar buttons are applied to the original image. Because you do not want to affect the appearance of the original image, you show Renee how to save the hardscape.jpg image file under a new filename so that you have two images: the original image and an edited image.

To resample and rename the hardscape.jpg image:

1. On the menu bar, click **View**, point to **Toolbars**, and then click **Pictures**.

   The Pictures toolbar appears, but with the exception of only one button, all the buttons on the toolbar are dimmed.

2. Click the **hardscape.jpg** image to select it.

   The buttons on the Pictures toolbar are no longer dimmed.

3. On the Pictures toolbar, click the **Resample** button.

   Although you might see only a slight change on the screen, the image is resampled.

4. Save the **lakenew.html** file. The Save Embedded Files dialog box opens, as shown in Figure 3-18.

Figure 3-18 The Save Embedded Files dialog box

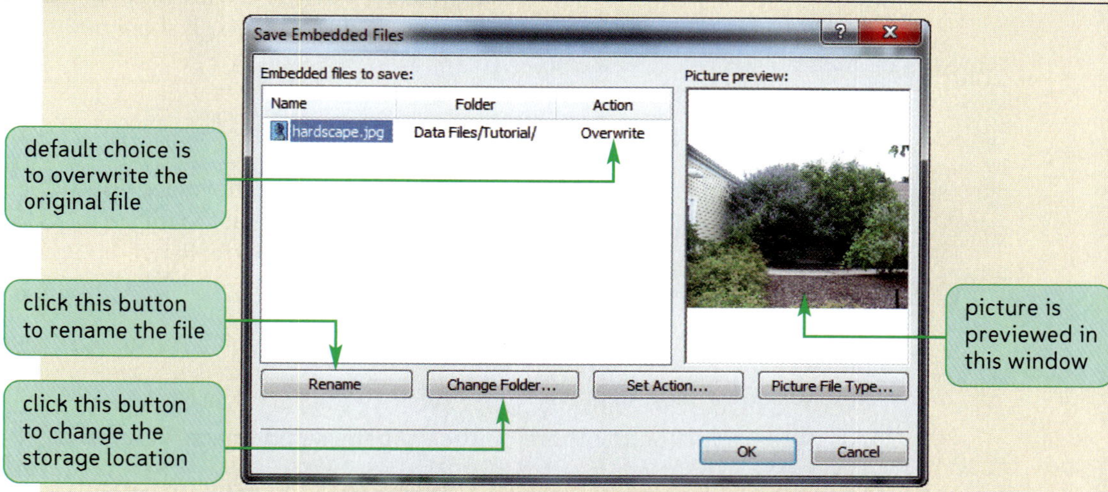

5. Click the **Rename** button.
6. Type **scapenew.jpg**, and then press the **Enter** key.

   The filename is now changed and the Action has been changed to Save, as shown in Figure 3-19.

Figure 3-19 Choices in the Save Embedded Files dialog box

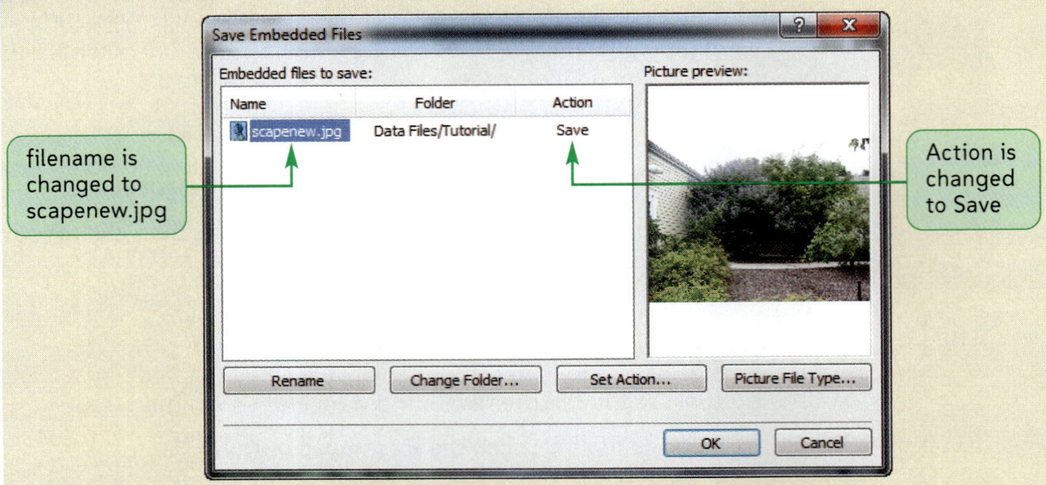

7. Click the **OK** button.

   The scapenew.jpg file is added to the list of files in the Folder List panel.

Now that you are working with a revised version of the original image, you are free to further revise the image without making those changes permanent to the original image. You'll first show Renee how to rotate an image, and then you'll show her how to flip an image.

Rotating and Flipping an Image

You can rotate an image in 90-degree increments so that the image appears sideways or upside down. Flipping an image is almost like looking at the image in a mirror—the image shown is the reverse of the original image. You'll show Renee how to rotate and flip an image using the Pictures toolbar.

To rotate and flip the scapenew.jpg image:

1. If necessary, click anywhere on the **scapenew.jpg** image to select it.
2. On the Pictures toolbar, click the **Rotate Left 90°** button.

   The image rotates to the left by 90 degrees.
3. Click the **Rotate Right 90°** button.

   The image rotates to the right by 90 degrees.
4. Click the **Flip Horizontal** button.

   The image inverts horizontally.
5. Click the **Flip Vertical** button.

   The image inverts vertically.
6. On the Pictures toolbar, click the **Restore** button (the last button on the right).

   The image is restored to its original appearance.

Next, you'll show Renee how to alter the image brightness.

Changing the Image Brightness

The More Contrast button brightens an image; the Less Contrast button darkens it. However, depending on the original contrast of the image, clicking these buttons might have little or no effect. Clicking the More Brightness button repeatedly causes an image to gradually fade. Clicking the Less Brightness button repeatedly darkens it gradually. You'll show Renee how to use these two buttons to affect the appearance of an image.

To change the brightness of an image:

1. With the scapenew.jpg image selected, on the Pictures toolbar, repeatedly click the **More Brightness** button.

   The image increasingly appears to grow brighter and wash out.

2. On the Pictures toolbar, repeatedly click the **Less Brightness** button.

   The image increasingly appears to darken as though night were falling.

3. On the Pictures toolbar, click the **Restore** button.

   The image is restored to its original appearance.

The Color button's name is somewhat misleading. You'll discuss the Color button with Renee next.

Removing Color

The Color button does not add color or change the colors of an image. Rather, the Color button allows you to choose between two effects: Grayscale and Wash Out. **Grayscale** is an image effect that removes all color from an image and turns the image into a black-and-white image. **Wash Out** is an image effect that fades the image. The Wash Out effect does not remove the color; instead, it makes the image appear as a watermark, a faded version of the original. You'll show Renee these two effects.

To remove the color and wash out an image:

1. With the scapenew.jpg image still selected, on the Pictures toolbar, click the **Color** button.
2. Click **Grayscale** on the drop-down menu, and then click outside the image.

   The image is now black and white only.

3. Click the **scapenew** image, and then click the **Restore** button.
4. With the image still selected, click the **Color** button.
5. Click **Wash Out** on the drop-down menu.

   The image loses most of its detail.

6. Click the **Restore** button.

   The image is restored to its original appearance.

You have already created borders for an image, but you'll next show Renee how to change the border so that it has a 3D effect and appears either sunken or raised.

Creating a Beveled Border

A **beveled border** is a border that has a 3D effect. A beveled border often appears as an **inset border**, where the border appears recessed, or as an **outset border**, where the border appears raised. The Pictures toolbar creates outset borders. You'll show Renee how to create an outset border for the hardscape.jpg image.

To create an outset beveled border:

1. With the scapenew.jpg image still selected, on the Pictures toolbar, click the **Bevel** button.

   A thick, sculpted border now surrounds the image.

2. Click the **Restore** button.

   The image is restored to its original appearance.

Finally, you'll show Renee how to crop an image.

Cropping an Image

You can use the **Crop tool** to eliminate portions of an image that have little or no content or to allow you to be selective about the image content. You can also use the Crop tool to eliminate a person or persons or unwanted objects from an image. When you **crop** an image, you select a desired rectangular portion from the image and delete the rest of the image content.

REFERENCE

Cropping an Image

- On the Pictures toolbar, click the Crop button.
- Click and drag a resize handle to resize the image, or click and drag to select an area of the image to be cropped.
- On the Pictures toolbar, click the Crop button.

For example, if you took a photo of a person and the left half of the photo did not have any content, you could crop the photo to include content from just the right side of the image. Image cropping does not reduce the resolution of the area cropped. If the image was of very high resolution, you could enlarge the image to focus on just the cropped portion of the original image.

Recall that resize handles are small rectangles that appear on the four corners and the sides of an image. Resize handles are also known as sizing handles. You can use the resize handles to crop an image. You can also crop any area of an image you want. You'll show Renee how to use the resize handles to select an area to crop.

TIP

Be sure to make a backup copy of an image you want to crop. If you save the image with the cropped changes, it might not be possible to undo the cropping.

To crop the image:

1. With the scapenew.jpg image selected, on the Pictures toolbar, click the **Crop** button.

   Although the crop marks are faint, a cropping graphic—a box with a dashed border—appears inside the image, as shown in Figure 3-20.

Figure 3-20 Crop marks

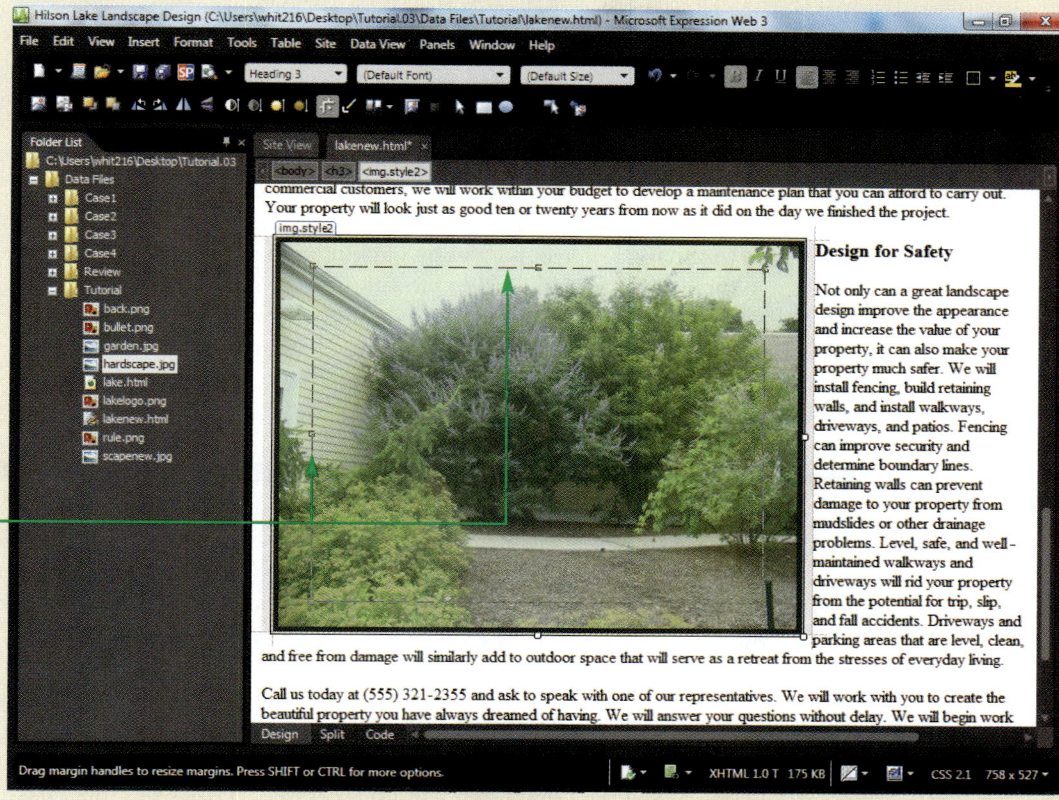

a dashed border indicates the area to be cropped

If you drag the pointer too far down, drag the pointer up again without releasing the mouse button.

2. Move the pointer over the **top resize handle**. When the insertion point turns into a **double-headed arrow**, ↕, click and drag down about half the height of the image.
3. On the Pictures toolbar, click the **Crop** button again.

   Only the area that was inside the cropping box remains, as shown in Figure 3-21.

Figure 3-21 The cropped image

the image has been resized to include only content within the cropped area

4. On the Pictures toolbar, click the **Restore** button.

   The image is restored to its original appearance.

Next, you'll show Renee how to resize an image manually.

Manually Resizing an Image

You have used the Picture Properties dialog box to resize an image. You can also manually resize an image in Design view by clicking and dragging any of the resize handles to change the image size. In Design view, an image has three resize handles: one on the right side, one on the bottom, and one in the lower-right corner. When you pass the mouse pointer over a resize handle, you see a ScreenTip that indicates the width and the height of the image. As you drag to resize the image, the ScreenTip displays the current width and height.

REFERENCE

Manually Resizing an Image

- Double-click the image.
- In the Picture Properties dialog box, click the Appearance tab.
- In the Size group, make sure the check boxes for Specify size and Keep aspect ratio are checked.
- Click in the Width and Height text boxes to change the width and height, respectively.
- Click the OK button.

or

- In Design view, click the image, and then click and drag the corner resize handle to set the desired size.

After you resize an image, it is a good idea to resample it, which restores the image to its fullest clarity at the specified size. You'll show Renee how to use the resize handles to manually resize an image, and then you'll have her resample the image. The image currently has a width of 500 pixels and a height of 375 pixels, so you'll show Renee how to resize the image to a width of 250 pixels and a height of 187 pixels.

To manually resize an image and resample the image:

1. Locate the corner resize handle, which is in the lower-right corner of the scapenew.jpg image.
2. With the scapenew.jpg image selected, drag the **corner resize handle** up and to the left until the image is approximately half its current size. (You do not have to be too precise.)
3. Release the **mouse button**.
4. Click anywhere outside the image. The image should now appear resized, as shown in Figure 3-22.

Figure 3-22 **Manual resize**

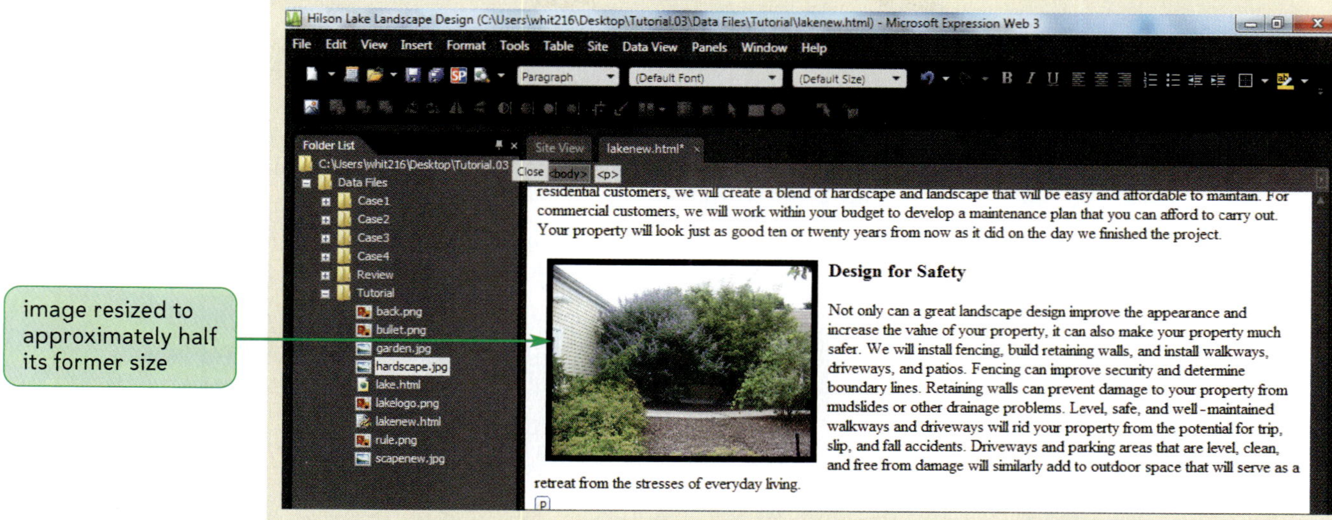

5. Right-click anywhere on the **scapenew.jpg** image.
6. Click **Reset Size** on the shortcut menu to restore the image to its original size.
7. Press and hold the **Shift** key while you click and drag the lower-right corner resize handle until the image is completely to the left of the "Design for Safety" heading and text, as shown in Figure 3-23.

   Based on your monitor's resolution, your screen might look different.

Figure 3-23 **Image resized to align with text**

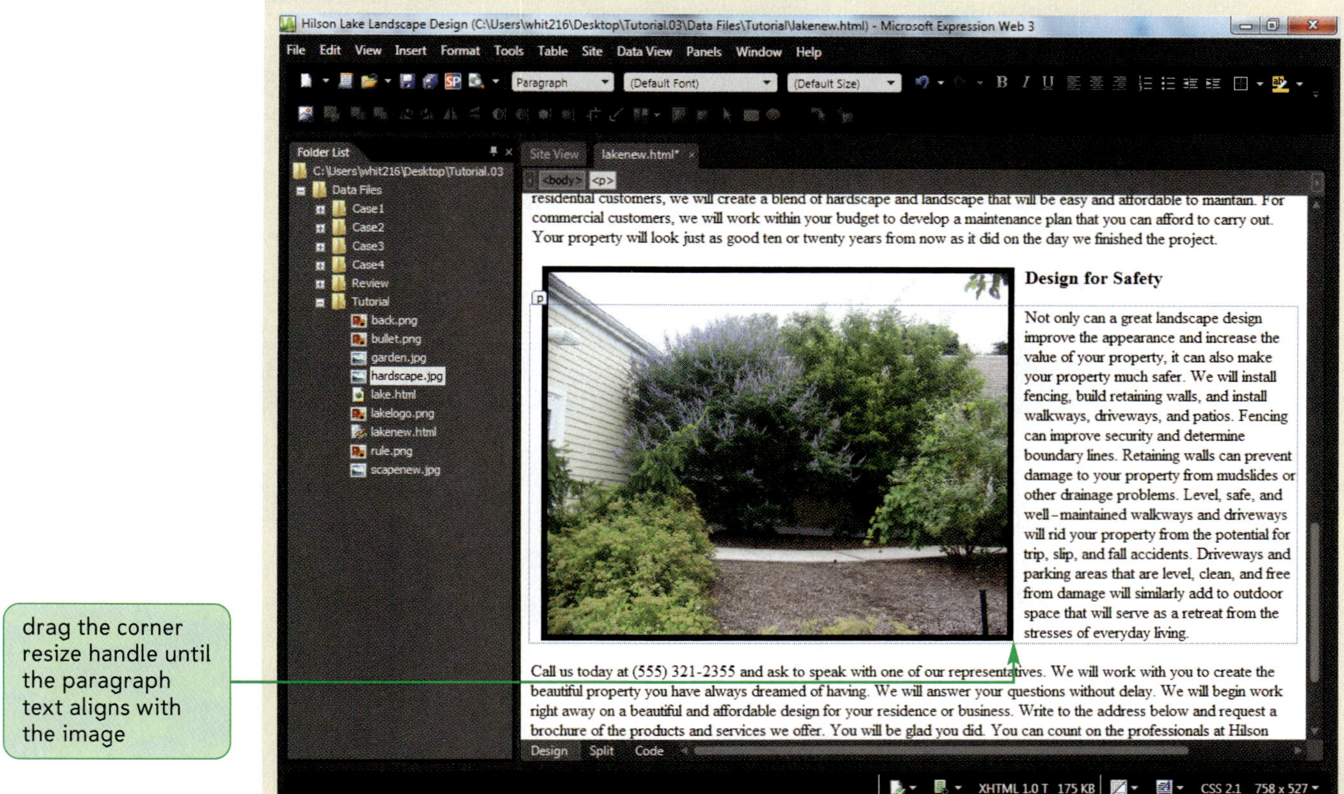

Renee wants some more margin space to the right of the image. She could set the margin space in the Picture Properties dialog box, but you'll show her how to manually add margin space selectively to an image.

To manually add margin space to the image:

1. If necessary, click the **scapenew.jpg** image to select it. Pass the pointer over any portion of the right border of the image except the resize handle until the pointer turns into a double-headed arrow ⟺.
2. Using the ScreenTip as your guide, click and drag the **arrow pointer** ⟺ to the right to add margin space so that there is 20 pixels of margin space to the right of the image.
3. Click anywhere outside the scapenew.jpg image. The image should appear as shown in Figure 3-24.

Figure 3-24 Margin space added to an image

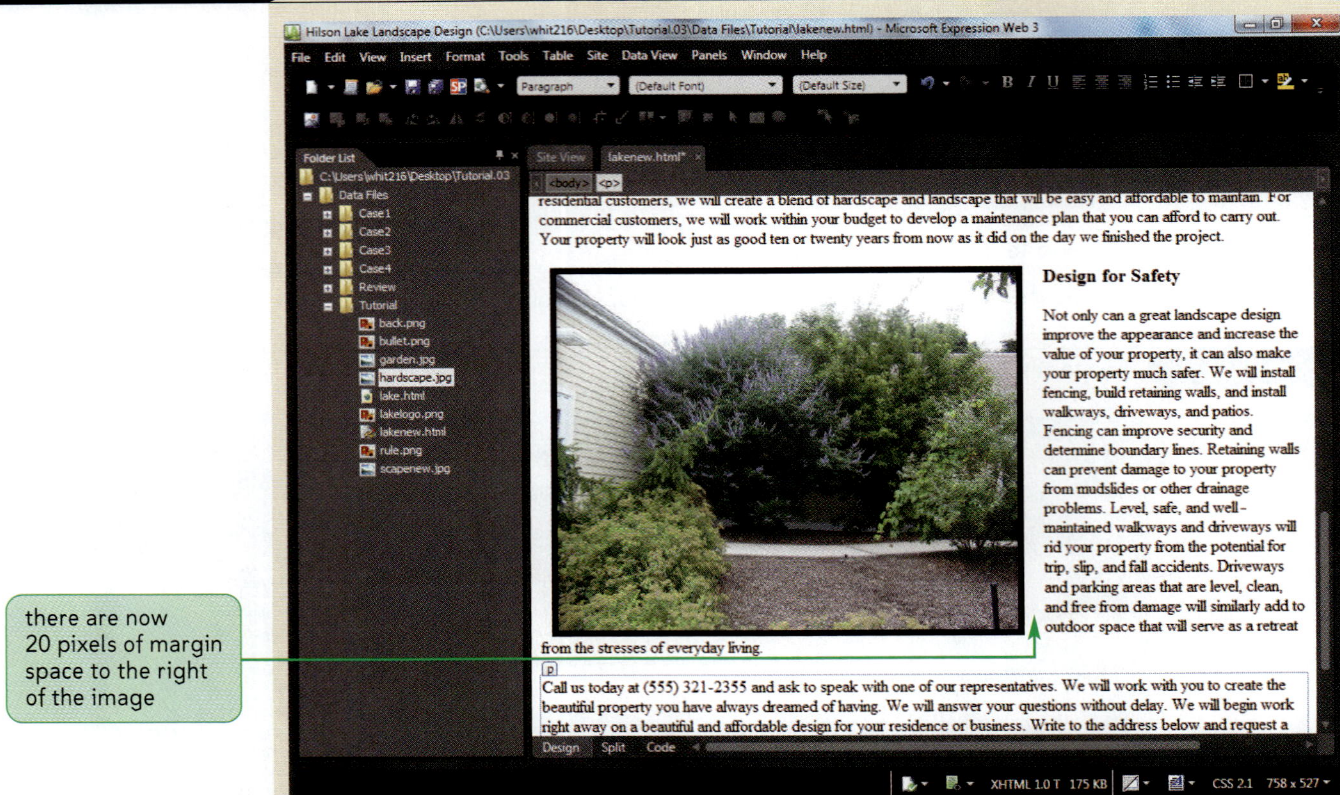

After you resize an image manually, you can also resample it by clicking the Picture Actions button, which appears below the image.

Renee is curious about the function of the Auto Thumbnail button. You'll next show Renee how to create an auto thumbnail image.

Creating Thumbnail Images

Because images can greatly increase Web page file size and thereby slow download times, Web designers often use thumbnail images. A **thumbnail image** is a small image that, when clicked, displays a new Web page with a larger version of the same image. Creating a thumbnail image does not modify the original image; it instead generates a new, but smaller, image.

An **image gallery** is a column-and-row grid of several thumbnail images. By creating an image gallery, you conserve screen space on your Web page. In addition, the image gallery gives Web page visitors the option of seeing images in a larger size if they want.

REFERENCE

Creating a Thumbnail Image

- Click anywhere on the image to select the image.
- On the Pictures toolbar, click the Auto Thumbnail button (or press the Ctrl+T keys).
- If necessary, move the thumbnail image to align the image with surrounding text.

TIP

You can convert an image into an auto thumbnail by right-clicking the image and then clicking Auto Thumbnail on the shortcut menu.

Expression Web automates the entire process of creating a thumbnail. Expression Web takes the original image, reduces it to a smaller size, creates a new viewing area to display the larger image, and creates a link from the thumbnail image to the viewing area. When a visitor to your Web site clicks the image, the viewing area (with the original image) appears. You'll show Renee how to create a thumbnail from the garden.jpg image using the Auto Thumbnail button on the Pictures toolbar.

To create the thumbnail image:

1. If necessary, scroll up to view the garden.jpg image. Click anywhere on the **garden.jpg** image.
2. On the Pictures toolbar, click the **Auto Thumbnail** button.

   The thumbnail image is much smaller, and a thin blue border has replaced the black border, as shown in Figure 3-25.

Figure 3-25 Creating an auto thumbnail image

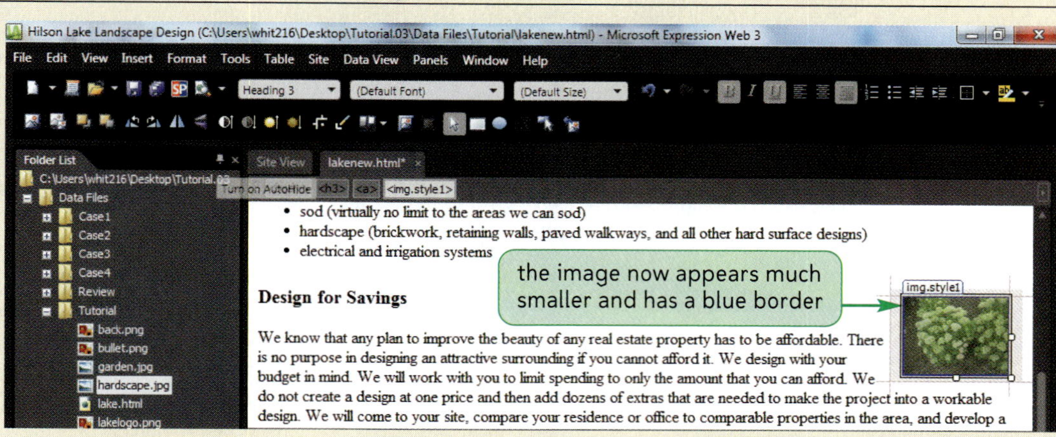

3. Save the file.

The Save Embedded Files dialog box opens. The image file has a new name, garden_small.jpg, as shown in Figure 3-26.

Figure 3-26 **Save Embedded Files dialog box**

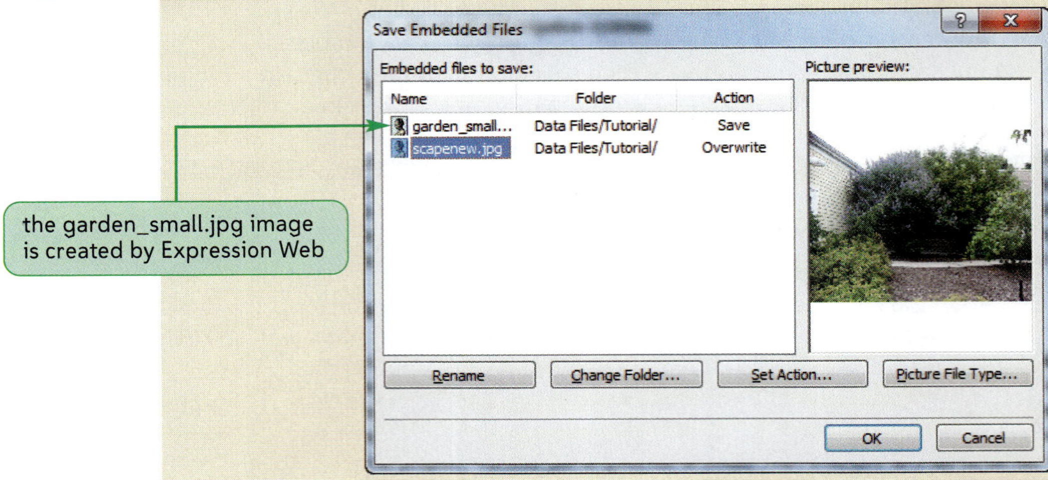

4. Click the **OK** button.

   The garden_small.jpg file is saved.

5. Press the **F12** key to view the page in the default browser.

6. In the browser, click the thumbnail image.

   The image appears in its original size in a separate viewing area, as shown in Figure 3-27.

Figure 3-27 **The viewing area for the thumbnail**

7. Click the browser's **Back** button to display the lakenew.html file again in the browser.

8. Close the browser window to return to Design view in Expression Web.

TIP

To restore a thumbnail image to its original size, right-click the image, click Hyperlink Properties on the shortcut menu, and then click the Remove Link button.

INSIGHT

Setting the Thumbnail Settings

The Auto Thumbnail settings in the Page Editor Options determine the size of the thumbnail picture. It is possible to change the default Auto Thumbnail Properties in Expression Web for a particular auto thumbnail. You might have noticed in the browser that the thumbnail image had a blue or purple border around it. In the Page Editor Options, you can change the width and the height of the thumbnail image: changing either one also changes the other for the same value. You can also change the border thickness—the default is 2 pixels, and the maximum width is 8 pixels. In addition, you can give the image a beveled border so that the border has a 3D design effect. The Auto Thumbnail options are specific to a single image; they are not applied globally to all thumbnail images. After you set the Auto Thumbnail options, Expression Web creates a style in the Apply Styles panel. You can modify the style as you want.

TIP

If you create a thumbnail image by mistake, press the Ctrl+Z keys to undo the action. You can also click Edit on the menu bar, and then click Undo Auto Thumbnail.

Next, you'll show Renee how to use Expression Web to insert an image as a horizontal line.

Using an Image as a Horizontal Line

Today, it is much more common to use an image as a horizontal line than it is to use the HTML <hr /> tag to create a horizontal line. To use an image as a horizontal line, you insert the image on the Web page as you would any other image. You do not use the <hr /> tag at all. Renee wants a horizontal line to follow the last sentence of the document. Images designed as horizontal lines are wide and short. To ensure that the image occupies the entire screen width, you'll also show her how to revise the appearance of the horizontal rule.

To insert an image as a horizontal rule:

1. If necessary, scroll down to the bottom of the page. In the last sentence of the document before the address, position the insertion point after the period that follows the word "Expo."
2. Press the **Enter** key to create a new paragraph.
3. In the Folder List task pane, click and drag the **rule.png** filename anywhere in the new paragraph you just created, and then release the mouse button.

   The Accessibility Properties dialog box opens.
4. For the alternate text, type **image as a horizontal line**.
5. Click the **OK** button to insert the rule.png file. A green gradient horizontal line now appears below the last paragraph.
6. Save the file.
7. Press the **F12** key to view the file in the browser, and then, if necessary, scroll down to view the image as a horizontal line. The new horizontal rule should appear as shown in Figure 3-28.

Figure 3-28 Using an image as a horizontal line

gradient green line serves as a horizontal rule

- **8.** Close the browser.

Depending on your browser and screen resolution, the rule.png line might not extend the full screen width. You'll show Renee how to correct that problem in the next set of steps.

To extend the rule across the entire screen width:

- **1.** Double-click anywhere on the **rule.png** image.
  The Picture Properties dialog box opens.
- **2.** Click the **Appearance** tab.
- **3.** Click in the **Width** box. Delete any value in the box, and then type **100**.
- **4.** Click the **in percent** option button.
- **5.** Click in the **Height** box. Delete any value in the box, and then type **10**.
- **6.** Click in the **Vertical margin** box. Delete any value in the box and then type **6**.
- **7.** Click the **OK** button.
  The rule should now be 100% of the screen width and have a height of 10 pixels.
- **8.** Save the file.
- **9.** Press the **F12** key to view the file in the browser. If necessary, scroll down to view the image as a horizontal line.
  The line extends from screen edge to screen edge, as shown in Figure 3-29.

Figure 3-29 The revised rule in the browser

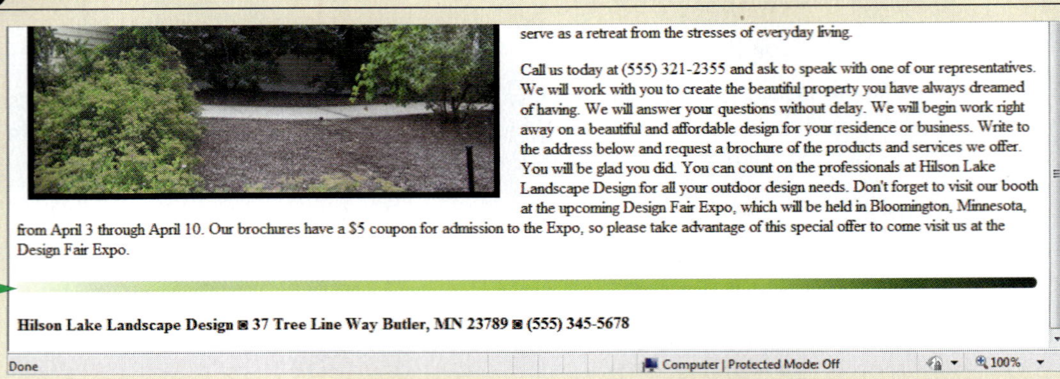

gradient green line now extends the full screen width

10. Close the browser.

Renee wants to create a list. She has seen images used as bullets on the Web, and she wonders if Expression Web can do the same. You'll show Renee how to create the list using an image as a bullet.

Using an Image as a Bullet

It is quite common today for Web pages to go beyond using just the default solid bullet, which is the list marker for unordered lists. Today, you are more likely to see an image used as a bullet. Certainly, an image used as a bullet has much more visual appeal than a solid black bullet. Expression Web makes it easy to use an image as a bullet.

REFERENCE

Using an Image as a Bullet

- Create the image in image-editing software, or obtain an appropriately sized image you want to use as a bullet.
- Create the list.
- Right-click on the list, and then on the shortcut menu, click List Properties.
- If necessary, click the Picture Bullets tab, and then click the Specify picture option button.
- Browse to the location of the image.
- Double-click the filename of the image file and then click the OK button.

Expression Web does not create the image for the bullet. You must use one of the other Expression Studio design programs, such as Expression Design, or similar illustration software. You have provided Renee with a pointer image named bullet.png. You'll show her how to use that image as a bullet for an unordered list.

To use an image as a bullet:

1. Press the **Ctrl+Home** keys to position the insertion point at the top of the page.
2. Select the **four lines** in the unordered list that follow the first paragraph.
3. Click the **Format** menu, and then click **Bullets and Numbering**.

   The List Properties dialog box opens.
4. Click the **Picture Bullets** tab.
5. Click the **Specify picture** option button.
6. Click the **Browse** button.

   The Select Picture dialog box opens, as shown in Figure 3-30.

Figure 3-30 **Select Picture dialog box**

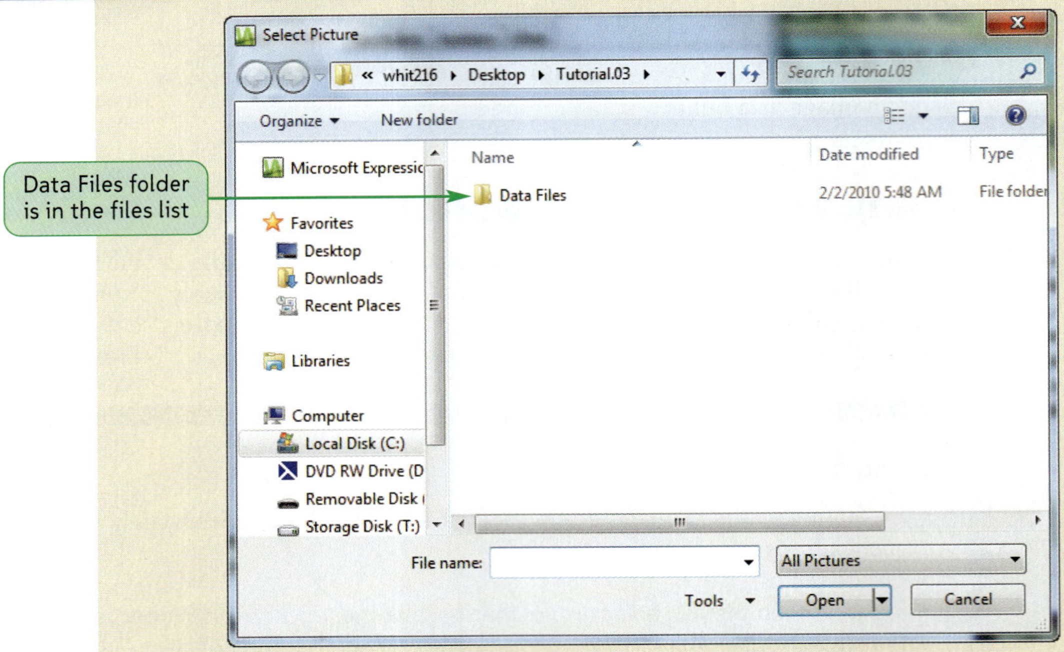

7. Double-click the **Data Files** folder, double-click the **Tutorial** folder, and then double-click the **bullet.png** filename.

   The List Properties dialog box reopens. The bullet.png filename is in the Specify picture box.

8. Click the **OK** button.

9. Click anywhere outside the bulleted list. Arrowheads appear instead of solid bullets, as shown in Figure 3-31.

Figure 3-31 **Images used as bullets**

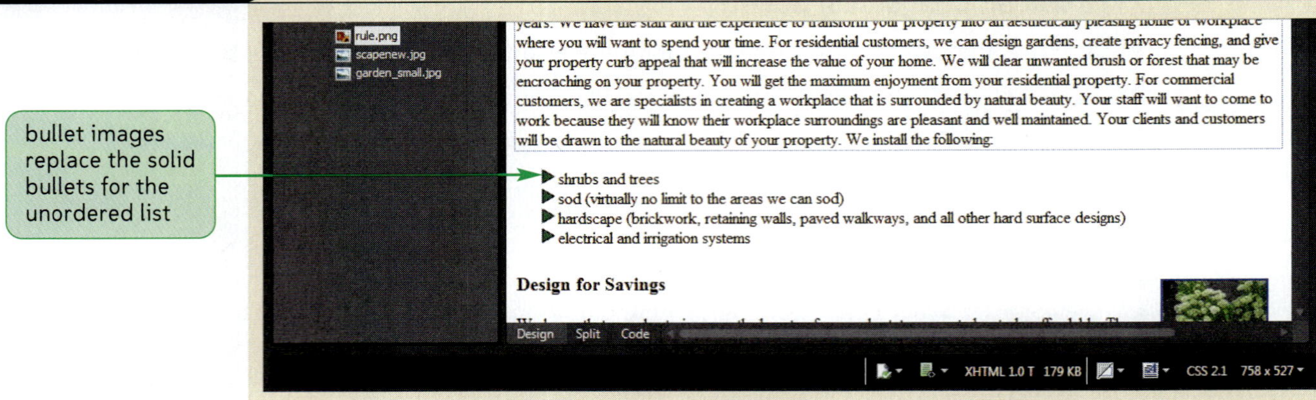

Because you no longer need to use the Pictures toolbar, you'll show Renee how to close it.

To close the Pictures toolbar:

1. Click anywhere in the editing window.
2. Click the **View** menu, point to **Toolbars**, and then click **Pictures**.

   The Common toolbar should now be the only toolbar on the screen.

PROSKILLS

Written Communication: Writing for a Web Page

When you compose text content for a Web page, perhaps the most important criterion to remember is your target audience. For example, if you are writing text for a newspaper, consider that your audience could be as young as elementary school students. If you use technical jargon, be sure to define any terms that might be unfamiliar to those people reading the page. On the other hand, if you intend your Web site audience to be a very narrow one, such as people involved in a particular profession, use the language of that industry without defining the terms. For example, if you intend for lawyers to read your Web page, it actually would be counterproductive and annoying if you defined legal jargon—your intended audience already knows these terms.

Irrespective of your audience, it is imperative that your text content be grammatically correct, factually accurate, and free of any typographical errors. These sorts of errors, even a single one, detract from the credibility of the Web site. When composing text for a Web page, always have zero tolerance for these types of errors. The success of your Web site depends on it.

Recall that you can specify a background color for a Web page. It is also possible to use an image as a Web page background. You'll show Renee how to design a page background.

Designing the Page Background

Currently, the lakenew.html Web page has a white background. It is possible to change the background color for the page and to use a background image for the page. You should always change the background color if you intend to use a background image. If there is a problem in loading the background image for the page, the background color takes its place. In choosing a background, it is very important to contrast the background with page text. Avoid bright, harsh colors, such as red, orange, or bright yellow. At all times, the readability of the page takes precedence over design issues.

INSIGHT

Using the Select Button to Choose a Color

When trying to choose a background color, the **eyedropper tool** is a useful feature that lets you pick from colors that are already present in images on the Web page. To use the eyedropper tool, click the Formatting tab in the Page Properties dialog box. In the Colors group, click the Background arrow, and then click More Colors. In the More Colors dialog box, click the Select button. As soon as you click the Select button, the pointer turns into an eyedropper icon. Drag the title bar of the More Colors dialog box out of the way if necessary, and then find a color on the page that you want to use as a background color. Click the eyedropper on that color. Click the OK button twice to display the editing window. The page background color will match the color you chose with the eyedropper tool. By using the eyedropper tool, you do not need to guess about a named color value or a hexadecimal value. The eyedropper lets you choose the exact color you want.

Renee wants to use a textured tan or beige background. You'll show Renee how to use an image, named back.png, for the page background and how to also set a background color for the page.

To use an image for the document background:

1. In Design view, right-click any area of the editing window, and then click **Page Properties**.

   The Page Properties dialog box opens.
2. Click the **Formatting** tab.
3. Click the **Background picture** check box, and then click the **Browse** button.
4. If necessary, navigate to the Tutorial.03\Tutorial folder, and then double-click the **back.png** filename.

   The Page Properties dialog box opens again.
5. In the Colors section, click the **Background** arrow.
6. Click **More Colors** and then click the light yellow colors until you see (Hex={#FF,FF,99}) in the Value box, as shown in Figure 3-32.

Figure 3-32 More Colors dialog box

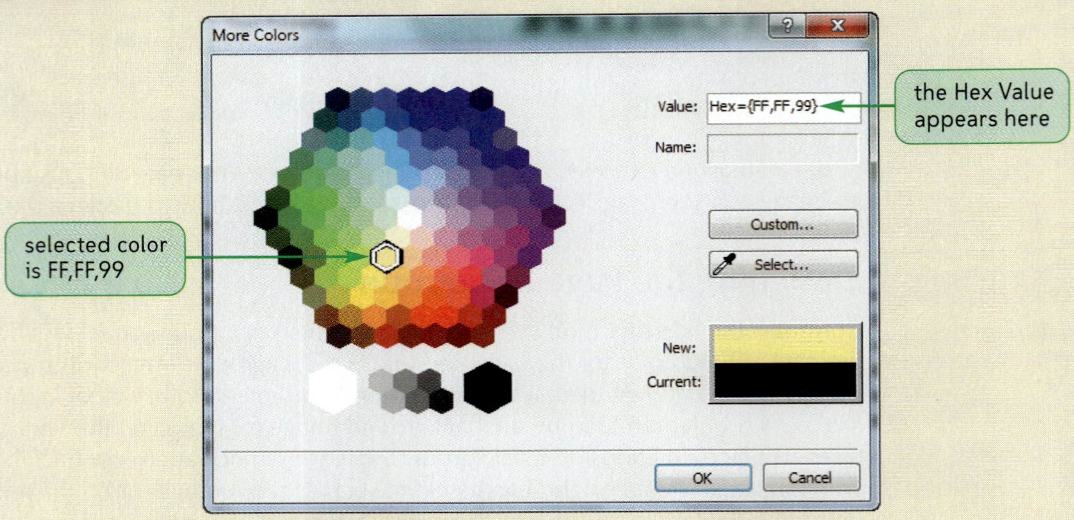

7. In the More Colors dialog box, click the **OK** button.

   The Page Properties dialog box reopens.
8. Click the **OK** button.

   The document has a beige background color, as shown in Figure 3-33. The texture confirms that the Web page is showing the background image you specified, rather than an untextured background color.

Figure 3-33 Background color is changed

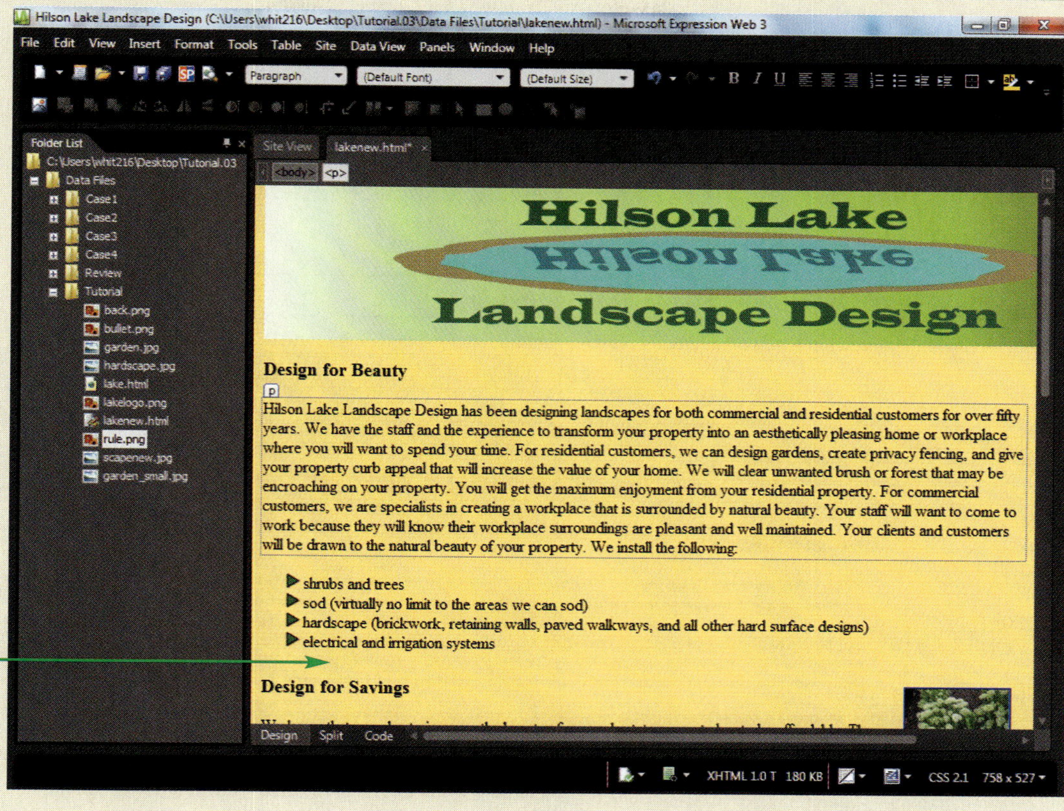

background color is beige

Last, you'll center the footer line and add some documentation to the page.

To center the footer line:

1. If necessary, scroll down to the bottom of the page, and then click anywhere in the address line.
2. On the Common toolbar, click the **Center** button.
3. Click anywhere outside the line. The line is centered, as shown in Figure 3-34.

Figure 3-34 The footer

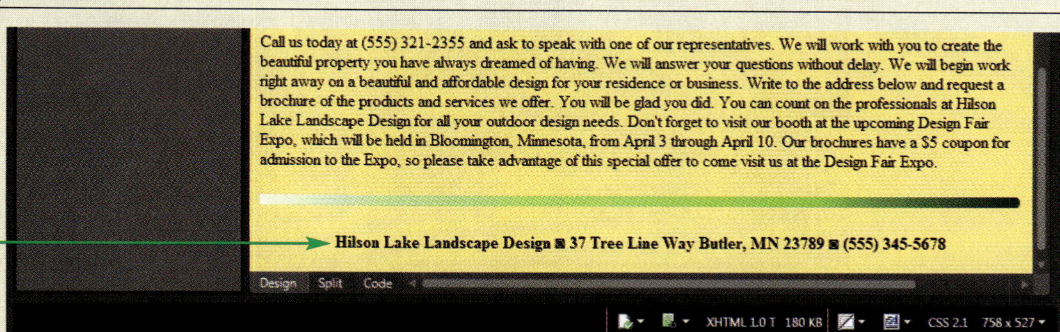

the footer is now centered

You'll now have Renee add some documentation to the page and view the completed file in the default browser.

To save the file and view it in the browser:

1. Press the **Ctrl+End** keys to position the insertion point at the end of the document.
2. Type your first and last name, press the **Shift+Enter** keys, and then type **Tutorial 3**.
3. Format the two lines you just typed as bold.
4. Save the file.
5. Press the **F12** key to view the completed lakenew.html Web page in the browser, as shown in Figure 3-35.

Figure 3-35 The completed file in the browser

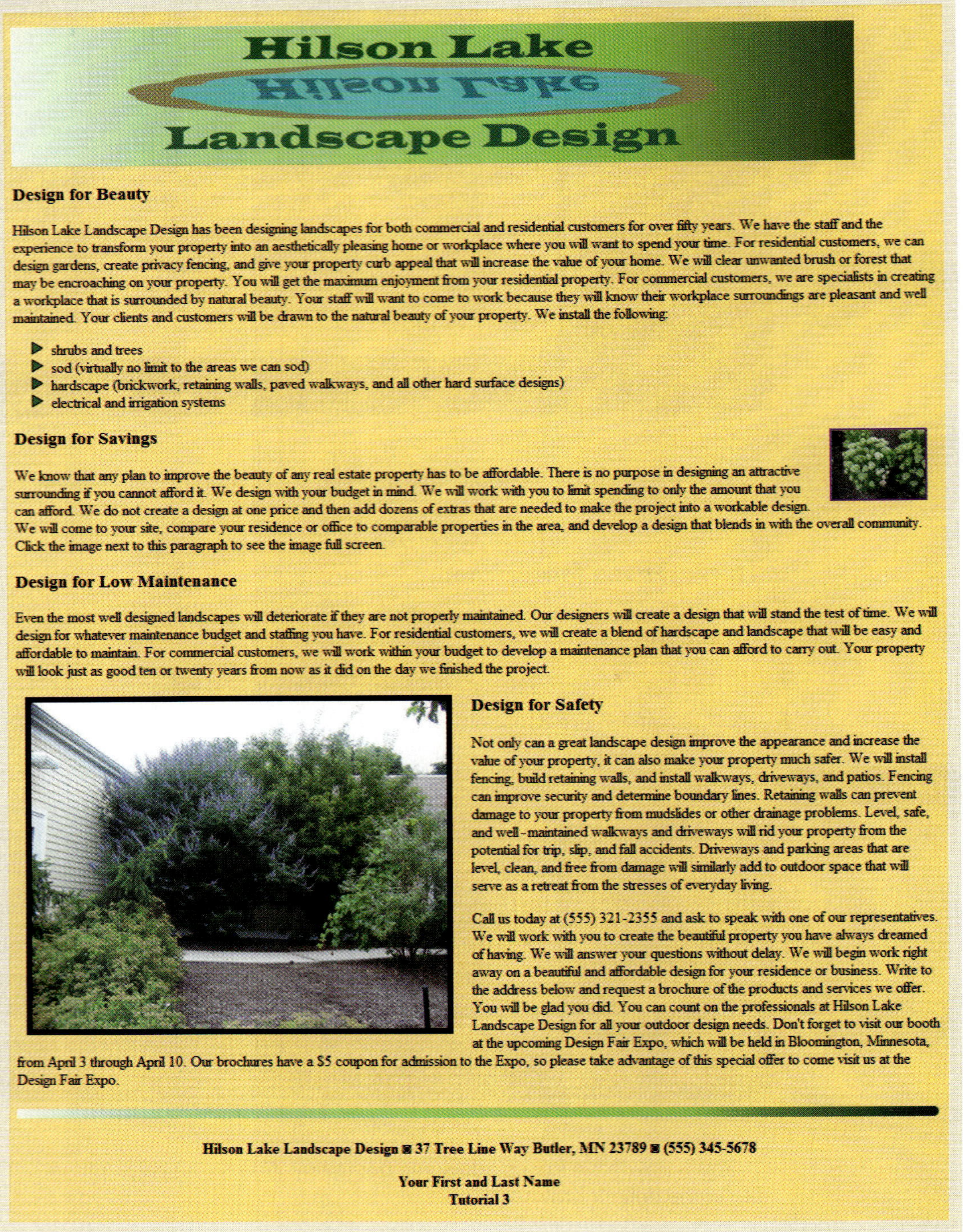

Hilson Lake Landscape Design

Design for Beauty

Hilson Lake Landscape Design has been designing landscapes for both commercial and residential customers for over fifty years. We have the staff and the experience to transform your property into an aesthetically pleasing home or workplace where you will want to spend your time. For residential customers, we can design gardens, create privacy fencing, and give your property curb appeal that will increase the value of your home. We will clear unwanted brush or forest that may be encroaching on your property. You will get the maximum enjoyment from your residential property. For commercial customers, we are specialists in creating a workplace that is surrounded by natural beauty. Your staff will want to come to work because they will know their workplace surroundings are pleasant and well maintained. Your clients and customers will be drawn to the natural beauty of your property. We install the following:

- shrubs and trees
- sod (virtually no limit to the areas we can sod)
- hardscape (brickwork, retaining walls, paved walkways, and all other hard surface designs)
- electrical and irrigation systems

Design for Savings

We know that any plan to improve the beauty of any real estate property has to be affordable. There is no purpose in designing an attractive surrounding if you cannot afford it. We design with your budget in mind. We will work with you to limit spending to only the amount that you can afford. We do not create a design at one price and then add dozens of extras that are needed to make the project into a workable design. We will come to your site, compare your residence or office to comparable properties in the area, and develop a design that blends in with the overall community. Click the image next to this paragraph to see the image full screen.

Design for Low Maintenance

Even the most well designed landscapes will deteriorate if they are not properly maintained. Our designers will create a design that will stand the test of time. We will design for whatever maintenance budget and staffing you have. For residential customers, we will create a blend of hardscape and landscape that will be easy and affordable to maintain. For commercial customers, we will work within your budget to develop a maintenance plan that you can afford to carry out. Your property will look just as good ten or twenty years from now as it did on the day we finished the project.

Design for Safety

Not only can a great landscape design improve the appearance and increase the value of your property, it can also make your property much safer. We will install fencing, build retaining walls, and install walkways, driveways, and patios. Fencing can improve security and determine boundary lines. Retaining walls can prevent damage to your property from mudslides or other drainage problems. Level, safe, and well-maintained walkways and driveways will rid your property from the potential for trip, slip, and fall accidents. Driveways and parking areas that are level, clean, and free from damage will similarly add to outdoor space that will serve as a retreat from the stresses of everyday living.

Call us today at (555) 321-2355 and ask to speak with one of our representatives. We will work with you to create the beautiful property you have always dreamed of having. We will answer your questions without delay. We will begin work right away on a beautiful and affordable design for your residence or business. Write to the address below and request a brochure of the products and services we offer. You will be glad you did. You can count on the professionals at Hilson Lake Landscape Design for all your outdoor design needs. Don't forget to visit our booth at the upcoming Design Fair Expo, which will be held in Bloomington, Minnesota, from April 3 through April 10. Our brochures have a $5 coupon for admission to the Expo, so please take advantage of this special offer to come visit us at the Design Fair Expo.

Hilson Lake Landscape Design ■ 37 Tree Line Way Butler, MN 23789 ■ (555) 345-5678

Your First and Last Name
Tutorial 3

5. Close the browser and return to Design view in Expression Web.
6. Close the **lakenew.html** file.
7. Submit the results of the lakenew.html file to your instructor, either in printed or electronic form, as requested.
8. Close the Web site.

REVIEW

Session 3.2 Quick Check

1. Which toolbar do you use to edit images?
2. What term describes eliminating part of an image that contains little or no content?
3. What is a beveled border?
4. What do you click and drag to change the size of an image?
5. What is a smaller representation of a larger image called?
6. What does it mean to scale an image?
7. When resizing an image, what must you maintain so that the image is resized in proportion to its original width and height?

Practice the skills you learned in the tutorial.

PRACTICE

Review Assignments

Data Files needed for this Review Assignment: field.html, lakelogo.png, sod.jpg

Renee was pleased with the lakenew.html Web page. Renee wants to add another page that calls attention to some of the other services available from Hilson Lake Landscape Design. Although your file might look somewhat different, a preview of the completed file appears in Figure 3-36.

Figure 3-36

Hilson Lake Landscape Design

Your Field, Your Dreams

Hilson Lake Landscape Design has been designing athletic fields for more than a quarter century. We have designed and maintained many of the collegiate football fields across the state. Our knowledge of design and horticulture has placed us in high demand when schools are considering installing or renovating professional-quality athletic fields. For residential customers, sod is a very practical alternative to seed lawns for a variety of reasons that are listed below.

Why Sod Gets the Nod

There are many advantages to using a sod lawn over a seed lawn.

- *Speed* - a sod lawn can be established in a few hours, rather than a few weeks
- *Dense, even coverage* - sod is much thicker than a seed lawn, which is especially important for athletic fields
- *Time* - you can install sod in any season
- *Irrigation* - sod lawns require less water than seed lawns
- *Traffic* - sod handles abuse and foot traffic much better than a seed lawn

Good for You and Good for the Planet

Sod just doesn't look good; it is good for the Earth. Grassy areas help to cool the surrounding area. Typically, a sod area can be 30 degrees cooler than an asphalt or brick area. Grassy areas also help to purify the air. Plants, such as grass, convert carbon dioxide to oxygen through a process known as photosynthesis. Because lawn grasses are so dense, compared to other foliage, lawns can absorb carbon dioxide from the atmosphere and release enough oxygen at a very high rate. It's common knowledge that grass also absorbs atmospheric pollutants from the air, such as sulfur dioxide and ozone. Grass also purifies the water system. Fortunately, grass has a very deep and complex root system, which makes grass particularly effective in cleaning water runoff as it enters into the ground, and grass roots act as a filter to rid the water of these harmful contaminants. Grass reduces water runoff into streams, lakes, and rivers. One of the greatest benefits of grass is that it is also a natural and self-renewing surface, unlike asphalt or brick. Asphalt is made from petroleum and it needs ongoing repair or replacement. Natural turf provides a safe, sanitary, self-renewing surface, while artificial turf may harbor harmful bacteria, retain dust and pollutants, and increase sports injuries. Lawns also help to make a neighborhood quieter. In addition, lawns absorb sound, while asphalt and concrete reflect sound.

Let Us Design for You

We are the experts in sod installation and maintenance. We also can install an irrigation system to keep your sod lawn looking beautiful for years to come. Do not leave a job as important as this to someone else who does not have the experience and knowledge to do the job right. Call us at the number below right away.

Hilson Lake Landscape Design ■ 37 Tree Line Way Butler, MN 23789 ■ (555) 345-5678

Your First and Last Name
Tutorial 3, Review Assignment

Complete the following:

1. If necessary, start Expression Web, close any open sites, and open the Tutorial.03 Web site. Reset the workspace layout.
2. If necessary, in the Folder List panel, expand the Data Files and Review folders to display the Review folder contents.
3. Open the **field.html** file and then save the file as **fieldnew.html** in the same folder.

4. In Design view, open the Page Properties dialog box. In the Title box, type **Hilson Lake Landscaping Athletic Field Design**. In the Page description box, type your first and last name, type a slash, type **Tutorial 3, Review Assignment**, and then close the dialog box.
5. Select the text in the first heading, "Your Field, Your Dreams," and format it as an h2 heading.
6. One by one, select the other headings, "Why Sod Gets the Nod," "Good for You and Good for the Planet," and "Let Us Design for You," and format those lines as h2 headings.
7. Show the Pictures toolbar.
8. Insert the lakelogo.png image at the top of the page. Use "Hilson Lake logo image" as the alternate text. Center the image.
9. Position the insertion point before the letter H in the first sentence of the first paragraph of the document. Insert the sod.jpg image. Use "photo of beautiful, green sod lawn" as the alternate text.
10. Change the Picture Properties for sod.jpg image on the Appearance tab as follows:
    - Change the Wrapping style to Left.
    - Change the Border thickness to 4 pixels.
    - Change the Horizontal margin to 4 pixels.
    - Change the Vertical margin to 4 pixels.
11. Make sure that the check boxes for Specify size and Keep aspect ratio are checked. Change the Width to 200 (let Expression Web determine the value for the Height), and then close the dialog box.
12. With the sod.jpg image selected, use the Pictures toolbar to resample the image.
13. With the sod.jpg image selected, move the image to just before the letter G in the h2 heading "Good for You and Good for the Planet."
14. Select the paragraphs from "Speed" through "Traffic" and make those items a bulleted list.
15. Click anywhere in the last line in the document (the address and phone number) and then center and bold that line.
16. Press the Ctrl+End keys to position the insertion point at the end of the document. Press the Enter key. Type your first and last name, press the Shift+Enter keys, and then type **Tutorial 3, Review Assignment**.
17. Save the **fieldnew.html** file. Save Embedded Files, if prompted.
18. Open the **fieldnew.html** file in your browser, as shown in Figure 3-36.
19. Close the browser. In Expression Web, close all open documents. If you will not be completing the next assignment, close the Web site and exit Expression Web.
20. Submit the completed files to your instructor, either in printed or electronic form, as requested.

Use the skills you learned in the tutorial to create a Web page for a seafood restaurant.

APPLY

Case Problem 1

Data Files needed for this Case Problem: burger.jpg, cake.jpg, and steer.html

The Swimming Steer The Swimming Steer is one of Texas's finest steak and seafood restaurants. Located in Hamilton Township, The Swimming Steer is less than a mile from the Gulf Coast. Although the restaurant is famous for its steaks and chops, The Swimming Steer is becoming just as famous for its other menu choices. Dan Gordon, the owner of The Swimming Steer, has asked for your help in updating the restaurant's home page. Although your file might look somewhat different, a preview of the completed file appears in Figure 3-37.

Figure 3-37

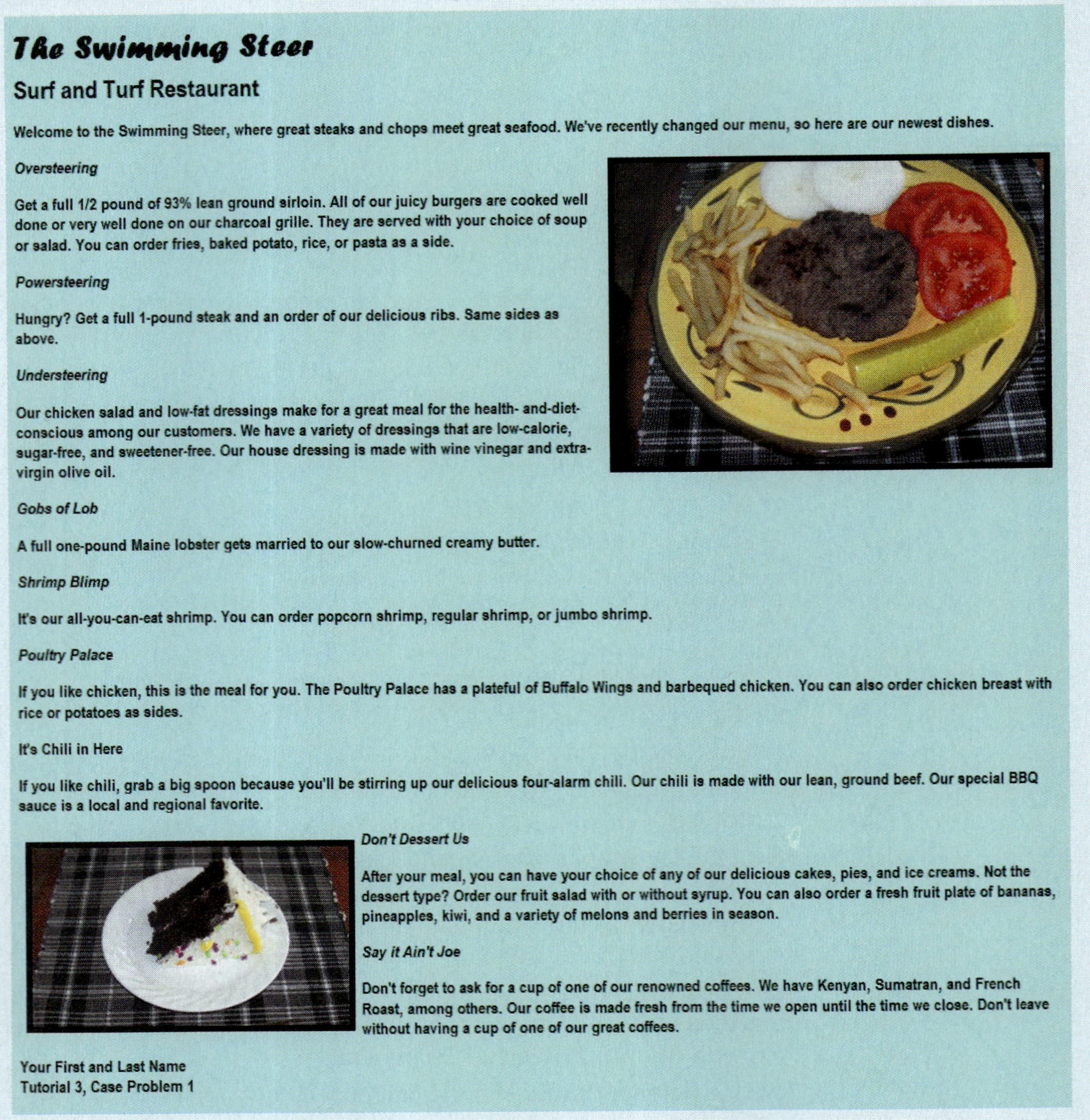

Complete the following:

1. If necessary, start Expression Web, close any open sites, and then open the Tutorial.03 Web site. Reset the workspace layout. If necessary, display the Pictures toolbar.
2. In the Folder List panel, expand the Data Files and Case1 folders to display the Case1 folder contents.
3. Open the **steer.html** file and then save the file as **steernew.html** in the same folder.
4. In Design view, open the Page Properties dialog box. In the Title box, type **The Swimming Steer Restaurant**.
5. In the Page description box, type your first and last name, type a slash, type **Tutorial 3, Case Problem 1**, and then close the dialog box.

6. From the Folder List panel, click and drag the burger.jpg filename to just before the word "Oversteering" near the top of the page, and then release the mouse button. For the alternate text, type **photo of delicious burger platter**, and then insert the image. Change the Picture Properties for the burger.jpg image as follows:
   - Set the Wrapping style to Right.
   - Set the Border thickness to 6 pixels.
   - Set the Horizontal margin to 6 pixels.
   - Set the Vertical margin to 6 pixels. (Make sure that the "Specify size" and "Keep aspect ratio" check boxes are checked.)
   - Change the width to 467 pixels (the height will be set automatically), and then close the dialog box.
7. With the burger.jpg image selected, crop the burger.jpg image so that the knife is no longer in the picture, and then set the crop.
8. If necessary, scroll down to see the "Don't Dessert Us" heading in the editing window. From the Folder List panel, click and drag the cake.jpg filename to just before the "Don't Dessert Us" heading in the editing window, and then release the mouse button. For the alternate text, type **photo of large slice of chocolate cake**, and then insert the image. Change the Picture Properties for the cake.jpg image as follows:
   - Set the Wrapping style to Left.
   - Create a Border thickness of 6 pixels.
   - Create a Horizontal margin of 6 pixels.
   - Create a Vertical margin of 10 pixels.
   - Scale the image to a width of 300 pixels (the height will adjust automatically), and then close the dialog box.
9. Crop the cake.jpg image so that the fork no longer shows in the image.
10. Press the Ctrl+End keys to position the insertion point at the end of the document. Type your first and last name, press the Shift+Enter keys, and then type **Tutorial 3, Case Problem 1**.
11. Save the **steernew.html** file, and in the Save Embedded Files dialog box, rename the burger.jpg file as burgernew.jpg, and rename the cake.jpg file as cakenew.jpg. Click OK to close the Save Embedded Files dialog box.
12. Open the **steernew.html** file in your browser. Your document should look similar to the one shown in Figure 3-37, although the background color on your screen may look slightly different than the color shown in the figure.
13. Close the browser. In Expression Web, close all open documents. If you will not be completing the next assignment, close the Web site and exit Expression Web.
14. Submit the completed files to your instructor, either in printed or electronic form, as requested.

Use the skills you learned in the tutorial to create and style a Web page for a historic mansion and garden.

APPLY

Case Problem 2

Data Files needed for this Case Problem: east.html, eastlogo.gif, hours.gif, pine.jpg, walkway.jpg

The Old Eastbrook Gardens George Collins is the manager of the Old Eastbrook Gardens, one of the largest landscaped gardens in Virginia. The Old Eastbrook Gardens is the site of the historic Eastbrook House, a mansion owned by the Eastbrook family for more than 100 years. In addition to tours of the mansion and gardens, Old Eastbrook Gardens has numerous activities for its visitors. George has composed some promotional copy for the Gardens Web site. He needs your help in creating a picture gallery that will provide visitors to the Web site with a quick means of seeing the wonderful beauty that is so common to the Gardens. Although your file might look somewhat different, a preview of the completed file appears in Figure 3-38.

Figure 3-38

Welcome to Old Eastbrook Gardens

26 East Glen Road
Old Eastbrook, VA 35699
Open All Year

Old Eastbrook Gardens, more than a century old, is a 500-acre oasis of landscaped gardens, virgin woodlands, ponds, streams, brooks, and lakes. Eastbrook House is a celebration of post-colonial America itself. Decorated with the finest antiques, Eastbrook House is itself an attraction worth visiting.

Join us at Old Eastbrook Gardens. We welcome visitors from all over the world of all ages all year. We have formal guided tours of the grounds and of Eastbrook House. We have school field trips year round. We have children's programs on the weekends, indoor and outdoor lectures, slide shows, and spring and summer concerts on the Great Lawn and by the Grainger Bandshell.

If you are looking for a class in gardening or horticulture in general, we have classes during the day, evening, and on weekends. We cater to all those people who, like us, have a love of and a devotion to art, literature, history, formal design, and nature. If you are one of those people, you certainly will enjoy coming to Old Eastbrook Gardens time after time.

Call our Visitors Center for hours and ticket prices at 1-818-765-4788. Ask about our new year-round Golden Visitors Pass, which offers reduced admission and discounts at all of our gift shops and restaurants. Take something home with you when you visit us. We have a gift shop, a souvenir shop, and a bookstore. You will want to remember your trip to Old Eastbrook Gardens, so take a part of us home with you so that you can treasure your visits here to our beautifully landscaped gardens and walkways. Other attractions on our grounds include the Garden Shoppe, where you can buy both flowers and plants, and the Mill Inn, where you can enjoy delicious coffee and tea right by the lake. The Mill Inn has an atrium, so you can enjoy a breakfast or lunch anytime of the day or any day of the year.

Picture Being Here as you stroll through our wooded paths and walkways. Walk among the pines and other evergreens. This is the place to go when you want to relax and get away from it all. The Eastbrook Gardens has prided itself on being a center where people can get in touch with nature and experience all the benefits that it has to offer. We at the Eastbrook Gardens feel that the best way to appreciate nature is to live it.

Current Hours
Visitors Center 9–5
Garden Shoppe 9–4
Eastbrook House 9–6
Mill Inn Coffee House 10–4
Book Shop 10–4

Your First and Last Name
Tutorial 3, Case Problem 2

Complete the following:

1. If necessary, start Expression Web, close any open sites, and then open the Tutorial.03 Web site. Reset the workspace layout. If necessary, display the Pictures toolbar.
2. In the Folder List panel, expand the Data Files and Case2 folders to display the Case2 folder contents.
3. Open the **east.html** file and then save the file as **eastnew.html** in the same folder.
4. In Design view, open the Page Properties dialog box, and then in the Title box, type **The Old Eastbrook Gardens**.
5. In the Page description box, type your first and last name, type a slash, type **Tutorial 3, Case Problem 2**, and then close the dialog box.
6. If necessary, display the Common toolbar. If necessary, drag the title bar of the Pictures toolbar so that the Pictures toolbar appears below the Common toolbar.
7. Press the Ctrl+Home keys to position the insertion point at the top of the page.

8. Drag the eastlogo.gif filename from the Folder List panel to the blank line at the top of the page. For the alternate text, type **The Old Eastbrook Gardens logo**, and then insert the image.
9. Click anywhere on the eastlogo image and then center the image.
10. Drag the walkway.jpg filename from the Folder List panel to the start of the third paragraph, which begins "If you are looking for. . ." For the alternate text, type **photo of walkway with trees and bushes**, and then insert the image.
11. In Design view, click anywhere inside the image. Increase the margin on the right border by approximately 40 pixels.
12. Press the Ctrl+End keys to position the insertion point at the bottom of the page. Drag the hours.gif filename to the blank line below the last paragraph of the document. For the alternate text, type **hours we are open**, and then insert the image.
13. Change the picture properties for the hours.gif file so that the image has a Wrapping style of Left.
14. Click and drag the pine.jpg filename from the Folder List panel to the right of the hours.gif image. For the alternate text, type **photo of pine trees**, and then insert the image.
15. Click anywhere on the pine.jpg image. Use the Pictures toolbar to make the pine.jpg file into an auto thumbnail image. If necessary, click and drag the thumbnail image so that it is in line with the hours.jpg image.
16. Press the Ctrl+End keys to position the insertion point at the end of the document. Type your first and last name, press the Shift+Enter keys, and then type **Tutorial 3, Case Problem 2**.
17. Save the **eastnew.html** file. Save the **pine_small.jpg** image in the Save Embedded Files dialog box.
18. Open the **eastnew.html** file in your browser. The document should look similar to the one shown in Figure 3-38.
19. In your browser, click the thumbnail link. View the result. Return to the eastnew.html page in your browser.
20. Close the browser. In Expression Web, close all open documents. If you will not be completing the next assignment, close the Web site and exit Expression Web.
21. Submit the completed files to your instructor, either in printed or electronic form, as requested.

Use what you've learned, and expand your skills, to create and style a Web page for a movie theater.

CHALLENGE

Case Problem 3

Data Files needed for this Case Problem: cola.jpg, movie.html, movielogo.gif, popcorn.jpg

The Eight Star Theatre and Entertainment Center Located in Lower Manhattan in New York City, the new Eight Star Theatre and Entertainment Center is designed for families and adults to have a day or an evening of fun. The Center boasts 16 movie screens, a miniature golf course, virtual reality arcades, three restaurants, a discotheque, and a food court. Evan Klein, the owner of the Center, has asked you to design a new Web page for the Center. Although your file might look somewhat different, a preview of the completed file appears in Figure 3-39.

Figure 3-39

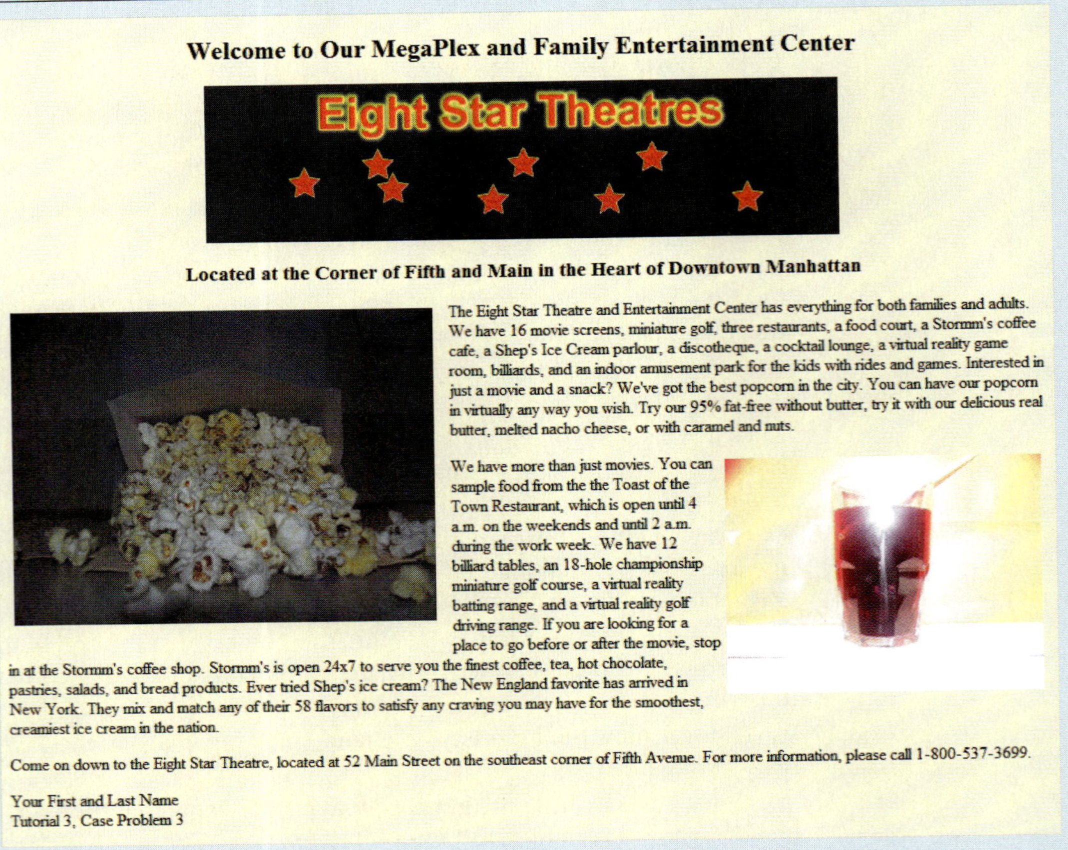

Complete the following:

1. If necessary, start Expression Web, close any open sites, and open the Tutorial.03 Web site. Reset the workspace layout. If necessary, display the Pictures toolbar.
2. In the Folder List panel, expand the Data Files and Case3 folders to display the Case3 folder contents.
3. Open the **movie.html** file and save the file as **movienew.html** in the same folder.
4. In Design view, right-click anywhere on the page. Open the Page Properties dialog box, and then in the Title box, type **Eight Star Movie Theatre and Entertainment Center**.
5. In the Page description box, type your first and last name, type a slash, type **Tutorial 3, Case Problem 3**, and then close the dialog box.
6. Click and drag the movielogo.gif filename from the Folder List panel to the empty paragraph below the h2 heading at the top of the page. For the alternate text, type **Movie Theatre and Entertainment Center logo**. Click the OK button to insert the image. Click the image and center it.
7. Click and drag the popcorn.jpg filename from the Folder List panel to just before the T in the first sentence of the first paragraph. For the alternate text, type **photo of box of popcorn**. Click the OK button to insert the image.
8. Open the Picture Properties dialog box for the popcorn.jpg image, and then set the Wrapping style to Left. Make sure that the Specify size and Keep aspect ratio check boxes are checked. Set the Width to 400 pixels (and the Height to 300 pixels), and then close the dialog box.
9. Click the right edge of the popcorn.jpg image, and then add about 15 pixels of margin space on the right side of the image.

EXPLORE 10. Click the bottom edge of the popcorn.jpg image, and then add about 30 pixels of margin space at the bottom of the image.

11. Click and drag the cola.jpg filename from the Folder List panel in front of the letter W in the paragraph that begins "We have more than just movies." For the alternate text, type **photo of glass of cola**, and then insert the image.

12. Open the Picture Properties dialog box for the cola.jpg image, and then do the following:
    - Set the Wrapping style to Right.
    - Set the Horizontal margin to 6 pixels.
    - Set the Vertical margin to 6 pixels.
    - Size the image to have a Width of 300 pixels and a Height of 225 pixels, and then close the dialog box.

EXPLORE 13. Right-click a blank area in the editing window, and open the Page Properties dialog box. On the Formatting tab, select *More Colors* for the Background, and then use the Select button eyedropper to sample any of the yellow area in the cola.gif image. Close the More Colors dialog box, and then close the Page Properties dialog box.

14. Press the Ctrl+End keys to position the insertion point at the end of the document. Type your first and last name, press the Shift+Enter keys, and then type **Tutorial 3, Case Problem 3**.

15. Save the **movienew.html** file.

16. Open the **movienew.html** file in your browser. The document should look similar to the one shown in Figure 3-39.

17. Close the browser. In Expression Web, close all open documents. If you will not be completing the next assignment, close the Web site and exit Expression Web.

18. Submit the completed files to your instructor, either in printed or electronic form, as requested.

Using the files provided, create and style a Web page for a travel agency.

CREATE

Case Problem 4

Data Files needed for this Case Problem: judd.gif, judd.html, london.gif, madrid.gif, paris.gif, rome.gif

Judd Travel Judd Travel, located just outside of Los Angeles, California, is a travel agency that specializes in sending celebrity couples on their honeymoons to exotic places around the world. Judd works with several of Hollywood's top talent agencies to ensure that the trip is discreet and the accommodations are luxurious. Malcolm Judd, the owner of the travel agency, has requested your assistance in creating a Web site for Judd Travel.

Complete the following:

1. If necessary, start Expression Web, close any open sites, and open the Tutorial.03 Web site. Reset the workspace layout. If necessary, display the Pictures toolbar.
2. In the Folder List panel, expand the Data Files and Case4 folders to display the Case4 folder contents.
3. Open the **judd.html** file in the Case4 folder and save the file as **juddnew.html** in the same folder.
4. In Design view, open the Page Properties dialog box, and then in the Title box, type **Judd Travel Agency**.
5. In the Page description box, type your first and last name, type a slash, type **Tutorial 3, Case Problem 4**, and then close the dialog box.
6. Insert the judd.gif image at the top of the page.

7. Using the judd.html file and the images provided for this Case Problem, insert at least three images into the judd.html file. Do the following:
   - Scale each of the images to an appropriate size.
   - Enter alternate text for each image.
   - Set the Wrapping style for each image so that the images alternate, with the first image wrapping left, the second image wrapping right, and so forth.
   - Make sure that each image has the appropriate horizontal and vertical margin space.
8. Press the Ctrl+End keys to position the insertion point at the end of the document, and then press Enter. Type your first and last name, press the Shift+Enter keys, and then type **Tutorial 3, Case Problem 4**.
9. Save the **juddnew.html** file.
10. Open the **juddnew.html** file in your browser. Correct the file as necessary.
11. Close the browser. In Expression Web, close all open documents. Close the Web site and exit Expression Web.
12. Submit the completed files to your instructor, either in printed or electronic form, as requested.

ENDING DATA FILES

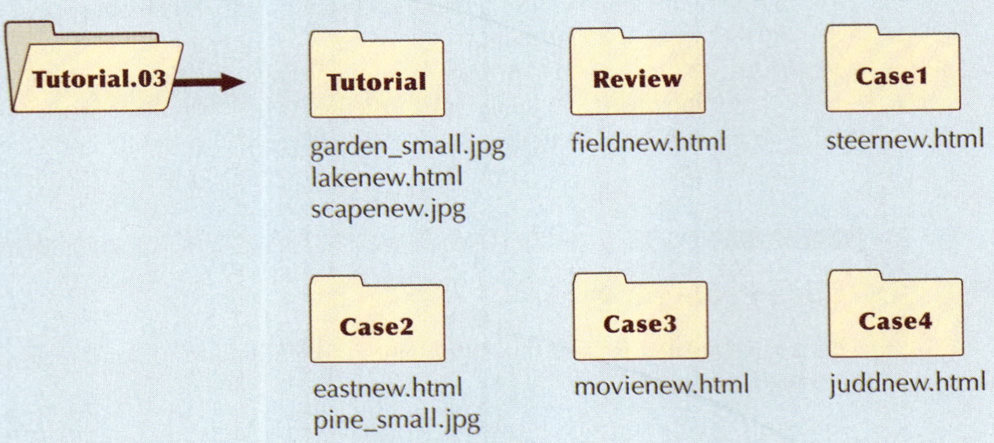

TUTORIAL 4

Working with Hyperlinks

Creating Bookmarks and Links

EXPRESSION WEB

OBJECTIVES

Session 4.1

- Place bookmarks on a Web page
- Create a link to a bookmark
- Create a link to another Web page
- Create a link to an external Web site
- Create an email link

Session 4.2

- Create a link to an image
- Construct an image map
- Create and modify hotspots
- Change link colors
- Edit a hyperlink

Case | *Purr Your Request*

Purr Your Request is a nonprofit organization located in Billings, Pennsylvania. Founded in 1985, the organization has become one of the largest pet adoption organizations in the state. Over the years, Purr Your Request has found homes for thousands of animals, mainly cats. Purr Your Request is part of the growing trend toward "no-kill" shelters, where pets are not euthanized unless it is a medical necessity. The organization screens all people who want to adopt a pet, with an aim toward finding lifelong, animal-loving friends who will take care of pets responsibly. Every three months, Purr Your Request has a weekend Adopt-a-Thon, which has proven to be very popular. By staging these events every few months, the organization ensures that it gets good coverage in the local print and electronic news media. To further ensure that the Adopt-a-Thon events are well attended, numerous celebrities have been invited and have participated in the Adopt-a-Thon events. You'll be working with Trevor McKnight, the organization's public relations director. Trevor has created a basic Web page, but he wants to use Expression Web to both create links and keep track of them on the organization's Web site. In this tutorial, you'll help Trevor create and organize links on his Web page.

STARTING DATA FILES

Tutorial.04 →

Tutorial	Review	Case1	Case2	Case3	Case4
adopt.png	cat.jpg	apple.html	info.gif	map.gif	antique.html
breeds.html	events.html	applelogo.gif	gantt.html	mapinfo.html	antiquelogo.gif
info.html	purrlogo.png	apples.jpg	pert.html	training.html	chair.html
kitten.html		granny.html	spiral.html		chair.jpg
main.html		red.html	techlogo.gif		dresser.html
pets.html		red.jpg			dresser.jpg
petcare.html					
puppy.html					
purrlogo.png					
uparrow.gif					

SESSION 4.1 VISUAL OVERVIEW

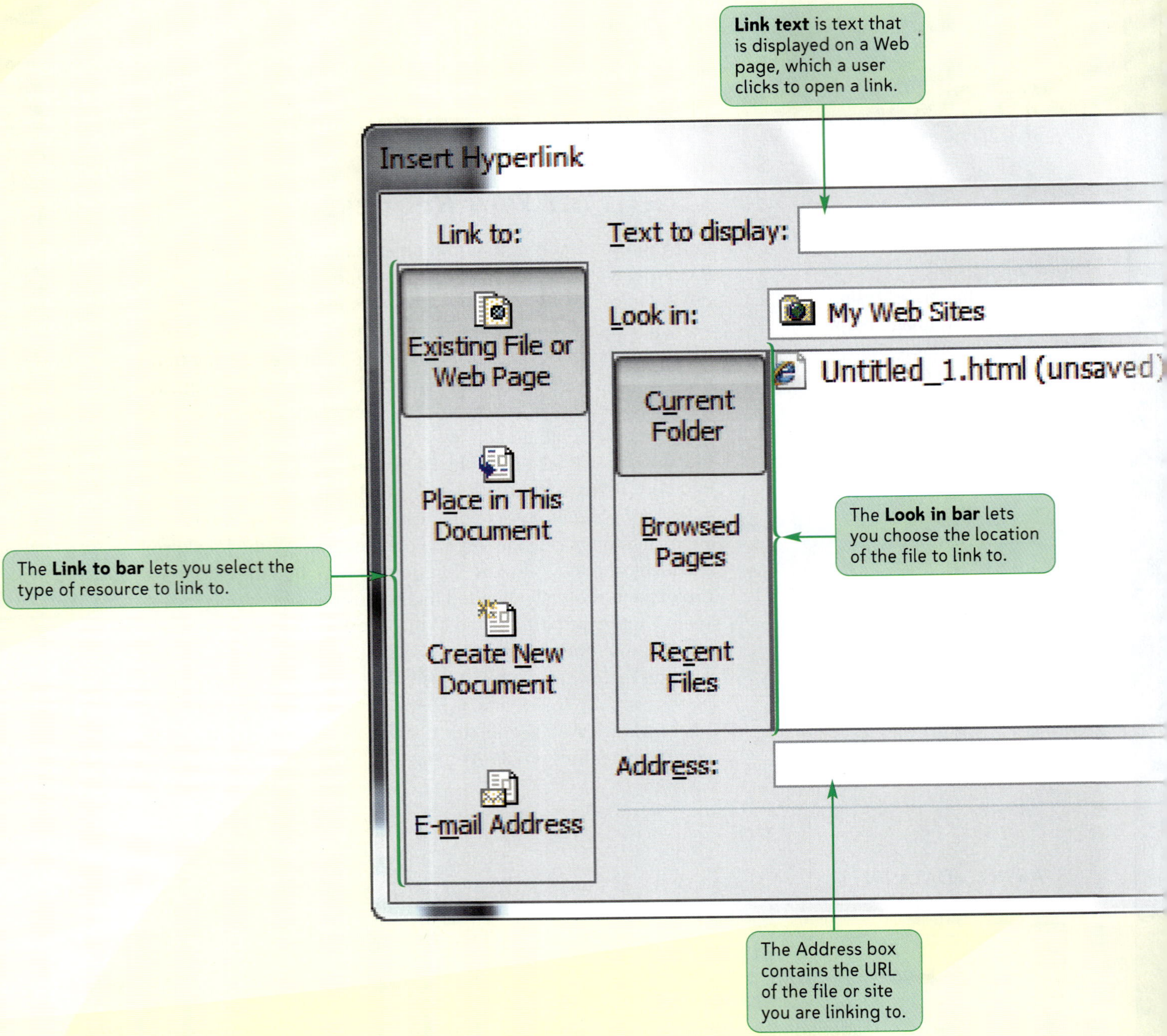

THE INSERT HYPERLINK DIALOG BOX

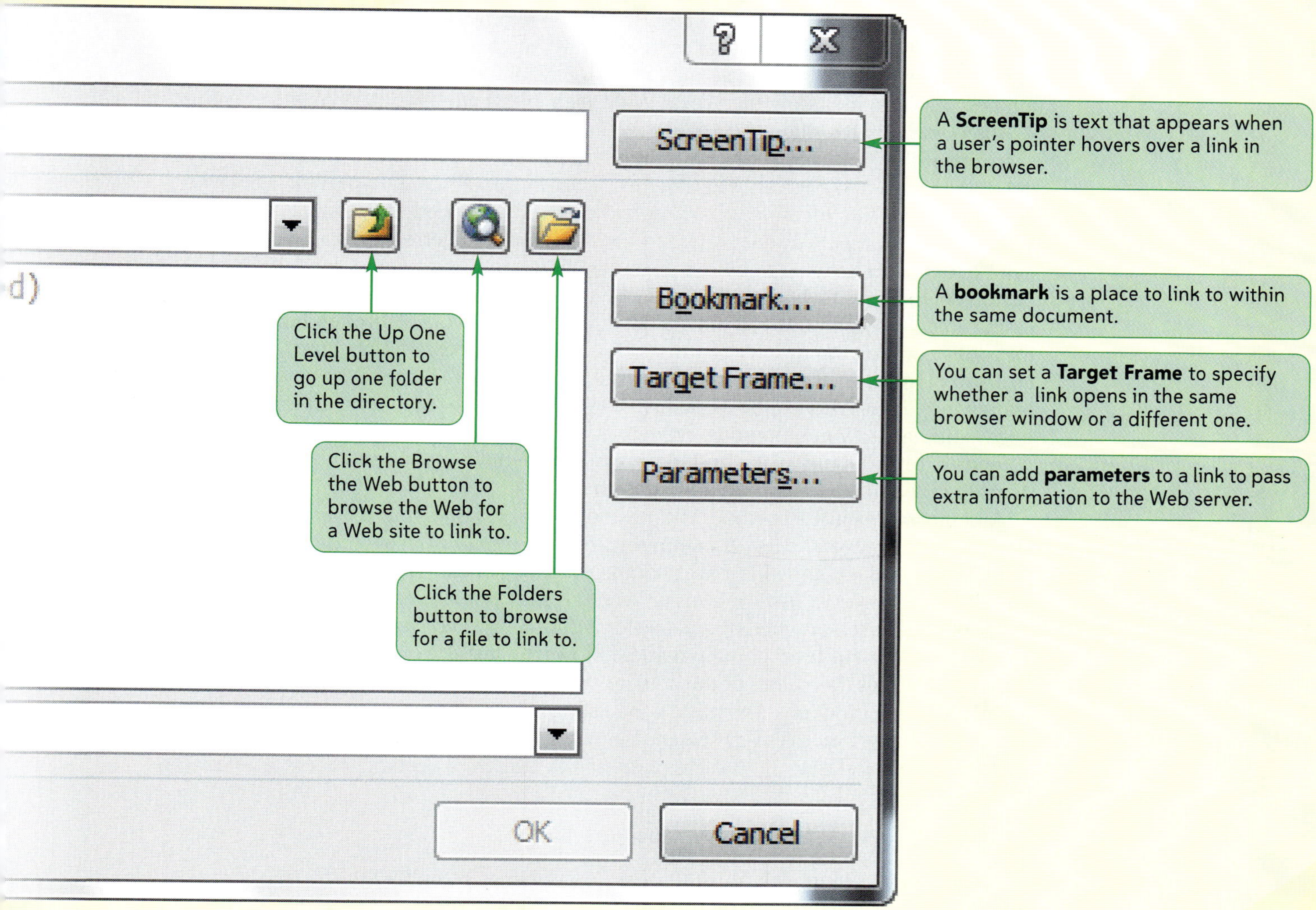

Working with Hyperlinks

The **Internet** is a global network of computers linked by high-speed data lines and wireless systems. The Internet was established in 1969 as a collaborative project between the Department of Defense and several large colleges on the West Coast. National security concerns during the Cold War era sparked interest in developing better communications systems. At that time, the concept of a local area network was a new one, and the idea of linking individual networks to create a "network of networks" was uncharted territory. During the '70s and '80s, the primary users of the Internet were educational and research institutions. They used the Internet to freely share and exchange research information, but they did so by sending and receiving email. Today, billions of people use this and other Internet services, including the **World Wide Web** (also called the **WWW** or the **Web**).

The popularity that the World Wide Web enjoys today comes largely from offering users the ability to locate and view online information in a **nonlinear** manner, without needing to read one page after another in a specific sequence. A **hyperlink** is HTML code that refers to a location within the same document, another Web page at the same Web site, or another Web site. A hyperlink is commonly referred to as a **link**. A link can be text or an image. On a Web page, text links are usually underlined. Visitors can click links in a nonlinear manner to choose topics that most interest them in any order. Unfortunately, sometimes you click a link and it doesn't work. A **broken link** is a link that does not function as intended or at all. Broken links have many causes, including errors in HTML code, relocation of the page that the link references, or deletion of the referenced file or Web site by its owner. A **Web server** is a computer that is used to send pages and data to your computer. Servers can also be used to receive data from your computer; for example, when you make a purchase online, you're sending data about items to buy and payment method to a Web server.

A **Uniform Resource Locator (URL)** is the complete address of a Web page. A URL is composed of several parts. A **communications protocol** is an agreed-to standard for sending voice, data, and video over communications lines. **Hypertext Transfer Protocol (HTTP)** is the protocol used to transfer Web pages. A **domain name** is the registered name of the file server where the pages for a particular Web site are stored. A **suffix**, also known as a **top-level domain name**, follows the last dot of a domain name, and it broadly identifies the nature of the activity at the Web site. Common suffixes include .com, .net, .edu, and .org. The **path** is the listing of one or more nested folders that contain the Web page on the Web server. When entering a URL in a browser's Address bar, you type forward slashes (/), not backslashes. A URL for a Web page has the following components:

protocol://service.domainname.suffix/path/filename

For example, Figure 4-1 illustrates the components in the URL *http://www.expressionusers.org/tutorials/default.html*.

Figure 4-1 **Components of a URL**

Component	What It Is
http	Protocol
www	Service
expressionusers	Domain name
org	Suffix
tutorials	Folder in the path
default.html	The Web page you are viewing

INSIGHT

Cybersquatting

A domain name can be registered for a few dollars a year. **Cybersquatting** is the registering, trafficking in, or use of a domain name with the sole intent to profit from a trademark belonging to someone else. The goal of a cybersquatter, therefore, is not to use the domain name for personal use, but rather to buy a domain name as an investment, and to later sell it at a profit. Cybersquatting was very popular in the last century, when the Web was still in the process of being discovered by much of the world. The English language adopts new phrases and words every day as science and popular culture affect our daily lives. These new words serve as an enticement for cybersquatters. Cybersquatters intend to profit from these new terms by registering domain names using these terms at little cost and then later selling these domain names to interested parties at a much higher cost. Cybersquatters sometimes also register variations of popular trademarked names, a technique which is known as **typosquatting**. The next time you enter a URL for a Web site and find yourself viewing an unfamiliar page, check for typos in the URL—you might have mistyped the URL and ended up at a typosquatter's site. Disputes among domain names are usually resolved by the Internet Corporation for Assigned Names and Numbers (ICANN). ICANN is responsible for managing the assignment of domain names and IP addresses.

Creating Links

Allowing readers to quickly find topics of interest is critical to the success of any Web site. Your goal as a Web designer is to get the reader to those places, pages, and sites of interest efficiently. Links can take your visitors to

- A specific place on the same Web page
- A different Web page at your Web site
- A different Web site

You can also use a link to connect to an email client, such as Microsoft Outlook, Google Gmail, or Yahoo! Mail. You can also link to a document other than a Web page. In addition to using text as a link, you can use an image.

You have created an Expression Web site for Trevor. You'll now show Trevor how to open the Tutorial.04 Web site and customize the workspace for working with multiple files.

To open the Tutorial.04 Web site and customize the workspace:

1. Start Expression Web and reset the workspace layout.
2. Click **Site** on the menu bar, and then click **Open Site**.

   The Open Site dialog box opens.
3. Click the **Browse** button, navigate to the Tutorial.04 folder included with your Data Files, click **Tutorial.04** to select it, and then click the **Open** button twice.

   The Tutorial.04 Web site opens. The Folder List panel shows the root folder and the Data Files folder. Your root folder name might be different.
4. Click the **+ sign** to the left of the Data Files folder, and then click the **+ sign** to the left of the Tutorial folder to display the contents of that folder.
5. In the Folder List panel, double-click **pets.html**.

   The pets.html file opens, as shown in Figure 4-2.

Figure 4-2 The pets.html page

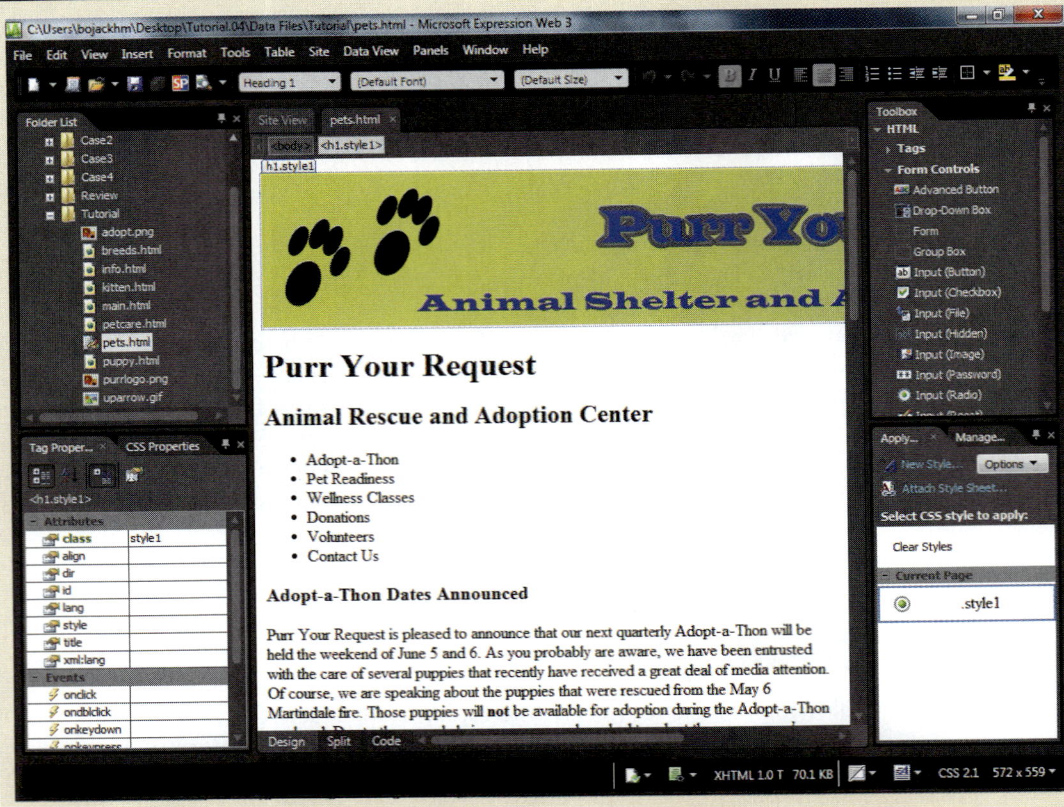

6. If necessary, click the **Design** button at the bottom of the editing window to display Design view.
7. If necessary, close any open toolbars other than the Common toolbar.
8. Click **Panels** on the menu bar and then click **AutoHide All Panels**.

   The workspace should appear similar to that shown in Figure 4-3.

Figure 4-3 Hidden panels and Toolbox

PROSKILLS

Decision Making: Building Team Consensus

Whether you are the moderator of a meeting or a participant at a meeting, it's important that everyone who wants to be heard be given a chance to speak. It is quite possible to become passionate about an issue or a proposal, especially one where you feel you are correct in your beliefs. However, you could be making the wrong decision if yours is the only voice that is heard. Listen to what others have to say, even those who disagree with you. Be open-minded and fair. Don't rush to judgment. Think about what everyone has said. A good technique is to write down what others have proposed on an easel board or as part of a PowerPoint slide. By having everyone's ideas "on the board" and visible for review, ideas won't get lost in the heat of discussion. This process can also help the group build on ideas that are shared. Above all, never feel that a decision has to be unanimous. As long as the idea has been thoroughly discussed and all sides have been heard, the team should make the best decision based upon the merits of the proposal.

You'll now have Trevor save the pets.html file under a new filename in the same file folder.

To save and rename the pets.html file:

1. Click **File** on the menu bar, and then click **Save As**.

   The Save As dialog box opens.
2. In the File name box, type **petsnew**.
3. Click the **Save** button.

   The file is saved as petsnew.html.

Creating Bookmarks

Most visitors to a Web page want to find what they're looking for right away. Forcing your visitors to scroll several screens down a page to find information is one sure way to lose their interest. Bookmarks help your Web page visitors locate a topic or a specific place on a Web page. A bookmark is a place within a document that can be used as a target for a link. Do not confuse Expression Web's bookmarks with the bookmarks or Favorites that you can create in your browser. Bookmarks in Internet Explorer, for example, are often just URLs that you frequently visit when you browse the Web.

Once you create a bookmark, you can create a link to the bookmark to help your visitors find what they are looking for easily and efficiently.

TIP

In HTML code, a bookmark is referred to as an anchor.

REFERENCE

Creating a Bookmark

- Select the text or element to be used as the bookmark.
- Click Insert on the menu bar, and then click Bookmark (or press the Ctrl+G keys).
- In the Bookmark dialog box, enter a name for the bookmark in the Bookmark name box.
- Click the OK button.

When you read a newspaper, it's common for you to fold the newspaper to make it easier to read the page and hold the newspaper. Similarly, in a Web browser, **the fold** is the bottom of the first screen of a Web page. The fold serves to divide the top screen of your page with the content below it. If your home page is several screens long, you should create bookmarks past the fold so that readers do not have to scroll to locate what they want. You should create bookmarks even for items that appear before the fold because it is possible that your bookmarks will be moved. What currently appears without difficulty at the top of the page might end up being moved to the middle or the bottom of the page.

TIP

To delete a bookmark, right-click the bookmark, click Bookmark Properties, and then click the Clear button.

If a Web page is several screens long, it is also helpful to include a link back to the top of the page so users don't have to scroll back up. You'll start adding bookmarks to Trevor's Web page with the first h3 heading, Adopt-a-Thon Dates Announced. A bookmark name should not contain spaces, so Expression Web converts spaces in the selected text with underscores when it creates a bookmark name.

To create the first bookmark:

1. Select the h3 heading text **Adopt-a-Thon Dates Announced**.
2. With those words still selected, click **Insert** on the menu bar, and then click **Bookmark**.

   The Bookmark dialog box opens. The words *Adopt-a-Thon_Dates_Announced* appear in the Bookmark name box, as shown in Figure 4-4. Expression Web has replaced the spaces between words in the bookmark name with underscores.

Figure 4-4 The Bookmark dialog box

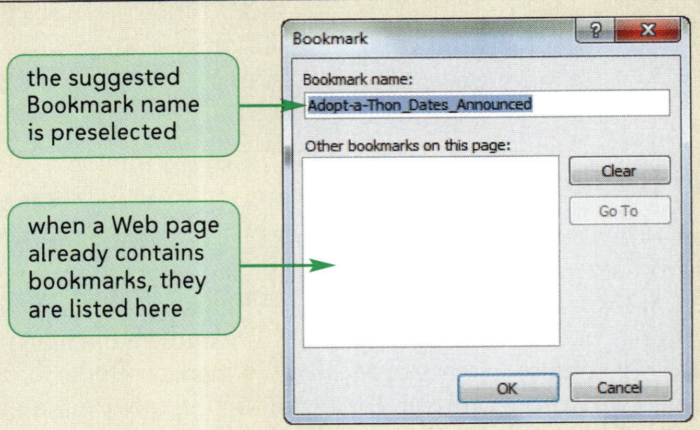

3. Click the **OK** button.

   The bookmark is created.
4. Click anywhere outside the bookmark.

   The bookmark appears, as shown in Figure 4-5.

Figure 4-5 First bookmark created

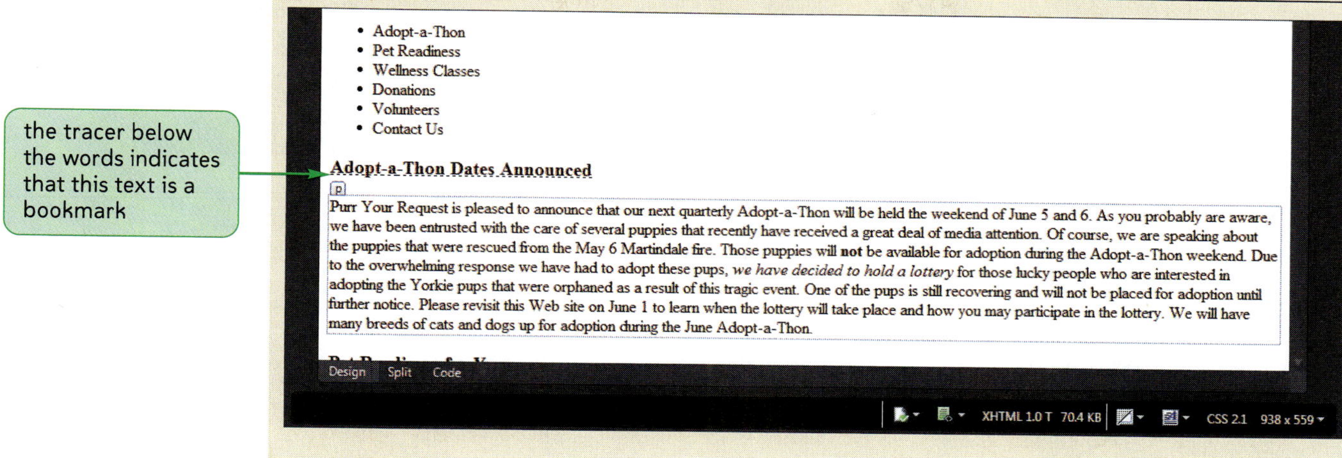

TIP

Alternatively, to create a bookmark, select the text and then press the Ctrl+G keys. Click the OK button to accept the bookmark name.

In Design view, a dashed underline known as a **tracer** appears below the words *Adopt-a-Thon Dates Announced,* indicating the location of a bookmark. Instead of using the menu bar to create the bookmark, you'll show Trevor how to use the Ctrl+G keyboard shortcut.

To create the other bookmarks:

1. Scroll down if necessary and then select the heading **Pet Readiness for You**.
2. Press the **Ctrl+G** keys.

   The Bookmark dialog box opens, displaying the bookmark you created earlier in the Other bookmarks on this page box.
3. Click the **OK** button to accept the default bookmark name.

   The bookmark is created.
4. Scroll down if necessary and one by one, repeat Steps 1 through 3 for each of the four remaining h3 headings: **Wellness Classes**, **New Options for Donations**, **Volunteers are Always Needed**, and **Contact Us**.
5. When you are done, click anywhere outside the Contact Us bookmark.

   Tracers appear beneath all six h3 headings on the Web page. The last three bookmarks should appear as shown in Figure 4-6.

Figure 4-6 **Bookmark formatting completed**

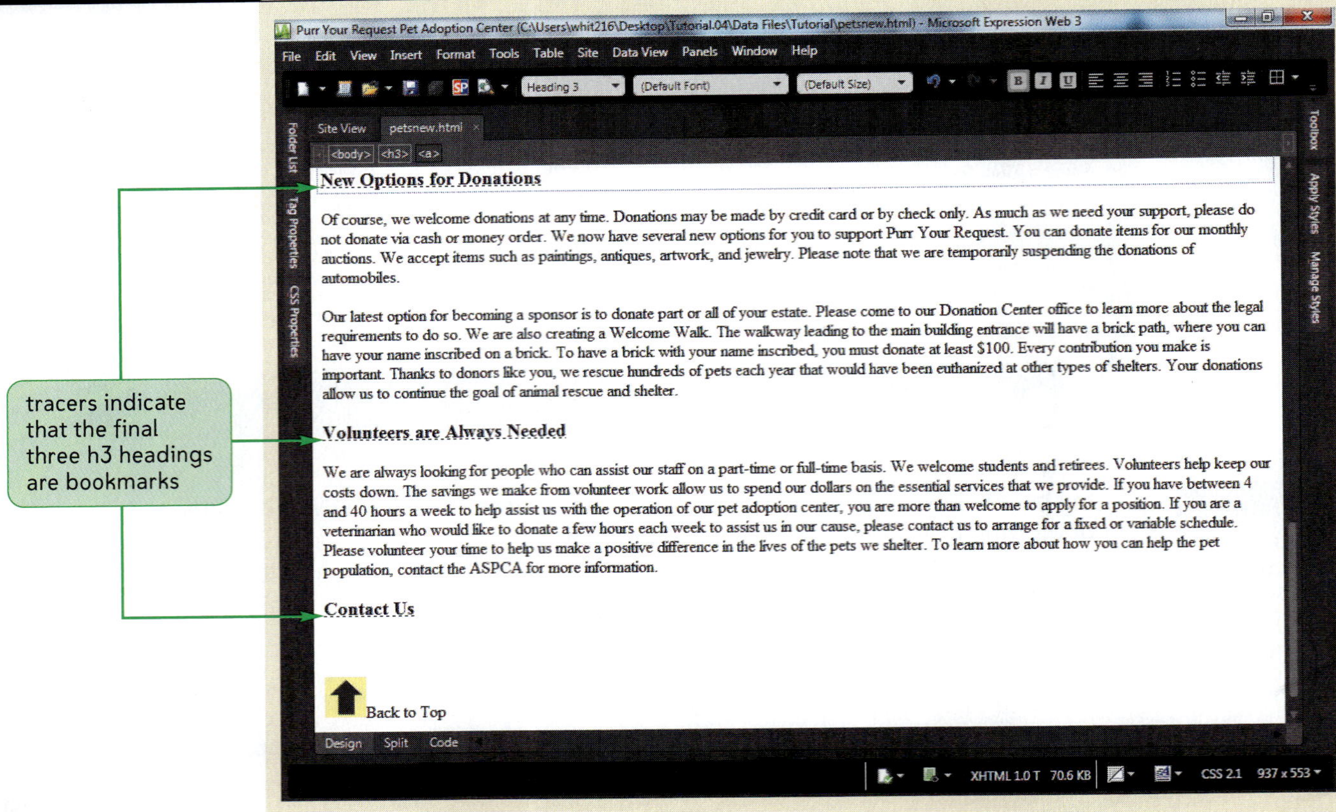

Now that you have created the bookmarks, you can create links to enable users to quickly navigate Trevor's page.

Linking to a Bookmark

You can create a link to a bookmark using text or an image. When a user clicks the link, the Web browser displays the portion of the page where the bookmark is located. This makes it easy for users to move from topic to topic on the Web page without a lot of scrolling.

REFERENCE

Linking to a Bookmark

- Select the text or image to be used as the link.
- Click Insert on the menu bar, and then click Hyperlink (or press the Ctrl+K keys).
- In the Insert Hyperlink dialog box, click Place in This Document in the Link to bar.
- In the Select a place in this document panel, click the name of the bookmark to which you want to link.
- To provide a ScreenTip for the link, click the ScreenTip button, enter the ScreenTip text in the Set Hyperlink ScreenTip dialog box, and then click the OK button.

You'll show Trevor how to use the first item in the bulleted list on his Web page to create a link to the Adopt-a-Thon bookmark.

To create the link to the Adopt-a-Thon bookmark:

1. Press the **Ctrl+Home** keys to position the insertion point at the top of the page.
2. In the bulleted list, select the words **Adopt-a-Thon**.
3. Click **Insert** on the menu bar, and then click **Hyperlink**.

   The Insert Hyperlink dialog box opens.
4. If necessary, in the Link to bar, click the **Place in This Document** button.
5. Below the words *Select a place in this document*, click **Adopt-a-Thon_Dates_Announced**, as shown in Figure 4-7.

Figure 4-7 The first bookmark is selected

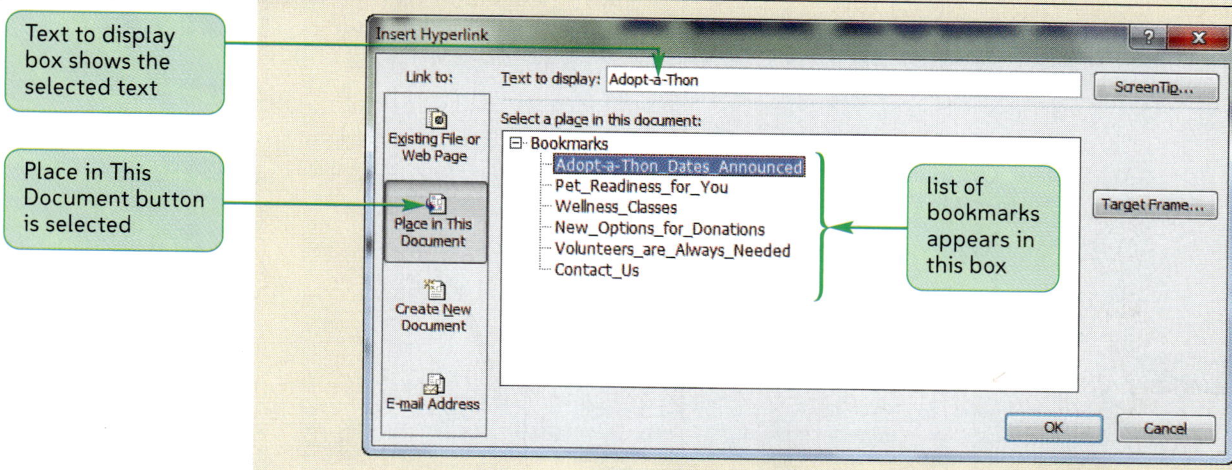

6. Click the **OK** button.
7. Click anywhere outside the link.

   In the bulleted list, "Adopt-a-Thon" now appears blue and underlined, indicating that these words are a link, as shown in Figure 4-8.

Figure 4-8 The first bookmark link

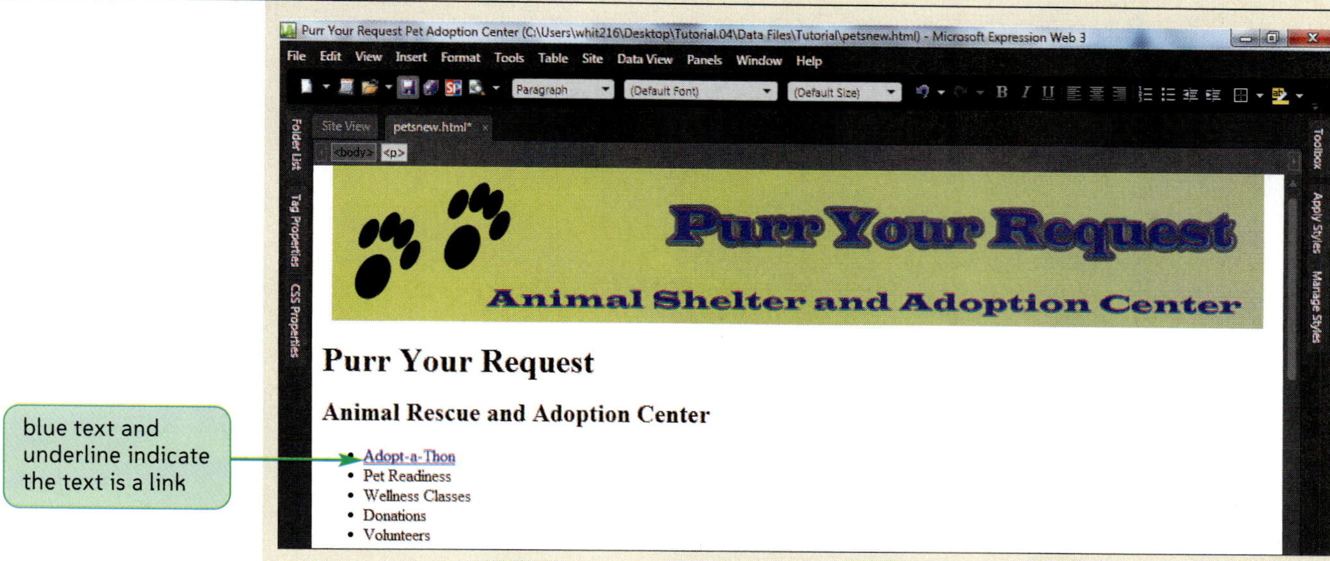

Text that links to a bookmark does not have to match the bookmark text, but it should be meaningful. Avoid expressions such as "click here" as link text. The best link text describes the section of the page that readers see when they click the link text. You'll use a keyboard shortcut to create the rest of the links.

To create links to the other bookmarks:

1. In the bulleted list, select the words **Pet Readiness**.
2. Press the **Ctrl+K** keys.

   The Insert Hyperlink dialog box opens.
3. In the Bookmarks list, click **Pet_Readiness_for_You**.
4. Click the **OK** button.

   In the bulleted list, the words *Pet Readiness* are now blue and underlined, indicating that the words are a link.
5. Repeat this procedure for the remaining four items in the bulleted list, linking **Wellness Classes** to the Wellness_Classes bookmark, **Donations** to New_Options_for_Donations, **Volunteers** to Volunteers_are_Always_Needed, and **Contact Us** to Contact_Us.
6. When you finish, click anywhere outside the bulleted list.

   The bulleted list items are all linked to bookmarks, as shown in Figure 4-9.

Figure 4-9 Link formatting completed

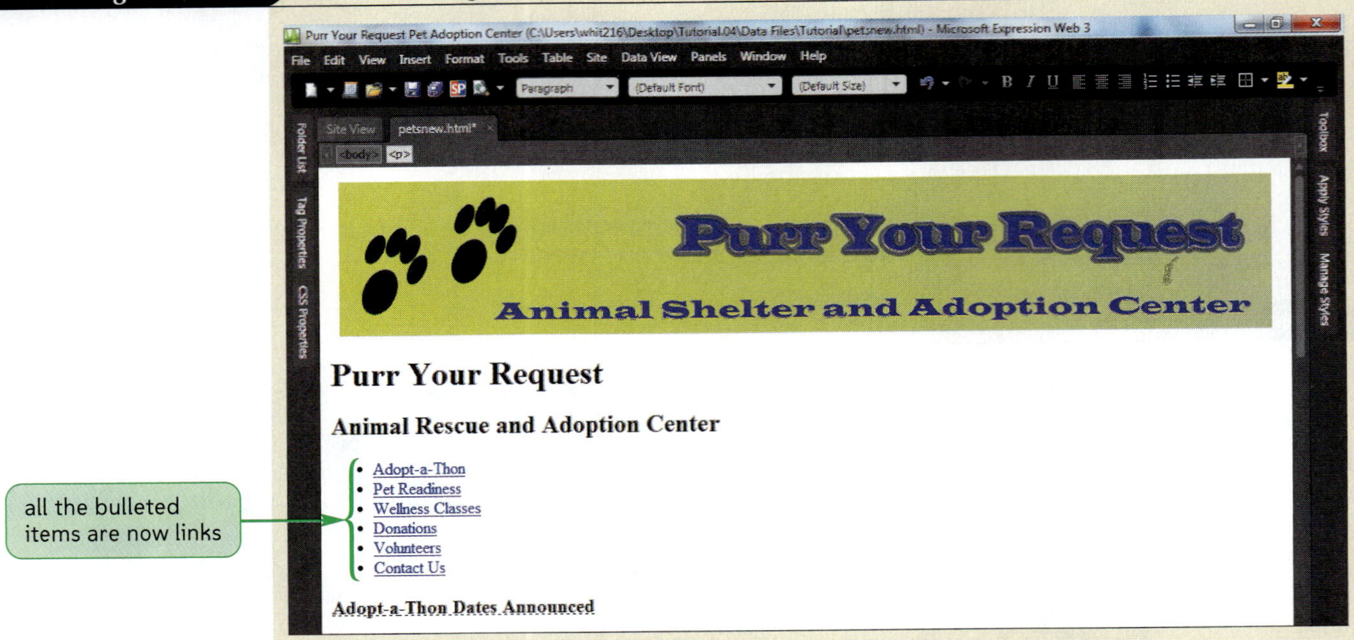

Trevor also wants to create a link using the words *Back to Top* at the bottom of the page that a user can click to return to the top of the page. You'll start by creating a bookmark at the top of the page and then linking the text to it.

To create the "Back to Top" link:

1. Press the **Ctrl+Home** keys to position the insertion point at the top of the page.
2. Press the **Ctrl+G** keys.

   The Bookmark dialog box opens.
3. In the Bookmark name box, type **top**, and then click the **OK** button.

   Next, you'll create the link to the Bookmark.
4. Press the **Ctrl+End** keys to position the insertion point at the bottom of the page.
5. Select the words **Back to Top**.
6. Press the **Ctrl+K** keys.

   The Insert Hyperlink dialog box opens.
7. If necessary, in the Link to bar, click the **Place in This Document** button.
8. In the Bookmarks list, click **top**.
9. Click the **OK** button.

   The words *Back to Top* are now blue and underlined, indicating that the words are a link.

TIP

Regardless of the order in which you create bookmarks, Expression Web lists the bookmarks in the Insert Hyperlinks dialog box in the order they appear on the page.

Now that you have created all the bookmarks and the links to the bookmarks, you'll test the links in the browser. If a bookmark is below the fold, the page view shifts to show the contents of where the bookmark is located, with the bookmark location at the top of the browser window.

To test the links in the browser:

1. Save the file.
2. Press the **F12** key to view the file in the default browser.
3. In the bulleted list, click the **Contact Us** link.

   The browser displays the bottom of the page.
4. Click the **Back to Top** link.

   The browser returns to the top of the page.
5. Click the remaining links to ensure that they work.
6. Close the browser.

Now that you have created links within the current page for Trevor, you'll next create links between Web pages in his Web site.

Creating Links to Other Pages

To link to another page, you use the Insert Hyperlink dialog box, just as you do to link to a bookmark. The page where the link is located is known as the **referring page**. The page that's opened by the link on the referring page is called the **target page**.

REFERENCE

Creating a Link to Another Page

- Select the link text.
- Click Insert on the menu bar, and then click Hyperlink (or press the Ctrl+K keys).
- Click Existing File or Web page in the Link to bar.
- Click Current Folder or Browsed Pages to locate the Web page.
- Select the target Web page.
- Click the OK button.

Next, you'll show Trevor how to create a link to another page by creating a link to the breeds.html page.

To create a link to another page:

1. Select the words **many breeds of cats and dogs** near the end of the last sentence of the paragraph below the Adopt-a-Thon Dates Announced heading.
2. Press the **Ctrl+K** keys.

   The Insert Hyperlink dialog box opens.
3. In the Link to bar, click the **Existing File or Web Page** button, and then if necessary, click the **Current Folder** button in the Look in bar, as shown in Figure 4-10.

Figure 4-10 **The Insert Hyperlink dialog box**

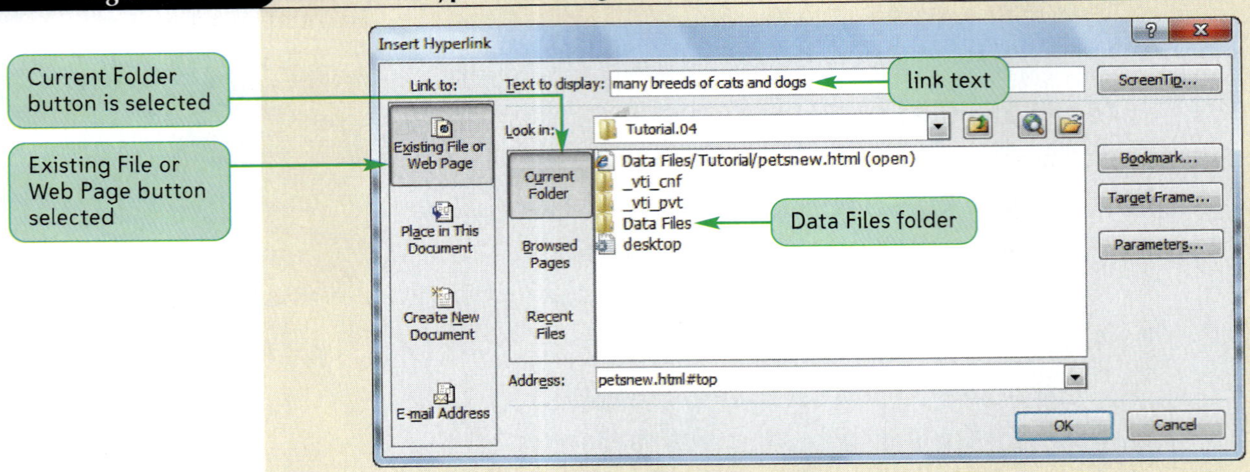

4. Double-click the **Data Files** folder.

   The dialog box displays the list of folders in the Tutorial.04 Web site.
5. Double-click the **Tutorial** folder.

   The dialog box displays the list of the files in the Tutorial folder.
6. Click the **breeds** page.

   Figure 4-11 shows the completed Insert Hyperlink dialog box.

Figure 4-11 The choice for breeds.html

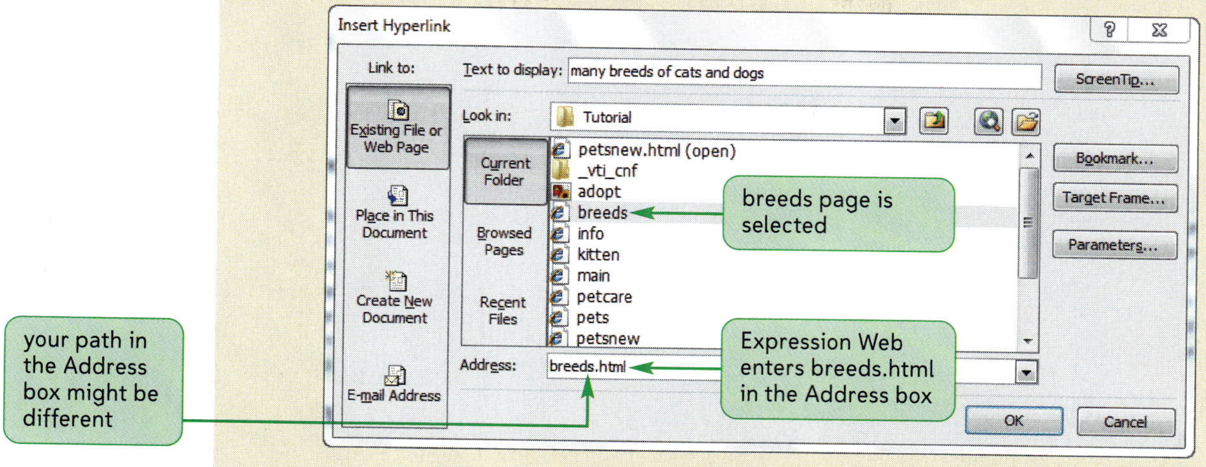

7. Click the **OK** button.

   The words *many breeds of cats and dogs* are now blue and underlined, and serve as a link to the breeds.html page.

Although some pages for the Web site already exist, such as the breeds.html page you just created a link to, as you first develop a Web site, it is common for other pages of the site not to exist yet. You can create links to such pages by creating **placeholder pages**, which are pages with little or no content. You merely create the pages, and then as you further develop the Web site, you can add content to the placeholder pages.

Expression Web has a great feature that allows you to create a placeholder page when you create a link to a page that has yet to be created. You'll show Trevor how to create a link to a placeholder page.

To create a link to a placeholder page:

1. Scroll down to the end of the last sentence of the Wellness Classes section and select the words **Pet Care Center**.
2. Press the **Ctrl+K** keys.

   The Insert Hyperlink dialog box opens.
3. In the Link to bar, click the **Create New Document** button.

   Expression Web prompts you to enter the name of the new document, as shown in Figure 4-12.

Figure 4-12 Choices for the Insert Hyperlink dialog box

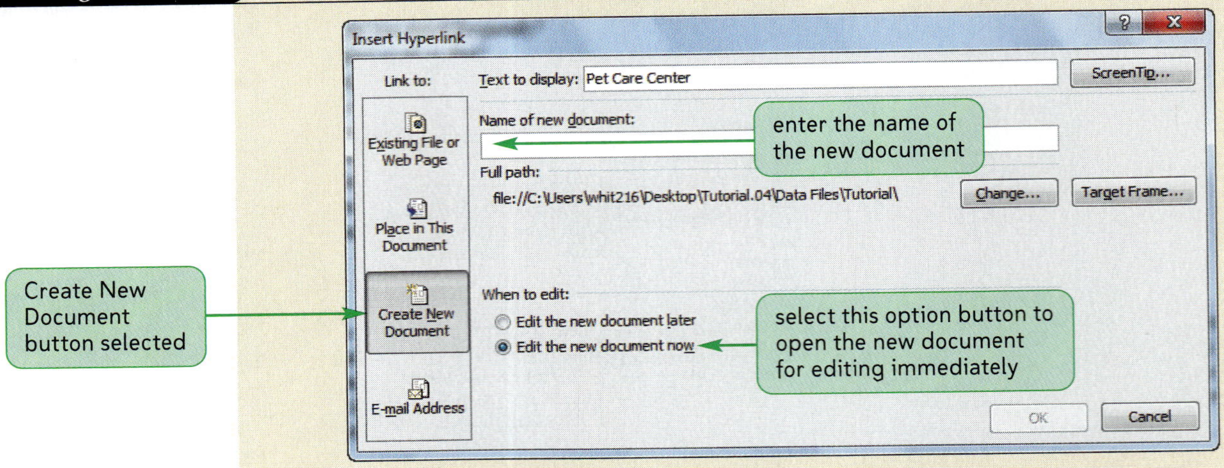

4. In the Name of new document box, type **centernew.html**.
5. If necessary, click the **Edit the new document now** radio button.
6. Click the **OK** button.

   Expression Web displays the new page. You're ready to enter some placeholder text in the new document.
7. In the centernew.html document, type **More information about our Pet Care Center will be added to this page at a later date**.
8. Right-click the **Document** tab for the centernew.html document and then click **Save**.
9. Right-click the **Document** tab for the centernew.html document, and then click **Close**.

   The document closes. Expression Web displays the petsnew.html document.

Next, you'll preview the petsnew file in your browser and test the two links to other pages.

To view the file in the browser and test the links:

1. Save the file.
2. Press the **F12** key. The document appears in the default browser.
3. Scroll down and click the **many breeds of cats and dogs** link.

   The breeds.html page opens in the browser, as shown in Figure 4-13.

Figure 4-13 The breeds page in the browser

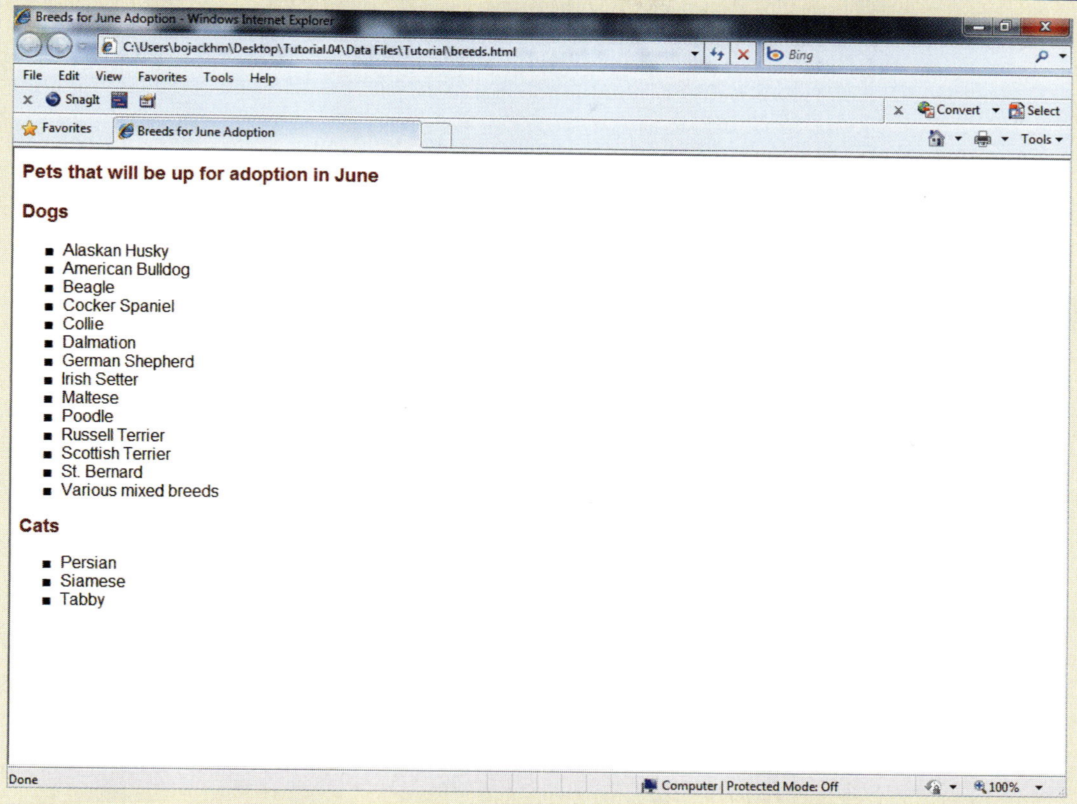

4. Click your browser's **Back** button.
5. Scroll down if necessary and click the **Pet Care Center** link.

   The centernew.html page opens in the browser, displaying the placeholder text you entered.
6. Close your browser.

It's impossible to provide your readers with all the information they need, so you also need to provide your visitors with links to related Web sites. Next, you'll create a link to an external Web site.

Creating External Links

In addition to creating bookmarks to help your visitors locate information on the current page or visit other pages at your own Web site, you also can create links to resources on other Web sites.

REFERENCE

Creating an External Link

- Select the text or image to be used as the link.
- Click Insert on the menu bar, and then click Hyperlink (or press the Ctrl+K keys).
- In the Insert Hyperlink dialog box, click Existing File or Web Page in the Link to bar.
- Click the Browse the Web button.
- Navigate to the Web site. Copy the URL in the Address bar. Close the browser.
- Paste the URL into the Address bar in the Insert Hyperlink dialog box.
- Click the OK button.

TIP

If you type the complete URL of a Web site in Design view, the URL will become link text.

Trevor wants to add a link to the Web site of the American Society for the Prevention of Cruelty to Animals (ASPCA), which has the URL *http://www.aspca.org*. You will show Trevor how to create a link to the ASPCA site.

To create a link to an external Web site:

1. Scroll down to view the last sentence of the paragraph below the Volunteers are Always Needed heading and then select the words **contact the ASPCA for more information**.
2. Press the **Ctrl+K** keys.

   The Insert Hyperlink dialog box opens.
3. In the Link to bar, click the **Existing File or Web Page** button.
4. If necessary, in the Address box, delete any existing text and then type **http://www.aspca.org**.

   The Insert Hyperlink dialog box should look similar to Figure 4-14.

Figure 4-14 Linking to an external Web site

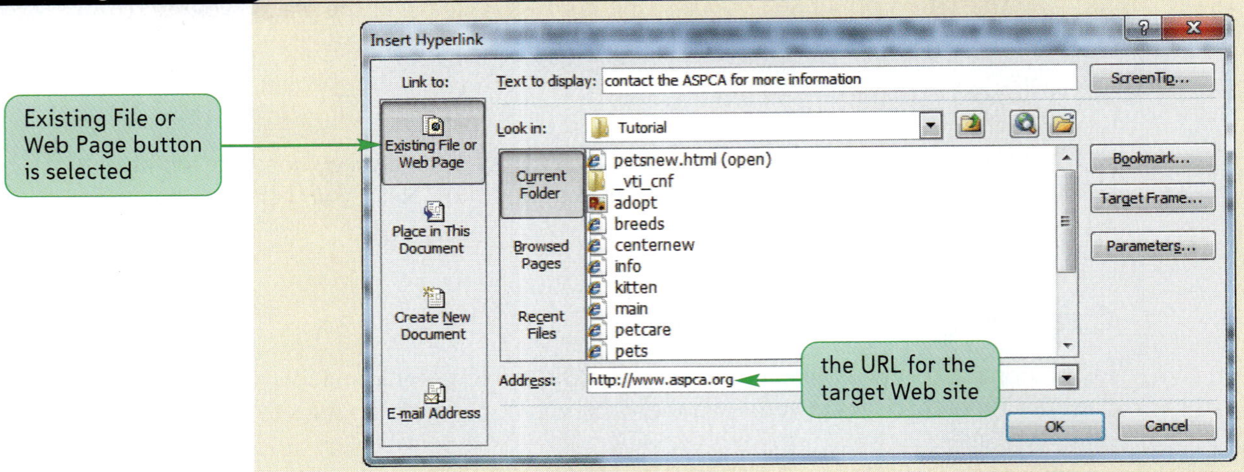

Trouble? If the AutoComplete function enters the protocol or attempts to complete the entry with different information, delete what AutoComplete enters and enter the correct URL.

5. Click the **OK** button.

   The words *contact the ASPCA for more information* are blue and underlined, indicating that they are a link.

If you don't know the URL of a Web page you want to link to, you can also use the Insert Hyperlink dialog box to temporarily leave Expression Web and find the page you want for the external link. Just click the Browse the Web button to open your default Web browser, and then locate the Web page. After you open the page in the browser, copy the URL from the browser's Location or Address bar. When you close the browser, you return to Expression Web, where you can paste or enter the URL in the Address box in the Insert Hyperlink dialog box.

Web pages commonly have an email link to the Webmaster at the bottom of the page. Trevor wants to see how an email link works, so you'll add one to his Web page and demonstrate its function for him.

Creating an Email Link

One common use of an email link is to provide a means for visitors to a Web site to contact the Webmaster. An email link to the Webmaster is often located in a Web page's footer. If you are creating an email link, it's wise not to use the email for an individual. Set up a dedicated address that will only receive responses to emails. Unfortunately, spammers scan Web pages for email addresses and then send unsolicited and unwanted mail to these email addresses.

REFERENCE

Creating an Email Link

- Select the link text on the Web page.
- Click Insert on the menu bar, and then click Hyperlink (or press the Ctrl+K keys).
- Click the E-mail Address button in the Link to bar.
- Enter the email address.
- Optionally, enter a subject.
- Click the OK button.

To send an email, you use the mailto protocol, rather than the http protocol used to open a Web page. As you type the email address, Expression Web automatically adds the mailto protocol to the beginning. You'll add an email link to the text in the Contact Us section of Trevor's Web page. Expression Web automatically adds the mailto: protocol when you type the email address.

To create an email link:

1. Click in the blank paragraph below the Contact Us heading, and then type **Please send your comments to the Webmaster**.
2. Select the line of text you just typed, and then press the **Ctrl+K** keys.

   The Insert Hyperlink dialog box opens.
3. In the Link to bar, click the **E-mail Address** button.
4. In the E-mail address box, type **purryourrequest@expression.org**.

   The mailto: protocol is added to the address automatically.
5. Click in the Subject box and type **feedback**.

   The dialog box should be similar to Figure 4-15.

Figure 4-15 **E-mail Address button is selected**

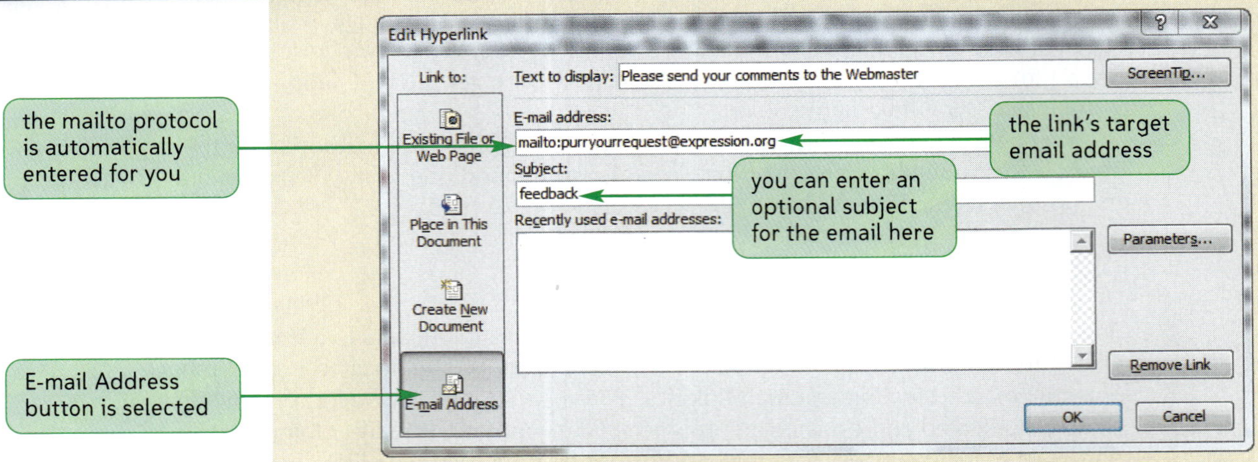

6. Click the **OK** button. The email link text is now underlined.

Next, you'll view the document in the browser and test the external link and the email link.

To view the file in the browser and test the links:

1. Save the file.
2. Press the **F12** key.

   The document opens in the default browser.
3. Scroll down and click the **contact the ASPCA for more information** link.

   The ASPCA Web site opens.
4. Click your browser's **Back** button.
5. Click the **Please send your comments to the Webmaster** link.

   If there is an email client installed on your computer, an email dialog box opens. For some email clients, such as Gmail, the associated Web site may open instead.
6. If your email client is open, close it without sending a message.

   Trouble? If an alert appears with the message "Could not perform this operation because the default mail client is not properly installed," click the OK button.
7. Close the browser.

In addition to using text, you can also use an image as a link to a bookmark, a Web page, or an email address. In the next session, you'll add image links to Trevor's Web site.

REVIEW

Session 4.1 Quick Check

1. What are hyperlinks more commonly called?
2. What is link text?
3. Where is "the fold" in the browser window?
4. Is it possible to create a link to a page that does not yet exist?
5. What do you need to enter in the Insert Hyperlink dialog box to create a link to another Web site?
6. What protocol is used for an email link?

SESSION 4.2 VISUAL OVERVIEW

The **Select** button is used to select a hotspot.

Use the **Rectangular Hotspot** button to create square and rectangular hotspots.

Use the **Circular Hotspot** button to create circles, ovals, and ellipses.

Use the **Polygonal Hotspot** button to create a hotspot of any size and shape.

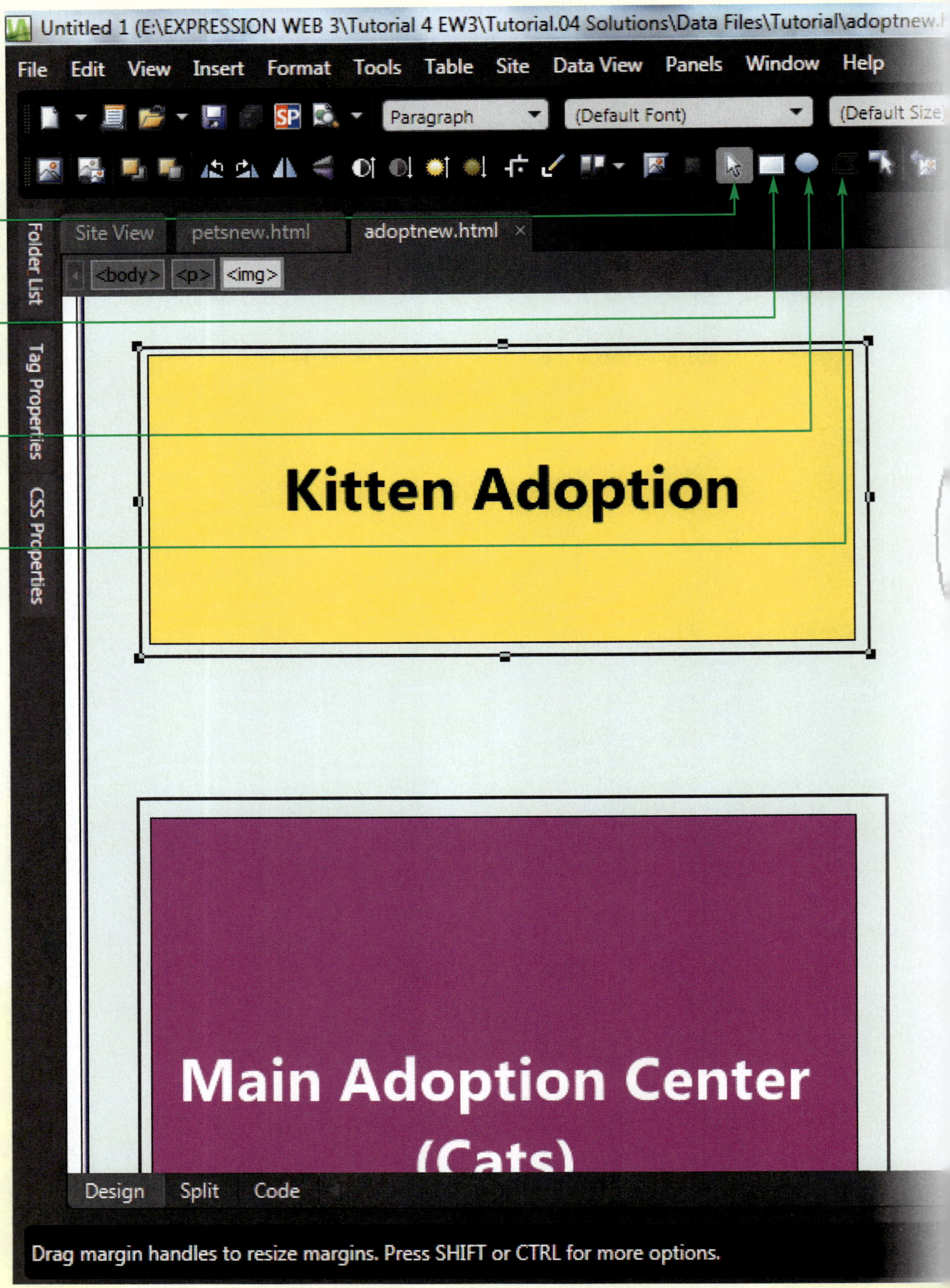

CREATING HOTSPOTS

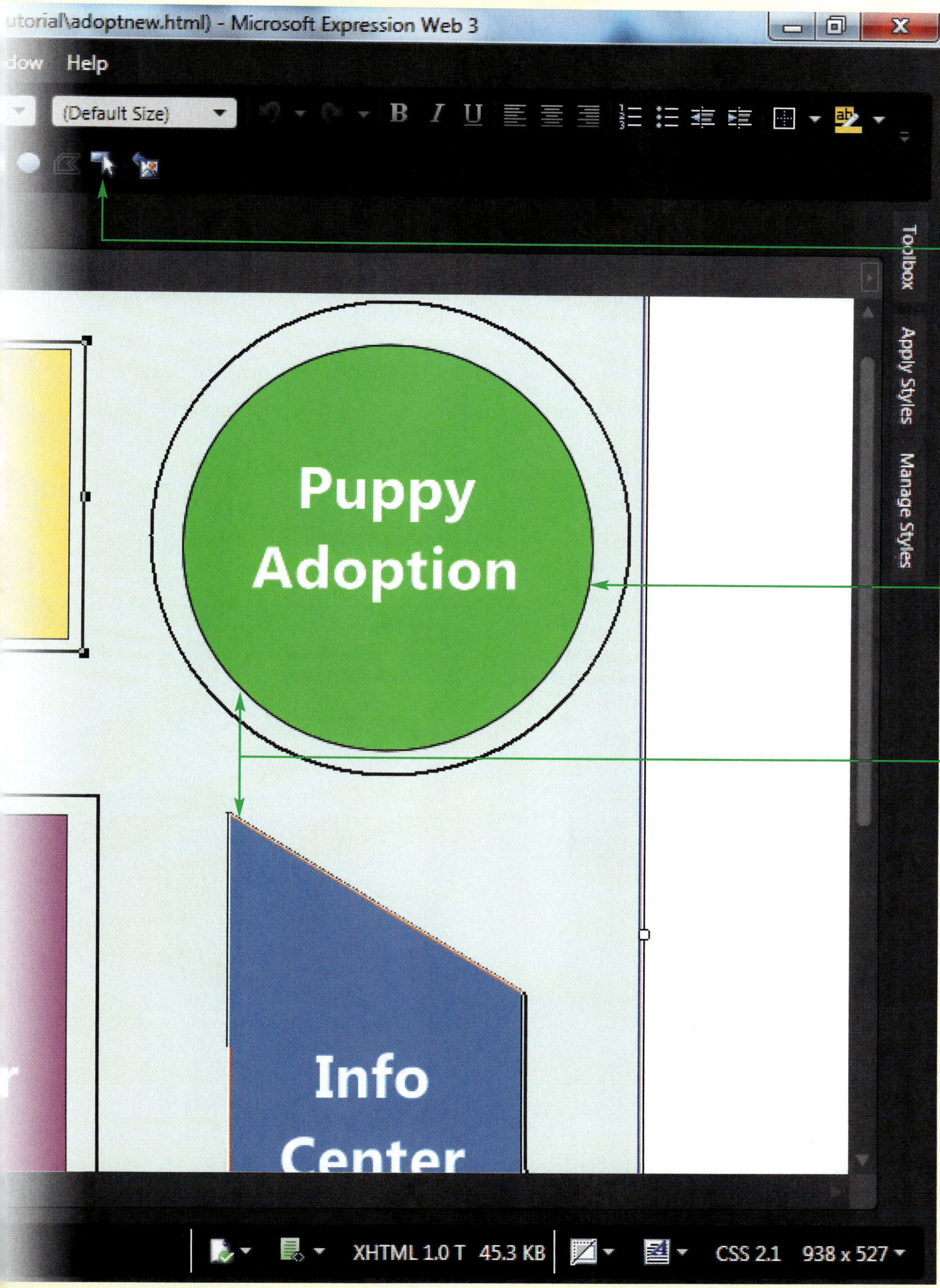

Use the **Highlight Hotspot** button to locate hotspots.

A hotspot does not need to match the corresponding image exactly.

You can use the hotspot tools to create hotspots with different geometric shapes.

Using Images with Links

In addition to linking text, you can add links to images. Images such as arrows and pointers are commonly used as navigational icons. A graphic image, such as an upward-pointing or left-pointing arrow, often appears at the bottom of a Web page to serve as a link back to the top of the page, the previous page, or the home page. When you use an image as a link, it's always a good idea to include some alternative text, just in case the user has set preferences in the browser not to display images. Earlier, you linked the words *Back to Top* on Trevor's Web page to a bookmark at the top of the page. Next, you'll add a link to an image of an upward-pointing arrow with the top of the page as its target.

To use an image as a link:

1. If you took a break after the previous session, make sure that the Tutorial.04 Web site and the petsnew.html file are open and then, if necessary, reset the workspace layout so all panels are visible.
2. Press the **Ctrl+End** keys to position the insertion point at the bottom of the page.
3. Click anywhere on the upward-pointing arrow image to select it, and then press the **Ctrl+K** keys.

   The Insert Hyperlink dialog box opens.
4. In the Link to bar, click the **Place in This Document** button.
5. In the Bookmarks list, click **top**. The Insert Hyperlink dialog box should appear as shown in Figure 4-16.

Figure 4-16 Creating the link to the top bookmark

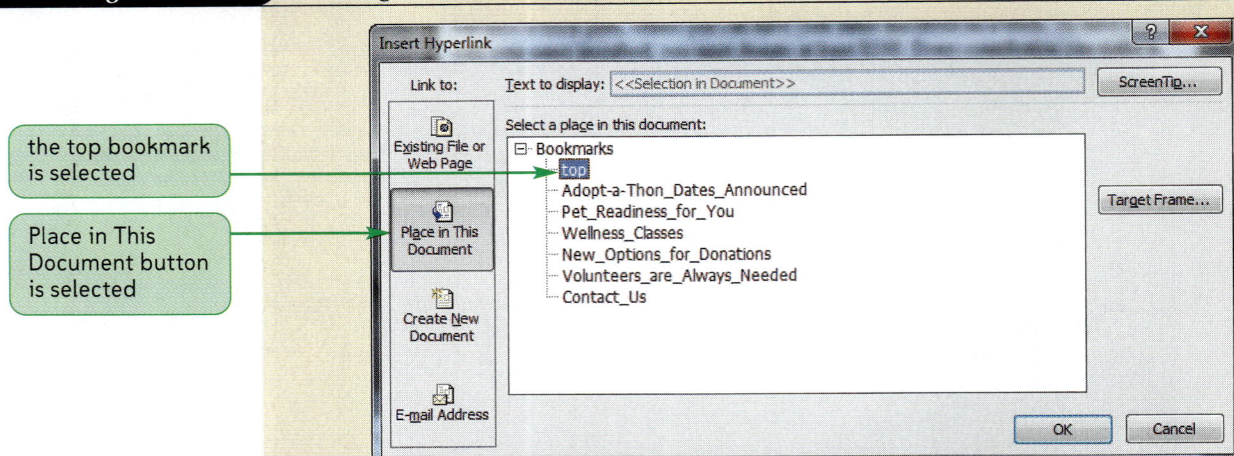

6. Click the **OK** button.
7. Save the file.

Formatting an Image Used as a Link

Note that the image and the text beside it, the words *Back to Top*, are right next to each other. By default, no white space appears between an image and the text beside it. To create some white space between the text and the image, you can use the margin property. Because this image appears at the left edge of the screen, it's a good idea to add some margin space above and to the right of the image. In HTML code, by default, a 2-pixel blue border is placed around an image used as a link. Most Web designers remove this blue border around the image. When you use an image as a link, Expression Web automatically creates and applies a style to remove the blue border. Also, by default, the bottom of the image is aligned with a line of text beside it. Although there are several values for vertical alignment, the three most widely supported values are top, middle, and bottom. You show Trevor how to center the image vertically with the text.

To format the image:

1. Double-click the **uparrow.gif** image.

   The Picture Properties dialog box opens.
2. Click the **Appearance** tab.
3. Click the **Alignment** arrow, scroll down the list, and then click **Middle**.
4. Click the **OK** button.

   The image is now aligned vertically, but the image is still too close to the link text.
5. With the image still selected, click **Format** on the menu bar, and then click **Borders and Shading**.

   The Borders and Shading dialog box opens.
6. In the Padding section, click in the **Right** box, delete the contents, and type **10**.
7. Click the **OK** button.
8. Click anywhere outside of the uparrow.jpg image.

   The arrow image should now appear as shown in Figure 4-17.

Figure 4-17 Positioning the uparrow image

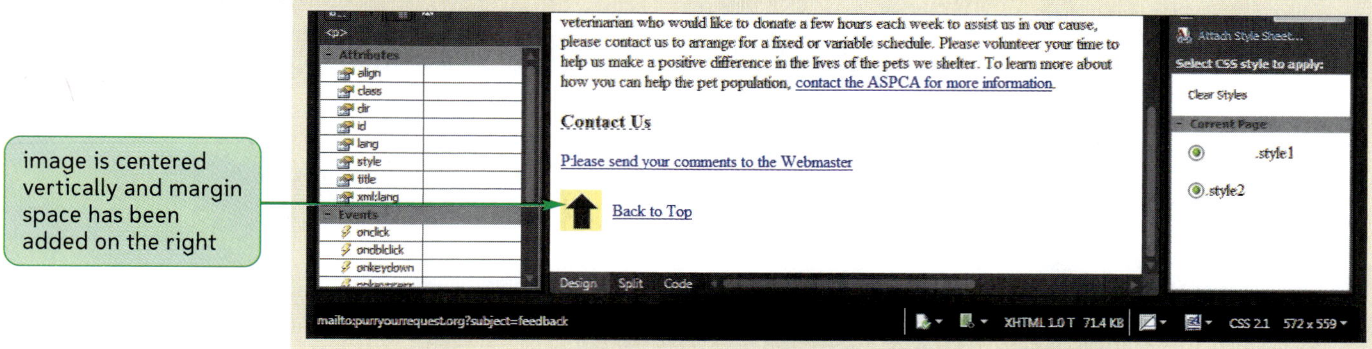

9. Save the file.

Next, you'll work with Trevor to link a single image to several Web pages.

Creating an Image Map

An **image map** is an image that is divided into sections known as hotspots, which allow the same image to serve as the location for several links. A user can click a hotspot to display the target page or Web site.

REFERENCE

Creating a Hotspot

- In Design view, drag the image that will be associated with the image map to the desired place in the editing window.
- If necessary, click View on the menu bar, point to Toolbars, and click Pictures to display the Pictures toolbar.
- Click the image to select it.
- On the Pictures toolbar, click either the Rectangular Hotspot button, the Circular Hotspot button, or the Polygonal Hotspot button.
- On the image, click and drag to draw the hotspot.
- In the Insert Hyperlink dialog box that opens, select the file to which you want to link and then click the OK button.

The image used with an image map can be any image—it doesn't have to be an image of a map, although it commonly is. For example, an image map could show the seating chart for an airliner or a movie theater.

Trevor has provided you with a map of the Adopt-a-Thon fairgrounds. You'll start by opening the Web page containing the image and customizing the Expression Web workspace for working with image maps.

To create a new page:

1. Click the **New Document** button on the Common toolbar.
2. Click the **Save** button on the Common toolbar. The Save As dialog box opens.
3. In the File name box, type **adoptnew**.
4. Press the **Enter** key. The adoptnew.html filename is added to the list of files in the Folder List panel.
5. If necessary, in the Folder List panel click and drag the **adoptnew.html** filename to just below the adopt.png filename in the Tutorial folder.

Now that the new page has been created, you'll show Trevor how to insert the adopt.png image into the adoptnew.html file.

To insert the adopt.png image:

1. In the Folder List panel, click the **adopt.png** filename, hold down the mouse button and drag the adopt.png filename to the top of the adoptnew.html page, and then release the mouse button.

   The Accessibility Properties dialog box opens.
2. For the Alternate text, type **image map for the Adopt-a-Thon fair**.
3. Click the **OK** button.

   The adopt.png image appears. The image is quite large.
4. Click the **Panels** menu and click **AutoHide All Panels** to hide all the panels and display panel tabs.
5. If necessary, drag the vertical scroll bar until you see the top of the adopt.png image.

6. The adopt.png image should appear similar to that shown in Figure 4-18. (Depending on your monitor size and screen resolution, you might not see the entire image.)

Figure 4-18 The page for the image maps

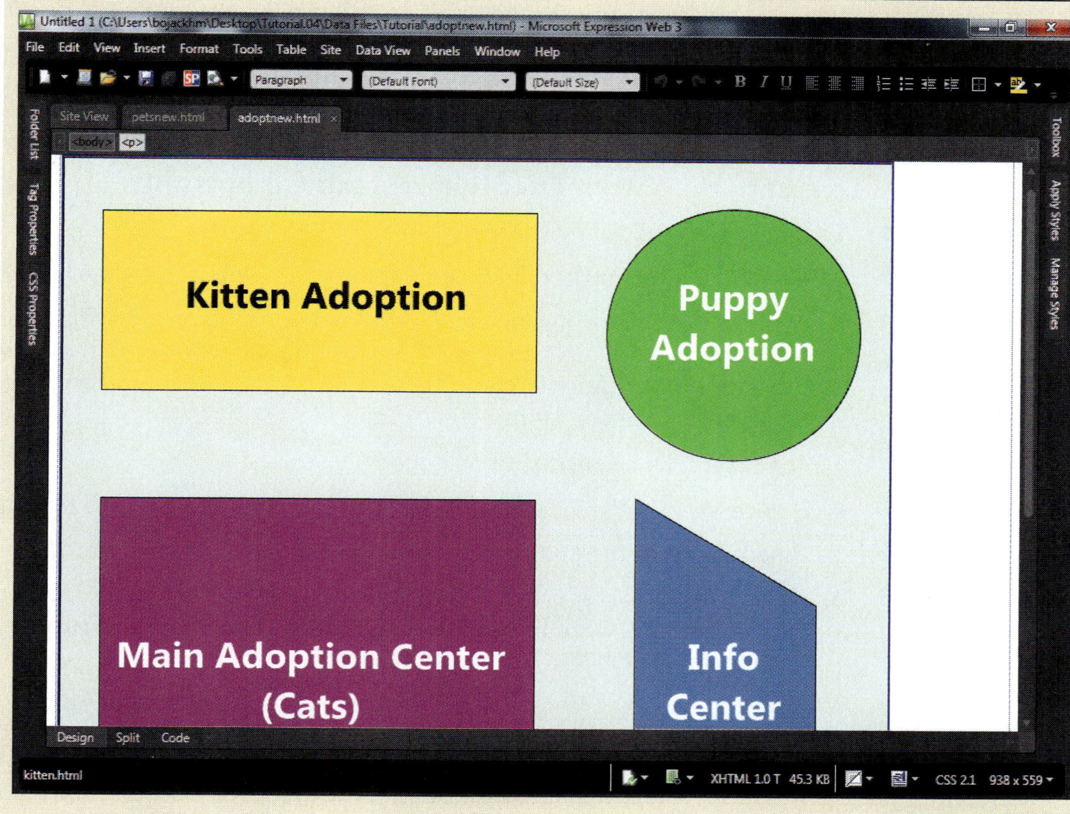

7. Save the **adoptnew.html** file.

The hotspots for the image are created by clicking buttons on the Pictures toolbar, so you'll have Trevor display the Pictures toolbar.

To view the Pictures toolbar:

1. Click **View** on the menu bar, point to **Toolbars**, and then click **Pictures**.
2. If the Pictures toolbar is not positioned below the Common toolbar, click and drag the Pictures toolbar until it is below the Common toolbar.

With the document open and the workspace optimized, you're ready to begin to create hotspots.

Creating Hotspots

The five buttons to the left of the Restore button on the Pictures toolbar, which are highlighted in the Visual Overview for this session, are tools for working with hotspots. When the image is selected, the hotspots are also selected; however, if you have clicked another button on the Pictures toolbar, you use the Select button to select hotspots. HTML recognizes only three types of shapes: rectangles, circles, and polygons (which are any shapes other than rectangles or circles). These categories encompass many other common geometric shapes: a square is considered a type of rectangle, an oval is considered a type of circle, and a triangle is considered a polygon.

TIP

It is okay if the hotspots overlap a little.

The adopt.png image contains four shapes: the Kitten Adoption section is a rectangle, the Puppy Adoption section is a circle, the Main Adoption Center shape is also a rectangle, and the irregularly shaped Info Center is a polygon. Trevor has provided you with four placeholder Web pages to serve as the targets of the hotspot links. You'll start by creating a hotspot for the Kitten Adoption rectangle.

To create the Kitten Adoption rectangular hotspot:

1. If necessary, click anywhere on the image to select it.
2. On the Pictures toolbar, click the **Rectangular Hotspot** button.
3. Position the pointer just above and to the left of the upper-left corner of the Kitten Adoption shape, click and drag the pencil pointer down and to the right until the entire Kitten Adoption section is contained in a rectangular outline, and then release the mouse button.

   The Insert Hyperlink dialog box opens.
4. If necessary, in the Link to bar, click the **Existing File or Web Page** button.
5. If necessary, in the Look in bar, click the **Current Folder** button.
6. If the Tutorial folder is not already open in the Insert Hyperlink dialog box , double-click the **Data Files** folder, and then double-click the **Tutorial** folder to display the files in the Tutorial folder.
7. If necessary, scroll down the list and then click the **kitten** filename.

   The kitten.html filename appears in the Address box, as shown in Figure 4-19.

Figure 4-19 **Selecting the target for the rectangular hotspot**

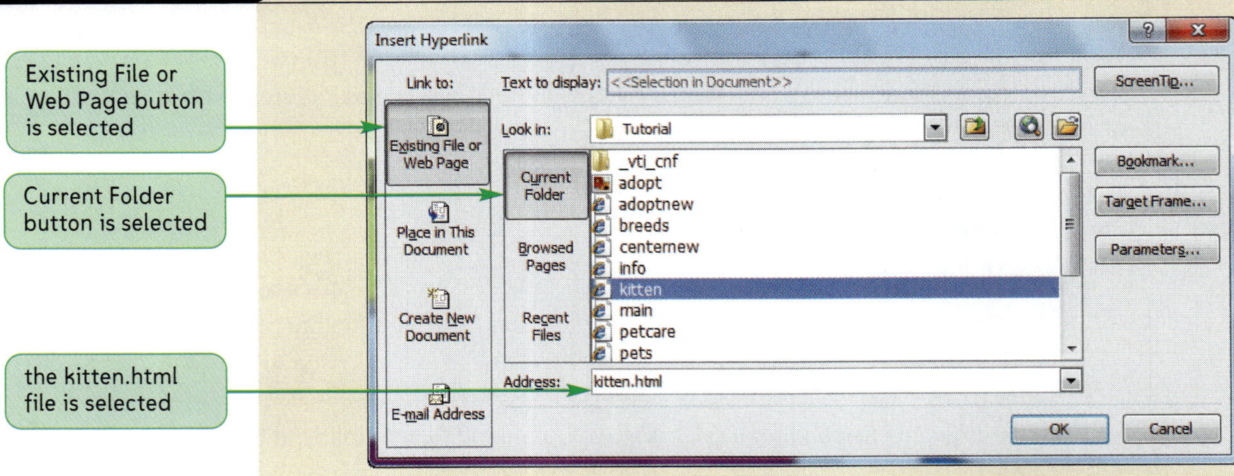

8. Click the **OK** button. A box with sizing handles now surrounds the Kitten Adoption shape, representing the hotspot, as shown in Figure 4-20.

Figure 4-20 Rectangular hotspot created

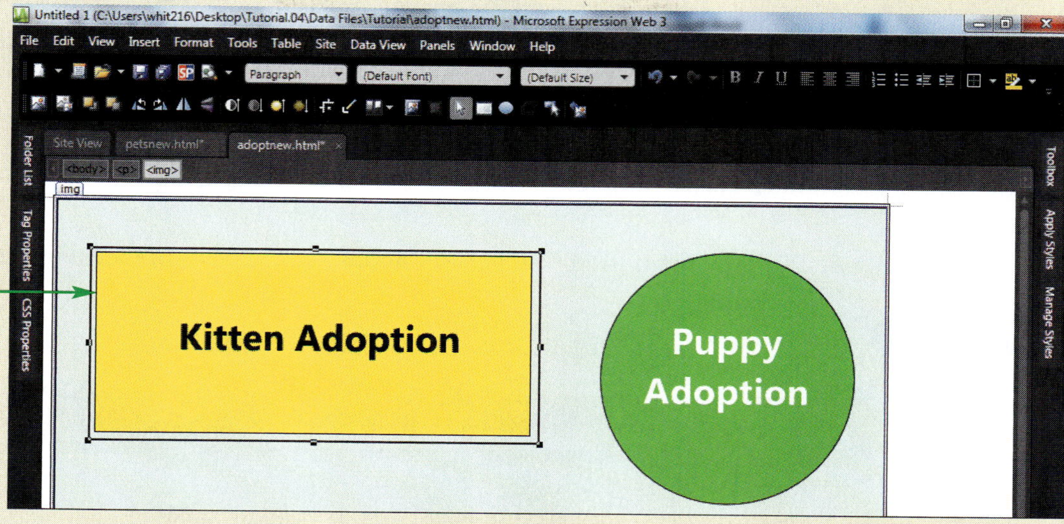

Trouble? If the hotspot is not correct, click and drag any of the sizing handles to adjust the shape of the hotspot.

9. Click on the image anywhere outside the rectangular hotspot.

   The hotspot you created no longer displays sizing handles, but the outline remains.

TIP

If hotspots overlap, the link to the first hotspot you drew prevails when a user clicks the overlap area.

Next, you'll save the file and then test the hotspot link in the default browser.

To test the hotspot:

1. Save the file.
2. Press the **F12** key.

   The document opens in the browser. The hotspot will not be visible until you pass the pointer over it.
3. Pass the pointer over the Kitten Adoption section.

   The icon becomes a pointing hand, indicating that this is a hotspot.
4. Click the **Kitten Adoption** hotspot.

   The kitten.html page opens.
5. Close the browser.

Now that you have created a rectangular hotspot, you'll create a circular hotspot for the Puppy Adoption section of the image.

To create the Puppy Adoption circular hotspot:

1. If necessary, scroll until you can see the entire green circle labeled "Puppy Adoption."
2. Verify that the adopt.png image is still selected, and then on the Pictures toolbar, click the **Circular Hotspot** button.

3. Position the pointer in the center of the Puppy Adoption circle.
4. Click and drag the pencil pointer downward until the Puppy Adoption circle is fully contained in a circular outline, and then release the mouse button.

   The Insert Hyperlink dialog box opens.
5. In the Look in box, scroll through the filename list if necessary and then select the **puppy** filename.

   The puppy.html filename now appears in the Address box.
6. Click the **OK** button. The hotspot appears as a circle, as shown in Figure 4-21.

Figure 4-21 **Circular hotspot created**

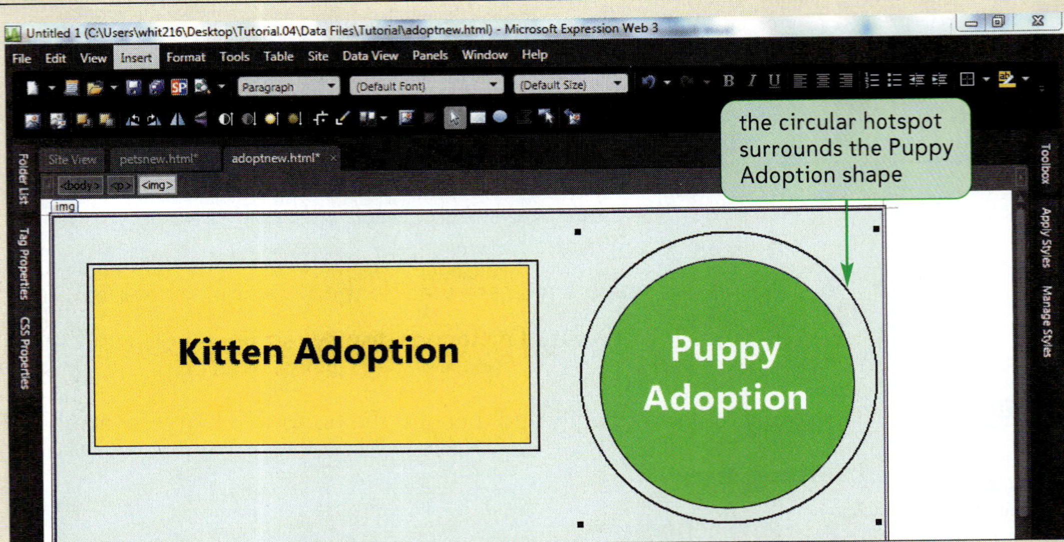

Trouble? If the hotspot is not correct, select the hotspot and use the arrow keys to reposition it. If using the arrow keys does not correct the hotspot, delete it, and return to Step 1 to re-create it.

7. Click a blank area of the image or the editing window to deselect the shape.

INSIGHT

Determining Hotspot Shape and Placement

Which shape to use for hotspots is determined by the image with which they are associated. Creating hotspots for a seating chart for an airplane or a theater might be best accomplished using the rectangle tool. If you had a map of cities in a country or on a continent, you could create circular hotspots for each of the major ones. For a national or regional map, though, the polygon tool would probably be best. Trouble might arise if hotspots are too close together. For example, on a map of the United States, the states in the Northeast are small and densely packed. For situations like this, consider including an inset (a larger image of a small area) in one of the four corners of the image map. You can then create another image map for the inset detail.

Next, you'll create a rectangular hotspot for the Main Adoption Center section of the image.

To create the Main Adoption Center rectangular hotspot:

1. If necessary, scroll down until you can see the entire Main Adoption Center purple rectangle.
2. Verify that the image is still selected, and then on the Pictures toolbar, click the **Rectangular Hotspot** button.
3. Position the pointer just above and to the left of the upper-left corner of the Main Adoption Center section of the map.
4. Click and drag the pencil pointer down and to the right until the entire Main Adoption Center purple rectangle is contained in an outline, and then release the mouse button. The Insert Hyperlink dialog box opens.
5. In the Link to box, click the **main** filename.

   The main.html filename appears in the Address box.
6. Click the **OK** button.

   The rectangular hotspot is shown in Figure 4-22.

Figure 4-22 Second rectangular hotspot created

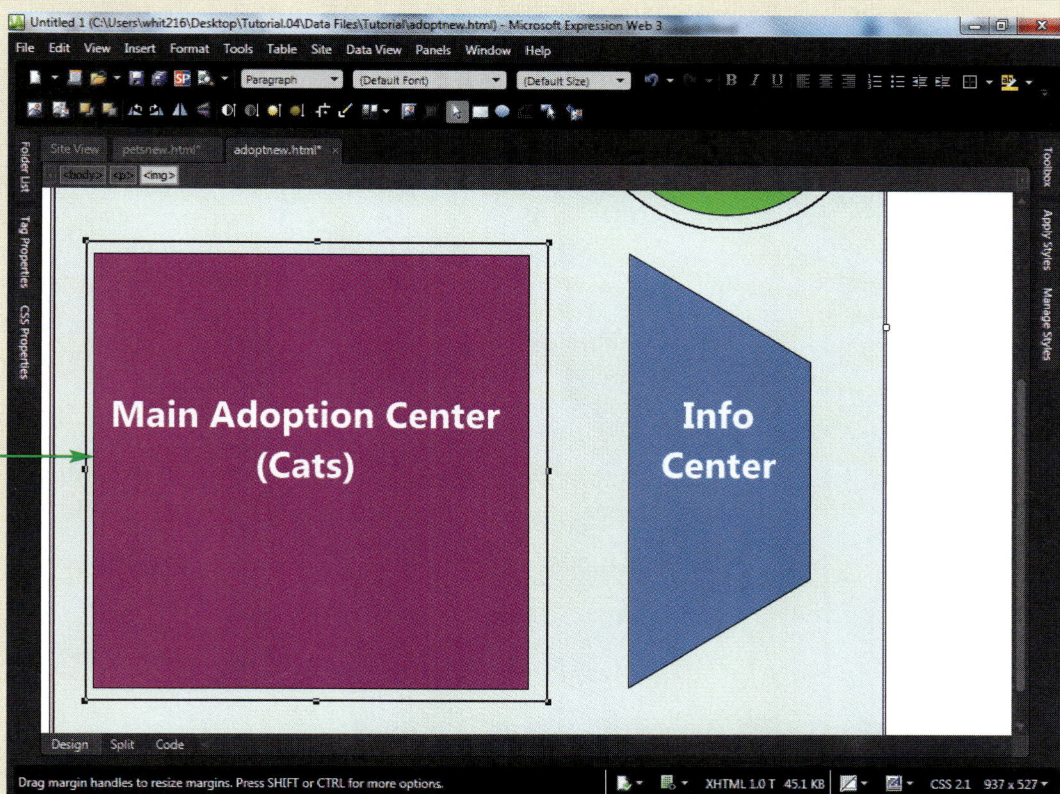

the rectangular hotspot surrounds the Main Adoption Center shape

Trouble? If the hotspot is not correct, select the hotspot and use the arrow keys to reposition the hotspot. If using the arrow keys does not correct the hotspot, delete the hotspot and return to Step 1 to re-create it.

7. Click a blank area of the image or the editing window to deselect the shape.

   The resizing handles for the Main Adoption Center rectangular hotspot section no longer appear.

TIP

When creating the target files, use filenames that are similar to (or abbreviated from) the hotspot name.

The last hotspot you need to create for Trevor is an irregularly shaped section, so you'll use the Polygonal Hotspot tool. Instead of simply clicking and dragging to create a shape, you'll click each corner point, or **vertex**, of the polygon. After you click all of the vertices, you'll click the starting point to complete the shape.

To create the Info Center polygonal hotspot:

1. Verify that the image is still selected, and then on the Pictures toolbar, click the **Polygonal Hotspot** button.
2. Click the upper-left corner of the Info Center shape.
3. Click the lower-left corner of the Info Center shape.
4. Click the lower-right corner of the shape.
5. Click the upper-right corner.
6. Click the starting point again.

   The Insert Hyperlink dialog box opens.
7. In the Link to box, click the **info** filename, and then click the **OK** button.

   The polygonal hotspot is created, as shown in Figure 4-23.

Figure 4-23 Polygonal hotspot created

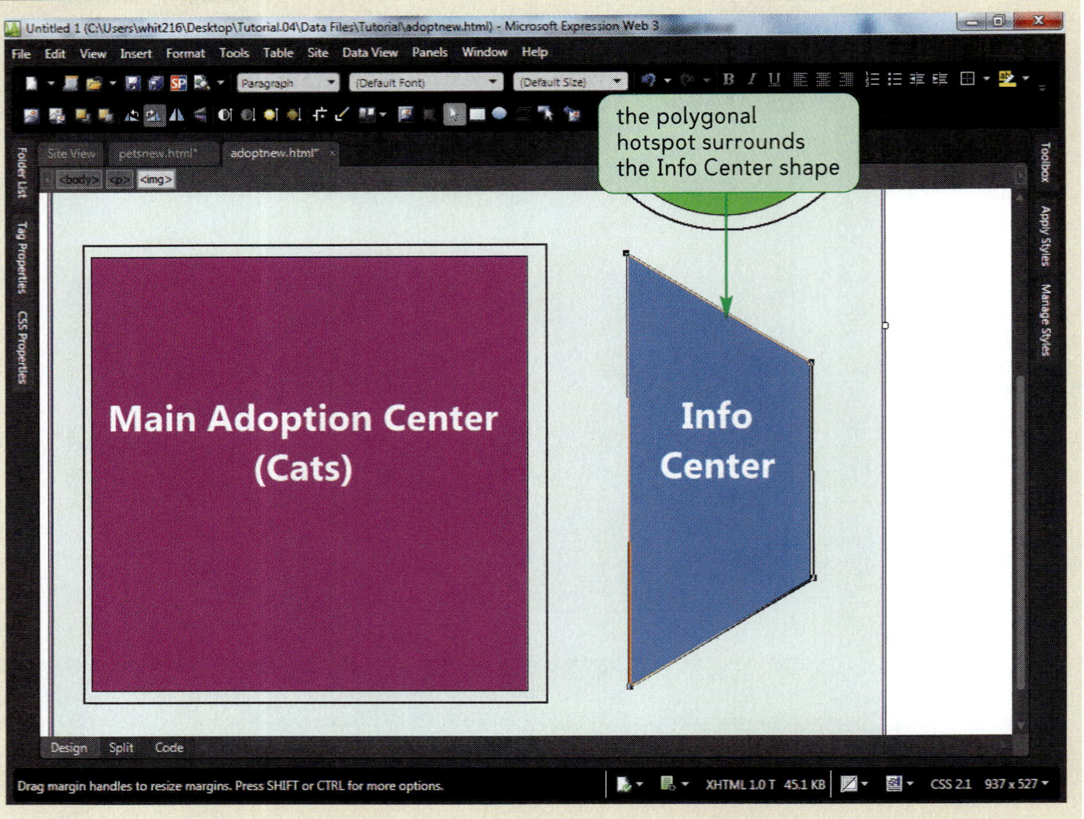

Trouble? If the Insert Hyperlink dialog box has not opened, you failed to completely close the polygon. Double-click to open the Insert Hyperlink dialog box. (It's okay if the polygon is not closed.)

8. Click a blank area of the image or the editing window to deselect the shape.

   Depending on how far from the outer edge of the shape the polygon is drawn, the border might still be visible.

PROSKILLS

Written Communications: Using Image Maps

One issue that surrounds the use of image maps is accessibility. Recall that every image should have alternate text that can be read aloud by screen reader software to an individual who is visually impaired. Although an image map serves as a link to several locations, you cannot create alternate text for a hotspot, only for the image itself. As a means of enhancing accessibility for the visually impaired, it's a good idea for each link to use the title attribute and a value that describes the hotspot area. The title attribute creates a ScreenTip that will appear in the browser. For example, if the image map were that of the United States, and you had hotspots linking each state to an individual Web page, assigning text such as "link to the New York State page" for the New York State hotspot would help visually impaired users better locate and identify each hotspot in the image map.

Expression Web has a useful feature that shows exactly where you have drawn the hotspots. Viewing the hotspot locations is particularly useful for locating the hotspots on an image map. For maps with many hotspots, it's also useful to verify that a hotspot has been created and where it is located on the map.

Viewing Hotspot Locations

Before you save the file and test the links in the browser, you can view just the hotspots to verify that all the hotspots have been entered and are in the desired shape and position. You can use the Highlight Hotspots button to display an outline of just the hotspot areas.

REFERENCE

Viewing a Hotspot

- In Design view, click anywhere on an image that contains one or more hotspots.
- Click the Highlight Hotspots button on the Pictures toolbar.
- Click inside a hotspot to highlight it as a reverse image.
- To return to Design view, click anywhere outside the image or click the Highlight Hotspots button again.

The Highlight Hotspots button is a toggle: you click the button to show the hotspots, and click it again to return to the standard view of the image. You can also turn off the hotspot highlights by clicking anywhere outside the image. You'll use the Highlight Hotspots button to locate the hotspots. You'll also edit a hotspot on Trevor's Web page to ensure that it has the correct target.

To locate the hotspots:

1. Click anywhere in the **Main Adoption Center** hotspot.
2. On the Pictures toolbar, click the **Highlight Hotspots** button.

   The currently selected hotspot appears in solid black, whereas the other hotspots are white with a black outline, as shown in Figure 4-24.

Figure 4-24 Viewing highlighted hotspots

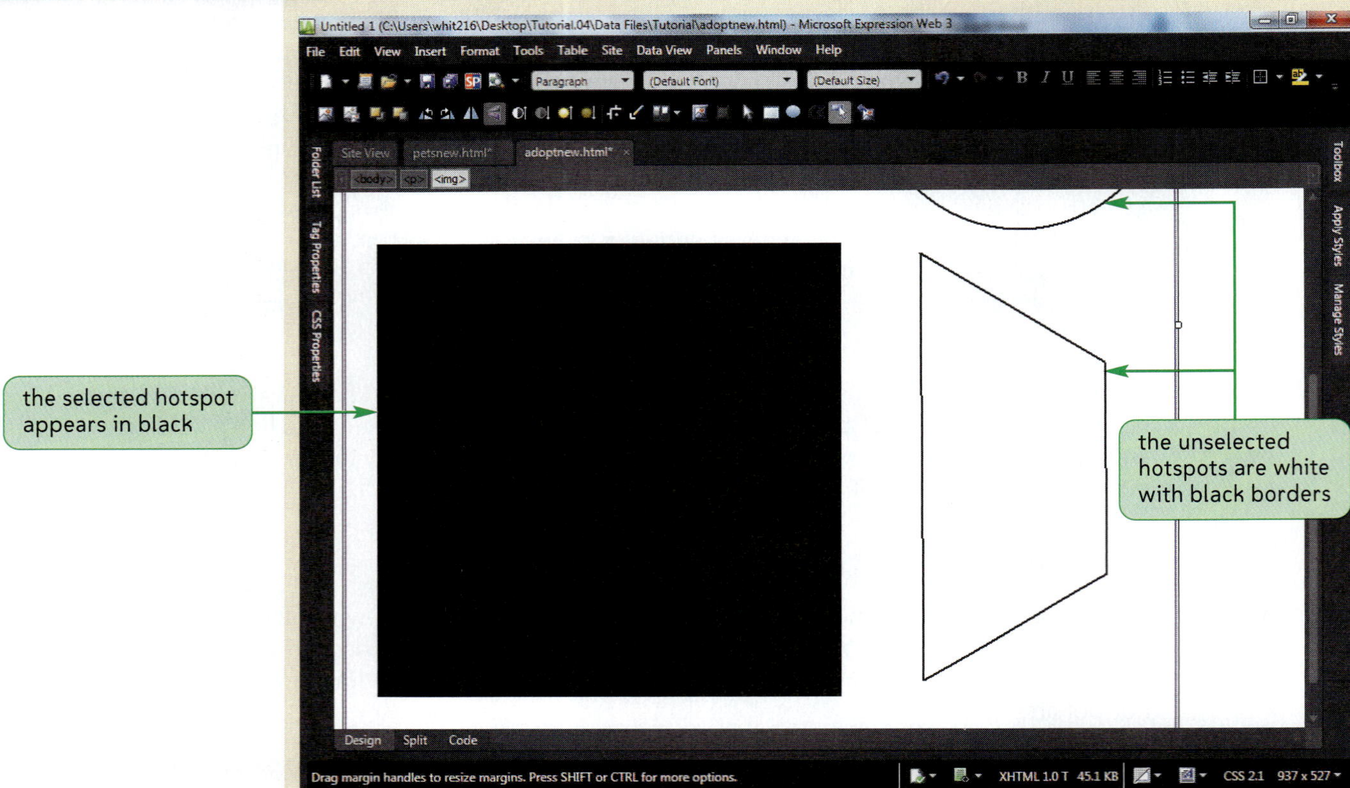

3. Click anywhere outside the image. The image map appears again.

TIP

You can't modify a hotspot while it is highlighted.

Now that you are sure that all the hotspots have been entered, you'll test the new hotspot links in the browser.

To test the hotspots:

1. Save the file.
2. Press the **F12** key.

   The Web page opens in the default browser. The hotspots are not visible on the page. You can verify a hotspot location by watching for the pointer to change into a pointing hand when you move it over a hotspot.
3. Move the pointer over the **Puppy Adoption** hotspot.
4. The hand cursor appears.

5. Click the **Puppy Adoption** hotspot.

   The puppy.html page opens.

6. Click the browser's **Back** button.

7. Test each of the remaining hotspots to verify that the hotspot works correctly, and then click your browser's **Back** button as necessary to return to the main page.

8. After you have verified all hotspots are correct, close the browser.

An image map can easily be modified. After selecting a hotspot, you can modify its shape using the sizing handles, move it, or delete it. Next, you'll show Trevor how to modify a hotspot shape.

Modifying a Hotspot

For a rectangular hotspot, sizing handles appear along each side and in the corner. As you pass the pointer over a resize handle, the pointer turns into the resize pointer (a double-headed arrow). You can click and drag the sizing handles to adjust the hotspot shape. When you click inside a circular hotspot, the circle is enclosed within a square. Each of the corners has a sizing handle that you can use to make the circle smaller or larger. When you click inside a polygonal hotspot, sizing handles appear at each vertex (corner) of the polygon shape. To resize the polygon, you can't just drag the sizing handle. You must wait until the move pointer appears, and then you can drag the sizing handle to change the polygon's shape.

REFERENCE

Modifying a Hotspot

- To move a hotspot, click within it and drag it to its new location.

or

- Use the arrow keys to reposition the hotspot.
- To resize a rectangular or circular hotspot, click within the hotspot, and then drag a sizing handle.
- To resize a polygonal hotspot, click a vertex to select it, and then click and drag the vertex to change the polygon shape.
- To modify a hotspot's hyperlink, double-click the hotspot, change the filename or URL in the Edit Hyperlink dialog box, and then click the OK button.
- To delete a hotspot, click the hotspot to select it, and then press the Delete key.

INSIGHT

Linking to Other File Types

Hyperlink targets are not limited to just Web pages. Any electronic file is a potential link target, including a Microsoft Word, Excel, or PowerPoint file or an Adobe PDF file. You should always include some text on your Web page that identifies the target of such a link as a non-HTML file and specify its file extension. This prevents visitors from expecting to see another Web page when they click the link, rather than a page that might require a download or the installation of a plug-in to view the document. If a plug-in is required to view a document that your Web page links to, you can assist visitors to your Web site in accessing the content by providing a link to download the plug-in.

To modify a Hotspot:

1. Click inside the Kitten Adoption hotspot to select that hotspot.
2. Use the sizing handles to increase the size of the hotspot until it is larger than the Kitten Adoption yellow rectangle.
3. Click inside the Puppy Adoption circle.
4. Use the sizing handles to increase the size of the hotspot until it is larger than the Puppy Adoption green circle.

Next, you'll show Trevor how to add some documentation to this image map page.

To add documentation to the file:

1. Press the **Ctrl+End** keys to position the insertion point at the end of the page.
2. Type your first and last name, press the **Ctrl+Enter** keys, and then type **Tutorial 4**, **Image Map**.
3. Save and then close the adoptnew.html file.

   The petsnew.html file appears again.

Trevor is happy with the work you've done so far on the Web page, but wonders if there's a way to customize the page's appearance a little more. You suggest changing the colors of linked text on the Web page, and Trevor likes the idea.

Changing Link Colors

By default, most browsers indicate links by underlining the link text and displaying the text in blue. After you click a link, it becomes a visited link, and the text and underline appear in purple. HTML allows you to change the colors of both unvisited and visited links, and Expression Web makes the changes easy to implement.

REFERENCE

Changing the Link Colors

- In Design view, right-click a blank area of the page, and then click Page Properties on the shortcut menu.
- In the Page Properties dialog box, click the Formatting tab.
- In the Colors section, click the Hyperlink arrow, select a color from the palette, and then repeat for Visited hyperlink, Active hyperlink, and Hovered hyperlink, in that order.
- Click More Colors to view color options in addition to the standard 16 Web-safe colors.

You also can change the color for an active hyperlink, which affects the moment when a visitor clicks the link. Generally, you want to use an attention-getting color for that purpose to attract the visitor to unvisited links. In addition, you can change the color of links when a user moves the pointer over them without clicking. This type of change is known as a **mouseover** or **rollover**, or **hover effect**.

You use the Page Properties dialog box to change the link colors for Trevor's Web page.

To change the link colors:

1. Right-click anywhere on the **petsnew.html** page.
2. Click **Page Properties** on the shortcut menu.

   The Page Properties dialog box opens.
3. Click the **Formatting** tab.
4. Click the **Hyperlink** arrow, and then click the **Maroon** swatch.
5. Click the **Visited hyperlink** arrow, and then click the **Olive** swatch.
6. Click the **Hovered hyperlink** arrow, and then click the **Teal** swatch.

   Your Page Properties dialog box should be similar to Figure 4-25.

Figure 4-25 **Customizing link colors**

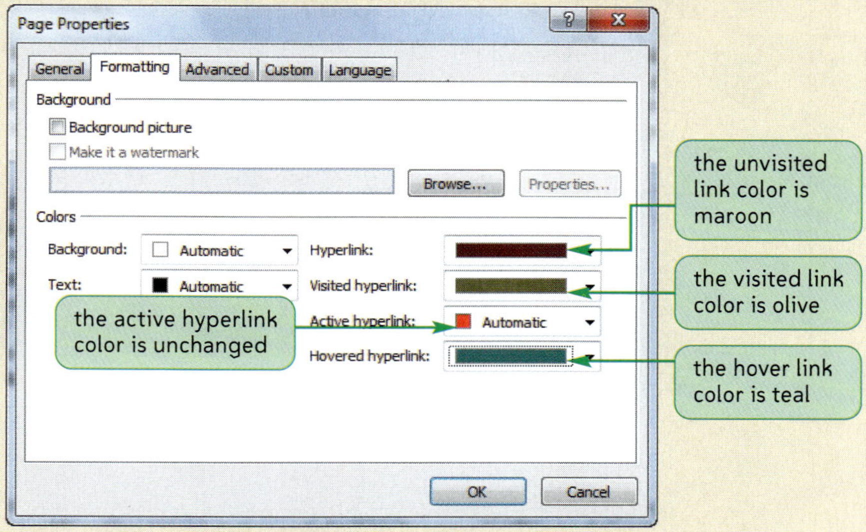

7. Click the **OK** button.
8. Press the **Ctrl+Home** keys to position the insertion point at the top of the page.

   All of the links, including the bookmark links, now appear in maroon, as shown in Figure 4-26.

Figure 4-26 **Hyperlink colors changed**

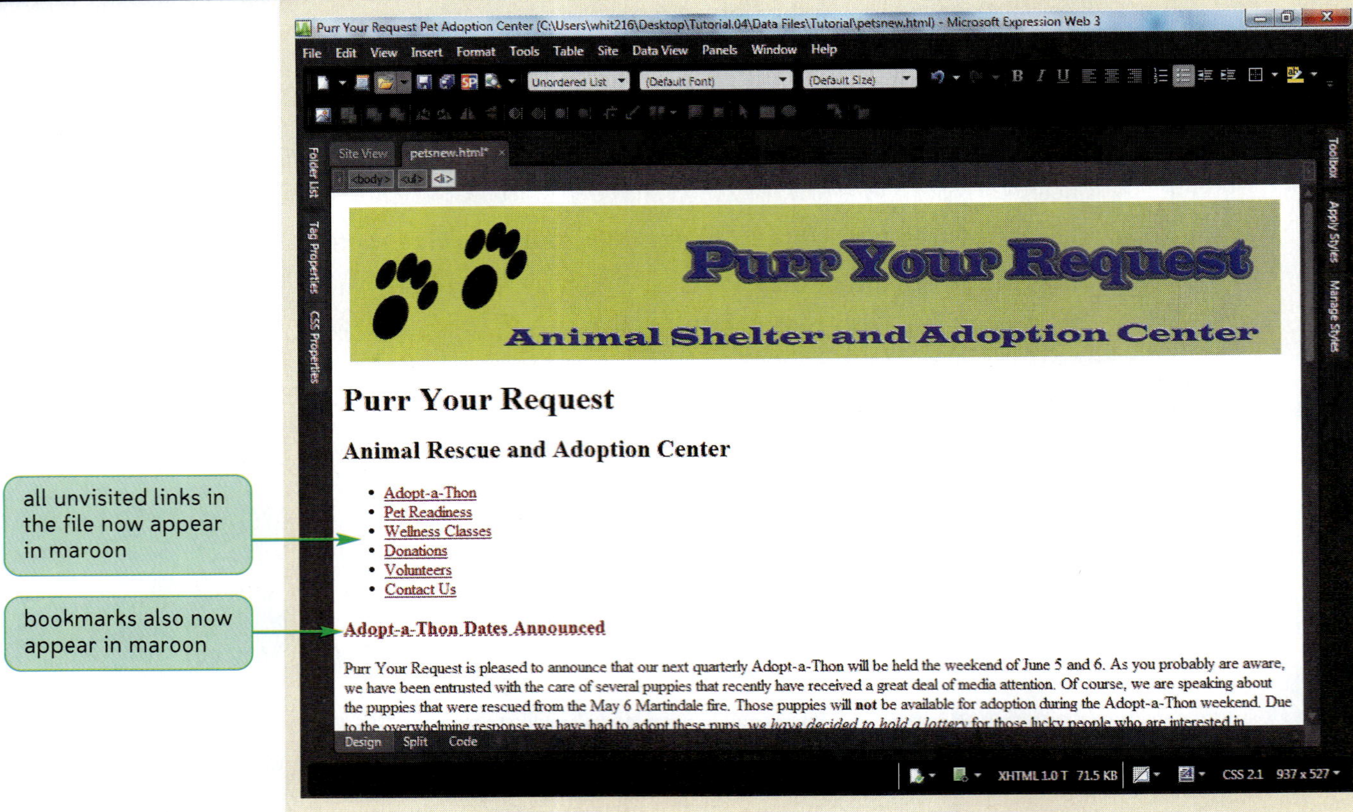

Next, you'll review your work on Trevor's Web page by opening the document in the browser.

To view the document in the browser:

1. Save the file.
2. Press the **F12** key.

   The document opens in the default browser.
3. Move the pointer over the links in the bulleted list.

   The color of each link changes to teal as long as the pointer hovers over it.
4. If necessary, scroll to the bottom of the page, and then click the **uparrow image** to test the link to the top of the page.
5. Press the **Ctrl+End** keys to position the insertion point at the bottom of the page in the browser.

   The link text "Back to Top" is now olive, which is the color you specified for visited link text.
6. Close the browser.

Occasionally, you might need to edit a hyperlink because some information about the hyperlink is incorrect or has changed. Over time, files are deleted or they are moved to other folders. New pages are added. Filenames might be changed. All of these maintenance issues could be quite time consuming and involve a great deal of detective work on your part to determine which files are linked to each other. Fortunately, Expression Web solves all of these file maintenance problems.

Next, you'll show Trevor how to edit a hyperlink.

Editing a Hyperlink

If you have created an Expression Web site, Expression Web keeps track of all the links for your Web pages. Should you move, delete, or rename a file using the Folder List panel, Expression Web automatically rewrites the HTML code to reflect the changes you have made to your Web site file structure. There's no need to determine which files are linked and how they are linked. You don't have to open each file, edit the HTML link code, and save the revised file. Expression Web keeps track of all your linked documents and does all the tedious code revision for you automatically in seconds.

The Edit Hyperlink dialog box can be used to change the link text, change the URL to which you want to link, and remove a link. Expression Web updates links automatically, saving you, the Web page developer, from spending a multitude of hours needlessly updating broken or revised links.

Trevor decided that a different page in his Web site would be a more appropriate link for users to read more about pet care, and he wants you to change the link. You'll change the link to direct the visitor to a different page about pet care. You'll also test a link in Design view.

To edit the hyperlink:

1. If necessary, scroll to view the Pet Care Center link, which is in the last sentence of the paragraph below the Wellness Classes heading, and then click anywhere in the **Pet Care Center** link text.
2. Press the **Ctrl+K** keys. The Edit Hyperlink dialog box opens.
3. In the file list, click the **petcare** filename.

   The petcare.html filename replaces the centernew.html filename in the Address box, as shown in Figure 4-27.

Figure 4-27 **Editing the hyperlink**

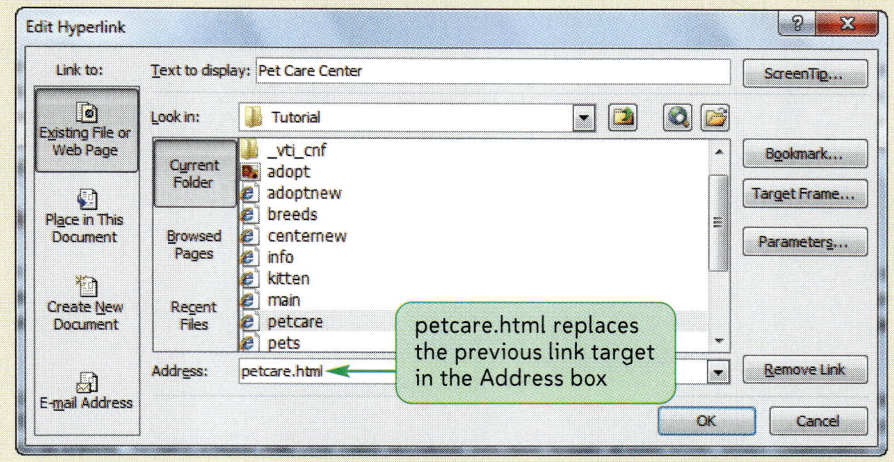

4. Click the **OK** button.
5. With the Pet Care Center text still selected, press and hold down the **Ctrl** key and click the **Pet Care Center** link text.

   The Petcare file opens.
6. Right-click the **petcare.html** Document tab, and then click **Close**.
7. Press the **Ctrl+End** keys to position the insertion point at the end of the petsnew.html page.
8. On two lines, type the following, substituting your name as appropriate, and pressing the **Shift+Enter** keys after you type your name:

   Your First and Last Name
   Tutorial 4

Finally, you'll view the completed file in the browser.

To review the final version of the file:

1. Save the file.
2. Press the **F12** key to open the file in the browser. Your document should look similar to that shown in Figure 4-28.

Figure 4-28 The completed file

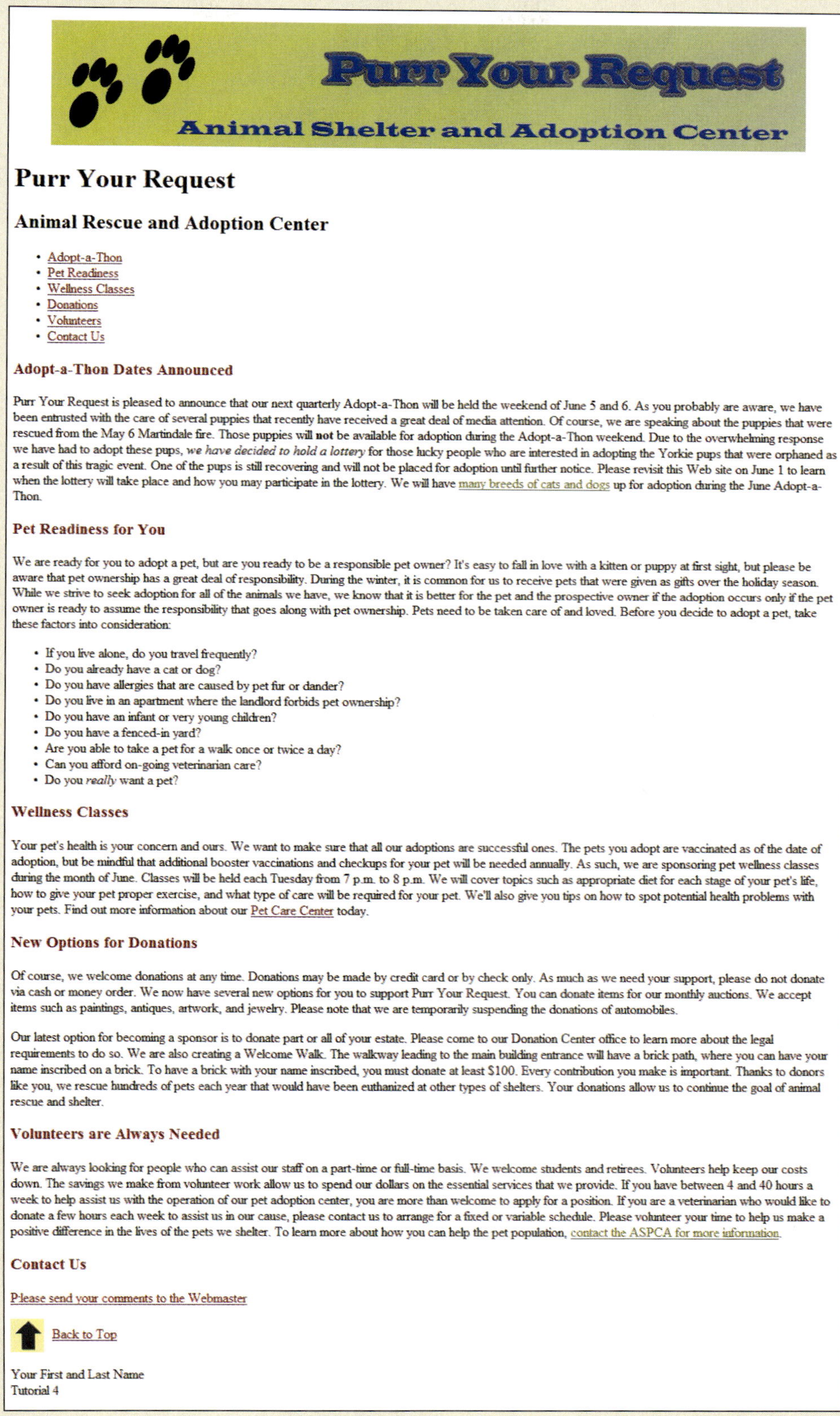

Purr Your Request
Animal Shelter and Adoption Center

Purr Your Request

Animal Rescue and Adoption Center

- Adopt-a-Thon
- Pet Readiness
- Wellness Classes
- Donations
- Volunteers
- Contact Us

Adopt-a-Thon Dates Announced

Purr Your Request is pleased to announce that our next quarterly Adopt-a-Thon will be held the weekend of June 5 and 6. As you probably are aware, we have been entrusted with the care of several puppies that recently have received a great deal of media attention. Of course, we are speaking about the puppies that were rescued from the May 6 Martindale fire. Those puppies will **not** be available for adoption during the Adopt-a-Thon weekend. Due to the overwhelming response we have had to adopt these pups, *we have decided to hold a lottery* for those lucky people who are interested in adopting the Yorkie pups that were orphaned as a result of this tragic event. One of the pups is still recovering and will not be placed for adoption until further notice. Please revisit this Web site on June 1 to learn when the lottery will take place and how you may participate in the lottery. We will have many breeds of cats and dogs up for adoption during the June Adopt-a-Thon.

Pet Readiness for You

We are ready for you to adopt a pet, but are you ready to be a responsible pet owner? It's easy to fall in love with a kitten or puppy at first sight, but please be aware that pet ownership has a great deal of responsibility. During the winter, it is common for us to receive pets that were given as gifts over the holiday season. While we strive to seek adoption for all of the animals we have, we know that it is better for the pet and the prospective owner if the adoption occurs only if the pet owner is ready to assume the responsibility that goes along with pet ownership. Pets need to be taken care of and loved. Before you decide to adopt a pet, take these factors into consideration:

- If you live alone, do you travel frequently?
- Do you already have a cat or dog?
- Do you have allergies that are caused by pet fur or dander?
- Do you live in an apartment where the landlord forbids pet ownership?
- Do you have an infant or very young children?
- Do you have a fenced-in yard?
- Are you able to take a pet for a walk once or twice a day?
- Can you afford on-going veterinarian care?
- Do you *really* want a pet?

Wellness Classes

Your pet's health is your concern and ours. We want to make sure that all our adoptions are successful ones. The pets you adopt are vaccinated as of the date of adoption, but be mindful that additional booster vaccinations and checkups for your pet will be needed annually. As such, we are sponsoring pet wellness classes during the month of June. Classes will be held each Tuesday from 7 p.m. to 8 p.m. We will cover topics such as appropriate diet for each stage of your pet's life, how to give your pet proper exercise, and what type of care will be required for your pet. We'll also give you tips on how to spot potential health problems with your pets. Find out more information about our Pet Care Center today.

New Options for Donations

Of course, we welcome donations at any time. Donations may be made by credit card or by check only. As much as we need your support, please do not donate via cash or money order. We now have several new options for you to support Purr Your Request. You can donate items for our monthly auctions. We accept items such as paintings, antiques, artwork, and jewelry. Please note that we are temporarily suspending the donations of automobiles.

Our latest option for becoming a sponsor is to donate part or all of your estate. Please come to our Donation Center office to learn more about the legal requirements to do so. We are also creating a Welcome Walk. The walkway leading to the main building entrance will have a brick path, where you can have your name inscribed on a brick. To have a brick with your name inscribed, you must donate at least $100. Every contribution you make is important. Thanks to donors like you, we rescue hundreds of pets each year that would have been euthanized at other types of shelters. Your donations allow us to continue the goal of animal rescue and shelter.

Volunteers are Always Needed

We are always looking for people who can assist our staff on a part-time or full-time basis. We welcome students and retirees. Volunteers help keep our costs down. The savings we make from volunteer work allow us to spend our dollars on the essential services that we provide. If you have between 4 and 40 hours a week to help assist us with the operation of our pet adoption center, you are more than welcome to apply for a position. If you are a veterinarian who would like to donate a few hours each week to assist us in our cause, please contact us to arrange for a fixed or variable schedule. Please volunteer your time to help us make a positive difference in the lives of the pets we shelter. To learn more about how you can help the pet population, contact the ASPCA for more information.

Contact Us

Please send your comments to the Webmaster

Back to Top

Your First and Last Name
Tutorial 4

3. Submit the completed files to your instructor either in printed or electronic form, as requested.
4. Close the browser and close all files.
5. If you will not be completing the Review Assignments, close the Web site.

REVIEW

Session 4.2 Quick Check

1. What is an image map?
2. What is a hotspot?
3. What are the three HTML hotspot shapes?
4. Which hotspot shape would you use to create a triangle? An oval? A square?
5. Which toolbar is used to create hotspots?
6. Which button can be used to view just an image's hotspots?
7. What is a vertex?

Practice the skills you learned in the tutorial using the same case scenario.

PRACTICE

Review Assignments

Data Files needed for this Review Assignment: cat.jpg, events.html, purrlogo.png

Trevor is creating another page for the Purr Your Request Web site that highlights the major events that have occurred in the organization over the last few years. He would like you to create bookmarks for all the sections of the page and link to them to make page navigation easier for visitors. A preview of the file is shown in Figure 4-29.

Figure 4-29 **The completed Purr Your Request Web page**

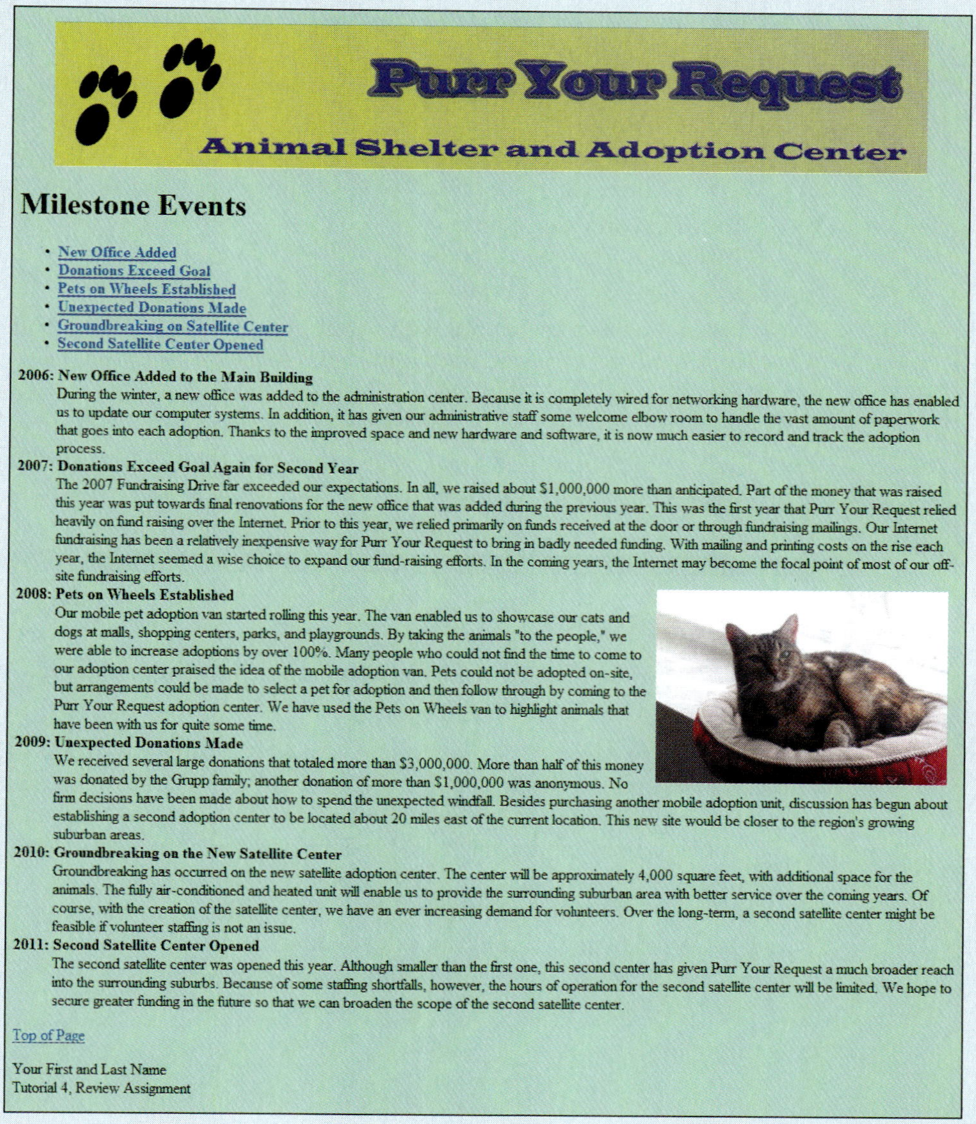

Purr Your Request

Animal Shelter and Adoption Center

Milestone Events

- New Office Added
- Donations Exceed Goal
- Pets on Wheels Established
- Unexpected Donations Made
- Groundbreaking on Satellite Center
- Second Satellite Center Opened

2006: New Office Added to the Main Building
During the winter, a new office was added to the administration center. Because it is completely wired for networking hardware, the new office has enabled us to update our computer systems. In addition, it has given our administrative staff some welcome elbow room to handle the vast amount of paperwork that goes into each adoption. Thanks to the improved space and new hardware and software, it is now much easier to record and track the adoption process.

2007: Donations Exceed Goal Again for Second Year
The 2007 Fundraising Drive far exceeded our expectations. In all, we raised about $1,000,000 more than anticipated. Part of the money that was raised this year was put towards final renovations for the new office that was added during the previous year. This was the first year that Purr Your Request relied heavily on fund raising over the Internet. Prior to this year, we relied primarily on funds received at the door or through fundraising mailings. Our Internet fundraising has been a relatively inexpensive way for Purr Your Request to bring in badly needed funding. With mailing and printing costs on the rise each year, the Internet seemed a wise choice to expand our fund-raising efforts. In the coming years, the Internet may become the focal point of most of our off-site fundraising efforts.

2008: Pets on Wheels Established
Our mobile pet adoption van started rolling this year. The van enabled us to showcase our cats and dogs at malls, shopping centers, parks, and playgrounds. By taking the animals "to the people," we were able to increase adoptions by over 100%. Many people who could not find the time to come to our adoption center praised the idea of the mobile adoption van. Pets could not be adopted on-site, but arrangements could be made to select a pet for adoption and then follow through by coming to the Purr Your Request adoption center. We have used the Pets on Wheels van to highlight animals that have been with us for quite some time.

2009: Unexpected Donations Made
We received several large donations that totaled more than $3,000,000. More than half of this money was donated by the Grupp family; another donation of more than $1,000,000 was anonymous. No firm decisions have been made about how to spend the unexpected windfall. Besides purchasing another mobile adoption unit, discussion has begun about establishing a second adoption center to be located about 20 miles east of the current location. This new site would be closer to the region's growing suburban areas.

2010: Groundbreaking on the New Satellite Center
Groundbreaking has occurred on the new satellite adoption center. The center will be approximately 4,000 square feet, with additional space for the animals. The fully air-conditioned and heated unit will enable us to provide the surrounding suburban area with better service over the coming years. Of course, with the creation of the satellite center, we have an ever increasing demand for volunteers. Over the long-term, a second satellite center might be feasible if volunteer staffing is not an issue.

2011: Second Satellite Center Opened
The second satellite center was opened this year. Although smaller than the first one, this second center has given Purr Your Request a much broader reach into the surrounding suburbs. Because of some staffing shortfalls, however, the hours of operation for the second satellite center will be limited. We hope to secure greater funding in the future so that we can broaden the scope of the second satellite center.

Top of Page

Your First and Last Name
Tutorial 4, Review Assignment

Complete the following:

1. If necessary, start Expression Web, close any open sites, and open the Tutorial.04 Web site. Reset the workspace layout.
2. If necessary, expand the Data Files folder and the Review folder to display the contents of the Review folder.

3. Open the **events.html** file and save the file as **eventsnew.html** in the same folder.
4. Locate the first bold heading below the bulleted list and then select the text *2006: New Office Added to the Main Building*.
5. Create a bookmark from the selected text using the default name.
6. Create bookmarks for the remaining headings in the document: *2007: Donations Exceed Goal Again for Second Year*, *2008: Pets on Wheels Established*, *2009: Unexpected Donations Made*, *2010: Groundbreaking on the New Satellite Center*, and *2011: Second Satellite Center Opened*.
7. Press the Ctrl+Home keys to position the insertion point at the top of the page.
8. Below the Purr Your Request logo, select the words *New Office Added*. Create a link to the New Office Added to the Main Building bookmark.
9. Create links to the remaining bookmarks you created earlier.
10. Press the Ctrl+Home keys to move to the top of the page, and create a bookmark named "pagetop."
11. At the bottom of the page, select the words *Top of Page* and create a link to the pagetop bookmark.
12. Press the Ctrl+End keys to position the insertion point at the end of the document. On two lines, type the following (substitute your name as appropriate):

    Your First and Last Name
    Tutorial 4, Review Assignment
13. Save the **eventsnew.html** file.
14. Open the **eventsnew.html** file in your browser. Test all links. Your document should look similar to the one shown in Figure 4-29.
15. Close all documents. If you are not completing the next assignment, close your browser, and then close the Web site.
16. Submit the completed file to your instructor, either in printed or electronic form, as requested.

Use the skills you learned in the tutorial to create a Web page for a produce supplier.

APPLY

Case Problem 1

Data Files needed for this Case Problem: apple.html, applelogo.gif, apples.jpg, granny.html, red.html, red.jpg

Mainly Maine Apples Mainly Maine Apples is a large regional distributor of apples. Headquartered near Lake Champlain, New York, the company supplies apples throughout the northeastern United States and eastern Canada. Iris Walters, marketing manager at Mainly Maine Apples, has approached you about creating an informational Web page about the company's products. She wants her customers to be aware of the many varieties of apples that are available in the marketplace from Mainly Maine Apples. You'll create a Web page that describes the benefits and characteristics of several of the most popular varieties of apples that Mainly Maine Apples sells. A preview of the file is shown in Figure 4-30.

Figure 4-30 **The completed Mainly Maine Apples Web page**

Mainly Maine Apples

Mainly Maine Apples is one of the largest sellers of apples in New England. We supply apples from New York, Vermont, New Hampshire, Massachusetts, and of course, the state of Maine. Apples are eaten all over the world. It may not be exactly true that "an apple a day keeps the doctor away," but apples certainly do provide health benefits in the form of fiber and nutrients. Depending on the variety and the size of the apple, most apples have fewer than 100 calories, and supply calcium, phosphorus, iron, potassium, foliate, and vitamins A and C. We stock all of the varieties described below.

When you think of an apple, you probably are thinking about a red delicious apple. Known for their deep red color and gloss, these apples have a crispness that's hard to match. Red delicious apples are grown big, probably because of their popularity as both a dessert and a snack. These apples are best when eaten raw, so they are not the best apples for baking. Truly a signature fruit if there ever was one, the red delicious apple is the traditional lunchbox snack for millions of American schoolchildren and many millions more worldwide.

Although you might think based on the name alone that golden delicious apples are similar to red delicious apples, they are not closely related. Golden delicious apples have a thinner skin than their red delicious namesakes. They are also firmer and quite a bit juicier than red delicious apples. While red delicious apples are more tubular and can have broad shoulders, golden delicious apples are round and tend to be wider than red delicious apples.

The key here, however, is in the texture: golden delicious apples stand up better to baking, so they are the ideal ingredient in strudels and pies. During baking, golden delicious apples tend not to shrivel, and although they lose their crispness, they don't lose any of their wonderful flavor. Can you think of a better way to top off a meal than with a slice of apple pie? Don't scrimp on the whipped cream or the ice cream in summer.

McIntosh apples were first developed by John McIntosh in the late 1800s, and are today the top-selling apples in North America. McIntosh apples are round and mostly red. At times it can be difficult to tell when they are actually ripe because they retain blushes of green when they ripen. Unlike red delicious apples, which have a beige tint to their flesh, the flesh of McIntosh apples is white. McIntosh apples produce plenty of juice, so this variety is a proven winner when it comes to making apple juice. Good for baking as well as snacking, there is no reason not to choose this apple for any purpose. It's delicious any month of the year.

Although there was a John McIntosh, there wasn't a Granny Smith who developed the Granny Smith apple. Bucking the trend towards red apples as emblems of what an apple should be, Granny Smith apples are green. Granny Smiths are probably one of the most successfully developed green apples ever to reach the North American marketplace. These apples are popular because their flavor strikes a balance between sweetness and tartness. In addition to being appreciated by people, Granny Smith apples are greatly appreciated by the food industry, as they can be refrigerated for several months before they reach the market. Granny Smith apples make their way into pies, but they are most well known for their use in applesauce.

The variety known as Rome apples is named for its birthplace, near Rome, Ohio. Although Rome apples don't have the deep red color of red delicious apples, many people prefer their blush of red over red delicious. Rome apples are known for their slightly tart taste. While not a snacking favorite, the flavor of Rome apples is ideal for making apple cider. Some people, however, do prefer to add nutmeg or cinnamon to their cider.

Gala apples are everything that their name suggests, with a golden skin flushed with red throughout. The flesh has a creamy yellow color. This is a great apple for snacking, rather than baking. Though gala apples certainly stand out on the basis of their appearance, some folks find it hard to discern when the apple is ripe: just look for a nice blend of both yellow and red throughout.

CONTACT US
Mainly Maine Applies | 25 Cloverdale Road | North Trevor, ME 04019
mainlymaine@freeport.net

Your First and Last Name
Tutorial 4, Case Problem 1

Complete the following:

1. If necessary, start Expression Web, close any open sites, and open the Tutorial.04 Web site. Reset the workspace layout.
2. If necessary, expand the Data Files folder and the Case1 folder to display the contents of the Case1 folder.
3. Open the **apple.html** file and save the file as **applenew.html** in the same folder.
4. In the first sentence of the second paragraph, select the words *red delicious apple*. Use those words as the link text to create a link to an existing Web page named red.html, which is also in the Case1 folder.
5. Open the **red.html** file. At the bottom of the page, select the words *Go to the Mainly Maine Apples Home Page* and link those words to the applenew.html page.
6. Save and close the red.html page.
7. In the applenew.html file, scroll down if necessary to the first sentence of the sixth paragraph, select the words *Granny Smith apple*, and then create a link to the Web page granny.html, which is also in the Case1 folder.

8. Open the **granny.html** file. Link the words *Go to the Mainly Maine Apples home page* to the applenew.html page.
9. Save and close the granny.html page.
10. In the last line of the document, use the text **mainlymaine@freeport.net** to create an email link to mainlymaine@freeport.net as the email address and **Maine Apples** as the subject.
11. EXPLORE Use the Page Properties to change the active link color to yellow.
12. Press the Ctrl+End keys to position the insertion point at the end of the document. Type the following on two lines, substituting your name as appropriate:
    Your First and Last Name
    Tutorial 4, Case Problem 1
13. Save **applenew.html**, open it in your browser, and then test all the links. Your document should look similar to the one shown in Figure 4-30.
14. Close all documents. If you are not completing the next assignment, close your browser, and then close the Web site.
15. Submit the completed files to your instructor, either in printed or electronic form, as requested.

Expand your skills while formatting a Web page about an information technology consulting company.

APPLY

Case Problem 2

Data Files needed for this Case Problem: gantt.html, info.gif, pert.html, spiral.html, techlogo.gif

Spiral-Technic Spiral-Technic provides information technology and systems consulting throughout the United States. You have been asked to create a new Web page for the company that outlines the different areas in which Spiral-Technic provides consulting services to its customers. A preview of the file is shown in Figure 4-31.

Figure 4-31 The completed Spiral-Technic Web page

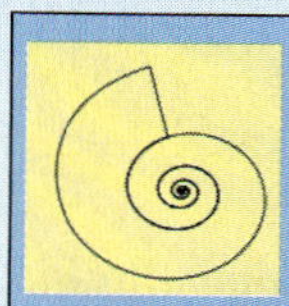

Spiral-Technic

We provide many services to the IT industry, such as Help Desk support, Internet and Intranet development, and database services and management. Below is a partial listing of the services we provide.

- Help Desk Support
- Internet and Intranet Development
- Networking and Security
- Database Management
- Project Management

Help Desk Support

Your help desk is a vital part of your company. Whenever someone in your company has become unproductive because of a technology issue, you are losing money every second that person can't perform his or her job. We provide help desk software to track common problems and determine if the problem relates to hardware, software, or training. If the problem relates to training, we provide on-site or off-site training for your staff. We even have online courses for those interested in using their true downtime or for "lunch and learn classes" and for before or after work seminars. If it's a hardware problem, we'll identify the nature of the problem right down to the individual part. If it's a software problem, we'll go in and rewrite the software subroutines if necessary to get the product to work as you intended. We provide all levels of support for help desk analysts and managers, system analysis, and technical trainers.

Typical tasks we perform in this area:

- Installing and debugging new software installations
- End user training

Internet and Intranet Development

Today, a company cannot survive without a Web presence. We will provide you with all the services you need regarding HTML/XTHML, XML (Extensible Markup Language), JavaScript, Java, and ASP (Active Server Pages). We can provide you with all the e-commerce tools you need to run your business successfully on the Web. We handle all aspects of client/server technology. We not only get your servers up and running, but we keep them that way with no downtime. We know that every second of lost business can have a negative effect on your bottom line. Our business is to keep you in business.

Typical tasks we perform in this area:

- Internet and intranet setup and maintenance
- Server installation and maintenance
- Software installation and maintenance

Networking and Security

Networking continues to be in high demand on all levels. In addition to installing new hardware and software to keep your network up to date, we also are deeply involved in maintaining network security. In this day of high-profile security breaches, the importance of having 100% reliable network security cannot be greater. We are experts at preventing network intrusion. We feel it is better to be proactive rather than reactive. In addition to the obvious and unnecessary loss of productivity from downtime because of computer intrusion or disruption, it's the intangible costs — the loss of reputation and consumer confidence in your company's ability to provide secure network transactions that are paramount. We can address all your security needs to identify threats both inside and outside your company.

Typical tasks we perform in this area:

- Local area network administration
- Network security and loss prevention
- Risk assessment

Database Management

Your business depends on its databases for its livelihood. We can provide you with database hardware and software installation. In addition, we can convert from legacy systems to contemporary database systems. We also have great expertise in setting up database software for human resources, sales management, contact management, asset management, inventory management, plant management, and e-commerce. Security is also of great concern with your databases, so we will train your staff in the software needed to lock up your data from intrusion.

Typical tasks we perform in this area:

- Software installation
- Legacy system conversions
- Database management

Project Management

We know that successful project management is critical to your company's success. We know that. From the initial planning session to the execution stage, you need to be able to determine whether your project is on task or not. We can provide you with the proper software for all aspects of project management, including **PERT and Gantt charts.**

More Info

Typical tasks we perform in this area:

- Proposal development
- Legacy project funding
- Project scheduling and time management
- All aspects of project management reporting

Please call us at: 890-204-3333

Back to Top of Page

Your First and Last Name
Tutorial 4, Case Problem 2

Complete the following:

1. If necessary, start Expression Web, close any open sites, and open the Tutorial.04 Web site. Reset the workspace layout.
2. If necessary, expand the Data Files folder and the Case2 folder to display the contents of the Case2 folder.
3. Open the **spiral.html** file and save the file as **spiralnew.html** in the same folder.
4. Create bookmarks for the following five h2 headings: Help Desk Support, Internet and Intranet Development, Networking and Security, Database Management, and Project Management.
5. Use the bulleted list at the top of the page and create links to the five bookmarks you just created.
6. Click before the *S* in *Spiral-Technic* in the h1 heading at the top of the page. Create a bookmark named *top*.
7. At the bottom of the page, link the words *Back to Top of Page* to the top bookmark.

EXPLORE

8. Below the Project Management section, use the info.gif image, which is an image of the words *More Info*, to create a link to a new document. Name the new document **infonew.html**.
9. On two lines, type the following, substituting your name as appropriate:

   Your First and Last Name
   Tutorial 4, Infonew Page
10. Save and then close the **infonew.html** file.
11. In the spiralnew.html document, in the last sentence of the paragraph below the Project Management heading, locate the phrase *PERT and Gantt charts*. Select the words *PERT and Gantt charts*, and create a link to the pert.html file, which is also in the Case2 folder.

EXPLORE

12. Open the pert.html page. Use the existing text to create a link to the home page (spiralnew.html) and to gantt.html. Save and close the pert.html file.

EXPLORE

13. Open the gantt.html page. Use the existing text to create a link to the home page (spiralnew.html) and to pert.html. Save and close the gantt.html file.
14. In the spiralnew.html file, press the Ctrl+End keys to position the insertion point at the end of the document. On two lines, type the following, substituting your name as appropriate:

    Your First and Last Name
    Tutorial 4, Case Problem 2
15. Save the **spiralnew.html** file.
16. Open the **spiralnew.html** file in your default browser. Test all links on all pages. Your spiralnew.html document should look similar to the one shown in Figure 4-31.
17. Close all documents. If you are not completing the next assignment, close your browser, and then close the Web site.
18. Submit the completed files to your instructor, either in printed or electronic form, as requested.

Use and expand on what you've learned to format a Web page for an athletic training facility.

APPLY

Case Problem 3

Data Files needed for this Case Problem: map.gif, mapinfo.html, training.html

Blue Lake Athletic Training Facility The Blue Lake Athletic Training Facility is one of the largest athletic training facilities in Colorado. Located about 30 miles east of Denver, the Blue Lake facility hosts many high school and college athletes who want to improve their skills in baseball, football, and soccer. Manuel Ramirez, the director of the Blue Lake facility, has asked for your help in adding links to an online map of Blue Lake's training facilities. The target pages will display more information about what the training camp has to offer, including detailed information about each building and training facility. A preview of the file is shown in Figure 4-32.

Figure 4-32 **The completed Blue Lake Web page**

Blue Lake Athletic Training Facility

Blue Lake Athletic Training Facility is ready this summer for baseball, basketball, soccer, and football camp. All participants in Summer Session A should report to Havner Dorm at 8 a.m. on June 1. Summer Session A lasts until June 28. Summer Session B participants should report to Parker Dorm at 8 a.m. on July 5. Summer Session B lasts until August 2. All registrants and guests should park in Parking Lot A for the first-day registration and orientation activities.

Please do not park near the athletic fields or by the Collins Gymnasium. There is special reserved parking for the first-day registration in Parking Lot A only.

There will be a welcoming reception brunch at 10 a.m. on your first day of camp. You may bring up to two guests with you to the brunch. Orientation and room assignments will be given out after the brunch. First-day practices will begin at 2 p.m. (weather permitting). In case of inclement weather, first-day practice will take place in the Collins Gymnasium.

Click on the map below to learn more information about the dining and dorm facilities.

For more sports information, *visit the ESPN Web site*.

Procedure for First Day Activities:

1. Sign in
2. Check bags and luggage
3. Report to dorm room
4. Attend first-day brunch
5. Attend first-day orientation
6. Practice begins at 2 p.m.

Back to Page Top

Your First and Last Name
Tutorial 4, Case Problem 3

Complete the following:

1. If necessary, start Expression Web, close any open sites, and open the Tutorial.04 Web site. Reset the workspace layout.
2. If necessary, expand the Data Files folder and the Case3 folder to display the contents of the Case3 folder.
3. Open the **training.html** file and save the file as **trainingnew.html** in the same folder.
4. EXPLORE Below the map image, select the words *visit the ESPN Web site*. Create a hyperlink to *http://www.espn.com*. In the Insert Hyperlink dialog box, click the ScreenTip button and create a ScreenTip with the text *visit the ESPN site*.
5. If necessary, display the Pictures toolbar, and then click anywhere on the map image.
6. Use the Pictures toolbar to create a hotspot for the Havner Dorm rectangle shape and link it to the mapinfo.html page.

7. Create a hotspot for the Perkins Dining Facility circle shape and link it to the mapinfo.html page.
8. Create a hotspot for the Parking Lot A polygonal shape and link it to the mapinfo.html page.
9. Create a hotspot for the Parker Dorm rectangle shape and link it to the mapinfo.html page.
10. Press the Ctrl+Home keys. At the top of the page, create a Bookmark named top.
11. Press the Ctrl+End keys. At the bottom of the page, link the words *Back to Page Top* to the top bookmark.
12. Press the Ctrl+End keys to position the insertion point at the end of the document. On two lines, type the following, substituting your name as appropriate:

    Your First and Last Name
    Tutorial 4, Case Problem 3
13. Save the **trainingnew.html** file.
14. Open the **trainingnew.html** file in your browser. Test all links. The document should be similar to the one shown in Figure 4-32. Pass the pointer over the hotspots and test the ScreenTips, but bear in mind that not all browsers support ScreenTips.
15. Close all documents. If you are not completing the next assignment, close your browser, and then close the Web site.
16. Submit the completed file to your instructor, either in printed or electronic form, as requested.

Use the figures provided to format a Web page for an antique shop.

CREATE

Case Problem 4

Data Files needed for this Case Problem: antique.html, antiquelogo.gif, chair.html, chair.jpg, dresser.jpg, dresser.html

Old for New Antique Shoppe The Old for New Antique Shoppe is an antique shop in Rawlings, New Hampshire. Antiquing is popular in New England, so the Old for New Antique Shoppe strives to differentiate itself by catering to newcomers to antiquing. The shop has an Antique Club that meets twice monthly to further promote interest in antiquing and the shop itself. Ted Harris, the shop owner, has asked you to create a Web page for the Old for New Antique Shoppe. Complete the following:

1. If necessary, start Expression Web, close any open sites, and open the Tutorial.04 Web site. Reset the workspace layout.
2. If necessary, expand the Data Files folder and the Case4 folder to display the contents of the Case4 folder.
3. Open the **antique.html** file and save the file as **antiquenew.html** in the same folder.
4. In the body of the document, add the following:
    - A bookmark
    - A link to a bookmark
    - A link to another page (use the text at the bottom of the page as the link text)
    - A link to an external Web site (use the text at the bottom of the page as the link text)
    - On the dresser and chair pages, create links back to the antiquenew home page
    - Customized hyperlink and hover hyperlink colors

5. Press the Ctrl+End keys to position the insertion point at the end of the document. On two lines, type the following, substituting your name as appropriate:
   Your First and Last Name
   Tutorial 4, Case Problem 4
6. Save your **antiquenew.html** file.
7. Open the **antiquenew.html** file in your browser. Test all links. If you notice any errors, return to Expression Web and correct them, and then retest the Web page in your browser.
8. Close the browser, close all documents, and then close the Web site.
9. Submit the completed files to your instructor, either in printed or electronic form, as requested.

ENDING DATA FILES

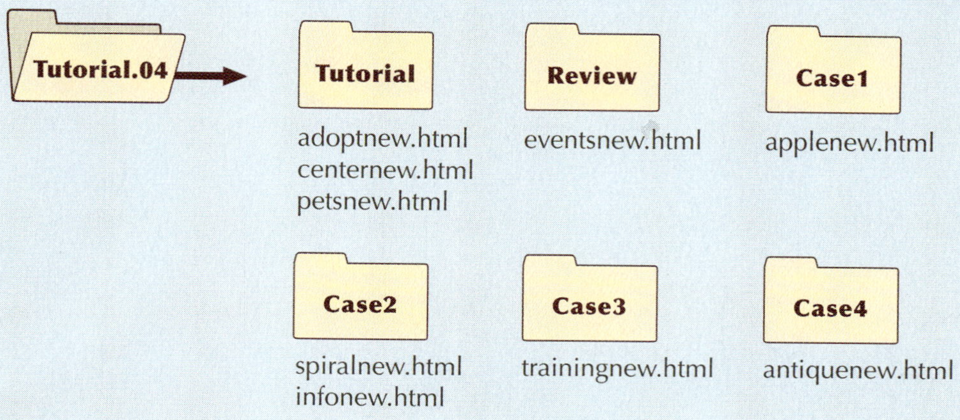

TUTORIAL 5

Formatting with CSS

Using CSS to Format Text and Pages

OBJECTIVES

Session 5.1
- Evaluate why CSS styles are used
- Determine where to write styles
- Create an element selector style
- Implement the font properties on a Web page

Session 5.2
- Create a style based on element, class, and ID selectors
- Apply and modify styles
- Create an external style sheet
- Attach a CSS style sheet to an HTML file
- Run a CSS report

Case | *Gasden Flooring*

Gasden Flooring is one of the nation's largest retailers of discount flooring. Headquartered in Gasden, Wisconsin, the company first began selling lumber and flooring more than 75 years ago. Gasden Flooring has flourished to become one of the major competitors in providing residential and commercial customers with numerous types of flooring. Each year, Gasden Flooring has a clearance sale to eliminate excess stock and discontinued items. The store places all items on sale, but its largest discounts are on discontinued items. Tyrell Johnson, the marketing manager at Gasden Flooring, wants you to develop a Web page that will provide its online customers with more information about this year's annual sale. You have started developing the Web page; you have also been provided with a logo image that you'll incorporate into the page.

STARTING DATA FILES

Tutorial.05 →

- **Tutorial**: gasden.html
- **Review**: gasdenlogo.png, rug.html, rug.jpg, rugstyles.css
- **Case1**: shoes.html
- **Case2**: move.html
- **Case3**: fonts.html
- **Case4**: site.html

SESSION 5.1 VISUAL OVERVIEW

Clicking the Apply new style to document selection check box immediately applies the style.

The **Selector** is the HTML element or class to be styled.

The **Define in** box determines the scope of the style.

The **Category bar** is used to select a group of CSS properties.

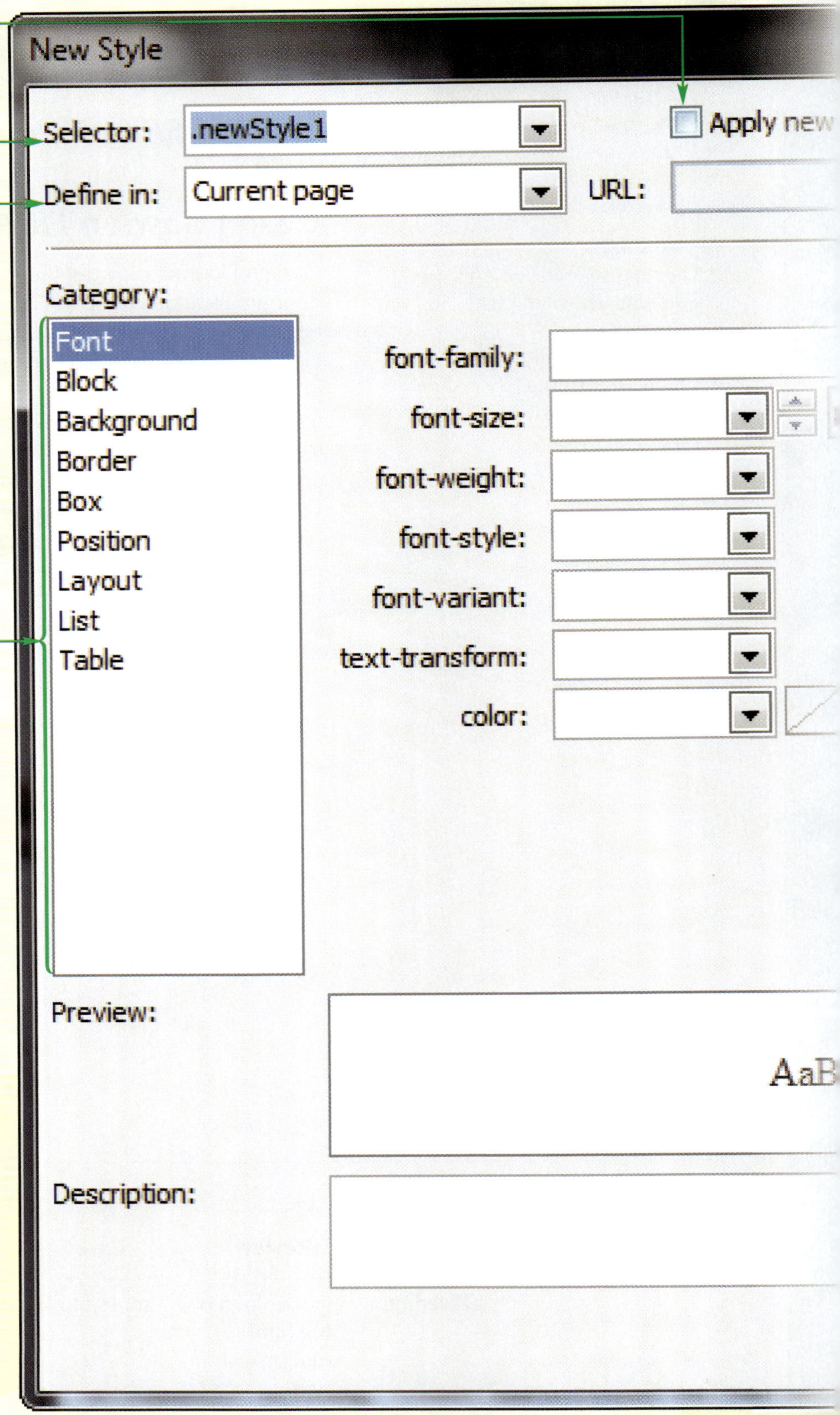

THE NEW STYLE DIALOG BOX

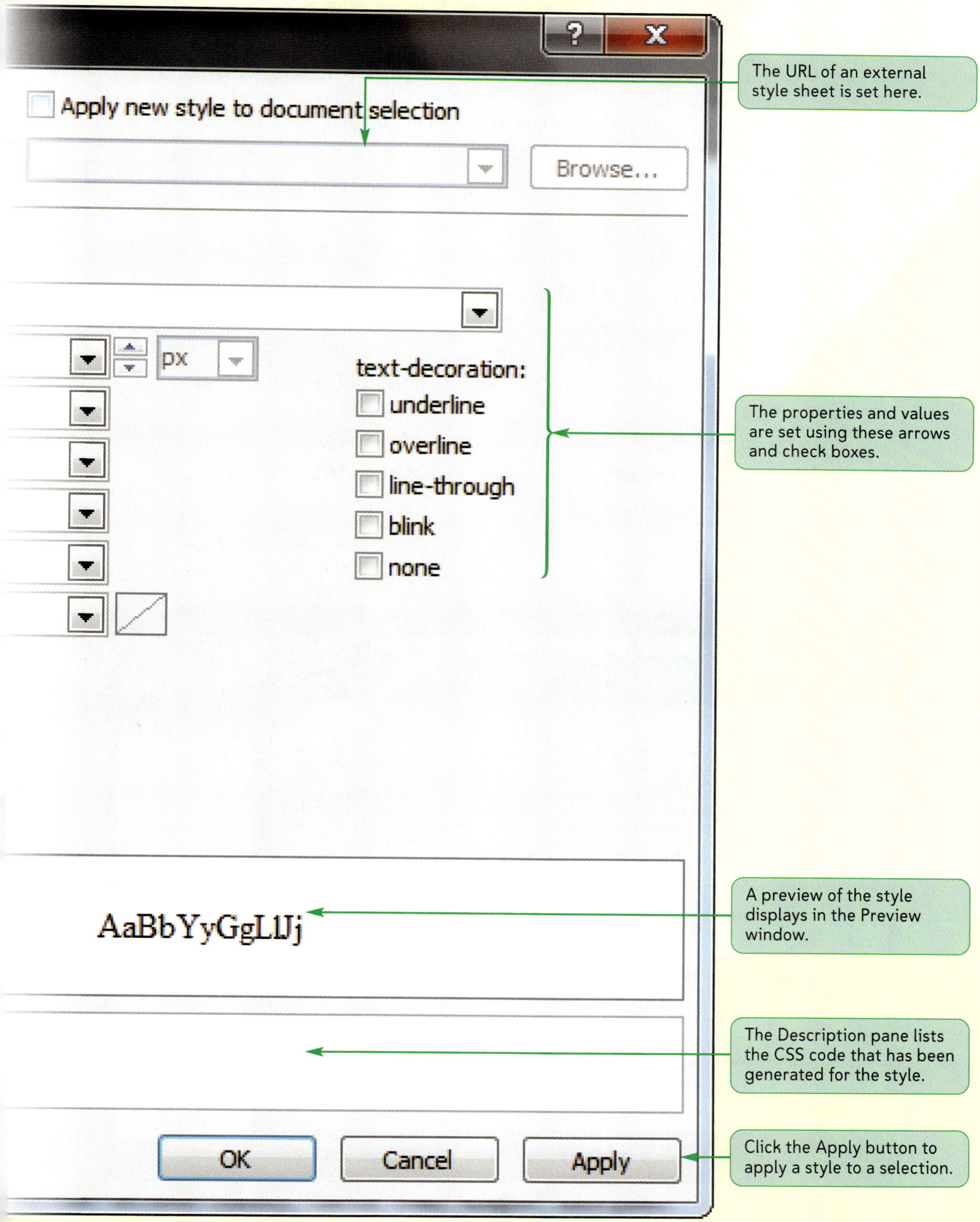

Introducing Cascading Style Sheets

Hypertext Markup Language (HTML) is the computer language used to create Web pages. Using HTML, Web page authors create code to describe the structure of a Web page in terms of paragraphs, lists, tables, forms, and so forth. **Cascading Style Sheets (CSS)** is the computer language used for describing the presentation of Web pages, such as the colors and the fonts you see when a Web page appears in the browser. By separating structure from presentation, it is easier to modify and share the CSS code so that the same code can be used to format many Web pages. In this tutorial, you'll learn how to use CSS to deliver the same presentation across multiple Web pages, rather than formatting a single Web page using the Common toolbar.

The Web page you are developing does not currently include any formatting. You'll start by opening the file in Expression Web.

To open the Tutorial.05 Web site:

1. If necessary, start Expression Web, reset the workspace layout, and then close any toolbars other than the Common toolbar.
2. Open the Tutorial.05 Web site and then expand the Data Files and Tutorial folders.
3. Open the **gasden.html** file and then save it as **gasdennew.html** in the same folder.
4. Close all panels other than the Apply Styles and Manage Styles panels.

   The workspace should appear as shown in Figure 5-1.

Figure 5-1 The gasden.html page

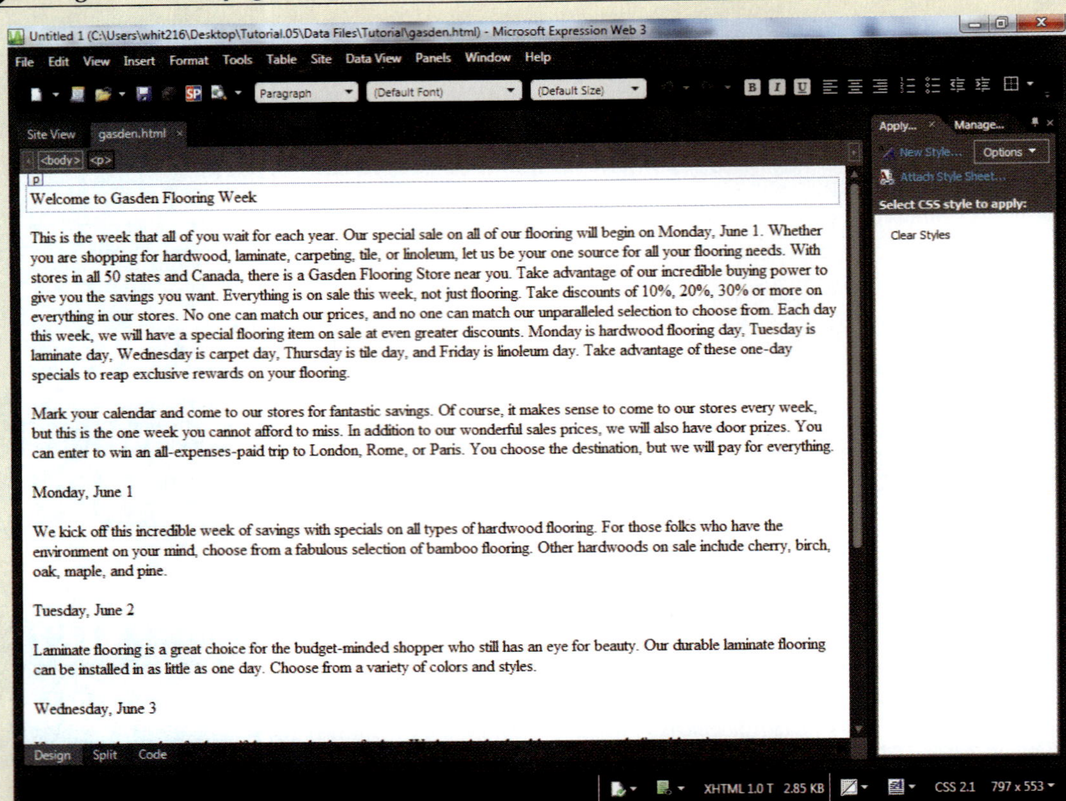

Next, you'll help Tyrell understand the importance of Cascading Style Sheets and their relationship to HTML.

Recognizing the Importance of CSS

In an earlier tutorial, you practiced formatting text for an individual Web page using the Common toolbar. You applied a principle called **direct formatting**, which is formatting text without the use of CSS styles. A Web site, however, can consist of hundreds, thousands, or even tens of thousands of pages. If you were to use direct formatting for all your Web pages, and you wanted to change the appearance of some or all of the pages on your Web site, you would have to open, revise, and save each one of those pages. What if your business required you to change the Web site's appearance every season, or every month, or even every day? To revise so many pages so often would be a very time-consuming task. This is where CSS comes to the rescue.

By using CSS, you can create one or more documents that control the appearance of some or all of the pages on your Web site. CSS can help you to format and revise an unlimited number of Web pages easily and efficiently. In addition, CSS offers many other advantages:

- *Greater consistency in your Web site*—You can apply styles you create in one document to some or all of the other pages in your Web site to ensure a consistent design.
- *Easily modified code*—When you modify code to change the style of one page, all of the pages in your Web site can change, saving you valuable development time.
- *More flexible formatting*—You can use CSS to format and position text in ways that you cannot when using HTML alone.
- *Greater functionality*—CSS provides access to many features common to word-processing programs that are unavailable in HTML, such as tab indents, line spacing, and margins.

Ideally, all browsers would provide **cross-browser support**, displaying all of the CSS properties and values in the same way. However, none of the major browsers, including Firefox, Safari, Opera, Chrome, and Internet Explorer, support all the features of CSS, and these browsers do not render the features they support in a consistent manner. The most recent versions of these browsers do the best job of displaying CSS features. However, you must expect that visitors to your Web site will view your Web pages using different browsers and different versions of each browser, so it's a good idea to test your pages in at least the current and prior version of each browser. If you see problems with a particular browser, try to address those issues.

Understanding How Styles Are Written

Using CSS, you can change how an HTML element appears in the browser. For example, the HTML *strong* element makes text appear as bold, but the strong element does not change the font, size, or color of the text. Using CSS, you can create a *style* for the strong element so that whenever you use that element, *you* control how the strong element displays text in the browser. For example, you could create a style to format any strong text on your Web page not just to appear in bold, but also to appear in the Arial font, in a larger type size, and in red.

A CSS **style** is a description of how to present Web page content. A CSS style is composed of three parts: a selector, a property, and a value. The **selector** identifies the element, class, or ID you are applying a style to. The **property** specifies the aspect of the selector to modify. The **value** indicates the manner or extent to which the selector is modified. When you create a style in Expression Web, the CSS code is generated automatically. For example, the CSS code to have all h1 elements appear in blue would look like this:

```
h1 {
  color: blue;
}
```

Determining Where to Write Styles

CSS styles can come from more than one source. You apply different source types to HTML code in different ways. Each browser has its own styles as well. A **style sheet** is a collection of styles, and is most often written in two places: within an HTML document or as a separate file that contains only CSS code. An **internal style sheet** is one where the HTML code and the CSS code are in the same HTML file. An **external style sheet** is a separate file that contains only CSS code.

Creating External Styles

External style sheets can format as few or as many pages as you want on your Web site. Therefore, external style sheets are the preferred method for writing CSS code. The style sheet code is usually preceded by a **CSS comment**, which documents the external style sheet. The comment might identify the author of the style sheet, the date the file was created or last modified, and the Web pages or categories of Web pages that the style sheet is intended to format. A CSS comment is created differently from an HTML comment. The text for the comment is preceded by /* and followed with */, as in the following example:

```
/* This is a CSS comment */
```

> **TIP**
> A CSS file has a different icon in the Folder List panel than an HTML file.

Only CSS code is contained in the CSS external style sheet. When you save your CSS file, the file must be named with the filename extension of .css, not .html. Do not include spaces in the filename, and do not begin the filename with a number. After the external style sheet has been written and saved as a CSS file, you must enter code in each of the HTML documents that will use the style sheet. The HTML **link element** is used to attach a CSS style sheet to an HTML file. Once a style sheet is attached, the HTML file uses the CSS code in the style sheet to format the contents of the HTML file. Expression Web creates the <link> tag code for you and uses the Folder List panel to keep track of the location of the CSS file.

Using Internal Styles

> **TIP**
> Expression Web can attach one or more style sheets to as few or as many files in your Web site as you want.

An **internal style** is a style in which the CSS code is entered in the <head> section of an HTML document. An internal style is also referred to as an **embedded style**. Internal styles are used only in the document in which they are written, and are placed using the style element. Expression Web writes most of your styles as internal styles, creating the code for the start <style> tag and the end </style> tag. The CSS code is written between these two tags. By developing your pages using internal styles, you have the code right at hand so that you can modify it as needed. Once the page is finalized and the code is the way you want it, you can use the Manage Styles panel to create an external style sheet and then move the internal styles to the external style sheet.

Using Inline Styles

An **inline style** is a style that is written in the <body> section of an HTML document. Inline styles format just a section of text. Using inline styles is similar to direct formatting, so you should use inline styles sparingly. To revise an inline style, you must find the style and then manually revise it, which can be quite tedious. The more inline styles you use, the more you defeat the goal of separating structure from presentation. Expression Web creates an inline style for the <body> element when you use the Page Properties dialog box to change the background color for the page. Figure 5-2 summarizes where styles are written and what they format.

Figure 5-2 Where styles are written

Type of CSS Style	Where You Write the CSS Code	Formats
External	In a document separate from the HTML document	Some or all of the pages in a Web site
Internal	In the <head> section of an HTML document	Only the document in which the styles are written
Inline	In the <body> section of an HTML document	A section of text within the document body

Creating Structure and Styles with the Common Toolbar

> **TIP**
> Depending on your monitor size and screen resolution, you might not see the words *Apply Styles* on the Apply Styles panel tab. Instead, you might see those words abbreviated as *Apply St....*

You might have noticed in prior tutorials that as you clicked buttons on the Common toolbar, the Apply Styles panel became populated with styles. Not all of the buttons on the Common toolbar create styles, however. The main purpose of the Common toolbar is to create structure on the Web page by entering HTML code. Some HTML elements create formatting along with structure, though. You'll begin showing Tyrell which buttons on the Common toolbar create structure alone and which buttons create both structure and styles.

To create structure using the Common toolbar:

1. Click anywhere in the *Welcome to Gasden Flooring Week* text at the top of the page, and then click the **p** Code tab above that text to select it.
2. Click the **Bold** button on the Common toolbar.

   The text is formatted in bold, but a style does not appear in the Apply Styles panel.
3. With the text still selected, click the **Italic** button on the Common toolbar.

   The text is now both bold and italic, but again a style has not been created.
4. Click the **Bold** button and then click the **Italic** button on the Common toolbar to restore the original formatting.
5. With the text still selected, click the **Center** button on the Common toolbar.

   The text is now centered, and the .style1 style now appears in the Apply Styles panel, preceded by a green bullet, as shown in Figure 5-3.

Figure 5-3 The first style

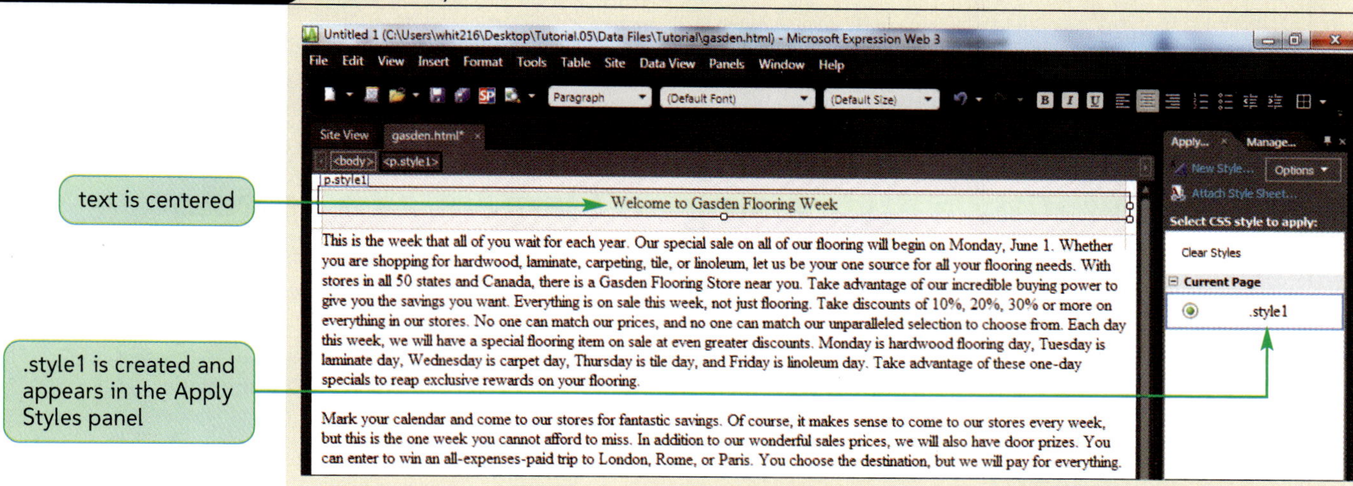

6. Again click the **Center** button on the Common toolbar to restore the original formatting.

The .style1 style no longer appears in the Apply Styles panel.

Figure 5-4 indicates whether a button on the Common toolbar creates a style.

Figure 5-4 **The Common toolbar and styles**

Button	Creates a Style
Align Text Left	Yes
Align Text Right	Yes
Bold	No
Bullets	No
Center	Yes
Decrease Indent Position	No
Font Color	Yes
Highlight	Yes
Increase Indent Position	Yes
Italic	No
Numbering	Yes
Outside Borders	Yes
Underline	Yes

When you click a button that creates a style, a green icon appears to the left of the style name. This icon, known as a **panel icon**, indicates what type of style is in use in the Apply Styles panel. The icons are blue, green, red, and yellow. Figure 5-5 describes the color or appearance of each panel icon.

Figure 5-5 **The panel icons**

Icon Color or Appearance	What It Means
Blue bullet icon	An element-based style rule
Green bullet icon	A class-based style rule
Red bullet icon	An ID-based style rule
Yellow bullet icon	An inline style rule
A circle around any bullet icon	A style rule applied to at least one HTML element on the page

Creating a Style Using an Element as a Selector

CSS has several kinds of selectors, but the three most common are element selectors, class selectors, and ID selectors. **Element selectors**, also known as **type selectors**, are used to format HTML elements. **Class selectors** are used to select a specific HTML element or format one or more elements on a Web page. **ID selectors** are used to uniquely format a single element on a Web page. The simplest type of selector is the element selector, in which you redefine the appearance of an HTML element, such as h1, p, or em. You don't have to assign a style for a characteristic the element already has. For example, by default, h1 headings appear as black, bold, and in 25-point type. You don't have to specify properties and values for those characteristics; they are that way by default.

INSIGHT

Understanding Specificity

Web pages do not have to be formatted exclusively by one type of style or style sheet. You can mix the use of internal, external, and inline styles and apply those styles to the same document. Recall that cascading is the process of applying multiple style sheets to a single HTML file. Because you can write styles as either inline, internal, or external styles, you need to know how CSS resolves conflicts between two styles. For example, let's say you formatted an h2 heading to be blue in an external style sheet, green in an internal style sheet, and red in an inline style. Which style wins out? In this instance, the winner is the inline style. The h2 heading would appear as red because inline styles prevail over both internal styles and external styles. Internal styles prevail over external styles.

Specificity determines priorities and uses a weighting method to calculate which style rule prevails if there are conflicting rules. Inline styles are the most specific type of styles, so a rule created by an inline style prevails over both an internal and an external style that attempt to format the same selector. If there is a conflict within the same style sheet, generally, *the style farthest down in the list prevails.*

Specificity only resolves style conflicts. In addition to knowing where a style is written, CSS also uses specificity to resolve style conflicts among different types of selectors. For example, what if there were conflicts between two styles in the same internal style or external style sheet?

The World Wide Web Consortium weighting methodology counts ID selectors the most, assigning them a value of 100. Class selectors have a value of 10, and element selectors have a value of 1. If two styles should conflict, these weighting values determine the calculation of which style prevails.

Tyrell would like to format the first line of the document as an h1 heading and then style the heading. You'll show Tyrell how to change the text in the first line to appear as an h1 heading. You'll show Tyrell how to create the h1 heading now.

To create an h1 heading:

1. At the top of the page, if necessary, select **Welcome to Gasden Flooring Week**.
2. Click the **Style** arrow on the Common toolbar.
3. Click **Heading 1 <h1>**. The first line is now formatted as an h1 heading.
4. Click anywhere outside the h1 heading. The text appears as shown in Figure 5-6.

Figure 5-6 The h1 heading

Tyrell would also like the subheadings Monday, June 1, Tuesday, June 2, and so forth to be styled as h2 headings. You'll show Tyrell how to create the h2 headings now.

To create the h2 headings:

1. Select the words **Monday, June 1**.
2. Click the **Style** arrow on the Common toolbar.
3. Click **Heading 2 <h2>**. The line is now formatted as an h2 heading.
4. Select the words **Tuesday, June 2**.
5. Click the **Style** arrow on the Common toolbar.
6. Click **Heading 2 <h2>**. The line is now formatted as an h2 heading.
7. Repeat this procedure to select the other days of the week and format those lines as h2 headings.
8. When you are done, click anywhere outside the headings.

   Your document should be similar to that shown in Figure 5-7.

Figure 5-7 The h2 headings

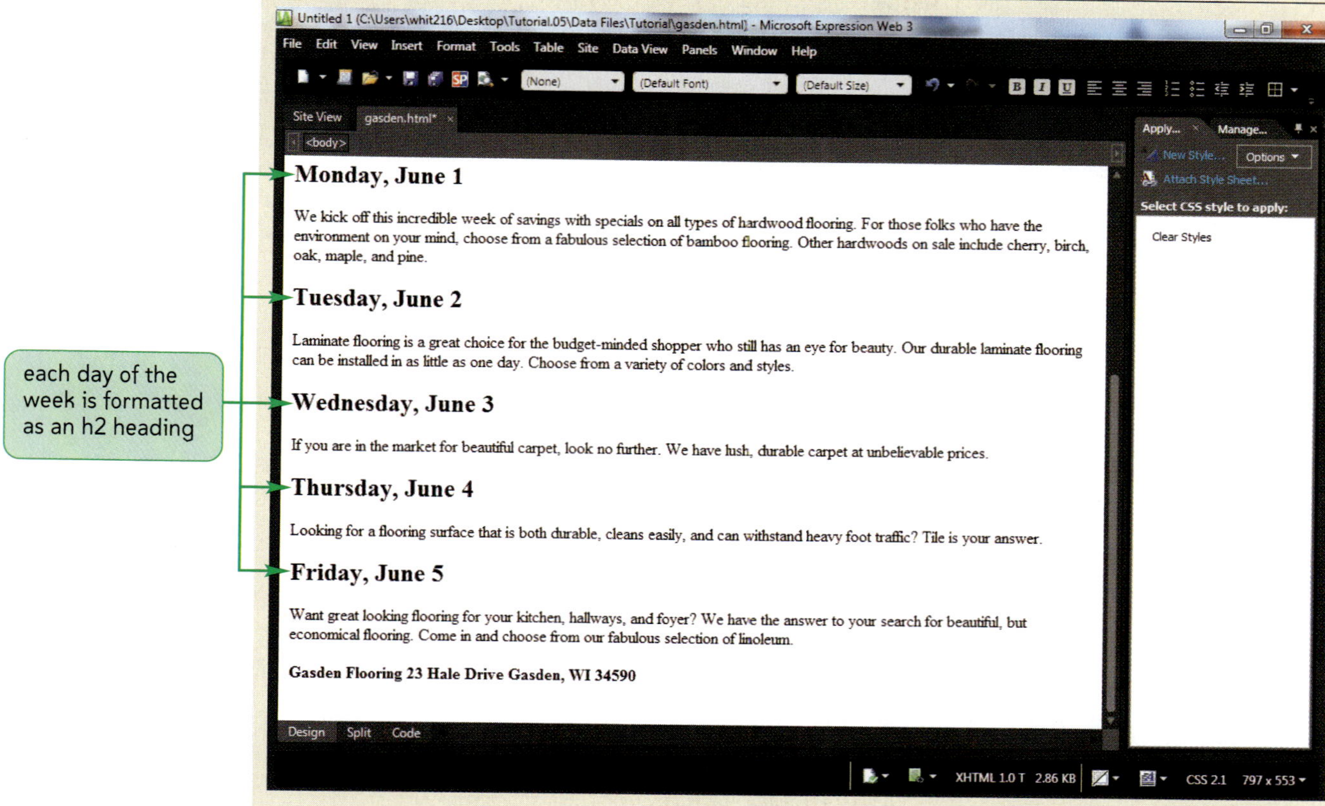

Now you'll work with Tyrell to show him some of the properties that are used to style documents. The font properties are very commonly used, so you'll start there.

Using the Font Properties

The **font properties** are used to change the appearance of text. The CSS font properties are font-family, font-size, font-style, font-weight, font-variant, and font. Figure 5-8 describes the font properties.

Figure 5-8 The Expression Web font properties

Font	ProprtyValues	What It Does	Comments
font-family	choose from the three default font families in Expression Web or create your own font family	Changes the font	Always end the list of font-family values with the name of one of the five generic font families: serif, sans-serif, monospace, cursive, or fantasy.
font-size	xx-small x-small small medium large x-large xx-large	Changes the size of type	For text, use keywords, em values, or percentage values. For print style sheets, use point values.
font-style	italic oblique normal	Makes text italic or not	Oblique is generally not supported.
font-variant	small-caps normal	Makes text appear in small capitals, generally 1 or 2 points smaller than the font size currently in effect	In larger point sizes, the first letter of each word should appear 1 or 2 points taller than the other letters in the word.
font-weight	bold bolder lighter normal *numeric value 100–900*	Makes text appear in bold or not	The keyword values *lighter* and *bolder* and the numeric values (100–900) are generally not supported.
text-transform	capitalize lowercase none uppercase	Changes the capitalization of text	The *capitalize* value is used to capitalize the first letter of each word.
color	a named color, an RGB triplet, or a hexadecimal value	Changes the color of text	Hexadecimal values are preferred.
text-decoration	underline overline line-through blink none	Generally used to underline text or not	Use underline only with links or together with overline to style headings. Do not use *blink*.

REFERENCE

Creating a CSS Style

- In the Apply Styles or Manage Styles panel, click New Style. Alternatively, click Format on the menu bar, and then click New Style.
- Choose a selector by typing or selecting it in the Selector box. For a class selector, precede the class name with a period. For an ID selector, precede the ID name with a # sign. For an inline style, choose inline style from the Selector box.
- Define the style in the current page (the default), or choose a different location in the Define in box.
- Choose an option in the Category bar, and then select choices in the appropriate boxes.
- When you have entered all the styles, click the OK button.

You'll show Tyrell how to create a CSS style that makes maximum use of the font properties. In this instance, you'll create a style for the h1 heading. Expression Web has several methods to create styles. You'll begin by showing Tyrell how to use the Apply Styles panel to open the New Style dialog box. In the New Style dialog box, the **Category bar** is the area used to group all of the available CSS properties in the Apply Style dialog box or Modify Style dialog box. The Category bar is on the left side of the New Style dialog box.

Creating a Font Family

TIP

HTML has five generic font families: serif, sans-serif, monospace, fantasy, and cursive.

The **font-family property** is used to identify the font that is currently in use. Expression Web has several predefined font families, but you can create your own font families. Tyrell would like an interesting font that will serve to catch the attention of Web site visitors, so you'll use the Gill Sans font for the h1 text. A very helpful feature of Expression Web is that as you create the style, you see a sample of the style in the New Style dialog box Preview window.

To create a font family:

1. Click anywhere in the h1 heading text at the top of the page.
2. Click the **h1** Code tab to select the h1 heading text.
3. In the Apply Styles panel, click **New Style**.

   The New Style dialog box opens. Take a moment to study the dialog box choices, as shown in Figure 5-9.

Figure 5-9 The New Style dialog box

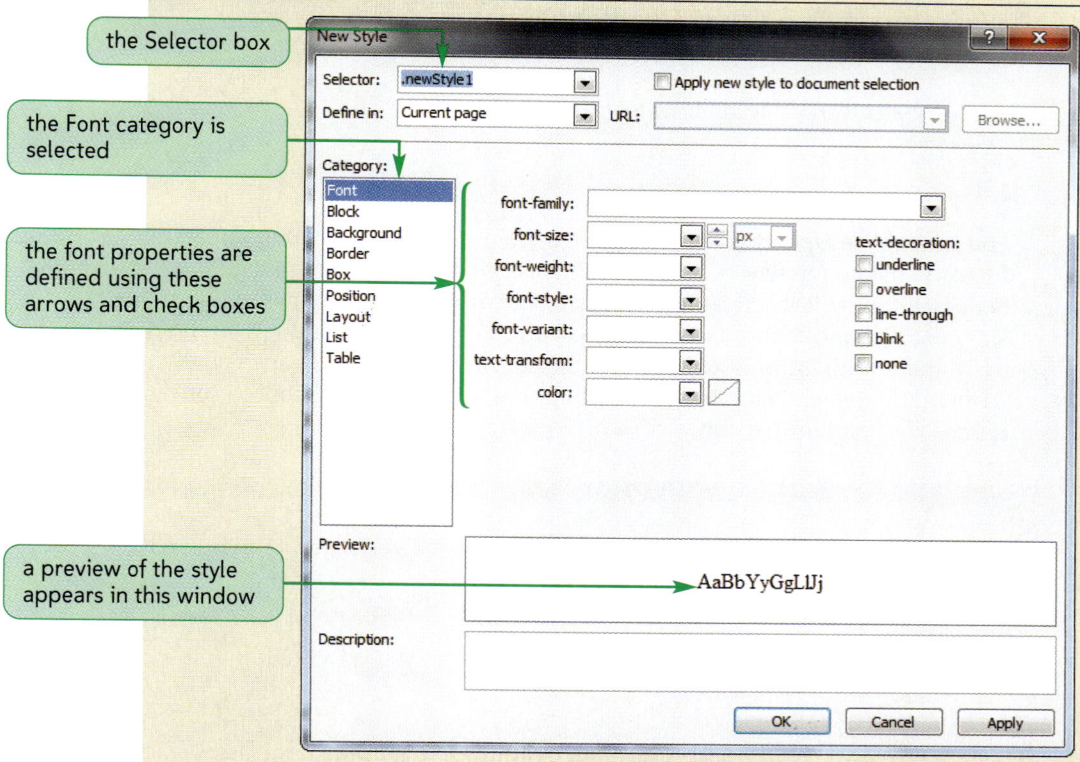

4. Click the **Selector** arrow, scroll down the list of elements, and then click **h1**.

5. In the New Style dialog box, click the **font-family** arrow.
6. Click **Gill Sans, Gill Sans MT, Calibri, Trebuchet MS, sans-serif**.

   The Preview window at the bottom of the dialog box illustrates how this style will appear on the Web page.

7. Click the **OK** button to return to Design view.

   The h1 text should appear as shown in Figure 5-10.The blue panel icon that appears before the h1 style in the Apply Styles panel indicates that this style is an element style.

Figure 5-10 Changing the font family

Next, you'll show Tyrell how to change the text size.

Changing the Text Size

The **font-size property** is used to change the text size. Although the headings h1 through h6 also change the size of text, the font-size property lets you change text size without also making the text a heading. The font-size property also allows you to make text any size, not just one of the six heading sizes. To avoid overwhelming your readers and to assist them in discerning what is truly most important, a Web page usually has only one h1 heading, which is the largest heading size. An h1 heading should serve to format banner text or headline text only.

REFERENCE

Modifying a Style

- In the Apply Styles or Manage Styles panel, right-click the style and then click Modify Style.
- In the Modify Style dialog box, modify styles as you want, and then click the OK button.

or

- To use the CSS Properties panel to modify a style, in the document window, click inside the text you want to modify, and then click in the value box for a style.
- Type the new value or choose from the list of values.

The values for font size should be expressed either as keywords, as em values, or as percentages. An **em value** is a CSS measurement equal to the default font size, usually 12-point text. A value of 2em, therefore, would be double the browser's default font size, or approximately 24 points. Percentage values work in the same way. A font-size property value of 200% would be twice the browser's default size, and equal to 2em.

PROSKILLS

Teamwork: Writing or Editing CSS Code

Although Expression Web generates CSS code, you, as a Web page developer, are always free to compose your own code. If you know how to write CSS code, you can click the Code view button and enter your own code as desired. Expression Web creates code using a very common style: the selector on one line, followed by the properties and values indented on separate lines, and ending with a closing brace. If you choose to type your own code, it's best to enter the code using the same layout, spacing, and indenting that Expression Web uses because other developers might work with your document at some point. It could be quite confusing to other developers working with the same document if you chose to enter the code in a manner that is not consistent with the way in which Expression Web generates CSS code.

Ordinarily, to format the h1 heading, you would make several formatting changes in the New Style dialog box and then click the OK button. However, as you work with Tyrell to create each of several style declarations, you want to show him the effect of each style change, so you'll have him create one style declaration at a time and then view the style effect in Design view. You'll begin by showing Tyrell how to change the font size for an h1 heading to a size that is slightly smaller than the default.

To change the font size:

1. In the Apply Styles panel, right-click the **h1** style.
2. On the shortcut menu, click **Modify Style**.

   The Modify Style dialog box opens.
3. In the Modify Style dialog box, click the **font-size** arrow.
4. If necessary, scroll down the list and click **x-large**.
5. Click the **OK** button.

   The font size decreases slightly, as shown in Figure 5-11.

Figure 5-11 **Changing the font size**

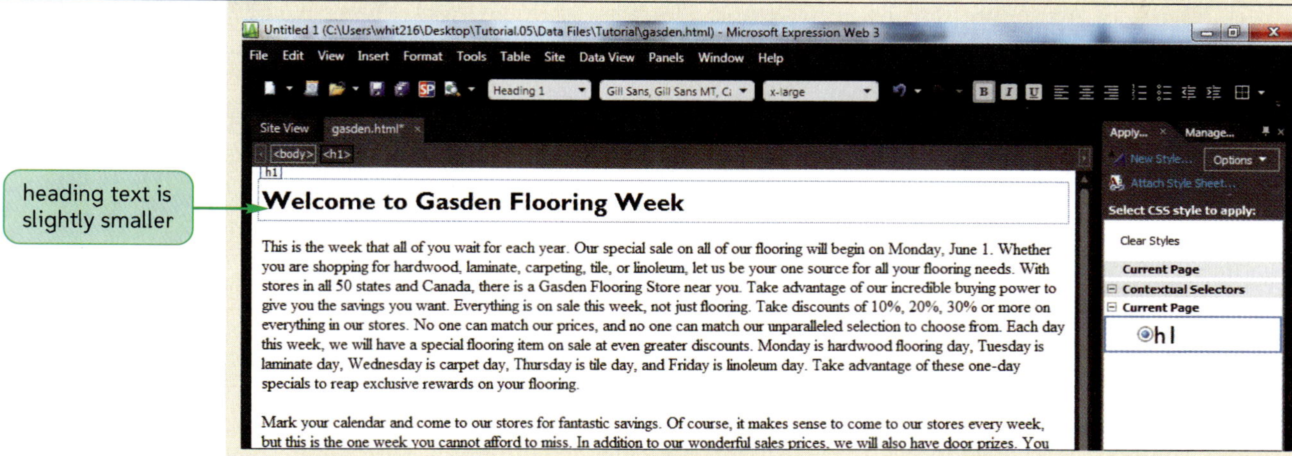

You have already used the Bold button on the Common toolbar to make text bold. Next, you'll show Tyrell how to use a style to make text bold.

Changing the Font Weight

The **font-weight property** is used to make text appear as bold text. The two most common values for the font-weight property are "bold" and "normal." The keywords "lighter" and "bolder" generally are not supported. The value of "bold" has a straightforward effect: it makes text bold. The value of "normal" does the opposite: it makes text not appear in bold.

You can also use numeric values ranging from 100 to 900 in increments of 100. A value of 100 should display text as bold text, but in a lighter bold. A value of 900 should display text as bold as possible. A value of 700 displays bold text as it normally would appear. Because each browser and browser version may display the font-weight properties somewhat differently, the numeric values might not display text lighter or darker when viewed in your browser. You'll now show Tyrell how to change the setting to the lightest font weight.

> **TIP**
> The "bold" value is equivalent to a numeric value of 700.

To change the value for the font-weight property:

1. In the Apply Styles panel, right-click the **h1** style.
2. Click **Modify Style**.

   The Modify Style dialog box opens.
3. In the Modify Style dialog box, click the **font-weight** arrow and then click **100**.
4. Click the **OK** button.

   The font weight decreases, making the heading appear less bold, as shown in Figure 5-12.

Figure 5-12 Changing the font weight

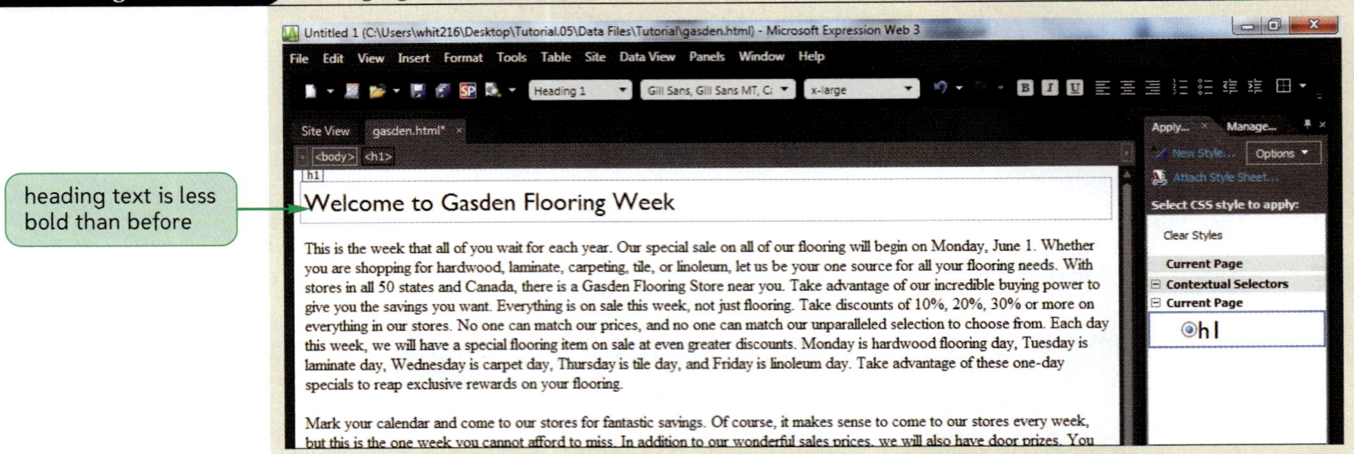

INSIGHT

Using IntelliSense

Instead of using the New Style dialog box to create CSS styles, you can enter CSS code directly in Code view. To assist you in entering valid CSS code, Expression Web uses its IntelliSense feature, which provides a pop-up menu with property and value choices. As you type code, IntelliSense determines what type of code you are entering and gives you a list of choices of valid commands. Using IntelliSense makes it faster and easier to enter code because you do not have to remember all of the values associated with a particular CSS property.

Now that you have shown Tyrell how to make text bold, you'll show him how to use the font-style property to have text appear in italic.

Making Text Italic

The **font-style property** is the property used to make text appear in italic. The font-style property has three values: "italic," "oblique," and "normal." Both italic and oblique make text appear slanted, though oblique text does so to a greater degree than italic text. The oblique value, however, is generally not supported. Normal text is text that is not italic; you use the normal value to remove italic from text that normally would appear in italic. Tyrell would like to display the h1 heading in italic, so you'll show him how to create a style declaration to do so.

To change the font style to italic for the h1 heading:

1. In the Apply Styles panel, right-click the **h1** style.
2. Click **Modify Style**.

   The Modify Style dialog box opens.
3. In the Modify Style dialog box, click the **font-style** arrow.
4. Click **italic**.
5. Click the **OK** button.

   The h1 heading text is now italic, as shown in Figure 5-13.

Figure 5-13 Changing the font style

heading text now appears as italic text

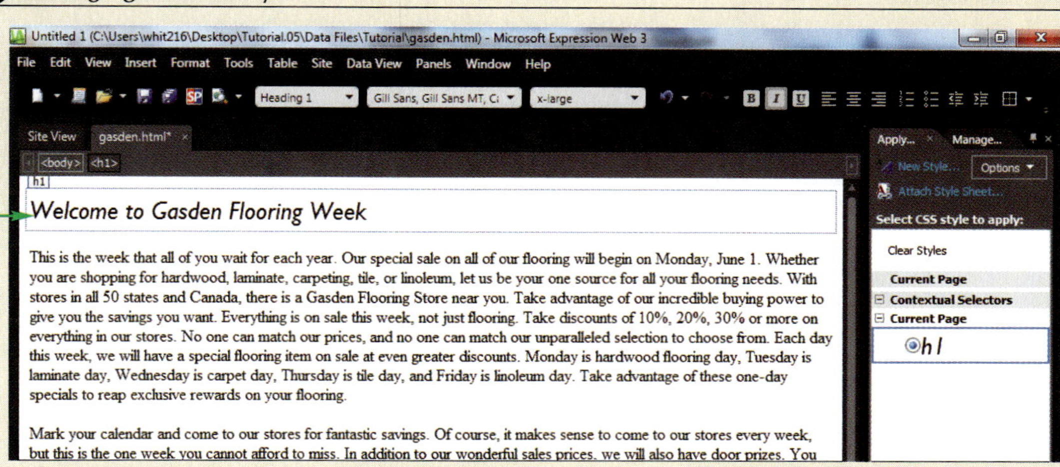

Next, you'll show Tyrell how to use the font properties to capitalize text. There are two CSS properties that capitalize text: the font-variant property and the text-transform property.

Working with Text Capitalization

The **font-variant property** displays text in small caps—text that appears in all capital letters, but slightly smaller than normal capitalized letters. The font-variant property has only two values: "normal" and "small-caps." The **text-transform property** is also used to change the capitalization of text, but this property does not make text appear in small-caps. The values for the text-transform property are shown in Figure 5-14.

Figure 5-14 **Values for the text-transform property**

Property	Function
capitalize	Capitalizes just the first letter of each word selected
lowercase	Makes text appear in all lowercase letters
none	Removes any value you have set for text-transform
uppercase	Makes text appear in all capitals, regardless of how you originally typed the text
inherit	Inherits the value of the text-transform property from the parent element, such as text within a paragraph

You'll have Tyrell use the text-transform property to make the h1 text appear in uppercase.

To have the h1 text appear in uppercase:

1. In the Apply Styles panel, right-click the **h1** style.
2. Click **Modify Style**.
3. In the Modify Style dialog box, click the **text-transform** arrow.
4. Click **uppercase**.
5. Click the **OK** button. The h1 text now appears in uppercase, as shown in Figure 5-15.

Figure 5-15 **Changing the text-transform value**

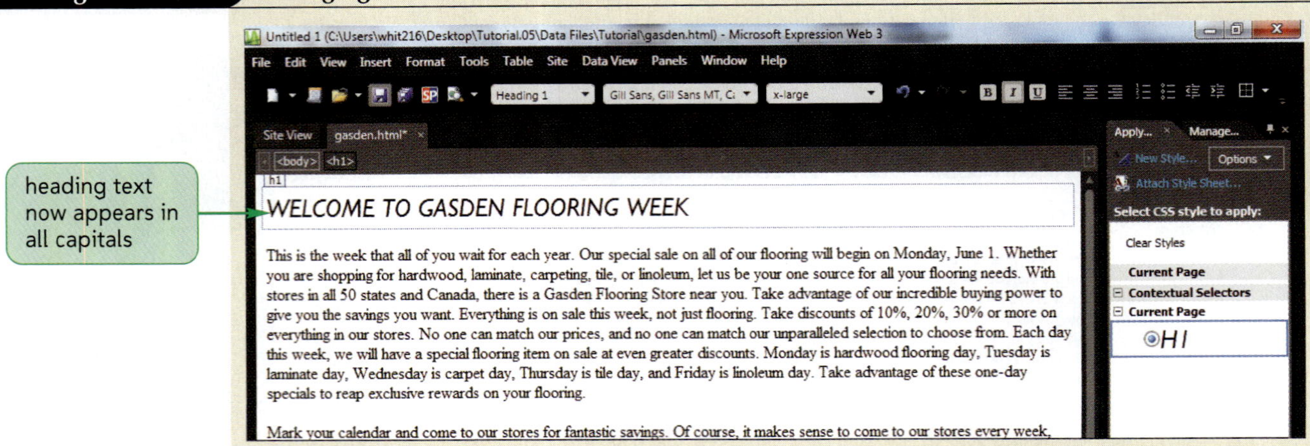

One other choice in the Font category is the **color property**, which determines the font color. You'll work with Tyrell to set a value for the color property.

Working with Color

In an earlier tutorial, you made choices for both the font color (the foreground color) and the highlight color (the background color) by clicking buttons on the Common toolbar. Expression Web also allows you to change the font color as part of the group of choices in the Font category. To change the color, you can click the color arrow and then choose from among 16 colors that are most commonly used on Web pages. If you want to use a color other than one of these 16 colors, you can click the Color Palette icon instead. This icon contains a small square with a diagonal line through it; it is located just to the right of the color arrow.

REFERENCE

Changing the Text Color

- In the Apply Styles or Manage Styles panel, click New Style.
- In the Font category, click the color arrow.
- Click one of the 16 predefined colors.

or

- Click More Colors, and then in the More Colors dialog box, click a color from the color palette.
- Click the OK button.

Colors can be represented in HTML code in several ways (for example, as a named color or as a hexadecimal value). When you select a color sample, Expression Web displays the hexadecimal value of the color in the Color box. It does not display the name of the color.

You'll show Tyrell how to change the font color for a style by clicking a color sample in the gallery.

To change the font color:

1. In the Apply Styles panel, right-click the **h1** style, and then click **Modify Style**.
2. Click the **color** arrow, and then click the **Teal** swatch (hex value #008080).
3. Click the **OK** button.

   The h1 heading text now appears in teal, as shown in Figure 5-16.

Figure 5-16 **Changing the font color style**

Last, you'll show Tyrell how to create a decorative border above and below the h1 heading text.

Creating Text Decoration

The **text-decoration property** determines if a line should appear over, under, or through text. The values for this property are "underline," "overline," "line-through," "blink," and "none." Because visitors to your Web site might mistake underlined text for a link, you should not underline text—italicize it instead. You can, however, use an underline together with an overline to create a decorative effect for a heading. The "overline" value is also used with math equations. The value of "line-through" scores a line through text to indicate a deletion. The value of "none" is commonly used to remove underlining in links that have already been visited. Do not use the value of "blink." Most visitors today consider blinking text annoying and amateurish.

You'll show Tyrell how to use underline and overline together to create a decorative effect for the h1 heading. In addition, you'll show him how to view a **style ScreenTip**, a pop-up window that reveals the style code when you hover the pointer over a style name in the Apply Styles panel.

To change the value for text decoration:

1. In the Apply Styles panel, right-click the **h1** style, and then click **Modify Style**.
2. In the Modify Style dialog box, in the check boxes for text-decoration, click the **underline** check box.
3. Click the **overline** check box.
4. Click the **OK** button.
5. Click anywhere outside the h1 text.

   The h1 heading text should appear similar to that shown in Figure 5-17. Note that because the insertion point is no longer within the h1 element style, the style no longer appears in the Apply Styles panel.

Figure 5-17 Creating text rules

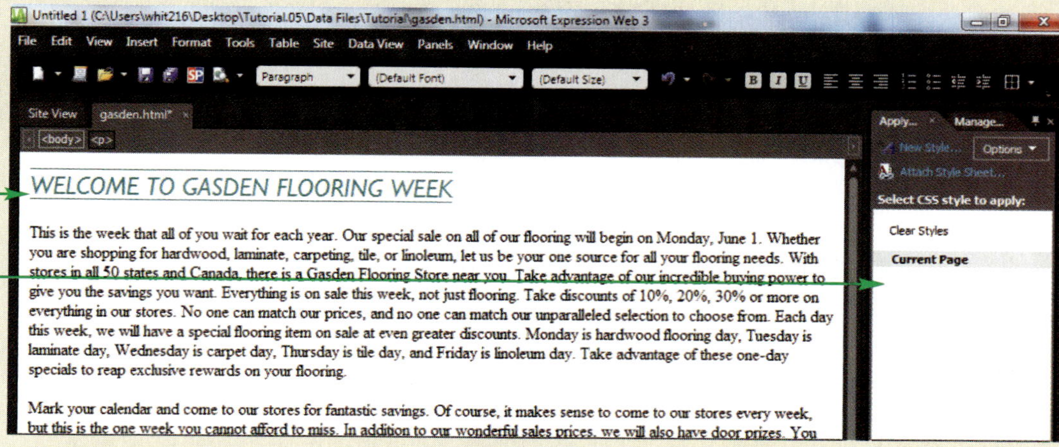

6. Click anywhere in the h1 heading text, hover the pointer over the h1 style in the Apply Styles panel until you see a style ScreenTip for the h1 style, and then take a moment to review the style declarations.
7. Click the **Split** button to display the document in Split view.
8. If necessary, scroll up through the top pane to see that the same CSS code that appeared in the ScreenTip has automatically been entered for you in the document code, as shown in Figure 5-18.

   Expression Web lets you specify the formatting without requiring you to type the CSS code.

Figure 5-18 The Split view screen

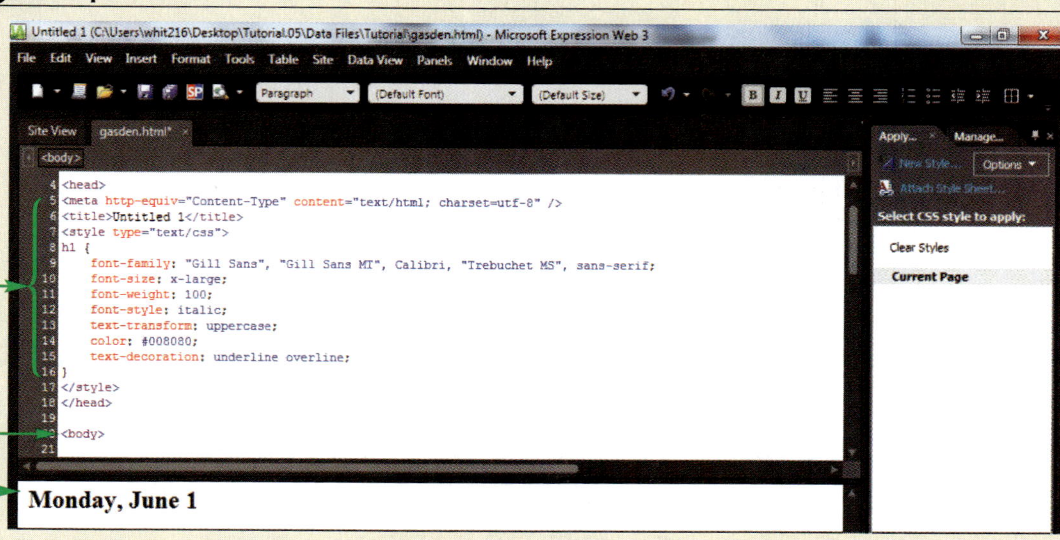

9. Click the **Design** button to display the document in Design view.

Next, you'll create a style for the h2 headings. Tyrell would like these headings to have a smaller font size and he would also like them to appear in maroon.

To create style declarations for the h2 headings:

1. In the Apply Styles panel, click the words **New Style**.

   The New Style dialog box opens.
2. Click the **Selector** arrow, scroll down the list of elements, and then click **h2**.
3. Click the **font-size** arrow, and then click **large**.
4. Click the **color** arrow, and then click **Maroon** (it's the fourth swatch in the top row and its hex value is #800000).
5. Click the **OK** button to return to Design view, and then scroll down if necessary to view all of the h2 headings.

   The h2 headings should now appear in maroon, as shown in Figure 5-19.

Figure 5-19 The h2 heading style

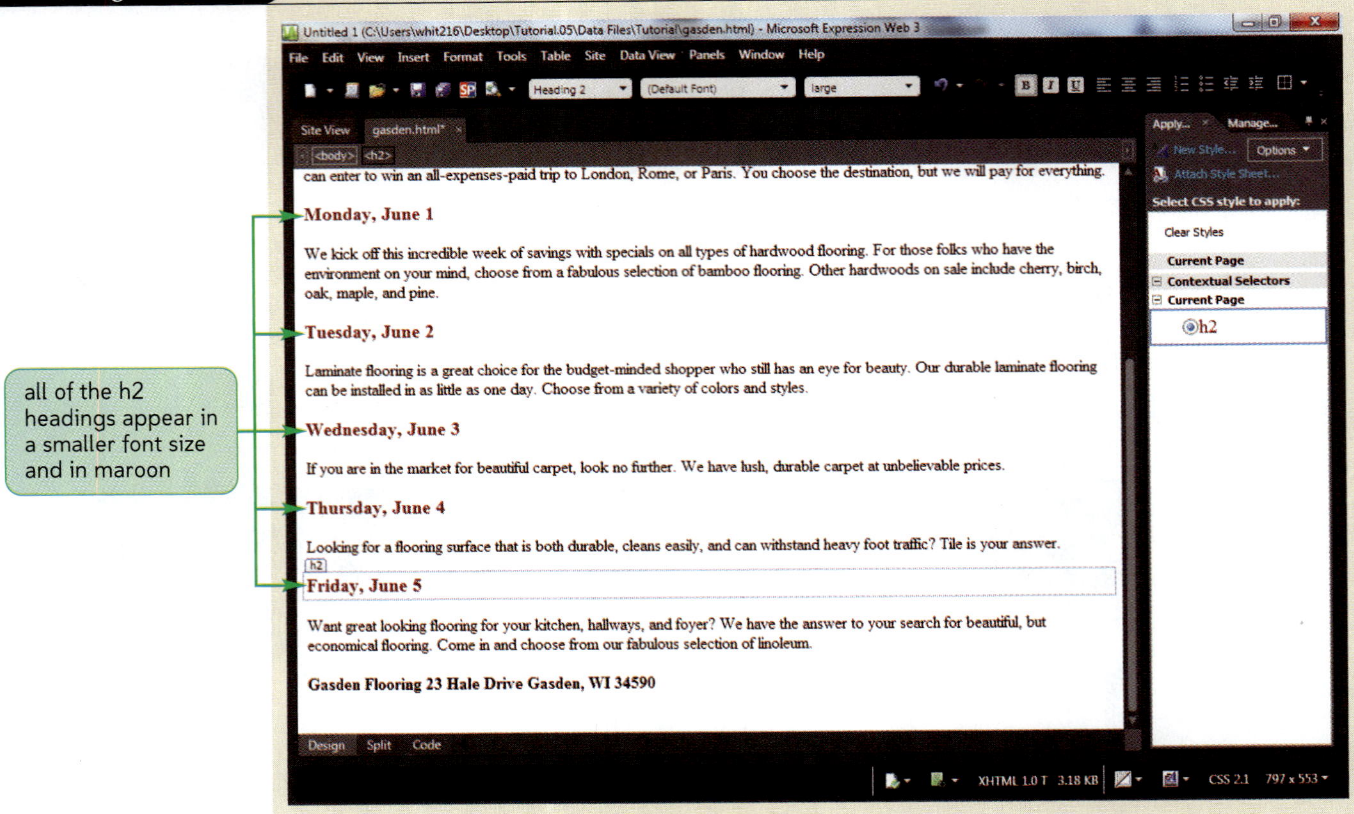

Finally, you'll show Tyrell how to save the file and preview it in the default browser.

To save the file and preview it in the default browser:

1. Save the file.
2. Press the **F12** key to display the document in the default browser.

   Your document should look similar to the one shown in Figure 5-20.

Figure 5-20 The document in the browser

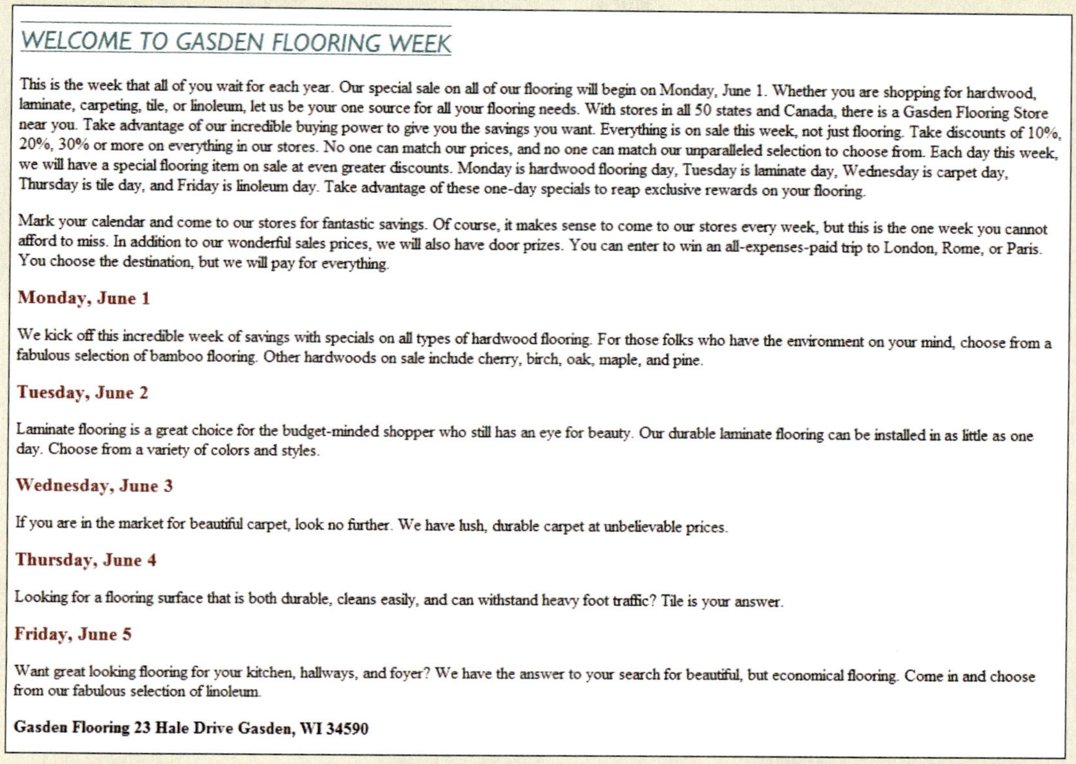
WELCOME TO GASDEN FLOORING WEEK

This is the week that all of you wait for each year. Our special sale on all of our flooring will begin on Monday, June 1. Whether you are shopping for hardwood, laminate, carpeting, tile, or linoleum, let us be your one source for all your flooring needs. With stores in all 50 states and Canada, there is a Gasden Flooring Store near you. Take advantage of our incredible buying power to give you the savings you want. Everything is on sale this week, not just flooring. Take discounts of 10%, 20%, 30% or more on everything in our stores. No one can match our prices, and no one can match our unparalleled selection to choose from. Each day this week, we will have a special flooring item on sale at even greater discounts. Monday is hardwood flooring day, Tuesday is laminate day, Wednesday is carpet day, Thursday is tile day, and Friday is linoleum day. Take advantage of these one-day specials to reap exclusive rewards on your flooring.

Mark your calendar and come to our stores for fantastic savings. Of course, it makes sense to come to our stores every week, but this is the one week you cannot afford to miss. In addition to our wonderful sales prices, we will also have door prizes. You can enter to win an all-expenses-paid trip to London, Rome, or Paris. You choose the destination, but we will pay for everything.

Monday, June 1

We kick off this incredible week of savings with specials on all types of hardwood flooring. For those folks who have the environment on your mind, choose from a fabulous selection of bamboo flooring. Other hardwoods on sale include cherry, birch, oak, maple, and pine.

Tuesday, June 2

Laminate flooring is a great choice for the budget-minded shopper who still has an eye for beauty. Our durable laminate flooring can be installed in as little as one day. Choose from a variety of colors and styles.

Wednesday, June 3

If you are in the market for beautiful carpet, look no further. We have lush, durable carpet at unbelievable prices.

Thursday, June 4

Looking for a flooring surface that is both durable, cleans easily, and can withstand heavy foot traffic? Tile is your answer.

Friday, June 5

Want great looking flooring for your kitchen, hallways, and foyer? We have the answer to your search for beautiful, but economical flooring. Come in and choose from our fabulous selection of linoleum.

Gasden Flooring 23 Hale Drive Gasden, WI 34590

Trouble? The headline on your screen might look slightly different from the one shown in Figure 5-20, depending on the fonts installed on your computer.

3. Close the browser.

REVIEW

Session 5.1 Quick Check

1. What is direct formatting?
2. What are four advantages to using CSS?
3. What is a CSS style?
4. What are the three most commonly used CSS selectors?
5. What are the three places where styles are written?
6. What CSS property is used to make text appear in italic?
7. What CSS property is used to make text appear in bold?
8. What CSS property is used to make text appear larger or smaller?

SESSION 5.2 VISUAL OVERVIEW

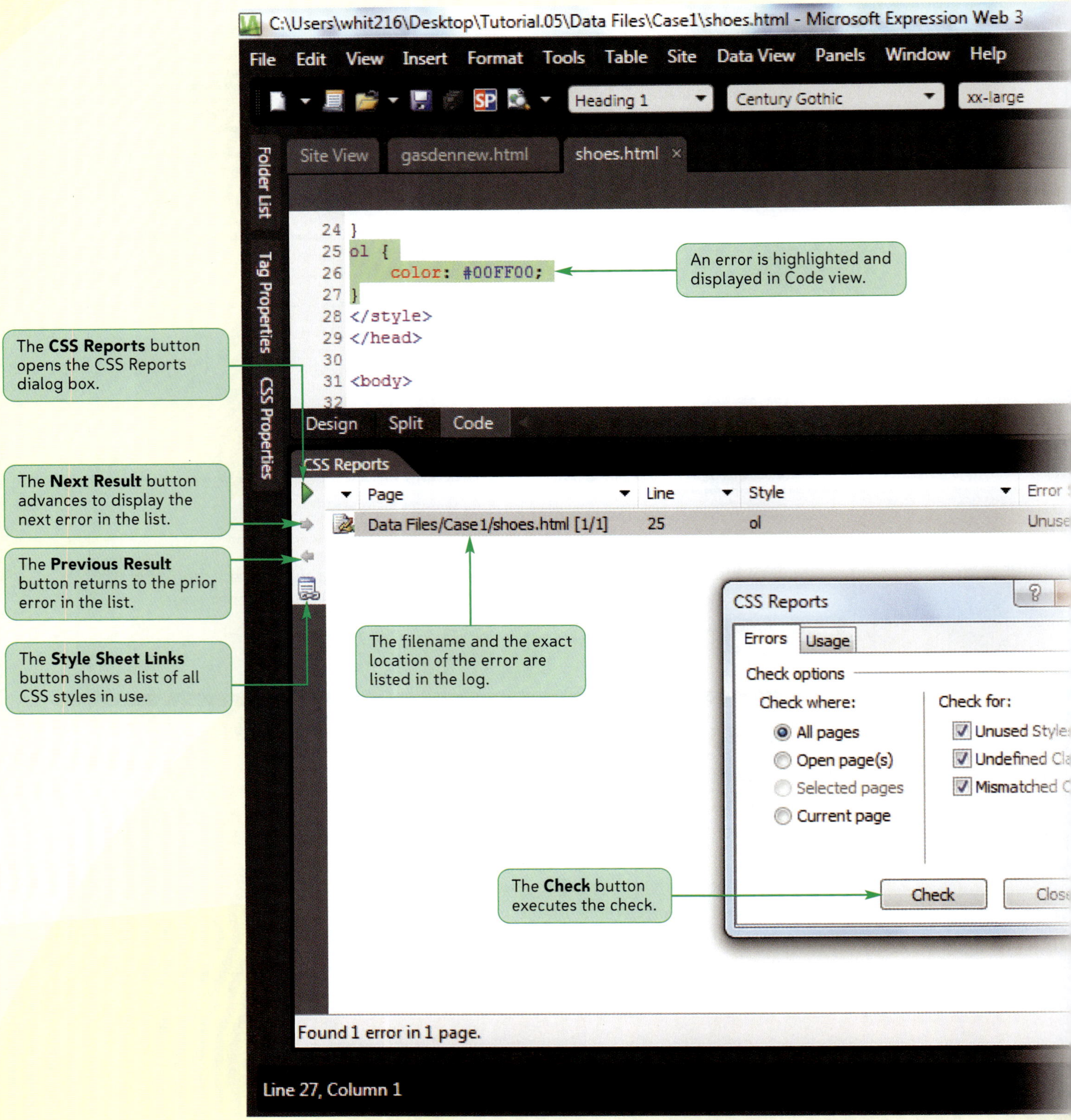

CREATING CSS REPORTS

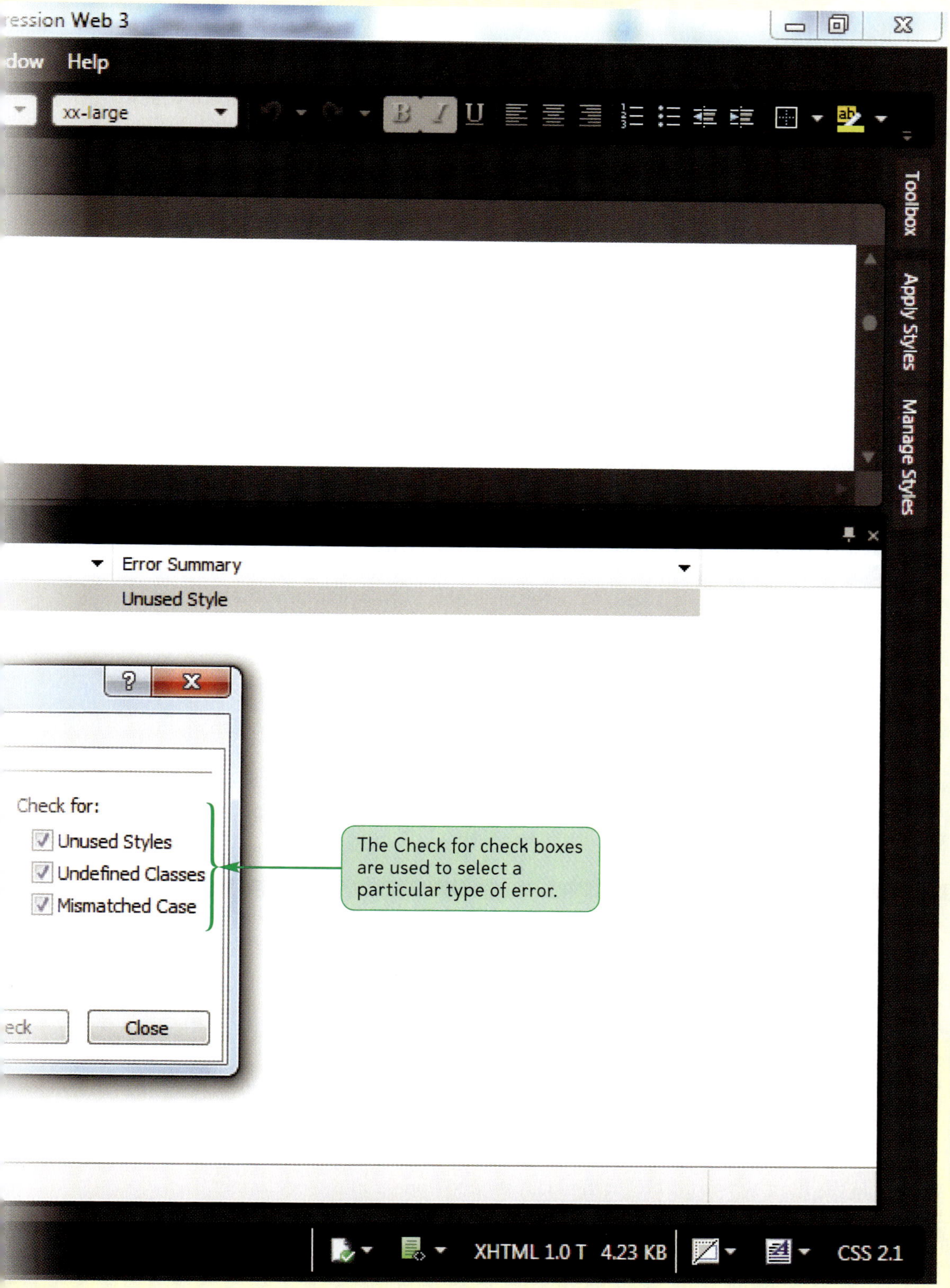

Using Class Selectors

Class selectors allow you to define the formatting characteristics of an element in more than one way. For example, let's say that you wanted some paragraphs to appear as single-spaced text, but you also wanted other paragraphs to be double-spaced. How do you style the paragraph element to display text in more than one way? You do so by creating classes. The selector for a class is indicated in HTML code by the element name and then the class name. For example, to create paragraphs that are double-spaced, you might name the class p.double.

In the code, the selector ("p") comes first, then a period, and then the name of the class. *You* get to name the class. If you do not name the class, by default, Expression Web names classes as .style1, .style2, and so forth, which is not very descriptive. For the class name, choose a short, one-word name that describes the purpose of the class.

A **dependent class** is a class that styles only one type of element. In this example, the p.double class creates styles for the paragraph element and no other. The style declarations you create for the p.double class style only paragraphs. If you tried to apply the p.double class to style any other HTML element, the style would not take effect, and you wouldn't see any result on the Web page.

Sometimes, though, you'll want to apply a class to different elements. Let's say, for example, you are creating an online training manual, and you want to use a style to call the reader's attention to some essentially important information, no matter whether the information is in a paragraph, a table, a heading, or any other page element. To solve this problem, you create **independent classes**, which are classes that can be used to style *any* HTML element. The syntax for an independent class is very similar to that of a dependent class, except that you do not specify an HTML element selector. The independent class begins with a period, followed by the class name, with no space in between. Once again, *you* get to name the class, so in this instance, you might name the class as .essential.

Applying Classes

TIP

Spaces are not allowed in either a dependent class or an independent class name.

When you created the element class for the h1 element, you did nothing more than create the style for the class. The class automatically styled the h1 element the moment you were done entering the code for the class and clicked the OK button in the New Style dialog box. In contrast, creating dependent or independent classes is a two-step process. First, you create the class, and then you *apply* the class.

REFERENCE

Applying a Class

- Select the content to which you want to apply the style.
- In the Apply Styles or Manage Styles panel, right-click the style.
- On the shortcut menu, click Apply Style.

or

- In the New Style dialog box, click the Apply new style to document selection check box.

You apply the class where you want the class style to appear in the document. The New Style dialog box has an option to both create and apply a style to selected text. Tyrell would like the text in the first paragraph of the document to be spaced a little farther apart and have a background color. You'll show him how to create a dependent class for the paragraph selector, which you'll name *p.intro*.

To create the p.intro dependent class selector:

1. If necessary, start Expression Web, close any other Web sites, and then open the Tutorial.05 Web site.
2. If necessary, expand the Data Files and the Tutorial folder, and then open the **gasdennew.html** file.
3. If necessary, close the Folder List, the Tag Properties, the CSS Properties, and the Toolbox panels.
4. In Design view, click anywhere in the first paragraph (it begins with the words *This is the week . . .*).
5. Click the **p** Code tab to select the paragraph.
6. In the Apply Styles panel, click **New Style**.

   The New Style dialog box opens.
7. With the default selector name highlighted in the Selector box, press the **Delete** key and then press the **Backspace** key to delete .newStyle1.
8. In the Selector box, type **p.intro**.
9. Click the **Apply new style to document selection** check box.

Now that you have named the style and made the choice to apply the style, you'll show Tyrell how to create the style declarations for the p.intro class.

To create the style declarations for the p.intro dependent class selector:

1. In the Category bar, click **Block**, and then examine the new set of properties that appears.
2. Click in the **line-height** box and then type **2em**.
3. In the Category bar, click **Background**, and then examine the new set of properties that appears. The word *Block* in the Category bar is now bold, which indicates that the category has been used.
4. To the right of the background-color arrow, click the **background color** gallery icon.

   The More Colors dialog box opens.
5. In the More Colors dialog box, click the choice for hex value FF,FF,99, as shown in Figure 5-21.

Figure 5-21 The More Colors dialog box

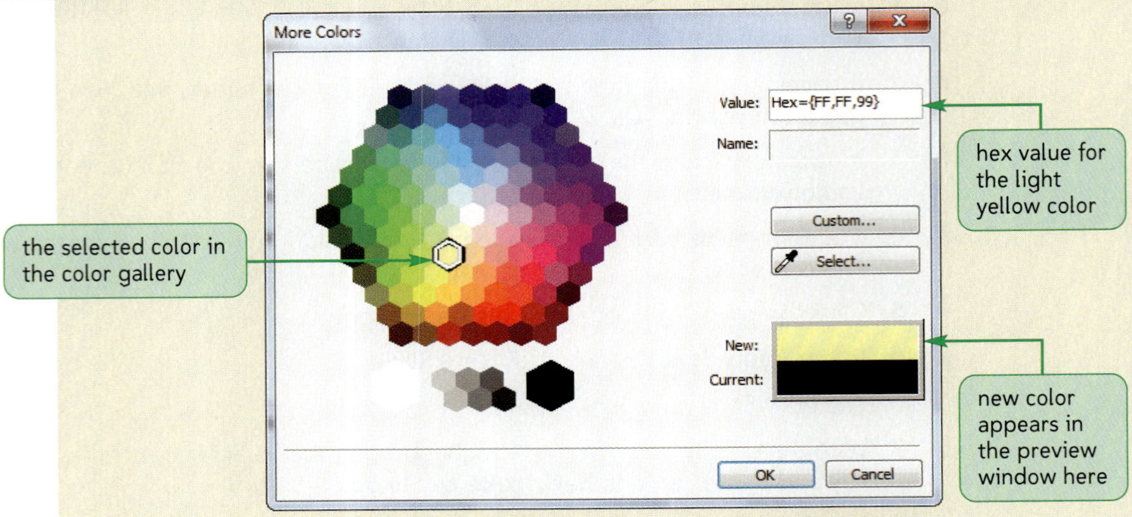

6. Click the **OK** button in the More Colors dialog box.
7. Click the **OK** button in the New Style dialog box to return to Design view.
8. Click anywhere outside of the first paragraph. The background color and the new setting for the line spacing should appear as shown in Figure 5-22.

Figure 5-22 Creating the p.intro style

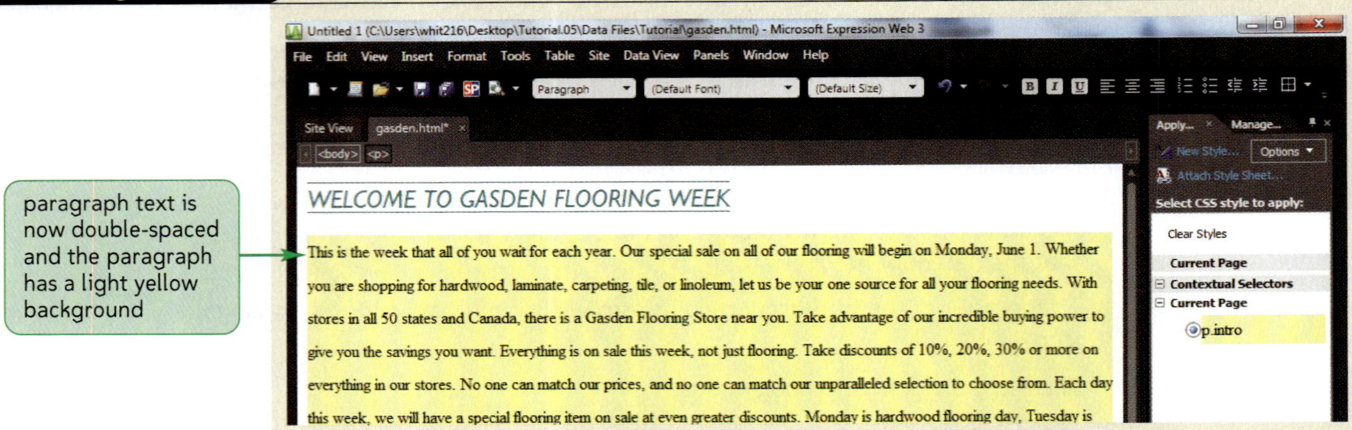

The p.intro class is a dependent class, so it can only be applied to paragraphs. If you click in any paragraph, the p.intro style appears in the Apply Styles panel. If you click in any element other than the p element, such as any of the h2 headings, the p.intro style does not appear in the Apply Styles panel. Tyrell would also like to apply the p.intro style to the second paragraph. When he created the p.intro style, you showed him that he could create and apply the style to selected text. Tyrell doesn't want to create a new style each time he wants to style some text, so you'll show him how to apply an existing style to text.

To apply the p.intro class style to the second paragraph:

1. Click anywhere inside the second paragraph.
2. In the Apply Styles panel, click the **p.intro** style.
3. Click anywhere outside of the second paragraph.

   The p.intro style is applied. The second paragraph should appear as shown in Figure 5-23.

Figure 5-23 Applying the p.intro style

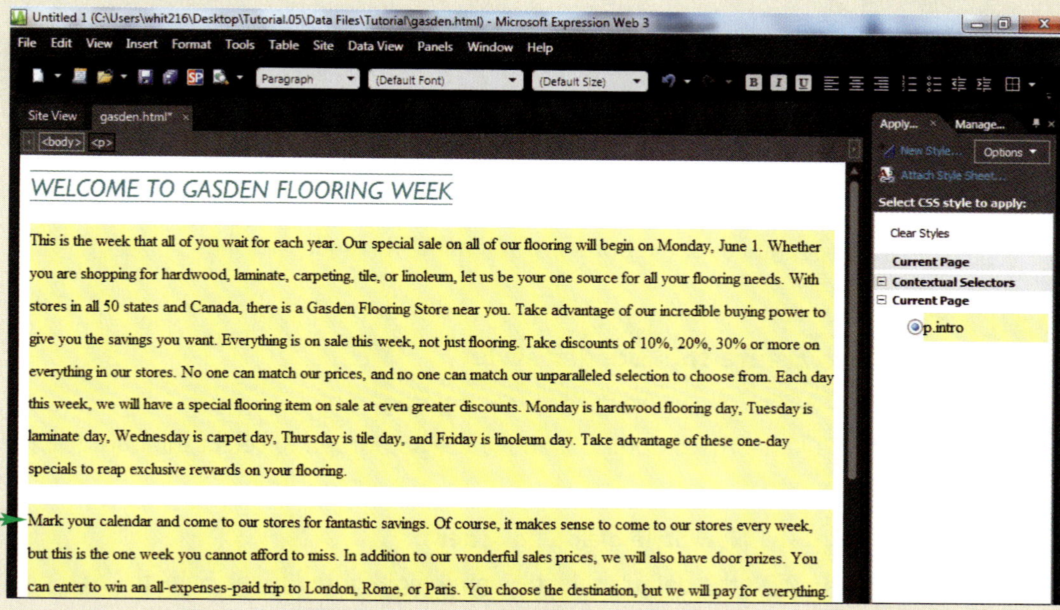

the second paragraph now has the same formatting as the first paragraph

Now that you have shown Tyrell how to create a dependent class selector, you'll show him how to create an independent class selector.

Creating an Independent Class Selector

Independent class selectors can be used to format any element. Tyrell would like to create a border around the second paragraph. He'd like only the first paragraph to have a yellow background. You'll show Tyrell how to clear a style using the Apply Styles panel and then create a new style for the second paragraph.

To clear the p.intro style from the second paragraph:

1. Click anywhere in the second paragraph. Click the **p.intro** Code tab above the second paragraph to select the paragraph.
2. In the Apply Styles panel, hover the pointer over the words *Clear Styles*.

   A ScreenTip appears alerting you that clicking Clear Styles removes the class-based styles and inline styles from selected text.
3. Click **Clear Styles**.
4. Click anywhere outside the second paragraph.

   The p.intro style has been removed, as shown in Figure 5-24.

TIP

You can clear only class-based styles (not element styles) by using the choice for Clear Styles in the Apply Styles panel.

Figure 5-24 **Clearing a style**

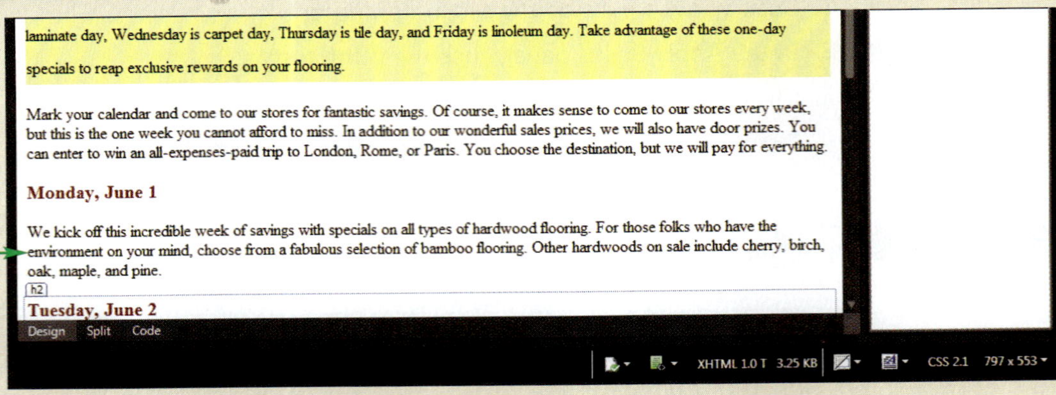

the second paragraph now has its original appearance

Now that the p.intro style has been cleared, you'll show Tyrell how to create and apply a new style to the second paragraph. Because this style will be used to create an appearance for the border, you'll name this style .border.

To create the .border style:

1. Click anywhere in the second paragraph.
2. Click the **p** Code tab above the paragraph to select the paragraph.
3. In the Apply Styles panel, click **New Style**.

   The New Style dialog box opens.
4. With the default selector name highlighted in the Selector box, press the **Delete** key to delete newStyle1. (Do not delete the period.)
5. Type **border**.

   The style should now be named as .border.
6. Click in the **Apply new style to document selection** check box.

Now that the style has been named, you'll show Tyrell how to create the style declarations for the .border style. You'll change the border style, the border width, and the border color. You'll also add padding to create some white space between the border and the text.

To create the style declarations for the .border style:

1. In the Category bar, click **Border**.

   The dialog box displays arrows for the border style, border width, and border color. The "same for all" check box is checked by default, which means that any value you enter in the top box is applied to all four borders: top, right, bottom, and left.
2. Click the **border-style** arrow, and then click **inset**.
3. Click the **border-width** arrow, and then click **medium**.

4. Click the **border-color** arrow, and click **Yellow** (hexadecimal code #FFFF00).

   The New Style dialog box should appear as shown in Figure 5-25.

Figure 5-25 **Creating the .border style**

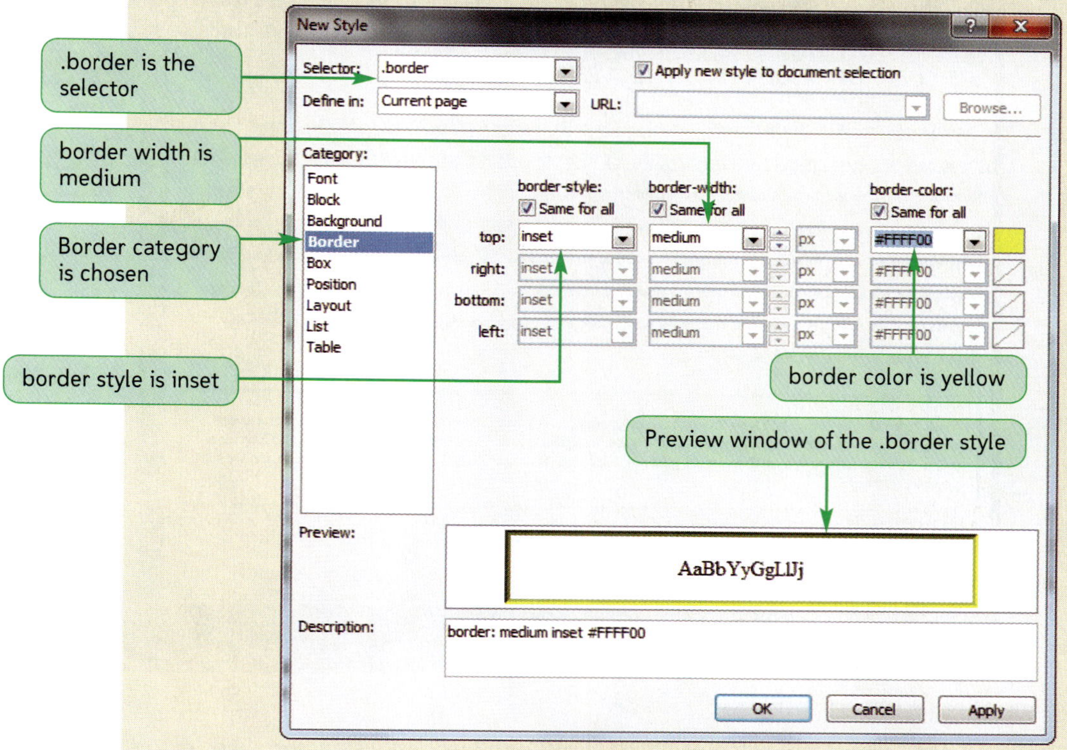

5. In the Category bar, click **Box**.
6. For padding, click in the **top** box and then type **1em**.
7. Click the **OK** button.

   The .border class appears in the Apply Styles panel. It has a green panel icon indicating it is a class selector style.
8. Click anywhere outside the second paragraph.

   The paragraph should appear as shown in Figure 5-26.

Figure 5-26 The border and padding are added to the paragraph

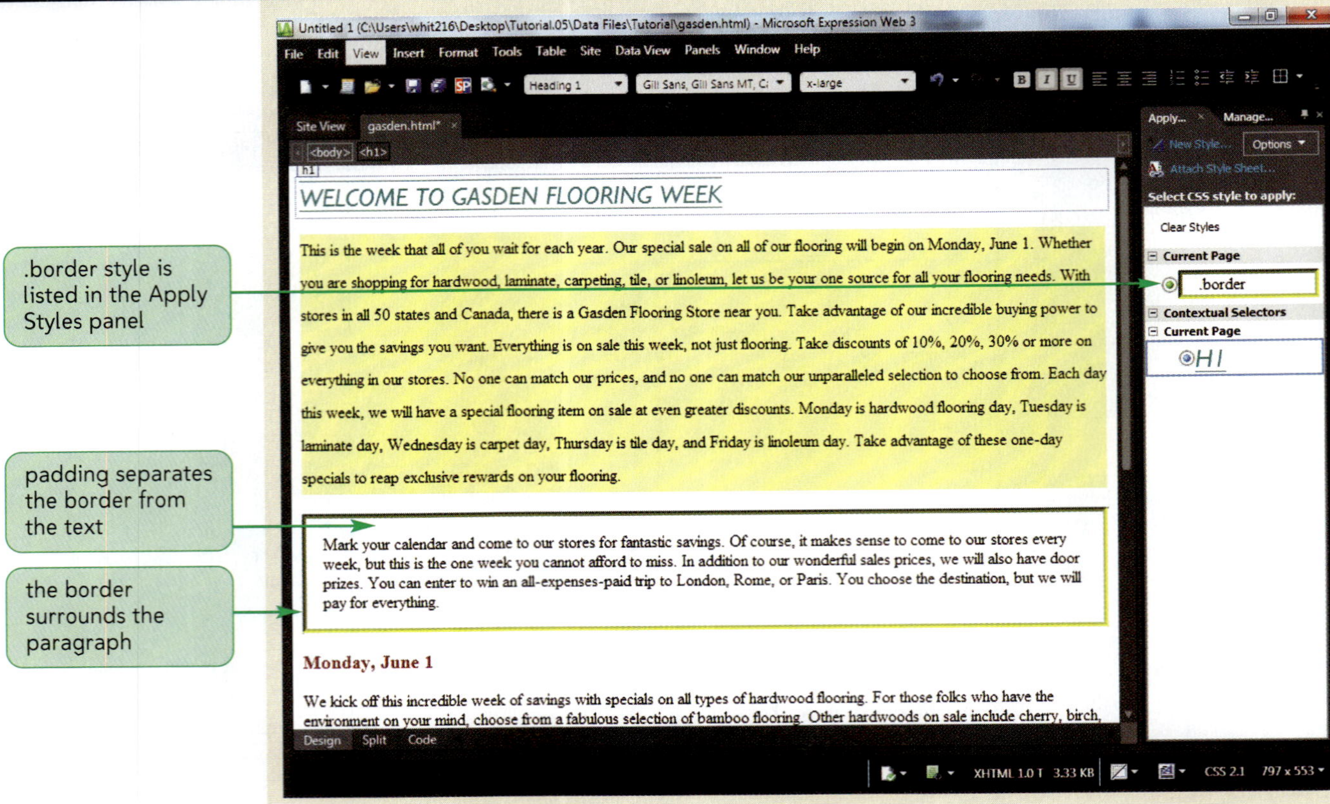

The last type of selector you'll show Tyrell is the ID selector. ID selectors will not be used extensively on the Gasden Flooring Web site, but later tutorials on Web page layout will use ID selectors extensively.

Creating an ID Selector

ID selectors function very similarly to independent classes. An **ID selector** can be used to style any HTML element, but only *once* on the Web page. ID selectors are most often used with the HTML <div> element, which is used to create formatting and positioning divisions on a Web page. The <div> element has no formatting of its own.

REFERENCE

Creating an ID Selector

- In either the Apply Styles or Manage Styles panel, click New Style.
- In the New Style dialog box, delete .newStyle1 in the Selector box.
- Type # followed by the name of the selector style.
- Specify styles for the ID selector.
- Click the OK button.

TIP

The # symbol is also known as a number sign, a hash, and the octothorpe character.

You'll work with the <div> element extensively as you build more complex Web sites. A pound symbol (#) precedes the ID selector name.

Tyrell would like the document's footer to have a unique appearance. Because the footer will be formatted differently from the rest of the document, you'll create and apply an ID selector style. You'll name the ID selector *#footer*.

To create the #footer ID selector:

1. If necessary, scroll down to the bottom of the page and click anywhere in the last line of text (the Gasden Flooring address).
2. Click the **p** Code tab to select the footer text.
3. Click the **OK** button to return to Design view.
4. In the Apply Styles panel, click **New Style**.

   The New Style dialog box opens.
5. In the Selector box, delete the period and the default text newStyle1.
6. In the Selector box, type **#footer**.
7. Click the **Apply new style to document selection** check box.
8. Click in the **font-size** box, and then type **1.2em**.

   Be sure not to type a space between 1.2 and em.

Make sure you do not leave a space between the # symbol and the word *footer*. If you did, delete the space.

Next, you'll show Tyrell how to use a style to center a line of text.

To use a style to center a line of text:

1. In the Category bar, click **Block**.
2. Click the **text-align** arrow, and then click **center**.
3. Click the **OK** button to return to Design view.
4. Click anywhere outside the footer line. The footer text should appear as shown in Figure 5-27.

Figure 5-27 Revisions to the footer

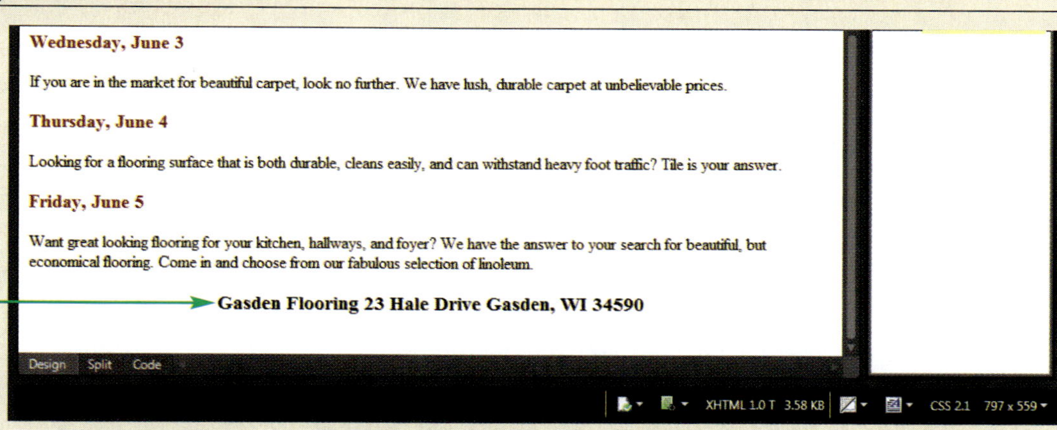

Tyrell would like to make the individual parts of the footer more clearly identifiable, so you'll insert several symbols into the footer line.

To insert symbols into the footer:

1. In the footer text, click before the number **2** in "23 Hale Drive."
2. Click **Insert** on the menu bar and then click **Symbol**.

   The Symbol dialog box opens.

3. If necessary, click the **from** arrow in the lower-right corner of the dialog box and then click **Unicode (hex)**.
4. Click in the **Character code** box, and then, if necessary, delete any contents.
5. Type **25D9**.

   In the lower-left corner of the dialog box, the words *INVERSE WHITE CIRCLE* appear, indicating that character code 25D9 will insert that character when you click the Insert button.
6. Click the **Insert** button and then click the **Close** button.
7. Press the **spacebar** once.
8. Repeat the same procedure as necessary to insert an inverse white circle symbol between the words *Drive* and *Gasden*, and between *WI* and *34590*.

   The footer should look like the one shown in Figure 5-28.

TIP

After you choose a symbol once, you can select it in the Recently used symbols section of the Symbol dialog box.

Figure 5-28 Inserting a symbol

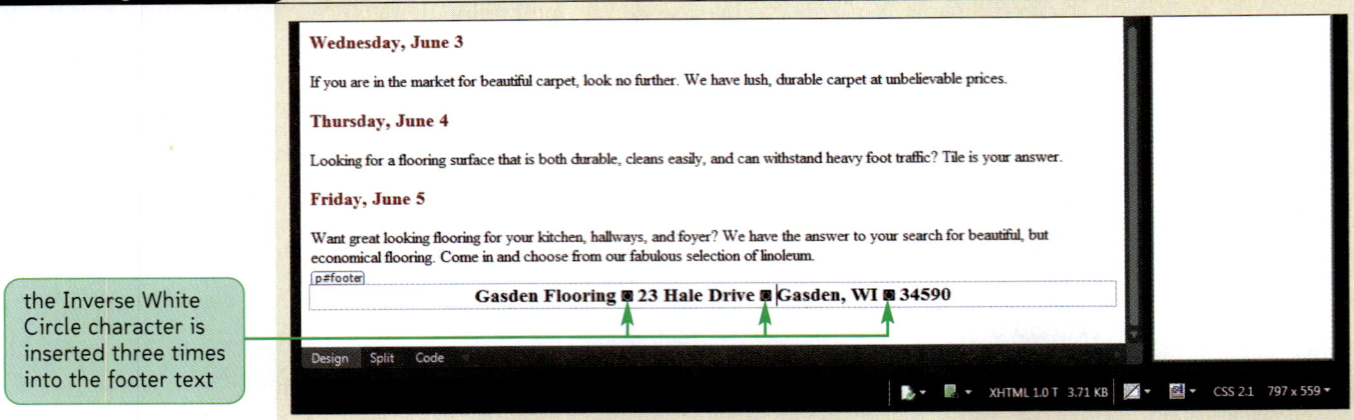

INSIGHT

Using the CSS Properties Panel

If you are familiar with CSS code, one quick way of modifying a style is to use the CSS Properties panel. The CSS Properties panel lists all of the CSS styles shown in the New Style dialog box. In the CSS Properties panel, the properties are listed in a column on the left, and any values that have been chosen appear in a column to the right. If the property has a red line through it, another rule has the same style declaration. Hover the pointer over the red line to see a ScreenTip. You can organize the properties in a number of different ways, using the four buttons at the top of the CSS Properties panel. The Show categorized list button is used to display the CSS Properties in categories. The Show alphabetized list button organizes all the CSS properties in alphabetical order. The Show set properties on top button places the properties and values that you have set on top of the list; the list shows all the other properties as well. The Summary button lists just the properties that you have set. Click the plus (+) sign to the left of the property to expand the list for that group of properties. You can also use the CSS Properties panel to modify an existing style.

Next, you'll show Tyrell how to modify an existing style and apply the style without having to select the text and use the Apply Styles panel.

Modifying and Applying an Existing Style

TIP

Never move a style manually by cutting and pasting in Code view. Always use the Manage Styles panel instead.

Tyrell is concerned about the .border style. He feels that the text and the border are too close together. You'll work with him to place some white space between the bottom border and the text for the paragraphs that follow. You'll also add some margin space below the second paragraph.

To create padding and margin space for the second paragraph:

1. In the Apply Styles panel, right-click the **.border** style.
2. Click **Modify Style**.

   The Modify Style dialog box opens.
3. In the Category bar, click **Box**.
4. In the margin section, click the **Same for all** check box to uncheck it.

   You can now type in all four of the margin boxes.
5. Click in the **bottom** box and then type **3em**.
6. Click the **OK** button and then, if necessary, scroll up to view the second paragraph.

   The bottom margin for the second paragraph has been increased, as shown in Figure 5-29.
7. Save the file.

Figure 5-29 Margin space added

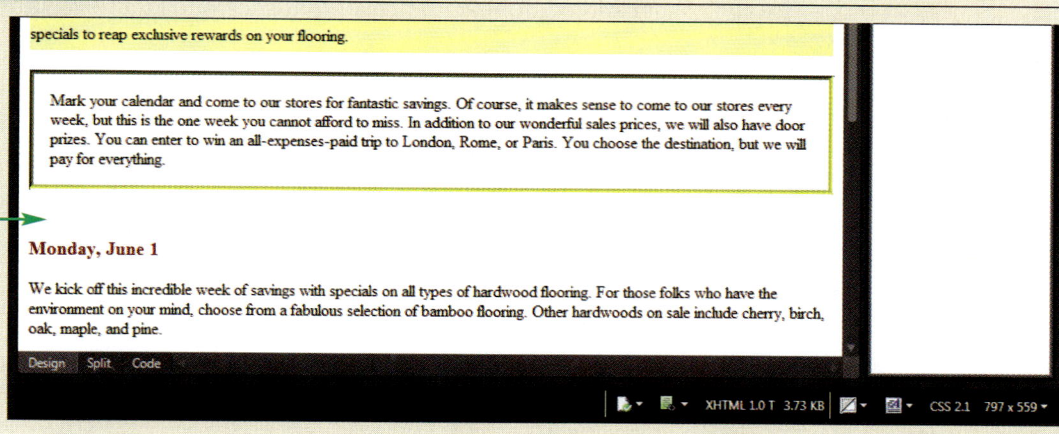

margin space is added below the second paragraph

Now that the styles are complete, you want to show Tyrell how to use an external style sheet. Using an external style sheet will allow the styles created in this document to be used in other documents as well.

Using External Styles

The true power of Cascading Style Sheets lies in external styles, which separate structure from presentation. Using an external style sheet, you can format many HTML documents at the same time. You'll start by creating an external style sheet for use with the gasdennew.html file, which Tyrell can later use to format all of the documents at the Gasden Web site.

REFERENCE

Creating an External Style Sheet File

- Click the File menu, point to New, and then click CSS.
- Enter an identifying CSS comment for the file.
- Enter the styles code.
- Save the file with the filename extension of .css.

Only CSS code, not HTML code, is typed in a CSS external style sheet. It's a good coding practice to type a CSS comment at the top of a CSS style sheet document. The code for a CSS comment begins with a forward slash and an asterisk. You then type the comment, followed by another asterisk and another forward slash. You'll start the Gasden Flooring external style sheet by entering a comment containing your first and last name.

To create the external style sheet:

1. Click **File** on the menu bar, point to **New**, and then click **CSS**.

   A blank page named Untitled_1.css opens.

2. Type **/* External Style Sheet created by**, type your first and last name, and then type ***/**.
3. Press the **Enter** key twice.

   The style sheet should appear similar to that shown in Figure 5-30.

Figure 5-30 Creating the external style sheet

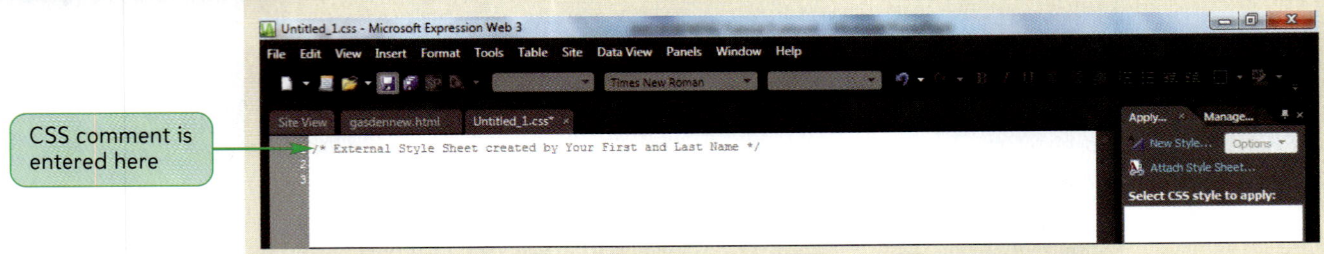

4. Right-click the **Untitled1.css** Document tab, and then click **Save**.

   The Save As dialog box opens.

5. In the Save As dialog box, navigate to the Tutorial folder and then, in the File name box, type **gasdenstylesnew.css**.
6. Click the **Save** button.
7. In the Save As dialog box, if necessary, navigate to the Tutorial folder and then click the Save button to save the file in the Tutorial folder.
8. Click the **gasdennew.html** Document tab.

   Trouble? If you receive an alert that the CSS file could not be attached, open the Folder List panel and then move the CSS file into the Tutorial folder.

   The gasdennew.html file now appears again in the editing window.

Next, you'll create two style declarations for the body element, which will affect the appearance of the entire page.

To create the body style and attach the gasdenstylesnew.css style sheet:

1. In the Apply Styles panel, click **New Style**.

   The New Style dialog box opens.
2. Click the **Selector** arrow and then click **body**.
3. Click the **Define in** arrow and then click **Existing style sheet**.
4. Click in the **URL** text box and type **gasdenstylesnew.css**.
5. Click the **font-family** arrow and then click **Arial, Helvetica, sans-serif**.
6. Click the **color** arrow, click **Navy** (the third swatch from the right in the top row), and then click the **OK** button to return to Design view.

No changes have occurred on the gasdennew.html Web page. You have to attach the style sheet, which you will do next.

To attach the gasdenstylesnew.css style sheet:

1. Press the **Alt+F1** keys to open the Folder List panel and then, if necessary, expand the Data Files and Tutorial folders.
2. In the Folder List panel, click and drag the **gasdenstylesnew.css** filename over any portion of the editing window, and then release the mouse button.

   The gasdenstylesnew.css file is attached to the gasdennew.html file and the document is formatted based on the styles created in the gasdenstylesnew.css file.
3. Press the **Alt+F1** keys again to close the Folder List panel.

   The gasdenstylesnew.css filename has been added in the Apply Styles panel. The gasdennew.html file should appear as shown in Figure 5-31.

Figure 5-31 The style sheet attached

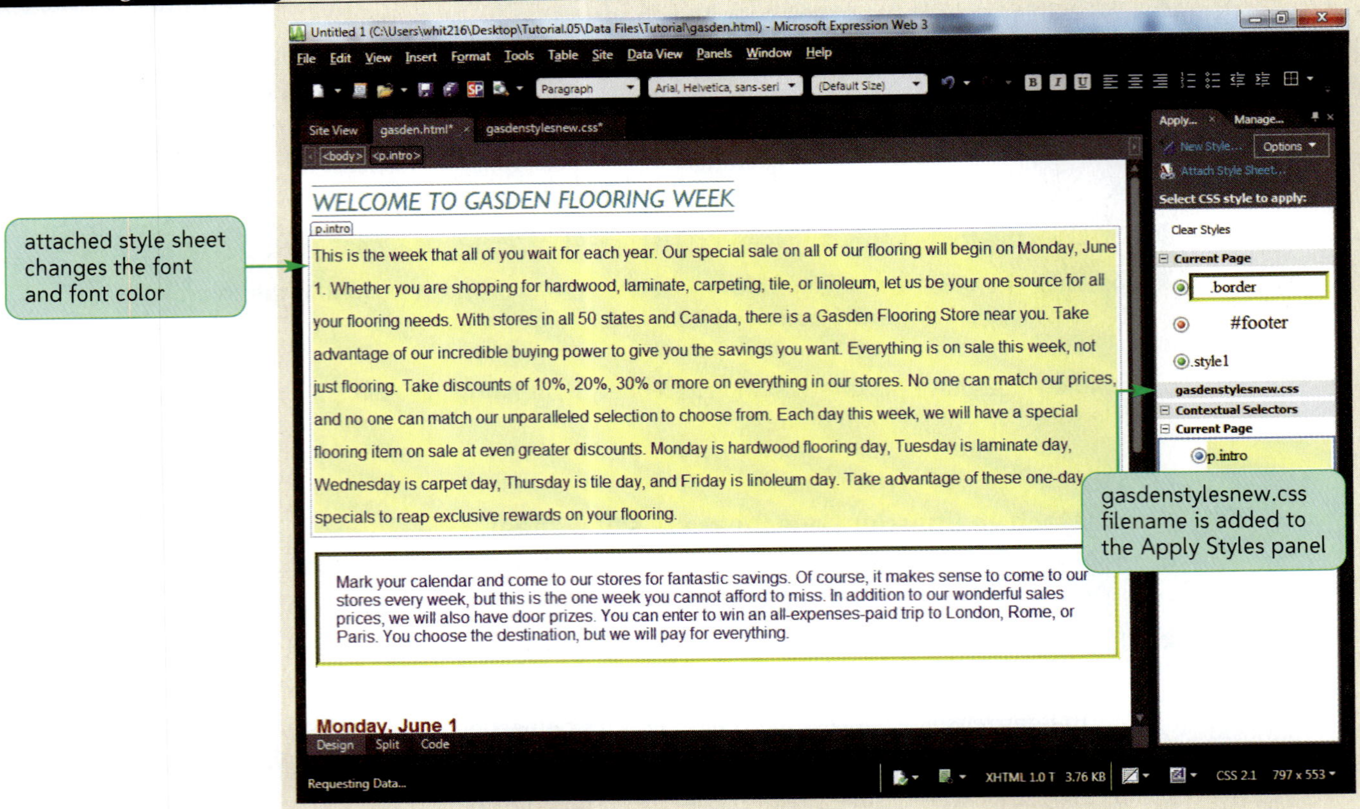

PROSKILLS

Written Communications: Using Styles Appropriately

When composing styles for your documents, don't get carried away with creating too many styles. Don't use too many fonts, colors, and borders. Too many changes in text appearance can actually detract from, rather than enhance, your message. You don't want your Web pages to look like a ransom note; instead, you want your readers to focus on what you have to say and not how you have said it. Don't use more than two fonts or more than two text colors on a Web page. If you change the text color and decide to use a background color as well, make sure that the foreground text and the background text complement each other, rather than compete with each other. Use bold or italic text only when you really need to draw attention to the most important points on your Web page. If you overuse bold or italic text, it becomes difficult for your readers to discern the ordinary from the important points in your document.

You have shown Tyrell how easy it is to attach a style sheet document. The real power of external styles, however, is the ability to attach a style sheet to more than one document. You want to show Tyrell a quick and efficient way to attach a style sheet to more than one document.

Detaching and Attaching an External Style Sheet

You can attach or detach an external style sheet using the Apply Styles panel or the Manage Styles panel. Both methods open the Attach Style Sheet dialog box, as shown in Figure 5-32.

Figure 5-32 The Attach Style Sheet dialog box

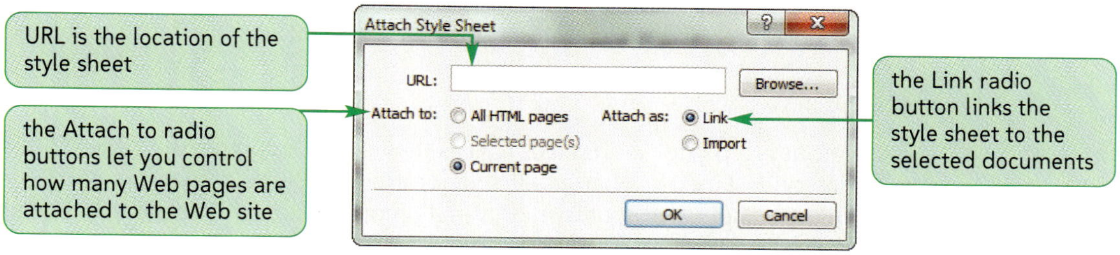

The URL box is used to specify the storage location of the CSS file. You have three options for Attach to:

- *All HTML pages*—This option attaches the external style sheet to all HTML pages in the Folder List panel.
- *Selected page(s)*—This option attaches a style sheet to several pages at once. To do so, before you attach the style sheet, hold down the Ctrl key and click the names of the files in the Folder List panel to which you want to attach the style sheet. Then, in the Apply Styles panel, click Attach Style Sheet.
- *Current page*—This option attaches the external style sheet to the file that is currently open on the screen.

REFERENCE

Attaching an External Style Sheet File

- Open the Web page to which you want to attach the external style sheet, go to the Apply Styles panel or the Manage Styles panel, and then click Attach Style Sheet.
- In the Attach Style Sheet dialog box, enter the URL of the style sheet file, or click the Browse button to navigate to the location of the file.

or

- Alternatively, to attach a style sheet, in Design view, click and drag a .css file from the Folder List panel onto the editing window.

TIP

To quickly find a style code, right-click the style name in the Apply Styles panel, and then click Go To Code on the shortcut menu.

The choice for *Attach as* has two options. Use the Link option to enter code for the link tag in the <head> section of your HTML document. Use the Import option to insert an @ import code instead of link code. The @import code imports—or makes use of—CSS code from another CSS external file. By importing the code, you do not have to spend time typing or cutting and pasting CSS code from another CSS file. You will use @import in later tutorials, but next you'll show Tyrell an easy way to detach the gasdenstylesnew.css file from the gasdennew.html document.

To detach the gasdenstylesnew.css style sheet:

1. In the Apply Styles panel, right-click the **gasdenstylesnew.css** filename, and then click **Remove Link** on the shortcut menu.

   An alert box appears asking you to confirm that you want to remove the link.

2. Click **Yes**.

3. In the Apply Styles panel, click **Attach Style Sheet**.

   The Attach Style Sheet dialog box opens. In the URL box, type **gasdenstylesnew.css**.

4. If necessary, click the option buttons for **Current page** and **Link**.

5. Click the **OK** button.

   The body style is again attached to the document and the font family and font color changes are made.

As you develop your Web pages and as they grow in complexity, you will likely create many styles. Finding a particular style or group of styles among many choices in the Apply Styles panel can become increasingly more tedious. Expression Web lets you organize your styles by order, by element, or by type. You'll show Tyrell how managing styles can make them easier to work with.

Managing Styles

You can control how you group and display styles using the Options buttons available in both the Apply Styles panel and the Manage Styles panel. The options are nearly the same in both panels, except that the Apply Styles panel allows you to preview a background color and automatically previews the appearance of styles, whereas the Manage Styles panel allows you to categorize the styles by element. You'll show Tyrell how to group and display styles in the Manage Styles panel, and you'll show him how to use the Manage Style options.

TIP

"Manage Styles" might be abbreviated as "Mana..." on the Manage Styles panel tab.

To view the Manage Styles options:

1. Click the **Manage Styles** panel tab to display the Manage Styles panel.

2. Click the **Options** button.

   A drop-down list opens.

3. Click **Categorize By Type**.

   The styles are now categorized by type, as shown in Figure 5-33.

Figure 5-33 Manage Styles list categorized by type

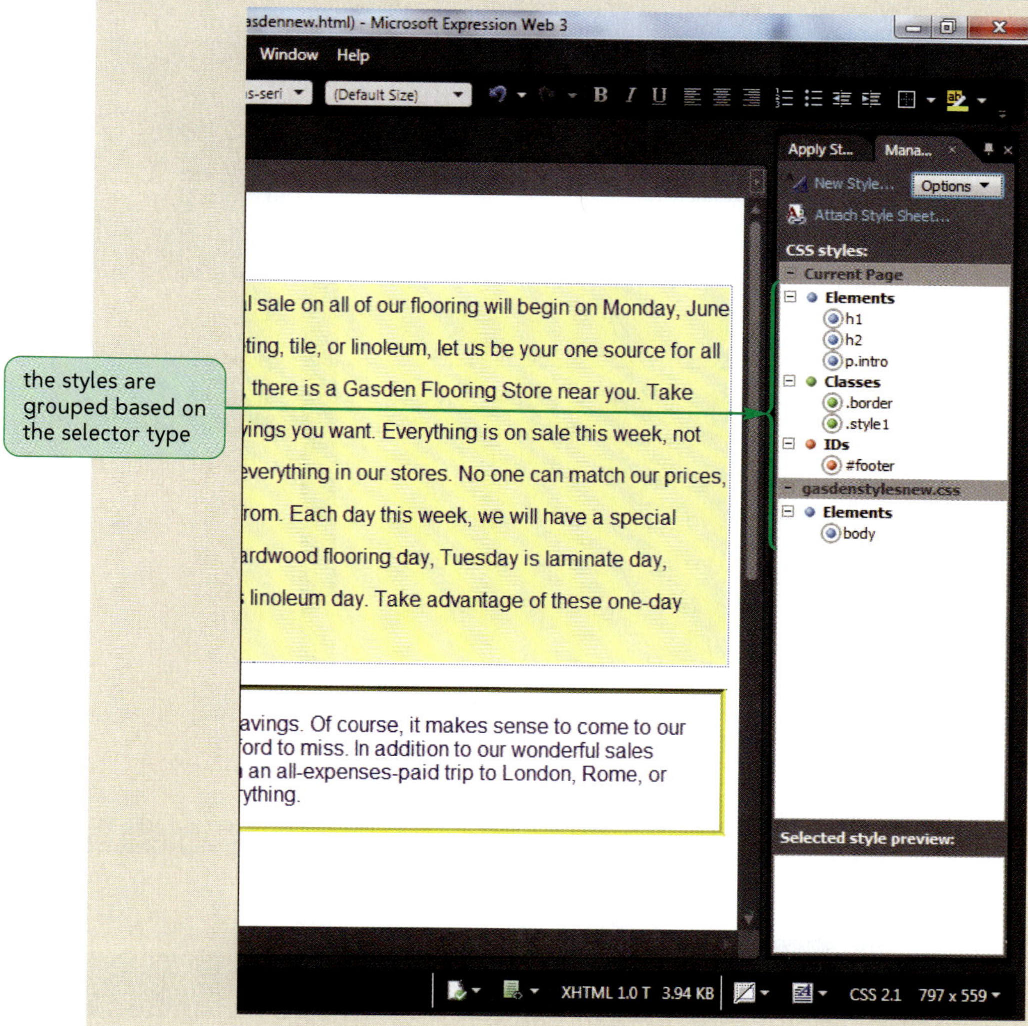

4. Click the **Options** button and then click **Categorize by Order**.

   The styles are now grouped by their order in the internal style sheet and in the external style sheet, as shown in Figure 5-34.

Figure 5-34 **Changing the style order**

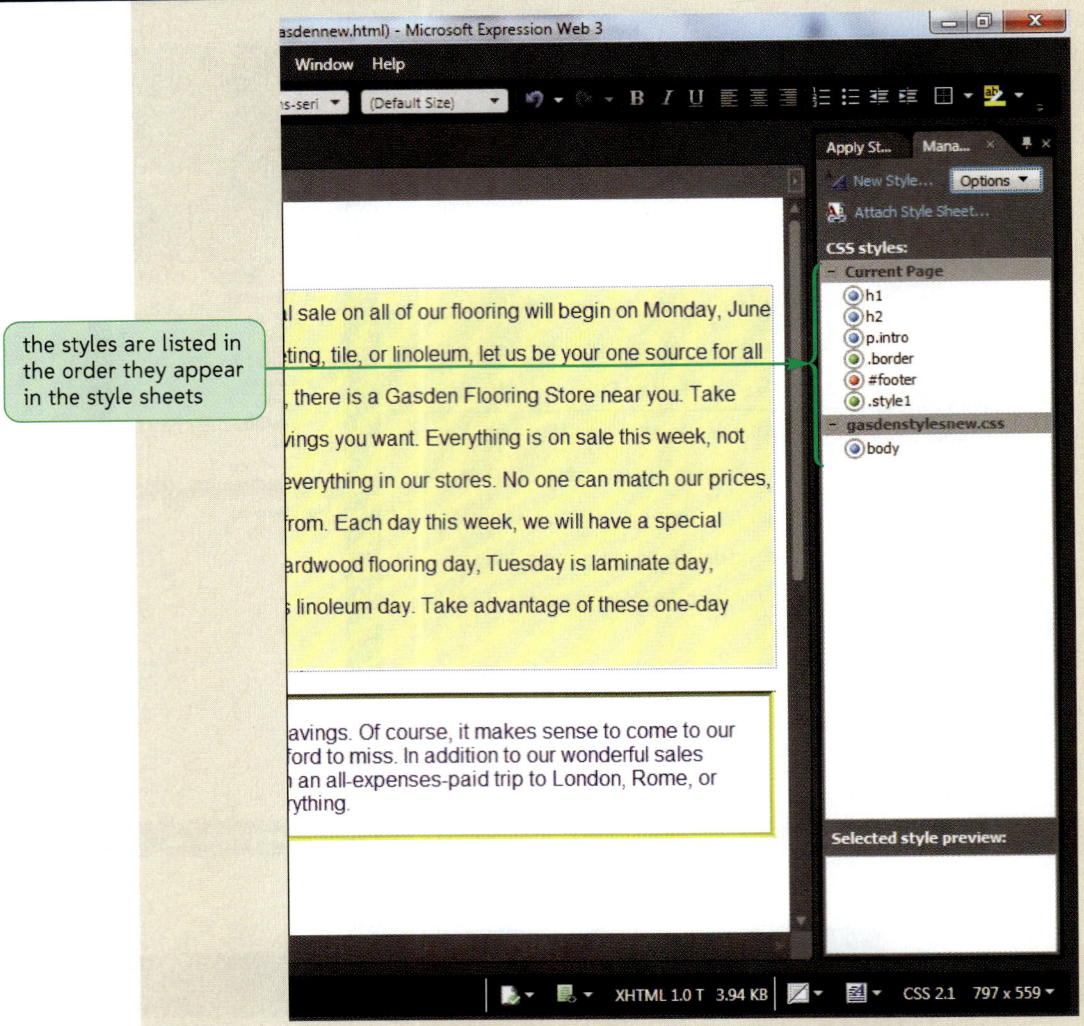

INSIGHT

Using the Options Button

Both the Apply Styles panel and the Manage Styles panel have an Options button. The options allow you to choose which styles appear in the style list in the panel and how they are displayed. The option for Categorize by Order lists the styles in the order in which they appear in the style sheet from top to bottom. The option for Categorize by Type lists each type of style based upon whether the style is an element style, a class style, or an ID style. The Manage Styles panel has a third option, the option for Categorize by Element. This option places all of the styles in alphabetic order, irrespective of what type of styles are in the style list.

Tyrell would like to center the h1 heading. To make this type of simple edit, you can use the Center button in the Common toolbar. However, using the Center button will generate a style. You'll have Tyrell center the line he wants, and then have him rename the style that Expression Web creates so that it has a more descriptive name.

Having a descriptive name serves to document the code so that the style name suggests the purpose of the style. You'll also have Tyrell rename an earlier style, .style1, which was created when the symbols were entered into the footer, to give this style a more descriptive name.

To center the h1 text and rename the style:

1. Click the **Apply Styles** panel tab to open the Apply Styles panel.
2. Click anywhere in the h1 heading at the top of the page and then click the **Center** button on the Common toolbar.
3. Right-click **.style2** in the Apply Styles panel and then click **Rename class "style2"**.

   The Rename Class dialog box opens.
4. In the New name box, type **center**, and then click the **OK** button.

   The style is renamed as .center.
5. Right-click **.style1** in the Apply Styles panel and then click **Rename class "style1"**.

   The Rename Class dialog box opens. You created the style1 class when you entered the Symbol code in the footer.
6. In the New name box, type **footer_symbol**, and then click the **OK** button. The style is renamed.

With the text content styled, you are ready to insert the logo image in the document. The image, named gasdenlogo.png, is located in the Review folder in the Folder List panel. You'll show Tyrell how to copy a file from one folder to another.

To copy the gasdenlogo.png image:

1. Press the **Alt+F1** keys to display the Folder List panel.
2. Click the **+** sign to the left of the Review folder to expand that folder.
3. Click the **gasdenlogo.png** filename.
4. Press and hold the **Ctrl** key, drag the **gasdenlogo.png** filename anywhere over the Tutorial folder, and then release the mouse button and the Ctrl key.

   The gasdenlogo.png file is copied into the Tutorial folder.
5. Click the **-** sign to the left of the Review folder to collapse that folder.

Now that the image file has been copied, you are ready to insert the logo image onto the page.

To insert the gasdenlogo.png image:

1. Click anywhere in the document and then press the **Ctrl+Home** keys to position the insertion point at the top of the page.
2. Press the **Enter** key and then click anywhere in the new blank line at the top of the page.
3. Click the **h1.center** Code tab for the new blank line (not the h1 heading below it).

4. On the Common toolbar, click the **Style** arrow and then click **Paragraph <p>**.
5. Click and drag the gasdenlogo.png filename from the Folder List panel to the new blank paragraph at the top of the page, and then release the mouse button.

   The Accessibility Properties dialog box opens.
6. In the Alternate box, type **Gasden Flooring logo image**.
7. Click the **OK** button.
8. On the Common toolbar, click the **Center** button to center the image.
9. Press the **Alt+F1** keys to hide the Folder List panel.

   The logo image should appear as shown in Figure 5-35.

Figure 5-35 The logo image

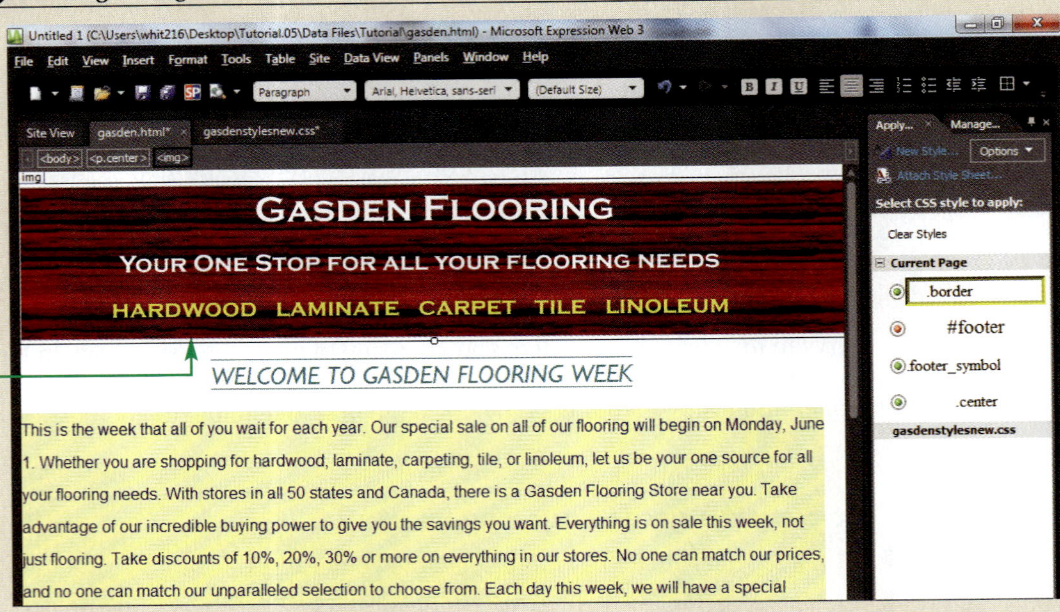

Now that the document is complete, your final task is to show Tyrell how to use the CSS Reports feature to check for errors.

Running CSS Reports

You use the CSS Reports feature in Expression Web to check for errors in CSS code in your Web pages and external CSS files. CSS reports are a very useful tool for determining if there are any errors in the CSS code on your Web site. You can check some or all of the pages for errors. You can find unused styles, undefined classes, and mismatched cases. If an error is found, you can double-click the error in the report list, and Expression Web will open the file in Code view and position the insertion point where the error occurs in the code.

REFERENCE

Running CSS Reports

- Click Tools on the menu bar and then click CSS Reports to open the CSS Reports dialog box.
- Select one of the *Check where* option buttons.
- Check the appropriate *Check for* check boxes.
- Click the Check button to open the CSS Reports window.
- When you finish reviewing the results, click the Close button.

You'll run a CSS report with Tyrell to check gasdennew.html and gasdenstylesnew.css for errors.

To run a CSS report:

1. Click **Tools** on the menu bar and then click **CSS Reports**.

   The CSS Reports dialog box opens.

2. Click the **All pages** option button and then, if necessary, click the Check for check boxes so all three are checked.

   The CSS Reports dialog box should look like the one shown in Figure 5-36.

Figure 5-36 **The CSS Reports dialog box**

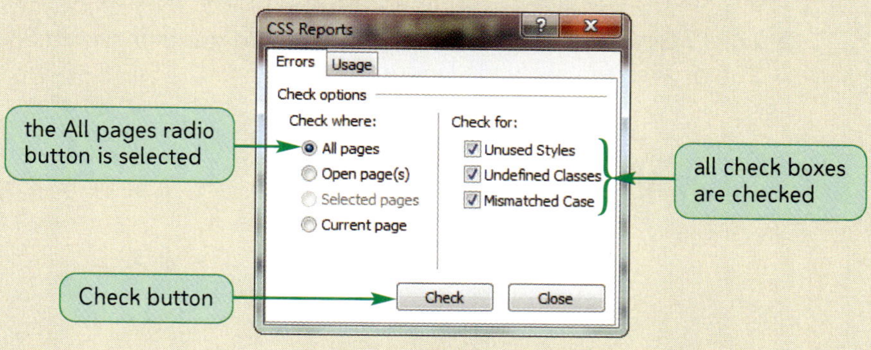

3. Click the **Check** button.

   Expression Web checks the file and displays the CSS Reports window, as shown in Figure 5-37. The report indicates that an unused style is present in the shoes.html file in the Case1 folder.

Figure 5-37 **The CSS Reports window**

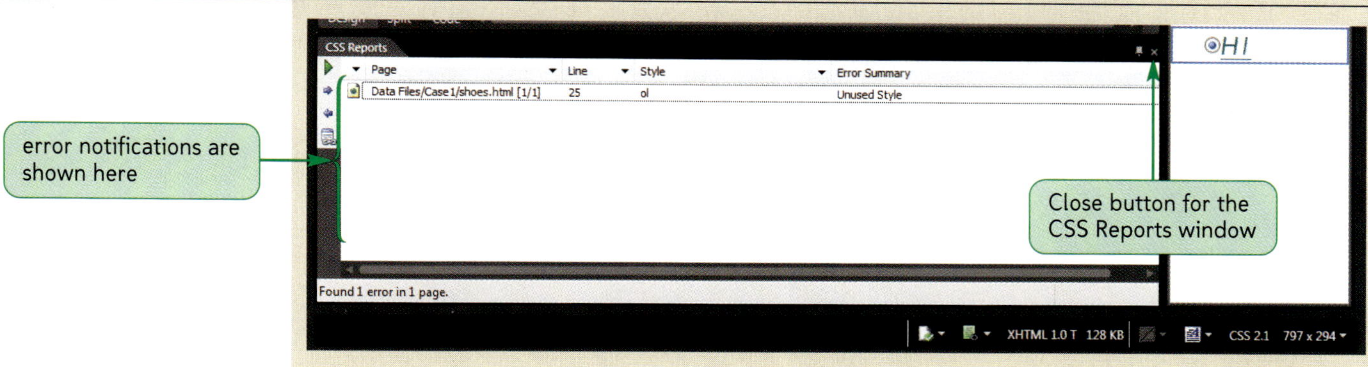

4. In the CSS Reports pane, double-click anywhere on the line with the error notification.

   Expression Web opens the file containing the error and positions the insertion point at the exact point in the code where the error is located. You will correct the error later.

5. In the upper-right corner of the CSS Reports window, click the **Close** button.
6. Close the **shoes.html** file.

You'll now add some documentation to the Web page file and then view the completed file in the browser.

To save all files and view the completed file in the browser:

1. Press the **Ctrl+End** keys to position the insertion point at the end of the document.
2. Type your first and last name.
3. Press the **Shift+Enter** keys and then type **Tutorial 5**.
4. If necessary, select the two lines of text you just typed and format those two lines as bold text.
5. Click **File** on the menu bar, click **Save All**, and then if the Save Embedded files dialog box opens, click the **OK** button.
6. Press the **F12** key to view the completed gasdennew.html file in the default browser, as shown in Figure 5-38.

Figure 5-38 The completed file in the browser

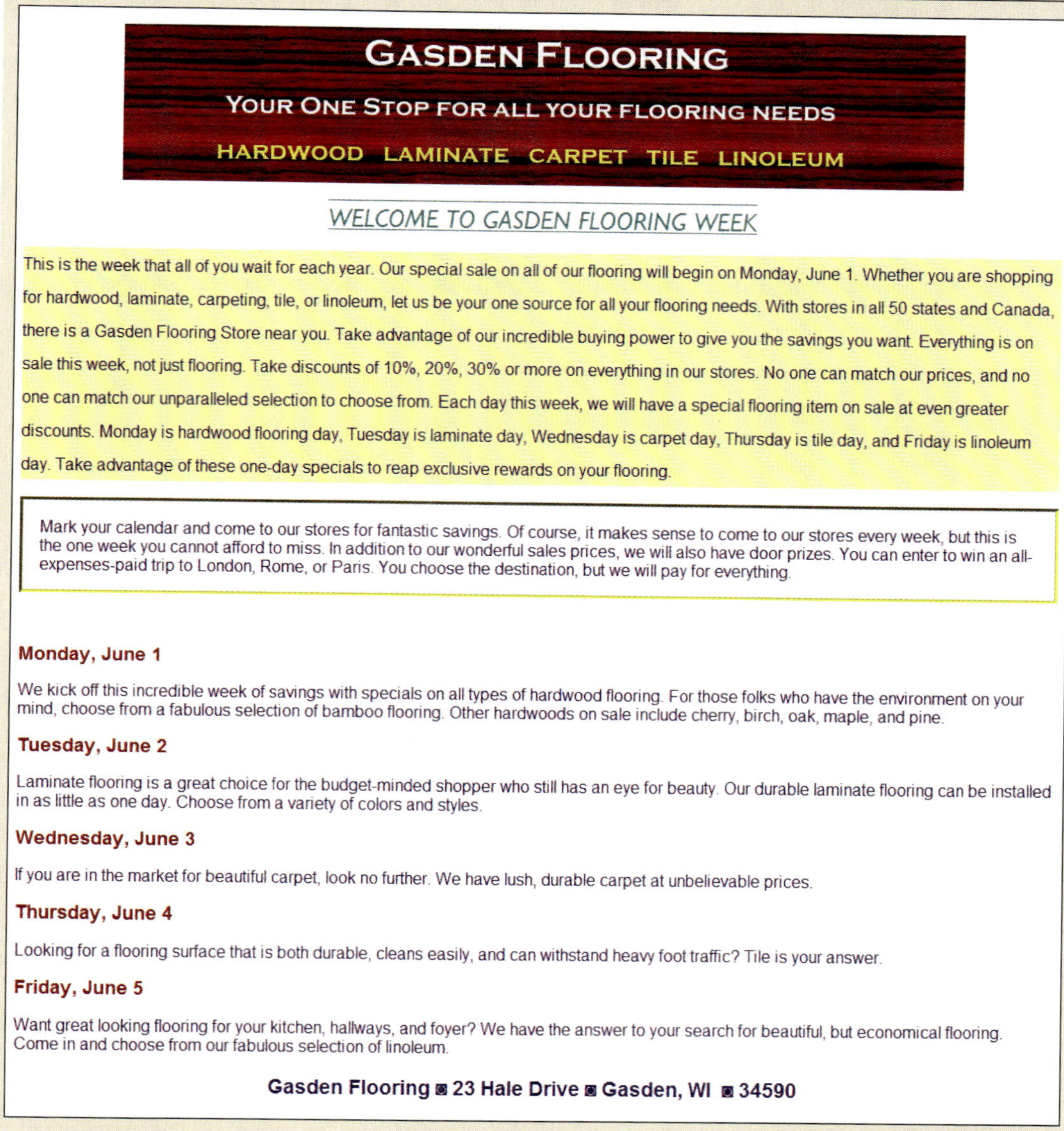

GASDEN FLOORING

YOUR ONE STOP FOR ALL YOUR FLOORING NEEDS

HARDWOOD LAMINATE CARPET TILE LINOLEUM

WELCOME TO GASDEN FLOORING WEEK

This is the week that all of you wait for each year. Our special sale on all of our flooring will begin on Monday, June 1. Whether you are shopping for hardwood, laminate, carpeting, tile, or linoleum, let us be your one source for all your flooring needs. With stores in all 50 states and Canada, there is a Gasden Flooring Store near you. Take advantage of our incredible buying power to give you the savings you want. Everything is on sale this week, not just flooring. Take discounts of 10%, 20%, 30% or more on everything in our stores. No one can match our prices, and no one can match our unparalleled selection to choose from. Each day this week, we will have a special flooring item on sale at even greater discounts. Monday is hardwood flooring day, Tuesday is laminate day, Wednesday is carpet day, Thursday is tile day, and Friday is linoleum day. Take advantage of these one-day specials to reap exclusive rewards on your flooring.

Mark your calendar and come to our stores for fantastic savings. Of course, it makes sense to come to our stores every week, but this is the one week you cannot afford to miss. In addition to our wonderful sales prices, we will also have door prizes. You can enter to win an all-expenses-paid trip to London, Rome, or Paris. You choose the destination, but we will pay for everything.

Monday, June 1

We kick off this incredible week of savings with specials on all types of hardwood flooring. For those folks who have the environment on your mind, choose from a fabulous selection of bamboo flooring. Other hardwoods on sale include cherry, birch, oak, maple, and pine.

Tuesday, June 2

Laminate flooring is a great choice for the budget-minded shopper who still has an eye for beauty. Our durable laminate flooring can be installed in as little as one day. Choose from a variety of colors and styles.

Wednesday, June 3

If you are in the market for beautiful carpet, look no further. We have lush, durable carpet at unbelievable prices.

Thursday, June 4

Looking for a flooring surface that is both durable, cleans easily, and can withstand heavy foot traffic? Tile is your answer.

Friday, June 5

Want great looking flooring for your kitchen, hallways, and foyer? We have the answer to your search for beautiful, but economical flooring. Come in and choose from our fabulous selection of linoleum.

Gasden Flooring ◙ 23 Hale Drive ◙ Gasden, WI ◙ 34590

7. Close the browser, and then in Expression Web, close all files.
8. Submit the completed files to your instructor, either in printed or electronic form, as requested.

REVIEW

Session 5.2 Quick Check

1. What are the two types of classes?
2. What character precedes an ID selector name?
3. After you create a class style, what must you also do to have that style take effect?
4. What filename extension must be given to a style sheet file?
5. What two panels are used to arrange styles so that you can see them in a different order?
6. What can you run to verify the accuracy of your CSS code?

Practice the skills you learned in the tutorial, using the same case scenario.

PRACTICE

Review Assignments

Data Files needed for this Review Assignment: rug.html, rug.jpg, rugstyles.css

Gasden Flooring is introducing a new line of rugs. Tyrell would like you to add another page to the Gasden Flooring Web site explaining the advantages of purchasing rugs from Gasden Flooring. A preview of the completed Web page appears in Figure 5-39.

Figure 5-39 Completed Gasden Flooring Rug Palace Web page

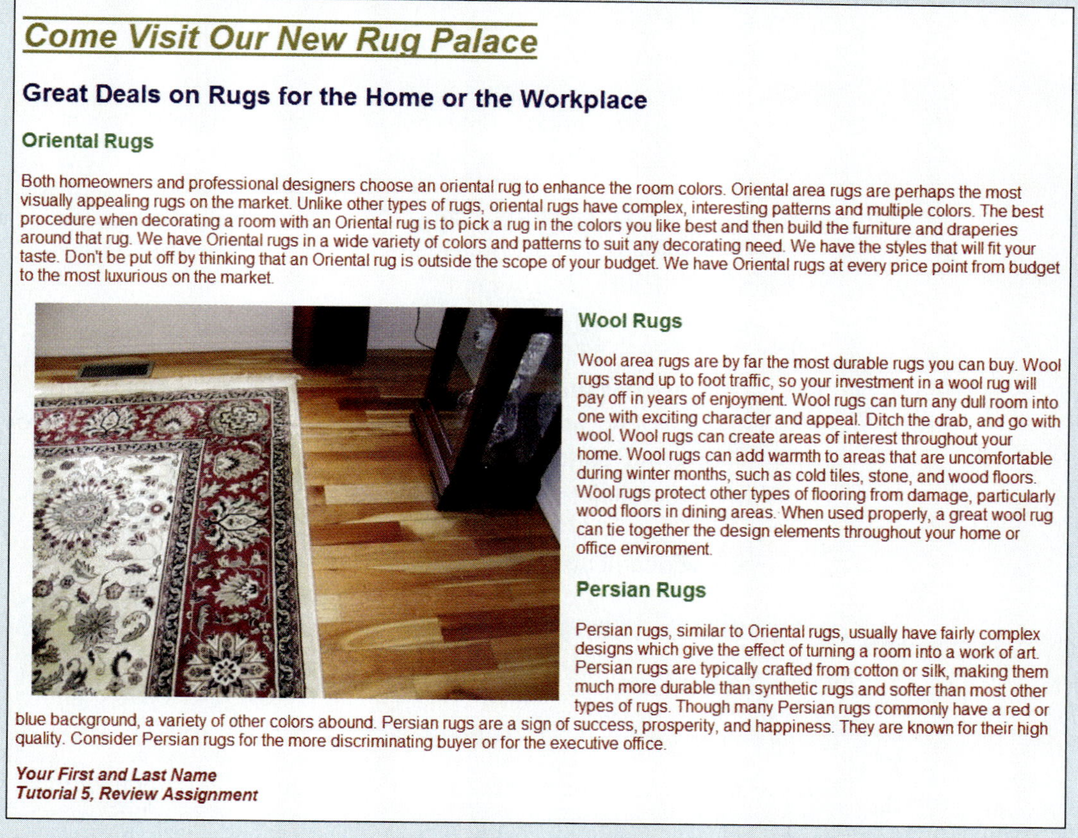
Come Visit Our New Rug Palace

Great Deals on Rugs for the Home or the Workplace

Oriental Rugs

Both homeowners and professional designers choose an oriental rug to enhance the room colors. Oriental area rugs are perhaps the most visually appealing rugs on the market. Unlike other types of rugs, oriental rugs have complex, interesting patterns and multiple colors. The best procedure when decorating a room with an Oriental rug is to pick a rug in the colors you like best and then build the furniture and draperies around that rug. We have Oriental rugs in a wide variety of colors and patterns to suit any decorating need. We have the styles that will fit your taste. Don't be put off by thinking that an Oriental rug is outside the scope of your budget. We have Oriental rugs at every price point from budget to the most luxurious on the market.

Wool Rugs

Wool area rugs are by far the most durable rugs you can buy. Wool rugs stand up to foot traffic, so your investment in a wool rug will pay off in years of enjoyment. Wool rugs can turn any dull room into one with exciting character and appeal. Ditch the drab, and go with wool. Wool rugs can create areas of interest throughout your home. Wool rugs can add warmth to areas that are uncomfortable during winter months, such as cold tiles, stone, and wood floors. Wool rugs protect other types of flooring from damage, particularly wood floors in dining areas. When used properly, a great wool rug can tie together the design elements throughout your home or office environment.

Persian Rugs

Persian rugs, similar to Oriental rugs, usually have fairly complex designs which give the effect of turning a room into a work of art. Persian rugs are typically crafted from cotton or silk, making them much more durable than synthetic rugs and softer than most other types of rugs. Though many Persian rugs commonly have a red or blue background, a variety of other colors abound. Persian rugs are a sign of success, prosperity, and happiness. They are known for their high quality. Consider Persian rugs for the more discriminating buyer or for the executive office.

Your First and Last Name
Tutorial 5, Review Assignment

Complete the following:

1. If necessary, start Expression Web, close any open sites, and open the Tutorial.05 Web site. Reset the workspace layout.
2. If necessary, expand the Data Files folder and the Review folder to display its contents.
3. Open the **rug.html** file from your Review folder and save the file as **rugnew.html** in the same folder.
4. In Design view, right-click anywhere on the page. On the shortcut menu, click Page Properties. In the Title box, type **Gasden Flooring Rugs**.
5. In the Page description box, type your own first and last name, type a forward slash, and type **Tutorial 5, Review Assignment**. Click the OK button.

6. In the Apply Styles panel, click New Style. Click the Selector arrow and click body. Click the font-family arrow and click Arial, Helvetica, sans-serif. Click the OK button to return to Design view.
7. In the Apply Styles panel, click New Style. Click the Selector arrow, scroll down the list, and click h1. Format the h1 style to display text in italic and olive (#808000). For text decoration, click the underline check box, and then click the overline check box. Click the OK button to return to Design view.
8. In the Apply Styles panel, click New Style. Click the Selector arrow, scroll down the list, and click h2. Format the h2 style to display text in Navy (#000080). Click the OK button to return to Design view.
9. In the Apply Styles panel, click New Style. Click the Selector arrow, scroll down the list, and click h3. Format the h3 style to display text in green (#008000). Click the OK button to return to Design view.
10. Click and drag the rugstyles.css file onto the rugnew.html file in the editing window to attach the rugstyles.css file.
11. Click and drag the rug.jpg filename before the Wool Rugs h3 heading and then release the mouse button. Enter **photo of rug** as the alternate text, and then click the OK button. Right-click the image and change the Picture Properties so that the wrapping style is set to Left. Set the horizontal margin to 15 px.
12. Press the Ctrl+End keys to position the insertion point at the end of the last sentence of the document. Type your first and last name. Press the Shift+Enter keys and type **Tutorial 5, Review Assignment**.
13. Select the two lines of text you just typed. Using the Common toolbar, format the text to appear in both bold and italic.
14. Save the **rugnew.html** file.
15. Open the **rugnew.html** file in your browser. The document should look similar to the one shown in Figure 5-39.
16. Submit the completed file to your instructor, either in printed or electronic form, as requested.
17. Close all documents, close your browser, and close the Web site.

Use the skills you learned in the tutorial to create a Web page for an online shoe store.

APPLY

Case Problem 1

Data File needed for this Case Problem: shoes.html

Choose Shoes Choose Shoes is a very successful seller of men's and women's shoes. Although the stores are located in many malls in the eastern United States, Choose Shoes relies on its Web site to target a broader market. You'll use CSS classes to style the Choose Shoes Web page. A preview of the completed file appears in Figure 5-40.

Figure 5-40 Completed Choose Shoes Web page

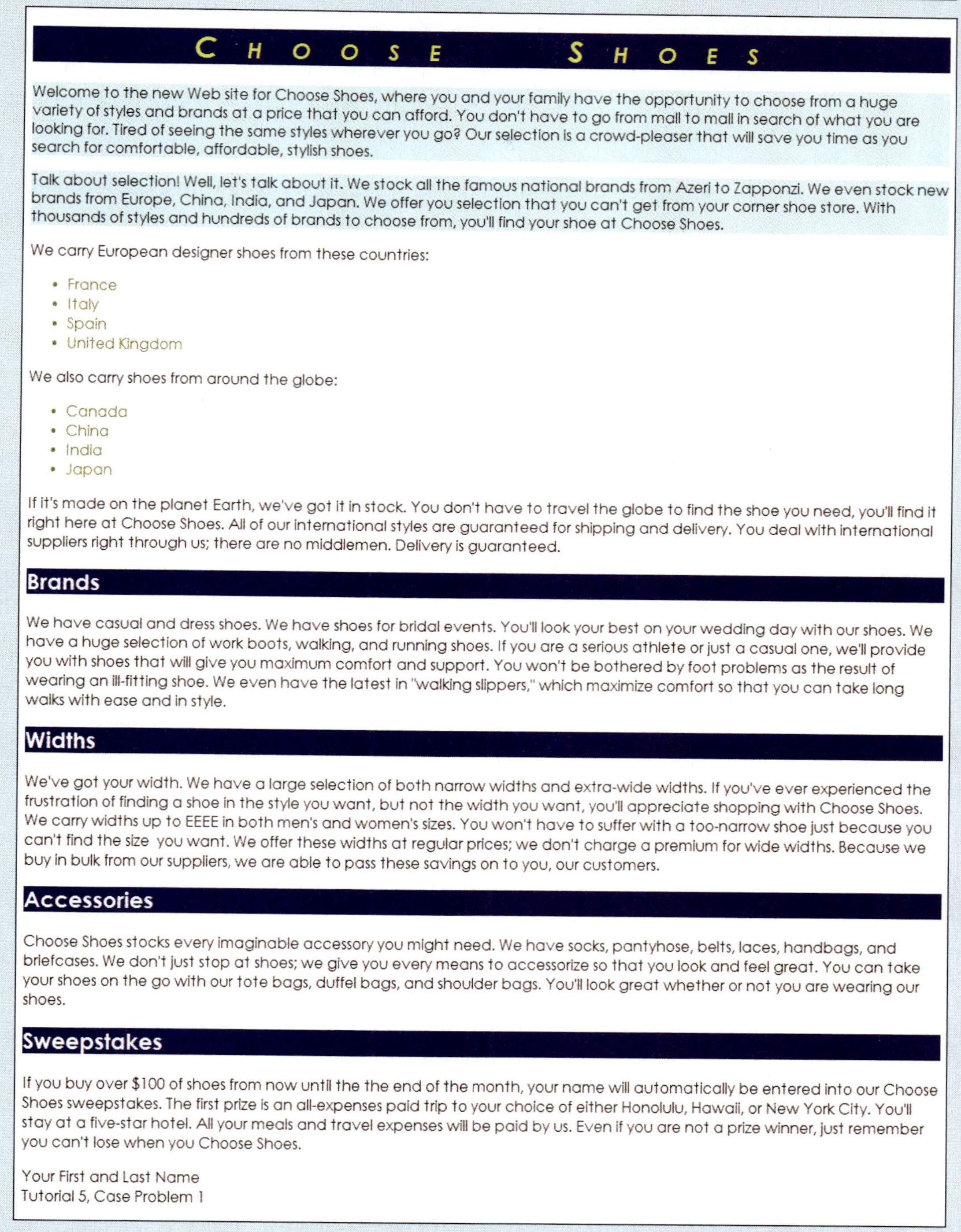

C H O O S E   S H O E S

Welcome to the new Web site for Choose Shoes, where you and your family have the opportunity to choose from a huge variety of styles and brands at a price that you can afford. You don't have to go from mall to mall in search of what you are looking for. Tired of seeing the same styles wherever you go? Our selection is a crowd-pleaser that will save you time as you search for comfortable, affordable, stylish shoes.

Talk about selection! Well, let's talk about it. We stock all the famous national brands from Azeri to Zapponzi. We even stock new brands from Europe, China, India, and Japan. We offer you selection that you can't get from your corner shoe store. With thousands of styles and hundreds of brands to choose from, you'll find your shoe at Choose Shoes.

We carry European designer shoes from these countries:

- France
- Italy
- Spain
- United Kingdom

We also carry shoes from around the globe:

- Canada
- China
- India
- Japan

If it's made on the planet Earth, we've got it in stock. You don't have to travel the globe to find the shoe you need, you'll find it right here at Choose Shoes. All of our international styles are guaranteed for shipping and delivery. You deal with international suppliers right through us; there are no middlemen. Delivery is guaranteed.

Brands

We have casual and dress shoes. We have shoes for bridal events. You'll look your best on your wedding day with our shoes. We have a huge selection of work boots, walking, and running shoes. If you are a serious athlete or just a casual one, we'll provide you with shoes that will give you maximum comfort and support. You won't be bothered by foot problems as the result of wearing an ill-fitting shoe. We even have the latest in "walking slippers," which maximize comfort so that you can take long walks with ease and in style.

Widths

We've got your width. We have a large selection of both narrow widths and extra-wide widths. If you've ever experienced the frustration of finding a shoe in the style you want, but not the width you want, you'll appreciate shopping with Choose Shoes. We carry widths up to EEEE in both men's and women's sizes. You won't have to suffer with a too-narrow shoe just because you can't find the size you want. We offer these widths at regular prices; we don't charge a premium for wide widths. Because we buy in bulk from our suppliers, we are able to pass these savings on to you, our customers.

Accessories

Choose Shoes stocks every imaginable accessory you might need. We have socks, pantyhose, belts, laces, handbags, and briefcases. We don't just stop at shoes; we give you every means to accessorize so that you look and feel great. You can take your shoes on the go with our tote bags, duffel bags, and shoulder bags. You'll look great whether or not you are wearing our shoes.

Sweepstakes

If you buy over $100 of shoes from now until the the end of the month, your name will automatically be entered into our Choose Shoes sweepstakes. The first prize is an all-expenses paid trip to your choice of either Honolulu, Hawaii, or New York City. You'll stay at a five-star hotel. All your meals and travel expenses will be paid by us. Even if you are not a prize winner, just remember you can't lose when you Choose Shoes.

Your First and Last Name
Tutorial 5, Case Problem 1

Complete the following:

1. If necessary, start Expression Web, close any open sites, and open the Tutorial.05 Web site. Reset the workspace layout.
2. If necessary, expand the Data Files folder and the Case1 folder to display its contents.
3. Open the **shoes.html** file from the Case1 folder and save the file as **shoesnew.html** in the same folder.
4. In Design view, right-click anywhere on the page. On the shortcut menu, click Page Properties. In the Title box, type **You Never Lose with Choose Shoes**.
5. In the Page description box, type your own first and last name, type a forward slash, and type **Tutorial 5, Case Problem 1**. Click the OK button.

EXPLORE

6. In the Apply Styles panel, click the Manage Styles tab to display the Manage Styles panel. An <ol> element style has been created in error. Right-click the ol style and click Delete on the shortcut menu to remove it. Click the Yes button to confirm deletion.
7. In the Manage Styles panel, right-click the h1 style. On the shortcut menu, click Modify Style.
8. In the Block category, click the arrow for the text-align property. Click center. Create 2em of word spacing and 1em of letter spacing.
9. In the Background category, change the background color to navy (#000080). Click the OK button to return to Design view.
10. In the Manage Styles panel, right-click the h2 style. On the shortcut menu, click Modify Style. In the Font category, change the color from Yellow to White (#FFFFFF). In the Background category, change the background color to Navy (#000080). Click the OK button to return to Design view.
11. In the Manage Styles panel, click New Style. In the New Style dialog box, delete .newStyle1 in the Selector box and type **p.intro** in the Selector box.
12. Click Block in the Category bar. Click in the line-height property text box and type **125%**.
13. Click Background in the Category bar. Click the background-color arrow and then click More Colors. Click any shade of light blue. Click the OK button twice to return to Design view.
14. In the Manage Styles panel, click New Style. In the New Style dialog box, delete .newStyle1 in the Selector box. You will be creating an independent class. In the Selector box, type **.bullets**. (Don't forget to type the period before *bullets*.)
15. In the Font category, change the text color to olive (#808000). Click the OK button to return to Design view.
16. If necessary, scroll up to display the first paragraph below the *Choose Shoes* heading. Click anywhere in the first paragraph. In the Manage Styles panel, right-click the p.intro style. On the shortcut menu, click Apply Style.
17. Click anywhere in the second paragraph. In the Manage Styles panel, right-click the p.intro style. On the shortcut menu, click Apply Style.
18. Select the list items France, Italy, Spain, and United Kingdom.
19. In the Manage Styles panel, right-click the bullets style. On the shortcut menu, click Apply Style.
20. Select the list items Canada, China, India, and Japan.
21. In the Manage Styles panel, right-click the bullets style. On the shortcut menu, click Apply Style. Click the Apply Styles tab to display the Apply Styles panel.

EXPLORE

22. Click Tools on the menu bar, and then click CSS Reports. In the CSS Reports dialog box, click the All pages option button. Click the Check button. Determine if there are any CSS errors in the Web site. Click the Close button at the right of the CSS Reports pane to close the CSS Reports pane.
23. In Design view, press the Ctrl+End keys to position the insertion point at the end of the last sentence of the document. Type your first and last name. Press the Shift+Enter keys and type **Tutorial 5, Case Problem 1**.
24. Save the **shoesnew.html** file.
25. Open the **shoesnew.html** file in your browser. The document should appear similar to the one shown in Figure 5-40.
26. Submit the completed file to your instructor, either in printed or electronic form, as requested.
27. Close all documents, close the browser, and close the Web site.

Use the skills you learned in the tutorial to create and style a Web page about the migration patterns of Americans.

CHALLENGE

Case Problem 2

Data File needed for this Case Problem: move.html

A Nation on the Move The United States is a nation in constant flux. In addition to new people continually entering the nation as new citizens, the current populace is in a state of migration from one part of the country to another. You'll style a Web page that offers moving advice. You'll create and apply several ID selectors to style the page. A preview of the completed file appears in Figure 5-41.

Figure 5-41 Completed Nation on the Move Web site

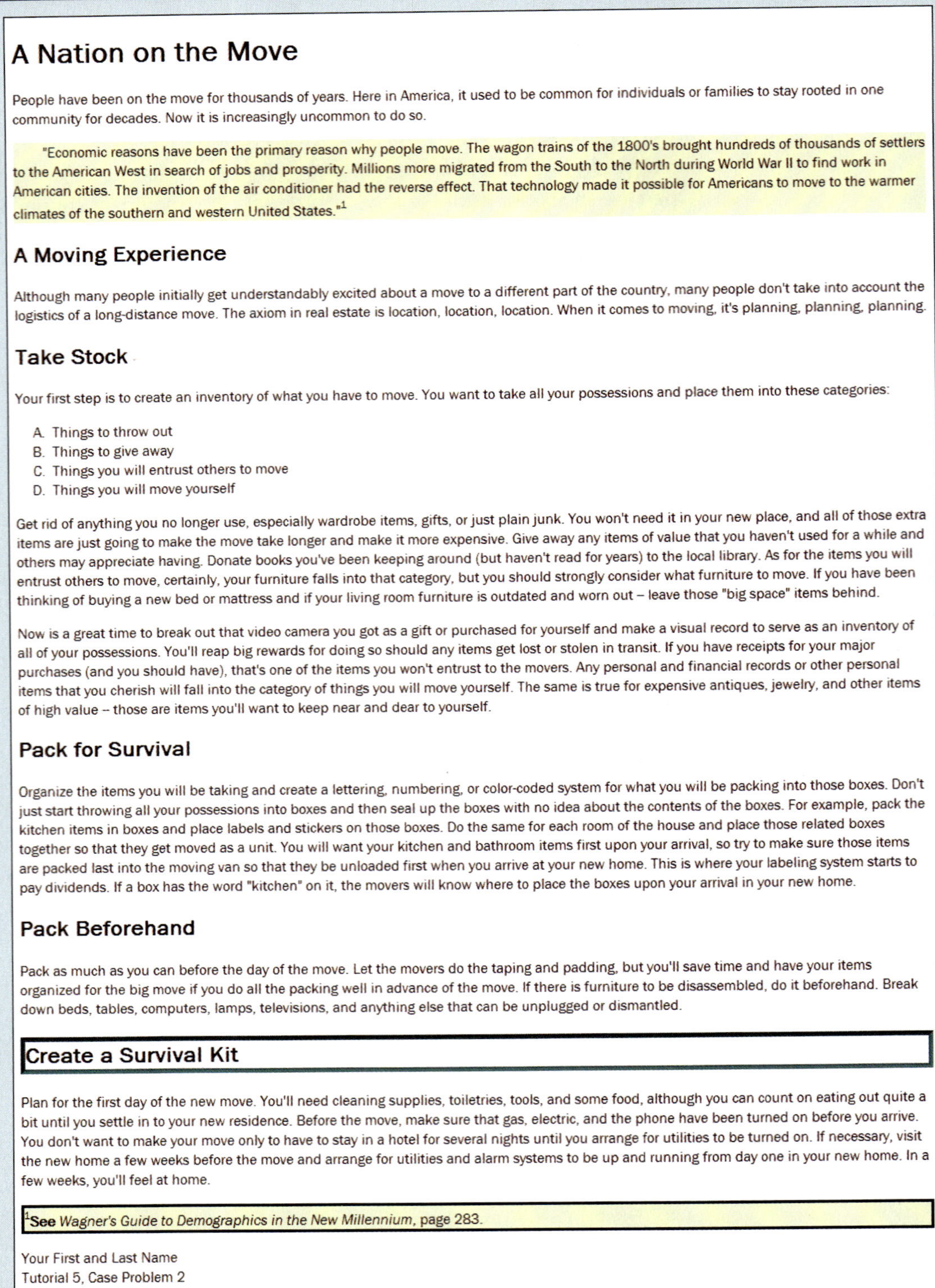

A Nation on the Move

People have been on the move for thousands of years. Here in America, it used to be common for individuals or families to stay rooted in one community for decades. Now it is increasingly uncommon to do so.

"Economic reasons have been the primary reason why people move. The wagon trains of the 1800's brought hundreds of thousands of settlers to the American West in search of jobs and prosperity. Millions more migrated from the South to the North during World War II to find work in American cities. The invention of the air conditioner had the reverse effect. That technology made it possible for Americans to move to the warmer climates of the southern and western United States."[1]

A Moving Experience

Although many people initially get understandably excited about a move to a different part of the country, many people don't take into account the logistics of a long-distance move. The axiom in real estate is location, location, location. When it comes to moving, it's planning, planning, planning.

Take Stock

Your first step is to create an inventory of what you have to move. You want to take all your possessions and place them into these categories:

A. Things to throw out
B. Things to give away
C. Things you will entrust others to move
D. Things you will move yourself

Get rid of anything you no longer use, especially wardrobe items, gifts, or just plain junk. You won't need it in your new place, and all of those extra items are just going to make the move take longer and make it more expensive. Give away any items of value that you haven't used for a while and others may appreciate having. Donate books you've been keeping around (but haven't read for years) to the local library. As for the items you will entrust others to move, certainly, your furniture falls into that category, but you should strongly consider what furniture to move. If you have been thinking of buying a new bed or mattress and if your living room furniture is outdated and worn out – leave those "big space" items behind.

Now is a great time to break out that video camera you got as a gift or purchased for yourself and make a visual record to serve as an inventory of all of your possessions. You'll reap big rewards for doing so should any items get lost or stolen in transit. If you have receipts for your major purchases (and you should have), that's one of the items you won't entrust to the movers. Any personal and financial records or other personal items that you cherish will fall into the category of things you will move yourself. The same is true for expensive antiques, jewelry, and other items of high value – those are items you'll want to keep near and dear to yourself.

Pack for Survival

Organize the items you will be taking and create a lettering, numbering, or color-coded system for what you will be packing into those boxes. Don't just start throwing all your possessions into boxes and then seal up the boxes with no idea about the contents of the boxes. For example, pack the kitchen items in boxes and place labels and stickers on those boxes. Do the same for each room of the house and place those related boxes together so that they get moved as a unit. You will want your kitchen and bathroom items first upon your arrival, so try to make sure those items are packed last into the moving van so that they be unloaded first when you arrive at your new home. This is where your labeling system starts to pay dividends. If a box has the word "kitchen" on it, the movers will know where to place the boxes upon your arrival in your new home.

Pack Beforehand

Pack as much as you can before the day of the move. Let the movers do the taping and padding, but you'll save time and have your items organized for the big move if you do all the packing well in advance of the move. If there is furniture to be disassembled, do it beforehand. Break down beds, tables, computers, lamps, televisions, and anything else that can be unplugged or dismantled.

Create a Survival Kit

Plan for the first day of the new move. You'll need cleaning supplies, toiletries, tools, and some food, although you can count on eating out quite a bit until you settle in to your new residence. Before the move, make sure that gas, electric, and the phone have been turned on before you arrive. You don't want to make your move only to have to stay in a hotel for several nights until you arrange for utilities to be turned on. If necessary, visit the new home a few weeks before the move and arrange for utilities and alarm systems to be up and running from day one in your new home. In a few weeks, you'll feel at home.

[1]See *Wagner's Guide to Demographics in the New Millennium*, page 283.

Your First and Last Name
Tutorial 5, Case Problem 2

Complete the following:

1. If necessary, start Expression Web, close any open sites, and open the Tutorial.05 Web site. Reset the workspace layout.
2. If necessary, expand the Data Files folder and the Case2 folder to display its contents.

3. Open the **move.html** file from the Case2 folder and save the file as **movenew.html** in the same folder.
4. In Design view, right-click anywhere on the page. On the shortcut menu, click Page Properties. In the Title box, type **A Nation on the Move**.
5. In the Page description box, type your own first and last name, type a forward slash, and type **Tutorial 5, Case Problem 2**. Click the OK button.

EXPLORE

6. At the end of the second paragraph, select the number *1* that follows the word *States*. Click Format on the menu bar, and then click Font. In the Font dialog box, click the Superscript check box. Click the OK button to return to Design view.
7. Press the Ctrl+End keys to position the insertion point at the bottom of the page. Repeat the method you used in the previous step to apply a superscript to the number *1* that precedes the word *See*. Click the OK button to return to Design view.
8. Scroll up to the *Take Stock* heading. Select the four items in the ordered list, from *Things to throw out* through *Things you will move yourself*.

EXPLORE

9. If necessary, click the Apply Styles tab to display the Apply Styles panel. In the Apply Styles panel, right-click .style1 and click Rename class "style1". In the Rename Class dialog box, type **uppercase_list**. Click the OK button to return to Design view.
10. In the Apply Styles panel, click New Style.
11. In the Selector box, delete .newStyle1 and type **#quotation**.
12. Click Block in the Category bar. Click in the text-indent property box and type **2em**.
13. Click Background in the Category bar. Click the background-color arrow and then click More Colors. Click any shade of light yellow. Click the OK button twice to return to Design view.
14. In the Apply Styles panel, click New Style.
15. In the Selector box, delete .newStyle1 and type **#closing**.

EXPLORE

16. Click Border in the Category bar. Click the top arrow for border-style and click inset. Click the top arrow for border-width and click thick. Click the top arrow for border-color and click teal (#008080). Click the OK button to return to Design view.
17. In the Apply Styles panel, click New Style. In the New Style dialog box, delete .newStyle1 in the Selector box, and type **#footer**.
18. Click Background in the Category bar. Click the background-color arrow and then click More Colors. Click any shade of light yellow. Click the OK button.
19. Click Border in the Category bar. For the border-style property, if necessary, click the Same for all check box to select it. Under border-style, click the top arrow and then click solid. Click the OK button to return to Design view.
20. Click anywhere in the second paragraph (the paragraph in quotes). In the Apply Styles panel, right-click #quotation and then click Apply Style.
21. Scroll down the page and click anywhere in the heading *Create a Survival Kit*. In the Apply Styles panel, right-click #closing and then click Apply Style.
22. Click anywhere in the last line of the document (the footnote). Click the p Code tab to select the paragraph. In the Apply Styles panel, right-click #footer and then click Apply Style.
23. Press the Ctrl+End keys to position the insertion point at the end of the document. Type your first and last name. Press the Shift+Enter keys and type **Tutorial 5, Case Problem 2**.
24. Save the **movenew.html** file.
25. Open the **movenew.html** file in your browser. The document should appear similar to the one shown in Figure 5-41.
26. Close all documents, close the browser, and close the Web site.
27. Submit the completed file to your instructor, either in printed or electronic form, as requested.

Use what you've learned, and expand your skills, to create and style a Web page for a printing services company.

APPLY

Case Problem 3

Data File needed for this Case Problem: fonts.html

LaMonte's Fonts and Print Shops The LaMonte's Fonts and Print Shops chain of stores is expanding its business to the Web. You'll create a Web site that makes use of an external style sheet. A preview of the completed file appears in Figure 5-42.

Figure 5-42 **Completed LaMonte's Fonts and Print Shops Web page**

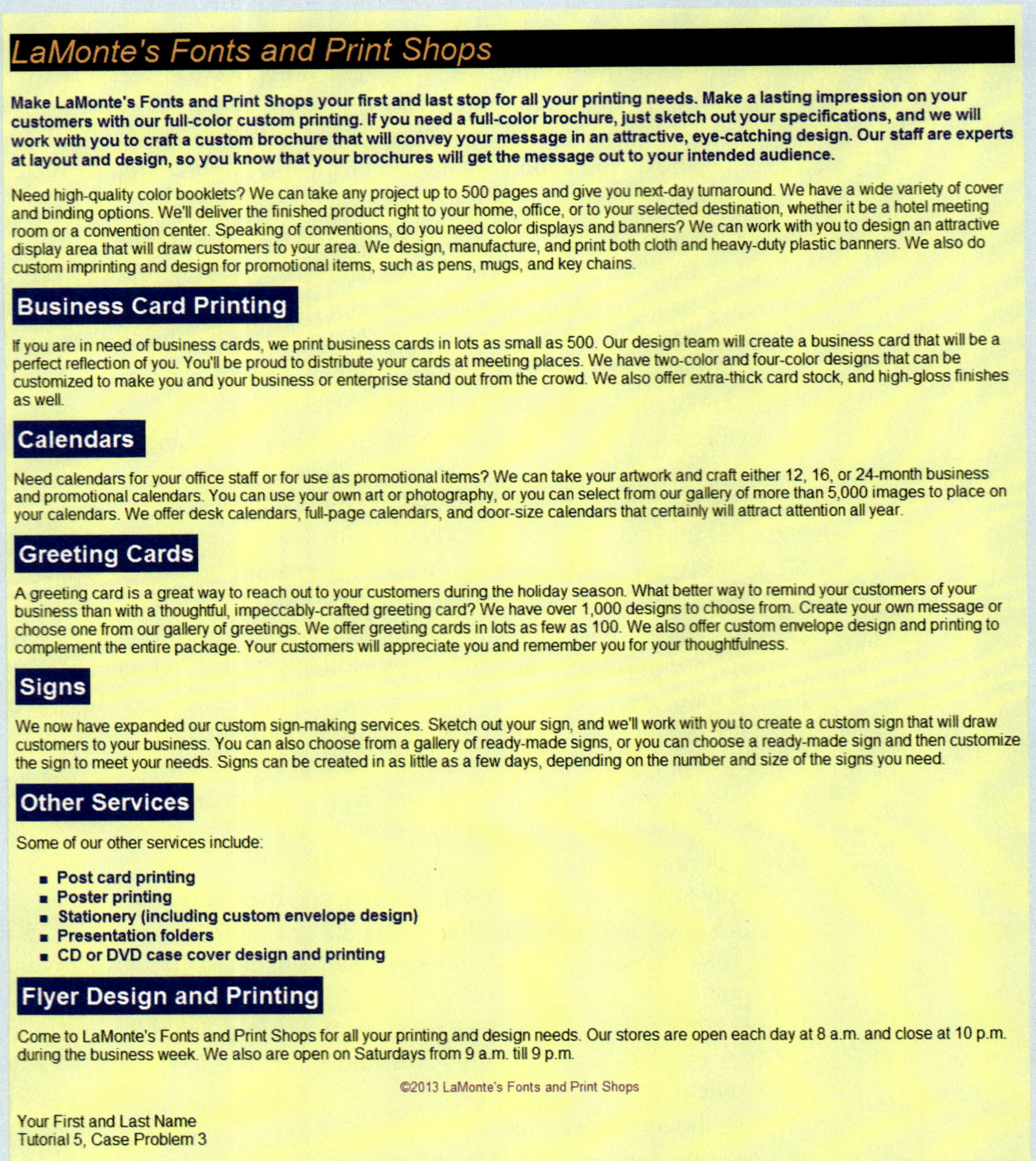

Complete the following:

1. If necessary, start Expression Web, close any open sites, and open the Tutorial.05 Web site. Reset the workspace layout.
2. If necessary, expand the Data Files folder and the Case3 folder to display its contents.

3. Open the **fonts.html** file from the Case3 folder and save the file as **fontsnew.html** in the same folder.
4. In Design view, right-click anywhere on the page. On the shortcut menu, click Page Properties. In the Title box, type **LaMonte's Fonts and Print Shops**.
5. In the Page description box, type your own first and last name, type a forward slash, and type **Tutorial 5, Case Problem 3**. Click the OK button.
6. Click File on the menu bar, point to New, and then click CSS. In the CSS file, type the following CSS comment (using your first and last name):

   /* Your First and Last Name */
7. Press the Enter key twice. Right-click the Untitled_1.css Document tab. Click Save. Save the file as **fontsnew.css** in the Case3 folder.
8. Click the fontsnew.html Document tab to display the fontsnew.html file.
9. From the Folder List panel, click and drag the fontsnew.css file anywhere over the fontsnew.html file and then release the mouse button.
10. In the Apply Styles panel, click the Manage Styles tab to display the Manage Styles panel.

EXPLORE

11. In the Manage Styles panel, click the body style and drag it from the Current Page list into the fontsnew.css list.
12. In the Manage Styles panel, click and drag the h1 style from the Current Page list into the fontsnew.css list.
13. One by one, in the Manage Styles panel, click and drag the other styles from the Current Page list into the fontsnew.css list.
14. In the Manage Styles panel, click and drag as necessary to organize the styles in the fontsnew.css window in this order: body, h1, h2, li, #footer, .intro, .copyright.
15. Click the Code button to switch to Code view.
16. Click the fontsnew.css Document tab. Verify that all styles have been moved to the fontsnew.css style sheet.
17. Right-click the fontsnew.css Document tab. Click Save on the shortcut menu. Right-click the fontsnew.css Document tab again and click Close on the shortcut menu.
18. Switch to Design view. Press the Ctrl+End keys to position the insertion point at the end of the document. Type your first and last name. Press the Shift+Enter keys and type **Tutorial 5, Case Problem 3**.
19. Save the **fontsnew.html** file. If you are prompted to Save Embedded Files, click the OK button.
20. Open the **fontsnew.html** file in your browser. The document should appear similar to the one shown in Figure 5-42.
21. Submit the completed files to your instructor, either in printed or electronic form, as requested.
22. Close all documents, close your browser, and close the Web site.

Create and style a Web page for a travel organization.

CREATE

Case Problem 4

Data File needed for this Case Problem: site.html

Site Sea-ers Site Sea-ers is a Seattle, Washington, group that organizes tours and outings for water enthusiasts and nature lovers. Site Sea-ers plans tours of local rivers, bays, lakes, and estuaries. They also organize and promote boating trips from Seattle to Vancouver Island. Complete the following:

1. If necessary, start Expression Web, close any open sites, and open the Tutorial.05 Web site. Reset the workspace layout.

2. If necessary, expand the Data Files folder and the Case4 folder to display its contents.
3. Open the **site.html** file from the Case 4 folder and save the file as **sitenew.html** in the same folder.
4. In Design view, right-click anywhere on the page. On the shortcut menu, click Page Properties. In the Title box, type **Site Sea-ers Tours**.
5. In the Page description box, type your own first and last name, type a forward slash character, and type **Tutorial 5, Case Problem 4**. Click the OK button.
6. In the body of the document, include examples of the following:
   - An element selector style
   - A dependent class selector style (and apply the selector)
   - An independent class selector style (and apply the selector)
   - An ID selector style (and apply the selector)
7. Create an external style sheet file. In the CSS file, enter this comment at the top of the page (use your first and last name as indicated):
   Your First and Last Name/Tutorial 5, Case Problem 4
8. Create a style for the body element in the external style sheet. Create a style to change the line height for the document to 2.0em.
9. Name the CSS file **sitenew.css**. Save the CSS file in the Case4 folder.
10. Attach the sitenew.css file to the sitenew.html file.
11. Create a bookmark at the top of the page. At the bottom of the page, create a link to the bookmark.
12. In the body text, create a link to an external Web site that will give visitors to the Web site more information about conservation and maintaining a clean environment.
13. Run a CSS report on the document. Correct any errors the report finds.
14. Press the Ctrl+End keys to position the insertion point at the end of the document. Type your first and last name. Press the Shift+Enter keys and type **Tutorial 5, Case Problem 4**.
15. Save your **sitenew.html** file.
16. Open the **sitenew.html** file in your browser. Observe the result. Correct any errors.
17. Submit the completed files to your instructor, either in printed or electronic form, as requested.
18. Close the browser, close all documents, and close the Web site.

ENDING DATA FILES

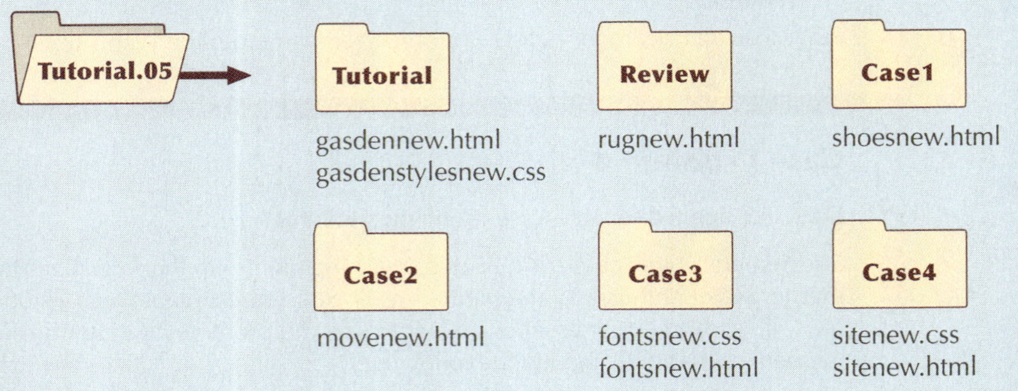

TUTORIAL 6

Creating Tables and CSS Layouts

Using Tables for Data and Organizing Page Content

EXPRESSION WEB

OBJECTIVES

Session 6.1
- Create a data table to display and organize data
- Modify table properties and layout
- Input data into a table
- Insert and delete rows and columns
- Merge table cells

Session 6.2
- Create a template layout
- Modify a layout
- Create a navigation bar
- Format a table using the Table AutoFormat feature

Case | *The Flew Line Bus Company*

The Flew Line Bus Company operates a bus fleet that provides rapid transit for passengers traveling along the East Coast. Although most of the Flew Line's routes travel the busy travel corridor between Boston, New York City, and Washington, D.C., the Flew Line operates as far south as Miami, Florida, and as far north as Bangor, Maine. The Flew Line competes both on price and speed. For example, the cost of a Flew Line ticket between New York City and Washington, D.C., is typically half that for other forms of travel. In addition, buses run nonstop between cities, so travel times are very competitive when compared with rail transit. Many people like taking the Flew Line because they do not have to deal with the protocols and delays that are a common part of traveling by commercial airliner. Michele McDavies, the marketing director at the Flew Line, has asked for your help in creating a Web page to summarize some of the special sales the company will be offering during the winter season, when both business and recreational travel is less common. You'll show Michele how to create a data table for the Flew Line Web site that will summarize the special sales that the Flew Line will be offering this winter.

STARTING DATA FILES

Tutorial.06 →

Tutorial	Review	Case1	Case2	Case3	Case4
crew.html flewlogo.png info.html rules.html seating.html terminals.html tickets.html	flewlogo.png	realty.html	year.html	content.html header.html left.html soccerlogo.gif	show.html

SESSION 6.1 VISUAL OVERVIEW

The (insert) **Column to the Right** button inserts a column to the right of the present cursor position.

The (insert) **Column to the Left** button inserts a column to the left of the present cursor position.

The (insert) **Row Above** button inserts a row above the present cursor position.

The (insert) **Row Below** button inserts a row below the present cursor position.

The **Delete Cells** button deletes one or more cells.

The **Merge Cells** button merges two or more cells.

The **Split Cells** button splits one or more cells.

The **Align Top** button aligns text with the top of the cell.

The **Center Vertically** button centers text vertically in the cell.

The **Align Bottom** button aligns text with the bottom of the cell.

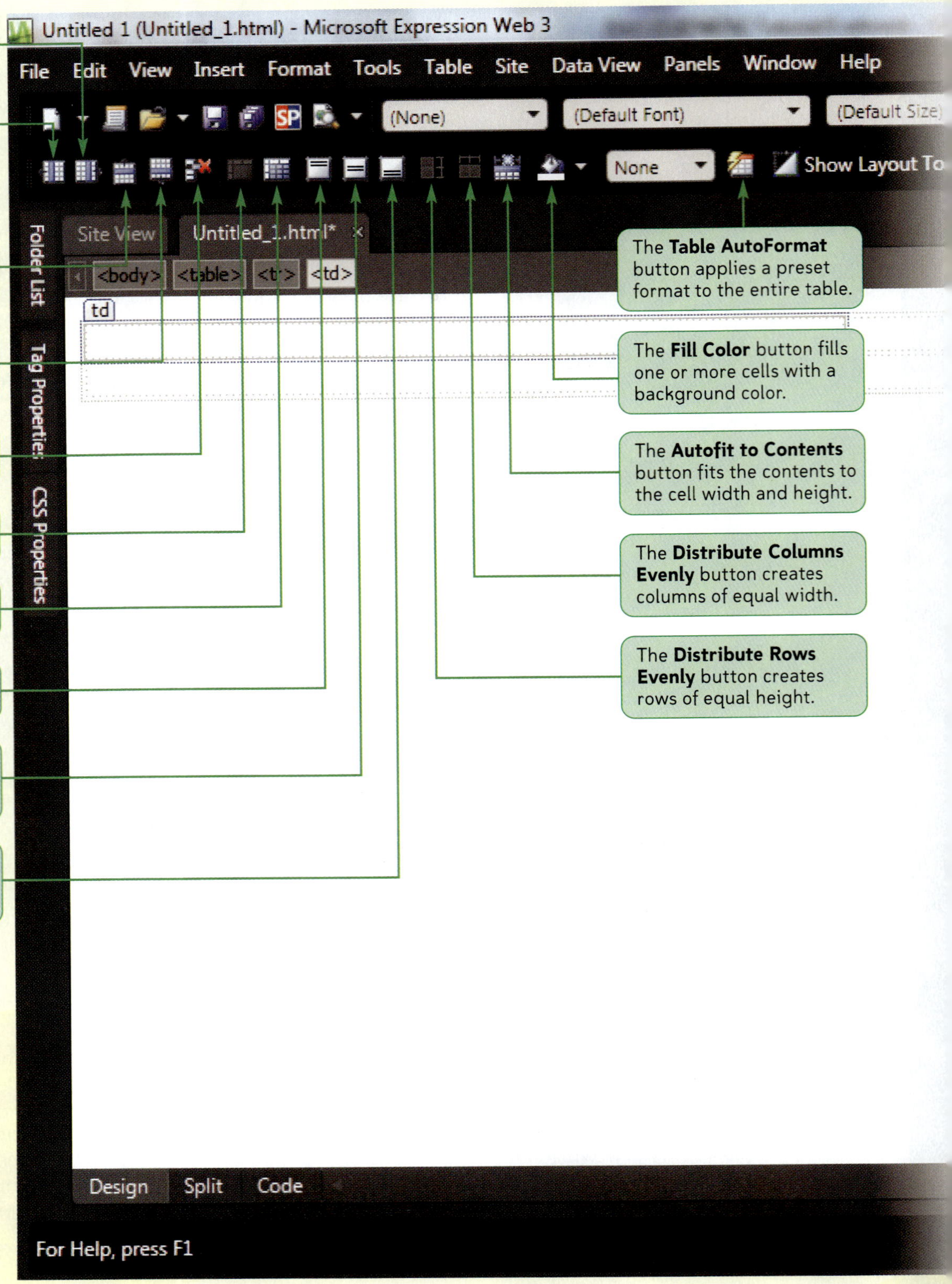

The **Table AutoFormat** button applies a preset format to the entire table.

The **Fill Color** button fills one or more cells with a background color.

The **Autofit to Contents** button fits the contents to the cell width and height.

The **Distribute Columns Evenly** button creates columns of equal width.

The **Distribute Rows Evenly** button creates rows of equal height.

CREATING A TABLE

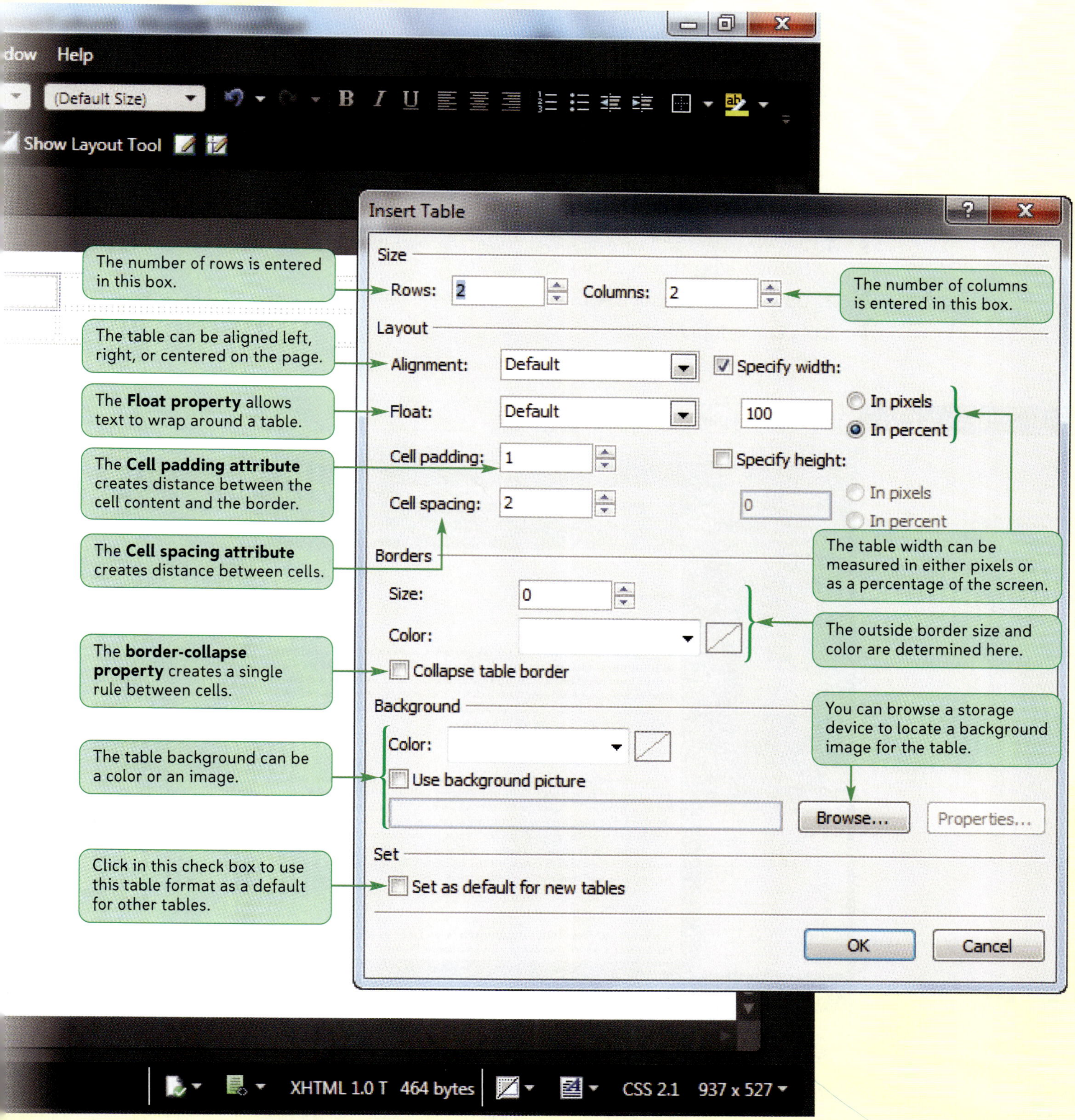

Working with Tables

Expression Web has several means of creating and modifying tables quickly and easily. Before you begin creating tables in Expression Web, you need to understand how tables traditionally have been used on the Web. Until recently, HTML tables were used both as a means for organizing data and for creating page layout. Although HTML tables are still used to organize data, CSS is now the preferred method for creating page layout.

To organize data, you create a **data table**, whose sole purpose is to align page content, such as text and numbers, in columns and rows. The table can occupy a small part of a page or an entire page. You'll start your work with Michele on the Flew Line data table by opening the Tutorial.06 Web site.

To open the Tutorial.06 Web site:

1. If necessary, start Expression Web, reset the workspace layout, and then close any toolbars other than the Common toolbar.
2. Open the **Tutorial.06** Web site and expand the **Data Files** and **Tutorial** folders.
3. Open the **info.html** file.

   The info.html file should appear as shown in Figure 6-1.

Figure 6-1 The info.html page

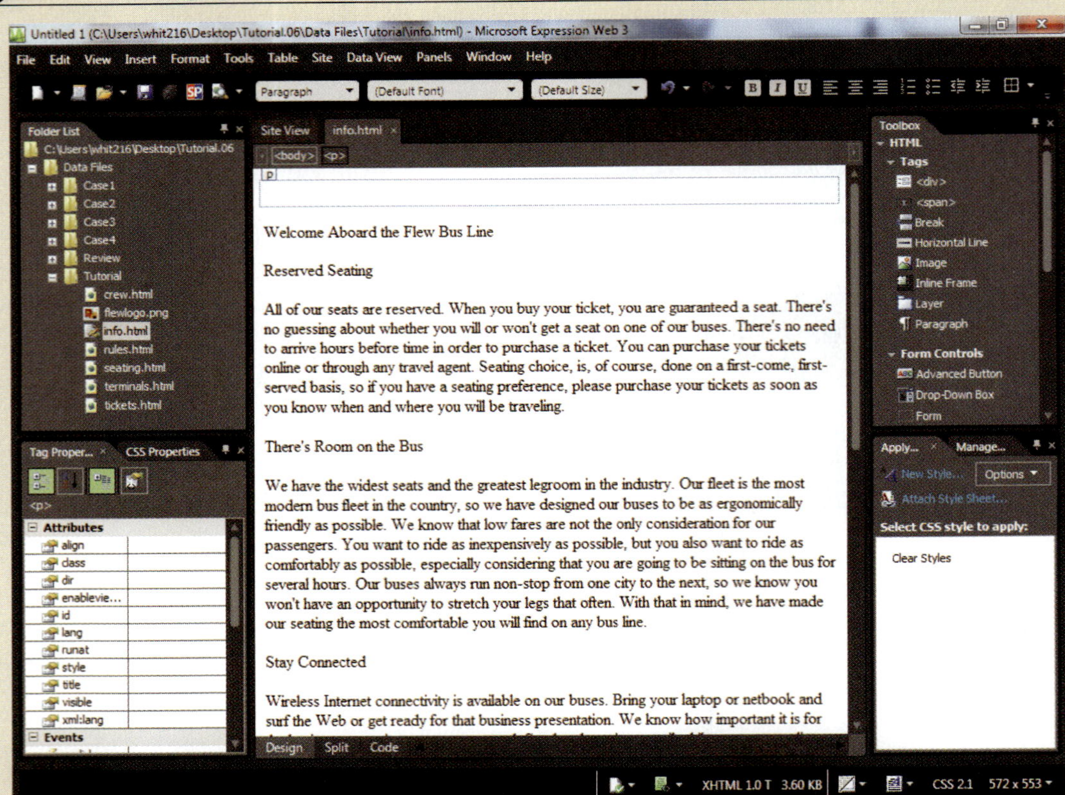

4. Save the file as **infonew** in the same folder.
5. Click the **Panels** menu and then click **AutoHide All Panels**. All panels are now hidden. Panel tabs take the place of the panels.

Next, you and Michele will begin creating the Flew Bus data table.

Creating Tables

A **cell** is the intersection between a table row and a table column. To create a table in HTML, a considerable amount of code is required to create each cell and each row. It's also quite challenging to merge table cells across columns or rows. Expression Web, however, makes it very easy to create, revise, and format data tables. As you create a table, Expression Web shows you table **tracer lines**, which are dotted lines that outline each of the table's cells.

REFERENCE

Creating a Table

- Click the Table menu, and then click Insert Table.
- In the Insert Table dialog box, enter the number of rows and columns for the table.
- Optionally, make choices for layout, borders, and background.
- Click the OK button.

or

- Click the Insert Table button on either the Common toolbar or the Standard toolbar.
- Move the pointer to specify the number of rows and columns for the table.
- Click to create the table.

You'll create the Flew Line data table using the Insert Table dialog box.

To create the data table:

1. In Design view, press the **Ctrl+End** keys to position the insertion point at the end of the document.

   The insertion point should be below the last line of the document, "Flew Line Winter Specials."

2. Click the **Table** menu, and then click **Insert Table**.

   The Insert Table dialog box opens, as shown in Figure 6-2.

Figure 6-2 **The Insert Table dialog box**

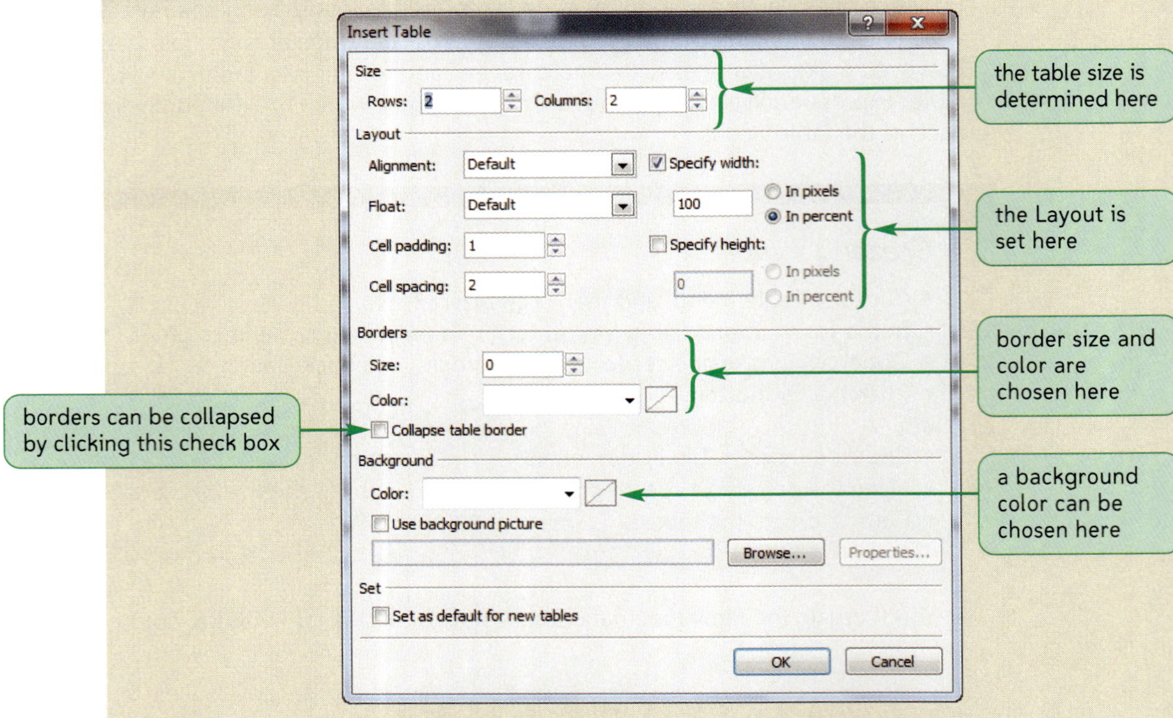

3. In the Rows box, type **6**.
4. Press the **Tab** key, and then in the Columns box, type **6**.
5. In the Borders group, click in the Size box, delete the contents of the box, and then type **6**.
6. Click the **OK** button.

   A table with 6 rows and 6 columns is created, as shown in Figure 6-3. If necessary, scroll down to see the table.

Figure 6-3 **The table is created**

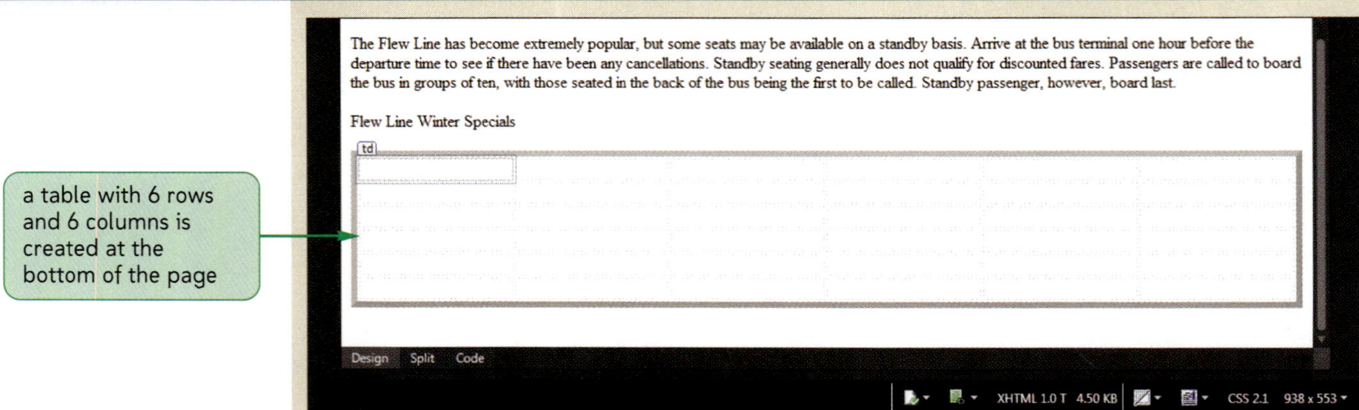

Trouble? If you do not see the table tracer lines, click the View menu, point to Visual Aids, and then click Show. If you still do not see the table tracer lines, click the View menu, point to Visual Aids, and then click Visible Borders.

7. Pass the mouse pointer over each of the HTML tags in the breadcrumb bar.

As you pass over each tag, a different section of the table is selected.

INSIGHT

Generating Table Code

When the table or any element of the table is selected, you'll see several HTML tags in the breadcrumb bar at the top of the editing window. In HTML code, a table begins with the start <table> tag. The end </table> tag follows the code for the table contents. Tables can be placed anywhere between the opening and closing <body> tags. Table rows are created by entering the start table row tag, <tr>, and the end table row tag, </tr>. The table cells are created by entering the start table data tag, <td>, and the end table data tag, </td>. Cells in the first row of a table can be formatted as column headings by placing contents between the opening <th> and closing </th> tags. These tags format the contents as both bold and centered.

TIP

If the choice for Visible Borders in Visual Aids is not enabled, you will not see the table tracer lines.

The table has been created, but you need to provide some formatting for the table and its cells so that the gridlines and text have more visual appeal. You'll work with Michele to set the table properties and improve the appearance of the table.

Setting the Table Properties

To access the table properties, you can either use the Table menu, or simply right-click anywhere on the table and then click Table Properties on the shortcut menu.

REFERENCE

Setting the Table Properties

- Click the Table menu, point to Table Properties, and then click either Table or Cell.

or

- Right-click anywhere on the table, and then click Table Properties on the shortcut menu.
- In the Table Properties dialog box, make choices in any or all of the sections, which include:
  - Size—Set the number of rows and columns.
  - Layout—Set your choices for alignment, float, cell padding, cell spacing, width, and height.
  - Borders—Set your choices for size, color, and collapsing the table border.
  - Background—Set your choices for color and background picture.
  - Set—Set whether to make the selected settings the default choices for new tables.
- Click the OK button.

TIP

By default, an Expression Web table occupies 100% of the screen width.

Table borders are the horizontal and vertical ruled lines both outside and inside the table. Table borders are often referred to as the **table gridlines** or the **table grid**. By default, a table does not show the gridlines in the browser. If you were to save a Web page file containing only a table with default settings and open it in the browser, the screen would appear blank. To see the table borders in a browser, you must create a border width of at least one pixel.

The Layout group in the Table Properties dialog box includes choices for Alignment, Float, Cell padding, and Cell spacing. If the table were less than 100% of the screen width, you could set the alignment of the table to be left, right, or center. You can enter a value of either Left or Right as the value for Float. The float effect is similar to what happens when you float an image. Entering a value of Left causes the table to appear at the left edge of the screen, and text to wrap around the table to the right. Entering a value of Right does the opposite; the table appears at the right edge of the screen and text wraps to the left of the table. The value of Default causes the table not to float either left or right. If the table is less than 100% of the screen width, leaving the value as Default sometimes creates undesirable white space to the right of the table.

PROSKILLS

Decision Making: Making Table Formatting and Layout Decisions

Before you include a data table on a Web page, consider what information you want to convey to your visitors. Visitors to your Web page probably do not want to be burdened with too much information. If you want to include one or more tables that have a significant amount of data, consider linking to them from the home page. On your home page, avoid incorporating a data table of more than six columns and ten rows. If the column content is not very wide, consider floating the table either left or right and wrapping the text accordingly to create a more attractive page layout. If there are several columns and quite a bit of data in each row, format the data table to occupy the entire screen width. If some white space appears to the right of the table, center the table horizontally. When you format the table for color and background color, be mindful of the use of the color red in particular; because red signifies danger and financial loss, you should think carefully about using red in your data table.

Cell padding is the white space that surrounds the contents of a cell. If you choose to display table gridlines, it is a good practice to include some cell padding in a table because the white space makes the cell contents more readable. **Cell spacing** is used to increase the distance between cells.

In addition to specifying a width for a table, you can also specify a height. The Specify height check box is not checked by default. In general, you do not want to specify a height for a table.

Next, you and Michele will enter values for some of the table properties.

To enter the table properties for size and layout:

1. Right-click anywhere in the table.
2. Click **Table Properties**.

   The Table Properties dialog box opens.
3. Click the **Alignment** arrow, and then click **Center**.
4. Click in the **Specify width** text box, delete the current contents, and then type **90**.
5. If necessary, click the **In percent** radio button.
6. Click in the **Cell padding** box, delete the current contents, and then type **4**.

   At this point, your choices in the Table Properties dialog box should look similar to those shown in Figure 6-4.

Figure 6-4 **Editing the Table Properties**

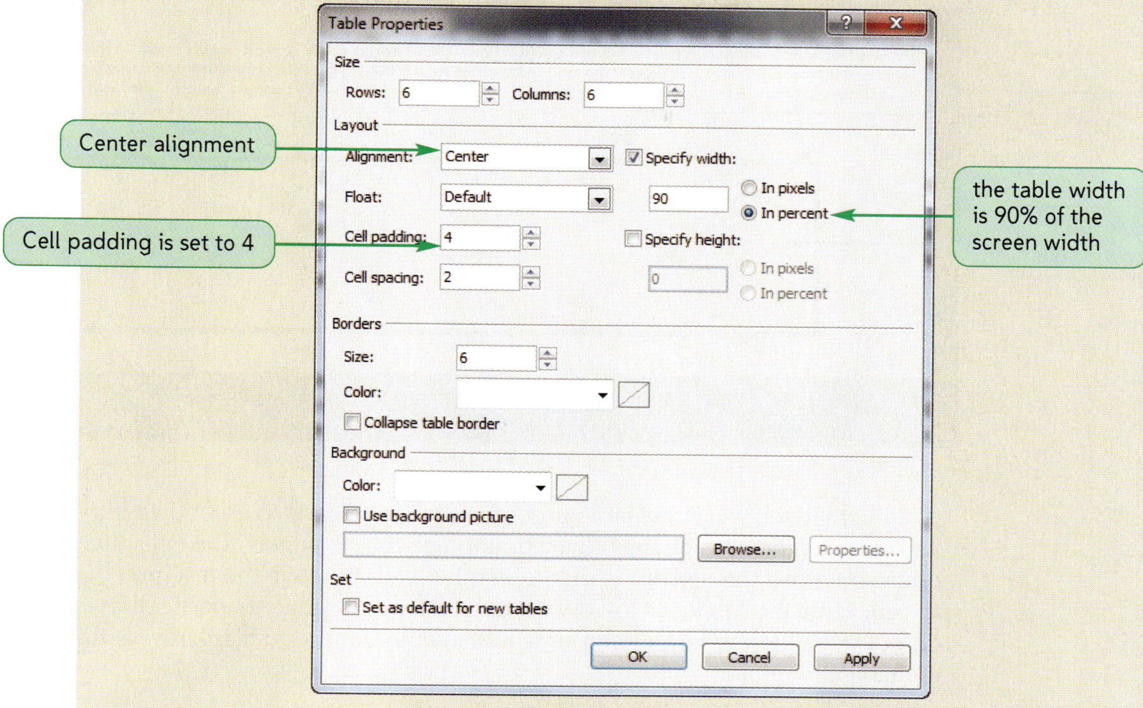

The Size value in the Borders group, which controls the size of the outside table borders, is currently set to 6. You also have the option of setting a color for the outside borders. If you check the Collapse table border check box, Expression Web uses the CSS border-collapse property to create a single ruled line, rather than a double ruled line, for the interior gridlines of the table. You can also change the background color of the entire table, or you can use a background picture for the table. The background color or background image should not compete with the text, though. Do not, for example, use a navy background with black text, which would make it very difficult to read the text. Likewise, do not use a background image that makes the text hard to read. You want visitors to your Web site to focus on the data in the table, not the background image. You'll work with Michele to make more changes to the table borders and to change the background color of the table.

To change the table borders:

1. In the Borders group, click the **Color** arrow, and then click **Olive**, which is the fifth color in the first row.
2. In the Borders group, click the **Collapse table border** check box.
3. In the Background group (not the Borders group), click in the **Color** box, and then type **#ffffcc**.
4. Click the **OK** button, and then click in the first cell of the table.

   Your table should look similar to that shown in Figure 6-5.

Figure 6-5 The table with an outside border and a background color

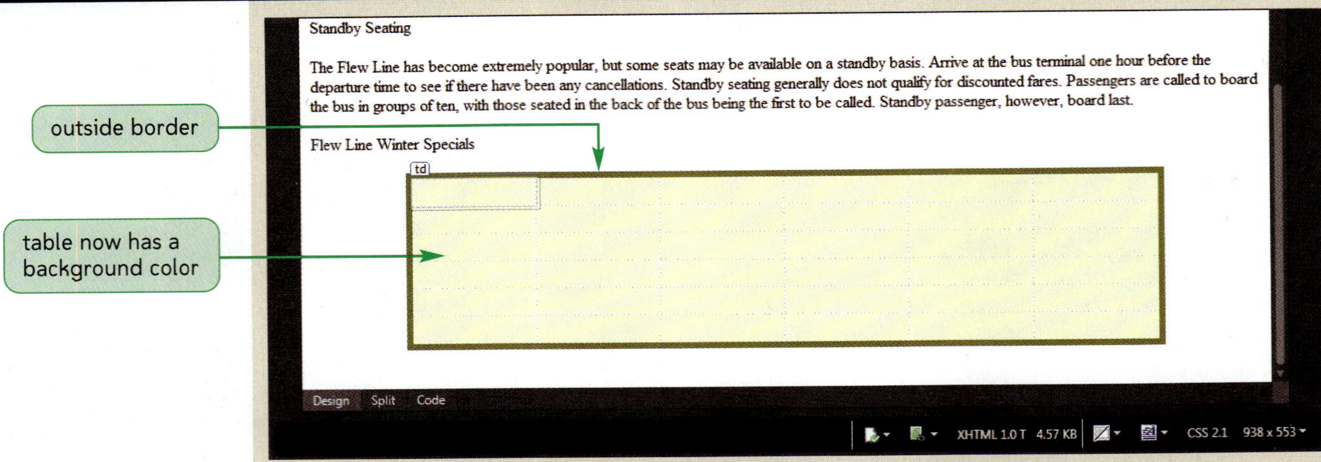

Now that you've set the table properties, you are ready to enter data into the table. As you type, the cells change to accommodate their contents. The cells then contract once you move the insertion point to another cell. To move the insertion point from cell to cell, press the Tab key. However, after you type data into the last cell in the table, do not press the Tab key. Doing so would add an unneeded blank row at the bottom of the table.

To type data into the table:

1. If necessary, click in the first cell of the table.
2. Type the text shown in Figure 6-6, using the Tab key to move the insertion point from cell to cell.

   Some cells remain blank. After you type *P122* in the last cell, do not press the Tab key. As you type, let the text wrap in each cell. Don't press the Enter key, for example, in the *Winter Is Special* cell.

Figure 6-6 The table data

Winter Is Special					
From	**To**	**Leave**	**Arrive**	**% Off Price**	**Trip Number**
New York	Washington	7:20 a.m.	12:35 p.m.	20	N45
New York	Philadelphia	7:30 a.m.	9:10 a.m.	25	N30
Washington	New York	6:30 a.m.	10:45 a.m.		W67
Philadelphia	New York	6:50 a.m.	8:30 a.m.		P122

Trouble? If you pressed the Tab key after typing "P122," press the Ctrl+Z keys to undo the last action.

Now that the data has been entered into the table, you'll modify the table layout to add and delete rows, which will accommodate some changes that need to be made to the table.

Modifying the Table Layout

Michele is impressed with the tables feature. However, she has just learned of three special trips that need to be added to the data table.

REFERENCE

Inserting a Row or Column

- Click to position the insertion point where you want to insert a row or column.
- Click the Table menu, point to Insert, and then choose one of the following:
  - Column to the Left
  - Column to the Right
  - Row Above
  - Row Below

or

- Right-click a table cell, point to Insert, and click any of the applicable choices on the shortcut menu to insert either a column or a row.

You'll insert rows to add the information about the three new trips that need to be added to the data table. You can insert rows above or below a row to insert a row; it's usually just a matter of preference.

To insert rows:

1. Click in the first cell of the second row, which contains the word *From*.
2. Click the **Table** menu, point to **Insert**, and then click **Row Below**.

   A new row is inserted below the insertion point.
3. Click in the first cell of the new row.
4. Type the data for the New York to Boston trip shown in bold in Figure 6-7.
5. In the From column, click in the cell containing the word *Washington*.
6. Click the **Table** menu, point to **Insert**, and then click **Row Above**.

   A new row is inserted above the insertion point.
7. Click in the first cell of the new row, and then type the data for the Boston to New York trip shown in bold in Figure 6-7.

   Not all cells in this row contain data.
8. Click anywhere in the last table cell of the table, which contains the text *P122*.
9. Press the **Tab** key.

   A new row is inserted at the end of the table.
10. Type the information for the Cleveland to Philadelphia trip shown in bold in Figure 6-7.

Figure 6-7 The text to be inserted

Winter Is Special					
From	**To**	**Leave**	**Arrive**	**% Off PriceTrip**	**Number**
New York	**Boston**	**7:10 a.m.**	**12:25 p.m.**	**15**	**N64**
New York	Washington	7:20 a.m.	12:35 p.m.	20	N45
New York	Philadelphia	7:30 a.m.	9:10 a.m.	25	N30
Boston	**New York**	**7:00 a.m.**	**12:15 p.m.**		**B33**
Washington	New York	6:30 a.m.	10:45 a.m.		W67
Philadelphia	New York	6:50 a.m.	8:30 a.m.		P122
Cleveland	**Philadelphia**	**5:45 a.m.**	**10:45 a.m.**		**C88**

TIP

To select the contents of the next table cell, press the Tab key; press Shift+Tab to select the contents of the preceding table cell.

Michele notes that the table has become more complex. She feels the table would be more readable if it included ruled lines. You'll change the table cell properties to add a colored border to the interior cells. To access the Cell properties dialog box, you can't click the table style tag in the breadcrumb bar, nor can you use the Table menu and then make the choice to select the table. Instead, you'll click and drag to select the table cells to format the interior table cells.

To display the interior grid:

1. Click in the first cell of the table, which contains the text *Winter Is Special*, and then click and drag down and to the right to select all the cells in the table.
2. Right-click anywhere in the table, and then click **Cell Properties** on the shortcut menu.

   The Cell Properties dialog box opens.
3. In the Borders group, click in the **Size** box and then type **3**.
4. In the Borders group (not the Background group), click the **Color** arrow and then click **Navy** (the third swatch from the right in the top row).

   Your choices should be similar to those shown in Figure 6-8.

Figure 6-8 **The Cell Properties dialog box**

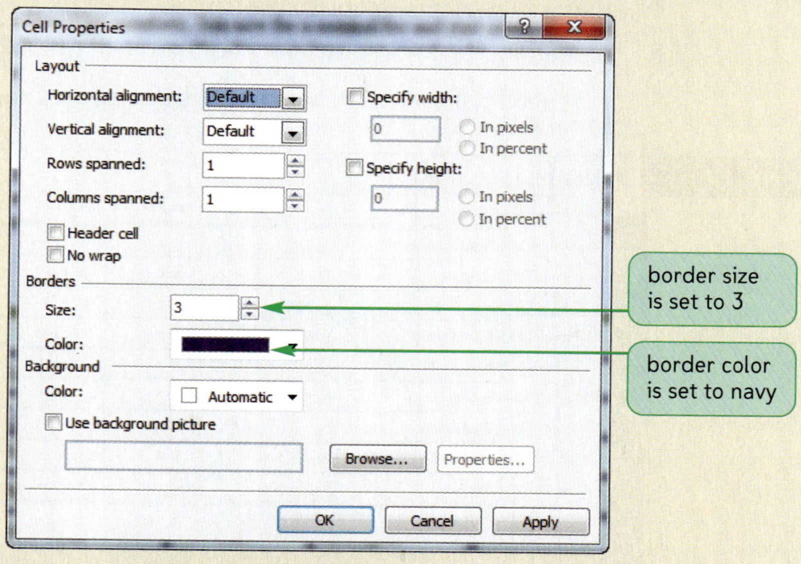

5. Click the **OK** button.
6. Click anywhere outside the table.

   The interior gridlines should appear as shown in Figure 6-9.

Figure 6-9 **The table with inside borders**

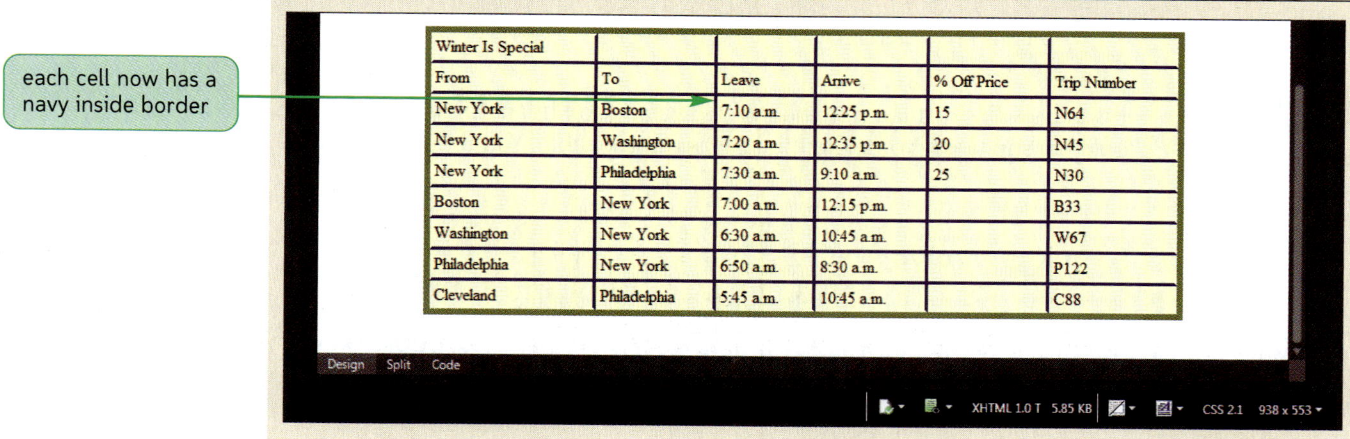

Winter Is Special					
From	To	Leave	Arrive	% Off Price	Trip Number
New York	Boston	7:10 a.m.	12:25 p.m.	15	N64
New York	Washington	7:20 a.m.	12:35 p.m.	20	N45
New York	Philadelphia	7:30 a.m.	9:10 a.m.	25	N30
Boston	New York	7:00 a.m.	12:15 p.m.		B33
Washington	New York	6:30 a.m.	10:45 a.m.		W67
Philadelphia	New York	6:50 a.m.	8:30 a.m.		P122
Cleveland	Philadelphia	5:45 a.m.	10:45 a.m.		C88

Now that the table gridlines are visible, you and Michele will insert a new column. This time, you'll make choices by right-clicking within a cell.

To change the number of columns:

1. Click anywhere in the **To** column.
2. Right-click, point to **Insert**, and then click **Column to the Right**.

   A new, but very narrow, column is inserted, as shown in Figure 6-10.

Figure 6-10 **Inserting a column**

a new column is inserted, but it is very narrow

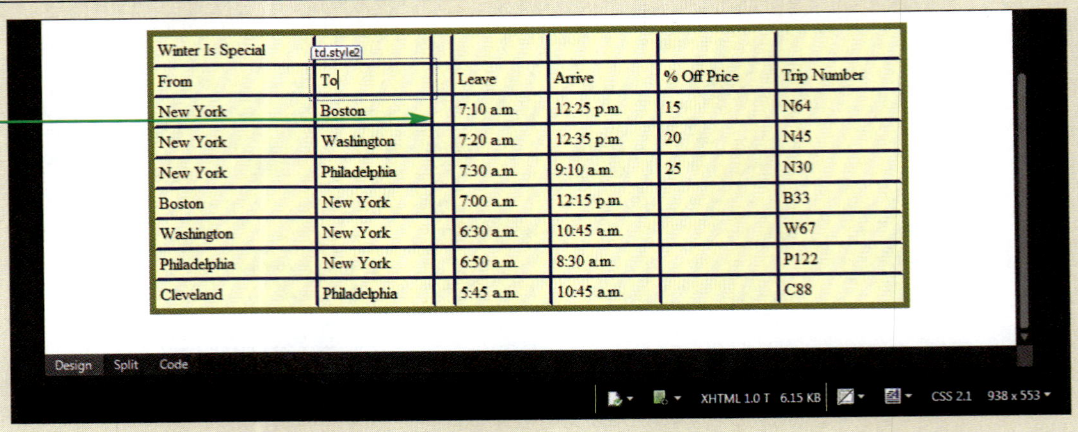

Michele prefers the previous table layout, so she wants to delete the column you just inserted.

3. Right-click in any cell in the new column you just inserted.
4. On the shortcut menu, point to **Delete**, and then click **Delete Columns**.

   The column is deleted.

TIP

Alternatively, to select a column, position the insertion point near the top border of the topmost cell. When the pointer changes to a downward-pointing arrow, click to select the column.

Michele has just learned that the Cleveland to Philadelphia trip should not be in this table, so she wants to delete the last row in the table. You'll delete the row.

To delete a row:

1. Right-click anywhere in the last row of the table.
2. On the shortcut menu, point to **Delete**, and then click **Delete Rows**.

   The row is deleted, as shown in Figure 6-11.

Figure 6-11 Deleting a row

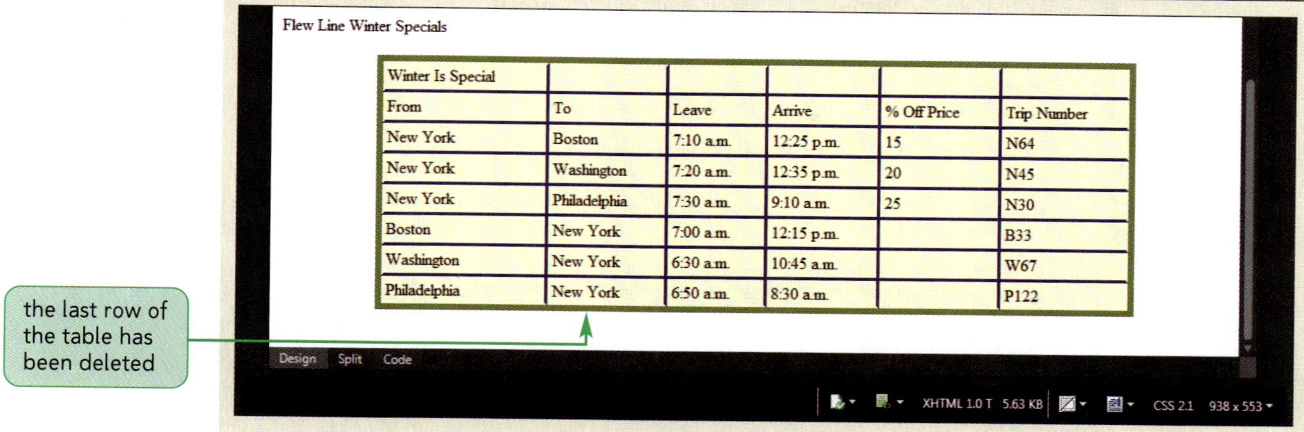

Three cells in the table in the % Off Price column are blank. The Expression Web Table Fill feature provides an easy way to fill in table cells with duplicate data. Depending on which cells are blank, you can fill to the right or you can fill down. You will fill in the three cells that do not have data for the % Off Price column.

To use the Table Fill feature:

1. In the % Off Price column, click anywhere in the cell with the number *25*.
2. Click and drag to select that cell and the three cells below it.
3. Click the **Table** menu, point to **Fill**, and then click **Down**.

   The previously empty cells now have data copied from the first cell you selected.
4. Click anywhere outside of the table. The table should appear as shown in Figure 6-12.

Figure 6-12 Creating a Fill

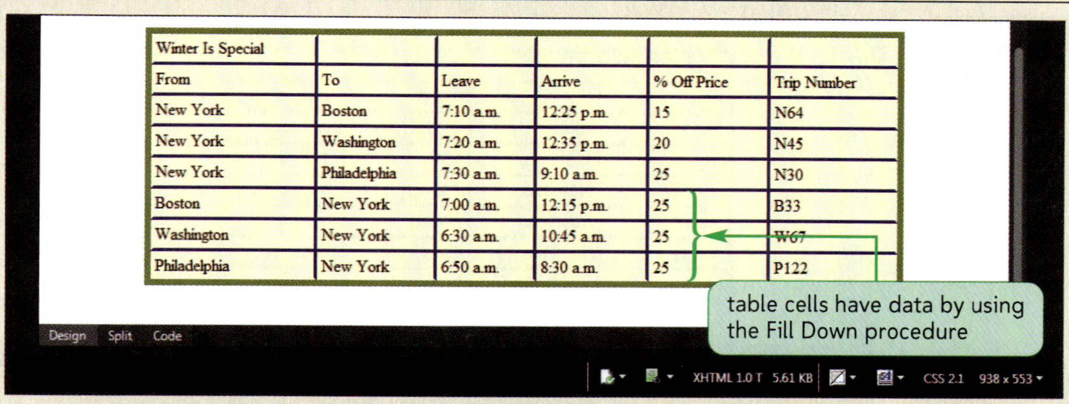

Michele is concerned about the appearance of the columns, which do not have a consistent width. She would like to adjust the column widths. You'll use the Expression Web Tables toolbar to make these changes. In this instance, you'll distribute the columns so that all of them have the same width. When you make the choice in the Tables toolbar to distribute columns evenly, the percentage width you set earlier (90%) will be converted to an equivalent pixel width based on your screen resolution.

To automatically adjust the column widths:

1. Click **View** on the menu bar, point to **Toolbars**, and then click **Tables**.

   The Tables toolbar appears.

2. Click anywhere inside the table to activate the Tables toolbar buttons.

   Figure 6-13 shows the Tables toolbar.

Figure 6-13 The Tables toolbar

Tables toolbar opens below the Common toolbar

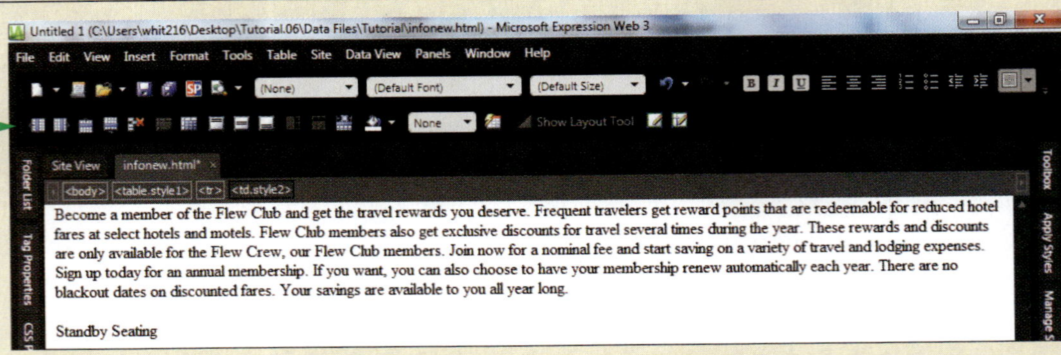

3. Pass the mouse pointer over the buttons on the Tables toolbar to familiarize yourself with their functions.
4. Click in the first cell of the second row of the table, which contains the word *From*, and then click and drag to the right to select the entire row.
5. On the Tables toolbar, click the **Distribute Columns Evenly** button.

   The column widths are distributed evenly.

6. Click anywhere outside of the selected cells.

   The table should appear as shown in Figure 6-14.

Figure 6-14 Distributing rows

all columns in the table now have the same width

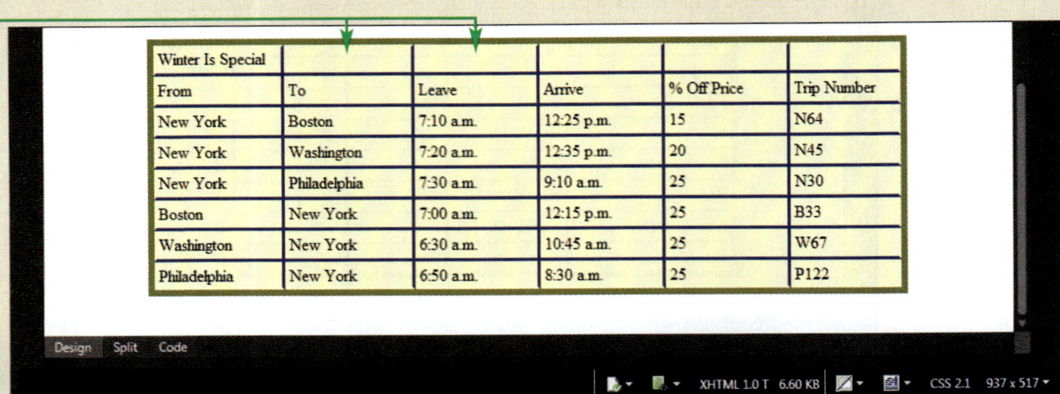

Winter Is Special					
From	To	Leave	Arrive	% Off Price	Trip Number
New York	Boston	7:10 a.m.	12:25 p.m.	15	N64
New York	Washington	7:20 a.m.	12:35 p.m.	20	N45
New York	Philadelphia	7:30 a.m.	9:10 a.m.	25	N30
Boston	New York	7:00 a.m.	12:15 p.m.	25	B33
Washington	New York	6:30 a.m.	10:45 a.m.	25	W67
Philadelphia	New York	6:50 a.m.	8:30 a.m.	25	P122

TIP

To select the contents of a row or a column, pass the pointer over the outside border of a row or a column. When the selection arrow appears, click the left mouse button.

Michele is troubled by the column width of the % Off Price column. The column heading is wide, but the cell contents are not. She would like *% Off* to be on one line and *Price* to be on the line below it. She would like to do the same for the Trip Number column, placing the word *Number* on its own line. You'll work with her to position cell contents on multiple lines.

To position text on two lines:

1. In the cell containing the text *% Off Price*, click at the end of the word *Off*.
2. Press the **Shift+Enter** keys.

   The word *Price* moves to a new line.
3. Press the **Delete** key. The space before the word *Price* is deleted.
4. In the *Trip Number* cell, click at the end of the word *Trip*.
5. Press the **Shift+Enter** keys.

   The word *Number* moves to a new line.
6. Press the **Delete** key. The space before the word *Number* is deleted.
7. Click anywhere outside the table. The table should appear as shown in Figure 6-15.

Figure 6-15 **Creating a two-line heading**

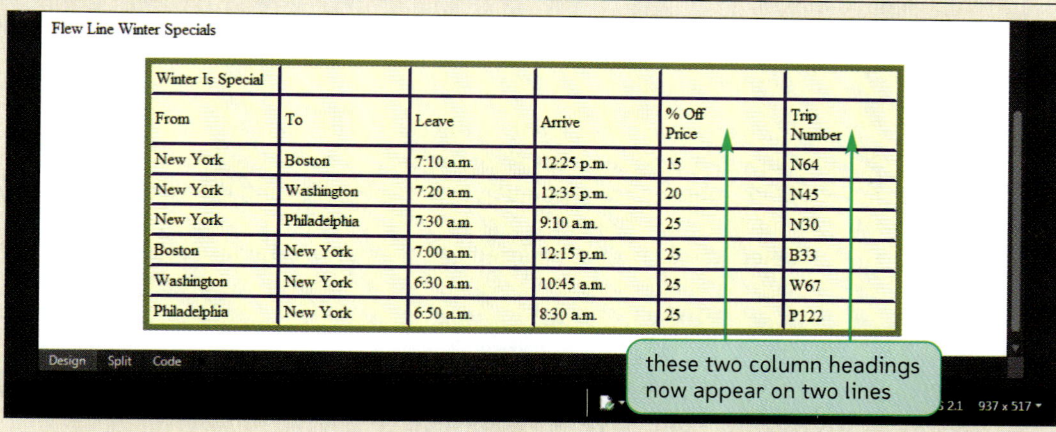

Flew Line Winter Specials

Winter Is Special					
From	To	Leave	Arrive	% Off Price	Trip Number
New York	Boston	7:10 a.m.	12:25 p.m.	15	N64
New York	Washington	7:20 a.m.	12:35 p.m.	20	N45
New York	Philadelphia	7:30 a.m.	9:10 a.m.	25	N30
Boston	New York	7:00 a.m.	12:15 p.m.	25	B33
Washington	New York	6:30 a.m.	10:45 a.m.	25	W67
Philadelphia	New York	6:50 a.m.	8:30 a.m.	25	P122

Now that the contents of the % Off Price column are narrower, Michele wonders if it's possible to widen both the From and the To columns. You can change the widths of individual columns by passing the pointer over a cell border and then clicking and dragging to the left or the right to resize the column as you want. As you click and drag, you'll see a ScreenTip indicating the width of the column in pixels. You can also be more precise in determining a column width by using the Cell Properties dialog box. You'll work with Michele to manually change the width of the first cell. You'll show her two methods for changing the column width. The first method allows her to use a ScreenTip to set the column width. The second method uses a dialog box to change the column width.

To manually change a column width:

1. Click in the first cell of the table, which contains the text *Winter Is Special*.
2. Pass the pointer over any portion of the right border of the cell. When you see the double-headed arrow, click and drag the border until the ScreenTip reports a column width of approximately 200 pixels wider than the original size.

3. Press the **Ctrl+Z** keys to undo the change.
4. Click in the first cell of the table, right-click the cell, and then click **Cell Properties** on the shortcut menu.
5. Click in the **Specify width** box and then type a number that is 100 pixels wider than the current value.
6. Click the **OK** button.
7. Press the **Ctrl+Z** keys to undo the change.

Merging and Splitting Cells

Michele wants to know if the text in the first cell can be combined with the other cells to its right. Combining cells in Expression Web is called **merging cells**. Dividing them is known as **splitting cells**. You show Michele how easy it is to merge cells in Expression Web.

REFERENCE

Merging Cells

- Click anywhere inside one of the cells to be merged.
- Click and drag to select all of the cells to be merged.
- Click Table on the menu bar, point to Modify, and then click Merge Cells.

or

- Select the cells to be merged and then on the Tables toolbar, click the Merge Cells button.

To merge cells across columns:

1. Click anywhere in the first cell of the table, which contains the text *Winter Is Special*.
2. Pass the pointer over the left border of the table, and then when you see the row selection arrow, click to select the entire row.
3. With the cells in the first row selected, click the **Merge Cells** button on the Tables toolbar.

   The cells are merged.
4. Click anywhere outside the merged cells.

   The table should appear as shown in Figure 6-16.

Figure 6-16 Merging cells across columns

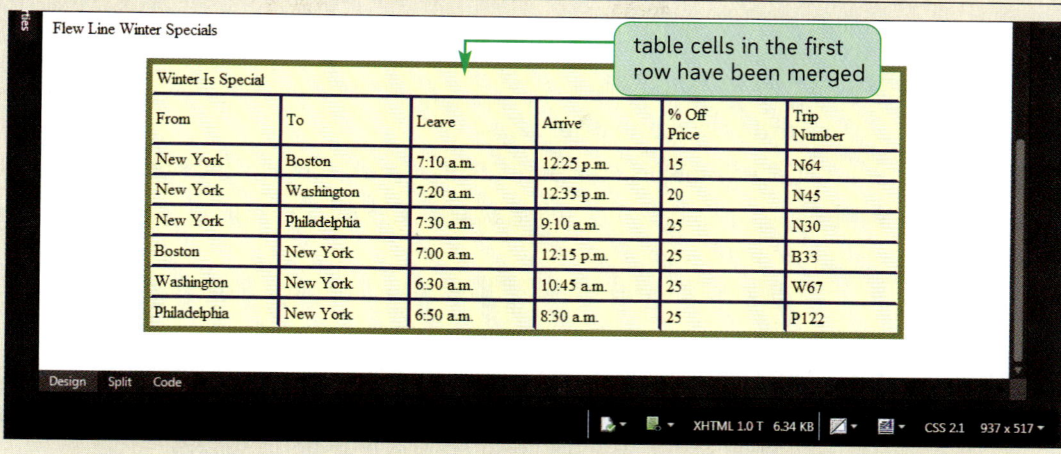

Winter Is Special					
From	To	Leave	Arrive	% Off Price	Trip Number
New York	Boston	7:10 a.m.	12:25 p.m.	15	N64
New York	Washington	7:20 a.m.	12:35 p.m.	20	N45
New York	Philadelphia	7:30 a.m.	9:10 a.m.	25	N30
Boston	New York	7:00 a.m.	12:15 p.m.	25	B33
Washington	New York	6:30 a.m.	10:45 a.m.	25	W67
Philadelphia	New York	6:50 a.m.	8:30 a.m.	25	P122

Michele is not sure if all the fares will be 25% off. She would like to substitute the text "TBD," which stands for To Be Determined, in place of the data (the number 15 and the number 20) in the first two cells of the % Off Price column. She also would like those cells to be merged across the rows. You'll show Michele how to merge those two cells across rows.

To merge cells across rows:

1. Click in the cell that contains the number 15.
2. Click and drag down one cell to select both the cell containing the number 15 and the cell containing the number 20 below it.
3. Press the **Delete** key.

   The numbers 15 and 20 are deleted.
4. With the cells still selected, on the Tables toolbar, click the **Merge Cells** button.
5. In the newly merged cell, type **TBD** and then click anywhere outside the table.

   The table should appear as shown in Figure 6-17.

Figure 6-17 Merging cells across rows

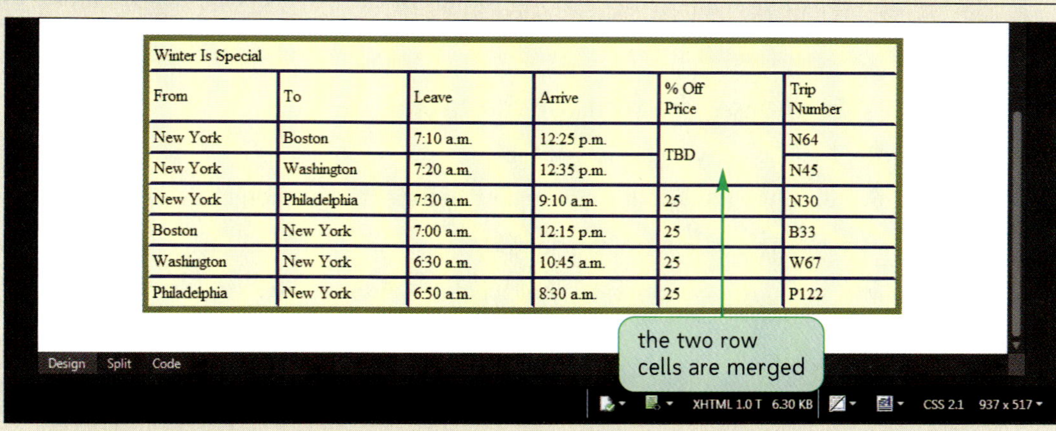

Winter Is Special					
From	To	Leave	Arrive	% Off Price	Trip Number
New York	Boston	7:10 a.m.	12:25 p.m.	TBD	N64
New York	Washington	7:20 a.m.	12:35 p.m.		N45
New York	Philadelphia	7:30 a.m.	9:10 a.m.	25	N30
Boston	New York	7:00 a.m.	12:15 p.m.	25	B33
Washington	New York	6:30 a.m.	10:45 a.m.	25	W67
Philadelphia	New York	6:50 a.m.	8:30 a.m.	25	P122

Michele would also like to format some rows and columns so that the data is centered. She wants the data in the first two rows to be centered horizontally. She also would like the data in some of the columns centered. You'll work with Michele to center the data in the cells.

To center data in the cells:

1. Click in the first cell of the table, which contains the text *Winter Is Special*.
2. Click and drag down and to the right to select all the data in the first two rows of the table.
3. Click the **Center** button on the Common toolbar.

   The data in the first two rows is centered.
4. Click in the cell containing the text *7:10 a.m.* in the Leave column, and then click and drag down and to the right to select all the cells below the headings in the Leave, Arrive, % Off Price, and Trip Number columns.
5. Click the **Center** button on the Common toolbar and then click anywhere outside the table.

   The table should appear as shown in Figure 6-18.

Figure 6-18 Centering text

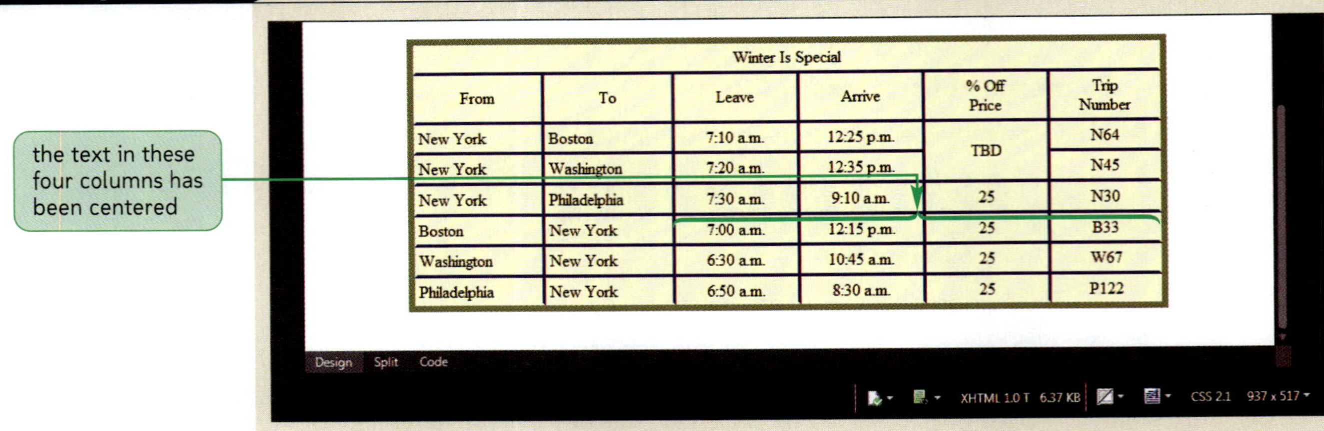

Winter Is Special					
From	To	Leave	Arrive	% Off Price	Trip Number
New York	Boston	7:10 a.m.	12:25 p.m.	TBD	N64
New York	Washington	7:20 a.m.	12:35 p.m.		N45
New York	Philadelphia	7:30 a.m.	9:10 a.m.	25	N30
Boston	New York	7:00 a.m.	12:15 p.m.	25	B33
Washington	New York	6:30 a.m.	10:45 a.m.	25	W67
Philadelphia	New York	6:50 a.m.	8:30 a.m.	25	P122

Michele would like to change the general appearance of the table. She wants the text to appear in a more modern font. You'll work with her to change the font for the table to Arial.

To change the font for the table:

1. Click anywhere in the table.
2. Click the **Table** menu, point to **Select**, and then click **Table**.

   The entire table is selected.
3. On the Common toolbar, click the **Font** arrow.

4. Click **Arial, Helvetica, sans-serif.**

   The font for the entire table is changed.

5. Click anywhere outside the table.

   The table should appear as shown in Figure 6-19.

Figure 6-19 Changing the font

the font for the entire table is changed to Arial

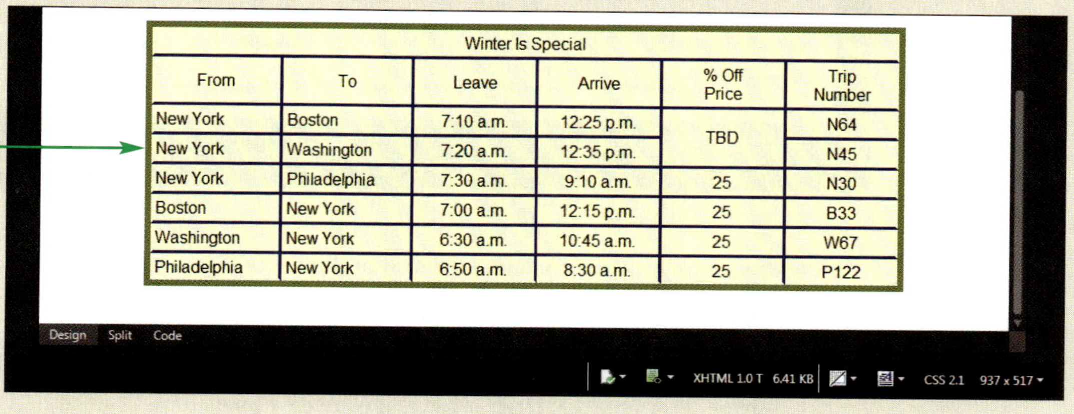

Winter Is Special					
From	To	Leave	Arrive	% Off Price	Trip Number
New York	Boston	7:10 a.m.	12:25 p.m.	TBD	N64
New York	Washington	7:20 a.m.	12:35 p.m.		N45
New York	Philadelphia	7:30 a.m.	9:10 a.m.	25	N30
Boston	New York	7:00 a.m.	12:15 p.m.	25	B33
Washington	New York	6:30 a.m.	10:45 a.m.	25	W67
Philadelphia	New York	6:50 a.m.	8:30 a.m.	25	P122

For the first and second rows, Michele wants to change the font size and format some of the text in bold and in a different color. For these sorts of multiple format changes, using the Font dialog box is the most efficient choice.

To change the formatting of the first row:

1. Select the text **Winter Is Special** in the first row of the table.
2. Click **Format** on the menu bar, and then click **Font**.

   The Font dialog box opens.

3. In the Font style list, click **Bold Italic**.
4. In the Size list, scroll down if necessary and then click **x-large (24 pt)**.
5. Click the **Color** arrow and then click **Navy**, which is the third swatch from the end in the first row.
6. In the Effects group, click the **All caps** check box.
7. Click the **OK** button and then click anywhere outside the table.

   The first row should appear as shown in Figure 6-20.

Figure 6-20 Formatting the first row

text in the first row is now bold, italic, 24 pt, navy, and all caps

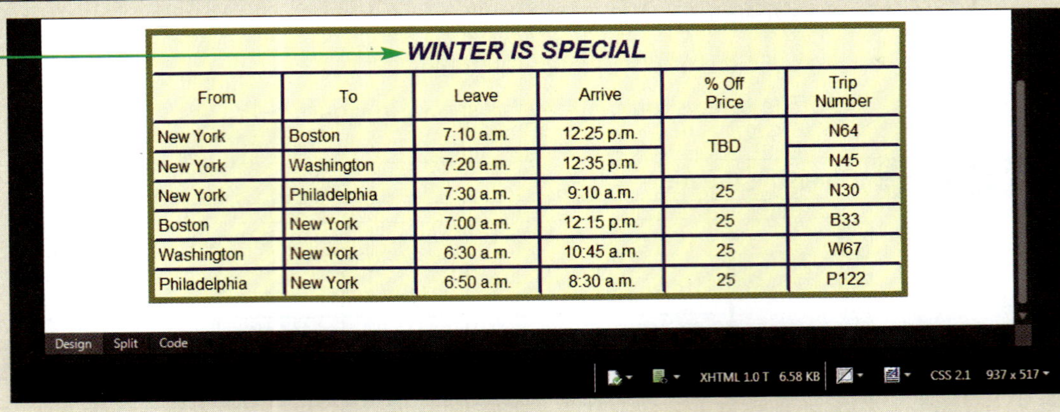

WINTER IS SPECIAL					
From	To	Leave	Arrive	% Off Price	Trip Number
New York	Boston	7:10 a.m.	12:25 p.m.	TBD	N64
New York	Washington	7:20 a.m.	12:35 p.m.		N45
New York	Philadelphia	7:30 a.m.	9:10 a.m.	25	N30
Boston	New York	7:00 a.m.	12:15 p.m.	25	B33
Washington	New York	6:30 a.m.	10:45 a.m.	25	W67
Philadelphia	New York	6:50 a.m.	8:30 a.m.	25	P122

Next, you'll work with Michele to format the second row of the table, which contains the column headings.

To change the formatting of the second row:

1. Click anywhere in the first cell of the second row, which contains the word *From*.
2. Pass the pointer over the left cell border and then when you see the row selection arrow, click to select the contents of the second row.
3. Click the **Format** menu and then click **Font**.

   The Font dialog box opens.
4. In the Size list, scroll down if necessary and then click **large (18 pt)**.
5. Click the **Color** arrow and then click **Maroon**, which is the fourth swatch in the first row.
6. In the Effects group, click the **All caps** check box and the **Strong** check box.
7. Click the **OK** button.
8. Click anywhere outside the table.

   The row should appear as shown in Figure 6-21.

Figure 6-21 Formatting the column headings

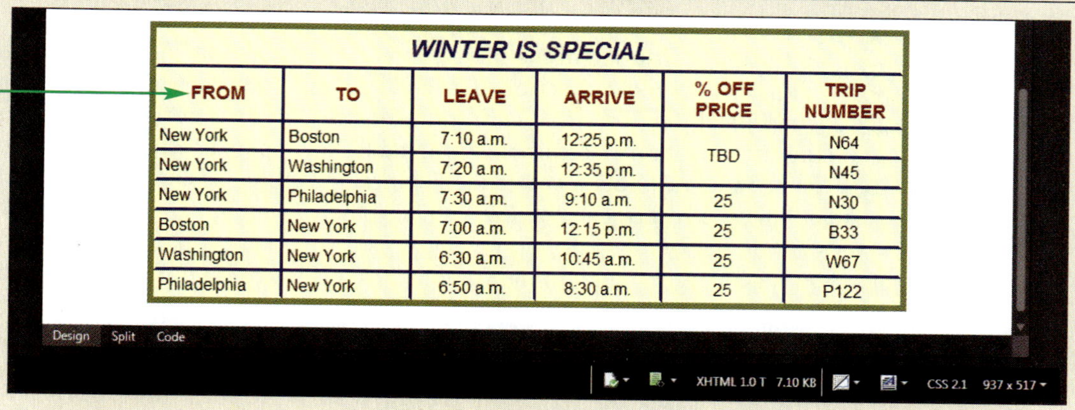

WINTER IS SPECIAL					
FROM	TO	LEAVE	ARRIVE	% OFF PRICE	TRIP NUMBER
New York	Boston	7:10 a.m.	12:25 p.m.	TBD	N64
New York	Washington	7:20 a.m.	12:35 p.m.		N45
New York	Philadelphia	7:30 a.m.	9:10 a.m.	25	N30
Boston	New York	7:00 a.m.	12:15 p.m.	25	B33
Washington	New York	6:30 a.m.	10:45 a.m.	25	W67
Philadelphia	New York	6:50 a.m.	8:30 a.m.	25	P122

Now, you'll work with Michele to change the text color and the background color in the second row using the Borders and Shading dialog box.

To change the foreground and background colors:

1. Select all of the cells in the second row.
2. Click the **Format** menu, and then click **Borders and Shading**.

   The Borders and Shading dialog box opens.
3. Click the **Shading** tab.
4. Click the **Background color** arrow.
5. Click **Teal**, which is the last swatch in the second row.
6. Click the **Foreground color** arrow.
7. Click **White**, which is the second swatch in the first row.
8. Click the **OK** button and then click anywhere outside the table.

   The cells in the second row now appear as shown in Figure 6-22.

Figure 6-22 Changing the foreground and background color

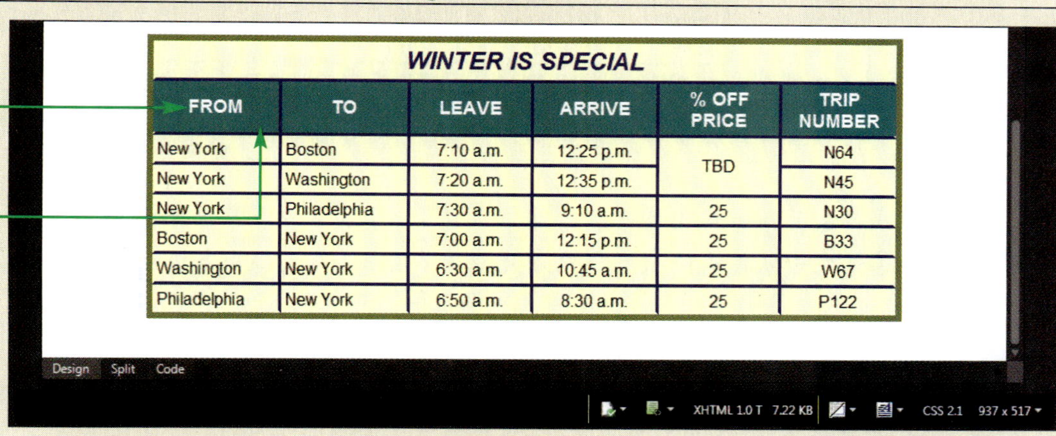

WINTER IS SPECIAL					
FROM	TO	LEAVE	ARRIVE	% OFF PRICE	TRIP NUMBER
New York	Boston	7:10 a.m.	12:25 p.m.	TBD	N64
New York	Washington	7:20 a.m.	12:35 p.m.		N45
New York	Philadelphia	7:30 a.m.	9:10 a.m.	25	N30
Boston	New York	7:00 a.m.	12:15 p.m.	25	B33
Washington	New York	6:30 a.m.	10:45 a.m.	25	W67
Philadelphia	New York	6:50 a.m.	8:30 a.m.	25	P122

INSIGHT

Creating a Table Caption

It's common to give a table a caption, which is displayed in the browser and serves as a brief description of the table contents. Caption text can be as brief as the words "Figure 1," or more descriptive, such as "Profit and Loss Statement for the Last Two Quarters of the Current Fiscal Year." A table caption is optional, but it helps to identify the data in a table—especially if the table is complex and has a great deal of numeric data. You can create a caption in Expression Web by clicking Table on the menu bar, pointing to Insert, clicking Caption, and then entering the caption text. To position the caption below the table, right-click anywhere in the caption. Click Caption Properties on the shortcut menu. In the Caption Properties dialog box, click the Bottom of table radio button, and then click the OK button. Caption positioning is not supported by all browsers and browser versions, so if you are positioning the caption below the table, test the page in several versions of contemporary browsers.

To check your work, you'll save the file and then display the file in the browser.

To display the file in the browser:

1. Save the file.
2. Press the **F12** key to display the file in the default browser.

   If necessary, scroll down to view the table, which should look similar to the one shown in Figure 6-23.

Figure 6-23 **The table in the browser**

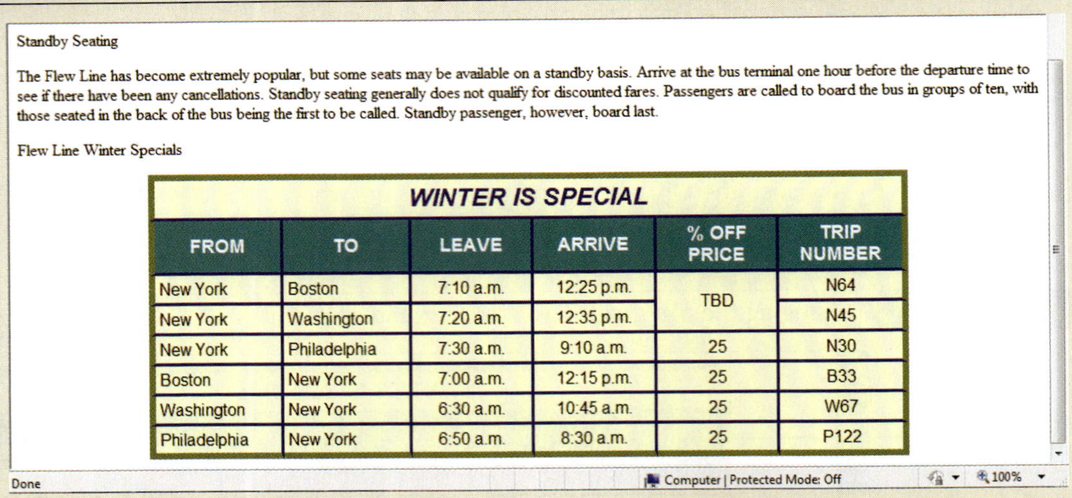

Standby Seating

The Flew Line has become extremely popular, but some seats may be available on a standby basis. Arrive at the bus terminal one hour before the departure time to see if there have been any cancellations. Standby seating generally does not qualify for discounted fares. Passengers are called to board the bus in groups of ten, with those seated in the back of the bus being the first to be called. Standby passenger, however, board last.

Flew Line Winter Specials

WINTER IS SPECIAL

FROM	TO	LEAVE	ARRIVE	% OFF PRICE	TRIP NUMBER
New York	Boston	7:10 a.m.	12:25 p.m.	TBD	N64
New York	Washington	7:20 a.m.	12:35 p.m.		N45
New York	Philadelphia	7:30 a.m.	9:10 a.m.	25	N30
Boston	New York	7:00 a.m.	12:15 p.m.	25	B33
Washington	New York	6:30 a.m.	10:45 a.m.	25	W67
Philadelphia	New York	6:50 a.m.	8:30 a.m.	25	P122

Done Computer | Protected Mode: Off 100%

3. Close the browser.
4. If you will not be completing the next session, close the Web site.

REVIEW

Session 6.1 Quick Check

1. What is the name for a table that aligns page content in rows and columns?
2. What is created by the intersection of a column and a row?
3. What are table gridlines?
4. What are tracer lines?
5. What are two ways you can create tables?
6. What is cell padding? What is cell spacing?

SESSION 6.2 VISUAL OVERVIEW

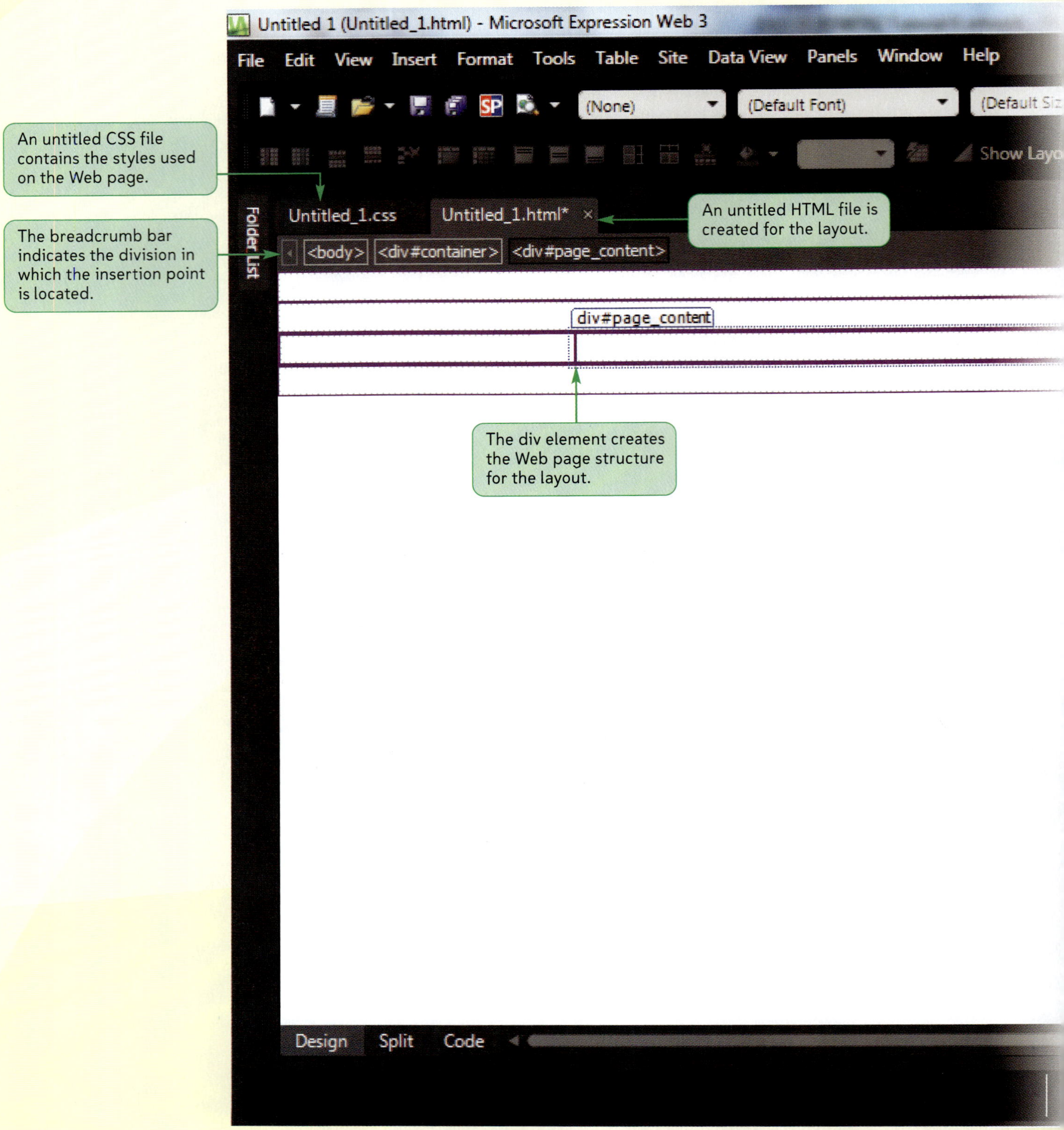

USING CSS LAYOUTS

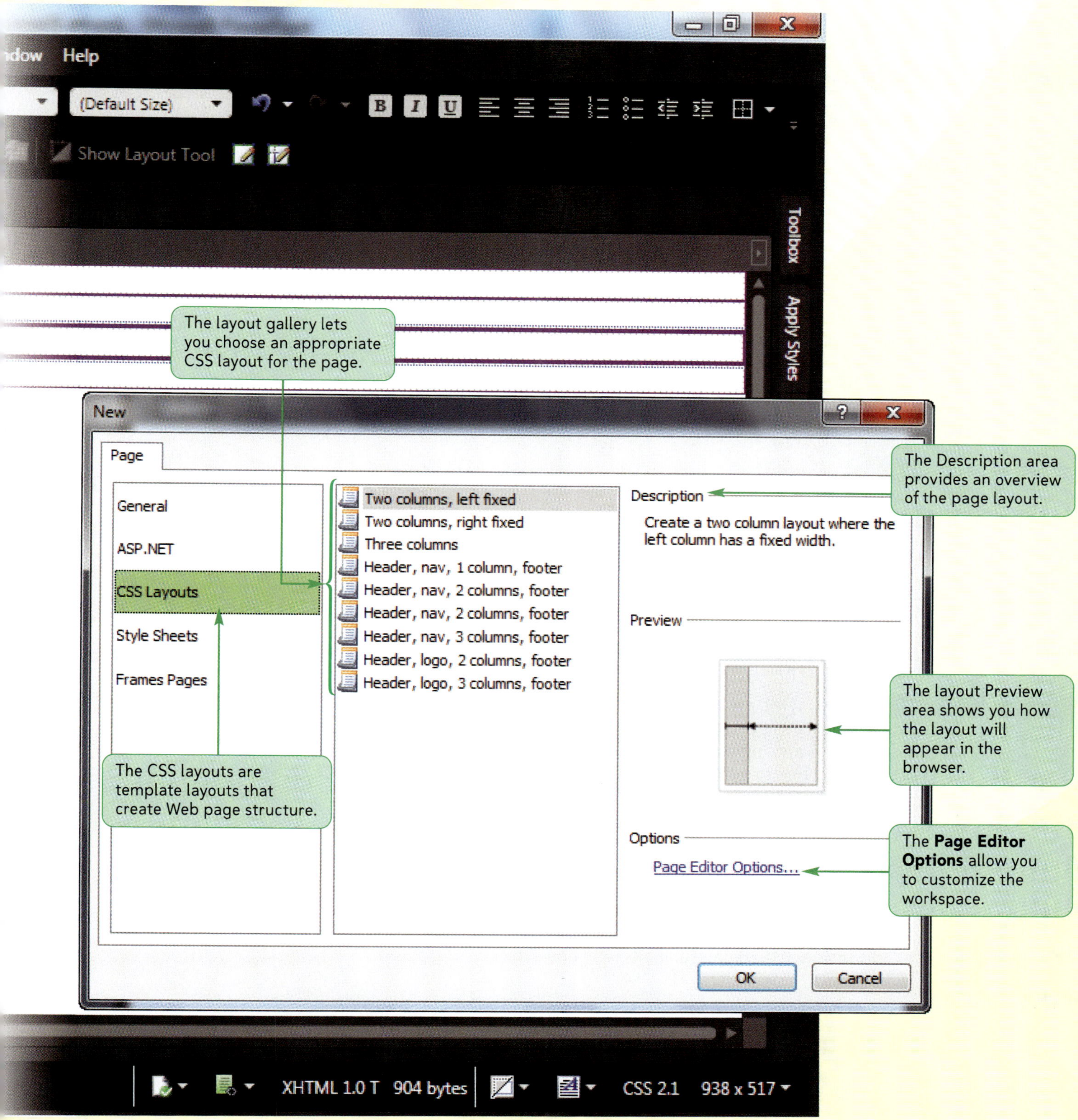

Creating Web Page Layouts

Michele has sketched the structure she'd like to use for the Flew Line Web page, which is shown in Figure 6-24. Several years ago, it was common to use tables not only to organize data, but also to structure Web page layouts. Today, CSS is used instead to lay out Web pages. Expression Web makes it easy to create your own layouts using CSS.

Figure 6-24 **The layout sketch**

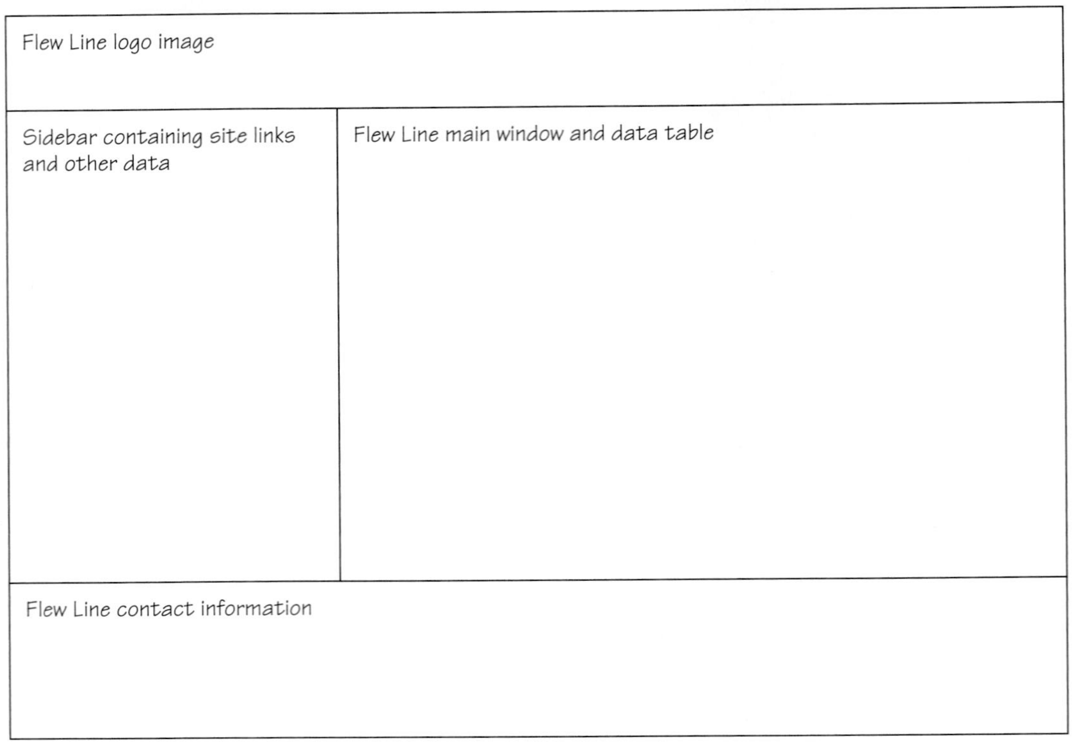

Working with the Div Element

TIP

The div element is also known as the division element.

The HTML **div element** is an important tool for creating layouts using CSS. Unlike elements that you have worked with so far, such as the heading elements, the div element does not apply any formatting to text. The sole purpose of the div element is to provide structure to a Web page. Div elements are formatted using the CSS ID selector, which always begins with a pound sign (#). An ID selector is used to create unique formatting on a Web page.

Template layouts are predefined page layouts created by Expression Web that create page divisions using the div element. Once the divisions are created, you can add content to each one. Alternatively, you can insert the divisions by selecting the content for a division, right-clicking the <div> tag button in the Toolbox panel, and clicking Wrap on the shortcut menu. You'll work with Michele to use an Expression Web template layout to create a Web page and alter its appearance.

REFERENCE

Creating a Template-Based Document

- Click File on the menu bar, point to New, and then click Page.
- In the New dialog box, click CSS Layouts.
- Click a template from one of the template layouts in the list box.
- Click the OK button.
- Enter content into each of the divisions that has been created.
- Optionally, style an ID class selector for each division.

Expression Web includes nine template Web page layouts from which to choose. You'll work with Michele to use a template Web layout to create a CSS template-based layout, even with little knowledge of CSS.

To reset the workspace layout:

1. If necessary, start Expression Web, close any other Web sites, and open the Tutorial.06 Web site.
2. If necessary, make the choice to AutoHide all panels and then, if necessary, display the Tables toolbar.
3. If necessary, press the **Alt+F1** keys to unhide the Folder List panel, open the **infonew.html** file, and then press the **Alt+F1** keys to hide the Folder List panel.

Now, you'll show Michele how to use Expression Web to create a CSS layout based on one of the several templates that are available in Expression Web.

To create a template-based CSS layout:

1. Click the **File** menu, point to **New**, and then click **Page**.

   The New dialog box opens.
2. Click **CSS Layouts**.

   A list of template layouts appears. The Preview window illustrates the currently chosen layout design, as shown in Figure 6-25.

Figure 6-25 The New dialog box

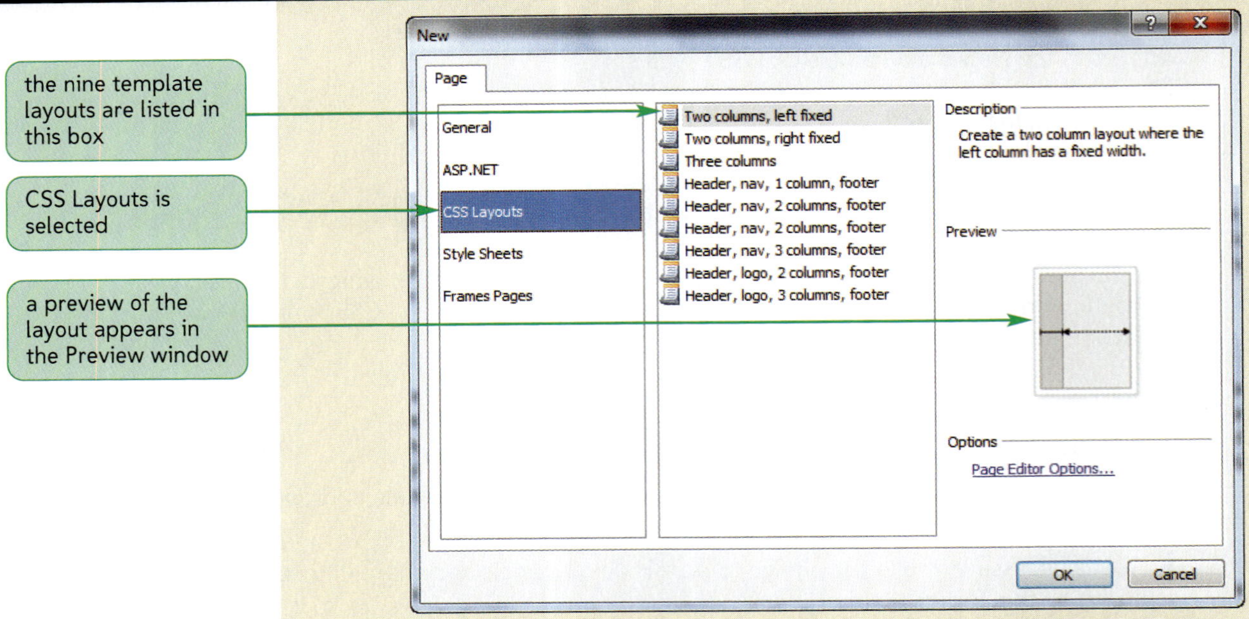

3. In the list of layout designs, click **Three columns**.

   The Preview window now illustrates a three-column layout.

4. Click the *first* instance of **Header, nav, 2 columns, footer**.

   Make sure that you have clicked the first, not the second, instance of Header, nav, 2 columns, footer.

5. Click the **OK** button.

   Expression Web creates two files: Untitled_1.css and Untitled_1.html.

6. Right-click the **Untitled_1.css** Document tab.

   Observe the CSS code that Expression Web has created.

7. Click **Save**.

   The Save As dialog box opens.

8. In the File name box, type **stylesnew.css**, and then click the **Save** button.
9. Right-click the **stylesnew.css** Document tab and then click **Close** on the shortcut menu.

Next, you'll save and rename the new HTML file.

To save and rename the Untitled_1.html file:

1. Right-click the **Untitled_1.html** Document tab.
2. Click **Save**.
3. In the File name box, type **layoutnew**.
4. Click the **Save** button.

   The file is saved as **layoutnew.html**.

You want to make sure that Michele has saved both the stylesnew.css file and the layoutnew.html file in the Tutorial folder, so you'll show her how to open the Folder List panel, and if need be, move those two files into the Tutorial folder.

To move the files into the Tutorial folder:

1. Pass the pointer over the **Folder List** panel tab to display the Folder List panel.
2. If the two files you just created are not in the Tutorial folder, click the **layoutnew.html** filename, hold down the **Shift** key, and then click the **stylesnew.css** filename to select both files.
3. Right-click either of the two selected filenames, and then on the shortcut menu, click **Cut**.
4. Right-click the **Tutorial** folder, and then on the shortcut menu, click **Paste**.

   The files are moved.
5. Click in the lower-right corner of the editing window.

   The Folder List panel collapses to a panel tab at the left edge of the screen.

Next, you'll work with Michele to change the page properties for the layoutnew.html file.

To set the page properties for the layoutnew file:

1. Right-click any area in the editing window and then click **Page Properties** on the shortcut menu.

   The Page Properties dialog box opens.
2. In the Title box, type **Flew Line Bus Company**.
3. Click in the Page description box and then type **The Flew Line is the fastest and most economical bus line on the East Coast**.
4. Click in the Keywords box and then type **flew flue flu line bus company**.

   Your screen should be similar to that shown in Figure 6-26.

Figure 6-26 The Page Properties dialog box

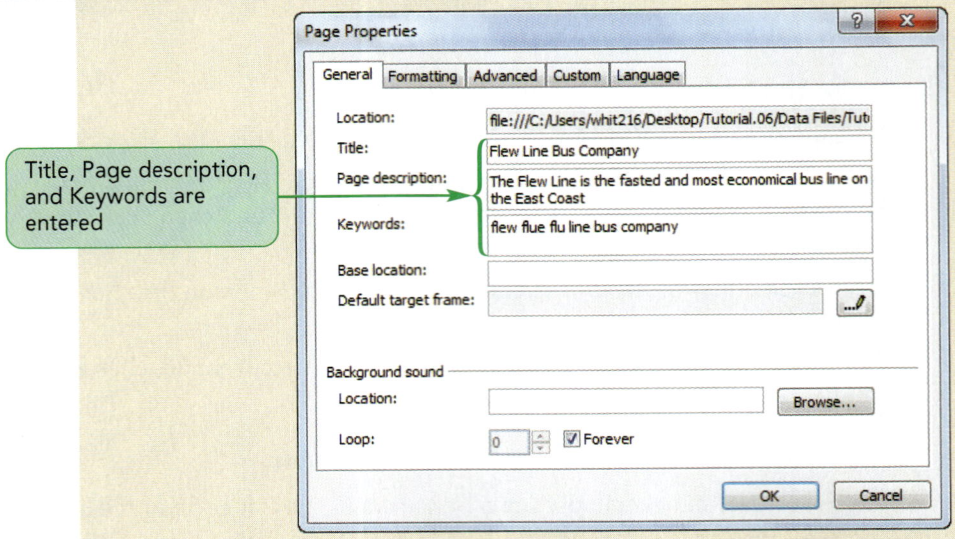

5. Click the **OK** button.
6. Save the file.

INSIGHT

Creating Borders for Page Divisions

When you create a CSS layout, tracer lines appear that serve to outline each of the page divisions (the div elements) on the Web page used to create the page layout. Recall that when you created a table, you also changed the border width to make tracer lines easier to see. You can do the same for a CSS layout. Create a style for the CSS div element. Change the border so that the border appears as solid, thin (or 1 or 2 pixels), and blue (or any color other than black), so that the border color does not compete with text content in the layout. Some of the inside borders might appear thicker than others, but the borders will provide you with an outline of where the structural elements are in your page layout.

TIP

Use the breadcrumb bar to identify on which page division the insertion point is currently located.

Now that the layout has been established, you are ready to work with Michele to add content to the Web page. The stylesnew.css file has created several divisions on the page. In Design view, it's not easy to see the borders of the divisions, though. You will have Michele create a border style for the div element so that you can clearly see the divisions.

To create the border style for the div element:

1. Pass the pointer over the **Apply Styles** panel tab until the Panel appears and then click **New Style**.

   The New Style dialog box opens.

2. Click the **Selector** arrow, scroll down the list of selectors, and then click **div**.
3. In the Category bar, click **Border**.
4. For the border-style, click the **top** arrow, and then click **solid**.
5. For the border-width, click in the **top** box, and then type **1**.
6. For the border-color, click the **top** arrow, and then click **Purple**, which is the second-to-last swatch in the top row.
7. Click the **OK** button. The page should now appear similar to the one shown in Figure 6-27.

Figure 6-27 The div style

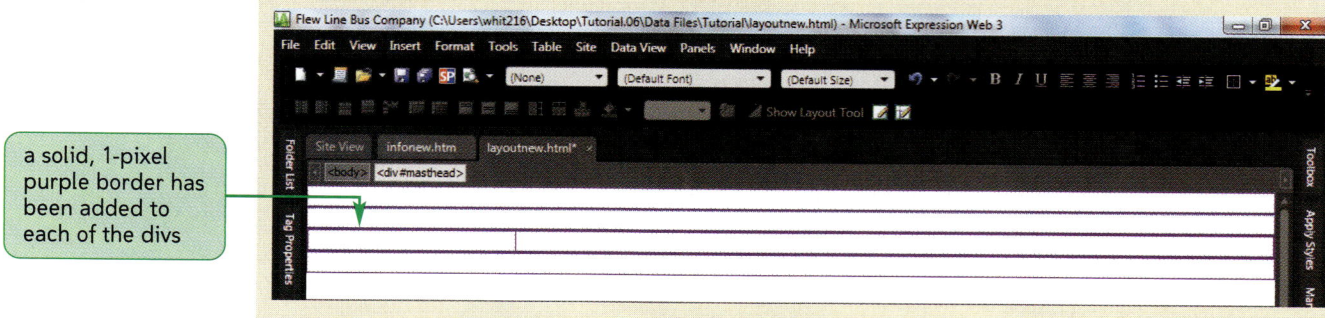

8. Save the file.

Next, you'll work with Michele to add content to the first page division, the layout. You'll begin with the masthead div at the top of the page, which will contain the Flew Line logo.

To add the logo image to the masthead div:

1. Pass the pointer over the Folder List panel tab to unhide the Folder List panel.
2. In the Folder List panel, click and drag the **flewlogo.png** image filename into the first row, and then release the mouse button.

   The Accessibilities Properties dialog box opens.
3. For the alternate text, type **Flew Bus Line logo**.
4. Click the **OK** button. The logo image is inserted, as shown in Figure 6-28.

Figure 6-28 The Flew Bus Line logo

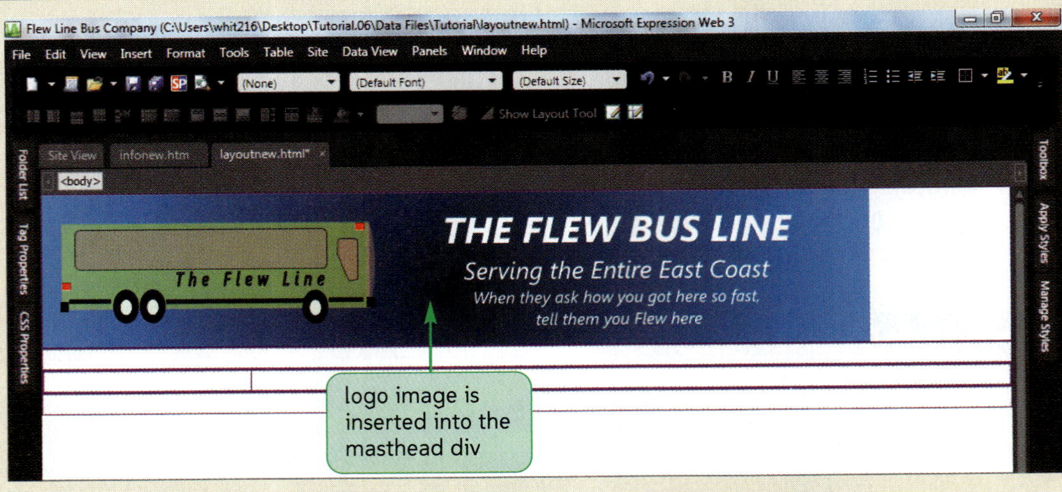

Michele's sketch places links in the sidebar. However, the template you're using includes a navigation bar below the masthead. You'll work with Michele to delete this division, which is named top_nav.

To delete the top_nav div:

1. Click anywhere in the row that is just below the masthead div.

   The div#top_nav code tab appears above the div.
2. Click the **div#top_nav** Code tab.

   The div is selected.
3. Press the **Delete** key.

   The div#top_nav div is deleted.
4. Click anywhere on the **flewlogo.png** image.
5. Press the **Down arrow** key twice.

   The insertion point should now be in the right column, which is the div#page_content div.

Next, you and Michele will copy and paste the promotional copy about the Flew Bus line into the page content div.

To copy and paste the text:

1. Click the **infonew.html** Document tab to display that document.
2. Press the **Ctrl+A** keys to select all of the page contents.
3. Press the **Ctrl+C** keys to copy the text.

4. Right-click the **infonew.html** Document tab and then click **Close**.

   The layoutnew.html document appears again.

5. With the insertion point in the div#page_content div, press the **Ctrl+V** keys to paste the text.

   The table should appear as shown in Figure 6-29. If necessary, scroll down to see the table.

Figure 6-29 The copied and pasted text

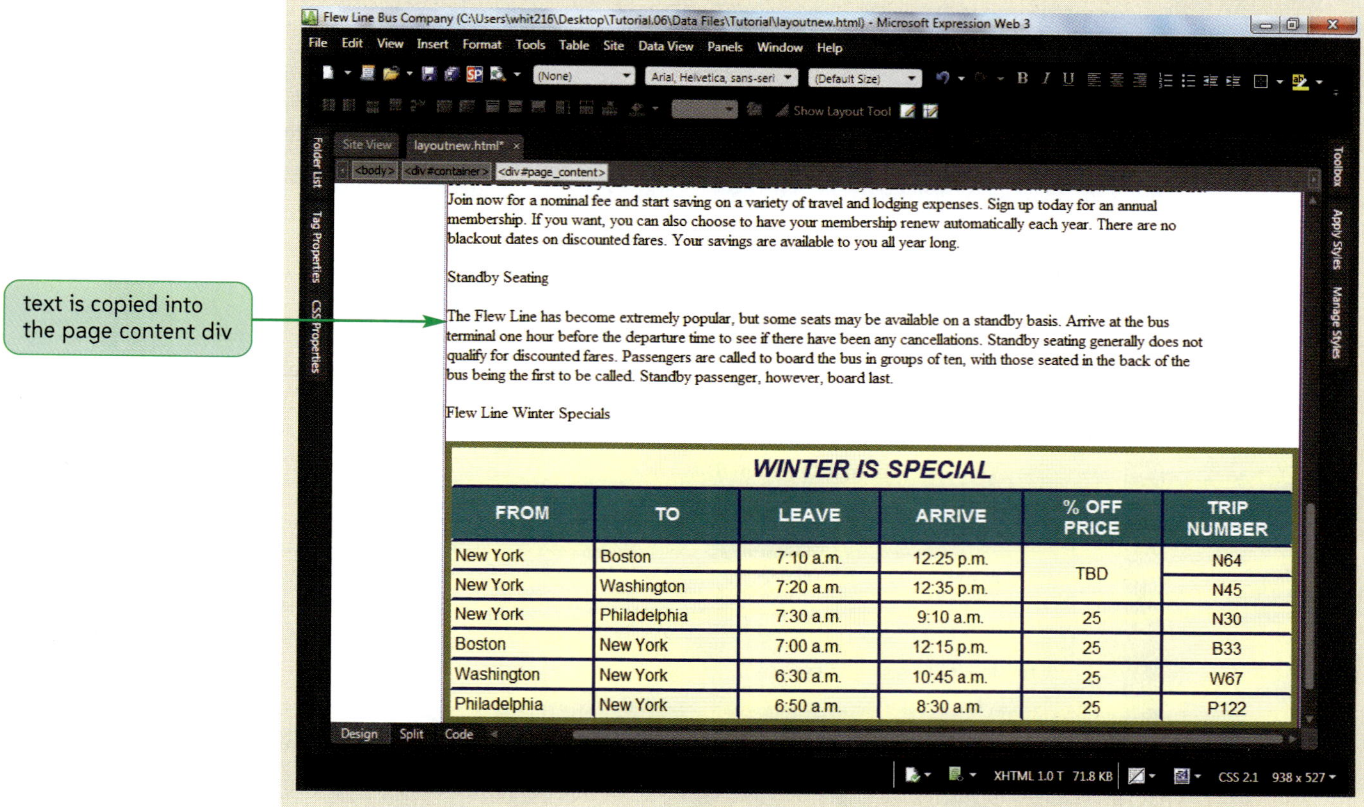

Michele wants to format the text in the document body, so you'll start by creating h1, h2, and h3 headings.

To format the first line as an h1 heading:

1. Press **Ctrl+Home** to position the insertion point at the top of the page, press the **Down arrow** key twice to position the insertion point in the blank paragraph, and then type **Tell Them You Flew Here**.
2. Click the **Style** arrow on the Common toolbar.
3. Click **Heading 1 <h1>**.
4. Click anywhere in the words **Welcome Aboard the Flew Bus Line**.
5. Click the **Style** arrow on the Common toolbar.
6. Click **Heading 2 <h2>**.

7. Click anywhere in the **Reserved Seating** side heading.
8. Click **Heading 3 <h3>**.
9. Use the same procedure to format the following headings as h3: *There's Room on the Bus*, *Stay Connected*, *Join the Flew Crew*, *Standby Seating*, and *Flew Line Winter Specials*.
10. Save the file, and then scroll up to the top of the page.

    The document should look similar to Figure 6-30.

Figure 6-30 Formatting headings

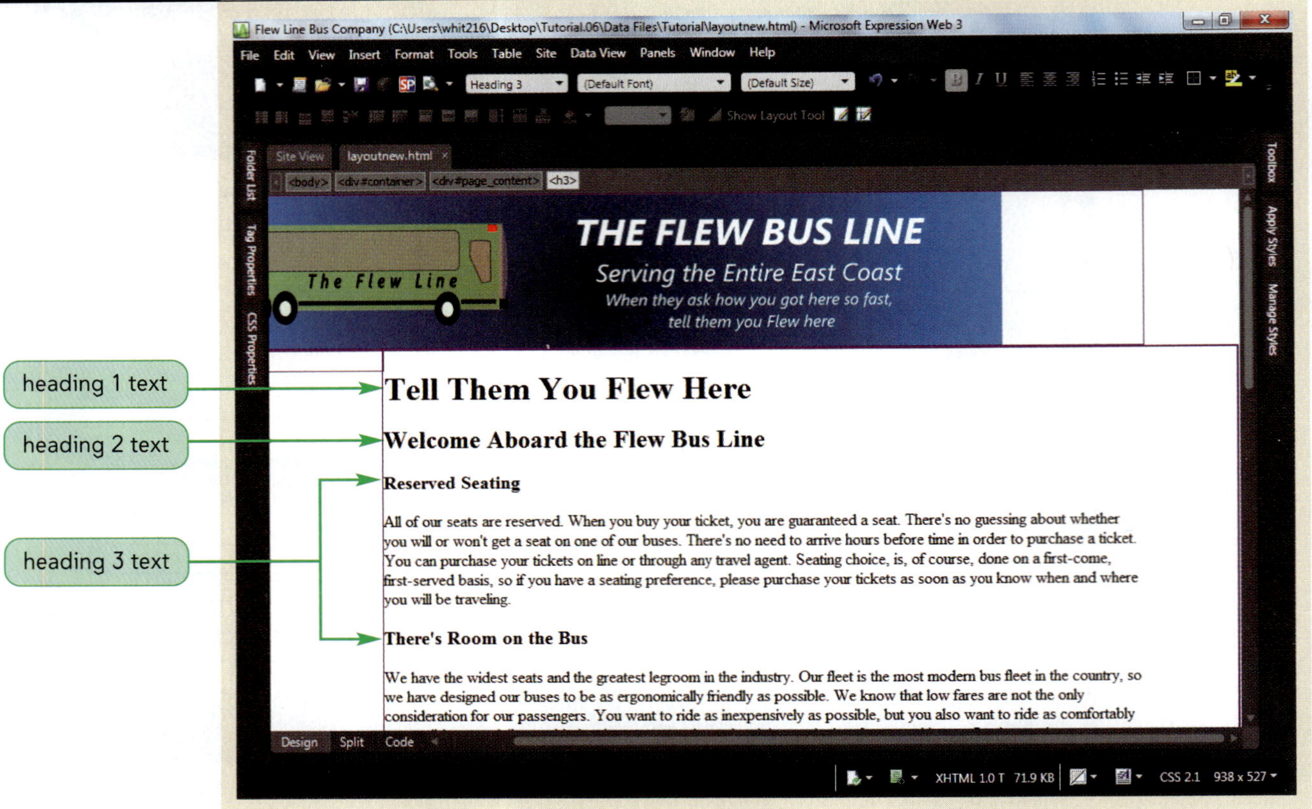

Next, you'll add some information to the footer cell.

To enter the footer information:

1. Scroll down to the bottom of page. Click anywhere in the div#footer row beneath the table at the bottom of the page.

    The **div#footer** Code tab appears.
2. Type **Contact the Flew Bus Line at flewbuslines@comlink.net**.

3. In the e-mail address you just typed, select **flewbuslines@comlink.net**.
4. Press the **Ctrl+C** keys to copy the e-mail address.
5. Press the **Ctrl+K** keys.

   The Insert Hyperlink dialog box opens.
6. In the Link to bar, click **E-mail Address**.
7. In the E-mail address box, press the **Ctrl+V** keys to paste the copied e-mail address. Note the mailto protocol is automatically added to the e-mail address in the address box.
8. Click the **OK** button.

   The e-mail address is now blue and underlined, indicating that the text is a link.
9. With the insertion point in the e-mail address, click the **Center** button on the Common toolbar.

   The footer text is centered, as shown in Figure 6-31.

Figure 6-31 **The footer text**

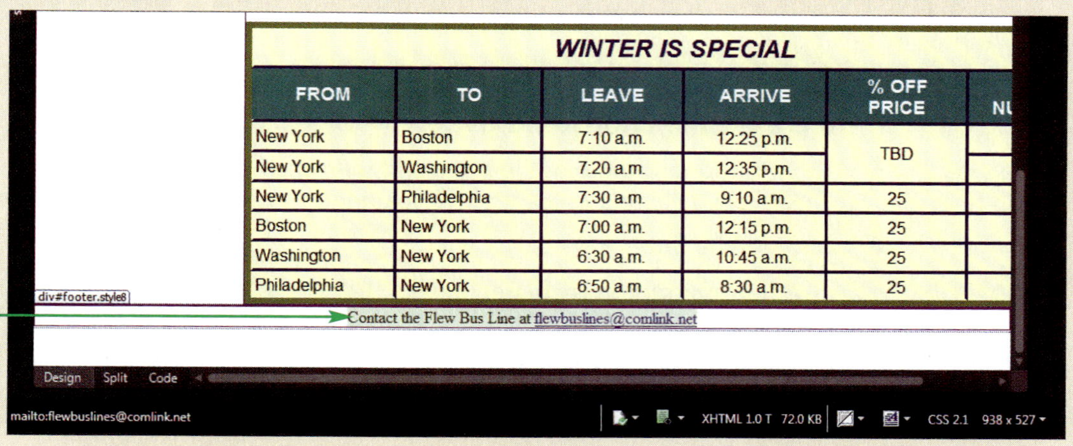

an e-mail link is created in the footer and the footer is centered

PROSKILLS

Problem Solving and Decision Making: Choosing a Web Page Layout

Expression Web includes several choices of template layouts. Expression Web does not, however, instruct you which layout is the best for a particular Web page. For a very simple Web page, you might consider using the two-column layout. This layout is especially useful if you have many links. You can place the links column either on the left or the right and have plenty of room for the main content division. If you want your pages to resemble those of a newspaper or magazine, the three-column layout is an ideal choice. If you want to include a navigation bar in your layout, choose any of the three layouts that include header, nav, columns, and footer. If you want to include a logo as well as a navigation bar, choose either of the two layouts that include header, logo, columns, and footer. For any layouts using a navigation bar, include buttons for only the most popular pages. You want your visitors to locate the links to those pages easily. If you want, you can include a more detailed list of links in the footer.

Now that the masthead, page content, and footer divs have content, you'll work with Michele to add content to the div#left_col div. This div will contain a series of interactive buttons.

Creating a Navigation Bar for the Left Column

The left column will have links to other pages in the Web site. You'll create an unordered list.

REFERENCE

Creating a Navigation Bar Using a List

- Type the text as paragraphs on separate lines.
- Select the text and convert the paragraphs to a bulleted list.
- Select a bulleted item, and then press the Ctrl+K keys to open the Insert Hyperlink dialog box.
- Enter an address for the link.
- Click the OK button.

To create a list that's formatted correctly, you'll have to type the list in the body of the document and then cut and paste it into the left column div.

To create the unordered list:

1. Scroll up to the top of the page and then click after the letter *g* in the words *Reserved Seating* in the first h3 heading.
2. Press the **Enter** key.

   A new paragraph is created.
3. Type the following text and press the Enter key at the end of each line except the last one:

   Buy Tickets

   View Our Terminals

   Seating Availability

   Safe Travel Rules

   The Flew Crew
4. Select the five lines of text you just typed.
5. Click the **Bullets** button on the Common toolbar.

   The five lines are now a bulleted list.
6. With the list still selected, press the **Ctrl+X** keys to cut the bulleted list.
7. Click anywhere in the div#left_col div, which is just below the left side of the logo image.

   The div#left_col code tab appears.
8. Press the **Ctrl+V** keys to paste the bulleted list.
9. Click anywhere outside the left column div and then, if necessary, scroll up to see the entire list.

   The left column div content should appear as shown in Figure 6-32.

Figure 6-32 Content for the left column div

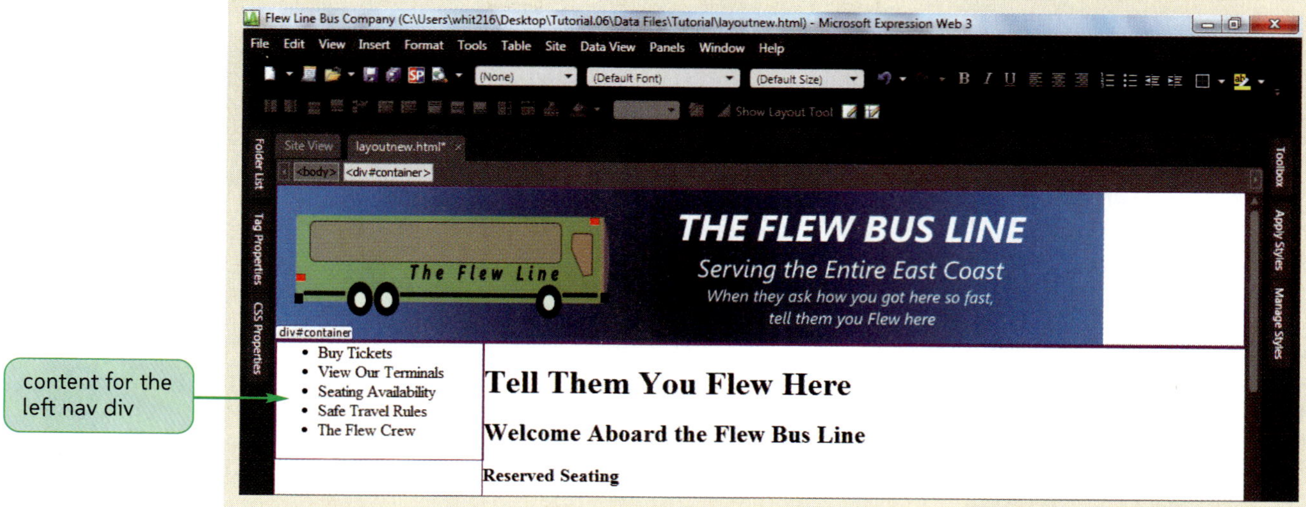

Now, you'll use the text you entered as link text to create links to the other five pages at the Flew Line Web site: tickets.html, terminals.html, seating.html, rules.html, and crew.html.

To create the links:

1. In the left column div, select the words **Buy Tickets**.
2. Press the **Ctrl+K** keys.

   The Insert Hyperlink dialog box opens.
3. If necessary, in the Link to bar, click the **Existing File or Web Page** button.
4. In the Insert Hyperlink dialog box, double-click the **Data Files** folder and then double-click the **Tutorial** folder.
5. If necessary, scroll down the list of files and then click **tickets**.
6. Click the **OK** button.

   The first link is created.
7. Repeat the same procedure to create links to the other four Web pages, as shown in Figure 6-33.

Figure 6-33 Creating the links

Text	Link to this File
View Our Terminals	terminals.html
Seating Availability	seating.html
Safe Travel Rules	rules.html
The Flew Crew	crew.html

8. When you are done, click anywhere outside the left column div.

   The links should appear as shown in Figure 6-34.

Figure 6-34 Creating links

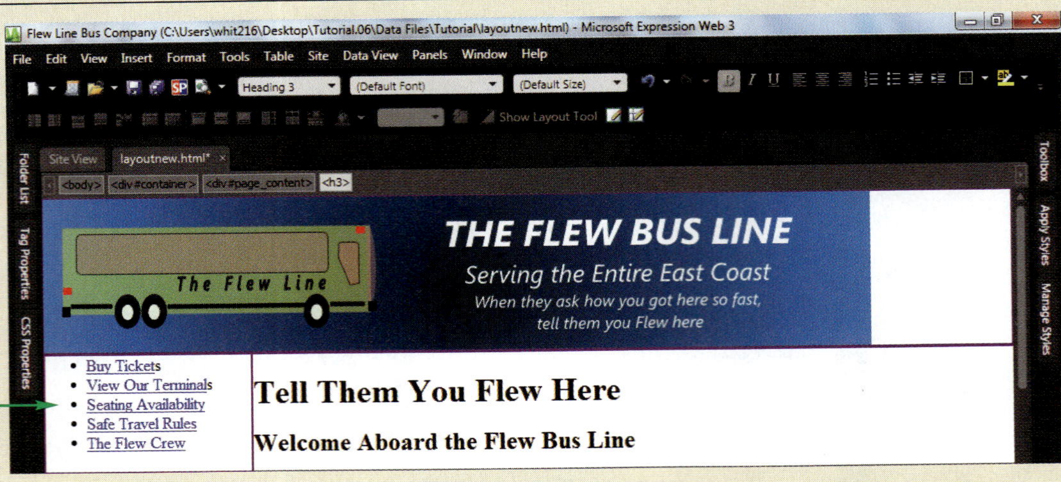

each bulleted list item links to a different page at the Flew Line Web site

Next, you'll work with Michele to create some visual interest for the links and add a hover effect.

Creating Link Styles

Michele wants to explore changing the page's link styles. In a previous tutorial, you used the Page Properties dialog box to change the link colors. In this instance, however, you want to remove the underscore for unvisited links, and make the underscore appear only when the pointer passes over the link. You can't achieve those effects by using the Page Properties dialog box.

You'll first work with Michele to change the style for unvisited links, and then you'll create a style for hovered links, which will change the appearance of links when a user's mouse pointer hovers over them.

To create the style for unvisited links:

1. Click the **Format** menu and then click **New Style**.

   The New Style dialog box opens.

2. Click the **Selector** arrow and then click **a:link**.
3. Click the **font-weight** arrow, and then click **bold**.
4. In the text-decoration area, click the **none** check box.
5. Click the **OK** button.

   The underscoring for the links is removed.

TIP

Don't change the font size for the hover effect. You don't want the text to shift when the pointer passes over the link text.

Next, you'll create a style for the hover effect. You want the underline to appear when the pointer passes over a link. To catch your visitors' attention, you will also change the text color to green when the pointer passes over the link. If you pass the mouse pointer over the link text in the editing window, you won't see any effect, so you'll test your style by opening the page in your browser.

To create the hover style:

1. Click the **Format** menu and then click **New Style**. The New Style dialog box opens.
2. Click the **Selector** arrow and then click **a:hover**.
3. Click the **color** arrow, and then click **Green**, which is the third swatch in the first row.
4. In the text-decoration section, click the **underline** check box.
5. Click the **OK** button.
6. Save the file.
7. Press the **F12** key to open the file in the default browser.
8. Pass the pointer over the links.

   As you pass the pointer over a link, the link text should appear in green and underlined, as shown in Figure 6-35.

Figure 6-35 **The hover effect in the browser**

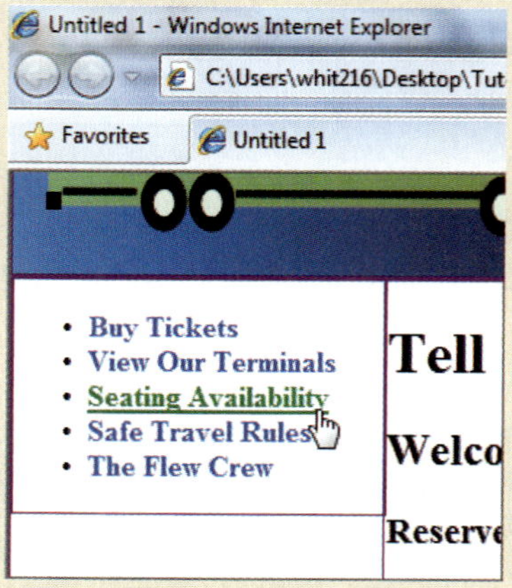

9. Close the browser.

Michele would still like a few more changes to the page, including adding another small table. You'll set it up using the Table AutoFormat feature.

Using the Table AutoFormat Feature

In the first session, you manually changed the appearance of a table. If you do not want precise control over a table's format, however, you can use the Table AutoFormat feature of Expression Web to quickly format the table appearance. The **Table AutoFormat** feature is a quick method to set the formatting for a table by choosing a set of table styles from a gallery of template styles.

REFERENCE

Using the Table AutoFormat Feature

- Click anywhere in the table.
- Click Table on the menu bar, point to Modify, and then click Table AutoFormat.
- In the Table AutoFormat dialog box, in the Formats list box, click the format you want to apply to the table.
- Click the OK button.

TIP

The Table AutoFormats in Expression Web are similar to those found in Microsoft Word.

Instead of individually styling the HTML table elements, such as table, td, th, or tr, you simply choose a design template from those available in the Table AutoFormat feature. You'll work with Michele to create the new table.

To create a new table:

1. Click at the end of the Flew Crew link.
2. Press the **Enter** key twice.
3. Click **Table** on the menu bar, and then click **Insert Table**.
4. In the Insert Table dialog box, click in the **Columns** box, delete the number in the box, and then type **1**.
5. Click the **OK** button.

   The table is created, as shown in Figure 6-36.

Figure 6-36 The new table

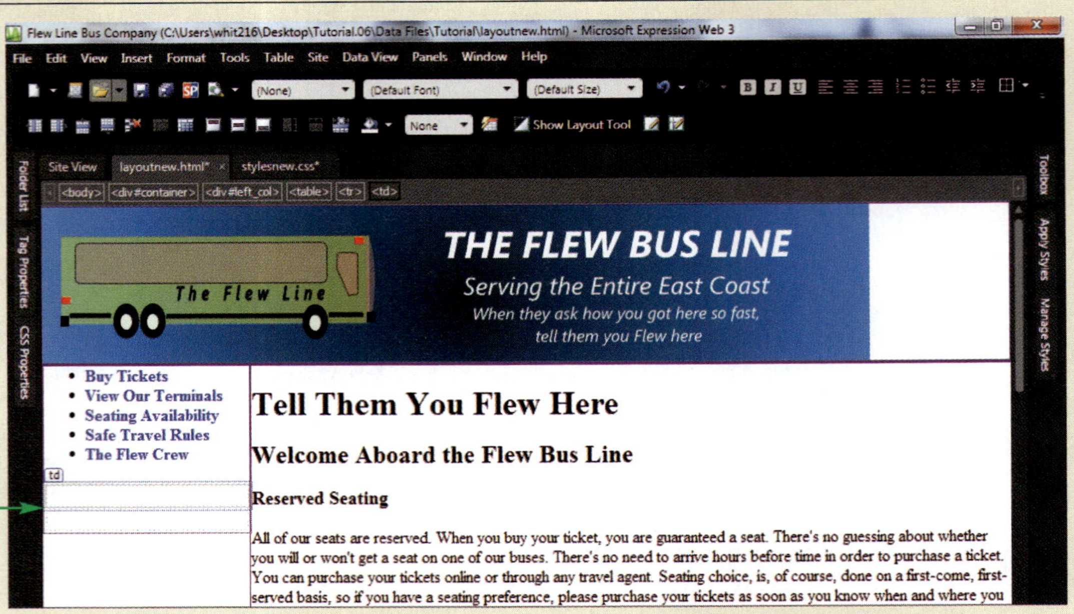

Now that the new table has been created, you'll format it using the Table AutoFormat feature, which will automatically apply a table style from a list of template styles. When you use the AutoFormat feature, it's important to apply an AutoFormat template before you enter the data into the table. Depending on the template you choose, the AutoFormat feature may change the font and point size, which could cause the table to expand or contract. You should also save the table before applying the AutoFormat template. This allows you to revert to the saved original in case you're not happy with the result of the AutoFormat.

To apply the Table AutoFormat:

1. With the insertion point still within the new table, click the **Table AutoFormat** button on the Tables toolbar.

   The Table AutoFormat dialog box opens displaying a list of table design templates. The Preview window shows you the appearance of the Simple 1 style, as shown in Figure 6-37.

Figure 6-37 The Table AutoFormat dialog box

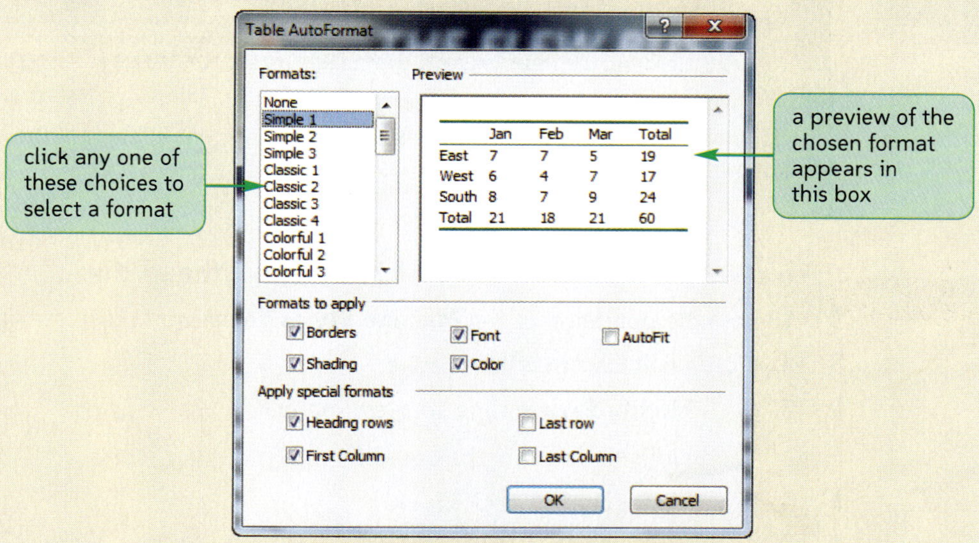

2. Under Formats, scroll down and then click **List 4**.
3. Click the **OK** button.

   The List 4 template style is applied to the new table.
4. In the first row of the table, type **Ticket Information**.
5. In the second row of the table, type **(631) 420-2755**.
6. Select both rows of the table.
7. Click the **Center** button on the Common toolbar.
8. Click anywhere outside the table.

   The table should appear as shown in Figure 6-38.

Figure 6-38 The text for the table

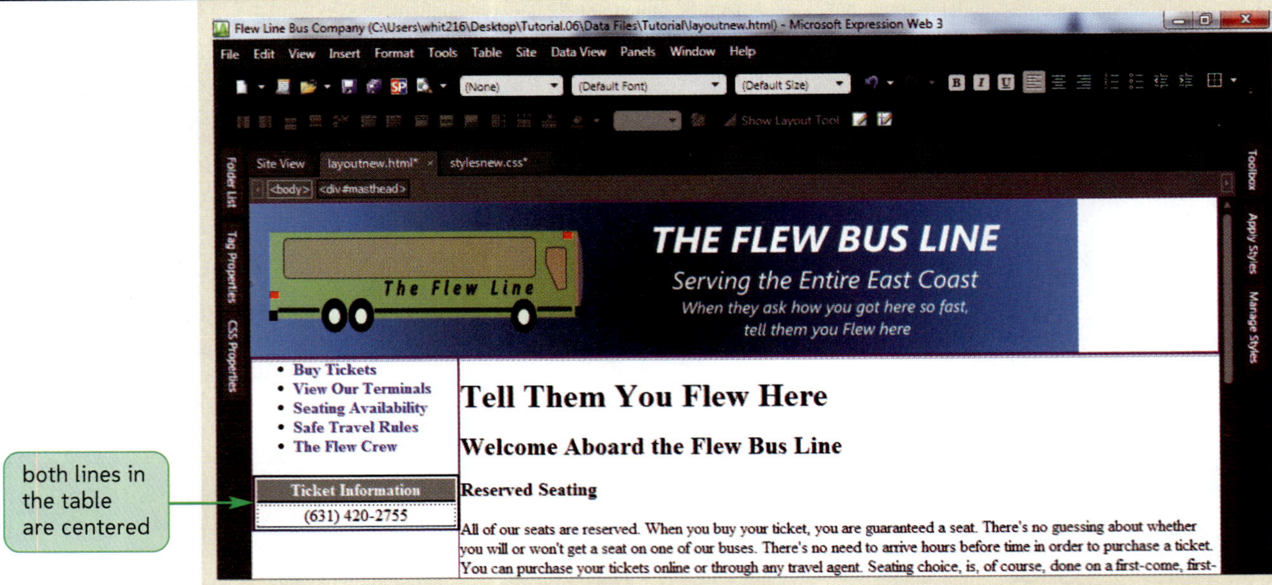

Finally, you'll improve the appearance of the content in each of the divs. You'll start by adding a background color to the masthead div.

To create a background color for the masthead div:

1. Pass the pointer over the **Manage Styles** panel tab to display that panel.
2. Right-click the **#masthead** style.
3. Click **Modify Style** on the shortcut menu.

   The Modify Style dialog box opens.
4. In the Category list, click **Block**.
5. Click the **text-align** arrow and then click **center**.
6. In the Category list, click **Background**.
7. Click the **background-color** arrow, and then click **Blue**, which is the second-to-last swatch in the second row.
8. Click the **OK** button.

   The masthead should look similar to that shown in Figure 6-39.

Figure 6-39 Creating styles for the masthead

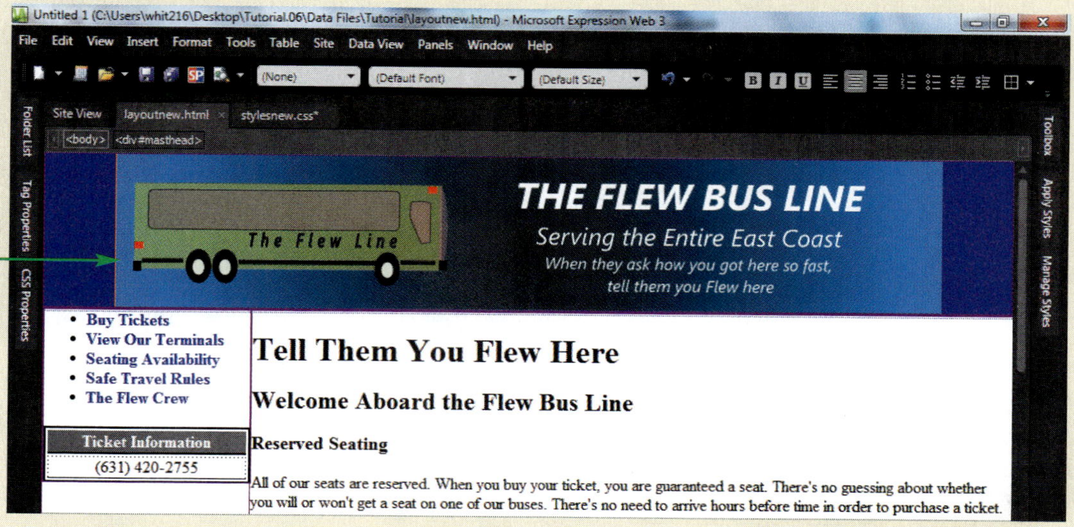

the logo image is centered and a blue background is applied to the masthead div

Michele would like you to make two changes to the page content div. First, she'd like to use a different font. She'd also like a little more space between the text and the edge of the div itself. You'll change the font and add some padding to the page content div.

To modify the page content style:

1. If necessary, pass the pointer over the **Manage Styles** panel tab to display that panel.
2. Right-click the **#page_content** style.
3. Click **Modify Style** on the shortcut menu.

   The Modify Style dialog box opens.
4. Click the **font-family** arrow and then click **Arial, Helvetica, sans-serif**.
5. In the Category list, click **Box**.
6. In the padding group, click in the **top** box, and then type **10px**.
7. Click the **OK** button. The text should look similar to that shown in Figure 6-40.

Figure 6-40 Formatting the page content div

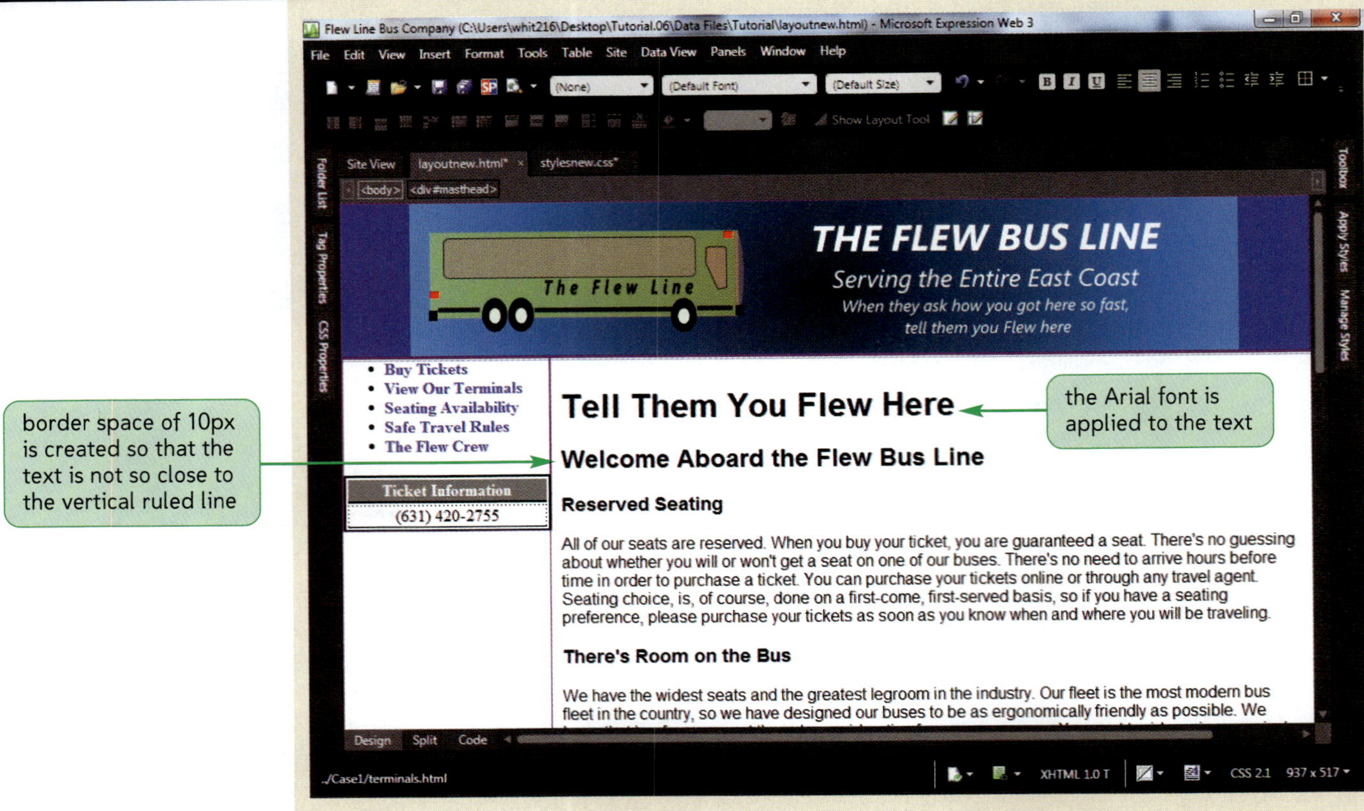

Michele also wants to format the footer div differently. She would like to use the same font as in the body text, and she also wants to specify a text color and background color.

To format the footer div style:

1. If necessary, pass the pointer over the **Manage Styles** panel tab to display that panel.
2. Right-click the **#footer** style.
3. Click **Modify Style** on the shortcut menu.

   The Modify Style dialog box opens.
4. Click the **font-family** arrow, and then click **Arial, Helvetica, sans-serif**.
5. Click the **color** arrow and then click **Navy**, which is the third swatch from the end in the first row.
6. In the Category list, click **Background**.
7. Click the **background-color** arrow and then click **Yellow**, which is the first swatch in the second row.
8. Click the **OK** button.
9. If necessary, scroll down to see the footer.

   The footer text is now navy on a yellow background, as shown in Figure 6-41.

Figure 6-41 Creating styles for the footer

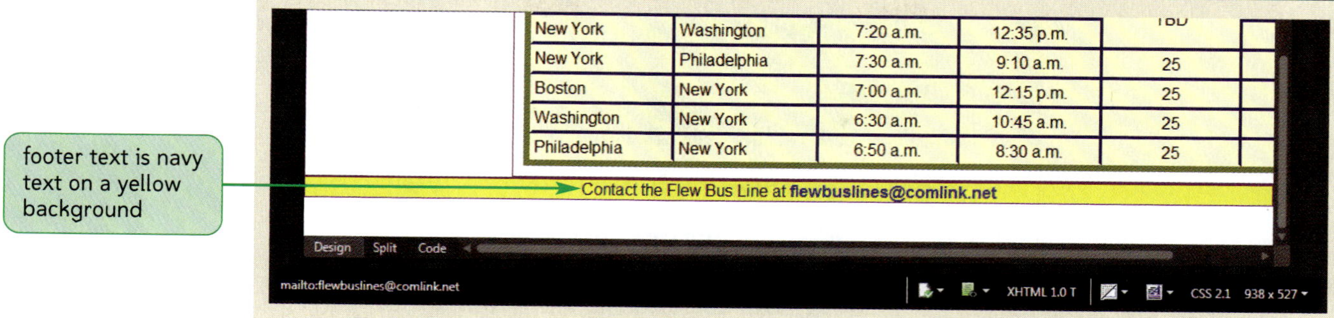

Finally, you'll add some documentation and view the file in the browser.

To view the file in the browser:

1. Press the **Ctrl+End** keys to position the insertion point at the end of the document.
2. Type your first and last name.
3. Press the **Shift+Enter** keys.
4. Type **Tutorial 6**.
5. Select the two lines of text you just typed and format them as bold.
6. Save the file and then if the Save Embedded files dialog box opens, click the **OK** button.
7. Press the **F12** key to view the file in the default browser. Your file should look similar to the one shown in Figure 6-42.

Figure 6-42 The completed file

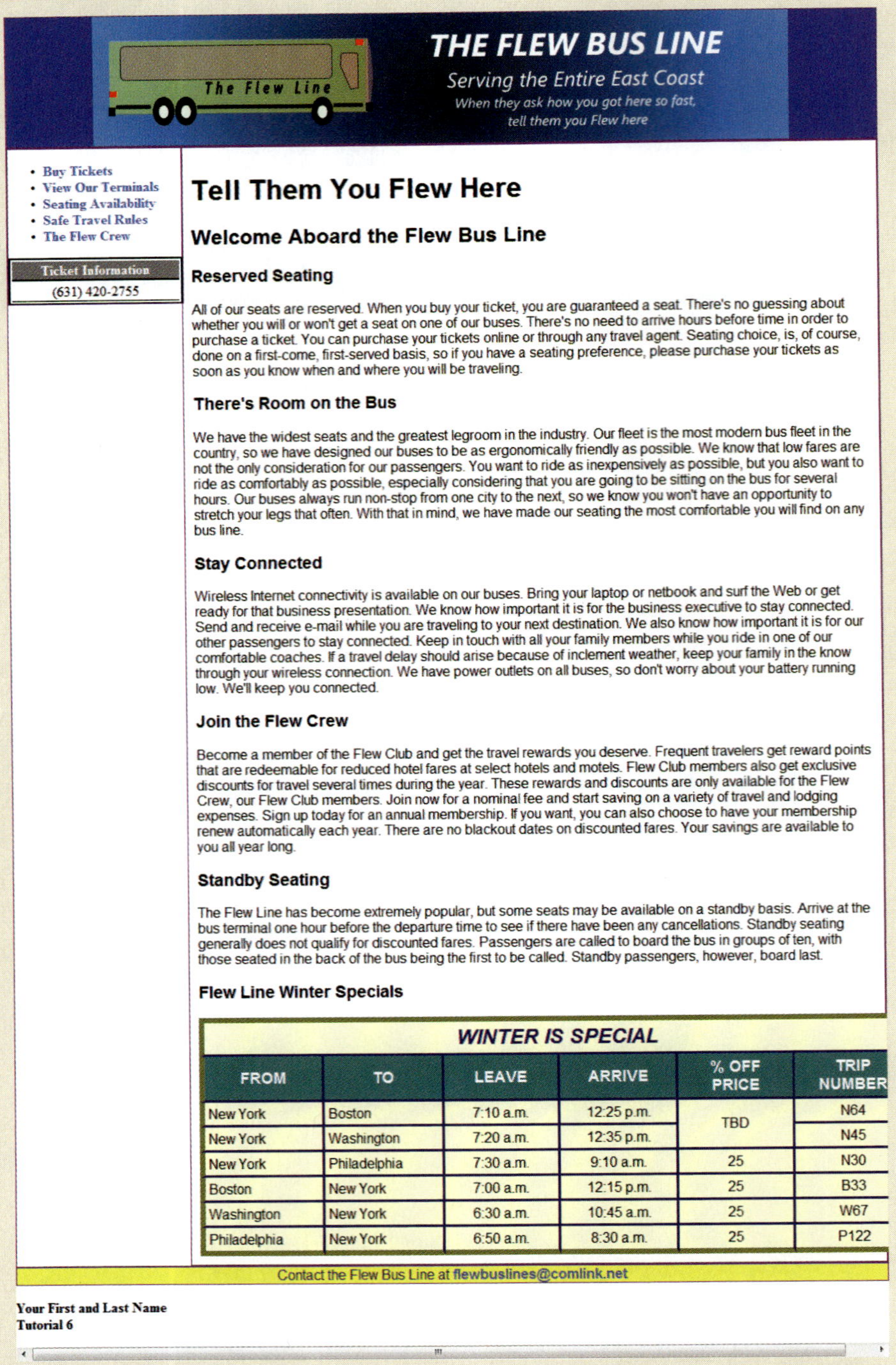

8. Close the browser.

9. Submit the results of the preceding steps to your instructor, either in printed or electronic form, as requested.

REVIEW

Session 6.2 Quick Check

1. Are tables still used for layout?
2. What HTML element is used to create structure only?
3. Which selector is used to format a div?
4. What is a template layout?
5. What should you do if there's a part of a CSS layout you do not need?
6. Which Expression Web feature automatically formats a table?

Practice the skills you learned in the tutorial using the same case scenario.

PRACTICE

Review Assignments

Data Files needed for this Review Assignment: flewlogo.png

Michele is pleased with the new Flew Line home page. She would like to add another page about the bus line that lists the cities along the East Coast that Flew Line serves. A preview of the completed file appears in Figure 6-43.

Figure 6-43

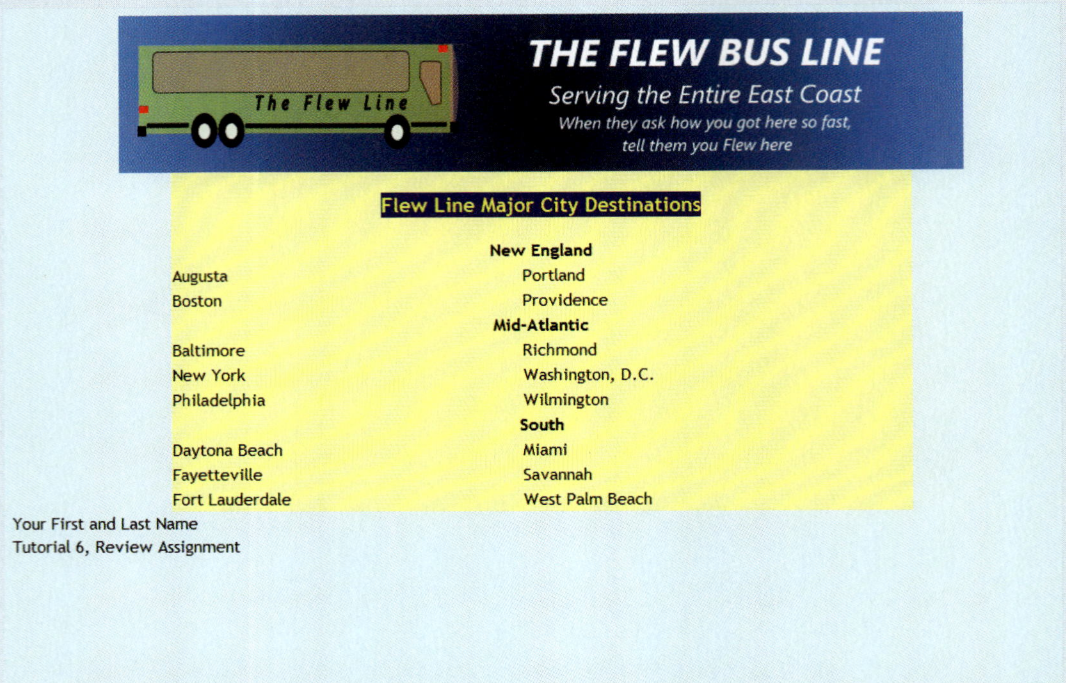

Complete the following:

1. If necessary, start Expression Web, close any open sites, and then open the Tutorial.06 Web site. Reset the workspace layout.
2. If necessary, expand the Data Files folder and the Review folder to display the contents of the Review folder.
3. Click File, point to New, and then click Page. Click CSS Layouts. Click Header, nav, 1 column, footer. Click the OK button to create the page layout.
4. In the Untitled_1.html page, right-click anywhere on the page. Click Page Properties. In the Page Properties dialog box, in the Title box type **Flew Bus Line City Destinations**. In the Page description box, type your first and last name, a slash, and **Tutorial 6, Review Assignment**. Click the OK button.
5. Click and drag the flewlogo.png image into the div#masthead section at the top of the page and then release the mouse button. For the alternate text, type **Flew Logo image**. Click the OK button. Center the image.

6. Press the down arrow key twice to position the insertion point within the page content div. Create the following table with 13 rows and 2 columns. Format the table as follows:
   - The table alignment should be set to center.
   - The table should occupy 70% of the screen width.
   - The table borders should be collapsed.
   - The background color of the table should be #FFFF99.

Flew Line Major City Destinations	
New England	
Augusta	Portland
Boston	Providence
Mid-Atlantic	
Baltimore	Richmond
New York	Washington, D.C.
Philadelphia	Wilmington
South	
Daytona Beach	Miami
Fayetteville	Savannah
Fort Lauderdale	West Palm Beach
TBD	

7. Select both cells in the first row. Apply the following formatting to the first row:
   - Merge the cells.
   - Make the text appear as an h3 heading.
   - Center the text.
   - Change the font color to yellow (#FFFF00).
   - Change the background color of the heading to navy (#000080).
8. In the rows containing the text New England, Mid-Atlantic, and South, do the following:
   - Merge the cells.
   - Center the text.
   - Make the text bold.
9. Delete the last row of the table.
10. Using the body element as the selector, create a style for the body so that the text appears in the Trebuchet MS font and has a background color of #CCFFFF.
11. Press the Ctrl+End keys to position the insertion point at the end of the document. Press the Up arrow key until the insertion point is within the div#footer section. Type your first and last name. Press the Shift+Enter keys and type **Tutorial 6, Review Assignment**.
12. Right-click the Untitled_1.html Document tab. Click Save. Save this file as **citynew.html** in the Review folder. Save the Untitled_1.css file as **citystylesnew.css** in the Review folder.
13. Open the **citynew.html** file in your default browser. Your document should look similar to the one shown in Figure 6-43.
14. Submit the completed files to your instructor, either in printed or electronic form, as requested.

Use the skills you learned in the tutorial to create a Web page for a realty investment company.

APPLY

Case Problem 1

Data Files needed for this Case Problem: realty.html

Flairboard Realty, Inc. Flairboard Realty and Investment Properties, Inc., located in Fort Taxson, Florida, specializes in acquiring, renovating, and reselling investment properties. Flairboard has done very well over the last 10 years during times of market growth. Even with the recent downturn in the housing market, Flairboard continues to achieve impressive growth. You have been asked to create a Web page for the Flairboard Realty intranet, the company's own internal Web site, which is viewed only by employees within the company. The new page will give more detail about the recent acquisitions and their investment potential. A preview of the completed file appears in Figure 6-44.

Figure 6-44

Flairboard Realty and Investment Properties, Inc.

May - June Acquisitions

Flairboard is pleased to announce that we have acquired properties totaling nearly $3 million during the past two months. The property at Smith Street is in excellent condition and was acquired at a price that was significantly below market value despite the residence being in mint condition. The sellers were highly motivated, as they were forced to relocate to another part of the country in order to capitalize on a very lucrative investment opportunity of their own.

The Granville property is in very good condition, and we believe it will need only modest repairs. We expect to put that house on the market shortly. The only concern about that property is the possibility of some development further down the block that might compete with the resale of this home. Otherwise, this appears to be a rather sound investment for us.

The Peachtree Avenue property, we believe, will turn out to be a very good investment. The property was acquired at very low cost, this time as a result of a death in the family. The home is in excellent condition and should require minimal, if any, renovation in order to prepare the property for resale. The homeowner was very motivated and seemed eager to sell the property well below market value. We foresee this property as a major money maker for us, with the potential for at least a 50% return on investment.

The Bernard Blvd. property was our most expensive acquisition this term. The home is in fair condition, but that is the result more of owner neglect than there being any structural defects in the property. The property is located in a prime area, and although this home will require substantial capital for renovation, we feel this is a sound venture that will yield us a 100% return on investment. The neighborhood is stable, and the surrounding homes generally are valued at $1 million or more. The renovation of this property will be in keeping with the competing homes in the neighborhood.

The Meyers Street property, albeit in poor condition, was purchased far below its potential market value. The home will be razed and a new home will be constructed on the site. Neighboring homes sell in the average of $750,000 or more, so we feel that if we can keep the construction costs to $300,000 or less, we should have a sizable return on investment for this property. The neighborhood is stable, and the home is near an elementary school.

The Priscilla Way property is in good condition. There is some structural damage as a result of the recent storms in the area, but other than that, the property is in good shape. The home is situated near a river, and it is possible to build a bulkhead or a dock that would lead to a private boat slip or landing. The construction of a boat slip or landing would be a substantial cost, but we feel that it would make the home more competitive with the surrounding homes and allow us to increase the asking price for the home. We feel that we can recoup any investment costs in this home.

FLAIRBOARD REALTY

Property	Seller	Date Acquired	Value	Condition	Taxes Due
24 Smith Street	Jones	May 4	456,000	Excellent	Yes
345 Granville Blvd.	Hanson	May 18	567,000	Very Good	Yes
2 Peachtree Ave.	Jones	May 29	351,000	Excellent	No
17 Bernard Blvd.	Greer	June 1	678,000	Fair	Yes
38 Meyers Street	McMann	June 11	232,000	Poor	No
116 Priscilla Way	Jones	June 27	544,000	Good	No

Your First and Last Name
Tutorial 6, Case Problem 1

Complete the following:

1. If necessary, start Expression Web, close any open sites, and open the Tutorial.06 Web site. Reset the workspace layout.
2. If necessary, expand the Data Files folder and the Case1 folder to display the contents of the Case1 folder.
3. Open the **realty.html** file in the Case1 folder and save the file as **realtynew.html** in the same folder.

4. In Design view, right-click anywhere on the page, and then click Page Properties. In the Title box, type **Flairboard Realty and Investment Properties, Inc.**
5. In the Page description box, type your **first** and **last name**, type a slash, and type **Tutorial 6, Case Problem 1**. Click the OK button.
6. If necessary, scroll down to display the Flairboard Realty table. In the table, delete the three rows that have no content.
7. Delete the column that has no content.
8. Insert a new column to the right of the Property column. Starting with the second row of the new column, type the following text in the cells:

   Seller

   Jones

   Hanson

   Jones

   Greer

   McMann

   Jones
9. Insert a new column to the right of the Condition column. Starting with the second row of the new column, type the following text in the cells:

   Taxes Due

   Yes

   Yes

   No

   Yes

   No

   No
10. Merge the cells in the first row. Center and bold the words *FLAIRBOARD REALTY*.
11. Right-click anywhere in the table, and then click Table Properties on the shortcut menu. Format the table as follows, and then click the OK button when you are done:
    - Set the table alignment to center.
    - Specify a width of 80%.
    - Change the cell padding to 4 and the cell spacing to 4.
    - Change the border size to 3.
    - Change the border color to Navy.
    - Collapse the table borders.
12. Display the Tables toolbar. Click anywhere inside the table to activate the Tables toolbar.
13. Select the cells in the row containing the column headings. Use the Tables toolbar to distribute the columns evenly.
14. If necessary, click and drag the border between the first two columns (the Property and the Seller columns) until all of the addresses in the first column appear on one line.
15. Make the column headings centered, bold, and olive (hex value #808000).
16. Right-click anywhere in the table. Click Table Properties on the shortcut menu. If the width of the table is now specified as a value in pixels, specify a width of 80%. Click the OK button.
17. Close the Tables toolbar.
18. Select all the cells in the table below the column headings. Center the content of the cells.
19. Press the Ctrl+End keys to position the insertion point at the end of the document. Type your first and last name. Press the Shift+Enter keys and type **Tutorial 6, Case Problem 1**.

20. Save your **realtynew.html** file.
21. Open the **realtynew.html** file in your browser. Your document should look similar to the one shown in Figure 6-44.
22. Submit the completed file to your instructor, either in printed or electronic form, as requested.

Use the skills you learned in the tutorial to create and style a Web page for a national men's and women's apparel company.

APPLY

Case Problem 2

Data Files needed for this Case Problem: year.html

S. Wilson Belliard Clothiers S. Wilson Belliard Clothiers is a nationally recognized leader in men's and women's apparel. With stores operating coast to coast, Belliard's prides itself on providing top-notch service to its customers. Belliard's does not compete on price, but it does compete on quality, selection, and service. You have been asked to compose a Web page that indicates how well the company performed over the course of the fiscal year. A preview of the completed file appears in Figure 6-45.

Figure 6-45

S. Wilson Belliard Clothiers

Sales Statement					
Apparel	**Q1**	**Q2**	**Q3**	**Q4**	**% Gain/Loss**
Blouses	10.4	11.6	12.3	14.3	12.15
Women's Suits	7.7	5.5	2.2	1.2	4.15
Men's Suits	12.1	14.4	10.9	9.1	11.62
Shoes	-21.5	-23.4	-33.9	-28.1	-26.72
Coats	10.3	Not Applicable		14.7	12.5
Sweaters	4.3	Not Applicable		3.3	3.8
Men's Slacks	12.8	8.8	10.3	11.4	10.82
Skirts	8.3	4.5	5.6	9.0	6.85
Overall change [1]	**5.55**	**3.56**	**1.23**	**4.36**	**3.67**

[1] Represents percent increase or decrease over last year.

Summary Annual Report

S. Wilson Belliard Clothiers had a sound financial year. Increases in sales were reported across the board for both men's and women's apparel. Shoes, however, showed a decline, as we are phasing out the sale of men's and women's shoes in most of our stores in order to better focus on our apparel lines. We also have cleared our inventories of certain ancillary items, such as umbrellas, the sale of which has been discontinued.

In the coming year, we plan to introduce a much more focused sales strategy. We no longer will be offering all types of seasonal clothing based upon a single calendar date. For example, the starting date for the sale of coats and sweaters will be approximately six to eight weeks sooner in the colder climates, such as the Northeast and the Midwest. Similarly, we will introduce summer apparel about two to three months sooner in warmer climates in the country. In areas of the country where it is feasible to sell summer apparel year-round, such as the Southwest and the extreme Southeast, we will extend the selling dates for those items that are typically seasonal in nature throughout the rest of the country.

We also plan to launch a new market segment, leisure attire, with a heavy emphasis on those stores in warmer climates. We plan to sell all types of athletic wear, and we are considering offering athletic footwear as well. We hope this shift in sales strategy will replace some of the lost sales we experienced this year as a result of the discontinuance of other footwear items.

Our plans to expand into other markets are going forward. We are finalizing plans for our expansion into Canada, targeting British Columbia, Ontario, and Quebec. We want to open our first stores in Vancouver and Montreal by the end of the next fiscal year. Increased competition from the Mitchell Group may force us to rethink some of this strategy, but we feel that we should move forward with this expansion sooner rather than later.

Overall, the company had a sound financial year, bucking the trend of many retailers who saw either modest gain, no gain, or even severe declines in sales. We feel that our "service is first and foremost" strategy is working, as customers appear to appreciate getting value for their dollar. Sales over the Internet have increased substantially from last year as well. We shall be issuing an annual report on our Internet sales next month.

Your First and Last Name
Tutorial 6, Case Problem 2

Complete the following:

1. If necessary, start Expression Web, close any open sites, and open the Tutorial.06 Web site. Reset the workspace layout. If necessary, display the Tables toolbar.
2. If necessary, expand the Data Files folder and the Case2 folder to display the contents of the Case2 folder.
3. Open the **year.html** file in the Case2 folder and save the file as **yearnew.html** in the same folder.
4. In Design view, right-click anywhere on the page. Click Page Properties. In the Title box, type **S. Wilson Belliard Clothiers**.
5. In the Page description box, type your **first** and **last name**, type a slash, and type **Tutorial 6, Case Problem 2**. Click the OK button.

EXPLORE

6. Click anywhere in the table. Click Table on the menu bar, point to Select, and then click Table. Right-click and click Cut. Press the Enter key. Press the Up arrow key. Type **S. Wilson Belliard Clothiers**.
7. Press the Enter key. With the insertion point in the new paragraph, right-click and then click Paste. The table is pasted below the new line you inserted.
8. Format the words *S. Wilson Belliard Clothiers* as an h1 heading. Center the h1 heading. Below the table, format the words *Summary Annual Report* as an h2 heading.
9. In the first cell of the last row of the table, format the number *1* to appear as a superscript and in bold.
10. Similarly, immediately below the table, select the number *1* before the word *Represents*, and format the number to appear as a superscript and in bold.
11. Click in the first cell of the table. Select the cells in the first row and merge the cells. Center and bold the words *Sales Statement*.
12. In the table, delete the Umbrellas row.
13. Select the cells in the second row of the table. Use the Tables toolbar to distribute the columns evenly.
14. If necessary, click anywhere in the table. Use the Tables toolbar to apply the Grid 4 Table AutoFormat to the table. In the Apply special formats area of the Table AutoFormat dialog box, click the Last row check box.
15. Click in the Q2 cell for Coats. Select that cell and the cell to its right. Merge the two cells. In the newly merged cell, type **Not Applicable**. Click in the Q2 cell for Sweaters. Select that cell and the cell to its right. Merge the two cells. In the newly merged cell, type **Not Applicable**.
16. Click in the Q1 cell in the second row. Click and drag the pointer to select all the cells except the first row and the first column. Center the contents of the selected cells. Also center the word "Apparel" in the second row. Also have the text in the second row appear in blue (#0000FF). Bold all the column headings.
17. Press the Ctrl+End keys to position the insertion point at the end of the document. Type your first and last name. Press the Shift+Enter keys and type **Tutorial 6, Case Problem 2**.
18. Save your **yearnew.html** file.
19. Open the **yearnew.html** file in your browser. Your document should look similar to the one shown in Figure 6-45.
20. Submit the completed file to your instructor, either in printed or electronic form, as requested.

Use what you've learned, and expand your skills, to create and style a Web page for a women's soccer league.

CHALLENGE

Case Problem 3

Data Files needed for this Case Problem: content.html, header.html, left.html, soccerlogo.gif

Eastern Penn Women's Soccer League Jill Davies is the coach of the women's soccer team at Riversburgh College, located in the western part of New York State. Riversburgh College competes with other teams in western New York and eastern Pennsylvania. Jill would like to make a Web page that lists the current league standings, and she seeks your assistance. A preview of the completed file appears in Figure 6-46.

Figure 6-46

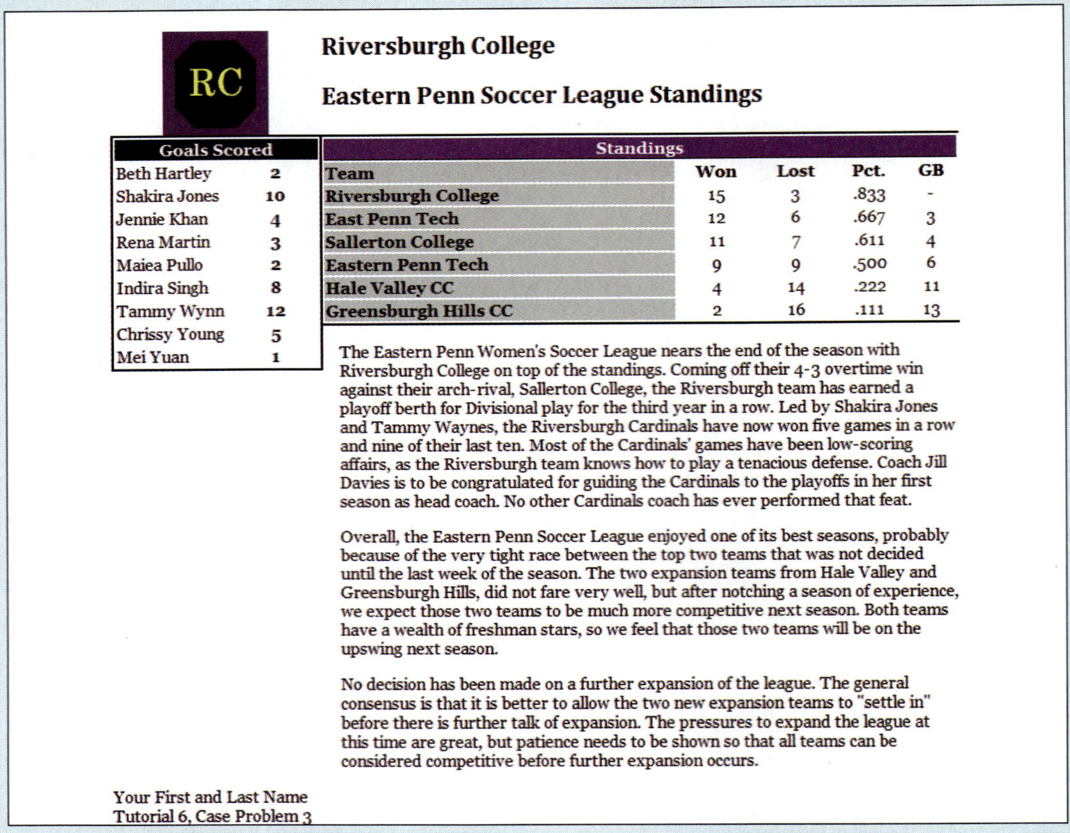

RC

Riversburgh College

Eastern Penn Soccer League Standings

Goals Scored	
Beth Hartley	2
Shakira Jones	10
Jennie Khan	4
Rena Martin	3
Maiea Pullo	2
Indira Singh	8
Tammy Wynn	12
Chrissy Young	5
Mei Yuan	1

Standings				
Team	**Won**	**Lost**	**Pct.**	**GB**
Riversburgh College	15	3	.833	-
East Penn Tech	12	6	.667	3
Sallerton College	11	7	.611	4
Eastern Penn Tech	9	9	.500	6
Hale Valley CC	4	14	.222	11
Greensburgh Hills CC	2	16	.111	13

The Eastern Penn Women's Soccer League nears the end of the season with Riversburgh College on top of the standings. Coming off their 4-3 overtime win against their arch-rival, Sallerton College, the Riversburgh team has earned a playoff berth for Divisional play for the third year in a row. Led by Shakira Jones and Tammy Waynes, the Riversburgh Cardinals have now won five games in a row and nine of their last ten. Most of the Cardinals' games have been low-scoring affairs, as the Riversburgh team knows how to play a tenacious defense. Coach Jill Davies is to be congratulated for guiding the Cardinals to the playoffs in her first season as head coach. No other Cardinals coach has ever performed that feat.

Overall, the Eastern Penn Soccer League enjoyed one of its best seasons, probably because of the very tight race between the top two teams that was not decided until the last week of the season. The two expansion teams from Hale Valley and Greensburgh Hills, did not fare very well, but after notching a season of experience, we expect those two teams to be much more competitive next season. Both teams have a wealth of freshman stars, so we feel that those two teams will be on the upswing next season.

No decision has been made on a further expansion of the league. The general consensus is that it is better to allow the two new expansion teams to "settle in" before there is further talk of expansion. The pressures to expand the league at this time are great, but patience needs to be shown so that all teams can be considered competitive before further expansion occurs.

Your First and Last Name
Tutorial 6, Case Problem 3

Complete the following:

1. If necessary, start Expression Web, close any open sites, and open the Tutorial.06 Web site. Reset the workspace layout. If necessary, display the Tables toolbar.
2. If necessary, expand the Data Files folder and the Case3 folder to display the contents of the Case3 folder.
3. Create a new page using the Header, logo, 2 columns, footer layout.
4. Save the Untitled_1.html file as **soccernew.html** in the Case3 folder. Save the Untitled_1.css file as **soccerstylesnew.css** in the same folder.
5. In the soccernew.html file, set the Page Properties to have **Riversburgh College Women's Soccer League** as the page title. For the description, type your first and last name, a slash, and **Tutorial 6, Case Problem 3**. Click the OK button.

6. In Design view, if necessary, use the arrow keys and the breadcrumb bar to locate the div#logo section. In the Folder List panel, click and drag the soccerlogo.gif image into the div#logo div, and then release the mouse button. For the alternate text, type **soccer league logo image**. Click the OK button.
7. Center the soccerlogo.gif image.
8. Open the header.html file. Select and copy the text. Right-click the header.html Document tab. Click Close.
9. In the soccernew.html file, click inside the layout and use the arrow keys and the breadcrumb bar to locate the div#header div. Paste the contents of the header.html file into the div#header div. If necessary, left align the two h2 headings above the table.
10. Open the left.html file, which contains the Goals Scored table. Click anywhere inside the table. Click Table, point to Select, and then click Table. Copy the table. Right-click the left.html Document tab. Click Close.
11. In the soccernew.html file, click inside the layout and locate the div#left_col div. Paste the Goals Scored table into the div#left_col div.
12. Open the content.html file. Select and copy the text, which includes the Standings table and the paragraphs below the table. Right-click the content.html Document tab. Click Close.
13. In the soccernew.html file, click inside the layout and locate the div#page_content div. Paste the contents of the content.html file into the div#page_content div.
14. In the Goals Scored table, click anywhere in the first row (the row with the words *Goals Scored*). Apply the Simple 3 Table AutoFormat to the table. Center the words *Goals Scored*. Select the numbers in the right column. Center and bold the numbers in that column.
15. In the Standings table, click anywhere in the first row of the table (the row with the word *Standings*).
16. Apply the Classic 2 Table AutoFormat to the table.
17. In the first row of the Standings table, center the word *Standings*.
18. In the Apply Styles panel, click New Style. Click the Selector arrow and click **p**. In the Category bar, click Box. In the margin area, click the Same for all check box to deselect it. In the left text box, type **1em**. Click the OK button.
19. Click in the cell with the word *Won* in the second row of the Standings table. Click and drag to select that cell and all cells to the right and below the Won cell. Center and bold the contents of the selected cells.
20. Create a style for the body element selector. For the font family, choose "Georgia, Times New Roman, Times, serif." Click the Box category. For margin, click the "Same for all" check box to uncheck that box. Set the right margin to auto. Set the left margin to auto. Click the Position category. In the width box, type 80%. Click the OK button.
21. Click in the div#footer section at the bottom of the layout. Type your first and last name. Press the Shift+Enter keys and type **Tutorial 6, Case Problem 3**.
22. Save your **soccernew.html** file. If prompted, save the embedded CSS file.
23. Open the **soccernew.html** file in your browser. The document should look similar to the one shown in Figure 6-46.
24. Submit the completed files to your instructor, either in printed or electronic form, as requested.

Create and style a Web page for a theater.

CREATE

Case Problem 4

Data Files needed for this Case Problem: show.html

The James Theater The James Theater, located in Austin, Texas, has been creating a Web page that tabulates attendance figures for some of its more popular shows. You have been asked to style the page so that the table appears in an attractive format. Complete the following:

1. Open sites, and open the Tutorial.06 Web site. Reset the workspace layout.
2. Open the **show.html** file in the Tutorial.06\Case4 folder and save the file as **shownew.html** in the same folder.
3. In Design view, right-click anywhere on the page. Click Page Properties. In the Title box, type **The James Theater Attendance Figures**.
4. In the Page description box, type your first and last name, type a slash, and type **Tutorial 6, Case Problem 4**. Click the OK button.
5. In the shownew.html file, delete any unused columns or rows.
6. Without using the Table AutoFormat feature, implement examples of the following:
   - Merged cells
   - Center-align the table
   - Cell padding and cell spacing (changed from the default)
   - Collapsed table border
   - Table width changed to 70%
   - Border size and color
   - Centered text and bold text
   - Font family changed for the entire table (create a style for the table selector)
   - Background color changed for the entire table (create a style for the table selector)
7. Press the Ctrl+End keys to position the insertion point below the table. Type your first and last name. Press the Shift+Enter keys and type **Tutorial 6, Case Problem 4**.
8. Save the **shownew.html** file.
9. Open the **shownew.html** file in your browser. Observe the result. Correct any errors.
10. Submit the completed file to your instructor, either in printed or electronic form, as requested.

ENDING DATA FILES

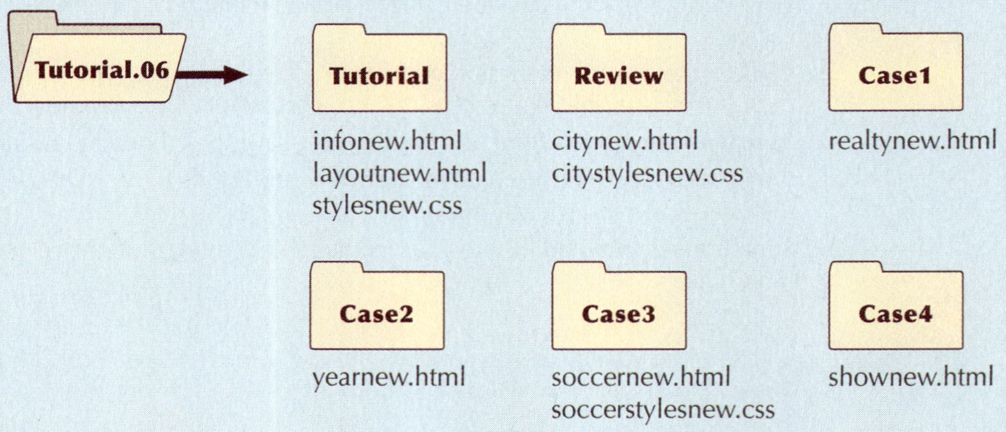

ProSkills

Written Communication

Creating an Effective Online Resume

Effective writing is a valuable tool whether you're creating an online blog about a local festival, a published report on the funding for public parks, or an informational Web site on the upcoming attractions in your town. Your written communications show your audience how prepared, informed, and detail-oriented you are. When searching for a job, the ability to write clearly and effectively is essential and can be a truly distinguishing factor that will set you apart from the crowd. In most cases, your first contact with a company is your resume and, increasingly, companies are requesting printed and online versions. To make the best possible impression, consider the following elements when communicating online.

Identify Your Audience

Who will read your Web page? What do they already know about your subject? It is safe to assume that your audience is made up of busy people who will only take the time to read what is important and relevant to them. In the case of a resume, your audience is typically one or more professional people who don't know you. The goal of your resume should be to introduce yourself quickly and efficiently.

State Your Purpose

At the beginning of the document, explain why you created a Web page. Are you trying to relay information or do you want the reader to take action? Traditionally, a cover letter accompanies the resume. This is where you can clearly state that you are writing to apply for a job, and then explain exactly what job you are applying for. This might sound obvious, but many job applicants forget about directness in their efforts to come across as clever or interesting. Remember, time is valuable and a clear, direct explanation of your intentions is best. In an online resume, the cover letter can be the home page of your Web site or a separate Web page.

Write Succinctly

Use as few words as possible. Don't indulge in long, complicated words and sentences because you think they make you sound smart. The most intelligent writing is often short and to the point. This is especially important online, when most or all of the content of the resume will be available on one page. Using unnecessary words and sentences can make the page look cluttered and difficult to read. Keep in mind that hiring a new employee is a very time-consuming process. In small companies, people in charge of hiring often have to do it while performing their regular duties. Thus, the more succinct your resume and cover letter, the greater the chances that a potential employer will actually read both documents.

Use the Right Tone

Be professional and courteous. In the case of building an online resume, don't make the mistake of being overly friendly, as it might indicate to the reader that you're not taking the job seriously. Your online resume will convey two things: first, your professional experience and interest in the job, and second, your Web page development and design skills.

ProSkills

Proofread and Revise

After you finish any Web page, set it aside for a while, and then proof it when it's no longer fresh in your mind. Even a small grammar or punctuation error can cause a potential employer to set aside your resume in favor of a more polished one with no errors. Remember, the best writers in the world seek out readers who can provide constructive suggestions, so consider having a friend or colleague read it and provide feedback. If someone points out an unclear passage, make every attempt to improve it.

PROSKILLS

Create a Web Page for Your Resume

You've now learned how to design and develop professional and interesting Web pages for several different companies using Expression Web 3. The skills you've learned will be useful to you in many areas of your life. For example, you could build a Web site with product pages for a new business, or create a photo album Web page for your family and friends. In the following exercise, you'll create a cover letter and resume for a specific job application. Research a career and job opportunity you are interested in and use that as your basis for this exercise.

1. Create a new Web page for your online resume and cover letter.
2. Set an anchor at the top of the page that will be used for a link to the bottom of the page.
3. Create a link at the bottom of the page back to the anchor at the top of the page.
4. Use at least two different sizes for section headings, such as <h1> or <h2>.
5. Apply both bold and italic formatting to some of the text. Keep in mind that your resume needs to be easy to read.
6. Include at least five separate paragraphs or entries of text.
7. Insert a headshot photo of yourself and make it a link.
8. Add a link to another page; for example, you might add a link to your LinkedIn page.
9. Include a minimum of three external links that provide examples of your interests and hobbies.
10. Create an ordered or unordered list (change the list style type or use a list style image).
11. Apply an independent class named "emphasis" that emphasizes text by changing its color and point size to some text on your home page.
12. Be sure to include and style all of the elements in your Web page, for example: <h1>, <h2>, <h3>; <p>, a:link, a:visited, and a:hover.
13. Review your Web page and save the files as <*yourlastname*>_resume.htm. Submit the completed file and printouts to your instructor as requested.

APPENDIX A

Colors by Name and Hexadecimal Value

EXPRESSION WEB

In the following table, the 17 Web-safe colors are in bold.

Named Color	Hexadecimal Code
aliceblue	#F0F8FF
antiquewhite	#FAEBD7
aqua	**#00FFFF**
aquamarine	#7FFFD4
azure	#F0FFFF
beige	#F5F5DC
bisque	#FFE4C4
black	**#000000**
blanchedalmond	#FFEBCD
blue	**#0000FF**
blueviolet	#8A2BE2
brown	#A52A2A
burlywood	#DEB887
cadetblue	#5F9EA0
chartreuse	#7FFF00
chocolate	#D2691E
coral	#FF7F50
cornflowerblue	#6495ED
cornsilk	#FFF8DC
crimson	#DC143C
cyan	**#00FFFF**
darkblue	#00008B
darkcyan	#008B8B
darkgoldenrod	#B8860B
darkgray	#A9A9A9
darkgreen	#006400
darkkhaki	#BDB76B
darkmagenta	#8B008B

STARTING DATA FILES

There are no starting Data Files needed for this appendix.

Named Color	Hexadecimal Code
darkolivegreen	#556B2F
darkorange	#FF8C00
darkorchid	#9932CC
darkred	#8B0000
darksalmon	#E9967A
darkseagreen	#8FBC8F
darkslateblue	#483D8B
darkslategray	#2F4F4F
darkturquoise	#00CED1
darkviolet	#9400D3
deeppink	#FF1493
deepskyblue	#00BFFF
dimgray	#696969
dodgerblue	#1E90FF
firebrick	#B22222
floralwhite	#FFFAF0
forestgreen	#228B22
fuchsia	**#FF00FF**
gainsboro	#DCDCDC
ghostwhite	#F8F8FF
gold	#FFD700
goldenrod	#DAA520
gray	**#808080**
green	**#008000**
greenyellow	#ADFF2F
honeydew	#F0FFF0
hotpink	#FF69B4
indianred	#CD5C5C
indigo	#4B0082
ivory	#FFFFF0
khaki	#F0E68C
lavender	#E6E6FA
lavenderblush	#FFF0F5
lawngreen	#7CFC00
lemonchiffon	#FFFACD
lightblue	#ADD8E6
lightcoral	#F08080
lightcyan	#E0FFFF
lightgoldenrodyellow	#FAFAD2
lightgray	#D3D3D3
lightgreen	#90EE90
lightpink	#FFB6C1
lightsalmon	#FFA07A
lightseagreen	#20B2AA

Named Color	Hexadecimal Code
lightskyblue	#87CEFA
lightslategray	#778899
lightsteelblue	#B0C4DE
lightyellow	#FFFFE0
lime	**#00FF00**
limegreen	#32CD32
linen	#FAF0E6
magenta	#FF00FF
maroon	**#800000**
mediumaquamarine	#66CDAA
mediumblue	#0000CD
mediumorchid	#BA55D3
mediumpurple	#9370DB
mediumseagreen	#3CB371
mediumslateblue	#7B68EE
mediumspringgreen	#00FA9A
mediumturquoise	#48D1CC
mediumvioletred	#C71585
midnightblue	#191970
mintcream	#F5FFFA
mistyrose	#FFE4E1
moccasin	#FFE4B5
navajowhite	#FFDEAD
navy	**#000080**
oldlace	#FDF5E6
olive	**#808000**
olivedrab	#6B8E23
orange	#FFA500
orangered	#FF4500
orchid	#DA70D6
palegoldenrod	#EEE8AA
palegreen	#98FB98
paleturquoise	#AFEEEE
palevioletred	#DB7093
papayawhip	#FFEFD5
peachpuff	#FFDAB9
peru	#CD853F
pink	#FFC0CB
plum	#DDA0DD
powderblue	#B0E0E6
purple	**#800080**
red	**#FF0000**
rosybrown	#BC8F8F
royalblue	#4169E1

Named Color	Hexadecimal Code
saddlebrown	#8B4513
salmon	#FA8072
sandybrown	#F4A460
seagreen	#2E8B57
seashell	#FFF5EE
sienna	#A0522D
silver	**#COCOCO**
skyblue	#87CEEB
slateblue	#6A5ACD
slategray	#708090
snow	#FFFAFA
springgreen	#00FF7F
steelblue	#4682B4
tan	#D2B48C
teal	**#008080**
thistle	#D8BFD8
tomato	#FF6347
turquoise	#40E0D0
violet	#EE82EE
wheat	#F5DEB3
white	**#FFFFFF**
whitesmoke	#F5F5F5
yellow	**#FFFF00**
yellowgreen	#9ACD32

APPENDIX B

Named Character Entities

The following table lists the name, syntax, and description of the named character entities. If the browser does not support the named character entity, use the numeric character entity in its place (see Appendix C).

Name	Syntax	Description
	´	Acute accent
	&	Ampersand
	¦	Broken vertical bar
	¸	Cedilla
	¢	Cent sign
	©	Copyright symbol
	¤	General currency symbol
	°	Degree sign
	½	Fraction one-half
	¼	Fraction one-quarter
	&fract34;	Fraction three-fourths
	>	Greater than sign
	¡	Inverted exclamation mark
	¿	Inverted question mark
	«	Left angle quotation mark
	<	Less than sign
	&macron;	Macron
	µ	Micro sign
	·	Middle dot
		Nonbreaking space
	¬	Not sign
	ª	Feminine ordinal
	º	Masculine ordinal
	¶	Paragraph sign
	±	Plus minus symbol
	"	Double quotation mark
	»	Right angle quotation mark
	®	Registered trademark

STARTING DATA FILES

There are no starting Data Files needed for this appendix.

Name	Syntax	Description
	§	Section sign
		Soft hyphen
	¹	Superscript 1
	²	Superscript 2
	³	Superscript 3
	™	Trademark symbol
	¨	Umlaut
	¥	Yen sign
Aacute	Á	Capital A, acute accent
Agrave	À	Capital A, grave accent
Acirc	Â	Capital A, circumflex accent
Atilde	Ã	Capital A, tilde
Aring	Å	Capital A, ring
Auml	Ä	Capital A, dieresis or umlaut mark
AElig	Æ	Capital AE, dipthong (ligature)
Ccedil	Ç	Capital C, cedilla
Eacute	É	Capital E, acute accent
Egrave	È	Capital E, grave accent
Ecirc	Ê	Capital E, circumflex accent
Euml	Ë	Capital E, dieresis or umlaut mark
Capital I, acute accent	Ì	Capital I, grave accent
Icirc	Î	Capital I, circumflex accent
Iuml	Ï	Capital I, dieresis or umlaut mark
ETH	Ð	Capital ETH, Icelandic
Ntilde	Ñ	Capital N, tilde
Oacute	Ó	Capital O, acute accent
Ograve	Ò	Capital O, grave accent
Ocirc	Ô	Capital O, circumflex accent
Otilde	Õ	Capital O, tilde
Ouml	Ö	Capital O, dieresis or umlaut mark
Oslash	Ø	Capital O, slash
Uacute	Ú	Capital U, acute accent
Ugrave	Ù	Capital U, grave accent
Ucirc	Û	Capital U, circumflex accent
Uuml	Ü	Capital U, dieresis or umlaut mark
Yacute	Ý	Capital Y, acute accent
szlig	ß	Small sharp s, German (sz ligature)
aacute	&aacute	Small a, acute accent
agrave	à	Small a, grave accent
acirc	â	Small a, circumflex accent
atilde	ã	Small a, tilde
auml	ä	Small a, dieresis or umlaut mark
aelig	æ	Small ae dipthong (ligature)

Name	Syntax	Description
ccedil	ç	Small c, cedilla
eacute	é	Small e, acute accent
egrave	è	Small e, grave accent
ecirc	ê	Small e, circumflex accent
euml	ë	Small e, dieresis or umlaut mark
iacute	í	Small i, acute accent
igrave	ì	Small i, grave accent
icirc	î	Small i, circumflex accent
iuml	ï	Small i, dieresis or umlaut mark
eth	ð	Small eth, Icelandic
ntilde	ñ	Small n, tilde
oacute	ó	Small o, acute accent
ograve	ò	Small o, grave accent
ocirc	ô	Small o, circumflex accent
otilde	õ	Small o, tilde
ouml	ö	Small o, dieresis or umlaut mark
oslash	ø	Small o, slash
uacute	ú	Small u, acute accent
ugrave	ù	Small u, grave accent
ucirc	û	Small u, circumflex accent
uuml	ü	Small u, dieresis or umlaut mark
yacute	ý	Small y, acute accent
thorn	þ	Small thorn, Icelandic
yuml	ÿ	Small y, dieresis or umlaut mark

APPENDIX C

Numeric Character Entities

EXPRESSION WEB

The following table lists the numeric character references and corresponding descriptions.

Reference	Description
&#00;–&#08;	Unused
	Tab
Line feed
&#11;–&#31;	Unused
	Space
!	Exclamation mark
"	Quotation mark (does not work in IE)
#	Number (pound) sign
$	Dollar sign
%	Percent sign
&	Ampersand
'	Apostrophe
(	Left parenthesis
)	Right parenthesis
*	Asterisk
+	Plus sign
,	Comma
-	Hyphen
.	Period
/	Forward slash
0–9	Digits 0–9
:	Colon
;	Semicolon
<	Less than symbol
=	Equal sign
>	Greater than
?	Question mark
@	Commercial at sign
A–Z	Letters A–Z

STARTING DATA FILES

There are no starting Data Files needed for this appendix.

Reference	Description
[	Left square bracket
\	Backslash
]	Right square bracket
^	Caret
_	Horizontal bar (underscore)
`	Acute accent
a–z	Letters a–z
{	Left curly brace
		Vertical bar
}	Right curly brace
~	Tilde
&#127;–	Unused
‚	Comma
ƒ	Function sign (florin)
„	Quotation mark (curly)
…	Ellipsis
†	Dagger
‡	Double dagger
ˆ	Circumflex
‰	Permille
Š	Capital S with hacek
‹	Left single angle
Œ	Capital OE ligature
–	Unused
‘	Single beginning quote
’	Single ending quote
“	Double beginning curly quote
”	Double ending curly quote
•	Bullet
–	En dash
—	Em dash
˜	Tilde
™	Trademark (tm)
š	Small s with hacek
›	Right single angle
œ	Lowercase oe ligature
–ž	Unused
Ÿ	Capital Y with umlaut
	Nonbreaking space
¡	Inverted exclamation
¢	Cent sign
£	Pound sterling
¤	General currency sign
¥	Yen sign
¦	Broken vertical bar

Reference	Description
§	Section sign
¨	Umlaut (dieresis)
©	Copyright
ª	Feminine ordinal
«	Left angle quote
¬	Not sign
	Soft hyphen
®	Registered trademark (R)
¯	Macron accent
°	Degree sign
±	Plus or minus
²	Superscript two
³	Superscript three
´	Acute accent
µ	Micro sign
¶	Paragraph sign
·	Middle dot
¸	Cedilla
¹	Superscript one
º	Masculine ordinal
»	Right angle quote
¼	Fraction one-fourth
½	Fraction one-half
¾	Fraction three-fourths
¿	Inverted question mark
À	Capital A, grave accent
Á	Capital A, acute accent
Â	Capital A, circumflex accent
Ã	Capital A, tilde
Ä	Capital A, umlaut
Å	Capital A, ring
Æ	Capital AE (ligature)
Ç	Capital C, cedilla
È	Capital E, grave accent
É	Capital E, acute accent
Ê	Capital E, circumflex accent
Ë	Capital E, umlaut
Ì	Capital I, grave accent
Í	Capital I, acute accent
Î	Capital I, circumflex accent
Ï	Capital I, umlaut
Ð	Capital ETH, Icelandic
Ñ	Capital N, tilde
Ò	Capital O, grave accent

Reference	Description
Ó	Capital O, acute accent
Ô	Capital O, circumflex accent
Õ	Capital O, tilde
Ö	Capital O, umlaut
×	Multiplication sign
Ø	Capital O, slash
Ù	Capital U, grave accent
Ú	Capital U, acute accent
Û	Capital U, circumflex accent
Ü	Capital U, umlaut
Ý	Capital Y, acute accent
Þ	Capital Thorn, Icelandic
ß	Small sharp s, German (sz ligature)
à	Small a, grave accent
á	Small a, acute accent
â	Small a, circumflex accent
ã	Small a, tilde
ä	Small a, umlaut
å	Small a, ring
æ	Small ae (ligature)
ç	Small c, cedilla
è	Small e, grave accent
é	Small e, acute accent
ê	Small e, circumflex accent
ë	Small e, umlaut
ì	Small i, grave accent
í	Small i, acute accent
î	Small i, circumflex accent
ï	Small i, umlaut
ð	Small eth, Icelandic
ñ	Small n, tilde
ò	Small o, grave accent
ó	Small o, acute accent
ô	Small o, circumflex accent
õ	Small o, tilde
ö	Small o, umlaut
÷	Division sign
ø	Small o, slash
ù	Small u, grave accent
ú	Small u, acute accent
û	Small u, circumflex accent
ü	Small u, umlaut
ý	Small y, acute accent
þ	Small thorn, Icelandic
ÿ	Small y, umlaut

APPENDIX D

HTML Elements

EXPRESSION WEB

The following table lists the HTML elements by name and provides a description of each.

Name	Description
a	Anchor
abbr	Abbreviated form
acronym	Abbreviation using initial letters of a phrase
address	By convention, the italicized address of the Web site or Webmaster
area	Client-side image map area
b	Bold text
base	Designates a default target
blockquote	Block-level element for a long quotation
body	Document body
br	Forced line break
button	Button
caption	Table caption
center	Center text (deprecated)
cite	Citation
code	Computer code
col	Table column
colgroup	Table column group
dd	Definition description
div	Generic style container
dl	Definition list
dt	Definition term
em	Emphasis
fieldset	Form control group
form	Interactive form
frame	Identifies window frame document
frameset	Window division
h1	Heading level 1
h2	Heading level 2
h3	Heading level 3
h4	Heading level 4

STARTING DATA FILES

There are no starting Data Files needed for this appendix.

Name	Description
h5	Heading level 5
h6	Heading level 6
head	Document head
hr	Horizontal rule
html	Document root element
iframe	Inline frame
img	Embedded image
input	Form control
kbd	Monospace type
label	Form field label text
legend	Fieldset legend
li	List item
link	A media-independent link
map	Client-side image map
meta	Generic meta information
noframes	Designates substitute text for frames
object	Generic embedded object
ol	Ordered list
optgroup	Option group
option	Selectable choice
p	Paragraph
pre	Preformatted text
q	Short, inline quotation
samp	Sample program output
select	Option selector
span	Generic language/style container
strong	Strong emphasis (bold)
style	Style information
sub	Subscript
sup	Superscript
table	Document table
tbody	Table body
td	Table data cell
textarea	Multiline text field
tfoot	Table footer
th	Table header cell
thead	Table header
title	Document title
tr	Table row
tt	Teletype (monospaced text)
u	Underlined text (deprecated)
ul	Unordered list
var	Variable

APPENDIX **E**

CSS 2.1 Properties and Values

EXPRESSION WEB

The following table lists the CSS 2.1 properties and the values available for each property. In the Values column, the default value is shown in bold. The Group column lists the group of which the property is a member.

Property	Description	Values	Group
background	The shorthand property for setting all background properties	background-attachment background-color background-image background-position background-repeat	background
background-attachment	Sets the position of a background image as fixed or scrolls as the insertion point moves down the page	fixed **scroll**	background
background-color	Sets the background color of an element	rgb value hex value short hex value named value **transparent**	background
background-image	Sets an image as the background	url (filename) **none**	background
background-position	Sets the position of a background image	top left top center top right center left **center center** center right bottom left bottom center bottom right x% y%	background
background-repeat	Determines whether a background image will be repeated	**repeat** repeat-x repeat-y no-repeat	background

STARTING DATA FILES

There are no starting Data Files needed for this appendix.

Property	Description	Values	Group
border	The shorthand property for setting all of the border properties	border-width border-style border-color	border
border-bottom	The shorthand property for setting all of the properties for the bottom border	border-bottom-width border-style border-color	border
border-bottom-color	Sets the color of the bottom border	border-color	border
border-bottom-style	Sets the style for the bottom border	border-style	border
border-bottom-width	Sets the width for the bottom border	thin **medium** thick length (in ems)	border
border-collapse	Determines whether a table border has a single or double rule	collapse **separate**	table
border-color	Sets the color for all four borders	rgb value hex value short hex value named value	border
border-left	The shorthand property for setting all of the properties for the left border	border-left-width border-style border-color	border
border-left-color	Sets the color for the left border	border-color	border
border-left-style	Sets the style for the left border	border-style	border
border-left-width	Sets the width for the left border	thin **medium** thick length (in ems)	border
border-right	The shorthand property for setting all of the properties for the right border	border-right-width border-style border-color	border
border-right-color	Sets the color for the right border	border-color	border
border-right-style	Sets the style for the right border	border-style	border
border-right-width	Sets the width for the right border	thin **medium** thick length (in ems)	border
border-style	Sets the style of the four borders	**none** hidden dotted dashed double groove inset outset ridge solid	border
border-top	The shorthand property for setting all of the properties for the top border	border-top-width border-style border-color	border

Property	Description	Values	Group
border-top-color	Sets the color for the top border	border-color	border
border-top-style	Sets the style for the top border	border-style	border
border-top-width	Sets the width for the top border	thin **medium** thick length (in ems)	border
border-width	A shorthand property for setting the width of the four borders in one declaration; can have from one to four values	thin **medium** thick length (in ems)	border
bottom	Determines how far from the bottom edge an element is from its parent element	**auto** length (in ems) %	positioning
caption-side	Determines the position of the table caption	**top** bottom left right	table
clear	Positions an element below another element	left right both none	classification
color	Determines text color	color in RGB, hex, short hex, or named values	text
display	Sets how and if an element is to be displayed	block inline list-item **none**	classification
empty-cells	Determines whether to show a table without content	**hide** show	table
float	Positions an element in relation to another element	left right **none**	classification
font	The shorthand property for setting all of the properties for a font	font-style font-variant font-weight font-size/line-height font-family	font
font-family	A list of font family names from specific to generic	font-family name generic-family name	font
font-size	Sets the size for the font	xx-small x-small small medium large x-large xx-large smaller pt values em values	font
font-style	Sets the style for the font	**normal** italic oblique	font

Property	Description	Values	Group
font-variant	Displays text in small caps or in a normal font	**normal** small caps	font
font-weight	Sets the weight of a font	**normal** bold bolder lighter 100 200 300 400 500 600 700 800 900	font
height	Sets the height of an element	**auto** length (in ems) %	dimension
left	Determines how far from the left edge an element is from its parent element	**auto** length (in ems) %	positioning
letter-spacing	Increases or decreases the space between characters	**normal** length (in ems)	text
line-height	Determines the white space between lines	**normal** number length (in ems) %	text
list-style	The shorthand property for setting all of the list-style properties	list-style-type list-style-position list-style-image	list
list-style-image	Sets an image to be used as a list-style marker	**none** url	list
list-style-position	Determines where the list-item marker will be positioned	inside **outside**	list
list-style-type	Determines the type of the list-item marker	circle decimal decimal-leading-zero **disc** lower-alpha lower-roman none square upper-alpha upper-roman	list
margin	The shorthand property for setting the margin properties	margin-top margin-right margin-bottom margin-left	margin
margin-bottom	Sets the bottom margin for an element	auto length (in ems) %	margin
margin-left	Sets the left margin for an element	auto length (in ems) %	margin

Property	Description	Values	Group
margin-right	Sets the right margin for an element	auto length (in ems) %	margin
margin-top	Sets the top margin for an element	auto length (in ems) %	margin
overflow	Determines the visibility of an element if the content exceeds the height of the containing box	auto hidden scroll **visible**	positioning
padding	The shorthand property for setting all of the padding properties	padding-top padding-right padding-bottom padding-left	padding
padding-bottom	Sets the bottom padding for an element	length (in ems) %	padding
padding-left	Sets the left padding for an element	length (in ems) %	padding
padding-right	Sets the right padding for an element	length (in ems) %	padding
padding-top	Sets the top padding for an element	length (in ems) %	padding
position	Positions an element	**static** relative absolute fixed	classification
position	Positions an element	absolute fixed relative **static**	positioning
right	Determines how far from the right edge an element is from its parent element	**auto** length (in ems) %	positioning
text-align	Aligns the text in an element horizontally	center justify **left** right	text
text-decoration	Adds a line above, through, or under text	line-through overline **none** underline	text
text-indent	Indents the first line of text in an element	length (in ems) %	text
text-transform	Determines the capitalization of text	capitalize lowercase **none** uppercase	text
top	Determines how far from the top edge an element is from its parent element	**auto** length (in ems) %	positioning

Property	Description	Values	Group
vertical-align	Sets the vertical alignment of an element	**baseline** bottom middle sub super text-bottom text-top top length %	positioning
visibility	Determines whether an element is visible	collapse hidden **visible**	classification
width	Sets the width of an element	**auto** % length (in ems)	dimension
word-spacing	Increases or decreases the space between words	**normal** length (in ems)	text
z-index	Determines the stacking order of an element (the greater the number, the higher the element is in the stack)	**auto** number	positioning

Pseudo-Classes

Pseudo-Class	Purpose
:active	Determines the style when a link is clicked
:focus	Determines the style when a link has the focus
:hover	Determines the style for mouse-over effect
:link	Determines the style for links that have not yet been visited
:visited	Determines the style for links that have been visited

Pseudo-Elements

Pseudo-Element	Purpose
:first-letter	Formats just the first letter of a word
:first-line	Formats just the first line of a paragraph
:before	Inserts white space before an element
:after	Inserts white space after an element

APPENDIX F

Expression Web 3.0 Keyboard Shortcuts

EXPRESSION WEB

Application Shortcuts

Task	Keyboard Shortcut
Cancel an action	Esc
Quit Expression Web	Alt+F4
Redo or repeat an action	Ctrl+Y or Shift+Alt+Backspace
Undo an action	Ctrl+Z or Alt+Backspace

Editing Tools Shortcuts

Task	Keyboard Shortcut
Check spelling	F7
Find text or code	Ctrl+F
Find the next occurrence of the current selection	Ctrl+F3
Find the next occurrence of the most recent search	F3
Find the previous occurrence of the current selection	Ctrl+Shift+F3
Find the previous occurrence of the most recent search	Shift+F3
Look up a word in the thesaurus	Shift+F7
Replace text or code	Ctrl+H

STARTING DATA FILES

There are no starting Data Files needed for this appendix.

Page Shortcuts

Task	Keyboard Shortcut
Close a Web page	Ctrl+F4
Create a new Web page	Ctrl+N
In Design view, show/hide Visual Aids	Ctrl+/
In Design view, show/hide formatting marks	Ctrl+Alt+/
Modify page properties	Alt+Enter
Move among Code, Design, and Split views	Ctrl+Page Down or Ctrl+Page Up
Move between Code and Design panes in Split view	Alt+Page Down or Alt+Page Up
Open a Web page	Ctrl+O
Preview a Web page in a Web browser	F12 or Ctrl+Shift+B
Print a Web page	Ctrl+P
Refresh a Web page, Code view changes in Design view, and the Folder List panel	F5
Rename the currently selected file in the Folder List panel	F2
Save a Web page	Ctrl+S
Show or hide the Folder List panel	Alt+F1
Switch between open Web pages	Ctrl+Tab
Switch between open Web pages in reverse order	Ctrl+Shift+Tab

SuperPreview Shortcuts

Task	Keyboard Shortcut
Add a new comparison browser slot	Ctrl+N
Clear baseline browser	Ctrl+Del
Clear selected browser	Del
Display a page in SuperPreview	Shift+F12
Open a Web page	Ctrl+O
Refresh the display	Ctrl+R or F5
Select baseline browser view	0
Select browser size	I
Select comparison browser slot 1	1
Select comparison browser slot 2	2
Select comparison browser slot 3	3
Select comparison browser slot 4	4
Select comparison browser slot 5	5
Select comparison browser slot 6	6
Select comparison browser slot 7	7
Select horizontal split layout view	S
Select overlay view	D
Select panning mode	H
Select selection mode	V
Select single browser view	F
Select the URL address bar	Alt+D or F4
Select vertical split layout view	A
Toggle guide display	Ctrl+;
Toggle lights-out display	L
Toggle ruler display	R
Toggle the thumbnail preview display	T
Zoom in	Ctrl+Plus Sign or Plus Sign
Zoom out	Ctrl+Minus Sign or Minus Sign
Zoom to 100%	Ctrl+1
Zoom to fit page	Ctrl+0

Text Formatting Shortcuts

Task	Keyboard Shortcut
Apply bold formatting	Ctrl+B
Apply italic formatting	Ctrl+I
Apply subscript formatting	Ctrl+Equal Sign
Apply superscript formatting	Ctrl+Plus Sign
Center a paragraph	Ctrl+E
Copy formatting	Ctrl+Shift+C
Copy text or graphics	Ctrl+C or Ctrl+Insert
Cut selected text or graphics	Ctrl+X or Shift+Delete
Decrease font size	Ctrl+Shift+<
Increase font size	Ctrl+Shift+>
Increase Indent Position	Ctrl+M
Decrease Indent Position	Ctrl+Shift+M
Insert a line break	Shift+Enter
Insert a nonbreaking space	Ctrl+Shift+spacebar
Left-align a paragraph	Ctrl+L
Paste formatting	Ctrl+Shift+V
Paste text or graphics	Ctrl+V or Shift+Insert
Remove manual formatting	Ctrl+Shift+Z or Ctrl+spacebar
Right-align a paragraph	Ctrl+R
Select the Font menu in the Common or Formatting toolbar	Ctrl+Shift+F
Select the Font Size menu in the Common or Formatting toolbar	Ctrl+Shift+P
Select the Style menu in the Common or Formatting toolbar	Ctrl+Shift+S

GLOSSARY/INDEX

Note: Boldface entries include definitions.

F

G

H

I

J

K

L

T

U

TASK REFERENCE

TASK	PAGE #	RECOMMENDED METHOD
All caps, format as	EW 80	Click Format, click Font, and then click the All caps check box
Blockquote, format as	EW 82	Click Format, click Paragraph, and then enter values for left and right indentation
Bookmark, create	EW 161	*See* Reference Window: Creating a Bookmark
Bookmark, link to	EW 164	*See* Reference Window: Linking to a Bookmark
Border, change style/color/width	EW 62	*See* Reference Window: Changing the Border, Style, Color, and Width
Border, create outside	EW 61	Click inside the text, click the Outside Borders list arrow in the Common toolbar, and then click the border style
Bullet type, change	EW 75	*See* the Reference Window: Changing the Bullet Type
Bulleted list, create	EW 72	*See* the Reference Window: Creating a Bulleted List
Cells, merge	EW 282	*See* Reference Window: Merging Cells
Character spacing, change	EW 83	*See* Reference Window: Changing the Character Spacing
Class, apply	EW 232	*See* Reference Window: Applying a Class
Column, insert	EW 275	*See* Reference Window: Inserting a Row or Column
Columns, distribute	EW 280	Click the Distribute Columns Evenly button on the Tables toolbar
CSS Report, run	EW 251	*See* Reference Window: Running CSS Reports
Definition list, create	EW 77	Click the Style arrow, and then click Defined term
E-mail link, create	EW 173	*See* Reference Window: Creating an E-Mail Link
Expression Web, exit	EW 18	Click File, and then click Exit
Expression Web, start	EW 5	Click the Start button on the taskbar, point to All Programs, point to Microsoft Expression Web 3, and then click Microsoft Expression Web 3
External style sheet, attach	EW 245	*See* Reference Window: Attaching an External Style Sheet File
External style sheet, create	EW 242	*See* Reference Window: Creating and Attaching an External Style Sheet File
File, print	EW 39	Press the Ctrl+P keys
File, save	EW 7	Click File, and then click Save As
File, view in the default browser	EW 32	*See* Reference Window: Previewing a File in the Browser
Font family, create	EW 219	Create a New Style, click the Font Category, and then click the font-family list arrow
Font, change	EW 59	*See* the Reference Window: Changing the Font
Font, change color	EW 66	Select the text; click the Font Color list arrow, and then select a color
Font, change size	EW 221	Click the Font Size arrow, and then click a font size
Font, change style	EW 223	In the New Style or Modify dialog box, click the font-style arrow, and then click a font style
Font, change weight	EW 222	In the New Style or Modify dialog box, click the font-weight arrow, and then click a font weight
Heading, apply	EW 58	Select the text, click the Style list arrow, and then click the heading size
Help, access	EW 37	Press the F1 key

TASK	PAGE #	RECOMMENDED METHOD
Highlight color, change	EW 66	Select the text, click the Highlight list arrow on the Common toolbar, and then select a color
Horizontal line, insert	EW 85	Double-click the Horizontal Line icon in the Toolbox
Hotspot locations, view	EW 187	*See* Reference Window: Viewing a Hotspot
Hotspot, create	EW 180	*See* Reference Window: Creating a Hotspot
Hotspot, modify	EW 189	*See* Reference Window: Modifying a Hotspot
Hyperlink, change colors	EW 190	*See* Reference Window: Changing Hyperlink Colors
Hyperlink, edit	EW 193	Right-click the link, and then click Hyperlink Properties
ID, create	EW 238	*See* Reference Window: Creating an ID Selector
Image, change brightness	EW 126	Click the image, and then click the More Brightness button or Less Brightness button on the Pictures toolbar
Image, create beveled border	EW 127	Click the image, and then click the Bevel button on the Pictures toolbar
Image, crop	EW 127	*See* Reference Window: Cropping an Image
Image, flip	EW 125	Click the image, and then click the Flip Horizontal button or the Flip Vertical button on the Pictures toolbar
Image, insert from Folder List panel	EW 106	*See* Reference Window: Inserting an Image from the Folder List panel
Image, manually resize	EW 129	*See* Reference Window: Manually Resizing an Image
Image, move	EW 112	*See* Reference Window: Moving an Image
Image, remove color from	EW 126	Click the image, click the Color button arrow on the Pictures toolbar, and click Grayscale
Image, resample	EW 124	Click the image, click the Resample button on the Pictures toolbar
Image, rotate	EW 125	Click the image and then click the Rotate Left 90° button or the Rotate Right 90° button on the Pictures toolbar
Image, scale	EW 119	Click the image, click Properties on the Format menu, click the Appearance tab, and then enter value(s) in the height and/or width text box(es)
Image, use as bullet	EW 137	*See* Reference Window: Using an Image as a Bullet
Layout, create	EW 293	*See* Reference Window: Creating a Template-Based Document
Line break, insert	EW 87	Press the Shift+Enter keys
Navigation bar, create	EW 301	*See* Reference Window: Creating a Navigation Bar Using a List
New page, create	EW 6	Click the New Document button
Page, change background color	EW 55	Right-click on a blank area of the page, click Page Properties, click the Formatting tab, click the Background list arrow, and then click a color
Page, change properties	EW 31	Right-click on a blank area of the page, click Page Properties
Page, close	EW 18	Click File, and then click Close
Panels, hide all	EW 16	Click Panels, and then click AutoHide All Panels
Picture, set properties	EW 109	*See* Reference Window: Setting Picture Properties
Row, insert	EW 275	*See* Reference Window: Inserting a Row or Column
Rulers, display vertical and horizontal	EW 12	*See* Reference Window: Displaying Rulers and Grids
Small caps, format as	EW 80	Click Format, click Font, and then click the Small caps check box

TASK	PAGE #	RECOMMENDED METHOD
Snapshot view, switch to	EW 33	Click Panels, and then click Snapshot
Spelling, check	EW 25	Press the F7 key
Style, clear	EW 235	Click Clear Styles in the Apply Styles Panel
Style, create	EW 218	*See* Reference Window: Creating a CSS Style
Style, modify	EW 220	*See* Reference Window: Modifying a Style
Subscript, format as	EW 80	Click Format, click Font, and then click the Subscript check box
SuperPreview, use	EW 34	*See* Reference Window: Using SuperPreview
Superscript, format as	EW 80	Click Format, click Font, and then click the Superscript check box
Symbol, insert	EW 86	Click Symbol on the Insert menu
Table AutoFormat, use	EW 305	*See* Reference Window: Using Table AutoFormat
Table, fill	EW 279	Select the cells, click Table, point to Fill, and then click the appropriate choice from the shortcut menu
Table properties, set	EW 271	*See* Reference Window: Setting the Table Properties
Table, create	EW 269	*See* Reference Window: Creating a Table
Text, change alignment	EW 60	Click inside the text, and then on the Common toolbar click the Align Text Left button, the Center button, or the Align Text Right button
Text, change color	EW 225	*See* Reference Window: Changing the Text Color
Text, change decoration	EW 226	In the New Style or Modify dialog box, in the Font category, click the underline or overline check box
Text, cut	EW 30	Select the text, right-click, and then click Cut
Text, emphasize	EW 68	*See* Reference Window: Emphasizing Text
Text, find and replace	EW 26	*See* Reference Window: Using the Editing Tools
Text, indent	EW 81	Click inside the text, and then on the Common toolbar, click either the Increase Indent Position button or the Decrease Indent Position button
Text, paste	EW 30	Right-click, and then click Paste
Thesaurus, use	EW 26	*See* Reference Window: Using the Editing Tools
Thumbnail image, create	EW 133	*See* Reference Window: Creating a Thumbnail Image
Views, change	EW 9	*See* Reference Window: Changing Views
Web page, link to	EW 168	*See* Reference Window: Creating a Link to Another Page
Web site, create	EW 90	*See* Reference Window: Creating a Web Site
Web site, link to	EW 172	*See* Reference Window: Creating an External Link
Web site, open	EW 50	Click Site, and then click Open Site
Workspace layout, reset	EW 6	Click Panels, and then click Reset Workspace Layout